5. LLYN LLYDAW AND SNOWDON
The Snowdonia region, like many highland areas in Scotland and Wales, is characterized by deep glacial erosion resulting in a dramatic landscape and scenery which has attracted tourism.

6. RIVER SPEY (GRAMPIAN)
In this picture the River Spey flows over an area of glacial deposition, which is characteristically flat. The river meanders within a belt of natural vegetation suggesting that its course is too unstable to risk cultivating the nearby floodplain.

7. EGLWYSEG MOUNTAINS (CLWYD)
This south-west facing limestone scarp is formed by differential weathering of the rocks. The poor soils and lack of surface water on the limestone plateau make this a poor farming area so that cultivation is restricted to the lowland areas.

8. RUMPS POINT (CORNWALL)
The processes of erosion and deposition on the hard rock of these promontories have resulted in the formation of near vertical cliffs and sandfilled bays, including a treacherous bank of sand across the estuary of the River Camel which hindered the development of the port at Padstow.

Philips' CERTIFICATE Atlas

George Philip

London · Melbourne · Milwaukee

Edited by

B. M. Willett, B.A., *Cartographic Editor*

H. Fullard, M.Sc., *Consultant Cartographer*

D. Gaylard, *Assistant Cartographic Editor*
  George Philip and Son, Ltd.

Maps and index produced by

G. Atkinson, B.A., Prudence Davson, B.Sc., Margaret Emslie, B.Sc., D. Fairbairn, B.A., N. Harris, B.A., P. Pearce, B.Sc., Elizabeth Prince-Smith, B.Sc., Mary Spence, M.A., R. Smith, B.Sc., S. Smith, B.A., Helen Stenhouse, B.Sc., and the Cartographic Staffs of George Philip Printers Ltd., London, Cartographic Services (Cirencester) Ltd., Fairey Surveys Ltd., and David L. Fryer & Company.

and prepared under the direction of

A. G. Poynter, M.A., *Director of Cartography*

First Edition 1979
Reprinted 1981
Second Edition 1983
Third Edition 1984

ISBN 0 540 05483 6 (General Edition)
   0 540 05484 4 (Educational Edition)

© **1984 George Philip & Son, Ltd., London**

Printed in Great Britain by George Philip Printers Ltd.

Preface

The prime function of a map is to portray an objective reality – topographical details and the patterns of human occupance that have developed upon it. In the tight limits of a school atlas, this requires a fine balance to show what is essential and yet maintain precision, legibility and a pleasing whole.

A school atlas must not be solely an arid enumeration of local detail and names. This century has seen an unparalleled expansion in the demand for specialized map information of all types and maps are expected to be not only more accurate and more detailed but also more interesting and more easily understood. The atlas should break new ground in the presentation and portrayal of essential facts of geography. It must give information on the matters which affect our environment and our daily lives. It must enable students to visualize landscape and understand the complex natural and human interrelationships which are the basis of regional, national and world problems. It must provide data for effective comparison of our own country and society with that of others in the world and between rich, poor and developing nations.

Philips' Certificate Atlas attempts to fulfil these aims by including topographic maps at various scales and on various projections, thematic maps, tables of statistics, diagrams, cross-sections, graphs, satellite, air and land photographs and an index. Every attempt has also been made to include up-to-date information, otherwise difficult to obtain by hard-pressed teachers and students, and to keep pace with the present-day greater rate of change of economies and societies.

The content is arranged with the world scene as the opening chapter followed by continental and regional studies.

Because many of the decisions which vitally affect our daily lives are taken at state government level, the world chapter starts with summary tables of the principal countries and cities of the world giving their areas and populations. Thematic maps, diagrams and graphs provide an overall view of the composition of the earth, and its surrounding atmosphere, its topography and climate, leading to a series of maps and graphics of spatial patterns of water and food resources, minerals and power resources, population and political organizations.

As befits an atlas intended for U.K. schools, there is emphasis on Great Britain and Ireland with thematic maps of the topography, geology, climate, land use, industry, power resources and population distribution. This is not, however, allowed to detract from a proper emphasis on our neighbouring countries in Europe and, in particular, on the E.E.C.

Throughout the regional and continental studies, topographic maps are complemented by thematic maps, diagrams and illustrations, which attempt to epitomise the character and problems of each country or region. For example, in West Germany, the importance of Ruhr industry and the significance of Rhine traffic, regional contrasts in Italy, the phenomenal industrial growth of Japan, the primary products of Australia and New Zealand, the economic production of North America.

Following the map section, there are tables of the production and trade of the principal countries and climatic statistics for representative stations throughout the world. A list of geographical terms precedes the index which gives the latitude and longitude co-ordinates for approximately 11 000 names.

H. FULLARD

Contents

Contents

Back Endpapers: The Earth from Space

* *Based upon Ordnance Survey Maps with the permission of Her Majesty's Stationery Office. Crown Copyright Reserved.*

Principal Countries of the World

Country or Dependency	Area in thousands of square km	Population in thousands	Density of population per sq. km.	Capital Population in thousands
Afghanistan	647	16 786	26	Kabul (1036)
Albania	29	2 858	99	Tiranë (198)
Algeria	2 382	20 293	9	Algiers (1 503)
Angola	1 247	7 452	6	Luanda (475)
Anguilla (U.K)	0.09	6	64	The Valley (2)
Antigua & Barbuda	0.44	77	175	St. John's (24)
Argentina	2 767	28 432	10	Buenos Aires (9 927)
Australia	7 687	15 175	2	Canberra (220)
Austria	84	7 571	90	Vienna (1 516)
Bahamas	14	218	16	Nassau (130)
Bahrain	0.62	330	532	Manama (114)
Bangladesh	144	92 619	643	Dhaka (3 459)
Barbados	0.43	269	626	Bridgetown (88)
Belgium	31	9 845	318	Brussels (995)
Belize	23	171	7	Belmopan (3)
Benin	113	3 618	32	Porto-Novo (132)
Bermuda	0.053	55	1 038	Hamilton (3)
Bhutan	47	1 355	29	Thimphu (60)
Bolivia	1 099	5 916	5	Sucre (63) La Paz (635)
Botswana	600	859	1	Gaborone (61)
Brazil	8 512	126 806	15	Brasilia (1 306)
Brunei	6	250	42	Bandar Seri Begawan (58)
Bulgaria	111	9 107	82	Sofia (1 052)
Burma	677	37 065	55	Rangoon (2 276)
Burundi	28	4 460	159	Bujumbura (157)
Cameroon	475	8 865	19	Yaoundé (314)
Canada	9 976	24 625	2	Ottawa (718)
Central African Rep.	623	2 405	4	Bangui (302)
Chad	1.284	4 643	4	Ndjamena (303)
Chile	757	11 487	15	Santiago (3 831)
China	9 597	1 020 673	106	Peking (9 231)
Colombia	1 139	28 776	25	Bogota (2 855)
Congo	342	1 621	5	Brazzaville (422)
Costa Rica	51	2 324	46	San José (265)
Cuba	115	9 782	85	Havana (1 924)
Cyprus	9	645	72	Nicosia (161)
Czechoslovakia	128	15 369	120	Prague (1 184)
Denmark	43	5 118	119	Copenhagen (1 382)
Djibouti	22	332	15	Djibouti (150)
Dominica	0.75	86	115	Roseau (17)
Dominican Republic	49	5 744	117	Santo Domingo (1 103)
Ecuador	284	8 945	31	Quito (844)
Egypt	1 001	44 673	45	Cairo (5 074)
El Salvador	21	4 999	238	San Salvador (366)
Equatorial Guinea	28	381	14	Rey Malabo (37)
Ethiopia	1 222	32 775	27	Addis Abeba (1 277)
Fiji	18	658	37	Suva (68)
Finland	337	4 824	14	Helsinki (483)
France	547	54 221	99	Paris (9 863)
French Guiana	91	64	1	Cayenne (39)
Gabon	268	563	2	Libréville (186)
Gambia	11	635	58	Banjul (109)
Germany, East	108	16 864	156	East Berlin (1 158)
Germany, West	249	61 638	248	Bonn (288)
Ghana	239	12 244	51	Accra (738)
Greece	132	9 793	74	Athens (3 027)
Greenland	2 176	52	0.02	Godthåb (10)
Grenada	0.34	113	332	St. George's (31)
Guadeloupe	1.8	331	184	Basse Terre (15)
Guatemala	109	7 699	71	Guatemala (793)
Guinea	246	5 285	21	Conakry (526)
Guinea-Bissau	36	594	17	Bissau (109)
Guyana	215	922	4	Georgetown (187)
Haiti	28	5 201	186	Port-au-Prince (888)
Honduras	112	3 955	35	Tegucigalpa (473)
Hong Kong	1	5 233	5 233	Hong Kong (1 184)
Hungary	93	10 702	115	Budapest (2 060)
Iceland	103	236	2	Reykjavik (84)
India	3 288	711 664	216	Delhi (5 729)
Indonesia	2 027	153 032	75	Jakarta (4 576)
Iran	1 648	40 240	24	Tehran (4 496)
Iraq	435	13 997	32	Baghdad (2 969)
Ireland	70	3 483	50	Dublin (525)
Israel	21	4 022	192	Jerusalem (407)
Italy	301	56 276	187	Rome (2 831)
Ivory Coast	322	8 568	27	Abidjan (850)
Jamaica	11	2 253	205	Kingston (671)
Japan	372	118 449	318	Tokyo (8 349)
Jordan	98	3 489	36	Amman (649)
Kampuchea	181	6981	39	Phnom Penh (400)
Kenya	583	17 864	31	Nairobi (835)
Korea, North	121	18 747	155	Pyongyang (1 500)
Korea, South	98	39 331	401	Seoul (8 367)
Kuwait	18	1 562	87	Kuwait (775)
Laos	237	3 902	16	Vientiane (90)
Lebanon	10	2 739	274	Beirut (702)
Lesotho	30	1 409	47	Maseru (45)
Liberia	111	2 113	19	Monrovia (204)
Libya	1 760	3 224	2	Tripoli (551)
Luxembourg	3	357	119	Luxembourg (79)
Madagascar	587	9 233	16	Antananarivo (400)
Malawi	118	6 267	53	Lilongwe (103)
Malaysia	330	14 765	45	Kuala Lumpur (938)
Mali	1 240	7 342	6	Bamako (419)
Malta	0.3	360	1 200	Valletta (14)
Martinique	1.1	326	296	Fort-de-France (99)
Mauritania	1 031	1 730	2	Nouakchott (135)
Mauritius	2	983	492	Port Louis (146)
Mexico	1 973	73 011	37	Mexico (14 750)
Mongolia	1 565	1 764	1	Ulan Bator (419)
Monserrat	0.098	12	122	Plymouth (3)
Morocco	447	21 667	48	Rabat (597)
Mozambique	783	11 052	14	Maputo (384)
Namibia	824	852	1	Windhoek (61)
Nepal	141	15 020	107	Katmandu (210)
Netherlands	41	14 310	349	Amsterdam (936)
Netherlands Antilles	0.96	267	278	Willemstad (146)
New Zealand	269	3 158	12	Wellington (321)
Nicaragua	130	2 918	22	Managua (608)
Niger	1 267	5 646	4	Niamey (130)
Nigeria	924	82 392	89	Lagos (1 477)
Norway	324	4 115	13	Oslo (624)
Oman	212	948	4	Muscat (25)
Pakistan	804	87 125	108	Islamabad (77)
Panama	76	2 043	27	Panama (655)
Papua New Guinea	462	3 094	7	Port Moresby (123)
Paraguay	407	3 370	8	Asunción (602)
Peru	1 285	18 790	15	Lima (4 601)
Philippines	300	50 740	169	Manila (1 479)
Poland	313	36 227	116	Warsaw (1 612)
Portugal	92	10 056	109	Lisbon (818)
Puerto Rico	9	3 952	439	San Juan (1 086)
Qatar	11	248	23	Doha (130)
Reunion	2.5	503	201	St-Deris (104)
Romania	238	22 638	95	Bucharest (2 090)
Rwanda	26	5 276	203	Kigali (90)
St. Kitts-Nevis	0.26	44	168	Basseterre (15)
St. Lucia	0.62	122	197	Castries (45)
St. Vincent	0.39	99	254	Kingstown (23)
Saudi Arabia	2 150	9 684	5	Riyadh (667)
Senegal	196	5 968	30	Dakar (799)
Sierra Leone	72	3 672	51	Freetown (214)
Singapore	0.6	2 472	4 120	Singapore (2 443)
Somali Republic	638	5 116	8	Mogadishu (400)
South Africa	1 221	31 008	25	Pretoria (563) Cape Town (1 107)
Spain	505	37 935	75	Madrid (3 159)
Sri Lanka	66	15 189	230	Colombo (1 412)
Sudan	2 506	19 451	8	Khartoum (561)
Suriname	163	407	2	Paramaribo (151)
Swaziland	17	585	34	Mbabane (23)
Sweden	450	8 325	19	Stockholm (1 387)
Switzerland	41	6 478	158	Berne (289)
Syria	185	9 660	52	Damascus (1 156)
Taiwan	36	18 458	513	Taipei (2 271)
Tanzania	945	19 111	20	Dar-es-Salaam (757)
Thailand	514	48 450	94	Bangkok (4 871)
Togo	56	2 747	49	Lomé (247)
Trinidad and Tobago	5	1 202	240	Port of Spain (66)
Tunisia	164	6 672	41	Tunis (944)
Turkey	781	46 312	59	Ankara (2 204)
Uganda	236	14 057	60	Kampala (332)
United Arab Emirates	84	790	9	Abu Dhabi (449)
U.S.S.R.	22 402	269 994	12	Moscow (8 203)
United Kingdom	245	55 782	228	London (6 696)
United States	9 363	232 057	25	Washington (3 061)
Upper Volta	274	6 360	23	Ouagadougou (173)
Uruguay	178	2 947	17	Montevideo (1 173)
Venezuela	912	14 714	16	Caracas (2 849)
Vietnam	330	56 205	170	Hanoi (2 571)
Virgin Is.	0.34	116	341	Charlotte Amalie (12)
Western Samoa	3	159	53	Apia (32)
Yemen, North	195	6 077	31	Sana (448)
Yemen, South	288	2 093	7	Aden (285)
Yugoslavia	256	22 646	88	Belgrade (775)
Zaïre	2 345	26 377	11	Kinshasa (2 242)
Zambia	753	6 163	8	Lusaka (641)
Zimbabwe	391	7 540	19	Harare (686)

Principal Cities of the World

The population figures used are from censuses or more recent estimates and are given in thousands for towns and cities over 500 000. Where possible the population of the metropolitan areas is given e.g. Greater London, Greater New York, etc.

AFRICA

ALGERIA (1974)
Algiers 1 503

EGYPT (1976)
Cairo 5 074
Alexandria 2 314
El Giza 1 230

ETHIOPIA (1980)
Addis Abeba 1 277

GUINEA (1972)
Conakry 526

IVORY COAST (1976)
Abidjan 850

LIBYA (1973)
Tripoli 551

MOROCCO (1973)
Casablanca 1 753
Rabat-Salé 596

NIGERIA (1975)
Lagos 1 477
Ibadan 847

SENEGAL (1976)
Dakar 799

SOUTH AFRICA (1970)
Johannesburg 1 441
Cape Town 698
Durban 737
Pretoria 545

TANZANIA (1978)
Dar-es-Salaam ... 757

TUNISIA (1976)
Tunis 944

ZAIRE (1975)
Kinshasa 2 242

ZAMBIA (1980)
Lusaka 641

ZIMBABWE (1981)
Harare 686

ASIA

AFGHANISTAN (1979)
Kabul 1 036

BANGLADESH (1982)
Dhaka 3 459
Chittagong 1 388
Khulna 623

BURMA (1977)
Rangoon 2 276

CHINA (1970)
Shanghai (1982) .. 11 860
Peking (1982) 9 231
Tientsin (1982) ... 7 746
Shenyang 2 800
Wuhan 2 560
Canton 2 400
Chungking 2 400
Nanking 1 750
Harbin 1 670
Luta 1 650
Sian 1 600
Lanchow 1 450
Taiyuan 1 350
Tsingtao 1 300
Chengtu 1 250
Changchun 1 200
Kunming 1 100
Tsinan 1 100
Fushun 1 080
Anshan 1 050
Chengchow 1 050
Hangchow 960
Tangshan 950
Paotow 920
Tzepo 850
Changsha 825
Shihkiachwang ... 800
Tsitsihar 760
Soochow 730
Kirin 720
Suchow 700
Foochow 680
Nanchang 675
Kweiyang 660

Wusih 650
Hofei 630
Hwainan 600
Penki 600
Loyang 580
Nanning 550
Huhehot 530
Sining 500
Wulumuchi 500

HONG KONG (1981)
Kowloon 2 450
Hong Kong 1 184
Tsuen Wan 599

INDIA (1981)
Calcutta 9 194
Bombay 8 243
Delhi 5 729
Madras 4 289
Bangalore 2 922
Ahmadabad 2 548
Hyderabad 2 546
Pune 1 686
Kanpur 1 639
Nagpur 1 302
Jaipur 1 015
Lucknow 1 008
Coimbatore 920
Patna 919
Surat 914
Madurai 908
Indore 829
Varanasi 797
Jabalpur 757
Agra 747
Vadodara 744
Cochin 686
Dhanbad 678
Bhopal 671
Jamshedpur 670
Allahabad 650
Ulhasnagar 649
Tiruchchirapalli .. 610
Ludhiana 606
Srinagar 606
Vishakhapatnam . 604
Amritsar 595
Gwalior 556
Calicut 546
Vijawada 543
Meerut 537
Dharwad 527
Trivandrum 520
Salem 519
Solapur 515
Jodhpur 506
Ranchi 503

INDONESIA (1971)
Jakarta 4 576
Surabaya 1 556
Bandung 1 202
Semarang 647
Medan 636
Palembang 583

IRAN (1976)
Tehran 4 496
Esfahan 672
Mashhad 670
Tabriz 599

IRAQ (1970)
Baghdad 2 969

ISRAEL (1981)
Tel Aviv-Jaffa ... 335

JAPAN (1980)
Tokyo 8 349
Yokohama 2 774
Osaka 2 648
Nagoya 2 088
Kyoto 1 473
Sapporo 1 402
Kobe 1 367
Fukuoka 1 089
Kitakyushu 1 065
Kawasaki 1 041
Hiroshima 899
Sakai 810
Chiba 746
Sendai 665
Okayama 546
Kumamoto 526

KAMPUCHEA (1981)
Phnom Penh 400

KUWAIT (1975)
Kuwait 775

LEBANON (1980)
Beirut 702

PAKISTAN (1972)
Karachi 3 499
Lahore 2 165
Faisalabad 822
Hyderabad 628
Rawalpindi 615
Multan 542

PHILIPPINES (1975)
Manila 1 479
Quezon City 957

SAUDI ARABIA (1974)
Riyadh 667
Jedda 561

SINGAPORE (1981)
Singapore 2 443

SRI LANKA (1981)
Colombo 1 412

SYRIA (1979)
Damascus 1 156
Aleppo 919

TAIWAN (1981)
Taipei 2 271
Kaohsiung 1 227
Taichung 607
Tainan 595

THAILAND (1979)
Bangkok 4 871

TURKEY (1980)
Istanbul 2 854
Ankara 2 204
Izmir 754
Adana 569

VIETNAM (1973-79)
Ho Chi Minh City .. 3 420
Hanoi 2 571
Haiphong 1 279

AUSTRALASIA

AUSTRALIA (1981)
Sydney 3 205
Melbourne 2 723
Brisbane 1 029
Adelaide 932
Perth 899

NEW ZEALAND (1981)
Auckland 770

EUROPE

AUSTRIA (1981)
Vienna 1 516

BELGIUM (1983)
Brussels 989

BULGARIA (1980)
Sofia 1 052

CZECHOSLOVAKIA (1982)
Prague 1 184

DENMARK (1981)
Copenhagen 1 382

FINLAND (1979)
Helsinki 893

FRANCE (1975)
Paris 9 863
Lyon 1 152
Marseille 1 004
Lille 929
Bordeaux 591

GERMANY, EAST (1981)
East Berlin 1 158
Leipzig 562
Dresden 517

GERMANY, WEST (1980)
West Berlin 1 896
Hamburg 1 645
München 1 299
Cologne 977
Essen 648
Frankfurt am Main ... 629

Dortmund 608
Düsseldorf 590
Stuttgart 581
Duisburg 558
Bremen 555
Hannover 535

GREECE (1981)
Athens 3 027
Thessaloniki ... 707

HUNGARY (1980)
Budapest 2 060

IRISH REPUBLIC (1981)
Dublin 525

ITALY (1981)
Rome 2 831
Milano 1 635
Napoli 1 211
Torino 1 104
Genova 760
Palermo 700

NETHERLANDS (1983)
Rotterdam 1 025
Amsterdam 936
s'Gravenhage ... 674

NORWAY (1980)
Oslo 624

POLAND (1981)
Warsaw 1 612
Lódz 843
Kraków 723
Wroclaw 622
Poznań 558

PORTUGAL (1981)
Lisbon 818
Oporto 330

ROMANIA (1980)
Bucharest 2 090

SPAIN (1981)
Madrid 3 159
Barcelona 1 753
Valencia 745
Sevilla 646
Zaragoza 572
Malaga 502

SWEDEN (1980)
Stockholm 1 387
Göteborg 693

SWITZERLAND (1982)
Zürich 705

U.S.S.R. (1981)
Moskva 8 203
Leningrad 4 676
Kiyev 2 248
Tashkent 1 858
Kharkov 1 485
Gorkiy 1 367
Novosibirsk ... 1 343
Minsk 1 333
Sverdlovsk 1 239
Kuybyshev 1 238
Dnepropetrovsk . 1 100
Tbilisi 1 095
Odessa 1 072
Chelyabinsk ... 1 055
Yerevan 1 055
Baku 1 046
Omsk 1 044
Donetsk 1 040
Perm 1 018
Kazan 1 011
Ufa 1 009
Alma-Ata 975
Rostov 957
Volgograd 948
Saratov 873
Riga 850
Krasnoyarsk ... 820
Zaporozhye ... 812
Voronezh 809
Lvov 688
Krivoy Rog ... 663
Yaroslavl 608
Karaganda 583
Krasnodar 581
Novokuznetsk . 581
Izhevsk 574
Irkutsk 568

Vladivostok ... 565
Frunze 552
Barnaul 549
Khabarovsk ... 545
Kishinev 539
Togliatti 533
Tula 521
Zhdanov 511
Dushanbe 510
Vilnius 503
Penza 500

UNITED KINGDOM (1981)
London 6 696
Birmingham ... 920
Glasgow 762
Liverpool 510

YUGOSLAVIA (1971)
Belgrade 775
Zagreb 602

NORTH AMERICA

CANADA (1981)
Toronto 2 999
Montréal 2 828
Vancouver 1 268
Ottawa 718
Edmonton 657
Calgary 593
Winnipeg 585
Québec 576
Hamilton 542

COSTA RICA (1978)
San José 563

CUBA (1981)
Havana 1 924

DOMINICAN REPUBLIC (1978)
Santo Domingo ... 1 103

GUATEMALA (1979)
Guatemala City ... 793

HAITI (1982)
Port-au-Prince ... 888

JAMAICA (1980)
Kingston 671

MEXICO (1979)
Mexico City ... 14 750
Guadalajara ... 2 468
Netzahualcóyotl .. 2 331
Monterrey 2 019
Puebla de Zaragoza . 711
Ciudad Juárez .. 625
León de los Aldamas . 625

NICARAGUA (1979)
Managua 608

PANAMA (1981)
Panama 655

PUERTO RICO (1980)
San Juan 1 086

UNITED STATES OF AMERICA (1980)
New York 16 121
Los Angeles ... 11 498
Chicago 7 870
Philadelphia ... 5 548
San Francisco .. 5 180
Detroit 4 618
Boston 3 448
Houston 3 101
Washington ... 3 061
Dallas 2 975
Cleveland 2 834
Miami 2 644
St. Louis 2 356
Pittsburgh 2 264
Baltimore 2 174
Minneapolis-St Paul 2 114
Seattle 2 093
Atlanta 2 030
San Diego 1 817
Cincinnati 1 660
Denver 1 621
Milwaukee 1 570
Tampa 1 569
Phoenix 1 509

Kansas City ... 1 327
Indianapolis ... 1 306
Portland (Oreg.) .. 1 243
Buffalo 1 243
New Orleans .. 1 187
Providence ... 1 096
Columbus (Ohio) . 1 093
San Antonio ... 1 072
Sacramento ... 1 014
Dayton 1 014
Rochester 971
Salt Lake City .. 936
Memphis 913
Louisville 906
Nashville 851
Birmingham ... 847
Oklahoma 834
Greensboro ... 827
Norfolk 807
Albany (N.Y.) .. 795
Toledo 792
Honolulu 763
Jacksonville (Fla.) . 738
Hartford 726
Orlando 700
Tulsa 689
Syracuse 643
Scranton 640
Charlotte 637
Allentown 635
Richmond 632
Grand Rapids .. 602
Omaha 570
Greenville 569
West Palm Beach . 577
Austin 537
Tucson 531
Springfield (Mass.) . 531
Youngstown ... 531
Raleigh 531
Flint 522
Fresno 515

SOUTH AMERICA

ARGENTINA (1980)
Buenos Aires ... 9 927
Córdoba 982
Rosario 955
Mendoza 597
La Plata 560

BOLIVIA (1970)
La Paz 720

BRAZIL (1980)
São Paulo 8 732
Rio de Janeiro .. 5 539
Belo Horizonte . 1 937
Salvador 1 502
Recife 1 433
Fortaleza 1 307
Brasilia 1 306
Pôrto Alegre .. 1 221
Nova Iguaçu .. 1 184
Curitiba 943
Belém 934
Goiânia 680
Duque de Caxias .. 666
São Gonçalo .. 660
Santo André .. 634
Campinas 587

CHILE (1982)
Santiago 3 831

COLOMBIA (1973)
Bogotá 2 855
Medellin 1 159
Cali 990
Barranquilla ... 692

ECUADOR (1981)
Guayaquil 1 169
Quito 844

PARAGUAY (1978)
Asunción 602

PERU (1981)
Lima 4 601

URUGUAY (1975)
Montevideo ... 1 173

VENEZUELA (1979)
Caracas 2 849
Maracaibo 874

Map Projections

As the Earth is spherical in shape, it cannot be represented on a plane surface without some distortion. The map projection is a system for attempting to represent the sphere on a two-dimensional plane. A projection has certain properties: the representation of correct area, true shape or true bearings. The preservation of one property can only be secured at the expense of the other qualities.

Azimuthal

Cylindrical

Conical

An Azimuthal projection is constructed by the projection of part of the globe onto a plane tangential to a pole, the equator, or any other single point on the globe. The zenithal gnomonic projection shown below (A), has a plane touching the pole. It is ideal for showing polar air-routes because the shortest distance between any two points is a straight line. Air-route distances from one point (e.g. Capetown) are best shown by the Oblique Zenithal Equidistant (B).

Cylindrical projections are constructed by projecting a portion of the globe onto a cylinder tangential to the globe. The cylinder may be tangential to the equator. The tangential line is the only one true to scale, with distortion of size and shape increasing towards the top and bottom of the cylinder. The Mercator projection below (A) is a modification of a cylindrical projection. It avoids distortion of shape by making an increase in scale along the parallels. There is still size distortion, but its great use is for navigation since bearings can be plotted as straight lines. The Mollweide projection (B) is a 'conventional' cylindrical projection on which the meridians are no longer parallel. This is an equal area projection, useful for mapping distributions. In this case, it has been 'interrupted'.

Conical projections use the projection of the globe onto a cone which is tangential to a parallel (or any other small circle) on the globe. The scale is correct along this tangential line and can be made to be correct along the parallel or the meridians. In the simple conic (A) below, the scale is correct along the parallel indicated and the meridians. Bonnes projection (B) is equal area, the parallels being correctly divided, although there is shape distortion, especially at the edges.

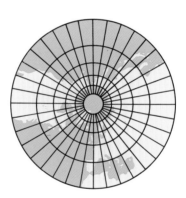

(A) Zenithal Gnomonic

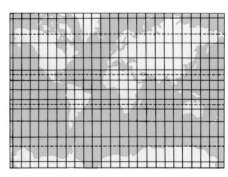

(A) Mercator

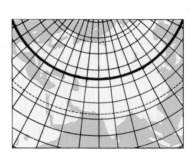

(A) Simple Conic

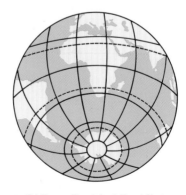

(B) Oblique Zenithal Equidistant

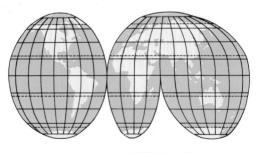

(B) Interrupted Mollweide

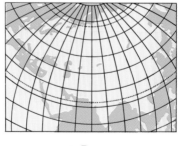

(B) Bonne

Many projections can be obtained if the surface onto which the graticule is developed cuts the sphere, rather than being tangential to it. These Projections, called secant, can reduce distortion.
The choice of map projection depends largely on the property required — correct area, scale, shape or bearings.
The area and location to be covered is also important. Conical projections cannot cover the entire globe and are most suited for temperate areas of large longitudinal extent. Azimuthal projections are best for larger scale maps of small areas so that distortion around the edges is not too great. Cylindrical projections are best to map the whole world.

KEY TO SYMBOLS

These are the symbols used in the general maps in the atlas. The thematic symbols are explained in a key alongside each map and an attempt has been made to keep them consistent throughout the atlas.

Settlement

⬡ **BERLIN**   ⬡ DETROIT   ■ Fukuoka   ⬤ Rosario   ⊙ Gaza   ⊚ Kananga   ⊙ Berhampur   ○ Laurel   ○ Riverton

⬟ **BIRMINGHAM**   ▣ **Derby**   ⊙ **Swansea**   ○ Greenock   ○ Herne Bay   ○ Minehead

The settlement symbols and their related type are decided upon by the population of the town or city for each area mapped. These limits vary from one map to another so the population size for each group is not given in this table.

Administration

———————— International Boundaries

– – – – – – – International Boundaries
(Undemarcated or undefined)

— — — — — Internal Boundaries

∴ Sites of Archaeological or Historical Importance

⬚ National Parks

International boundaries are drawn to show the 'de facto' situation where there are rival claims to territory.

Communications

——M4—— Motorways

– – – – – – Motorways under construction

———————— Principal roads

– – – – – – – Tracks, seasonal and other roads

⊣– – – –⊢ Road tunnels

———————— Principal railways

———————— Other railways

· · · · · · · · · · Railways under construction

⊣– – – –⊢ Railway tunnels

⤳‿⤸ Passes

· · ·+· · · Principal canals

·—+—+—· Principal oil pipelines

✿ ✈ Principal airports

Hydrology

〜 Perennial streams

〜 Seasonal streams

┣━ Dams

🞄 Perennial lakes

🞄 Seasonal lakes

🌿🌿🌿🌿 Swamps and marshes

❄ Permanent ice

˅ Wells in desert

Relief

The coloured height reference is repeated on the edge of the page.

▲ 4507 Height above sea level in metres   ▼ 1710 Depth below sea level in metres   *1134* Height of lakes

Abbreviations of measures used;   mm { Millimetres ; Millimeters   m { Metres ; Meters   km { Kilometres ; Kilometers   mb Millibars ;   tons Metric Tonnes ;   M.S.L. Mean Sea Level

The origin of the earth is still open to much conjecture although the most widely accepted theory is that it was formed from a solar cloud consisting mainly of hydrogen. Under gravitation the cloud condensed and shrank to form our planets orbiting around the sun. Gravitation forced the lighter elements to the surface of the earth where they cooled to form a crust while the inner material remained hot and molten. Earth's first rocks formed over 3 500 million years ago but since then the surface has been constantly altered.

Until comparatively recently the view that the primary units of the earth had remained essentially fixed throughout geological time was regarded as common sense, although the concept of moving continents has been traced back to references in the Bible of a break up of the land after Noah's floods. The continental drift theory was first developed by Antonio Snider in 1858 but probably the most important single advocate was Alfred Wegener who, in 1915, published evidence from geology, climatology and biology. His conclusions are very similar to those reached by current research although he was wrong about the speed of break-up.

The measurement of fossil magnetism found in rocks has probably proved the most influential evidence. While originally these drift theories were openly mocked, now they are considered standard doctrine.

The jigsaw
As knowledge of the shape and structure of the earth's surface grew, several of the early geographers noticed the great similarity in shape of the coasts bordering the Atlantic. It was this remarkable similarity which led to the first detailed geological and structural comparisons. Even more accurate fits can be made by placing the edges of the continental shelves in juxtaposition.

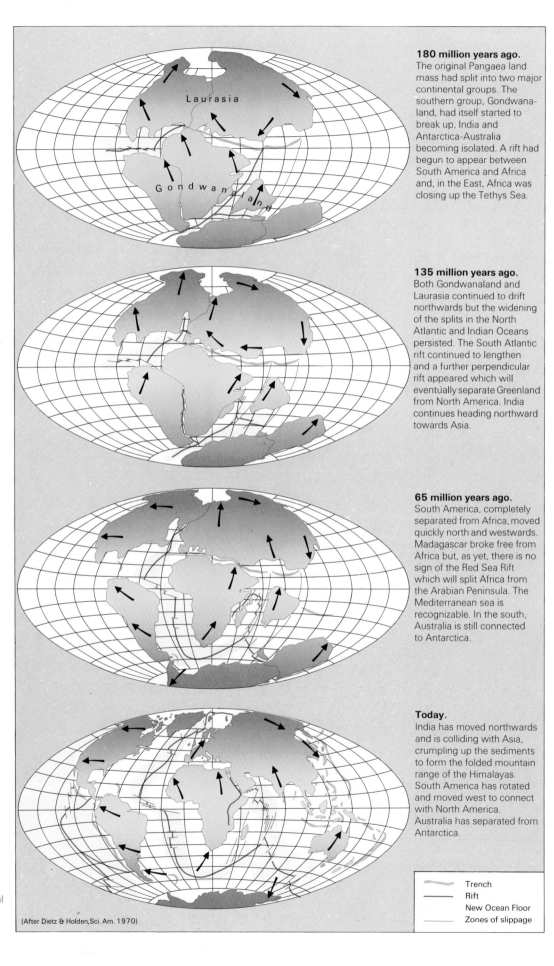

180 million years ago.
The original Pangaea land mass had split into two major continental groups. The southern group, Gondwana-land, had itself started to break up, India and Antarctica-Australia becoming isolated. A rift had begun to appear between South America and Africa and, in the East, Africa was closing up the Tethys Sea.

135 million years ago.
Both Gondwanaland and Laurasia continued to drift northwards but the widening of the splits in the North Atlantic and Indian Oceans persisted. The South Atlantic rift continued to lengthen and a further perpendicular rift appeared which will eventually separate Greenland from North America. India continues heading northward towards Asia.

65 million years ago.
South America, completely separated from Africa, moved quickly north and westwards. Madagascar broke free from Africa but, as yet, there is no sign of the Red Sea Rift which will split Africa from the Arabian Peninsula. The Mediterranean sea is recognizable. In the south, Australia is still connected to Antarctica.

Today.
India has moved northwards and is colliding with Asia, crumpling up the sediments to form the folded mountain range of the Himalayas. South America has rotated and moved west to connect with North America. Australia has separated from Antarctica.

(After Dietz & Holden, Sci. Am. 1970)

	Trench
	Rift
	New Ocean Floor
	Zones of slippage

Plate tectonics

The original debate about continental drift was only a prelude to a more radical idea; plate tectonics. The basic theory is that the earth's crust is made up of a series of rigid plates which float on a soft layer of the mantle and are moved about by convection currents in the earth's interior. These plates converge and diverge along margins marked by earthquakes, volcanoes and other seismic activity. Plates diverge from mid-ocean ridges where molten lava pushes upwards and forces the plates apart at a rate of up to 30 mm a year. Converging plates form either a trench, where the oceanic plate sinks below the lighter continental rock, or mountain ranges where two continents collide. This explains the paradox that while there have always been oceans none of the present oceans contain sediments more than 150 million years old.

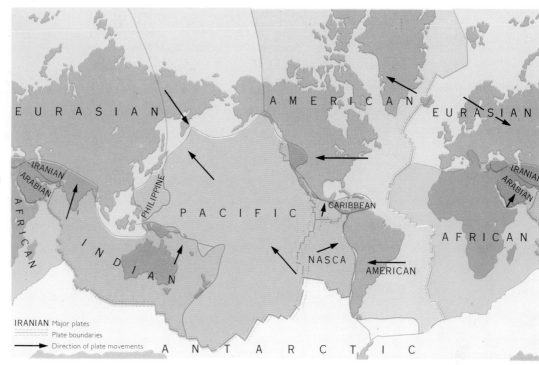

IRANIAN Major plates
Plate boundaries
→ Direction of plate movements

Trench boundary

The present explanation for the comparative youth of the ocean floors is that where an ocean and a continent meet the ocean plate, dips under the less dense continental plate at an angle of approximately 45°. All previous crust is then ingested by downward convection currents. In the Japanese trench this occurs at a rate of about 120 mm a year.

Transform fault

The recent identification of the transform, or transverse, fault proved to be one of the crucial preliminaries to the investigation of plate tectonics. They occur when two plates slip alongside each other without parting or approaching to any great extent. They complete the outline of the plates delineated by the ridges and trenches and demonstrate large scale movements of parts of the earth's surface

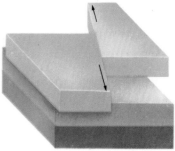

Ridge boundary

Ocean rises or crests are basically made up from basaltic lavas for although no gap can exist between plates, one plate can ease itself away from another. In that case hot, molten rock instantly rises from below to fill in the incipient rift and forms a ridge. These ridges trace a line almost exactly through the centre of the major oceans.

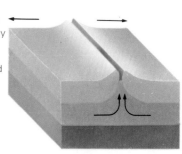

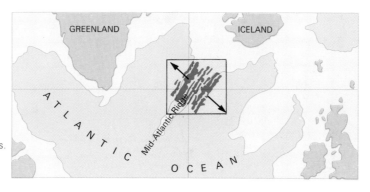

Destruction of ocean plates.

As the ocean plate sinks below the continental plate some of the sediment on its surface is scraped off and piled up on the landward side. This sediment is later incorporated in a folded mountain range which usually appears on the edge of the continent, such as the Andes. Similarly if two continents collide the sediments are squeezed up into new mountains.

Sea floor spreading

Reversals in the earth's magnetic field have occured throughout history. As new rock emerges at the ocean ridges it cools and is magnetised in the direction of the prevailing magnetic field. By mapping the magnetic patterns either side of the ridge a symmetrical stripey pattern of alternating fields can be observed (see inset area in diagram). As the dates of the last few reversals are known the rate of spreading can be calculated.

The earth's surface is slowly but continually being rearranged. Some changes such as erosion and deposition are extremely slow but they upset the balance which causes other more abrupt changes often originating deep within the earth's interior. The constant movements vary in intensity, often with stresses building up to a climax such as a particularly violent volcanic eruption or earthquake.

The crust (below and right)
The outer layer or crust of the earth consists of a comparatively low density, brittle material varying from 5 km to 50 km deep beneath the continents. This consists predominately of silica and aluminium; hence it is called 'sial'. Extending under the ocean floors and below the sial is a basaltic layer known as 'sima', consisting mainly of silica and magnesium.

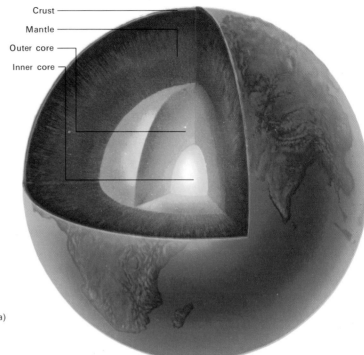

Crust
Mantle
Outer core
Inner core

Continental crust   Ocean crust

Sediment
Granite rock (sial)
Basaltic layer (sima)
Mantle

Volcanoes (right, below and far right)
Volcanoes occur when hot liquefied rock beneath the crust reaches the surface as lava. An accumulation of ash and cinders around a vent forms a cone. Successive layers of thin lava flows form an acid lava volcano while thick lava flows form a basic lava volcano. A caldera forms when a particularly violent eruption blows off the top of an already existing cone.

The mantle (above)
Immediately below the crust, at the mohorovicic discontinuity line, there is a distinct change in density and chemical properties. This is the mantle - made up of iron and magnesium silicates - with temperatures reaching 1 600 °C. The rigid upper mantle extends down to a depth of about 1 000 km below which is the more viscous lower mantle which is about 1 900 km thick.

The core (above)
The outer core, approximately 2 100 km thick, consists of molten iron and nickel at 2 000 °C to 5 000 °C possibly separated from the less dense mantle by an oxidised shell. About 5 000 km below the surface is the liquid transition zone, below which is the solid inner core, a sphere of 2 740 km diameter where rock is three times as dense as in the crust.

Shield volcano   Cinder cone   Hornit cone   Caldera

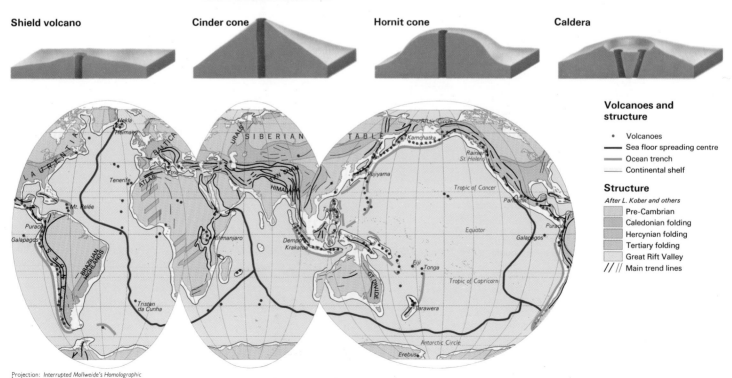

Volcanoes and structure

- Volcanoes
— Sea floor spreading centre
▬ Ocean trench
— Continental shelf

Structure
After L. Kober and others

Pre-Cambrian
Caledonian folding
Hercynian folding
Tertiary folding
Great Rift Valley
/// // Main trend lines

Projection: Interrupted Mollweide's Homolographic

Major earthquakes in the last 100 years and numbers killed

Year	Location	Killed
1896	Japan (tsunami)	22 000
1906	San Francisco	destroyed
1906	Chile, Valparaiso	22 000
1908	Italy, Messina	77 000
1920	China, Kansu	180 000
1923	Japan, Tokyo	143 000
1930	Italy, Naples	2 100
1931	New Zealand, Napier	destroyed
1931	Nicaragua, Managua	destroyed
1932	China, Kansu	70 000
1935	India, Quetta	60 000
1939	Chile, Chillan	20 000
1939/40	Turkey, Erzincan	30 000
1948	Japan, Fukui	5 100
1956	N. Afghanistan	2 000
1957	W. Iran	10 000
1960	Morocco, Agadir	12 000
1962	N.W. Iran	10 000
1963	Yugoslavia, Skopje	1 000
1966	U.S.S.R., Tashkent	destroyed
1970	N. Peru	66 800
1972	Nicaragua, Managua	7 000
1974	N. Pakistan	10 000
1976	China, Tangshan	650 000
1978	Iran, Tabas	11 000
1980	Algeria, El Asnam	20 000

World distribution of earthquakes

- Major earthquake zones
- Areas experiencing frequent earthquakes

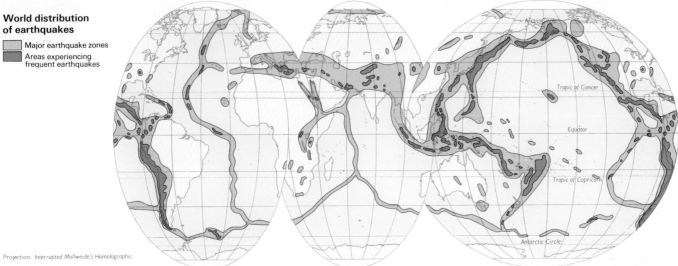

Projection: Interrupted Mollweide's Homolographic

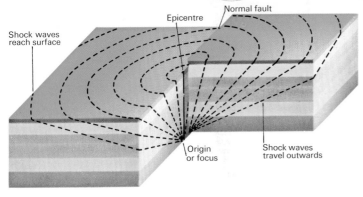

Earthquakes (right and above)
Earthquakes are a series of rapid vibrations originating from the slipping or faulting of parts of the earth's crust when stresses within build up to breaking point. They usually happen at depths varying from 8 km to 30 km. Severe earthquakes cause extensive damage when they take place in populated areas destroying structures and severing communications. Most loss of life occurs due to secondary causes i.e. falling masonry, fires or tsunami waves.

Alaskan earthquake, 1964

Seismic Waves (right)
The shock waves sent out from the focus of an earthquake are of three main kinds each with distinct properties. Primary (P) waves are compressional waves which can be transmitted through both solids and liquids and therefore pass through the earth's liquid core. Secondary (S) waves are shear waves and can only pass through solids. They cannot pass through the core and are reflected at the core-mantle boundary taking a concave course back to the surface. The core also refracts the P waves causing them to alter course, and the net effect of this reflection and refraction is the production of a shadow zone at a certain distance from the epicentre, free from P and S waves. Due to their different properties P waves travel about 1,7 times faster than S waves. The third main kind of wave is a long (L) wave, a slow wave which travels along the earth's surface, its motion being either horizontal or vertical.

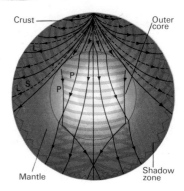

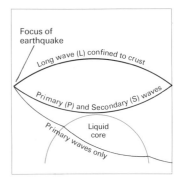

Tsunami waves (left)
A sudden slump in the ocean bed during an earthquake forms a trough in the water surface subsequently followed by a crest and smaller waves. A more marked change of level in the sea bed can form a crest, the start of a Tsunami which travels up to 60 km/h with waves up to 60 m high. Seismographic detectors continuously record earthquake shocks and warn of the Tsunami which may follow it.

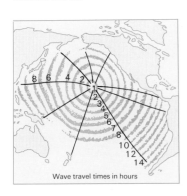

Wave travel times in hours

Principles of seismographs (left)
M = Mass
D = Drum
P = Pivot
S = Spring

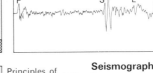

Seismographs
are delicate instruments capable of detecting and recording vibrations due to earthquakes thousands of kilometres away. P waves cause the first tremors. S the second, and L the main shock.

Its surface

Highest point on the earth's surface: Mt. Everest, Tibet-Nepal boundary 8 848 m

Lowest point on the earth's surface: The Dead Sea, Jordan below sea level 395 m

Greatest ocean depth, Challenger Deep, Mariana Trench 11 022 m

Average height of land 840 m

Average depth of seas and oceans 3 808 m

Dimensions

Superficial area	510 000 000 km²
Land surface	149 000 000 km²
Land surface as % of total area	29,2 %
Water surface	361 000 000 km²
Water surface as % of total area	70,8 %
Equatorial circumference	40 077 km
Meridional circumference	40 009 km
Equatorial diameter	12 756,8 km
Polar diameter	12 713,8 km
Equatorial radius	6 378,4 km
Polar radius	6 356,9 km
Volume of the Earth	1 083 230 x 10⁶ km³
Mass of the Earth	5,9 x 10²¹ tons

The Figure of Earth

An imaginary sea-level surface is considered and called a geoid. By measuring at different places the angles from plumb lines to a fixed star there have been many determinations of the shape of parts of the geoid which is found to be an oblate spheriod with its axis along the axis of rotation of the earth. Observations from satellites have now given a new method of more accurate determinations of the figure of the earth and its local irregularities.

Land and Sea Hemispheres.

About 85% of the total land area is contained in the hemisphere centred on a point between Paris and Brussels.

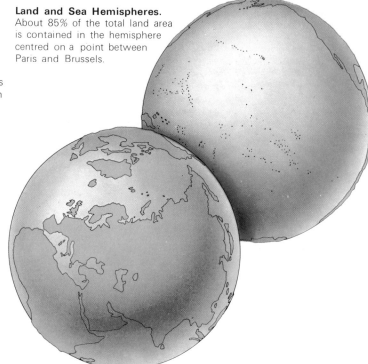

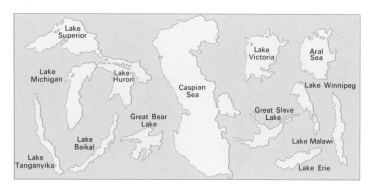

Oceans and Seas
Area in 1000 km²

Pacific Ocean	165 721	North Sea	575
Atlantic Ocean	81 660	Black Sea	448
Indian Ocean	73 442	Red Sea	440
Arctic Ocean	14 351	Baltic Sea	422
Mediterranean Sea	2 966	Persian Gulf	238
Bering Sea	2 274	St. Lawrence, Gulf of	236
Caribbean Sea	1 942	English Channel & Irish Sea	179
Mexico, Gulf of	1 813	California, Gulf of	161
Okhotsk, Sea of	1 528		
East China Sea	1 248		
Hudson Bay	1 230		
Japan, Sea of	1 049		

Lakes and Inland Seas
Areas in 1000 km²

Caspian Sea, Asia	424,2	Lake Ontario, N.America	19,5
Lake Superior, N.America	82,4	Lake Ladoga, Europe	18,4
Lake Victoria, Africa	69,5	Lake Balkhash, Asia	17,3
Aral Sea (Salt), Asia	63,8	Lake Maracaibo, S.America	16,3
Lake Huron, N.America	59,6	Lake Onega, Europe	9,8
Lake Michigan, N.America	58,0	Lake Eyre (Salt), Australia	9,6
Lake Tanganyika, Africa	32,9	Lake Turkana (Salt), Africa	9,1
Lake Baikal, Asia	31,5	Lake Titicaca, S.America	8,3
Great Bear Lake, N.America	31,1	Lake Nicaragua, C.America	8,0
Great Slave Lake, N.America	28,9	Lake Athabasca, N.America	7,9
Lake Malawi, Africa	28,5	Reindeer Lake, N.America	6,3
Lake Erie, N.America	25,7	Issyk-Kul, Asia	6,2
Lake Winnipeg, N.America	24,3	Lake Torrens (Salt), Australia	6,1
Lake Chad, Africa	20,7	Koko Nor (Salt), Asia	6,0
		Lake Urmia, Asia	6,0
		Vänern, Europe	5,6

Longest rivers

	km.
Nile, Africa	6 690
Amazon, S.America	6 280
Mississippi-Missouri, N. America	6 270
Yangtze, Asia	4 990
Zaïre, Africa	4 670
Amur, Asia	4 410
Hwang Ho (Yellow), Asia	4 350
Lena, Asia	4 260
Mekong, Asia	4 180
Niger, Africa	4 180
Mackenzie, N.America	4 040
Ob, Asia	4 000
Yenisey, Asia	3 800

The Highest Mountains and The Greatest Depths

Mount Everest defied the world's greatest mountaineers for many years and in 1953 the first successful attempt was made. The world's highest mountains have now been climbed but there are many as yet unexplored in the Himalaya.

The greatest depths are the ocean trenches representing less than 2% of the total area of the sea-bed. They are of great interest as lines of structural weakness in the earth's crust where earthquakes are frequent.

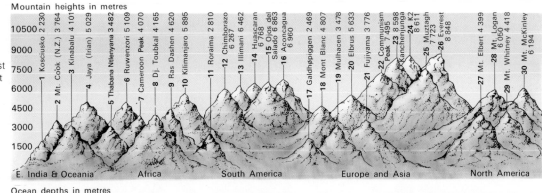

Mountain heights in metres

1 Kosciusko 2 230
2 Mt. Cook (N.Z.) 3 764
3 Kinabalu 4 101
4 Jaya (Irian) 5 029
5 Thabana Ntlenyana 3 482
6 Ruwenzori 5 109
7 Cameroon Peak 4 070
8 Dj. Toubkal 4 165
9 Ras Dashen 4 620
10 Kilimanjaro 5 895
11 Roraima 2 810
12 Chimborazo 6 267
13 Illimani 6 462
14 Huascaran 6 768
15 Ojos del Salado 6 863
16 Aconcagua 6 960
17 Galdhøppigen 2 469
18 Mont Blanc 4 807
19 Mulhacen 3 478
20 Elbrus 5 633
21 Fujiyama 3 776
22 Communism Peak 7 495
23 Kanchenjunga 8 598
24 K2 8 611
25 Muztagh 7 723
26 Everest 8 848
27 Mt. Elbert 4 399
28 Mt. Logan 6 050
29 Mt. Whitney 4 418
30 Mt. McKinley 6 194

E. India & Oceania   Africa   South America   Europe and Asia   North America

Ocean depths in metres

Sea level

31 Mauritius basin 6 400
32 W. Australian basin 6 459
33 Java trench 7 450
34 Mindanao trench 10 497
35 Mariana trench 11 022
36 Japan trench 10 554
37 Bougainville deep 9 140
38 Kuril trench 10 542
39 Aleutian trench 7 822
40 Kermadec trench 10 047
41 Tonga trench 10 822
42 Cayman trough 7 680
43 Puerto Rico trough 9 200
44 S. Sandwich trench 8 428
45 Romanche deep 7 758

Indian Ocean   Pacific Ocean   Atlantic Ocean

High mountains in the Himalayas

Waterfall in Iceland

Highest Waterfalls	height in metres
Angel, Venezuela	980
Tugela, South Africa	853
Yosemite, California	738
Mardalsfossen, Norway	655
Sutherland, New Zealand	579
Reichenbach, Switzerland	548
Wollomombi, Australia	518
Ribbon, California	491
Gavarnie, France	422
Tyssefallene, Norway	414
Krimml, Austria	370
King George VI, Guyana	366
Silver Strand, California	356

Highest Dams	height in metres
Africa	
Cabora Bassa, Zambezi R.	168
Akosombo Main Dam, Volta R.	141
Asia	
Nurek, Vakhsh R., U.S.S.R.	317
Bhakra, Sutlej R., India	226
Europe	
Grand Dixence, Switzerland	284
Vajont, Vajont R., Italy	261
America	
Oroville, Feather R.	235
Hoover, Colorado R.	221
Australasia	
Warragamba, N.S.W., Australia	137

Dam in Switzerland

The World: Physical

The numbers on the map refer to the mountains and ocean depths named in the above diagrams

Projection: Hammer Equal Area

Earth's thin coating *(right)*

The atmosphere is a blanket of protective gases around the earth providing insulation against otherwise extreme alternations in temperature. The gravitational pull increases the density nearer the earth's surface so that 80% of the atmospheric mass is in the first 15 km. It is a very thin layer in comparison with the earth's diameter of 12 680 km, like the cellulose coating on a globe.

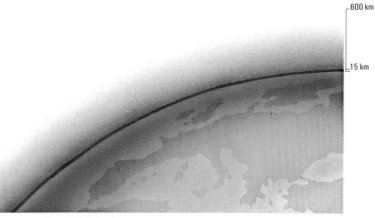

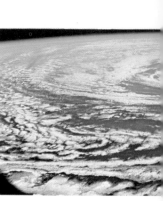

Exosphere*(1)*

The exosphere merges with the interplanetary medium and although there is no definite boundary with the ionosphere it starts at a height of about 600 km. The rarified air mainly consists of a small amount of atomic oxygen up to 600 km and equal proportions of hydrogen and helium with hydrogen predominating above 2 400 km.

Ionosphere*(2)*

Air particles of the ionosphere are electrically charged by the sun's radiation and congregate in four main layers, D, E, F1 and F2, which can reflect radio waves. Aurorae, caused by charged particles deflected by the earth's magnetic field towards the poles, occur between 65 km and 965 km above the earth. It is mainly in the lower ionosphere that meteors from outer space burn up as they meet increased air resistance.

Stratosphere*(3)*

A thin layer of ozone contained within the stratosphere absorbs ultra-violet light and in the process gives off heat. The temperature ranges from about -55°C at the tropopause to about -60°C in the upper part, known as the mesosphere, with a rise to about 2°C just above the ozone layer. This portion of the atmosphere is separated from the lower layer by the tropopause.

Troposphere*(4)*

The earth's weather conditions are limited to this layer which is relatively thin, extending upwards to about 8 km at the poles and 15 km at the equator. It contains about 85% of the total atmospheric mass and almost all the water vapour. Air temperature falls steadily with increased height at about 1°C for every 100 metres above sea level.

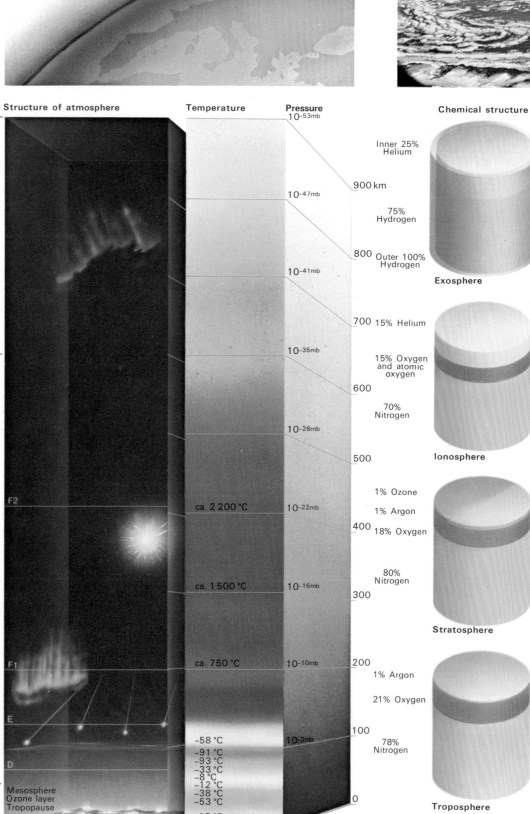

Structure of atmosphere

Temperature

Pressure

Chemical structure

600 km

15 km

10⁻⁵³mb

10⁻⁴⁷mb

10⁻⁴¹mb

10⁻³⁵mb

10⁻²⁸mb

10⁻²²mb

10⁻¹⁶mb

10⁻¹⁰mb

10⁻³mb

10³mb

900 km

800 Outer 100% Hydrogen

700 15% Helium

600

500

400

300

200

100

0

ca. 2 200 °C

ca. 1 500 °C

ca. 750 °C

−58 °C

−91 °C

−93 °C

−33 °C

−8 °C

−12 °C

−38 °C

−53 °C

15 °C

F2

F1

E

D

Mesosphere
Ozone layer
Tropopause

1

2

3

4

Exosphere

Inner 25% Helium

75% Hydrogen

Ionosphere

15% Oxygen and atomic oxygen

70% Nitrogen

Stratosphere

1% Ozone

1% Argon

18% Oxygen

80% Nitrogen

Troposphere

1% Argon

21% Oxygen

78% Nitrogen

Pacific Ocean
Cloud patterns over the Pacific show the paths of prevailing winds.

Circulation of the air

30°N

Equator

30°S

Circulation of the air
Owing to high temperatures in equatorial regions the air near the ground is heated, expands and rises producing a low pressure belt. It cools, causing rain, spreads out then sinks again about latitudes 30° north and south forming high pressure belts.

High and low pressure belts are areas of comparative calm but between them, blowing from high to low pressure, are the prevailing winds. These are deflected to the right in the northern hemisphere and to the left in the southern hemisphere (Coriolis effect). The circulations appear in three distinct belts with a seasonal movement north and south following the overhead sun.

Cloud types

Clouds form when damp air is cooled, usually by rising. This may happen in three ways: when a wind rises to cross hills or mountains; when a mass of air rises over, or is pushed up by another mass of denser air; when local heating of the ground causes convection currents.

Cirrus *(1)* are detached clouds composed of microscopic ice crystals which gleam white in the sun resembling hair or feathers. They are found at heights of 6 000 to 12 000 metres.

Cirrostratus *(2)* are a whitish veil of cloud made up of ice crystals through which the sun can be seen often producing a halo of bright light.

Cirrocumulus *(3)* is another high altitude cloud formed by turbulence between layers moving in different directions.

Altostratus *(4)* is a grey or bluish striated, fibrous or uniform sheet of cloud producing light drizzle.

Altocumulus *(5)* is a thicker and fluffier version of cirro cumulus, it is a white and grey patchy sheet of cloud.

Nimbostratus *(6)* is a dark grey layer of cloud obscuring the sun and causing almost continuous rain or snow.

Cumulus *(7)* are detached heaped up, dense low clouds. The sunlit parts are brilliant white while the base is relatively dark and flat.

Stratus *(8)* forms dull overcast skies associated with depressions and occurs at low altitudes up to 1500 metres.

Cumulonimbus *(9)* are heavy and dense clouds associated with storms and rain. They have flat bases and a fluffy outline extending up to great altitudes.

High clouds

Middle clouds

Low clouds

Thousands of metres

1 Cirrus

2 Cirrostratus

3 Cirrocumulus

4 Altostratus

5 Altocumulus

6 Nimbostratus

7 Cumulus

8 Stratus

9 Cumulonimbus

1:190 000 000

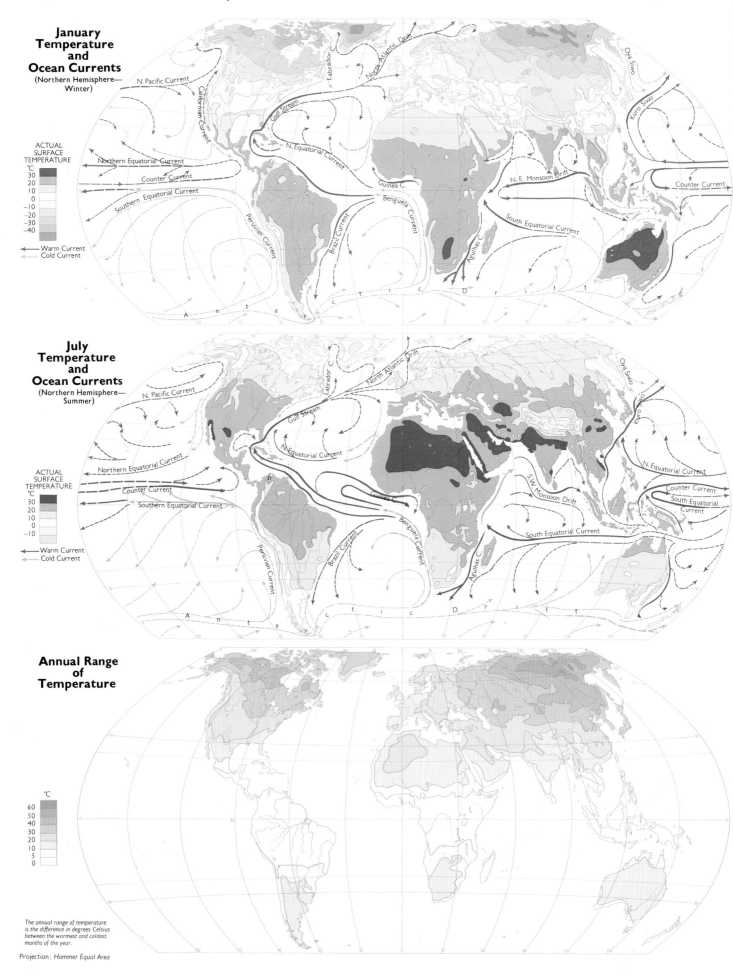

January Temperature and Ocean Currents
(Northern Hemisphere—Winter)

ACTUAL
SURFACE
TEMPERATURE
°C
30
20
10
0
−10
−20
−30
−40

→ Warm Current
→ Cold Current

July Temperature and Ocean Currents
(Northern Hemisphere—Summer)

ACTUAL
SURFACE
TEMPERATURE
°C
30
20
10
0
−10

→ Warm Current
→ Cold Current

Annual Range of Temperature

°C
60
50
40
30
20
10
5
0

The annual range of temperature is the difference in degrees Celsius between the warmest and coldest months of the year.

Projection: *Hammer Equal Area*

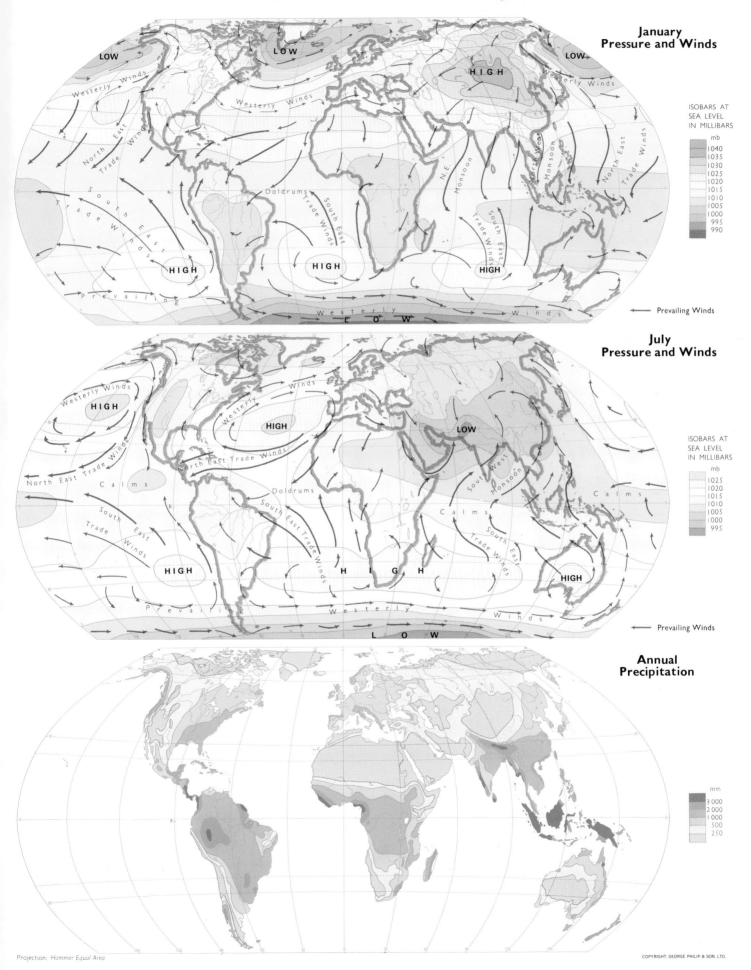

January
Pressure and Winds

ISOBARS AT
SEA LEVEL
IN MILLIBARS

mb
1040
1035
1030
1025
1020
1015
1010
1005
1000
995
990

⟵ Prevailing Winds

July
Pressure and Winds

ISOBARS AT
SEA LEVEL
IN MILLIBARS

mb
1025
1020
1015
1010
1005
1000
995

⟵ Prevailing Winds

**Annual
Precipitation**

mm
3 000
2 000
1 000
500
250

All weather occurs over the earth's surface in the lowest level of the atmosphere, the troposphere. Weather has been defined as the condition of the atmosphere at any place at a specific time with respect to the various elements: temperature, sunshine, pressure, winds, clouds, fog, precipitation. Climate, on the other hand, is the average of weather elements over previous months and years.

Climate graphs *right*

Each graph typifies the climatic conditions experienced in the related coloured region on the map. The red columns show the mean monthly temperature range; the upper limit is the mean monthly maximum and the lower limit the mean monthly minimum. From these the mean monthly median temperature can be determined as the mid-point of the column. The blue columns show the average monthly rainfall.

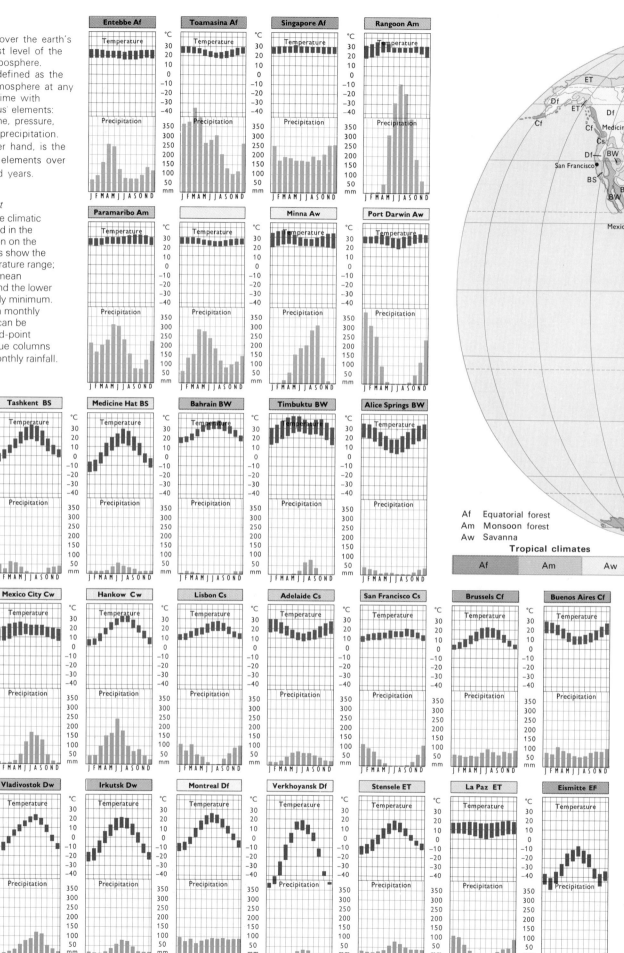

Af   Equatorial forest
Am   Monsoon forest
Aw   Savanna
Tropical climates

| Af | Am | Aw |

Map labels (climate regions and stations):

EF Eismitte · ET · ET · Df · ET · Df Verkhoyansk · ET

Df · ET · Cf · Cf Stensele · Df · Dw · Df

Df Montreal · Cs · Cf Brussels · Df · BS · Irkutsk · ET · Vladivostok

Cs · BS · Df · Cf · BW Tashkent · Dw · Df · Cw Hankow · Cf

Lisbon BS · Cs · BS · Df Cs · BW · Df · BS · ET · Cw

Am · BS · BS · BW · Bahrain · BS · Cw

BS BW · BW Timbuktu · BS · BW · Cw · Am Rangoon · Aw · Am

Af · Am Paramaribo · Minna · Cw · BS · Af Cf · Af

Cw · Af · Aw Am · Af Entebbe · Cw · Cf Singapore · Af · Cf

ET Cw La Paz · Aw · Aw · Aw · Af · Aw

BS · Cw · Cw · Af Toamasina * · Aw Port Darwin

BW · BS · Cw Buenos Aires · Salvador* · Af · Cw · BS · Alice Springs · Aw

Cs · BW Kimberley Johannesburg Cw · BS Adelaide · Cf · Aw

BW · Cs · BS · Cs · Cf

Cf · EF · Cf Wellington

ET · EF · EF

Legend:

BS Steppe	Dw Dry winters
BW Desert	Df Rain at all seasons
Cw Dry winters	ET Tundra
Cs Dry summers	EF Polar
Cf Rain at all seasons	

* These stations are marginal and show characteristics of two or more climatic groups

Dry climates — **Warm temperate climates** — **Cool temperate climates** — **Cold climates**

| BS | BW | Cw | Cs | Cf | Dw | Df | ET | EF |

Tropical storm tracks *below*

A tropical cyclone, or storm, is designated as having winds of gale force (16 m/s) but less than hurricane force (33 m/s). It is a homogenous air mass with upward spiralling air currents around a windless centre, or eye. An average of 65 tropical storms occur each year, over 50% of which reach hurricane force. They originate mainly during the summer over tropical oceans.

Extremes of climate & weather *right*

Tropical high temperatures and polar low temperatures combined with wind systems, altitude and unequal rainfall distribution result in the extremes of tropical rain forests, inland deserts and frozen polar wastes. Fluctuations in the limits of these extreme zones and extremes of weather result in occasional catastrophic heat-waves and drought, floods and storms, frost and snow.

Hurricane devastation ; Darwin

Hot desert ; Morocco

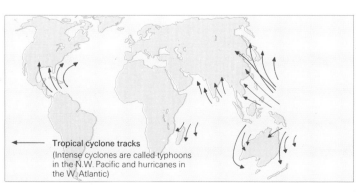

← Tropical cyclone tracks
(Intense cyclones are called typhoons in the N.W. Pacific and hurricanes in the W. Atlantic)

Tornado ; South East U.S.A.

Arctic dwellings ; Greenland

Water resources and vegetation

Fresh water is essential for life on earth and in some parts of the world it is a most precious commodity. On the other hand it is very easy for industrialised temperate states to take its existence for granted, and man's increasing demand may only be met finally by the desalination of earth's 1250 million cubic kilometres of salt water. 70% of the earth's fresh water exists as ice.

The hydrological cycle

Water is continually being absorbed into the atmosphere as vapour from oceans, lakes, rivers and vegetation transpiration. On cooling the vapour either condenses or freezes and falls as rain, hail or snow. Most precipitation falls over the sea but one quarter falls over the land of which half evaporates again soon after falling while the rest flows back into the oceans.

Distribution of water

Oceans and seas 97,29%
Ice caps and glaciers 2,09%
Underground aquifers 0,6054%
Lakes and rivers 0,01362%
Atmosphere 0,00094%
Biosphere 0,00004%

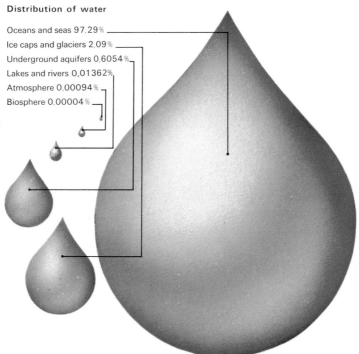

Tundra

Mediterranean scrub

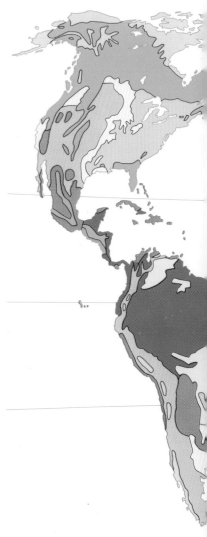

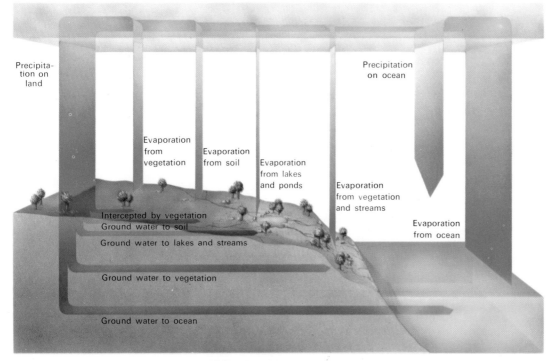

Precipitation on land

Precipitation on ocean

Evaporation from vegetation

Evaporation from soil

Evaporation from lakes and ponds

Evaporation from vegetation and streams

Evaporation from ocean

Intercepted by vegetation
Ground water to soil

Ground water to lakes and streams

Ground water to vegetation

Ground water to ocean

Domestic consumption of water

An area's level of industrialisation, climate and standard of living are all major influences in the consumption of water. On average Europe consumes 636 litres per head each day of which 180 litres is used domestically. In the U.S.A. domestic consumption is slightly higher at 270 litres per day. The graph (right) represents domestic consumption in the U.K.

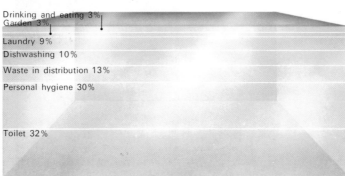

Drinking and eating 3%
Garden 3%
Laundry 9%
Dishwashing 10%
Waste in distribution 13%
Personal hygiene 30%
Toilet 32%

Coniferous forest

Broad-leaved forest

Tropical rain forest

Monsoon forest

Grassland

Savanna

Steppe and semi-desert

Desert

Natural vegetation

Tundra & ice
Coniferous forest
Broadleaf forest
Mediterranean scrub
Grassland
Savanna
Sub tropical forest
Dry tropical scrub & thorn forest
Monsoon forest
Tropical rain forest
Scrub, steppe and semidesert
Desert

Wheat

The most important grain crop in the temperate regions though it is also grown in a variety of climates e.g. in Monsoon lands as a winter crop.

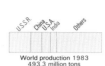

U.S.S.R.	China	U.S.A.	India	Others

World production 1983
493.3 million tons

Oats

Widely grown in temperate regions with the limit fixed by early autumn frosts. Mainly fed to cattle. The best quality oats are used for oatmeal, porridge and breakfast foods.

U.S.S.R.	U.S.A.	Canada	Poland	Australia	Others

World production 1983
44.5 million tons

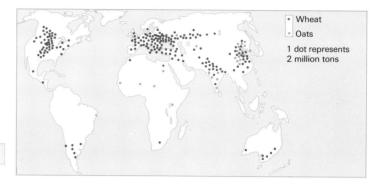

- Wheat
- Oats

1 dot represents
2 million tons

Rye

The hardiest of cereals and more resistant to cold, pests and disease than wheat. An important foodstuff in Central and E. Europe and the U.S.S.R.

U.S.S.R.	Poland	E. Germany	W. Germany	Others

World production 1983
33.1 million tons

Maize (or Corn)

Needs plenty of sunshine, summer rain or irrigation and frost free for 6 months. Important as animal feed and for human food in Africa, Latin America and as a vegetable and breakfast cereal.

U.S.A.	China	Brazil	Others

World production 1983
337.5 million tons

- Rye
- Maize

1 dot represents
2 million tons

Barley

Has the widest range of cultivation requiring only 8 weeks between seed time and harvest. Used mainly as animal-feed and by the malting industry.

U.S.S.R.	U.K.	W. Germany	France	Others

World production 1983
169.3 million tons

Rice

The staple food of half the human race. The main producing areas are the flood plains and hill terraces of S. and E. Asia where water is abundant in the growing season.

China	India	Indonesia	Others

World production 1983
435.7 million tons

- Barley
- Rice

1 dot represents
2 million tons

Millets

The name given to a number of related members of the grass family, of which sorghum is one of the most important. They provide nutritious grain.

India	China	Nigeria	Others

World production 1983
29.6 million tons

Potatoes

An important food crop though less nutritious weight for weight than grain crops. Requires a temperate climate with a regular and plentiful supply of rain.

U.S.S.R.	Poland	China	U.S.A.	Others

World production 1983
258.7 million tons

- Millets
- Potatoes

1 dot represents
2 million tons

Vegetable oilseeds and oils

Despite the increasing use of synthetic chemical products and animal and marine fats, vegetable oils extracted from these crops grow in quantity, value and importance. Food is the major use- in margarine and cooking fats.

Groundnuts are also a valuable subsistence crop and the meal is used as animal feed. Soya-bean meal is a growing source of protein for humans and animals. The Mediterranean lands are the prime source of olive oil.

Groundnut

Soya bean

Sunflower

- Groundnuts
- Soya beans
- Sunflower seed

1 dot represents
1 million tons

Tea and cacao

Tea requires plentiful rainfall and well-drained, sloping ground, whereas cacao prefers a moist heavy soil. Both are grown mainly for export.

Coffee

Prefers a hot climate, wet and dry seasons and an elevated location. It is very susceptible to frost, drought and market fluctuations.

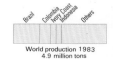

Sugar beet

Requires a deep, rich soil and a temperate climate. Europe produces over 90% of the world's beets mainly for domestic consumption.

Sugar cane

Also requires deep and rich soil but a tropical climate. It produces a much higher yield per hectare than beet and is grown primarily for export.

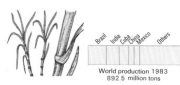

Fruit

With the improvements in canning, drying and freezing, and in transport and marketing, the international trade and consumption of deciduous and soft fruits, citrus fruits and tropical fruits has greatly increased. Recent developments in the use of the peel will give added value to some of the fruit crops.

Fish

Commercial fishing requires large shoals of fish of one species within reach of markets. Freshwater fishing is also important. A rich source of protein, fish will become an increasingly valuable food source.

Beef cattle

Australia, New Zealand and Argentina provide the major part of international beef exports. Western U.S.A. and Europe have considerable production of beef for their local high demand.

Dairy cattle

The need of herds for a rich diet and for nearby markets result in dairying being characteristic of densely-populated areas of the temperate zones – U.S.A., N.W. Europe, and S.E. Australia.

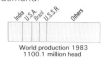

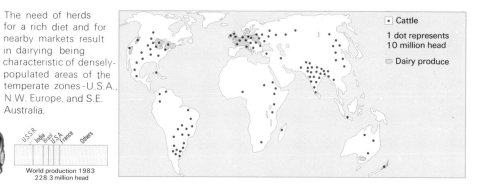

Sheep

Raised mostly for wool and meat, their skins and the cheese from their milk are important products in some countries. The merino yields a fine wool and crossbreeds are best for meat.

Pigs

Can be reared in most climates from monsoon to cool temperate. They are abundant in China, the Corn Belt of the U.S.A. N.W. and C. Europe, Brazil and U.S.S.R.

Production of ferro-alloy metals ·

Steel is refined iron with the addition of other minerals and ferro-alloys. The ferro-alloys give the steel their own special properties; for example resistance to corrosion (chromium and nickel), hardness (tungsten and vanadium), elasticity (molybdenum), magnetic properties (cobalt), high tensile strength (manganese) and high ductility (molybdenum).

Chromium
South Africa | U.S.S.R. | Zimbabwe | Finland | Philippines | Turkey | Others
World production 1982 4.2 million tons

Nickel
U.S.S.R. | Canada | Australia | New Caledonia | Others
World production 1982 620,000 tons

Manganese
U.S.S.R. | S. Africa | China | Brazil | India | Gabon | Others
World production 1981 7.84 million tons

Tungsten
China | U.S.S.R. | U.S.A. | Bolivia | Others
World production 1981 49,100 tons

Molybdenum
U.S.A. | Chile | Canada | U.S.S.R. | Others
World production 1981 108,000 tons

Vanadium
S. Africa | U.S.S.R. | U.S.A. | China | Others
World production 1981 33,400 tons

Production of non-ferrous metals and diamonds

Tin
Malaysia | Indonesia | Bolivia | Thailand | Others
World production 1982 222,500 tons

Gold
South Africa | U.S.S.R. | Canada | Others
World production 1981 1,270 tons

Copper
U.S.S.R. | U.S.A. | Zambia | Zaire | Canada | Others
World production 1982 8.2 million tons

Zinc
Canada | U.S.S.R. | Australia | Peru | U.S.A. | Others
World production 1982 6.5 million tons

Silver
U.S.S.R. | Peru | Mexico | Canada | U.S.A. | Others
World production 1982 11,531 tons

Lead
U.S.S.R. | U.S.A. | Australia | Canada | Others
World production 1982 3,572 million tons

Bauxite
Australia | Guinea | Jamaica | U.S.S.R. | Brazil | Others
World production 1982 78.1 million tons

Diamonds
U.S.S.R. | South Africa | Zaire | Botswana | Others
World production 1981 38.5 million carats

World production of pig iron and ferro-alloys

World production 1979 527,0 million tons

- Others 8,5%
- Netherlands 1%
- Mexico 1%
- Spain 1,5%
- S. Africa 1,5%
- Australia 1,5%
- India 1,5%
- Czechoslovakia 2%
- Belgium 2%
- Canada 2%
- Poland 2%
- Italy 2%
- U.K. 2,5%
- France 4%
- W. Germany 6%
- China 7%
- U.S.A. 15%
- U.S.S.R. 23%
- Japan 16%

Growth of world production of pig iron and ferro-alloys

million tons

1938 | 1946 | 1951 | 1956 | 1961 | 1966 | 1979

World production of iron ore (Fe content)

World production 1981 510.0 million tons

U.S.S.R. 20% | Australia 12% | U.S.A. 9% | Brazil 9% | China 7% | Canada 6% | India 5% | S. Africa 3% | Sweden 3% | Liberia 2% | Venezuela 2% | France 2% | Others 12%

World consumption of non-ferrous metals

Copper
1949/51 | 1963/65 | 1978/80 — 37% from scrap

Lead
1949/51 | 1963/65 | 1978/80 — 50% from scrap

Zinc
1949/51 | 1963/65 | 1978/80 — 23% from scrap

Nickel
1949/51 | 1963/65 | 1978/80

Tin
1949/51 | 1963/65 | 1978/80 — 19% from scrap

Aluminium (from Bauxite)
1949/51 | 1963/65 | 1978/80 — 25% from scrap

Principal sources of iron ore and ferro-alloys

- ■ Iron ore
- ◪ Chromium
- △ Cobalt
- □ Manganese
- ◪ Molybdenum
- ● Nickel
- + Tungsten
- ◹ Vanadium
- ⸺ Iron ore trade flow

Principal sources of non-ferrous metals and other minerals

Base metals
- ▲ Antimony
- ◤ Copper
- ▬ Lead
- ◓ Mercury
- ● Tin
- ◆ Zinc

Light metals
- ● Bauxite
- ▽ Beryllium
- ▪ Lithium
- ▼ Titanium

Rare metals
- ◆ Uranium

Precious metals
- ▲ Gold
- △ Platinum
- ▽ Silver

Precious stones
- △ Diamonds

Mineral fertilizers
- ◓ Nitrates
- ● Phosphates
- ● Potash
- ◆ Sulphur
- ▣ Pyrites

Other industrial minerals
- ▲ Asbestos
- △ Mica

Structural regions

- Pre-Cambrian shields
- Sedimentary cover on Pre-Cambrian shields
- Primary (Caledonian and Hercynian) folding
- Sedimentary cover on Primary folding
- Secondary folding
- Sedimentary cover on Secondary folding
- Tertiary (Alpine) folding
- Sedimentary cover on Tertiary folding

Tropic of Cancer

Equator

Tropic of Capricorn

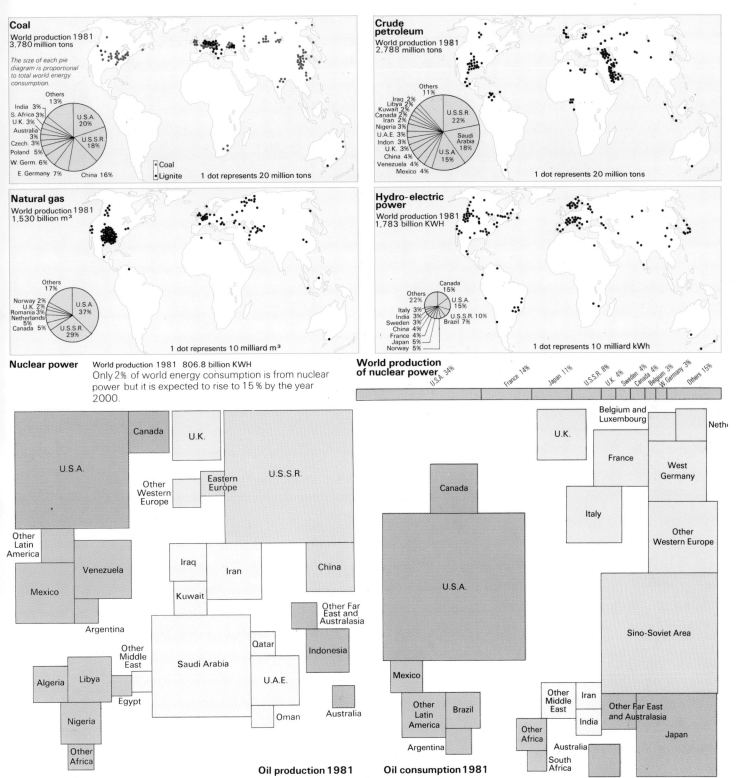

Coal

World production 1981
3,780 million tons

The size of each pie diagram is proportional to total world energy consumption.

Pie diagram:
- U.S.A. 20%
- U.S.S.R. 18%
- China 16%
- E. Germany 7%
- W. Germ. 6%
- Poland 5%
- Czech. 3%
- Australia 3%
- U.K. 3%
- S. Africa 3%
- India 3%
- Others 13%

☐ Coal
● Lignite

1 dot represents 20 million tons

Crude petroleum

World production 1981
2,788 million tons

Pie diagram:
- U.S.S.R. 22%
- Saudi Arabia 18%
- U.S.A. 15%
- Mexico 4%
- Venezuela 4%
- China 4%
- U.K. 3%
- Indon 3%
- U.A.E. 3%
- Nigeria 3%
- Iran 2%
- Canada 2%
- Kuwait 2%
- Libya 2%
- Iraq 2%
- Others 11%

1 dot represents 20 million tons

Natural gas

World production 1981
1,530 billion m³

Pie diagram:
- U.S.A. 37%
- U.S.S.R. 29%
- Canada 5%
- Netherlands 5%
- Romania 3%
- U.K. 2%
- Norway 2%
- Others 17%

1 dot represents 10 milliard m³

Hydro-electric power

World production 1981
1,783 billion KWH

Pie diagram:
- Canada 15%
- U.S.A. 15%
- U.S.S.R. 10%
- Brazil 7%
- Norway 5%
- Japan 4%
- France 4%
- China 4%
- Sweden 3%
- India 3%
- Italy 3%
- Others 22%

1 dot represents 10 milliard kWh

Nuclear power

World production 1981   806.8 billion KWH

Only 2% of world energy consumption is from nuclear power but it is expected to rise to 15% by the year 2000.

World production of nuclear power

U.S.A. 34% | France 14% | Japan 11% | U.S.S.R. 8% | U.K. 4% | Sweden 4% | Canada 4% | Belgium 3% | W. Germany 3% | Others 15%

Oil production 1981 (countries scaled):
U.S.A., Canada, U.K., Other Western Europe, Eastern Europe, U.S.S.R., China, Other Latin America, Venezuela, Mexico, Argentina, Iraq, Kuwait, Iran, Other Far East and Australasia, Qatar, Indonesia, Algeria, Libya, Egypt, Other Middle East, Saudi Arabia, U.A.E., Oman, Australia, Nigeria, Other Africa

Oil consumption 1981 (countries scaled):
Canada, U.K., Belgium and Luxembourg, Neth., France, West Germany, Italy, Other Western Europe, U.S.A., Sino-Soviet Area, Mexico, Other Latin America, Brazil, Argentina, Other Middle East, Iran, India, Other Far East and Australasia, Japan, Other Africa, Australia, South Africa

Oil's new super-powers *above*

When countries are scaled according to their production and consumption of oil they take on new dimensions. At present, large supplies of oil are concentrated in a few countries of the Caribbean, the Middle East and North Africa, except for the vast indigenous supplies of the U.S.A. and U.S.S.R. The Middle East, with 55% of the world's reserves, produces 37% of the world's supply and yet consumes less than 3%. The U.S.A., despite its great production, has a deficiency of nearly 300 million tons a year, consuming 30% of the world's total. Estimates show that Western Europe, at present consuming 747 million tons or 27% of the total each year, may by 1980 surpass the U.S. consumption. Japan is the largest importer of crude oil with an increase in consumption of 440% during the period 1963-73.

Energy balance

millions of tons of coal equivalent

- −500 to −200
- −200 to −50
- −50 to 0
- 0 to +50
- +50 to +200
- +200 to +500

The figures indicate whether a surplus or deficit exists between home production and home consumption.

Population distribution
(right and lower right)
People have always been unevenly distributed in the world. Europe has for centuries contained nearly 20% of the world's population but after the 16-19th century explorations and consequent migrations this proportion has rapidly decreased. In 1750 the Americas had 2% of the world's total: in 2000 AD they are expected to contain 16%.

The most densely populated regions are in India, China and Europe where the average density is between 100 and 200 per km² although there are pockets of extremely high density elsewhere. In contrast South West Africa has only 1,0 persons per km². The countries in the lower map have been redrawn to make their areas proportional to their populations.

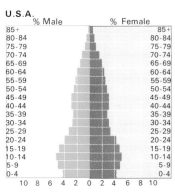

U.S.A.

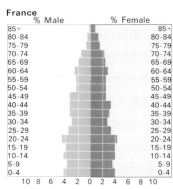

France

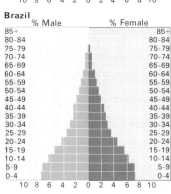

Brazil

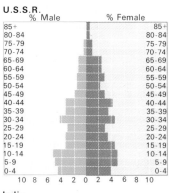

U.S.S.R.

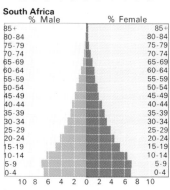

South Africa

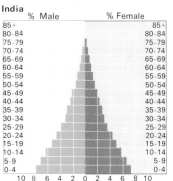

India

Age distribution
France shows many demographic features characteristic of European countries. Birth and death rates have declined with a moderate population growth - there are nearly as many old as young. In contrast, India and several other countries have few old and many young because of the high death rates and even higher birth rates. It is this excess that is responsible for the world's population explosion.

Increase in urbanisation in developed and developing countries

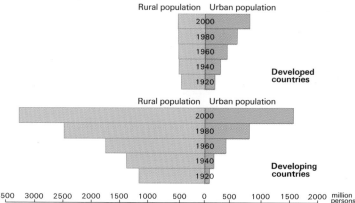

World population distribution

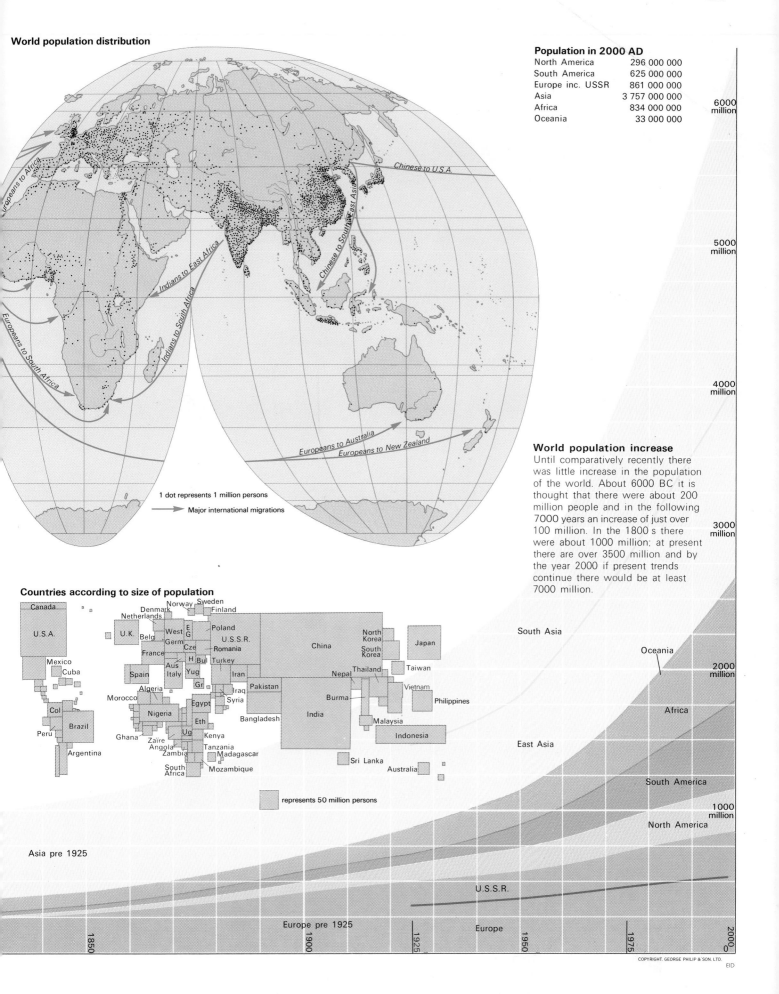

Europeans to Africa

Chinese to U.S.A

Chinese to South East Asia

Indians to East Africa

Europeans to South Africa

Indians to South Africa

Europeans to Australia

Europeans to New Zealand

1 dot represents 1 million persons

→ Major international migrations

Population in 2000 AD

North America	296 000 000
South America	625 000 000
Europe inc. USSR	861 000 000
Asia	3 757 000 000
Africa	834 000 000
Oceania	33 000 000

World population increase
Until comparatively recently there was little increase in the population of the world. About 6000 BC it is thought that there were about 200 million people and in the following 7000 years an increase of just over 100 million. In the 1800 s there were about 1000 million; at present there are over 3500 million and by the year 2000 if present trends continue there would be at least 7000 million.

Countries according to size of population

Canada
U.S.A.
Mexico
Cuba
Col
Peru
Brazil
Argentina

Denmark
Norway Sweden
Finland
Netherlands
U.K. West E G
Belg Germ
France Cze H Bul
Spain Aus Italy Yug
Algeria Gr
Morocco Egypt Syria
Nigeria Iraq
Ghana Eth
Ug Kenya
Zaïre
Angola Tanzania Madagascar
Zambia
South Africa Mozambique

Poland
U.S.S.R.
Romania
Turkey
Iran
Pakistan
Bangladesh
India
Sri Lanka

China
North Korea
South Korea
Nepal Thailand
Burma
Vietnam
Malaysia
Indonesia
Australia

Japan
Taiwan
Philippines

□ represents 50 million persons

South Asia

Oceania

East Asia

Africa

South America

North America

Asia pre 1925

Europe pre 1925

Europe

U.S.S.R.

6000 million
5000 million
4000 million
3000 million
2000 million
1000 million
0

1850 1900 1925 1950 1975 2000

COPYRIGHT. GEORGE PHILIP & SON. LTD.

EID

Political Associations

Capital cities of principal countries are underlined

	Arab League
	NATO
	Warsaw Pact

500 0 500 1000 1500 2000 2500 3000 3500 km

Economic Associations
see also page 29

OPEC is the Organisation of Petroleum Exporting Countries.
LAIA is the Latin American Integration Association.
Venezuela and Ecuador are also members of LAIA.
OECD is the Organisation for Economic Co-operation and Development
COMECON is the Council for Mutual Economic Assistance.

OPEC
LAIA
OECD
COMECON

• Colombo Plan Nations

Projection: *Hammer Equal Area*
COPYRIGHT. GEORGE PHILIP & SON. LTD.

1:20 000 000

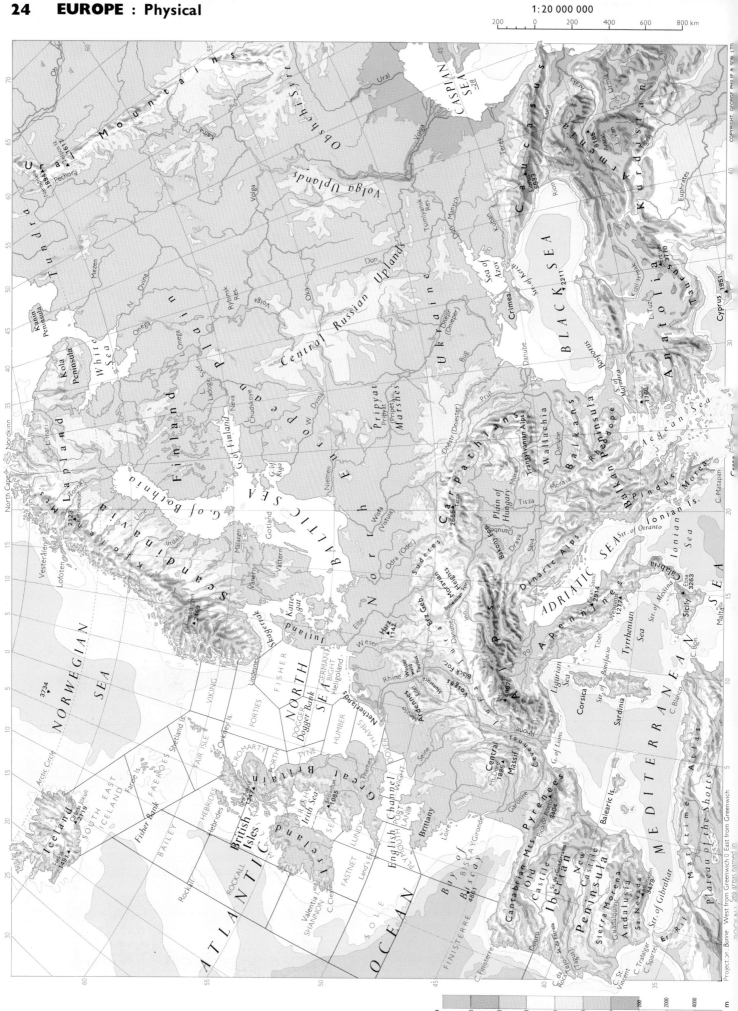

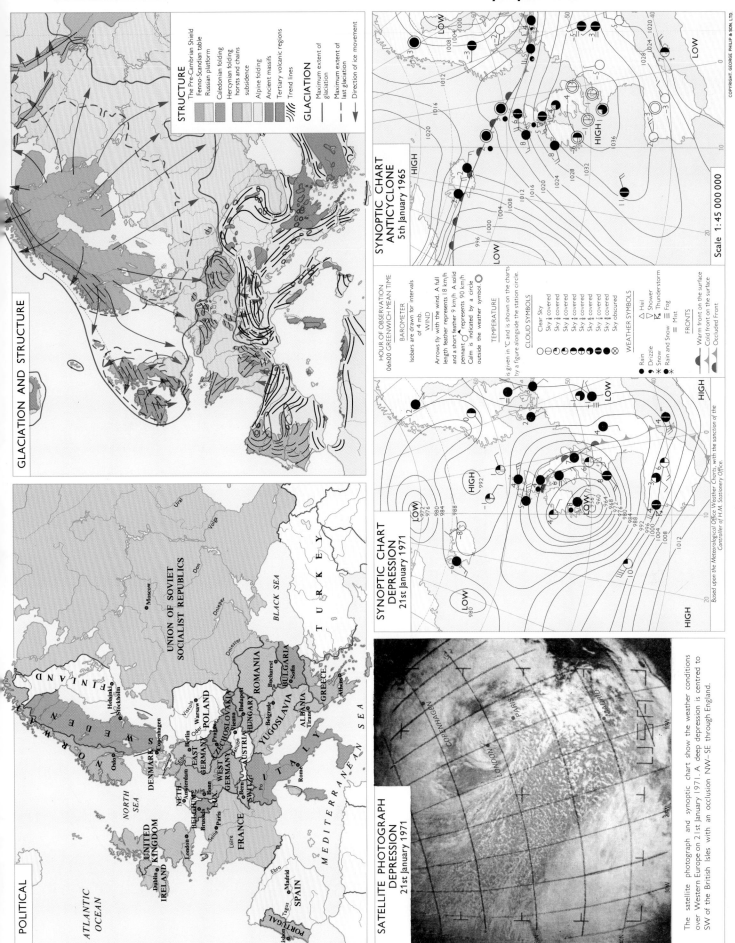

1:40 000 000

400   0   400   800   1200   1600 km

STRUCTURE
- The Pre-Cambrian Shield
- Fenno-Scandian table
- Russian platform
- Caledonian folding
- Hercynian folding
- horsts and chains
- subsidence
- Alpine folding
- Ancient massifs
- Tertiary volcanic regions
- Trend lines

GLACIATION
- Maximum extent of glaciation
- Maximum extent of last glaciation
- Direction of ice movement

GLACIATION AND STRUCTURE

POLITICAL

SYNOPTIC CHART ANTICYCLONE 5th January 1965

Scale 1:45 000 000

HOUR OF OBSERVATION 06h00 GREENWICH MEAN TIME

BAROMETER
Isobars are drawn for intervals of 4 mb.

WIND
Arrows fly with the wind. A full length feather represents 18 km/h and a short feather 9 km/h. A solid pennant represents 90 km/h Calm is indicated by a circle outside the weather symbol.

TEMPERATURE
is given in °C and is shown on the charts by a figure alongside the station circle.

CLOUD SYMBOLS
Clear Sky
Sky ½ covered
Sky ¼ covered
Sky ½ covered
Sky covered
Sky covered
Sky covered
Sky covered
Sky covered
Sky covered
Sky obscured

WEATHER SYMBOLS
- Rain
- Drizzle
- Snow
- Rain and Snow
- Hail
- Shower
- Thunderstorm
- Fog
- Mist

FRONTS
- Warm front on the surface
- Cold front on the surface
- Occluded Front

Based upon the Meteorological Office Weather Charts, with the sanction of the Controller of H.M. Stationery Office.

SYNOPTIC CHART DEPRESSION 21st January 1971

SATELLITE PHOTOGRAPH DEPRESSION 21st January 1971

The satellite photograph and synoptic chart show the weather conditions over Western Europe on 21st January 1971. A deep depression is centred to SW of the British Isles with an occlusion NW–SE through England.

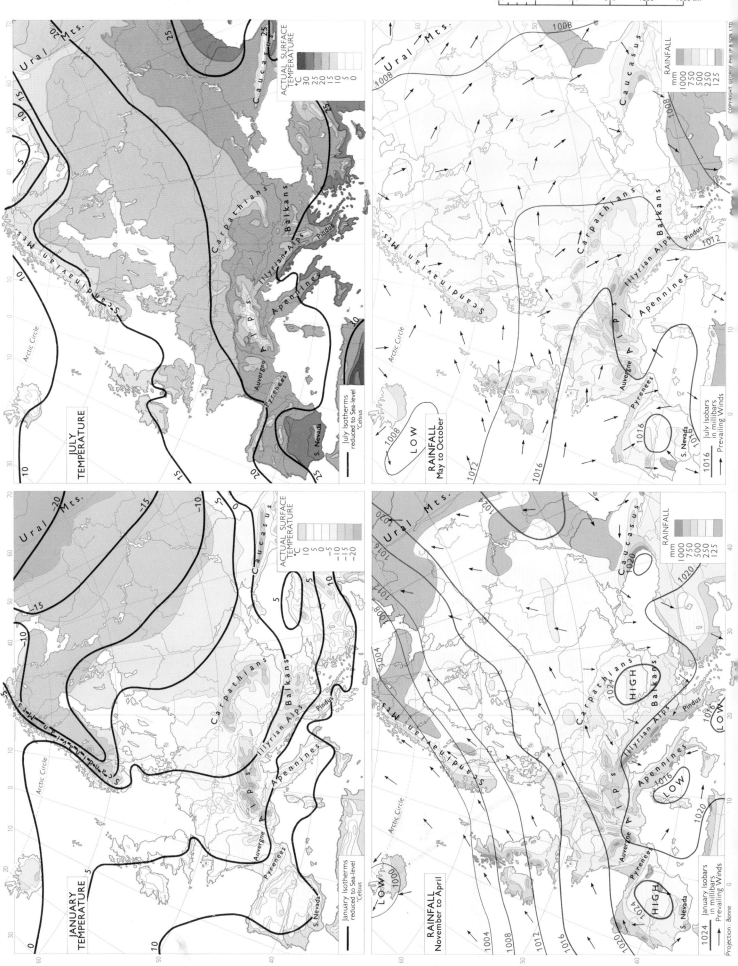

1 : 40 000 000

400 0 400 800 1200 1600 km

ACTUAL SURFACE
TEMPERATURE
°C
30
25
20
15
10
5
0

JULY
TEMPERATURE

July Isotherms
reduced to Sea-level
°Celsius

RAINFALL
mm
1000
750
500
250
125

LOW

RAINFALL
May to October

July Isobars
in millibars
Prevailing Winds

ACTUAL SURFACE
TEMPERATURE
°C
10
5
-5
-10
-15
-20

JANUARY
TEMPERATURE

January Isotherms
reduced to Sea-level
°Celsius

RAINFALL
mm
1000
750
500
250
125

RAINFALL
November to April

January Isobars
in millibars
Prevailing Winds

COPYRIGHT GEORGE PHILIP & SON LTD

Projection: Bonne

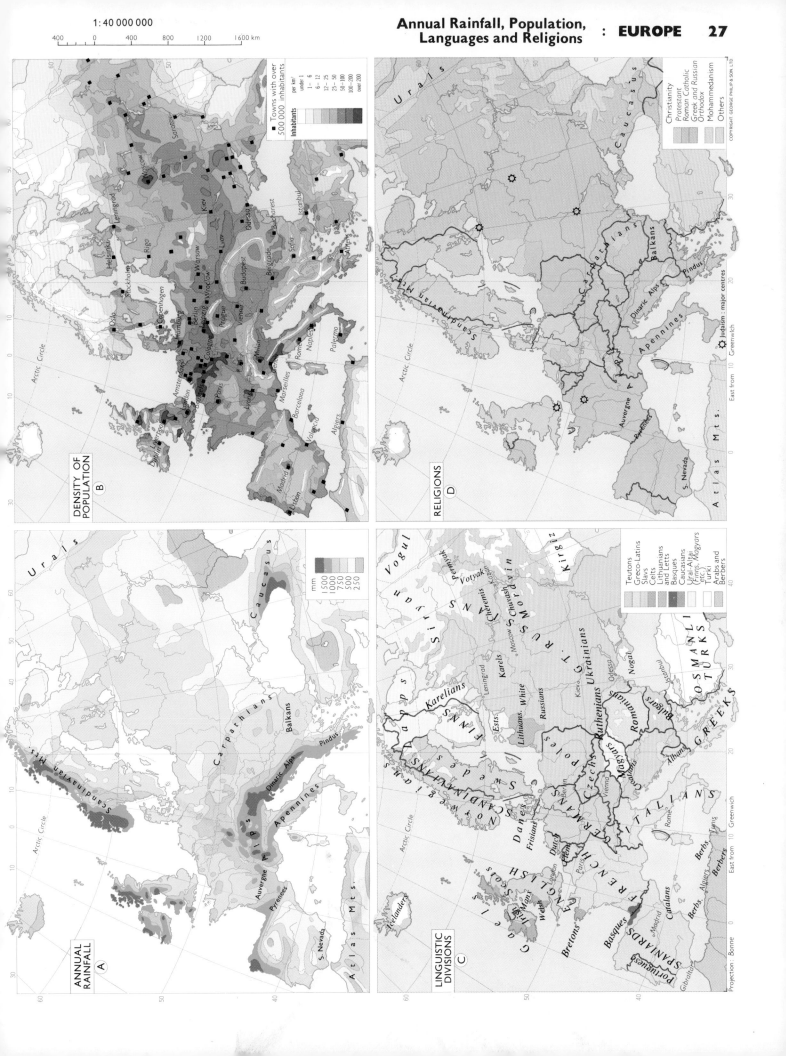

1:40 000 000

400 0 400 800 1200 1600 km

B DENSITY OF POPULATION

■ Towns with over 500 000 inhabitants

Inhabitants per km²
under 1 · 1–6 · 6–12 · 12–25 · 25–50 · 50–100 · 100–200 · over 200

D RELIGIONS

Christianity
Protestant
Roman Catholic
Greek and Russian Orthodox
Mohammedanism
Others

✡ Judaism : major centres

East from 10 Greenwich

A ANNUAL RAINFALL

mm
1500 · 1000 · 750 · 500 · 250

C LINGUISTIC DIVISIONS

Teutons
Greco-Latins
Slavs
Celts
Lithuanians and Letts
Basques
Caucasians
Ural-Altai (Finns, Magyars etc.)
Turki
Arabs and Berbers

Projection: Bonne

East from 10 Greenwich

1:40 000 000

400   0   400   800   1200   1600 km

ELECTRICITY
Sources of power, by percentage

	'000 millions of kWh generated 1980	Thermal	Hydro-electric	Nuclear
West Germany	368,8	84	5	11
U.K.	281,5	86	2	12
France	257,8	49	27	23
Italy	186,3	72	26	2
Poland	121,9	98	2	
Spain	110,2	67	28	5
East Germany	98,8	88	1	11
Sweden	96,3	13	64	22
Norway	84,0	1	99	
Czechoslovakia	74,1	88	6	6
Romania	67,5	82	18	
Netherlands	64,8	94		6
Yugoslavia	53,9	52	48	
Belgium	53,6	75		23
Switzerland	48,2	2	70	28

The burning of coal is still important for electricity generation but West European countries must import oil to meet their energy requirements. These imports will be reduced by the exploitation of North Sea oil and gas. Most of the potential sites for hydro-electric power have been harnessed and nuclear power is still in the development stages.

POWER STATION CAPACITY

Oil and gas	Nuclear
◨ > 500 MW	◆ > 500 MW
◪ < 500 MW	◇ < 500 MW
Coal and lignite	Hydro-electric
▣ > 500 MW	✳ > 500 MW
▨ < 500 MW	✲ < 500 MW

ELECTRICITY

LIGHT INDUSTRIAL PRODUCTS, 1981

TEXTILES

Cotton yarn '000 tons		Wool yarn '000 tons	
France	211,1	France	138,5
Poland	195,6	U.K.	110,4
Romania (1979)	175,2	Poland	88,8
Italy	174,6	Belgium	78,2
West Germany	146,4	Romania (1979)	70,8
Czechoslovakia	136,8	West Germany	51,9

MOTOR VEHICLES

Cars '000		Commercial vehicles '000	
West Germany	3 590	France	473
France	2 953	West Germany	312
Italy	1 388	U.K.	231
U.K.	953	Italy	178
Spain	862	Spain	127
Sweden	229	Czechoslovakia	85

ELECTRONICS
'000 televisions

West Germany	4 239
U.K.	2 417
France	1 913
Italy (1976)	1 813
Poland	972
Belgium	650

◯	Textiles
⊕	Electrical engineering
⬩	Motor vehicles

LIGHT INDUSTRY

MINERAL PRODUCTION, 1981
The tables show the leading producers of the industrially important minerals in Europe.

OIL '000 tons		NATURAL GAS* million m³	
U.K.	86 540	Netherlands	75 345
Norway	23 580	U.K.	37 857
Romania (1980)	11 496	Romania (1979)	34 014
West Germany	4 464	Norway	26 043
Yugoslavia	4 350	West Germany	19 174
Hungary	2 028	Italy	13 949

COAL '000 tons		LIGNITE '000 tons	
Poland	163 020	E.Germ. (1980)	258 000
U.K.	127 788	West Germany	130 620
West Germany	88 464	Czechoslovakia	95 220
Czechoslovakia	27 204	Yugoslavia	51 864
France	19 584	Poland	35 544
Spain	14 268	Bulgaria	28 980

IRON ORE '000 tons	
Sweden	23 220
France	21 576
Spain	8 412
Yugoslavia	4 788
Norway	4 068
Austria	3 048

⛏ Oil	▲ Salt	
⛏ Natural gas	▲ Potash	
◉ Coal	● Bauxite	
◗ Lignite	◆ Lead	
◯ Iron ore		

MINERALS

Upper Silesia
Ruhr
Lorraine
North Sea
South Yorkshire

HEAVY INDUSTRIAL PRODUCTS, 1981

CRUDE STEEL '000 tons		MERCHANT VESSELS '000 gross registered tons launched	
West Germany	42 156	West Germany	665
Italy	24 624	Spain	605
France	21 144	Sweden	363
Poland	15 720	Poland	350
U.K.	15 552	U.K.	342
Czechoslovakia	15 264	Finland	311

SULPHURIC ACID
'000 tons

West Germany	4 824
France	4 363
Spain (1979)	2 904
U.K.	2 860
Poland	2 776
Italy	2 405

Sulphuric acid is a fundamental basis for most branches of the chemical industry.

◗ Heavy engineering	
◣ Iron and steel plants	
⬥ Shipbuilding	
◥ Chemicals	

HEAVY INDUSTRY

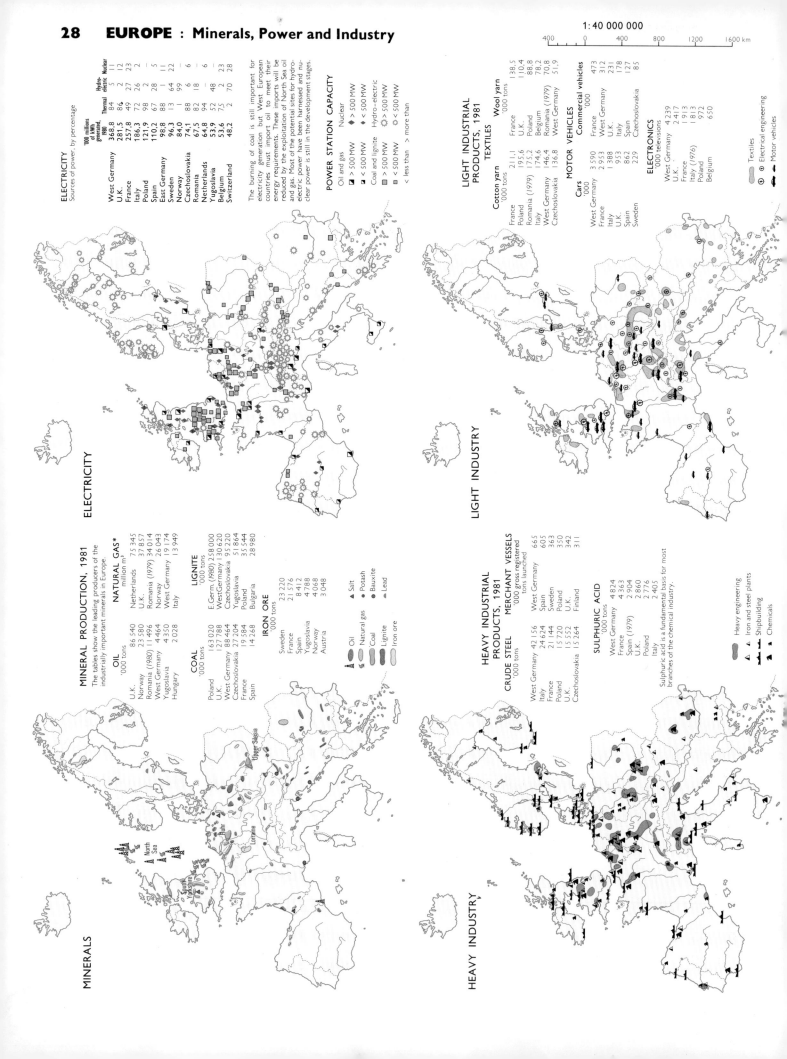

1 : 40 000 000

400　　0　　400　　800　　1200　　1600 km

COPYRIGHT GEORGE PHILIP & SON LTD.

TOURISM

Each proportional circle represents a country of arrival and shows the number (in millions) and nationality of visitors to that country.

Spain
Switzerland
U.K.
U.S.A.
West Germany
Yugoslavia
Rest of the world

Austria
Belgium
Denmark
France
Italy
Netherlands
Portugal

The Mediterranean coast with its consistently hot sun and clear skies make it the destination of many Europeans during the peak holiday months of July and August. Spanish hoteliers have developed the coastline to cater for packaged holiday makers who arrive by chartered aircraft from industrial Northern Europe.

RECEIPTS FROM TOURISM
$ US '000 million 1980

Italy	8.9
France	8.2
Spain	7.0
U.K.	6.9
West Germany	6.6
Austria	6.4
Switzerland	3.1
Belgium/Lux.	1.8
Greece	1.7
Netherlands	1.6
Denmark	1.3
Portugal	1.1
Sweden	1.0
Norway	0.7

SCANDINAVIA 15.17
12.67
1.51
0.46
0.53

WEST GERMANY 6.95
1.07
1.13
0.55
0.51
0.44
0.35

AUSTRIA 10.89
7.18
1.87
0.50
0.67
0.32

YUGOSLAVIA 5.46
1.63
2.35
0.58
0.57
0.33

GREECE 1.96
0.37
0.25
0.23
0.84
0.13 0.14

NETHERLANDS 2.68
0.71
0.37
0.89
0.36
0.13

ITALY 12.44
3.32
1.80
1.22
0.85
0.68
0.67
3.90

BELGIUM AND LUXEMBOURG 7.48
1.81
1.33
1.10
1.60
0.58

SWITZERLAND 6.22
1.73
0.84
0.73
0.45
0.37
1.79
0.37
9.10

U.K. 7.94
1.34
0.97
0.88
0.52
0.38 0.38
3.47

FRANCE 9.84
1.07
0.96
0.78
0.64
1.15
1.81
3.43

SPAIN 30.34
4.32
3.61
3.23
1.28
1.21
7.59

IRELAND 1.27
0.23
0.82
0.22

PORTUGAL 2.62
1.17
0.38
0.53
0.15
0.17
0.22

ECONOMIC DEVELOPMENT

ECONOMIC ACTIVITY

The circles are subdivided in proportion to the percentages of Gross Domestic Product contributed by each of the three economic activities. Gross Domestic Product is a measure of a country's total production of goods and services.(See note on P.113)

The per capita Gross Domestic Product of each country is stated in $ US 1978-80

Primary
Agriculture, forestry and fishing
Secondary
Manufacturing, mining and power industries
Tertiary
Services: wholesale and retail trade, transport and communications, finance and business services

FINLAND 8 701
SWEDEN 12 831
NORWAY 11 486
DENMARK 12 925
EAST GERMANY 4 034
POLAND 2 512
CZECHOSLOVAKIA 2 444
ROMANIA 1 240
BULGARIA 1 814
HUNGARY 2 184
GREECE 4 208
YUGOSLAVIA 1 917
AUSTRIA 9 294
SWITZERLAND 15 006
WEST GERMANY 9 845
NETHERLANDS 10 624
BELGIUM AND LUXEMBOURG
U.K. 7 192
IRELAND 4 412
FRANCE 10 720
ITALY 5 686
SPAIN 5 300
PORTUGAL 2 000
10 739

TRADE OF EEC COUNTRIES

WEST GERMANY

IMPORTS %		EXPORTS %
10.8	FOOD	4.8
22.6	FUELS	3.8
8.2	MATS.	2.5
18.8	MACH.	44.6
39.6	MANUFS.	44.3
185 922	TOTAL ($ US million)	191 647
IMPORTS FROM		EXPORTS TO
47.8	EEC	49.1
7.2	USA	6.1
3.2	ACP	1.9
41.8	REST	42.9

ITALY

IMPORTS %		EXPORTS %
12.0	FOOD	6.7
27.9	FUELS	5.6
11.0	MATS.	1.8
20.4	MACH.	32.1
28.7	MANUFS.	53.8
98 443	TOTAL ($ US million)	78 530
IMPORTS FROM		EXPORTS TO
44.3	EEC	49.0
7.0	USA	5.3
3.1	ACP	2.5
45.6	REST	43.2

DENMARK

IMPORTS %		EXPORTS %
10.3	FOOD	31.8
22.5	FUELS	3.5
6.7	MATS.	7.4
20.6	MACH.	24.0
39.9	MANUFS.	33.3
19 302	TOTAL ($ US million)	16 403
IMPORTS FROM		EXPORTS TO
49.1	EEC	50.5
6.7	USA	4.5
1.4	ACP	1.7
42.8	REST	43.3

BELG./LUX.

IMPORTS %		EXPORTS %
10.3	FOOD	9.0
17.4	FUELS	8.4
7.7	MATS.	3.0
22.5	MACH.	21.8
42.1	MANUFS.	57.8
71 186	TOTAL ($ US million)	63 960
IMPORTS FROM		EXPORTS TO
63.1	EEC	71.8
7.7	USA	3.4
3.3	ACP	2.2
25.9	REST	22.6

GREECE

IMPORTS %		EXPORTS %
8.0	FOOD	25.0
23.4	FUELS	15.5
7.0	MATS.	8.4
35.9	MACH.	3.0
25.7	MANUFS.	48.1
10 531	TOTAL ($ US million)	5 142
IMPORTS FROM		EXPORTS TO
39.7	EEC	47.6
4.6	USA	5.7
1.0	ACP	1.7
54.3	REST	45.0

NETHERLANDS

IMPORTS %		EXPORTS %
12.7	FOOD	18.9
24.2	FUELS	22.3
7.1	MATS.	6.2
19.9	MACH.	17.1
36.1	MANUFS.	35.5
76 411	TOTAL ($ US million)	73 335
IMPORTS FROM		EXPORTS TO
53.7	EEC	72.2
8.8	USA	2.5
5.5	ACP	2.5
32.0	REST	22.8

FRANCE

IMPORTS %		EXPORTS %
9.3	FOOD	15.5
26.7	FUELS	4.1
6.5	MATS.	4.2
21.4	MACH.	33.2
36.1	MANUFS.	43.0
134 328	TOTAL ($ US million)	110 865
IMPORTS FROM		EXPORTS TO
46.3	EEC	51.9
8.0	USA	4.4
5.1	ACP	5.8
40.6	REST	37.9

UNITED KINGDOM

IMPORTS %		EXPORTS %
12.1	FOOD	6.6
13.6	FUELS	13.0
7.6	MATS.	2.9
25.7	MACH.	34.6
41.0	MANUFS.	42.9
117 902	TOTAL ($ US million)	114 381
IMPORTS FROM		EXPORTS TO
38.7	EEC	42.7
13.4	USA	9.4
2.8	ACP	5.5
45.1	REST	42.4

IRELAND

IMPORTS %		EXPORTS %
11.6	FOOD	36.3
14.8	FUELS	0.6
3.6	MATS.	4.6
27.2	MACH.	18.5
42.8	MANUFS.	40.0
11 131	TOTAL ($ US million)	8 481
IMPORTS FROM		EXPORTS TO
74.5	EEC	74.9
7.8	USA	1.5
1.0	ACP	5.3
16.7	REST	18.3

For each country, the upper panel gives the total value of trade and the proportional breakdown of products, the lower gives the origins and destinations of imports and exports.

FOOD　Food, live animals, beverages and tobacco
FUELS　Mineral fuels, lubricants
MATS.　Crude materials, edible oils and fats
MACH.　Machinery and transport equipment
MANUFS.　Chemical, manufactured goods and miscellaneous transactions
ACP　Countries of Africa, Caribbean and Pacific

TRADING GROUPS

EUROPEAN TRADING GROUPS

The European Economic Community has ten member countries: Belgium, Denmark, France, West Germany, Greece, Ireland, Italy, Luxembourg, Netherlands and United Kingdom. These countries have a Common Market which has free trade in all goods.

The Warsaw Pact countries of Bulgaria, Czechoslovakia, East Germany, Hungary, Poland, Romania and U.S.S.R. are the European members of the Council for Mutual Economic Assistance (CMEA).

The European Free Trade Association consists of Austria, Iceland, Norway, Portugal, Sweden, Switzerland and Finland which is an associate member. EFTA has free trade in industrial products; it also has close trade links with the EEC.

	Imports $ US million 1981	Exports $ US million 1981
World	1 998 228	1 946 057
EEC	634 527	597 537
CMEA (incl. USSR)	163 965	158 672
EFTA	121 273	108 639
Other European Countries	49 379	31 455

1:40 000 000

400   0   400   800   1200   1600 km

DEMOGRAPHY

For each country, the Birth rate is recorded on the plus side of the diagram, the Death rate on the minus side, with the level of net migration contributing to either plus or minus totals. The mean annual percentage change is given on the right of each bar.

Births/deaths per 1 000

Yugoslavia
Belgium
Yugoslavia
Belgium

Birth rate
Death rate

1950 55 60 65 70 75

The graph shows comparative Birth and Death rate trends for two countries currently with marked differences in mean annual population increase.

30   40 Births/immigrants per 1 000

Albania 2.9
Ireland 1.2
Iceland 1.1
Luxembourg 1.0
Romania 1.0
Spain 1.0
Poland 0.9
Yugoslavia 0.9
France 0.8
Italy 0.8
Netherlands 0.8
Norway 0.7
Switzerland 0.7
Czechoslovakia 0.6
Greece 0.6
Bulgaria 0.5
Denmark 0.5
Finland 0.4
Germany, W. 0.4
Hungary 0.4
Sweden 0.4
Austria 0.3
Belgium 0.2
Portugal 0.2
United Kingdom -0.2
Germany, E.

Deaths/emigrants per 1 000

+
-

POPULATION OF SELECTED CITIES, 1960-75

	1960	1965	1970	1975
London	8 172	8 187	7 349	7 168
Madrid	2 260	2 765	3 146	3 520
Warsaw	1 136	1 241	1 274	1 316
Sofia	671	825	886	966
Stockholm	809	799	768	671

The cities are selected on grounds of position in Europe, size of population and the pattern of growth each has shown in recent years.

URBAN POPULATION

In many countries, considerable population change occurs within principal urban areas, which are too small to illustrate at this scale. Such change is usually one of decline in the more industrially-advanced countries where dispersal of industry and population is characteristic. Urban centres of the lesser-developed countries, particularly capital cities, where industrial activity is concentrated, tend to be marked by population increases.

Percentage population change in European regions, 1960-75

LOSS
% -20 -15 -10 -5   0   +5 +10 +15 +20 %
0   GAIN

POPULATION CHANGE, 1960-1975

UNEMPLOYMENT
1981 figures
Percentage of workforce

Ireland	13.5
Yugoslavia	12.0
Belgium	11.6
U.K.	11.3
Denmark	9.2
Netherlands	9.0
Italy	8.4
France	7.8
West Germany	5.5
Finland	5.3
Sweden	2.5
Austria	2.4
Norway	2.0

The circles are subdivided in proportion to each country's employable and dependent population. The "economically active" sector includes the currently unemployed, but excludes students, those occupied in domestic duties and retired persons.

The size of each national workforce is given in thousands.

Economically active population: male

Economically active population: female

Dependent population

POPULATION AND WORKFORCE, 1980

ICELAND 118
NORWAY 1 947
FINLAND 2 263
SWEDEN 4 318
DENMARK 2 624
IRELAND 1 222
U.K. 26 057
NETHERLANDS 5 206
BELGIUM 4 062
LUX. 160
EAST GERMANY 7 761
WEST GERMANY 26 154
POLAND 17 109
CZECHOSLOVAKIA 6 601
HUNGARY 5 062
AUSTRIA 3 116
SWITZERLAND 2 972
FRANCE 22 644
SPAIN 12 892
PORTUGAL 4 255
ITALY 22 269
YUGOSLAVIA 9 324
ROMANIA 10 320
BULGARIA 4 000
GREECE 3 451

Large scale flows of migrant workers to and within Western Europe arose during a period of rapid economic growth since 1950. Besides continued rural-urban migration within countries, the principal flows have been from the poorer regions of Europe, North Africa and the ex-colonies of European countries.

The bar-diagrams positioned in each recipient country represent the size of each immigrant workforce and its chief component nationalities. Totals are in thousands.

% workforce foreign
12
8
4
0

Migrant flows of greater than 100 000 (national totals in 000s)

Other
Commonwealth
Irish
N. Africans
Finns
S. Europeans
Yugoslavs
Turks

FOREIGN WORKERS IN EUROPE

Finland 115
SWEDEN 250
NETHS. 125
BELGIUM 250
U.K. 1 800
Ireland 455
West Indies 200
India and Pakistan 260
W. GERMANY 2 350
AUSTRIA 250
SWITZ. 1 050
FRANCE 1 900
Italy 705
Turkey 610
Yugoslavia 490
Greece 560
Algeria 446
Spain 474
Morocco 191
Portugal 574

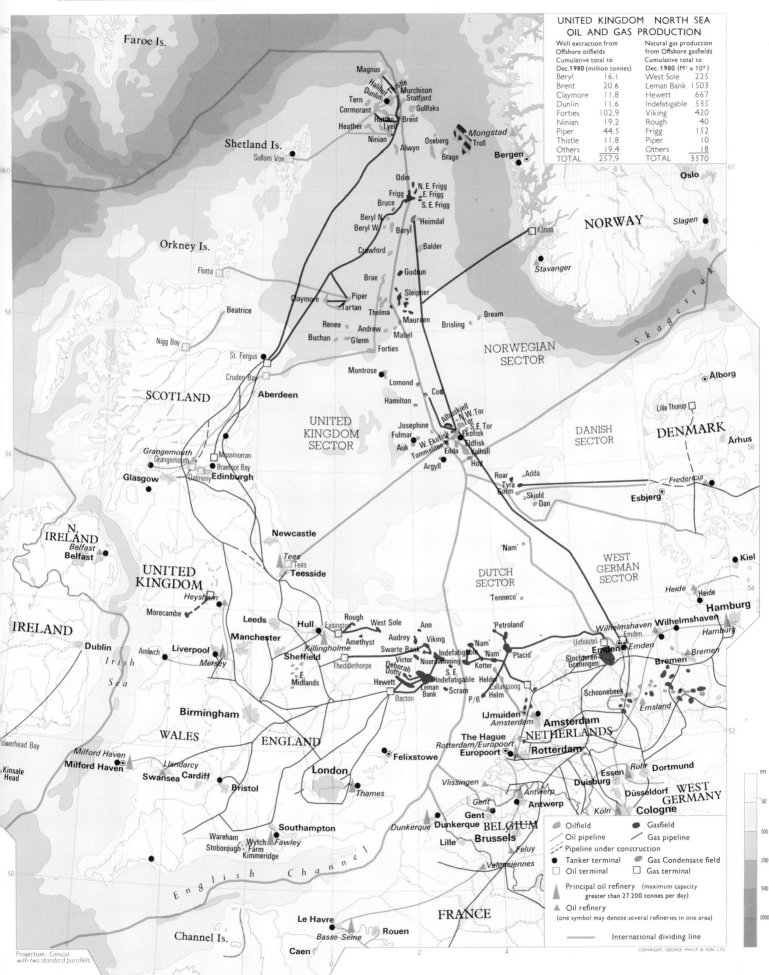

1:6 000 000

Projection: Conical with two standard parallels

UNITED KINGDOM NORTH SEA OIL AND GAS PRODUCTION

Well extraction from Offshore oilfields Cumulative total to Dec.1980 (million tonnes)		Natural gas production from Offshore gasfields Cumulative total to Dec.1980 (M³ x 10⁸)	
Beryl	16.1	West Sole	225
Brent	20.6	Leman Bank	1503
Claymore	11.8	Hewett	667
Dunlin	11.6	Indefatigable	535
Forties	102.9	Viking	420
Ninian	19.2	Rough	40
Piper	44.5	Frigg	152
Thistle	11.8	Piper	10
Others	19.4	Others	18
TOTAL	257.9	TOTAL	3570

Legend:
- Oilfield
- Gasfield
- Oil pipeline
- Gas pipeline
- Pipeline under construction
- Tanker terminal
- Gas Condensate field
- Oil terminal
- Gas terminal
- Principal oil refinery (maximum capacity greater than 27 200 tonnes per day)
- Oil refinery (one symbol may denote several refineries in one area)
- International dividing line

1:5 000 000

50   0   50   100   150   200   250 km

NATURAL VEGETATION
1:10 000 000

Natural vegetation is the plant cover associated with a particular environment, whose components, soil, climate, relief and drainage are unaffected by human activity.

NORTHUMBERLAND
HOLDERNESS
ESSEX
STRATH EARN
GLEN ORRIN
NEW FOREST
CHAT MOSS
TREGARON
ANTRIM
ATHLONE

The sectors represent the amounts of pollen contributed by different trees in peat at various sites. The cold and dry Boreal period favoured the pine and the oak and birch flourished during the mild and wet Atlantic period.

BOREAL PERIOD
Birch Pine Oak

ATLANTIC PERIOD
Birch Pine
Pine Oak

- Oakwood
- Beech and oakwood
- Ash and oakwood
- Birch and oakwood
- Scots Pine
- Heath and moorland
- Mountain tundra
- Water meadows, fen, bog and marsh

SOILS
1:10 000 000

- Calcareous brown earth
- Brown earth
- Acid brown earth
- Podsol
- Peaty podsol
- Grey-brown podsol
- Gley
- Basin peat and alluvial gleys
- Peaty gley and blanket peat

NORTH SEA

30m
Dogger Bank

238

Buchan Ness
Duncansby Hd.
Dunnet Hd.
C. Wrath
Butt of Lewis
Fair I.

Shetland Is.
Foula
Sumburgh Hd.

Orkney Is.
Pentland Firth

ATLANTIC OCEAN

Lewis
799
Outer Hebrides
North Uist
Skye
Ben More Assynt 998
Ben Wyvis 1045
Ben More 1182
Eigg
1009
L. Maree
North West Highlands
Rhum
Ardnamurchan Pt.
Mull
Firth of Lorn
Inner Hebrides
Coll
Islay
Jura
Mull of Kintyre
Arran
Firth of Clyde
Fair Hd.

Moray Firth
Ben Macdhui 1311
Dee
Deveron
Spey
Grampians
Ben Nevis 1343
Glen Mor
L. Ness
Don
Firth of Tay
Tay
Sidlaw Hills
Ochil Hills
Firth of Forth
Bass Rock
Fife Ness
974
Lomond
Forth
Clyde
Pentland Hills
Lammermuir Hills
Southern Uplands
Broad Law 840
Nith
Tweed
Cheviot Hills
Cheviot 816
Merrick 843
Mull of Galloway
St. Bee's Hd.
Eden
Solway Firth
Cross Fell 893
Scafell 978
Scafell 620

Duddon
North Channel
I. of Man

IRISH SEA

Morecambe Bay
Formby Pt.
Liverpool Bay
Gt. Ormes Hd.
Anglesey
Holy I.
Menai Str.
Cardigan Bay
St. George's Channel
Milford Haven
St. David's Hd.

Antrim Mts.
Bann
Neagh
Mourne Mts. 852
Giant's Causeway
Main Hd.
Tory I.
Errigal 752
Derryveagh Mts.
Donegal Bay
Erne
Errs Hd.
Achill Hd.
Mweelrea 819
Connemara
Galway Bay
L. Mask
L. Corrib
Shannon
Dunmore Hd.
Magillicuddy's Reeks 1041
Cork Harbour
Carnsore Pt.
C. Clear

CELTIC SEA

Isles of Scilly
Land's End

Snowdon 1085
Cambrian Mts.
892
Tywi
Brecon Beacons 752
Plynlimon
Wye
920
Golden Vale
Galty Mts. 920
Blackwater
Lee
Suir
Barrow
Slieve Bloom Mts.
Bog of Allen
Nore
Bann
Liffey
Boyne
Wicklow Mts. 926
Central Plain

Tees
N. York Moors
York Wolds
Yorkshire Wolds
Flamborough Hd.
Spurn Hd.
Humber
Holderness
Lincolnshire Wolds
Lincoln Heath
Witham
Trent
Derwent
Ouse
Swale
Wharfe
Aire
Vale of York
737
Pennines
The Peak 636
Cheshire Plain
Wrekin 407
Dee
Mersey
Weaver
Severn
Wye

The Wash
Breckland
The Fens
Nene
Welland
Gt. Ouse
The Naze
Stour
North Foreland
Thames
Lea
North Downs
The Weald
South Downs
Chiltern Hills
Berks Downs
Marlboro Downs
Hampshire Downs
Salisbury Plain
Cotswolds
Mendip Hills
Avon
Kennet
Thames
Cherwell
Severn
Perrett
N. Downs
N. Dorset Downs
Dorset Downs
Beachy Hd.
I. of Wight
Dungeness
Str. of Dover
FRANCE

Bristol Channel
Exmoor 520
Lundy
Hartland Point
Tamar
Yes Tor 618
Dartmoor
Bodmin Moor
Start Pt.
Portland Bill

English Channel

West from Greenwich 0 East from Greenwich

m
1000 400 200 100 0

0 100 200 400 600
m

Projection: Conical with two standard parallels

1:5 000 000

50   0   50   100   150   200   250 km

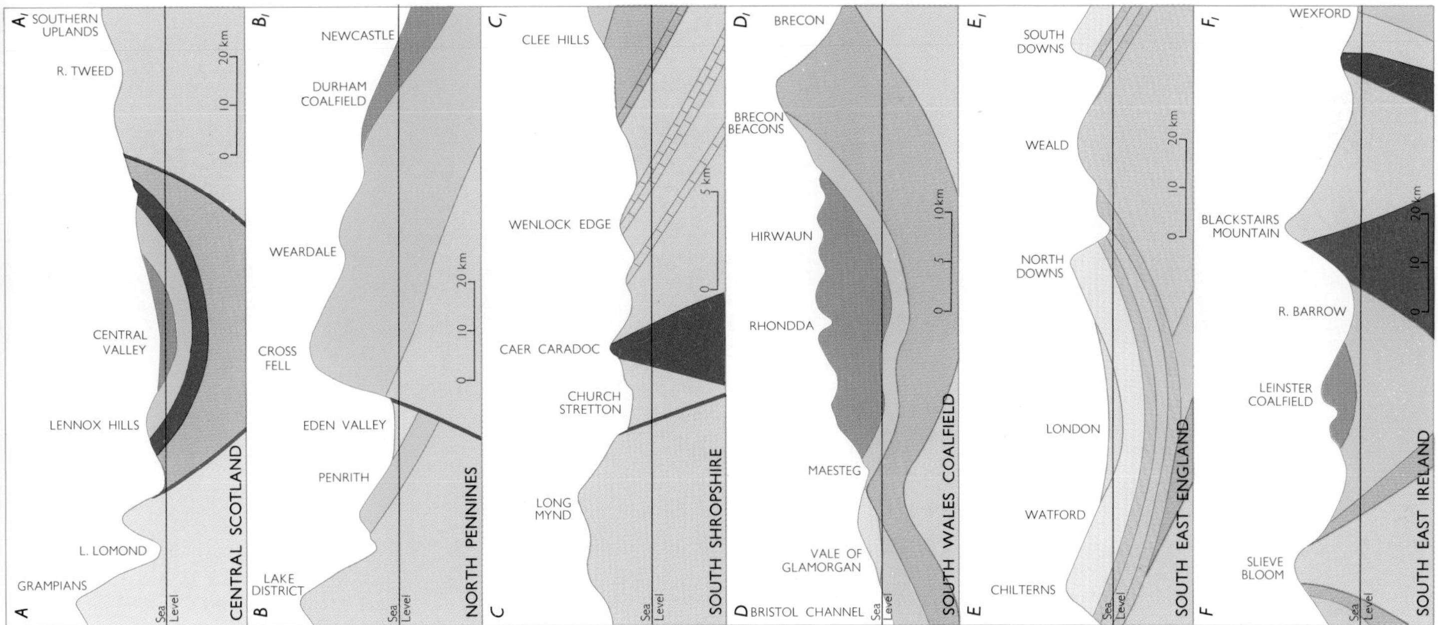

Cross sections (top panels):

A₁ SOUTHERN UPLANDS
R. TWEED
CENTRAL VALLEY
LENNOX HILLS
L. LOMOND
GRAMPIANS
A CENTRAL SCOTLAND
Sea Level
20 km

B₁ NEWCASTLE
DURHAM COALFIELD
WEARDALE
CROSS FELL
EDEN VALLEY
PENRITH
LAKE DISTRICT
B NORTH PENNINES
Sea Level
20 km

C₁ CLEE HILLS
WENLOCK EDGE
CAER CARADOC
CHURCH STRETTON
LONG MYND
C SOUTH SHROPSHIRE
Sea Level
5 km

D₁ BRECON
BRECON BEACONS
HIRWAUN
RHONDDA
MAESTEG
VALE OF GLAMORGAN
D BRISTOL CHANNEL
SOUTH WALES COALFIELD
Sea Level
10 km

E₁ SOUTH DOWNS
WEALD
NORTH DOWNS
LONDON
WATFORD
CHILTERNS
E SOUTH EAST ENGLAND
Sea Level
20 km

F₁ WEXFORD
BLACKSTAIRS MOUNTAIN
R. BARROW
LEINSTER COALFIELD
SLIEVE BLOOM
F SOUTH EAST IRELAND
Sea Level
20 km

Legend:

RECENT
Alluvium

TERTIARY (Cainozoic)
Sands and Clays

SECONDARY (Mesozoic)
Cretaceous–Chalk
Jurassic and Cretaceous –Clays and Sands
Jurassic–Oolitic Limestones
Liassic (Jur.), Triassic and Permian –Sandstones and Clays

PRIMARY (Palæozoic)
Carboniferous–Coal Measures,
Limestone and Millstone Grit
Old Red Sandstone and Devonian
Ordovician, Silurian and Cambrian

ANCIENT (Pre-Cambrian)
Torridonian, Longmyndian etc.
Metamorphic

IGNEOUS (Various ages)
Volcanic (e.g. Basalt)
Intrusive (e.g. Granite)

Major faults

Cross sections A —— A₁

Map labels:

Shetland Is.
Orkney Is.
Outer Hebrides
Skye
Mull
NORTH WEST HIGHLANDS
MOINE THRUST
GLEN MOR FAULT
BOUNDARY HIGHLAND FAULT
SOUTHERN UPLAND FAULT
Grampians
Southern Uplands
Cheviot Hills
Pennines
N. York Moors
Cumbrian Mts.
I. of Man
Lincolnshire Wolds
Antrim Mts.
Mourne Mts.
Central Plain
Derry Mts.
Connemara
Slieve Bloom Mts.
Galty Mts.
Mts. of Kerry
Wicklow Mts.
Anglesey
Cambrian Mts.
Cotswolds
Chilterns
North Downs
South Downs
I. of Wight
Exmoor
Dartmoor
SOUTHWARD LIMIT OF GLACIATION

West from Greenwich   0   East from Greenwich

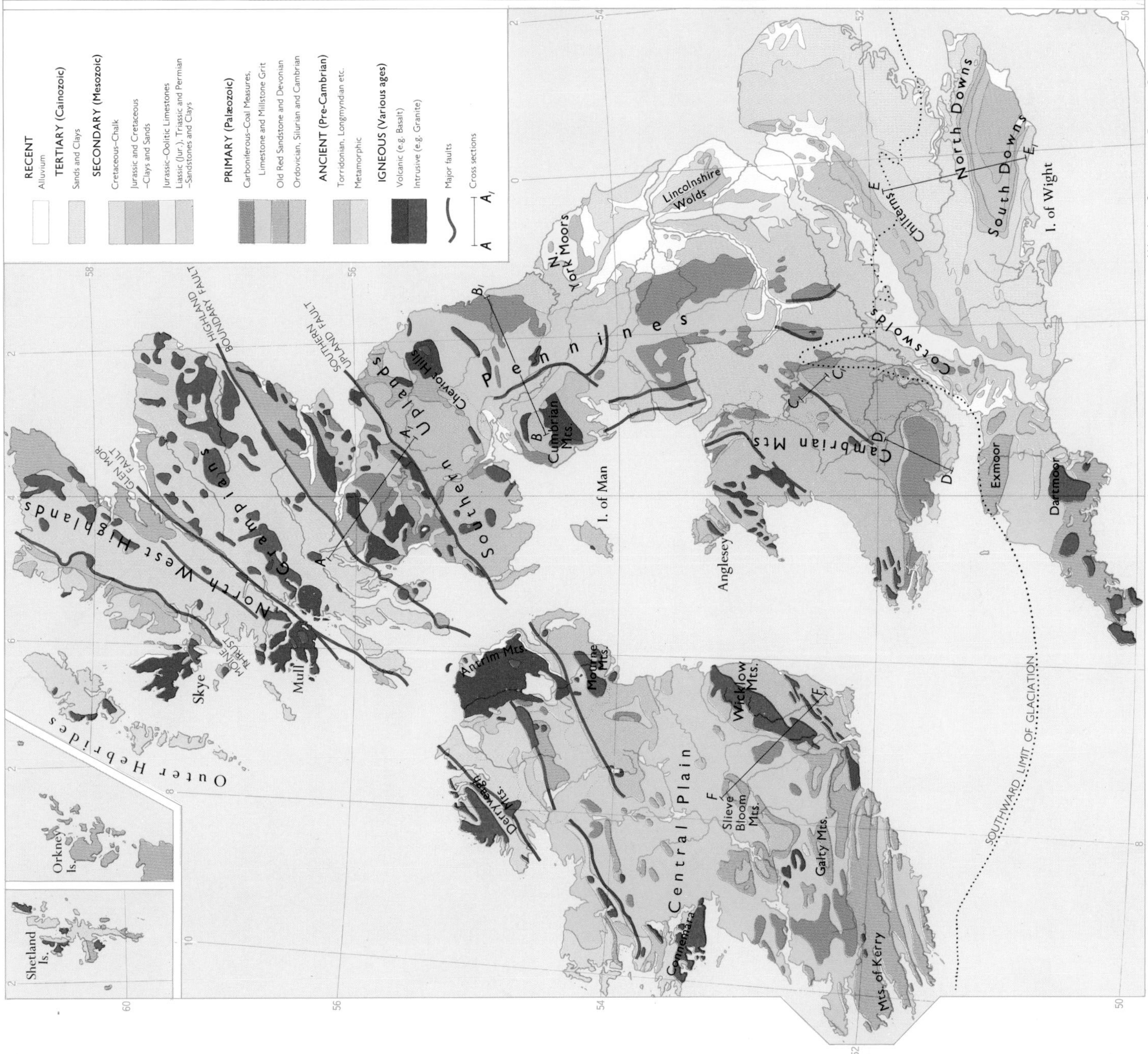

Projection: Conical with two standard parallels

1:10 000 000

100   0   100   200   300   400 km

WIND

% calms in a year
Direction the wind blows from
% frequency of wind from a direction
Force of wind (Beaufort scale)

BEAUFORT FORCE	SPEED (K.P.H.)	CATEGORY
1-3	1-20	Light breeze
4	21-29	Moderate breeze
5-6	30-50	Fresh to strong wind
7	51-61	Moderate gale
8-12	over 62	Gale, storm or hurricane

Lerwick 4.5
Wick 3.1
Dyce 15.
Stornoway 6.9
Tiree 6.8
Tynemouth 4.1
Turnhouse 15.2
Manby 6.5
Mildenhall 6.4
Dungeness 2.1
Heathrow 8.0
Elmdon 9.2
Ringway 9.2
Exeter 13.5
Aberporth 5.6
Aldergrove 5.0
Dublin 5.7
Rosslare 11.1
Belmullet 2.1
Shannon 2.3
Valentia 1.1

SNOW

Average number of mornings with snow cover per year

- more than 50
- 20-50
- 15-20
- 10-15
- 5-10
- less than 5

(after Manley, 1970)

RAIN DAYS

Average number of days per year in which 1mm or more of precipitation was recorded

- over 250 days
- 225-250 days
- 200-225 days
- 175-200 days
- less than 175 days

RAINFALL EXTREMES AND IRRIGATION

Average number of years in ten when irrigation is theoretically necessary for crops (in England and Wales only)

- over 9
- 8-9
- 7-8
- 6-7
- 5-6
- under 5

Regions of reliably high rainfall (more than 1250mm in at least 70% of the years)

Regions of occasionally low rainfall (less than 750mm in at least 30% of the years)

(after Pearl and others, 1954)

ANNUAL RAINFALL AND ISOBARS

mm
- 2500
- 2000
- 1500
- 1000
- 750
- 625

1012 mb.
1016 mb.
1008 mb.
1016 mb.
1013 mb.
1012 mb.
1016 mb.
1016 mb.

—— January Isobars
—— July Isobars

VARIABILITY OF RAIN

The percentage frequency with which rainfall varies from the normal rainfall regime in the year. The higher the percentage figure, the more variable the rainfall

- over 20%
- 18-20%
- 16-18%
- 14-16%
- 12-14%
- 10-12%
- under 10%

(after Gregory, 1955)

Rainfall is least variable in the wetter northern and western areas and most variable in the drier eastern and southern areas

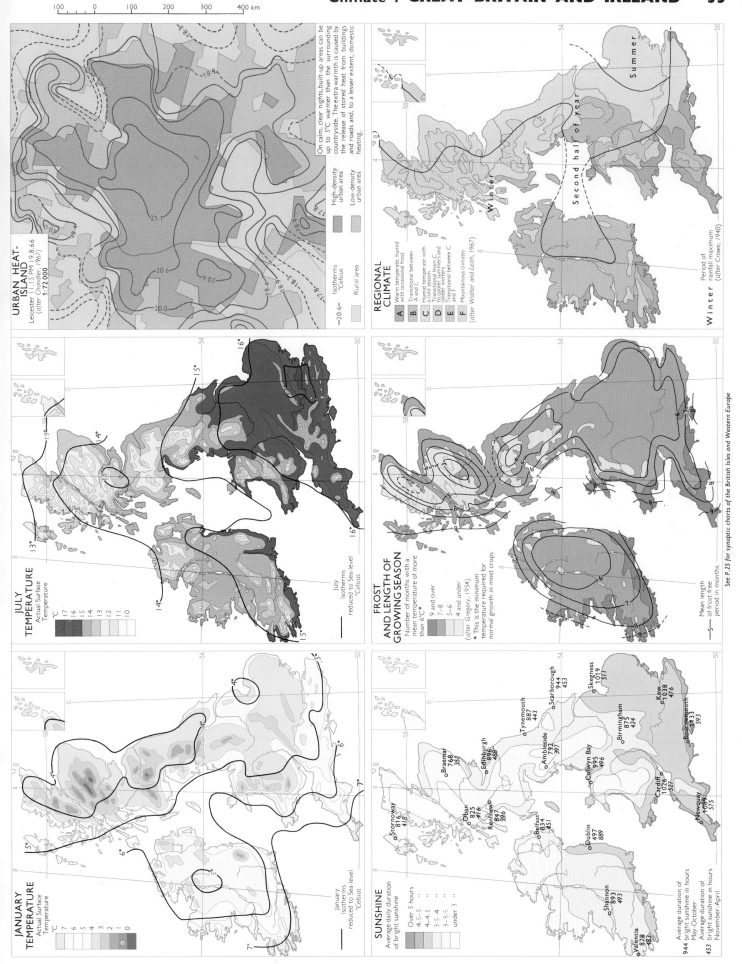

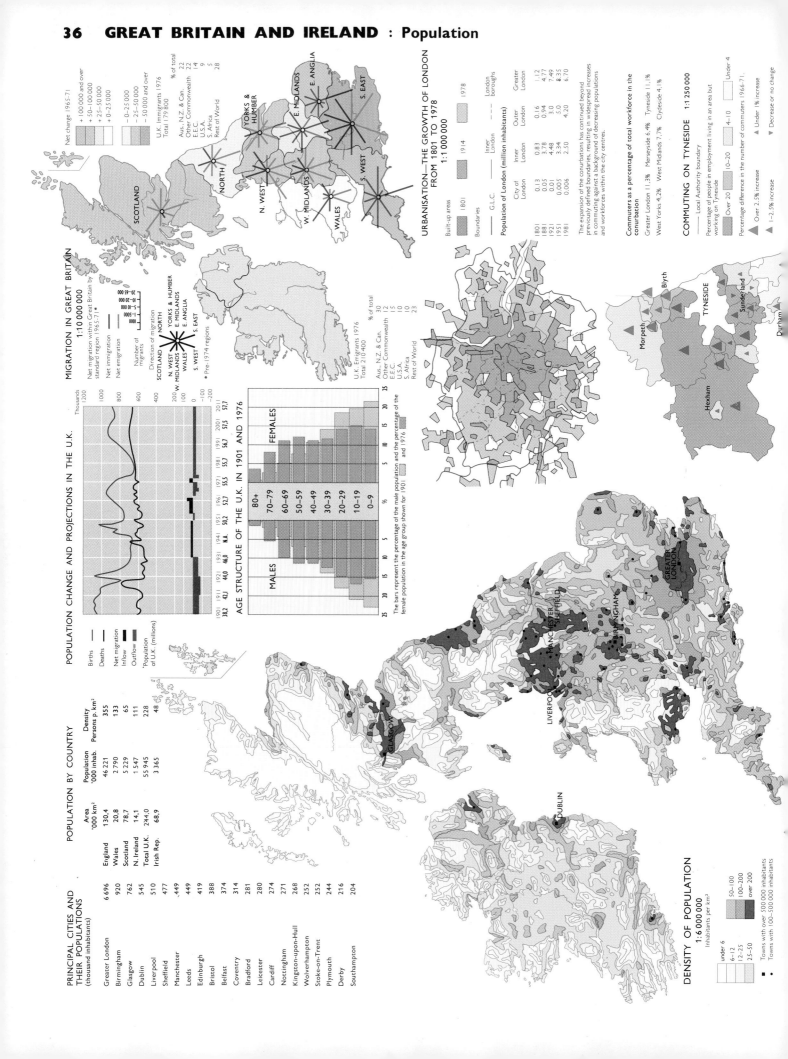

Net change 1965-71
- + 100 000 and over
- + 50–100 000
- + 25–50 000
- 0–25 000
- – 0–25 000
- – 25–50 000
- – 50 000 and over

U.K. Immigrants 1976 Total 179 800	% of total
Aus., N.Z. & Can.	22
Other Commonwealth	22
E.E.C.	14
U.S.A.	9
S. Africa	5
Rest of World	28

SCOTLAND
NORTH
YORKS & HUMBER
N. WEST
E. MIDLANDS
W. MIDLANDS
E. ANGLIA
WALES
S. WEST
S. EAST

URBANISATION—THE GROWTH OF LONDON FROM 1801 TO 1978
1:1 000 000

Built-up areas
- 1801
- 1914
- 1978

Boundaries
- G.L.C.
- Inner London
- London boroughs

Population of London (million inhabitants)	City of London	Inner London	Outer London	Greater London
1801	0.13	0.83	0.16	1.12
1881	0.05	3.78	0.94	4.77
1921	0.01	4.48	3.0	7.49
1951	0.005	3.34	5.0	8.35
1981	0.006	2.50	4.20	6.70

The expansion of the conurbations has continued beyond previously defined boundaries, resulting in widespread increases in commuting against a background of decreasing populations and workforces within the city centres.

Commuters as a percentage of total workforce in the conurbation

Greater London 11.3%   Merseyside 6.4%   Tyneside 11.1%
West Yorks 4.2%   West Midlands 7.7%   Clydeside 4.1%

COMMUTING ON TYNESIDE   1:1 250 000

- Local Authority boundary

Percentage of people in employment living in an area but working on Tyneside
- Over 20
- 10–20
- 4–10
- Under 4

Percentage difference in the number of commuters 1966-71.
- Over 2.5% increase
- Under 1% increase
- Decrease or no change
- – 1–2.5% increase

TYNESIDE
Blyth
Morpeth
Sunderland
Hexham
Durham

MIGRATION IN GREAT BRITAIN
1:10 000 000

Net migration within Great Britain by standard region 1965-71 *
- Net immigration
- Net emigration

Number of migrants
- 20–65 000
- 10–20 000
- 5–10 000
- 1–5 000
- 1000

Direction of migration
SCOTLAND   NORTH
N. WEST   YORKS & HUMBER
W. MIDLANDS   E. MIDLANDS
WALES   E. ANGLIA
S. WEST   S. EAST

* Pre-1974 regions

U.K. Emigrants 1976 Total 210 400	% of total
Aus., N.Z. & Can.	30
Other Commonwealth	12
E.E.C.	15
U.S.A.	10
S. Africa	10
Rest of World	23

POPULATION CHANGE AND PROJECTIONS IN THE U.K.

Thousands
1200 1000 800 600 400 200 0 –100 –200

- Births
- Deaths

Net migration
- Inflow
- Outflow

Population of U.K. (millions)

1901 1911 1921 1931 1941 1951 1961 1971 1981 1991 2001 2011

AGE STRUCTURE OF THE U.K. IN 1901 AND 1976

MALES   FEMALES

- 80+
- 70–79
- 60–69
- 50–59
- 40–49
- 30–39
- 20–29
- 10–19
- 0–9

	1901	1911	1921	1931	1941	1951	1961	1971	1981	1991	2001	2011
	38,2	42,1	44,0	46,0	N.A.	50,2	52,7	55,5	55,7	56,7	57,3	57,7

The bars represent the percentage of the male population and the percentage of the female population in the age group shown for 1901 and 1976

POPULATION BY COUNTRY

	Area '000 km²	Population '000 inhab.	Density Persons p. km²
England	130,4	46 221	355
Wales	20,8	2 790	133
Scotland	78,7	5 229	65
N.Ireland	14,1	1 547	111
Total U.K.	244,0	55 945	228
Irish Rep.	68,9	3 365	48

PRINCIPAL CITIES AND THEIR POPULATIONS
(thousand inhabitants)

Greater London	6 696
Birmingham	920
Glasgow	762
Dublin	545
Liverpool	510
Sheffield	477
Manchester	449
Leeds	449
Edinburgh	419
Bristol	388
Belfast	374
Coventry	314
Bradford	281
Leicester	280
Cardiff	274
Nottingham	271
Kingston-upon-Hull	268
Wolverhampton	252
Stoke-on-Trent	252
Plymouth	244
Derby	216
Southampton	204

DENSITY OF POPULATION
1:6 000 000

Inhabitants per km²
- under 6
- 6–12
- 12–25
- 25–50
- 50–100
- 100–200
- over 200

- ● Towns with over 500 000 inhabitants
- ● Towns with 100–500 000 inhabitants

GLASGOW
LIVERPOOL
MANCHESTER
SHEFFIELD
BIRMINGHAM
GREATER LONDON
DUBLIN

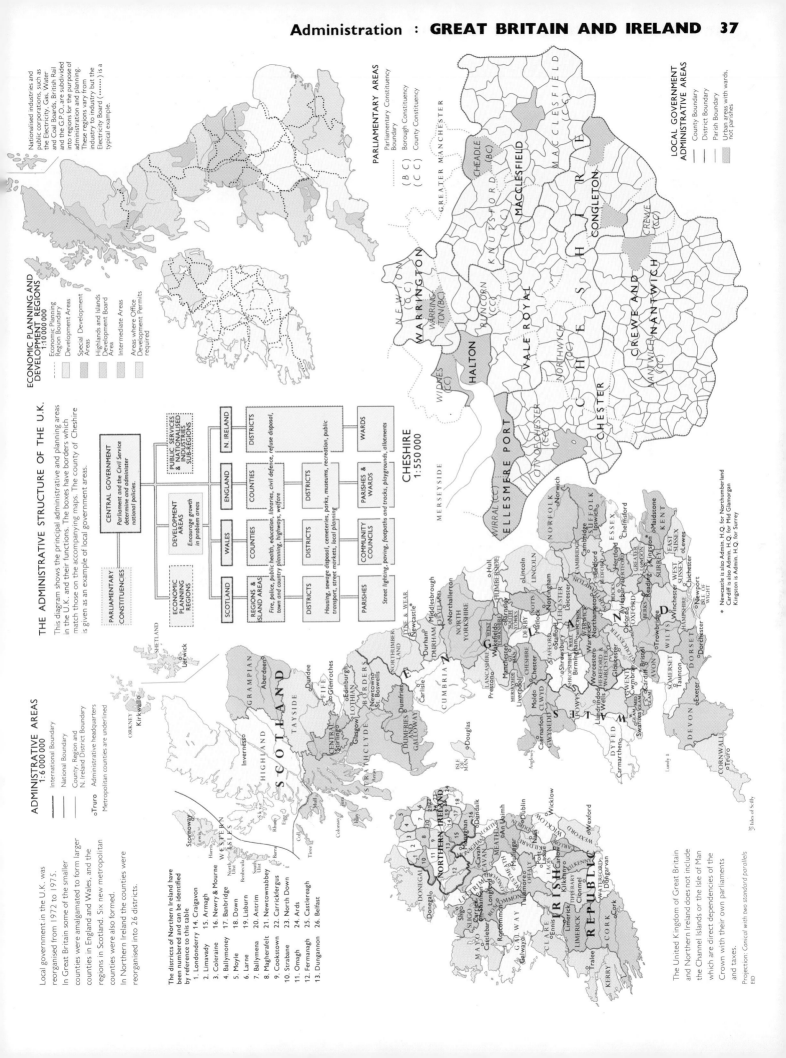

Nationalised industries and public corporations, such as the Electricity, Gas, Water and Coal Boards, British Rail and the G.P.O., are subdivided into regions for the purpose of administration and planning. These regions vary from industry to industry but the Electricity Board (·······) is a typical example.

PARLIAMENTARY AREAS

Parliamentary Constituency Boundary
Borough Constituency
County Constituency
(B C)
(C C)

LOCAL GOVERNMENT ADMINISTRATIVE AREAS

County Boundary
District Boundary
Parish Boundary
Urban areas with wards, not parishes

ECONOMIC PLANNING AND DEVELOPMENT REGIONS
1:10 000 000

Economic Planning Region Boundary
National Boundary
Development Areas
Special Development Areas
Highlands and Islands Development Board Area
Intermediate Areas
Areas where Office Development Permits required

THE ADMINISTRATIVE STRUCTURE OF THE U.K.

This diagram shows the principal administrative and planning areas in the U.K. and their functions. The boxes have borders which match those on the accompanying maps. The county of Cheshire is given as an example of local government areas.

CENTRAL GOVERNMENT
Parliament and the Civil Service determine and administer national policies.

PUBLIC SERVICES & NATIONALISED INDUSTRIES SUB-REGIONS.

PARLIAMENTARY CONSTITUENCIES

DEVELOPMENT AREAS
Encourage growth in problem areas

ECONOMIC PLANNING REGIONS

N. IRELAND	ENGLAND	WALES	SCOTLAND
DISTRICTS	COUNTIES	COUNTIES	REGIONS & ISLAND AREAS
	DISTRICTS	DISTRICTS	DISTRICTS
WARDS	PARISHES & WARDS	COMMUNITY COUNCILS	PARISHES

Fire, police, public health, education, libraries, civil defence, refuse disposal, town and country planning, highways, welfare

Housing, sewage disposal, cemeteries, parks, museums, recreation, public transport, street markets, local planning

Street lighting, paving, footpaths and tracks, playgrounds, allotments

CHESHIRE 1:550 000

ADMINISTRATIVE AREAS
1:6 000 000

International Boundary
National Boundary
County, Region and N. Ireland District Boundary
oTruro Administrative headquarters

Metropolitan counties are underlined

Local government in the U.K. was reorganised from 1972 to 1975.
In Great Britain some of the smaller counties were amalgamated to form larger counties in England and Wales, and the regions in Scotland. Six new metropolitan counties were also formed.
In Northern Ireland the counties were reorganised into 26 districts.

The districts of Northern Ireland have been numbered and can be identified by reference to this table.

1. Londonderry
2. Limavady
3. Coleraine
4. Ballymoney
5. Moyle
6. Larne
7. Ballymena
8. Magherafelt
9. Cookstown
10. Strabane
11. Omagh
12. Fermanagh
13. Dungannon
14. Craigavon
15. Armagh
16. Newry & Mourne
17. Banbridge
18. Down
19. Lisburn
20. Antrim
21. Newtownabbey
22. Carrickfergus
23. North Down
24. Ards
25. Castlereagh
26. Belfast

The United Kingdom of Great Britain and Northern Ireland does not include the Channel Islands or the Isle of Man which are direct dependencies of the Crown with their own parliaments and taxes.

Projection: Conical with two standard parallels
EID

* Newcastle is also Admin. H.Q. for Northumberland
Cardiff is also Admin. H.Q. for Mid Glamorgan
Kingston is Admin. H.Q. for Surrey

1:10 000 000

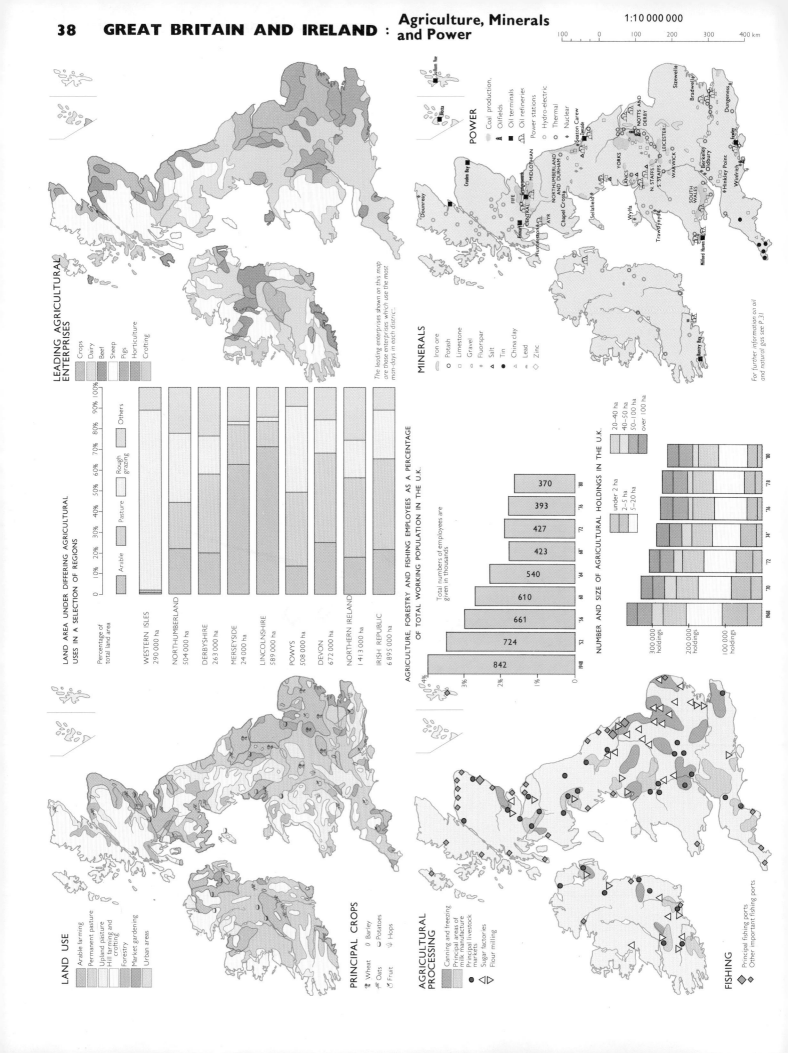

LEADING AGRICULTURAL ENTERPRISES

Crops
Dairy
Beef
Sheep
Pigs
Horticulture
Crofting

The leading enterprises shown on this map are those enterprises which use the most man-days in each district.

POWER

Coal production
Oilfields
Oil terminals
Oil refineries

Power stations
Hydro-electric
Thermal
Nuclear

For further information on oil and natural gas see P.31

MINERALS

Iron ore
Potash
Limestone
Gravel
Fluorspar
Salt
Tin
China clay
Lead
Zinc

LAND AREA UNDER DIFFERING AGRICULTURAL USES IN A SELECTION OF REGIONS

Percentage of total land area

Arable | Pasture | Rough grazing | Others

WESTERN ISLES 290 000 ha
NORTHUMBERLAND 504 000 ha
DERBYSHIRE 263 000 ha
MERSEYSIDE 24 000 ha
LINCOLNSHIRE 589 000 ha
POWYS 508 000 ha
DEVON 672 000 ha
NORTHERN IRELAND 1 413 000 ha
IRISH REPUBLIC 6 895 000 ha

AGRICULTURE, FORESTRY AND FISHING EMPLOYEES AS A PERCENTAGE OF TOTAL WORKING POPULATION IN THE U.K.

Total numbers of employees are given in thousands

'80	370
'76	393
'72	427
'68	423
'64	540
'60	610
'56	661
'52	724
1948	842

NUMBER AND SIZE OF AGRICULTURAL HOLDINGS IN THE U.K.

under 2 ha
2–5 ha
5–20 ha
20–40 ha
40–50 ha
50–100 ha
over 100 ha

'80
'78
'76
'74
'72
'70
1968

300 000 holdings
200 000 holdings
100 000 holdings

LAND USE

Arable farming
Permanent pasture
Upland pasture
Hill farming and crofting
Forestry
Market gardening
Urban areas

PRINCIPAL CROPS

Wheat
Oats
Barley
Potatoes
Fruit
Hops

AGRICULTURAL PROCESSING

Canning and freezing
Principal areas of milk manufacture
Principal livestock markets
Sugar factories
Flour milling

FISHING

Principal fishing ports
Other important fishing ports

1:16 000 000

IRON AND STEEL

TEXTILES
Cotton
Wool
Synthetic fibres
Silk
Linen and Jute

SHIPBUILDING AND MARINE ENGINEERING
Shipbuilding
Marine Engineering

MOTOR VEHICLES
Car Manufacture
Lorry Manufacture
Component Manufacture
Steel Strip Mills

TOTAL NUMBER OF EMPLOYEES IN EACH INDUSTRY

Paper, Printing and Publishing
Timber and Furniture
Bricks, Pottery, Glass, Cement
Clothing and Footwear
Leather goods
Textiles
Motor Vehicles
Shipbuilding, Marine Engineering
Electrical Engineering
Instrument Engineering
Mechanical Engineering
Other metals e.g. Copper
Aluminium
Iron and Steel
Chemicals
Food, Drink and Tobacco

1 000 000
800 000
600 000
400 000
200 000
0

ELECTRICAL ENGINEERING

ALUMINIUM
Aluminium Processing
Aluminium Smelting
Aluminium Production

Boundaries on all maps denote Standard U.K. Planning Regions. These are coloured to show the number of people employed in a region as a percentage of national employment in that industry. Figures for the Irish Republic are not available.

0–5%
5–10%
10–20%
over 20%

Primary (Agriculture, Mining and Fishing)
Secondary (Manufacturing)
Tertiary (Services and Government)

EMPLOYMENT BY REGION

7 000 000 people
5 000 000
2 500 000
1 000 000
500 000

SCOTLAND
NORTH
YORKSHIRE AND HUMBERSIDE
EAST MIDLANDS
EAST ANGLIA
SOUTH EAST
WEST MIDLANDS
WALES
NORTH WEST
SOUTH WEST
NORTHERN IRELAND
IRISH REPUBLIC

MECHANICAL ENGINEERING

CHEMICALS

PAPER, PRINTING AND PUBLISHING
Paper manufacture
Printing and Publishing

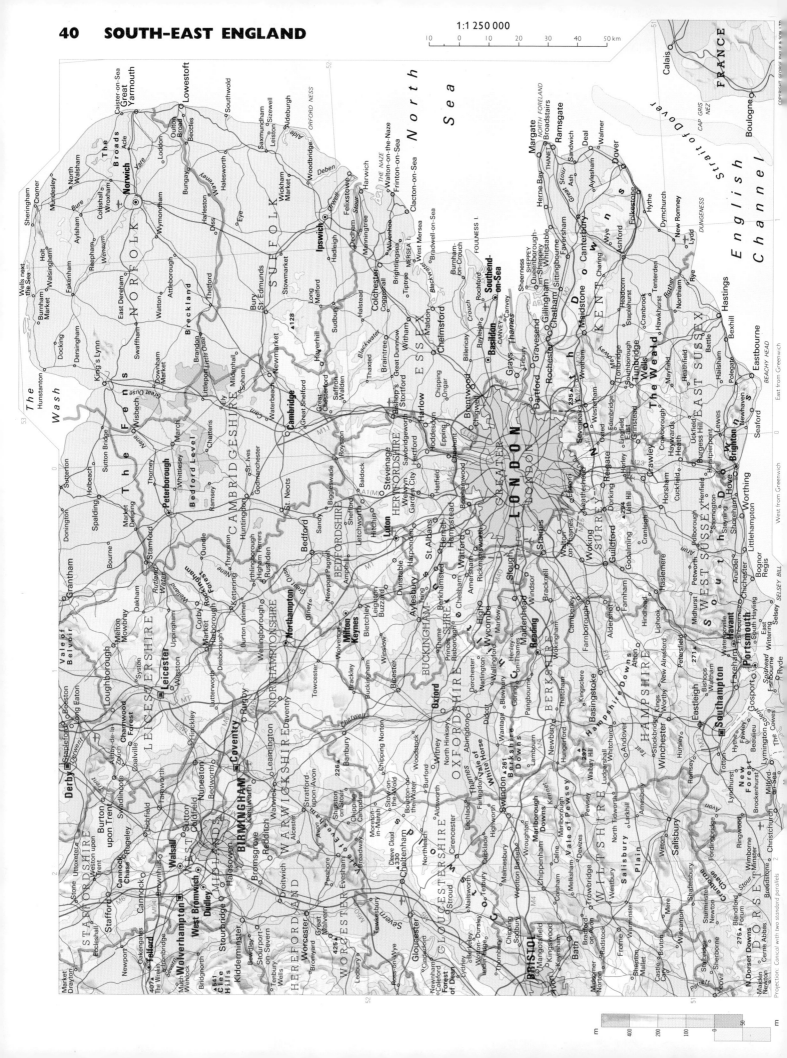

1:1 250 000

10   0   10   20   30   40   50 km

LIVERPOOL

Irish Sea

Cardigan Bay

Bristol Channel

ISLE OF MAN

Nottingham · **Derby** · **Leicester** · **BIRMINGHAM** · **Coventry** · **Oxford**

Stoke-on-Trent · **Wolverhampton** · **West Bromwich** · **Dudley** · Walsall

BRISTOL · **Cardiff** · **Newport** · **Swansea**

DERBYSHIRE · LEICESTERSHIRE · STAFFORDSHIRE · WARWICKSHIRE · WEST MIDLANDS · OXFORDSHIRE · BERKSHIRE · HAMPSHIRE

CHESHIRE · SHROPSHIRE · HEREFORD AND WORCESTER · GLOUCESTERSHIRE · WILTSHIRE · AVON

CLWYD · GWYNEDD · POWYS · DYFED · GWENT · MID GLAMORGAN · SOUTH GLAMORGAN · WEST GLAMORGAN · GLAMORGAN

ANGLESEY · Snowdonia · Brecon Beacons · Exmoor · Mendip Hills · Salisbury Plain · Berkshire Downs · Marlborough Downs

Holyhead · Caernarfon · Bangor · Aberystwyth · Cardigan · Haverfordwest · Milford Haven · Pembroke · Tenby · Carmarthen · Llanelli · Neath · Port Talbot · Bridgend · Barry

Shrewsbury · Telford · Hereford · Worcester · Cheltenham · Gloucester · Bath · Weston-super-Mare

m 1000 800 600 400 200 0   50 100

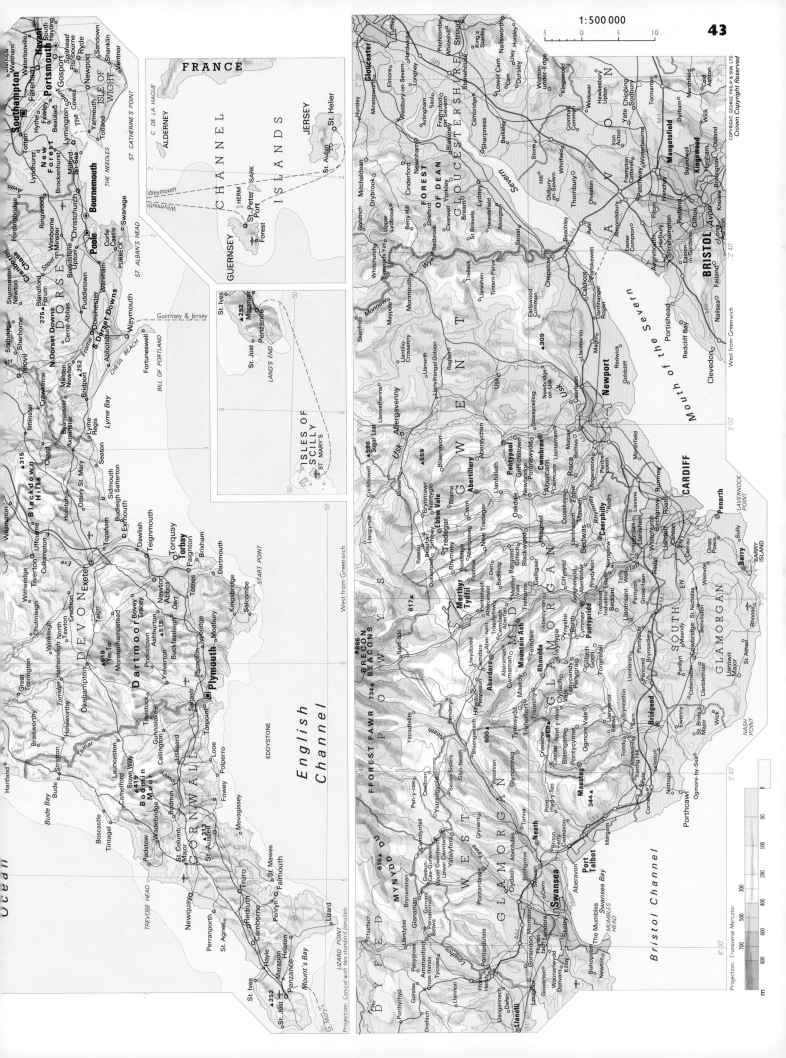

1:1 250 000
10   0   10   20   30   40   50 km

1:500 000

NORTHUMBERLAND

Blyth
Whitley Bay
Tynemouth
South Shields
SUNDERLAND
NEWCASTLE-UPON-TYNE
Gateshead
Jarrow
Hebburn
Wallsend
Washington
Boldon
Seaham
Chester-le-Street
Stanley
Consett
DURHAM
Durham
Houghton-le-Spring
Peterlee
Spennymoor
Bishop Auckland
Newton Aycliffe
Shildon
Hartlepool
CLEVELAND
TEESSIDE
Middlesbrough
Stockton-on-Tees
Thornaby-on-Tees
Billingham
Darlington

North Sea

Wells next the Sea

HUMBERSIDE
Kingston-upon-Hull
Beverley
Scunthorpe
Great Grimsby
Cleethorpes
Goole
LINCOLNSHIRE
Lincolnshire Wolds
Caistor
Market Rasen
Louth
Mablethorpe
Skegness
Lincoln
Newark
Gainsborough

North Sea

NORTHUMBERLAND
Kielder Forest
Kielder Reservoir
Carlisle
CUMBRIA
Cumbrian Mts.
Lake District
Scafell Pikes
Workington
Whitehaven
Keswick
Ullswater
Windermere
Kendal
Barrow-in-Furness
Morecambe Bay
Morecambe
Lancaster
Fleetwood
Blackpool
Lytham St. Annes
Southport
Liverpool Bay
LIVERPOOL
Birkenhead
MERSEYSIDE
Irish Sea

Newcastle-upon-Tyne
Gateshead
Sunderland
Tyne & Wear
South Shields
Tynemouth
Whitley Bay
Blyth
Ashington
Morpeth
DURHAM
Durham
Consett
Bishop Auckland
Newton Aycliffe
Darlington
Hartlepool
CLEVELAND
Teesside
Middlesbrough
Stockton-on-Tees
Redcar
Saltburn-by-the-Sea
Whitby
Scarborough
Filey
Bridlington
North York Moors
Cleveland Hills
Hambleton Hills
Vale of York
York
Harrogate
Ripon
Yorkshire Wolds
Pocklington
Market Weighton
Selby
LEEDS
Bradford
Wakefield
Pontefract
Castleford
Huddersfield
WEST YORKSHIRE
SOUTH YORKSHIRE
Barnsley
Rotherham
SHEFFIELD
Doncaster
Workshop
Retford
Mansfield
NOTTINGHAMSHIRE
Chesterfield
DERBYSHIRE
Peak District
Buxton
MANCHESTER
GREATER MANCHESTER
Stockport
Bolton
Bury
Rochdale
Oldham
Warrington
Widnes
Runcorn
CHESHIRE
Chester
Crewe
Macclesfield
Stoke-on-Trent
Newcastle-under-Lyme
Cheshire Plain
CLWYD
Wrexham
Clwydian Ra.
Denbigh
Rhyl

PENNINE
LANCASHIRE
Preston
Blackburn
Burnley
Accrington
Forest of Bowland
Wigan
St. Helens
Wensleydale
Wharfedale
Skipton
Keighley
Ilkley
Airedale

North Sea

Irish Sea

DUMFRIES AND GALLOWAY
Solway Firth

m
1000 800 600 400 200 100 0 50

1:500 000

45

1:1 250 000

10   0   10   20   30   40   50 km

North Sea

COPYRIGHT GEORGE PHILIP & SON LTD.

Major labels and regions:

HIGHLAND · TAYSIDE · CENTRAL · FIFE · LOTHIAN · STRATHCLYDE · BORDERS · DUMFRIES AND GALLOWAY · CUMBRIA · NORTHUMBERLAND · DURHAM · ULSTER

SOUTHERN UPLANDS · Sidlaw Hills · Ochil Hills · Lennox Hills · Lammermuir Hills · Moorfoot Hills · Pentland Hills · Cheviot Hills · Lowther Hills · Sandybar Hills · Galloway · Carrick · Kyle · Cunninghame · Knapdale · Kintyre · Mts. of Antrim · Rannoch Moor · Merse · Teesdale

Firths and waters:
Firth of Forth · Firth of Clyde · Firth of Tay · Firth of Lorn · Solway Firth · North Channel · Loch Lomond · Loch Katrine · Loch Awe · Loch Etive · Loch Fyne · Loch Long · Loch Doon · Loch Rannoch · Loch Earn · Loch Tay · Loch Leven · Sound of Jura · Sound of Mull · Luce Bay · Wigtown Bay

Cities and towns (selection):
EDINBURGH · GLASGOW · BELFAST · Dundee · Perth · Stirling · Newcastle-upon-Tyne · Gateshead · Durham · Carlisle · Dumfries · Stranraer · Ayr · Kilmarnock · Paisley · Greenock · Dumbarton · Falkirk · Motherwell · Hamilton · Coatbridge · Airdrie · Kirkcaldy · Dunfermline · St. Andrews · Arbroath · Montrose · Forfar · Brechin · Crieff · Callander · Oban · Campbeltown · Rothesay · Brodick · Berwick-upon-Tweed · Galashiels · Hawick · Jedburgh · Kelso · Melrose · Selkirk · Peebles · Lanark · Lockerbie · Annan · Gretna · Kirkcudbright · Newton Stewart · Girvan · Maybole · Troon · Prestwick · Irvine · Saltcoats · Ardrossan · Largs · Alloa · Alva · Dollar · Kinross · Cupar · Leven · Methil · Buckhaven · Haddington · Dunbar · Eyemouth · Coldstream · Duns · Lauder · Wooler · Alnwick · Morpeth · Ashington · Blyth · Hexham · Haltwhistle · Brampton · Penrith · Keswick · Cockermouth · Workington · Maryport · Silloth · Wigton · Langholm · Moffat · Sanquhar · Thornhill · Castle Douglas · Dalbeattie · Gatehouse of Fleet · Creetown · Wigtown · Whithorn · Port William · Glenluce · Portpatrick · Ballantrae · Dalmellington · Cumnock · New Cumnock · Muirkirk · Darvel · Strathaven · East Kilbride · Johnstone · Helensburgh · Gourock · Dunoon · Inveraray · Tarbert · Lochgilphead · Crinan · Bowmore · Port Ellen · Tobermory · Larne · Carrickfergus · Bangor · Newtownards · Holywood · Whitehead · Donaghadee

Heights (spot elevations shown):
Ben Lawers 1214 · Ben More 1174 · Ben Lui 1124 · Ben Cruachan 1126 · Ben Vorlich 942 · 1011 · 1098 · 4148 · Goat Fell 874 · The Cheviot 816 · Broad Law 840 · Merrick 843 · 710 · Trostan 554 · Mickle Fell 790 · Cross Fell 893 · Skiddaw 931 · Peel Fell 602 · 651

Islands:
MULL · JURA · ISLAY · ARRAN · BUTE · COLONSAY · ORONSAY · GIGHA · RATHLIN ISLAND · HOLY I. · FARNE IS. · AILSA CRAIG · STAFFA · IONA · INCHCAPE OR BELL ROCK · Paps of Jura

West from Greenwich

Projection: Conical with two standard parallels

m 1000 800 600 400 200 100 50 100

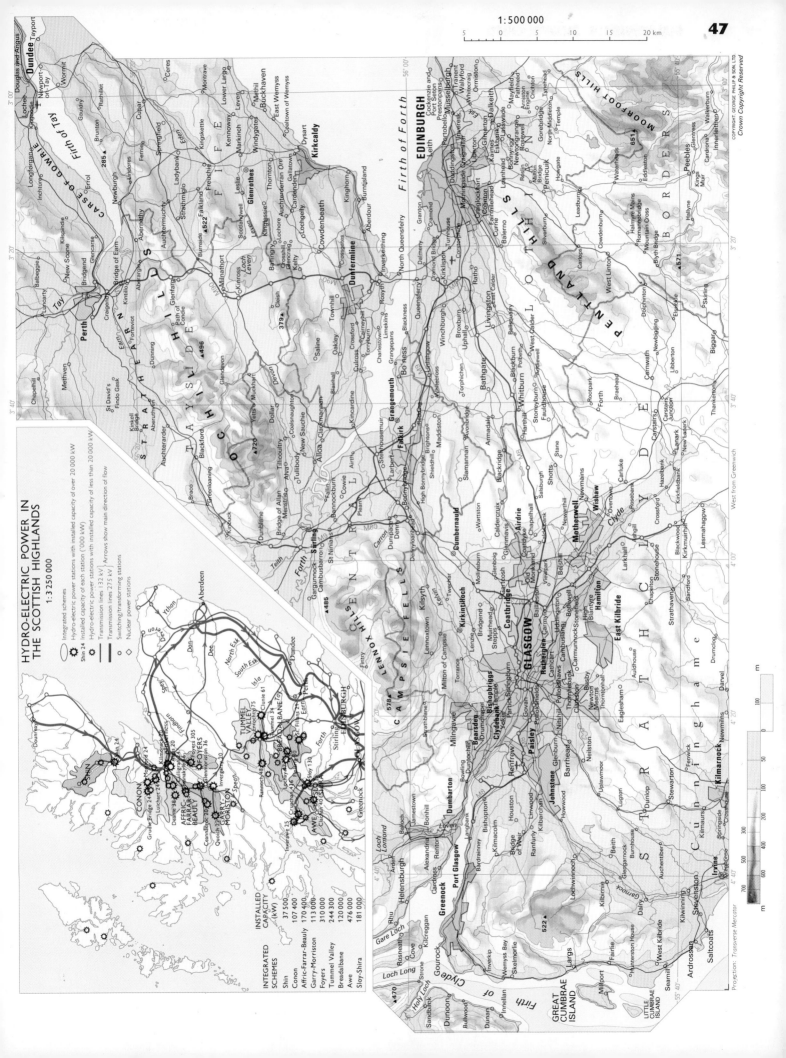

1:500 000

5 0 5 10 15 20 km

HYDRO-ELECTRIC POWER IN THE SCOTTISH HIGHLANDS
1:3 250 000

- ⬭ Integrated schemes
- ✿ Hydro-electric power stations with installed capacity of over 20 000 kW (1000 kW)
- Shin 24 Installed capacity of each station (1000 kW)
- ✿ Hydro-electric power stations with installed capacity of less than 20 000 kW
- Transmission lines (132 kV) Arrows show main direction of flow
- Transmission lines (275 kV)
- ○ Switching/transforming stations
- ◇ Nuclear power stations

INTEGRATED SCHEMES	INSTALLED CAPACITY (kW)
Shin	37 500
Conon	107 400
Affric-Farrar-Beauly	170 400
Garry-Morriston	113 000
Foyers	310 000
Tummel Valley	244 300
Breadalbane	120 000
Awe	476 000
Sloy-Shira	181 000

Projection: Transverse Mercator

West from Greenwich

COPYRIGHT GEORGE PHILIP & SON LTD.
Crown Copyright Reserved

1:1 250 000

10   0   10   20   30   40   50 km

North Sea

DUNCANSBY HEAD
John o'Groats
Duncansby
Mey
Castletown
Scrabster
Thurso
Dounreay
Halkirk
Wick
Lybster
Latheron
Mybster
Dunbeath
Morven ▲705
Kinbrace
Helmsdale
Brora
Golspie
Dornoch
Bonar Bridge
Lairg
Shin
Loch Shin
Strath of Kildonan
Melvich
Bettyhill
Tongue
Syre
Ben Klibreck ▲961
Ben Hope ▲927
Durness
Loch Eriboll
Laxford Bridge
Kylestrome
Scourie
Ben More Assynt ▲998
Ledmore
Loch nan Clar ▲763

DUNNET HEAD
STROMA
Caithness

CAPE WRATH
S U T H E R L A N D

Eddrachillis Bay
Unapool
Lochinver
Ben More ▲809
Enard Bay

Oykel
Ledmore
Squir Mor ▲1109
Achnasheen
▲981

H I G H L A N D

Durness
North Sea

North Minch

BUTT OF LEWIS
Port of Ness
EYE PENINSULA
Stornoway
Barvas
Carloway
Great Bernera
Scarp
Taransay
Clisham ▲798
Tarbert
Leverburgh
Rodel
Loch Seaforth
Scalpay
SHIANT IS.
RUBHA HUNISH

O U T E R   H E B R I D E S
W E S T E R N   I S L E S
L E W I S
H A R R I S
Sound of Harris
Lochmaddy

Little Minch

TARBAT NESS
Portmahomack
Tain
Dornoch Firth
Cromarty Firth
Invergordon
Evanton
Dingwall
Strathpeffer
Muir of Ord
Beauly
Beauly Firth
Inverness
North Kessock
Fortrose
Black Isle
Cromarty
Moray Firth
Nairn
Forres
Findhorn
Burghead
Lossiemouth
Elgin
Rothes
Fochabers
Buckie
Keith
Cullen Portsoy
Banff
Macduff
Aberchirder
Rosehearty
Fraserburgh
St. Combs
Peterhead
Boddam
Cruden Bay
Newburgh
Ellon
New Deer
Mintlaw
Old Meldrum
Inverurie
Kintore
Peterculter
Dyce
Aberdeen
Stonehaven
Inverbervie
Montrose
Arbroath
Carnoustie
Monifieth
Newport-on-Tay
Dundee

KINNAIRDS HEAD
B u c h a n
Turriff
Deveron
Fyvie
Yhan
Huntly
Rhynie
Alford
Aboyne
Banchory
Dee
Ballater
Crathie
Braemar
Glen Shee
Kirriemuir
Forfar
Brechin
Fettercairn
Laurencekirk

F o r m a r t i n e
S t r a t h b o g i e
G R A M P I A N
M a r
Strathspey

C a i r n g o r m   M t s.
▲1245
▲1311
Ben Macdhui ▲1309
Braeriach
Cairn Gorm
▲872
Glas Maol ▲1067
Braes
▲1154

M o n a d h l i a t h   M t s.
Aviemore
Carrbridge
Grantown-on-Spey
Tomintoul
Kingussie
Newtonmore
Dalwhinnie
Laggan
Loch Laggan
▲941
Spey

G R A M P I A N   M T S.
A t h o l l
Blair Atholl
Pitlochry
Tummel
Loch Tummel
▲1081
Loch Rannoch
Kinloch Rannoch
Rannoch Moor
Glen Lyon
Ben Lawers ▲1214
Loch Tay
Killin
Aberfeldy
Dunkeld
Blairgowrie
Coupar Angus
Alyth
Isla

B a d e n o c h
Loch Ericht
Ben Alder ▲1148
▲1128

T A Y S I D E

Sidlaw Hills
Melplash

S T R A T H C L Y D E
Crianlarich
Bridge of Orchy
Loch Awe
Dalmally
Ben Cruachan ▲1124
Oban
Taynuilt
Loch Etive
KERRERA
LISMORE

Fort William
Ben Nevis ▲1343
Spean Bridge
Loch Lochy
Loch Arkaig
Invergarry
Fort Augustus
Loch Ness
Loch Oich
Drumnadrochit
Invermoriston
Foyers
Inverfarigaig
Gle n M o re

L O C H A B E R
Glenfinnan
Glencoe
Kinlochleven
▲1148
▲1098
Ballachulish
Corran
Ardgour
Loch Linnhe
M o r v e r n
Sound of Mull
Tobermory
M U L L
Ben More ▲966
Salen
Craignure
ULVA
STAFFA
Lochaline
Kingairloch
POINT OF ARDNAMURCHAN

K n o y d a r t
Mallaig
Loch Nevis
Loch Morar
Morar
Arisaig
Loch Ailort
Lochailort
Glenuig
M o i d a r t
Loch Shiel
Acharacle
Salen
Strontian
Loch Sunart

W E S T E R   R O S S
Kinlochewe
Loch Maree
Gairloch
Poolewe
Loch Ewe
Gruinard Bay
Ullapool
Loch Broom
▲1053
Achnasheen
Torridon
Loch Torridon
▲1083
Shieldaig
Lochcarron
Loch Carron
Stromeferry
Kyle of Lochalsh
Plockton
Kyleakin
Broadford
SCALPAY
RAASAY
RONA
▲1009
Cuillins
Sligachan
SOAY
CANNA
RHUM
EIGG
MUCK
Armadale
Ardvasar
Sleat
Kyleakin
Loch Hourn
Loch Duich
Glen Shiel
Shiel Bridge
Loch Quoich
Glenelg
Arnisdale

S K Y E
Trotternish
Uig
Portree
Snizort
Loch Snizort
Dunvegan
Portnalong
Cuillin Sound
Point of Sleat
I N N E R   H E B R I D E S
COLL
Arinagour
TIREE
Scarinish
Sound of Arisaig

West from Greenwich

Projection: Conical with two standard parallels

COPYRIGHT GEORGE PHILIP & SON LTD.

m 1000 800 600 400 200 100 0   50 100 m

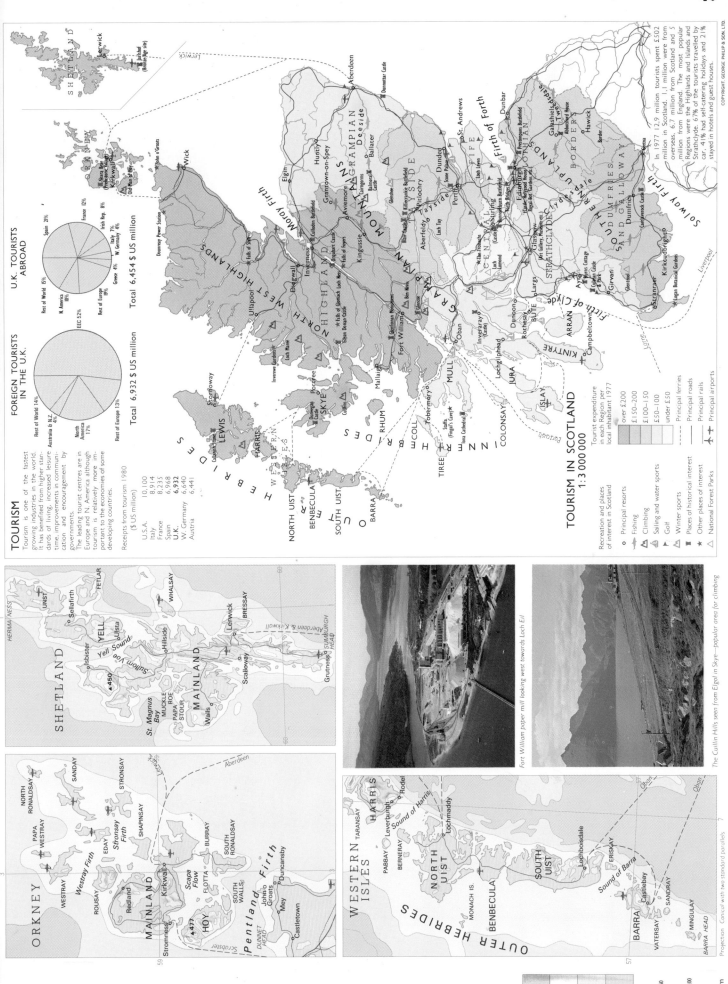

TOURISM

Tourism is one of the fastest growing industries in the world. It has benefited from higher standards of living, increased leisure time, improvements in communication and encouragement by governments.

The leading tourist centres are in Europe and N. America although tourism is relatively more important to the economies of some developing countries.

U.K. TOURISTS ABROAD

Rest of World 5%
Spain 21%
France 12%
N. America 10%
Irish Rep. 8%
Italy 7%
W. Germany 4%
Greece 4%
Rest of Europe 19%
EEC 52%

Total 6,454 $ US million

FOREIGN TOURISTS IN THE U.K.

Rest of World 14%
Australia & N.Z. 4%
North America 17%
Rest of Europe 13%

Total 6,932 $ US million

Receipts from tourism 1980 ($ US million)

U.S.A.	10,100
Italy	8,914
France	8,235
Spain	6,968
U.K.	**6,932**
W. Germany	6,640
Austria	6,441

In 1977 12.9 million tourists spent £502 million in Scotland. 1.1 million were from overseas, 6.7 million from Scotland and 5 million from England. The most popular Regions were the Highlands and Islands and Strathclyde. 67% of the tourists travelled by car, 41% had self-catering holidays and 2.1% stayed in hotels and guest houses.

COPYRIGHT GEORGE PHILIP & SON LTD.

TOURISM IN SCOTLAND
1:3 000 000

Recreation and places of interest in Scotland
○ Principal resorts
Fishing
Climbing
Sailing and water sports
Golf
Winter sports
★ Places of historical interest
Other places of interest
△ National Forest Parks

Tourist expenditure in each Region per local inhabitant 1977
over £200
£150–200
£100–150
£50–100
under £50

Principal ferries
Principal roads
Principal rails
✈ Principal airports

Fort William paper mill looking west towards Loch Eil

The Cuillin Hills seen from Elgol in Skye—popular area for climbing

SHETLAND

HERMA NESS
UNST
FETLAR
Sellafirth
WHALSAY
YELL
Isbister
Hillside
Ulsta
Yell Sound
SUMBURGH HEAD
Aberdeen & Kirkwall
Grutness
St. Magnus Bay
Sullom Voe
▲450
MUCKLE ROE
PAPA STOUR
Walls
MAINLAND
Scalloway
Lerwick
BRESSAY

ORKNEY

NORTH RONALDSAY
PAPA WESTRAY
SANDAY
WESTRAY
STRONSAY
ROUSAY
EDAY
SHAPINSAY
Westray Firth
Stronsay Firth
Redland
Kirkwall
MAINLAND
BURRAY
Stromness
HOY
▲477
Scapa Flow
FLOTTA
SOUTH RONALDSAY
SOUTH WALLS
Duncansby
John o'Groats
Mey
Castletown
DUNNET HEAD
Scrabster
Aberdeen
Pentland Firth

WESTERN ISLES / OUTER HEBRIDES

TARANSAY
Rodel
HARRIS
Leverburgh
Sound of Harris
PABBAY
BERNERAY
NORTH UIST
Lochmaddy
MONACH IS.
BENBECULA
Lochboisdale
SOUTH UIST
ERISKAY
Sound of Barra
BARRA
Castlebay
VATERSAY
SANDRAY
MINGULAY
BARRA HEAD
Oban

Projection Conical with two standard parallels

Map labels

SHETLAND
Lerwick
Jarlshof (Bronze-Age site)

ORKNEY
Skara Brae (Prehistoric Village)
Kirkwall
Old Man of Hoy
John o'Groats
Wick
Dounreay Power Station
Thurso

NORTH WEST HIGHLANDS
Ullapool
Inverewe Gardens
Loch Maree
Falls of Glomach
Eilean Donan Castle
Falls of Foyers
Urquhart Castle
Loch Ness
Inverness
Falls of Shin
Elgin
Moray Firth

WESTERN ISLES
LEWIS
Stornoway
Callanish Stones
HARRIS

SKYE
Portree
Dunvegan Castle
Cuillins
RHUM
COLL
TIREE
MULL
Tobermory
Staffa (Fingal's Cave)
Iona Cathedral
COLONSAY
JURA
ISLAY
Portaskaig
COLL
N

Mallaig
Glenfinnan Monument
Fort William
Glencoe
Ben Nevis
Oban
The Trossachs
Loch Awe
Inveraray (Castle)
Lochgilphead
KINTYRE
Campbeltown
BUTE
ARRAN
Rothesay
Dunoon
Largs
Firth of Clyde
Clyde

GRAMPIAN MOUNTAINS
Aberdeen
Dunnottar Castle
Huntly
Deeside
Grantown-on-Spey
Aviemore
Cairngorms
Kingussie
Balmoral Castle
Ballater
Glenshee
Braemar
Killiecrankie Battlefield
Pitlochry
Blair Castle
Aberfeldy
Loch Tay
Perth
Scone Palace
Glamis Castle
Dundee
St. Andrews
TAYSIDE
FIFE
Firth of Forth
Dunbar

CENTRAL
Stirling
Bannockburn Battlefield
Loch Lomond
Glasgow
Art Gallery, Museum etc.
Prestonpans Battlefield
Edinburgh
Castle, Holyrood House, Royal Bot. Garden etc.
LOTHIAN
Galashiels
Abbotsford House
Tweed
BORDER
Hawick
Border
Cupar

STRATHCLYDE
Clydesdale
Ayr
Burns Cottage
Culzean Castle & Park
Girvan
Glentrool
Logan Botanical Garden
Stranraer
Kirkcudbright
Cardoness Castle
Dumfries
SOUTHERN UPLANDS
DUMFRIES AND GALLOWAY
NITHSDALE
Solway Firth
Liverpool

HIGHLAND
NORTH WEST HIGHLANDS
GRAMPIAN MOUNTAINS

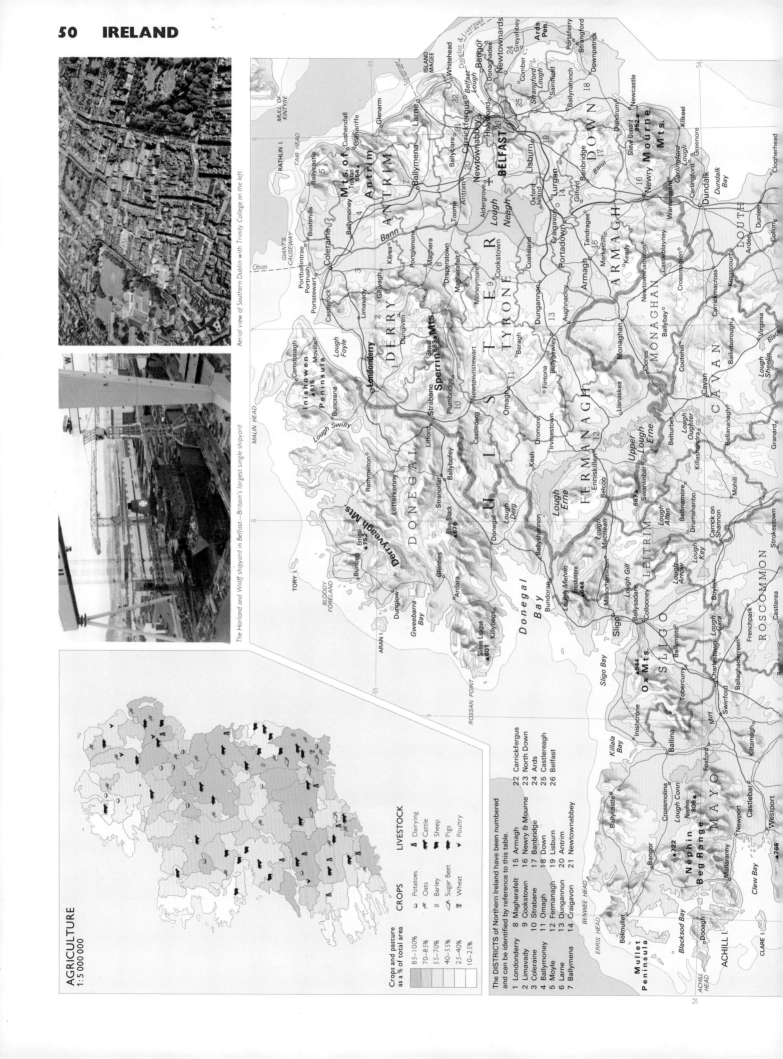

Aerial view of Southern Dublin with Trinity College on the left

The Harland and Wolff shipyard in Belfast—Britain's largest single shipyard

AGRICULTURE
1:5 000 000

Crops and pasture as a % of total area
- 85–100%
- 70–85%
- 55–70%
- 40–55%
- 25–40%
- 10–25%

CROPS
- Potatoes
- Oats
- Barley
- Sugar Beet
- Wheat

LIVESTOCK
- Dairying
- Cattle
- Sheep
- Pigs
- Poultry

The DISTRICTS of Northern Ireland have been numbered and can be identified by reference to this table.

1 Londonderry
2 Limavady
3 Coleraine
4 Ballymoney
5 Moyle
6 Larne
7 Ballymena
8 Magherafelt
9 Cookstown
10 Strabane
11 Omagh
12 Fermanagh
13 Dungannon
14 Craigavon
15 Armagh
16 Newry & Mourne
17 Banbridge
18 Down
19 Lisburn
20 Antrim
21 Newtownabbey
22 Carrickfergus
23 North Down
24 Ards
25 Castlereagh
26 Belfast

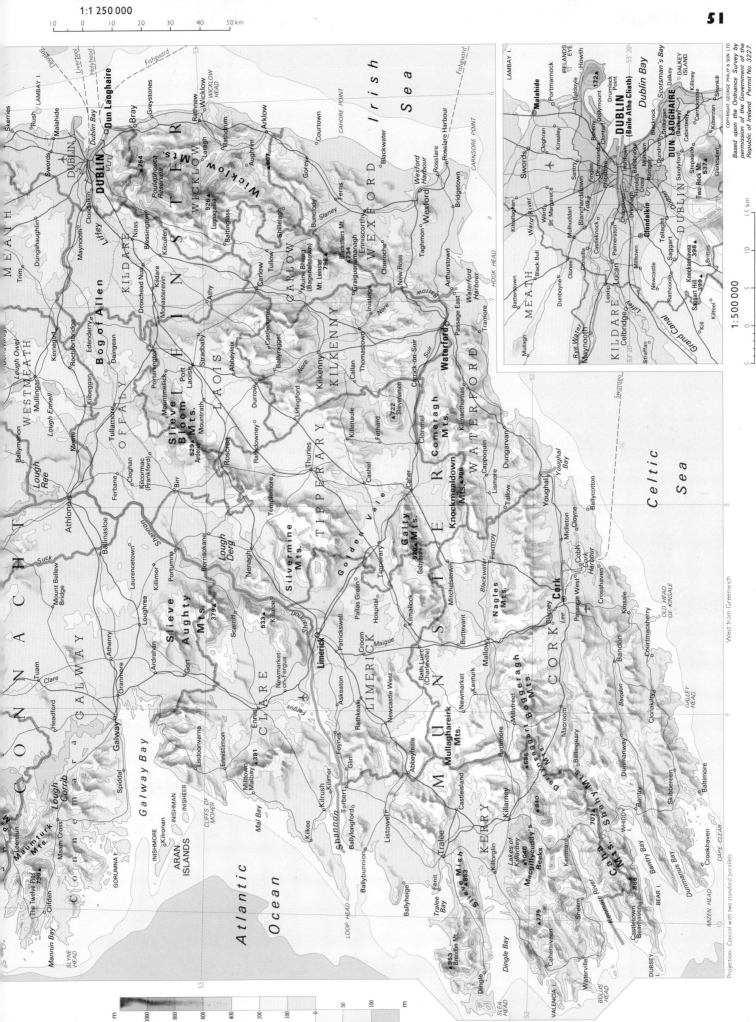

1:1 250 000

10 0 10 20 30 40 50 km

LAMBAY I.
Skerries
Rush
Malahide
Swords
Dun Laoghaire
DUBLIN
DUBLIN
Dublin Bay
Liverpool
Holyhead
Fishguard
Greystones
Bray
Wicklow
WICKLOW HEAD
Rathnew
Wicklow
Arklow
754
Paulabaoura Reservoir
926
Lugnaquilla
Laragh
Rathdrum
Aughrim
407
Courtown
MEATH
Dunshaughlin
Trim
Maynooth
Clondalkin
KILDARE
Naas
Blessington
Kilcullen
Kildare
Monasterevin
Athy
Carlow
Tullow
CARLOW
Muine Bheag
(Bagenalstown)
796
Mt. Leinster
Blackstairs Mt.
734
Gorey
Blackwater
CAHORE POINT
WEXFORD
Enniscorthy
Ferns
Bunclody
Shillelagh
Baltinglass
Slaney
CARNSORE POINT
Rosslare Harbour
Rosslare
Wexford
Wexford Harbour
Bridgetown
Taghmon
Wexford
New Ross
Arthurstown
HOOK HEAD
Waterford Harbour
Passage East
Cheekpoint
Tramore
Dunmore East

Irish Sea

WESTMEATH
Lough Owel
Mullingar
Lough Ennell
Kilbeggan
Edenderry
Rochfortbridge
Daingean
OFFALY
Tullamore
Portarlington
Port Laoise
Laoise
Stradbally
Abbeyleix
LAOIS
Durrow
Rathdowney
Ballyragget
KILKENNY
Kilkenny
Callan
Thomastown
Inistioge
Mullinavat
Carrick-on-Suir
WATERFORD
Waterford
Clonmel
Carrick-on-Suir

MEATH
Ballymahon
Lough Ree
Lough
Athlone
Ballinasloe
GALWAY
Laurencetown
Killimor
Portumna
Lough Derg
Borrisokane
Nenagh
TIPPERARY
Templemore
Thurles
Cashel
Caher
Golden Vale
Tipperary
Cahir
Clonmel
Comeragh Mts.
795
WATERFORD
Cappoquin
Dungarvan
Youghal Bay

CONNACHT
Suck
Mount Bellew
Bridge
Loughrea
Ardrahan
Gort
Slieve Aughty Mts.
379
Scarriff
533
Killaloe
Silvermine Mts.
Nenagh
Silvermine Mts.
Pallas Green
Hospital
Tipperary
Galtee Mts.
919
Galtymore
Kilmallock
Mitchelstown
Knockmealdown Mts.
795
Lismore
Tallow
Fermoy
Blackwater
Fermoy
Nagles Mts.
Mallow
Buttevant
CORK
Mitchelstown

Galway Bay
Galway
Oranmore
Clarinbridge
Kinvarra
Ballyvaughan
CLARE
Lisdoonvarna
CLIFFS OF MOHER
Ennistimon
Milltown
Malbay
391
Lahinch
Ennis
Newmarket-
on-Fergus
Fergus
Shannon
LIMERICK
Limerick
Patrickswell
Croom
Maigue
Bruff
Rath Luirc
(Charleville)
Newmarket
Kanturk
Millstreet
Boggeragh Mts.
Macroom
Blarney
Cork
Cork Harbour
Passage West
Crosshaven

ARAN ISLANDS
INISHMORE
INISHMAAN
INISHEER
Spiddal
GORUMNA
Costelloe
Galway Bay

Atlantic Ocean

LOOP HEAD
Kilkee
Kilrush
Killimer
Glin
Tarbert
Foynes
Askeaton
Shannon
Fergus
Abbeyfeale
Newcastle West
KERRY
Listowel
Ballybunnion
Tralee Bay
Fenit
Tralee
Slieve Mish Mts.
853
Castleisland
Castlemaine
Killorglin
Lakes of Killarney
Killarney
1040
Macgillycuddy's
Reeks
Mullaghareirk Mts.
486

Mal Bay
SLEA HEAD
Dingle
963
Brandon Mt.
Dingle Bay
Dingle
CAHERSIVEEN
VALENCIA I.
Waterville
BOLUS HEAD
Sneem
Kenmare
Kenmare River
DURSEY
BEAR I.
Castletown
Bearhaven
775
Caha Mts.
707
Bantry Bay
Bantry
Dunmanway
WHIDDY
Dunmanus Bay
MIZEN HEAD
Crookhaven
CAPE CLEAR
Skibbereen
Baltimore
Clonakilty
GALLEY HEAD
Courtmacsherry
Bandon
Kinsale
OLD HEAD OF KINSALE
Ballycotton
Cloyne
Midleton
Cobh
Youghal

Celtic Sea

West from Greenwich

Projection: Conical with two standard parallels

m 1000 800 600 400 200 100 50 0 50 100 m

1:500 000

15 km

DUBLIN
(Baile Átha Cliath)
Malahide
Portmarnock
Howth
IRELANDS EYE
LAMBAY I.
Baldoyle
Dollymount
172
Clontarf
DUN LAOGHAIRE
(Dunleary)
DALKEY ISLAND
DALKEY
Killiney
Shankill
537
Two Rock Mt.
Glencullen
Stepaside
Sandyford
Dundrum
Rathfarnham
Terenure
Tallaght
Clondalkin
398
Brittas
399
Saggart Hill
Saggart
Rathcoole
Newcastle
Lucan
Palmerston
Leixlip
Celbridge
Maynooth
KILDARE
MEATH
Dunboyne
Clonee
Black Bull
Batterstown
Dunshaughlin
Ratoath
Ashbourne
Swords
DUBLIN
Dublin Bay
Scotsman's Bay

COPYRIGHT GEORGE PHILIP & SON. LTD.
Based upon the Ordnance Survey by
permission of the Government of the
Republic of Ireland. Permit No. 3227.

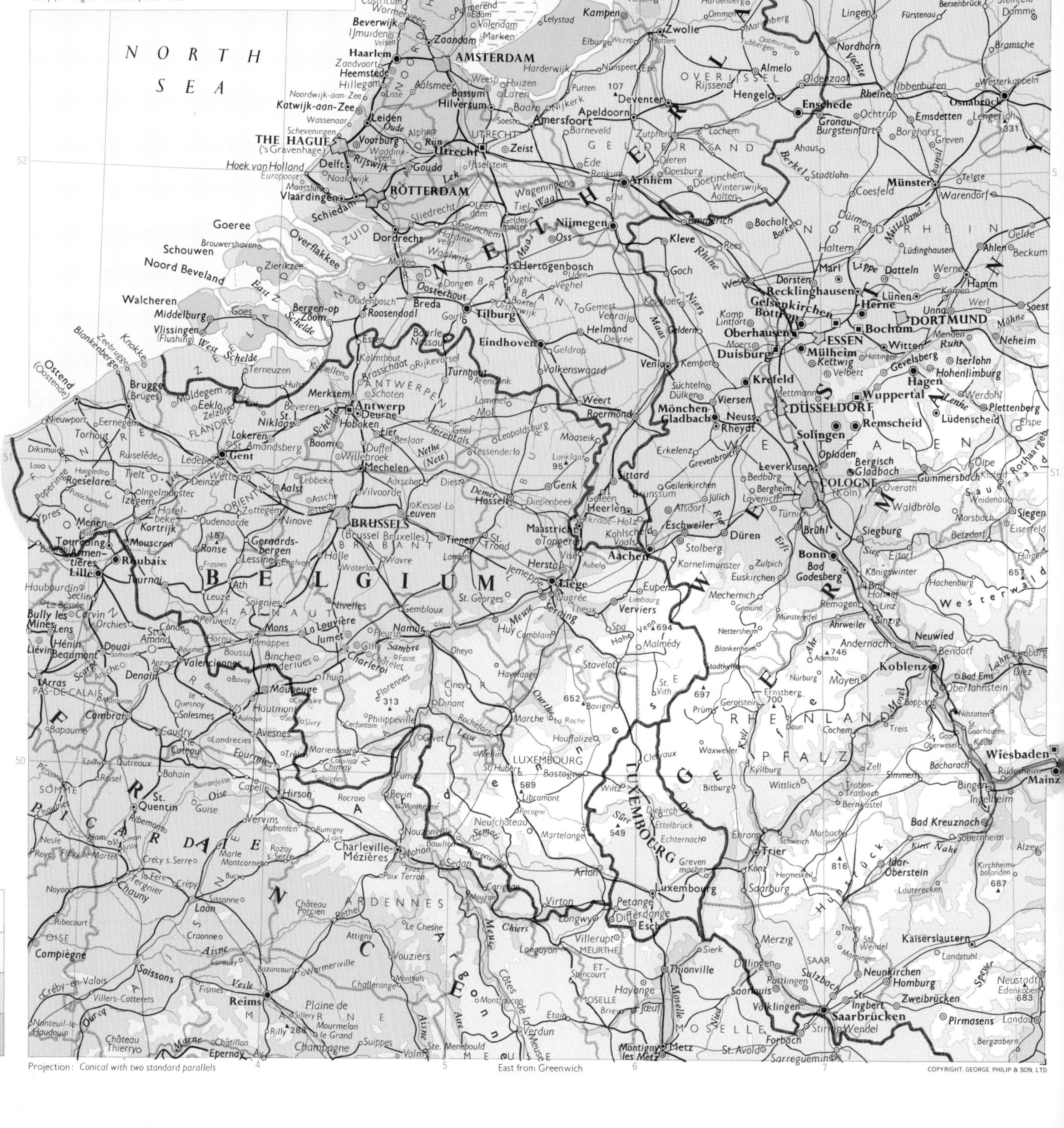

1:2 000 000

10 0 10 20 30 40 50 60 70 80 km

Dairy farming on Holland's polder lands

NORTH SEA

WESTFRISCHE EILANDEN

Ostfriesland

NETHERLANDS

FRIESLAND

DRENTHE

OVERIJSSEL

GELDERLAND

NOORD BRABANT

NIEDER SACHSEN

NORDRHEIN

WESTFALEN

RHEINLAND PFALZ

BELGIUM

HAINAU

BRABANT

FLANDRE

LUXEMBOURG

ARDENNES

PICARDIE

PAS-DE-CALAIS

SOMME

Major places: Schiermonnikoog, Ameland, Terschelling, Vlieland, Texel, Den Helder, Leeuwarden, Groningen, Emden, Oldenburg, Assen, Zwolle, Amsterdam, Haarlem, Leiden, THE HAGUE ('s Gravenhage), ROTTERDAM, Delft, Utrecht, Apeldoorn, Enschede, Münster, Osnabrück, Arnhem, Nijmegen, 's Hertogenbosch, Tilburg, Eindhoven, Breda, Venlo, Duisburg, ESSEN, DORTMUND, Bochum, Gelsenkirchen, Oberhausen, Krefeld, Mönchen-Gladbach, DÜSSELDORF, Wuppertal, Solingen, Remscheid, Hagen, COLOGNE (Köln), Aachen, Bonn, Bad Godesberg, Koblenz, Wiesbaden, Mainz, Antwerpen, Gent, BRUSSELS (Brussel Bruxelles), Mechelen, Leuven, Maastricht, Heerlen, Liège, Verviers, Namur, Charleroi, Mons, La Louvière, Roubaix, Lille, Tournai, Valenciennes, Maubeuge, LUXEMBOURG, Esch, Thionville, Metz, Trier, Saarbrücken, Kaiserslautern, Neunkirchen, Homburg, Zweibrücken, Pirmasens, Reims, Soissons, Laon, Compiègne, Charleville-Mézières, Sedan, Verdun

m
400
200
0

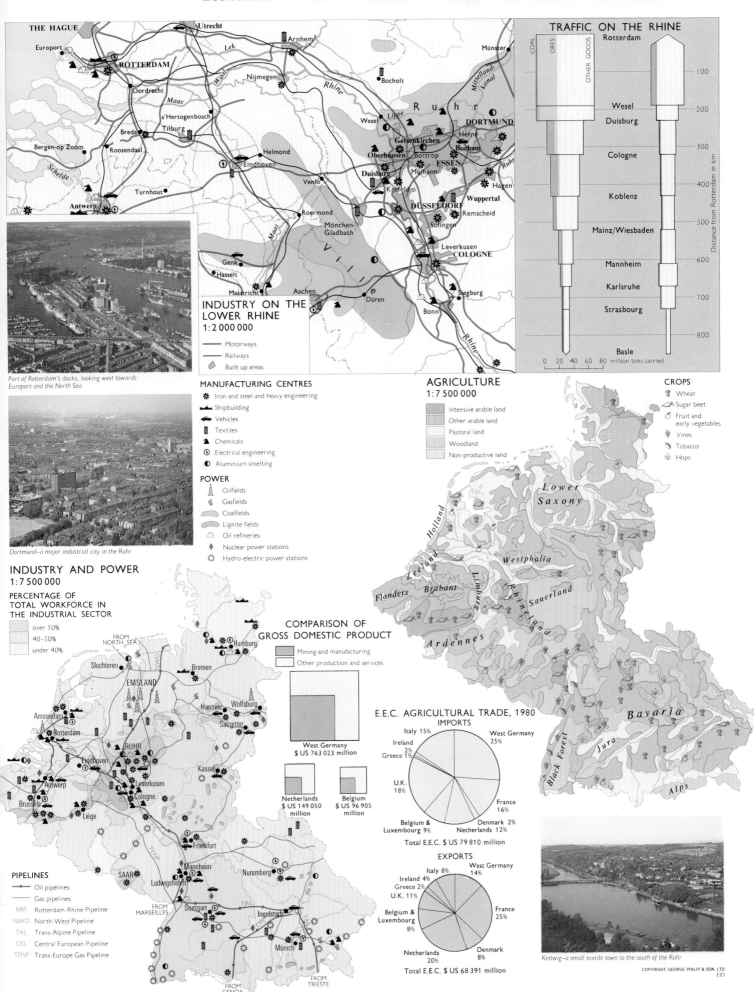

INDUSTRY ON THE LOWER RHINE
1 : 2 000 000

- Motorways
- Railways
- Built up areas

Part of Rotterdam's docks, looking west towards Europort and the North Sea

Dortmund—a major industrial city in the Ruhr

TRAFFIC ON THE RHINE

COAL — ORES — OTHER GOODS

Rotterdam
Wesel
Duisburg
Cologne
Koblenz
Mainz/Wiesbaden
Mannheim
Karlsruhe
Strasbourg
Basle

Distance from Rotterdam in km

0 20 40 60 80 million tons carried

MANUFACTURING CENTRES

- Iron and steel and heavy engineering
- Shipbuilding
- Vehicles
- Textiles
- Chemicals
- Electrical engineering
- Aluminium smelting

POWER

- Oilfields
- Gasfields
- Coalfields
- Lignite fields
- Oil refineries
- Nuclear power stations
- Hydro-electric power stations

AGRICULTURE
1 : 7 500 000

- Intensive arable land
- Other arable land
- Pastoral land
- Woodland
- Non-productive land

CROPS

- Wheat
- Sugar beet
- Fruit and early vegetables
- Vines
- Tobacco
- Hops

INDUSTRY AND POWER
1 : 7 500 000

PERCENTAGE OF TOTAL WORKFORCE IN THE INDUSTRIAL SECTOR

- over 50%
- 40–50%
- under 40%

COMPARISON OF GROSS DOMESTIC PRODUCT

- Mining and manufacturing
- Other production and services

West Germany
$ US 763 023 million

Netherlands
$ US 149 050 million

Belgium
$ US 96 905 million

E.E.C. AGRICULTURAL TRADE, 1980
IMPORTS

Italy 15%
Ireland 2%
Greece 1%
U.K. 18%
Belgium & Luxembourg 9%
Denmark 2%
Netherlands 12%
France 16%
West Germany 25%

Total E.E.C. $ US 79 810 million

EXPORTS

Italy 8%
Ireland 4%
Greece 2%
U.K. 11%
Belgium & Luxembourg 8%
Netherlands 20%
Denmark 8%
France 25%
West Germany 14%

Total E.E.C. $ US 68 391 million

PIPELINES

- Oil pipelines
- Gas pipelines

- RRP Rotterdam-Rhine Pipeline
- NWO North-West Pipeline
- TAL Trans-Alpine Pipeline
- CEL Central European Pipeline
- TENP Trans-Europe Gas Pipeline

Kettwig—a small textile town to the south of the Ruhr

NORTH SEA

BALTIC

NETHERLANDS

BELGIUM

LUX.

FRANCE

GERMANY

WEST GERMANY

EAST GERMANY

CZECHOSLOVAKIA

SWITZERLAND

AUSTRIA

ITALY

ADRIATIC SEA

Gulf of Genoa

Gulf of Venice

Flensburg · Schleswig · Kiel · Kiel Bay · Fehmarn · Lübeck Bay · Rostock · Stralsund · Rügen · Szczecin (Stettin)

Hamburg · Bremen · Bremerhaven · Hanover · Berlin · Potsdam · Magdeburg · Brandenburg · Leipzig · Dresden · Halle · Erfurt

Amsterdam · The Hague · Rotterdam · Utrecht · Haarlem · Groningen · Leeuwarden · Oldenburg

Antwerp · Brussels · Ghent · Bruges · Liège · Maastricht · Lille

Dortmund · Essen · Düsseldorf · Cologne · Bonn · Koblenz · Frankfurt · Wiesbaden · Mainz · Mannheim · Heidelberg · Karlsruhe · Stuttgart · Nuremberg · Würzburg · Munich · Augsburg · Regensburg · Ingolstadt

Luxembourg · Metz · Nancy · Strasbourg · Reims · Dijon · Besançon · Mulhouse · Freiburg

Prague · Plzeň (Pilsen) · Karl Marx Stadt (Chemnitz) · Zwickau · Brno (Brünn) · Bohemian Forest

Zürich · Bern · Geneva · Lausanne · Basle · Luzern · St. Gallen · Innsbruck · Salzburg · Vienna (Wien) · Linz · Graz · Klagenfurt

Milan · Turin · Genoa · Bologna · Venice · Verona · Padua · Trieste · Trento · Bolzano · Como · Bergamo · Brescia

Marseilles · Nice · Cannes · Lyons · Grenoble

Zagreb · Ljubljana · Maribor · Rijeka

Projection: Conical with two standard parallels · East from Greenwich

1:5 000 000

50   0   50   100   150   200 km

The Alps near Innsbruck in winter

COPYRIGHT. GEORGE PHILIP & SON. LTD

Countries and regions:
LITHUANIA S.S.R.
WHITE RUSSIA S.S.R.
P O L A N D
U K R A I N E   S.S.R.
U. S. S. R.
MOLDAVIA S.S.R.
S L O V A K I A
H U N G A R Y
R O M A N I A
Transylvania
Transylvanian Alps
Carpathians
Ruthenia
Moldavian Mountains
Wallachia
Banat
Dobrogea
B U L G A R I A
JUGOSLAVIA

Seas and bays:
Gdansk Bay
BLACK SEA
Pripyat Marshes
Masurian Lakes Plateau

Cities and towns:
Kaliningrad, Gdynia, Gdansk, Sopot, Elbląg, Malbork, Starogard, Grudziądz, Torun, Chełmno, Chełmża, Wabrzezno, Rypin, Lipno, Włocławek, Gniezno, Słupca, Konin, Kalisz, Turek, Kutno, Łęczyca, Łowicz, Łódź, Pabianice, Zduńska Wola, Ostrów Wielkopolski, Wieluń, Piotrków, Radomsko, Częstochowa, Tarnowskie Góry, Zabrze, Gliwice, Chorzów, Bytom, Sosnowiec, Katowice, Kraków, Bielsko-Biała, Wieliczka, Ostrava, Racibórz, Opole

Chernyakhovsk, Vilnius, Gusev, Alitus, Varena, Suwałki, Augustów, Grodno, Mosty, Lida, Novogrudok, Volkovysk, Slonim, Baranovichi, Bereza, Zhabinka, Brest, Kobrin, Pinsk, Kovel, Lutsk, Rovno, Dubno, Ostrog, Shepetovka, Zhitomir, Berdichev, Kazatin, Vinnitsa, Kiev, Borispol, Belaya Tserkov, Fastov, Korosten, Radomyshl, Zhmerinka, Uman, Pervomaisk, Kotovsk

Ketrzyn, Gizycko, Olsztyn, Mława, Ciechanów, Ostrów Mazowiecka, Ostrołęka, Łomża, Białystok, Sokółka, Hajnówka, Bielsk, Brańsk, Siemiatycze, Międzyrzec, Biała Podlaska, Łuków, Radzyń, Parczew, Włodawa, Chełm, Zamość, Krasnik, Lublin, Puławy, Radom, Kozienice, Pułtusk, Warsaw (Warszawa), Pruszków, Żyrardów, Grójec, Skierniewice, Otwock, Mińsk Mazowiecki, Siedlce, Legionowo

Kielce, Ostrowiec, Sandomierz, Tarnobrzeg, Stalowa Wola, Przeworsk, Jarosław, Przemyśl, Gorodok, Lvov, Zolochev, Ternopol, Khmelnitsky, Starokonstantinov, Chortkov, Buchach, Zaleshchiki, Kamenets Podolski, Khotin, Chernovtsy, Storozhinets, Snyatyn, Kolomyia, Ivano-Frankovsk, Nadvornaya, Sambor, Drogobych, Stry, Turka, Uzhgorod

Nowy Sącz, Jasło, Krosno, Sanok, Presov, Kosice, Mukachevo, Beregovo, Khust, Satu Mare, Sighet, Baia Mare, Carei, Debrecen, Oradea, Cluj, Turda, Alba-Iulia, Abrud, Sibiu, Medias, Sighisoara, Sfântu Gheorghe, Brasov, Fagaras, Câmpulung, Curtea, Pitesti, Târgoviste, Bucharest (Bucureşti), Ploesti, Buzau, Focsani, Ramnicu Sarat, Galati, Braila, Tulcea, Izmail, Kiliya

Ruzomberok, Zilina, Martin, Banska Bystrica, Zvolen, Kremnica, Lucenec, Nitra, Bratislava, Komárno, Győr, Esztergom, Tatabánya, Székesfehérvár, Veszprém, Dunaújváros, Budapest, Ujpest, Vác, Szolnok, Cegléd, Kecskemét, Kiskunfélegyháza, Kiskőrös, Kalocsa, Kiskunhalas, Baja, Szekszárd, Pécs, Mohács, Subotica, Senta, Kikinda, Zrenjanin, Pancevo, Belgrade (Beograd), Zemun, Novi Sad, Sremska Mitrovica, Osijek, Sarajevo

Miskolc, Tokaj, Nyíregyháza, Mezőkövesd, Eger, Gyöngyös, Hatvan, Jászberény, Karcag, Mezőtúr, Békéscsaba, Gyula, Szentes, Hódmezővásárhely, Szeged, Makó, Arad, Timişoara, Lugoj, Caransebes, Resita, Hunedoara, Deva, Orsova, Turnu-Severin, Craiova, Slatina, Caracal, Turnu Magurele, Giurgiu, Ruse (Ruschuk), Silistra, Cernavoda, Constanta, Mangalia

Rivers and features:
Wisła (Vistula), Warta, Pilica, Bug, Narew, Neman, Shchara, Pripyat, Styr, Sluch, Dnestr, Prut, Siret, Danube, Sava, Morava, Tisza, Drava, Iron Gate, Porta Orientalis, Mures, Cris, Olt, Arges, Ialomita, Sulina Mouth, St. George's Mouth, Portitei Mouth, Chilia Mouth, Trajan's Wall

Mountains/peaks:
High Tatra 2655, Low Tatra, West Beskids, East Beskids 550, Dukla P. 502, Slovakian Ore Mts., Bihor Mts., Mt. Bihor 1848, Mt. Negoiu 2535, Mt. Omul 2507, Parângul Mare 2518, Peleaga 2509, Retezat, Pietrosul 2305, Pietrosul 2102, 2061, 1881, 931, Tower 350, 309, 238, 390, 316, 384, 429, 467, 1346, 1725, 471

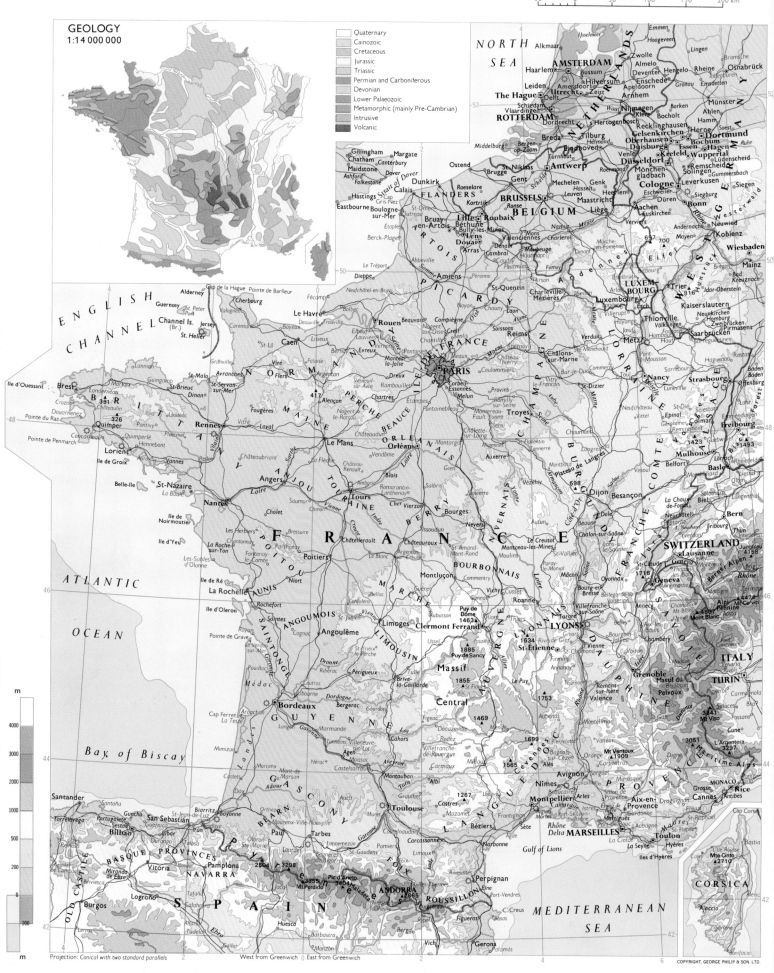

1:5 000 000

50   0   50   100   150   200 km

GEOLOGY
1:14 000 000

	Quaternary
	Cainozoic
	Cretaceous
	Jurassic
	Triassic
	Permian and Carboniferous
	Devonian
	Lower Palaeozoic
	Metamorphic (mainly Pre-Cambrian)
	Intrusive
	Volcanic

Projection: Conical with two standard parallels   West from Greenwich 0 East from Greenwich   COPYRIGHT. GEORGE PHILIP & SON. LTD.

AGRICULTURE

1 : 7 500 000

50   0   50   100   150   200   250   300 km

FRENCH PRODUCTION AS A PERCENTAGE OF E.E.C. PRODUCTION FOR SELECTED AGRICULTURAL GOODS

Wheat
Barley
Maize
Sugar beet
Wine
Beef

0   20%   40%   60%   80%   100%

LAND USE

- Arable land
- Permanent pasture
- Vineyards
- Woodland
- Rough grazing land
- Non-productive land
- —— Northern limit of the vine
- – – Northern limit of the olive

CROPS

- Wheat
- Oats
- Maize
- Sugar beet
- Potatoes
- Tobacco
- Fruit and early vegetables

Vineyard near Avignon in Provence

Paris looking eastwards from the roof of Notre Dame

INDUSTRY AND POWER

PERCENTAGE OF TOTAL WORKFORCE IN THE INDUSTRIAL SECTOR

- over 50%
- 40–50%
- 30–40%
- under 30%

FROM THE NETHERLANDS

Dunkirk, Lille, Valenciennes, Mauberge, NORD, Amiens, St. Quentin, Le Havre, Rouen, Caen, Paris, Longwy, Thionville, Hagondange, LORRAINE, Nancy, Strasbourg, TO WEST GERMANY, Brest, Rance, Brennilis, Rennes, Le Mans, Troyes, Orléans, Mulhouse, Besançon, Dijon, Montbeliard, St. Nazaire, Nantes, Chinon, Le Creusot, TO SWITZERLAND, La Rochelle, Limoges, Roanne, Angoulême, Clermont Ferrand, Lyons, St. Étienne, Grenoble, Bordeaux, *Massif Central*, Alps, Parentis, Lacq, Toulouse, Fos, Marseilles, FROM ALGERIA, Toulon

CORSICA

Pyrenées

INDUSTRY

- Iron and steel
- Heavy engineering
- Vehicles
- Shipbuilding
- Textiles
- Chemicals
- Electrical engineering
- Paper
- Iron ore

POWER

- Oilfields
- Gasfields
- Major coalfields
- Oil pipelines
- SEPL   South European Pipeline
- —— Gas pipelines
- Oil refineries
- Nuclear power stations
- Hydro-electric power stations

FRENCH PRODUCTION AS A PERCENTAGE OF E.E.C. PRODUCTION FOR SELECTED INDUSTRIAL GOODS

Steel
Cars
Cotton
Coal
Iron ore
Electricity production

0   20%   40%   60%   80%   100%

1 : 5 000 000

50   0   50   100   150   200 km

LIGURIAN SEA

CORSICA

Ajaccio

TYRRHENIAN SEA

SARDINIA

Cagliari

TUNISIA

Tunis

MEDITERRANEAN SEA

MALTA

Valletta

ADRIATIC SEA

YUGOSLAVIA

CROATIA

BOSNIA AND HERCEGOVINA

Zagreb

Sarajevo

IONIAN SEA

Str. of Otranto

G. of Taranto

Rome

Naples

Bari

Palermo

Catania

SICILY

Projection: Conical with two standard parallels   East from Greenwich

COPYRIGHT. GEORGE PHILIP & SON LTD.

Infra-red satellite photograph of Mt. Etna, Sicily
Vegetation shows as red, built-up areas grey and water and
bare rocks dark blue. Note the recent lava flows on Mt. Etna.

INDUSTRY AND POWER
1:8 000 000

MANUFACTURING CENTRES

⚙ Iron and steel and heavy engineering

⛴ Shipbuilding

🚗 Vehicles

▯ Textiles

▲ Chemicals

◑ Aluminium smelting

Varese
Bergamo
Trento
Milan
Marghera
Trieste
Venice
Turin
Genoa
Modena
La Spezia
Prato
Piombino
Rome
Naples
Taranto
Augusta

POWER

⛏ Oilfields

⬡ Gasfields

⊶ Oil pipelines

— Gas pipelines

CEL   Central European Pipeline

TAL   Trans-Alpine Pipeline

⌂ Oil refineries

◆ Nuclear power stations

⚙ Hydro-electric power stations

PERCENTAGE OF TOTAL WORKFORCE IN THE INDUSTRIAL SECTOR

over 50%
40–50%
30–40%
under 30%

SARDINIA

Cagliari

M E Z Z O G I O R N O

S I C I L Y

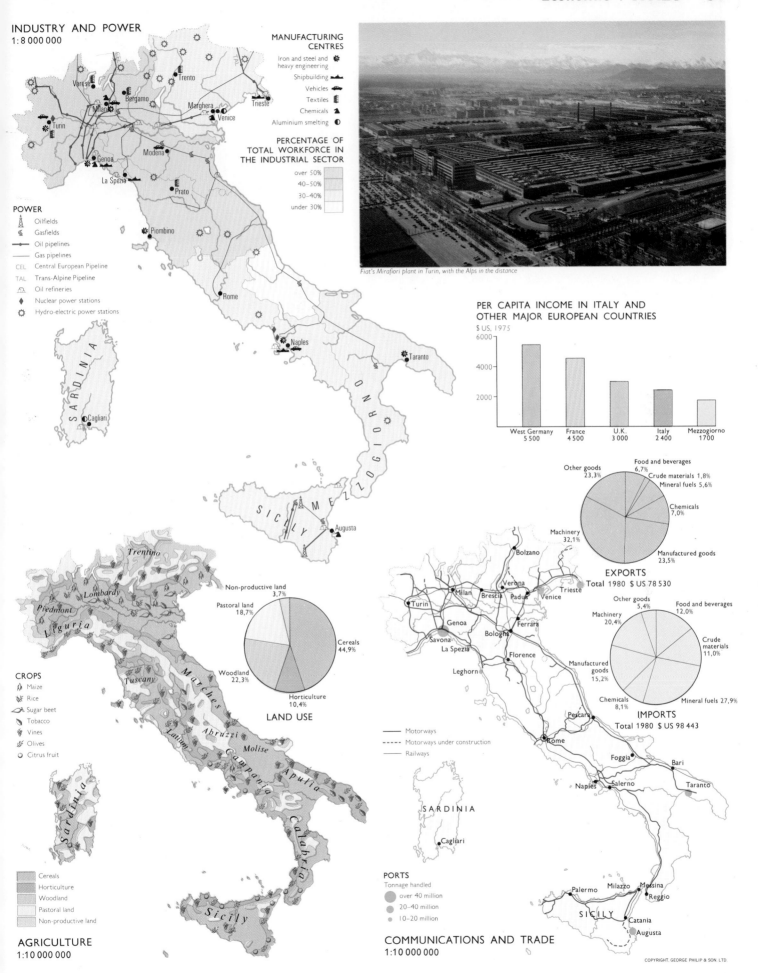

Fiat's Mirafiori plant in Turin, with the Alps in the distance

PER CAPITA INCOME IN ITALY AND OTHER MAJOR EUROPEAN COUNTRIES

$ US, 1975

West Germany	5 500
France	4 500
U.K.	3 000
Italy	2 400
Mezzogiorno	1 700

EXPORTS
Total 1980 $ US 78 530

Other goods 23,3%
Food and beverages 6,7%
Crude materials 1,8%
Mineral fuels 5,6%
Chemicals 7,0%
Manufactured goods 23,5%
Machinery 32,1%

IMPORTS
Total 1980 $ US 98 443

Other goods 5,4%
Food and beverages 12,0%
Machinery 20,4%
Crude materials 11,0%
Manufactured goods 15,2%
Chemicals 8,1%
Mineral fuels 27,9%

AGRICULTURE
1:10 000 000

Trentino
Lombardy
Piedmont
Liguria
Tuscany
Marches
Latium
Abruzzi
Molise
Campania
Apulia
Calabria
Sardinia
Sicily

CROPS

🌾 Maize

🌾 Rice

🌿 Sugar beet

🌱 Tobacco

🍇 Vines

🫒 Olives

◯ Citrus fruit

Cereals
Horticulture
Woodland
Pastoral land
Non-productive land

LAND USE

Non-productive land 3,7%
Pastoral land 18,7%
Cereals 44,9%
Woodland 22,3%
Horticulture 10,4%

COMMUNICATIONS AND TRADE
1:10 000 000

Bolzano
Verona
Milan
Brescia
Padua
Trieste
Turin
Venice
Genoa
Ferrara
Savona
Bologna
La Spezia
Florence
Leghorn
Pescara
Rome
Foggia
Bari
Naples
Salerno
Taranto
Palermo   Milazzo   Messina
Reggio
SICILY
Catania
Augusta

SARDINIA
Cagliari

— Motorways
--- Motorways under construction
— Railways

PORTS
Tonnage handled

◯ over 40 million
◯ 20–40 million
· 10–20 million

COPYRIGHT. GEORGE PHILIP & SON. LTD.

1:5 000 000

50   0   50   100   150   200 km

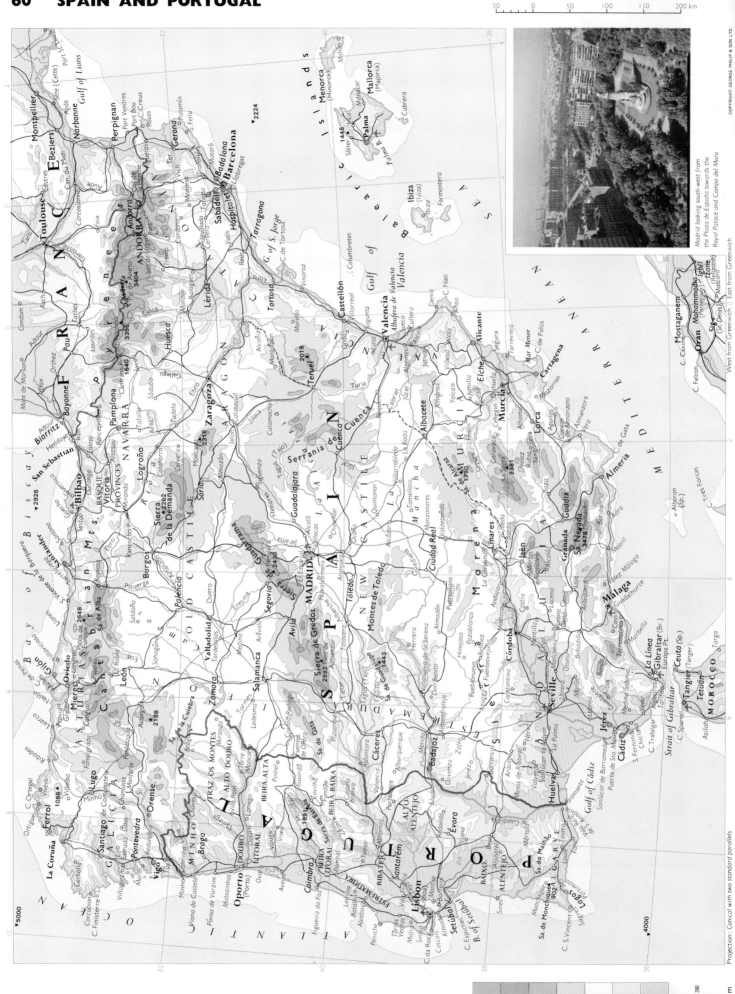

Madrid looking south-west from
the Plaza de España towards the
Royal Palace and Campo del Moro

COPYRIGHT GEORGE PHILIP & SON LTD.

West from Greenwich 0 East from Greenwich

Projection : Conical with two standard parallels

m
3000 2000 1500 1000 400 200 0 200
m

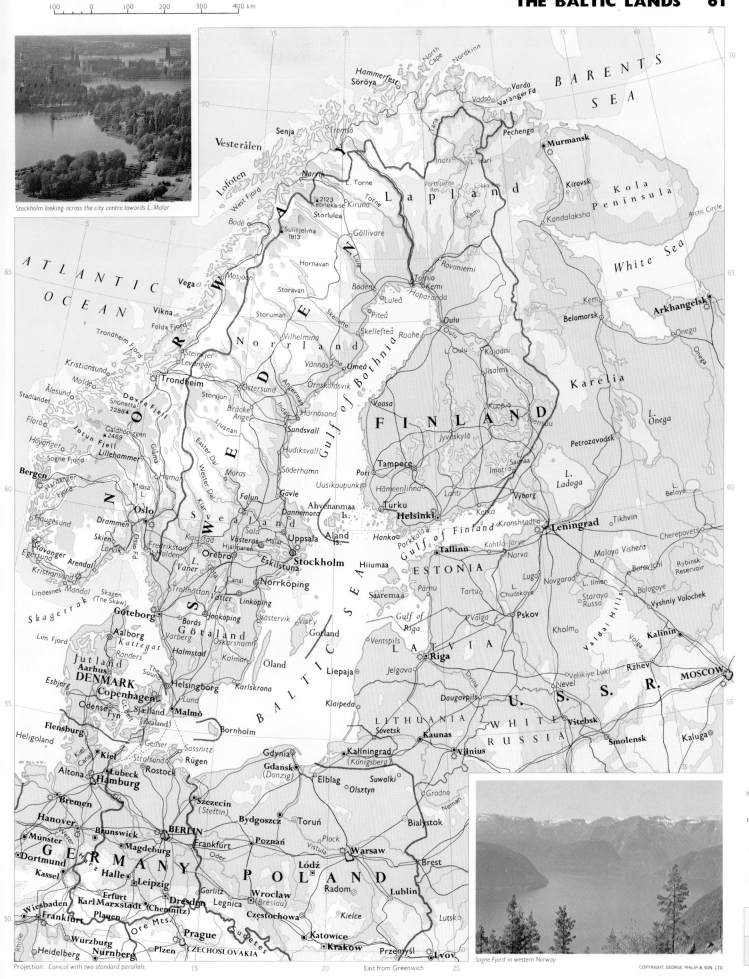

Stockholm looking across the city centre towards L. Mälar

Sogne Fjord in western Norway

Projection : Conical with two standard parallels

East from Greenwich

COPYRIGHT. GEORGE PHILIP & SON. LTD.

1:10 000 000

1:35 000 000

200 0 200 400 600 800 1000 1200 1400 km

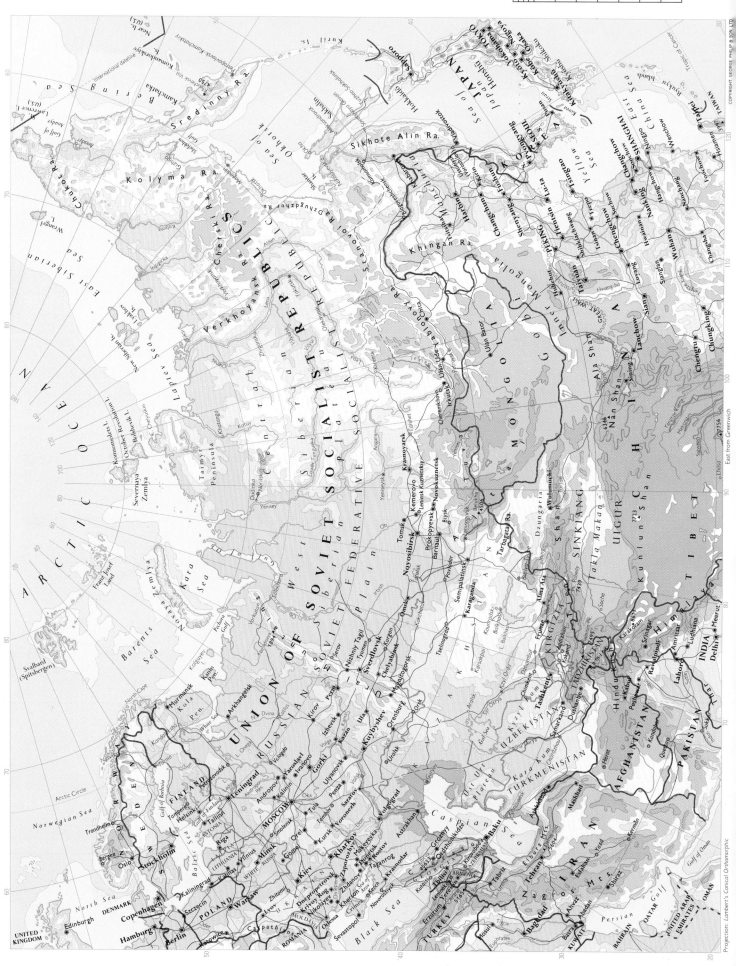

1 : 40 000 000

400 0 400 800 1200 1600 km

Moscow : The Red Square

NATIONALITIES OF THE U.S.S.R., 1979
(Population figures in millions)

Russians 137
Other nationalities 13
Chuvash 1
Latvians 1
Kirgiz 2
Germans 2
Jews 2
Lithuanians 2
Turkmen 2
Georgians 3
Moldavians 3
Tadzhiks 3
Azerbaijans 4
Armenians 4
Tartars 5
Kazakhs 6
White Russians 7
Uzbeks 9
Ukrainians 42

URBAN AND RURAL POPULATION STRUCTURE

URBAN POPULATION

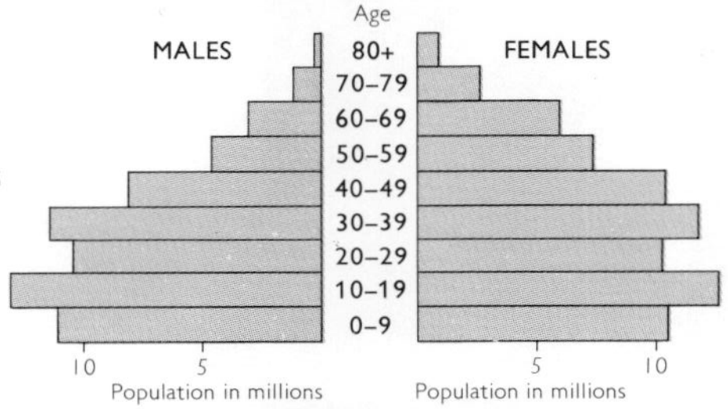

FEMALES

Age
80+
70–79
60–69
50–59
40–49
30–39
20–29
10–19
0–9

MALES

Population in millions 10 5 5 10

RURAL POPULATION

FEMALES

Age
80+
70–79
60–69
50–59
40–49
30–39
20–29
10–19
0–9

MALES

Population in millions 10 5 5 10

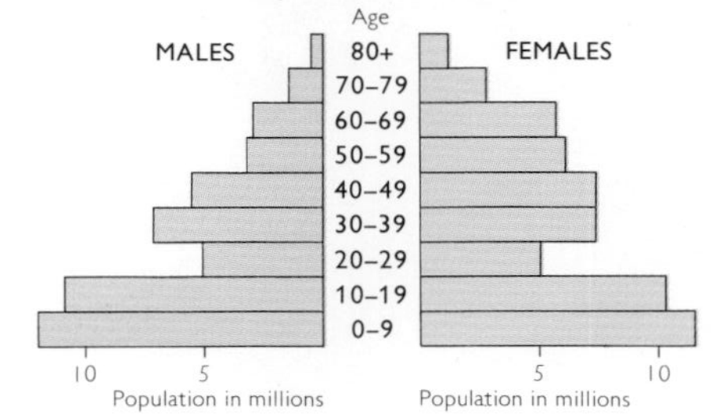

THE GROWTH OF POPULATION
within present boundaries
(Population figures in millions)

URBAN

RURAL

	1913	1940	1950	1959	1970	1980
Total	159.2	194.1	178.5	208.8	241.7	264.5
Urban %	18%	29%	38%	47%	56%	63%
Rural %	82%	71%	62%	53%	44%	37%

POPULATION OF CITIES AND TOWNS

■ Over 1 million inhabitants
● 500 000–1 million inhabitants
● 250 000–500 000 inhabitants
• 100 000–250 000 inhabitants

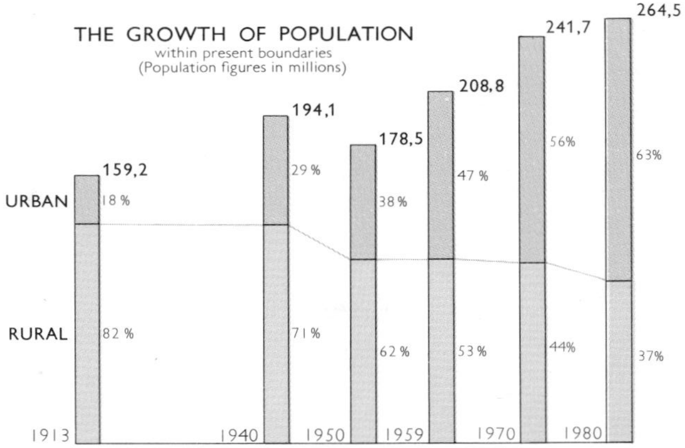

DENSITY OF POPULATION
inhabitants per km²

over 100
50–100
25–50
10–25
1–10
under 1
uninhabited

COPYRIGHT GEORGE PHILIP & SON, LTD

Leningrad
Minsk
Kiev
Odessa
Moscow
Gorki
Kharkov
Dnepropetrovsk
Donetsk
Kazan
Kuybyshev
Perm
Ufa
Sverdlovsk
Chelyabinsk
Omsk
Novosibirsk
Tashkent
Baku
Tbilisi
Yerevan

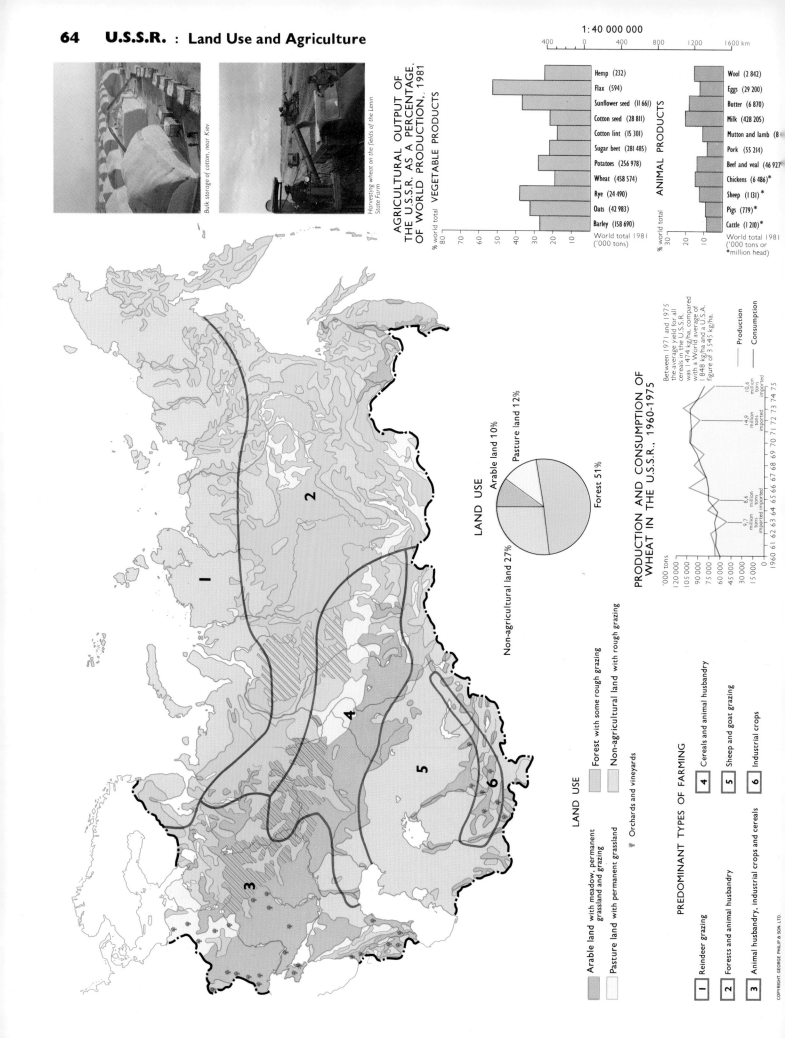

Bulk storage of cotton, near Kiev

Harvesting wheat on the fields of the Lenin State Farm

1 : 40 000 000

400   0   400   800   1200   1600 km

AGRICULTURAL OUTPUT OF THE U.S.S.R. AS A PERCENTAGE OF WORLD PRODUCTION, 1981

VEGETABLE PRODUCTS

Hemp (232)
Flax (594)
Sunflower seed (11 661)
Cotton seed (28 811)
Cotton lint (15 301)
Sugar beet (281 485)
Potatoes (256 978)
Wheat (458 574)
Rye (24 490)
Oats (42 983)
Barley (158 690)

% world total 80 70 60 50 40 30 20 10
World total 1981 ('000 tons)

ANIMAL PRODUCTS

Wool (2 842)
Eggs (29 200)
Butter (6 870)
Milk (428 205)
Mutton and lamb (8
Pork (55 214)
Beef and veal (46 927)
Chickens (6 486)*
Sheep (1 131)*
Pigs (779)*
Cattle (1 210)*

% world total 30 20 10
World total 1981 ('000 tons or *million head)

LAND USE

Arable land 10%
Pasture land 12%
Forest 51%
Non-agricultural land 27%

PRODUCTION AND CONSUMPTION OF WHEAT IN THE U.S.S.R., 1960-1975

Between 1971 and 1975 the average yield for all cereals in the U.S.S.R. was 1 474 kg/ha, compared with a World average of 1 848 kg/ha and a U.S.A. figure of 3 545 kg/ha.

Production
Consumption

10,6 million tons imported
14,9 million tons imported
8,6 million tons imported
9,7 million tons imported

'000 tons
120 000
105 000
90 000
75 000
60 000
45 000
30 000
15 000
0
1960 61 62 63 64 65 66 67 68 69 70 71 72 73 74 75

LAND USE

Arable land with meadow, permanent grassland and grazing

Pasture land with permanent grassland

Forest with some rough grazing

Non-agricultural land with rough grazing

Orchards and vineyards

PREDOMINANT TYPES OF FARMING

1 Reindeer grazing

2 Forests and animal husbandry

3 Animal husbandry, industrial crops and cereals

4 Cereals and animal husbandry

5 Sheep and goat grazing

6 Industrial crops

COPYRIGHT GEORGE PHILIP & SON, LTD.

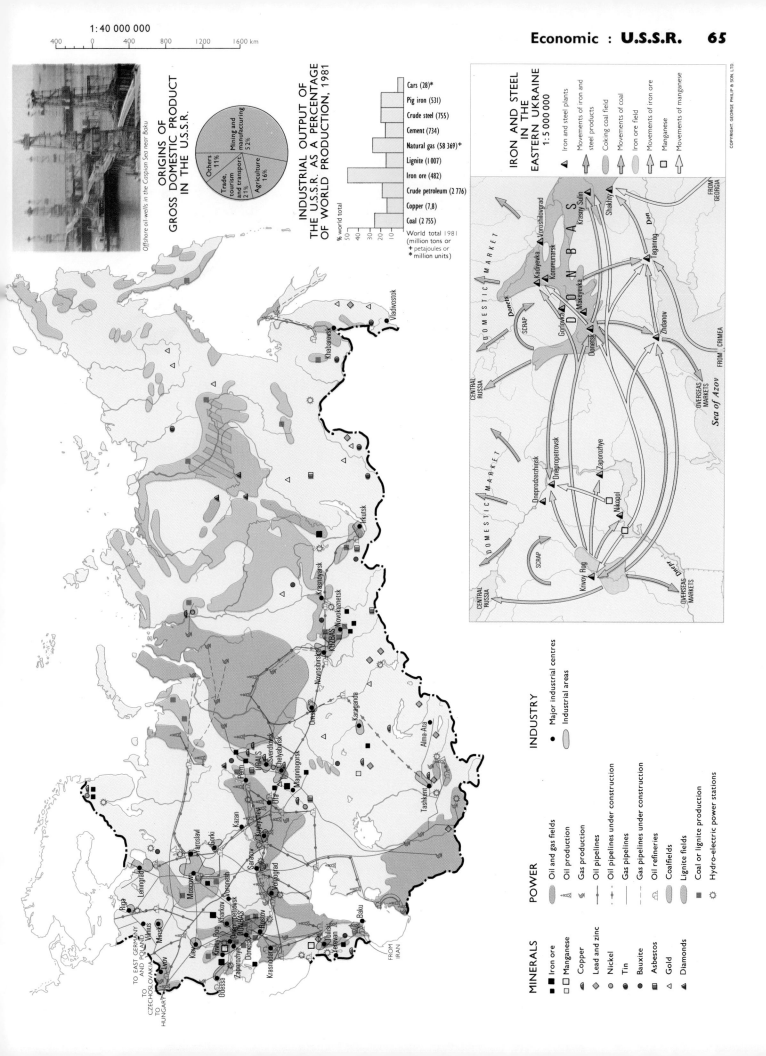

1 : 40 000 000

400   0   400   800   1200   1600 km

Offshore oil-wells in the Caspian Sea near Baku

ORIGINS OF GROSS DOMESTIC PRODUCT IN THE U.S.S.R.

Mining and manufacturing 52%

Others 11%

Trade, tourism and transport 21%

Agriculture 16%

INDUSTRIAL OUTPUT OF THE U.S.S.R. AS A PERCENTAGE OF WORLD PRODUCTION, 1981

Cars (28)*
Pig iron (531)
Crude steel (755)
Cement (734)
Natural gas (58 369)+
Lignite (1 007)
Iron ore (482)
Crude petroleum (2 776)
Copper (7,8)
Coal (2 755)

% world total
50   40   30   20   10

World total 1981 (million tons or + petajoules or * million units)

IRON AND STEEL IN THE EASTERN UKRAINE

1 : 5 000 000

▲ Iron and steel plants
⇨ Movements of iron and steel products
⬭ Coking coal field
⇨ Movements of coal
⬭ Iron ore field
⇨ Movements of iron ore
☐ Manganese
⇨ Movements of manganese

COPYRIGHT. GEORGE PHILIP & SON LTD.

INDUSTRY

• Major industrial centres
⬭ Industrial areas

POWER

⬭ Oil and gas fields
⚒ Oil production
⚒ Gas production
— Oil pipelines
–·– Oil pipelines under construction
— Gas pipelines
--- Gas pipelines under construction
⛽ Oil refineries
⬭ Coalfields
⬭ Lignite fields
■ Coal or lignite production
⚙ Hydro-electric power stations

MINERALS

■☐ Iron ore
☐☐ Manganese
◆ Copper
◆ Lead and zinc
● Nickel
● Tin
● Bauxite
■ Asbestos
△ Gold
▲ Diamonds

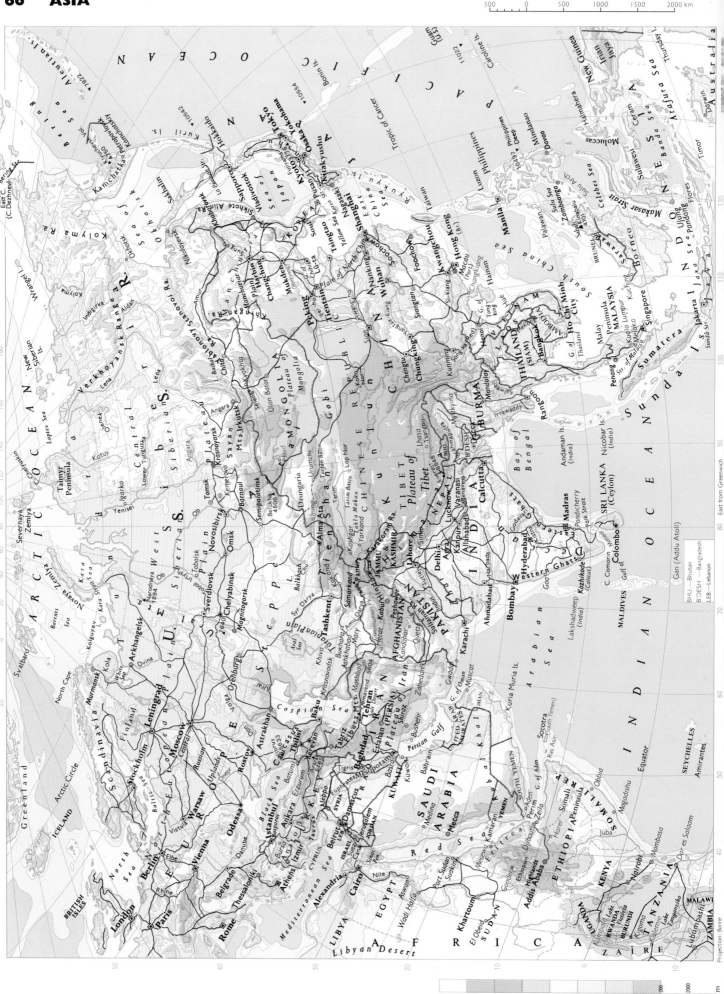

1 : 50 000 000

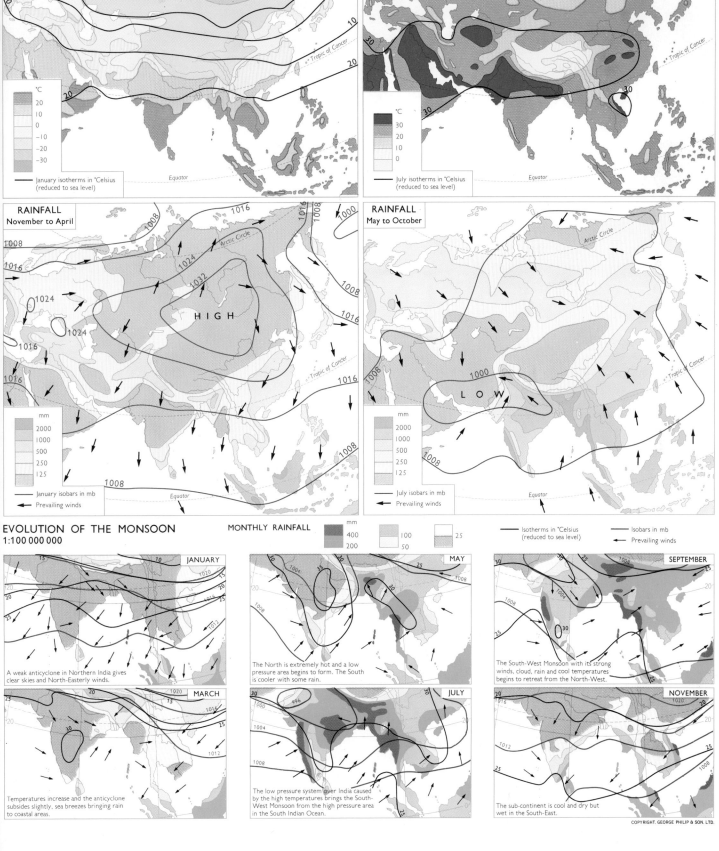

1:110 000 000

1000 0 1000 2000 3000 4000 km

JANUARY TEMPERATURE

Arctic Circle

Tropic of Cancer

Equator

°C
20
10
0
−10
−20
−30

January isotherms in °Celsius (reduced to sea level)

JULY TEMPERATURE

Arctic Circle

Tropic of Cancer

Equator

°C
30
20
10
0

July isotherms in °Celsius (reduced to sea level)

RAINFALL
November to April

Arctic Circle

HIGH

Tropic of Cancer

Equator

mm
2000
1000
500
250
125

January isobars in mb
Prevailing winds

RAINFALL
May to October

Arctic Circle

LOW

Tropic of Cancer

Equator

mm
2000
1000
500
250
125

July isobars in mb
Prevailing winds

EVOLUTION OF THE MONSOON
1:100 000 000

MONTHLY RAINFALL

mm
400
200
100
50
25

Isotherms in °Celsius (reduced to sea level)
Isobars in mb
Prevailing winds

JANUARY

A weak anticyclone in Northern India gives clear skies and North-Easterly winds.

MARCH

Temperatures increase and the anticyclone subsides slightly, sea breezes bringing rain to coastal areas.

MAY

The North is extremely hot and a low pressure area begins to form. The South is cooler with some rain.

JULY

The low pressure system over India caused by the high temperatures brings the South-West Monsoon from the high pressure area in the South Indian Ocean.

SEPTEMBER

The South-West Monsoon with its strong winds, cloud, rain and cool temperatures begins to retreat from the North-West.

NOVEMBER

The sub-continent is cool and dry but wet in the South-East.

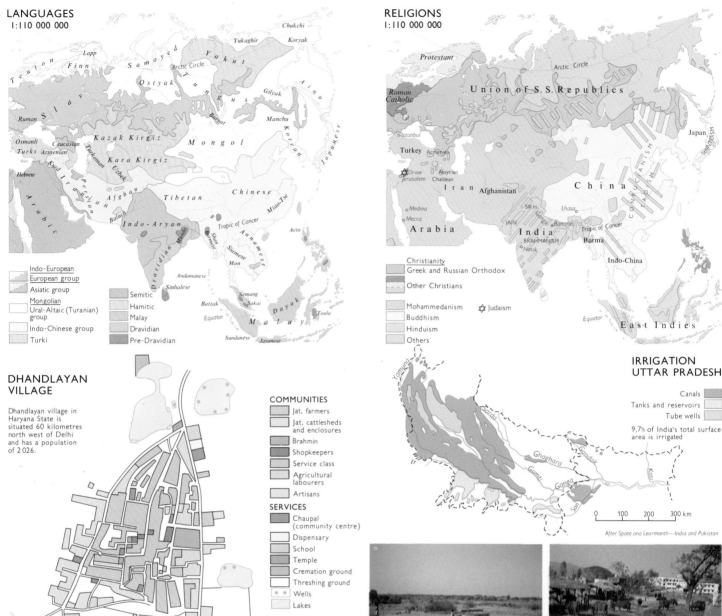

LANGUAGES
1:110 000 000

Indo-European
- European group
- Asiatic group

Mongolian
- Ural-Altaic (Turanian) group
- Indo-Chinese group
- Turki

- Semitic
- Hamitic
- Malay
- Dravidian
- Pre-Dravidian

RELIGIONS
1:110 000 000

Christianity
- Greek and Russian Orthodox
- Other Christians

- Mohammedanism
- Buddhism
- Hinduism
- Others

☆ Judaism

DHANDLAYAN VILLAGE

Dhandlayan village in Haryana State is situated 60 kilometres north west of Delhi and has a population of 2 026.

COMMUNITIES
- Jat, farmers
- Jat, cattlesheds and enclosures
- Brahmin
- Shopkeepers
- Service class
- Agricultural labourers
- Artisans

SERVICES
- Chaupal (community centre)
- Dispensary
- School
- Temple
- Cremation ground
- Threshing ground
- Wells
- Lakes

0   50   100 m

After Singh R. L.
India: A Regional Geography

IRRIGATION UTTAR PRADESH

- Canals
- Tanks and reservoirs
- Tube wells

9,7% of India's total surface area is irrigated

0   100   200   300 km

After Spate and Learmonth—India and Pakistan

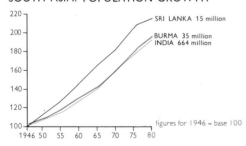

Rural industry; a clay pit for baking house bricks, Ranchi

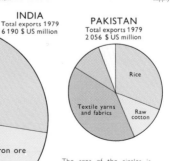

Urban agriculture; a small dairy to provide the local milk supply near Madras, Tamil Nadu

SOUTH ASIA: POPULATION GROWTH

- SRI LANKA 15 million
- BURMA 35 million
- INDIA 664 million

figures for 1946 = base 100

SOUTH ASIA: DEMOGRAPHY

	Population million	Birth rate per '000 population	Death rate per '000 population	Expectation of life at birth	Population density per km²
India	664	33,2	14,1	41,2	208
Bangladesh	89	47,0	17,6	35,8	616
Pakistan	82	36,0	12,0	51,3	103
Burma	35	38,6	14,3	50,1	52
Sri Lanka	15	28,5	6,6	65,8	223
Nepal	14	43,2	20,6	43,6	99

SOUTH ASIA: EXPORTS

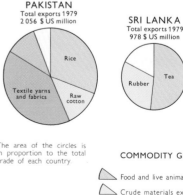

INDIA
Total exports 1979
6 190 $ US million

Textile yarns and fabrics
Iron ore

PAKISTAN
Total exports 1979
2 056 $ US million

Rice
Textile yarns and fabrics
Raw cotton

SRI LANKA
Total exports 1979
978 $ US million

Rubber
Tea

BANGLADESH
Total exports 1979
662 $ US million

Nuts
Tea
Jute

The area of the circles is in proportion to the total trade of each country.

Exports from selected South Asian countries are illustrated by proportional circles divided into principal commodity groups; the main goods in each group are shown.

COMMODITY GROUPS

- Food and live animals
- Crude materials excluding fuels
- Basic manufactures
- Machinery and other manufactures
- Others : beverages, mineral fuels, chemicals, edible oils and fats

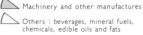

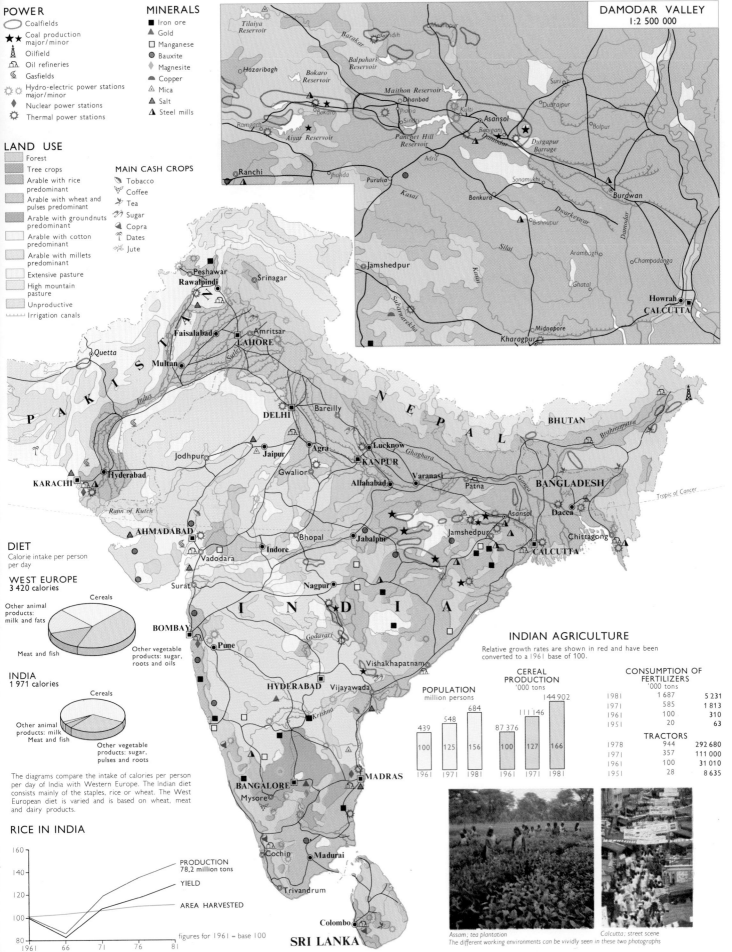

1:17 500 000

100 0 100 200 300 400 500 600 700 km

POWER
- ◯ Coalfields
- ★★ Coal production major/minor
- ⚑ Oilfield
- ⚙ Oil refineries
- ⬙ Gasfields
- ⚙⚙ Hydro-electric power stations major/minor
- ◆ Nuclear power stations
- ⚙ Thermal power stations

MINERALS
- ■ Iron ore
- ▲ Gold
- ☐ Manganese
- ◉ Bauxite
- ◆ Magnesite
- ● Copper
- △ Mica
- ▲ Salt
- △ Steel mills

LAND USE
- Forest
- Tree crops
- Arable with rice predominant
- Arable with wheat and pulses predominant
- Arable with groundnuts predominant
- Arable with cotton predominant
- Arable with millets predominant
- Extensive pasture
- High mountain pasture
- Unproductive
- Irrigation canals

MAIN CASH CROPS
- Tobacco
- Coffee
- Tea
- Sugar
- Copra
- Dates
- Jute

DIET
Calorie intake per person per day

WEST EUROPE 3 420 calories

Cereals
Other animal products: milk and fats
Meat and fish
Other vegetable products: sugar, roots and oils

INDIA 1 971 calories

Cereals
Other animal products: milk
Meat and fish
Other vegetable products: sugar, pulses and roots

The diagrams compare the intake of calories per person per day of India with Western Europe. The Indian diet consists mainly of the staples, rice or wheat. The West European diet is varied and is based on wheat, meat and dairy products.

RICE IN INDIA

160
140
120
100
80

PRODUCTION 78,2 million tons
YIELD
AREA HARVESTED

figures for 1961 = base 100

1961   66   71   76   81

DAMODAR VALLEY
1:2 500 000

INDIAN AGRICULTURE
Relative growth rates are shown in red and have been converted to a 1961 base of 100.

POPULATION million persons

439	548	684
100	125	156
1961	1971	1981

CEREAL PRODUCTION '000 tons

87 376	111 146	144 902
100	127	166
1961	1971	1981

CONSUMPTION OF FERTILIZERS '000 tons

1981	1 687	5 231
1971	585	1 813
1961	100	310
1951	20	63

TRACTORS

1978	944	292 680
1971	357	111 000
1961	100	31 010
1951	28	8 635

Assam; tea plantation
Calcutta; street scene
The different working environments can be vividly seen in these two photographs

1 : 20 000 000

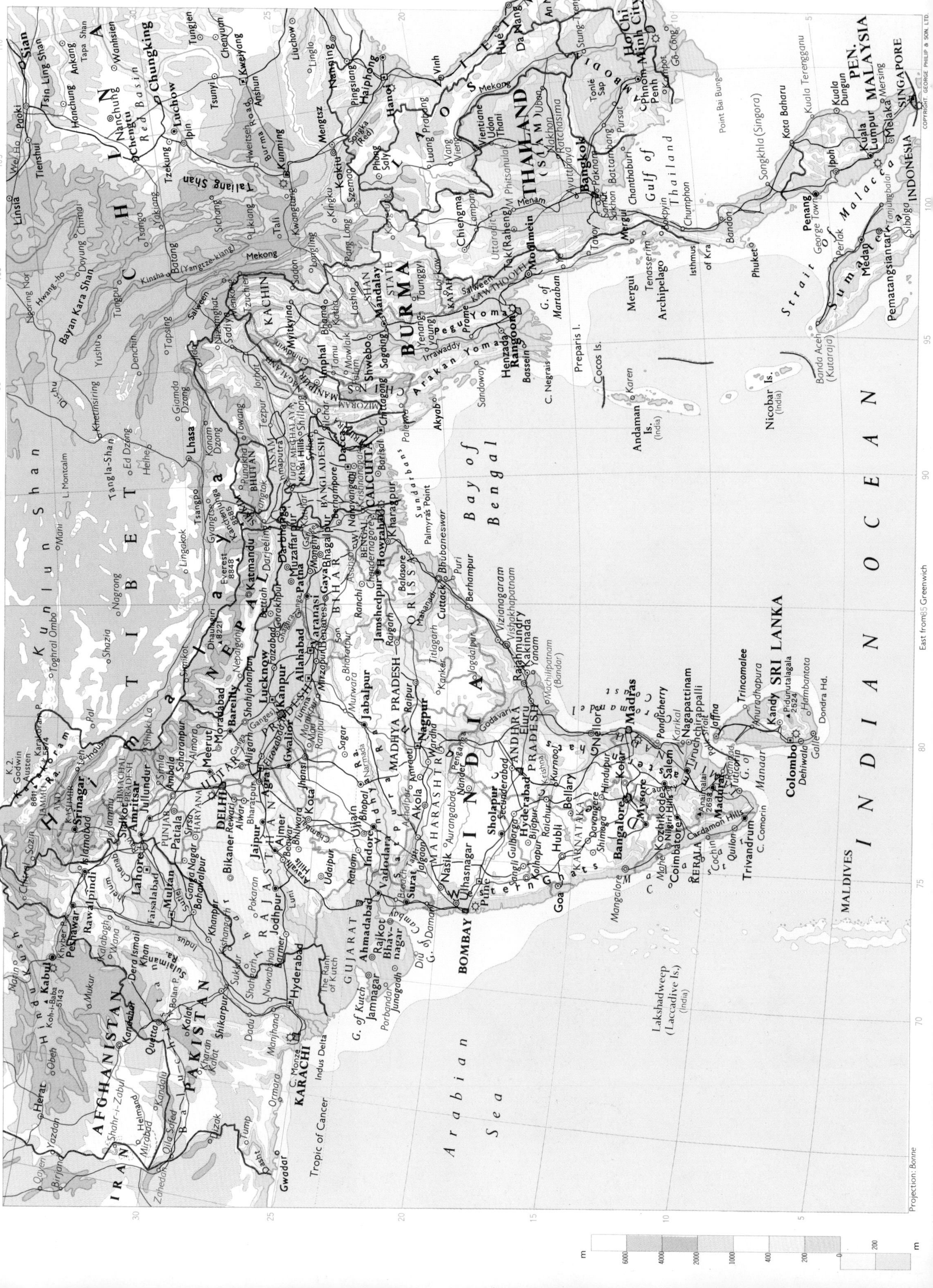

200   0   200   400   600   800 km

CHINA

TIBET

Kunlun Shan

Tsin Ling Shan

Red Basin

Talang Shan

Mekong

Tsangpo

Himalaya

NEPAL

BHUTAN

ASSAM

BANGLADESH

BURMA

KACHIN

SHAN STATE

Irrawaddy

Arakan Yoma

Pegu Yoma

THAILAND (SIAM)

LAOS

VIETNAM

KAMPUCHEA

Gulf of Thailand

Mekong

Tonle Sap

Ho Chi Minh City

Phnom Penh

Bangkok

Hanoi

Haiphong

Rangoon

Mandalay

Mergui Archipelago

Tenasserim

Isthmus of Kra

PEN. MALAYSIA

Kuala Lumpur

SINGAPORE

INDONESIA

Sumatra

Strait of Malacca

Penang

Phuket

Andaman Is. (India)

Nicobar Is. (India)

Cocos Is.

Preparis I.

Bay of Bengal

CALCUTTA

Howrah

BIHAR

ORISSA

WEST BENGAL

Patna

Varanasi

Allahabad

Lucknow

Kanpur

UTTAR PRADESH

DELHI

Agra

Gwalior

MADHYA PRADESH

Nagpur

MAHARASHTRA

BOMBAY

Pune

Hyderabad

ANDHRA PRADESH

Madras

KARNATAKA

Bangalore

Mysore

KERALA

TAMIL NADU

Trivandrum

C. Comorin

SRI LANKA

Colombo

Kandy

Trincomalee

Jaffna

MALDIVES

Lakshadweep (Laccadive Is.) (India)

Arabian Sea

KARACHI

Indus Delta

PAKISTAN

RAJASTHAN

GUJARAT

Ahmadabad

Surat

Jaipur

Jodhpur

PUNJAB

HARYANA

Lahore

Amritsar

Rawalpindi

Srinagar

JAMMU AND KASHMIR

Karakoram

K.2 (Godwin Austen)

Hindu Kush

Kabul

AFGHANISTAN

Herat

Kandahar

Quetta

IRAN

Suleiman Ra.

Tropic of Cancer

INDIAN OCEAN

INDIA

Ganges

Brahmaputra

Everest 8848

Tropic of Cancer

East from 5° Greenwich

Projection: Bonne

COPYRIGHT GEORGE PHILIP & SON LTD.

m 6000 4000 2000 1000 400 200 0 200 m

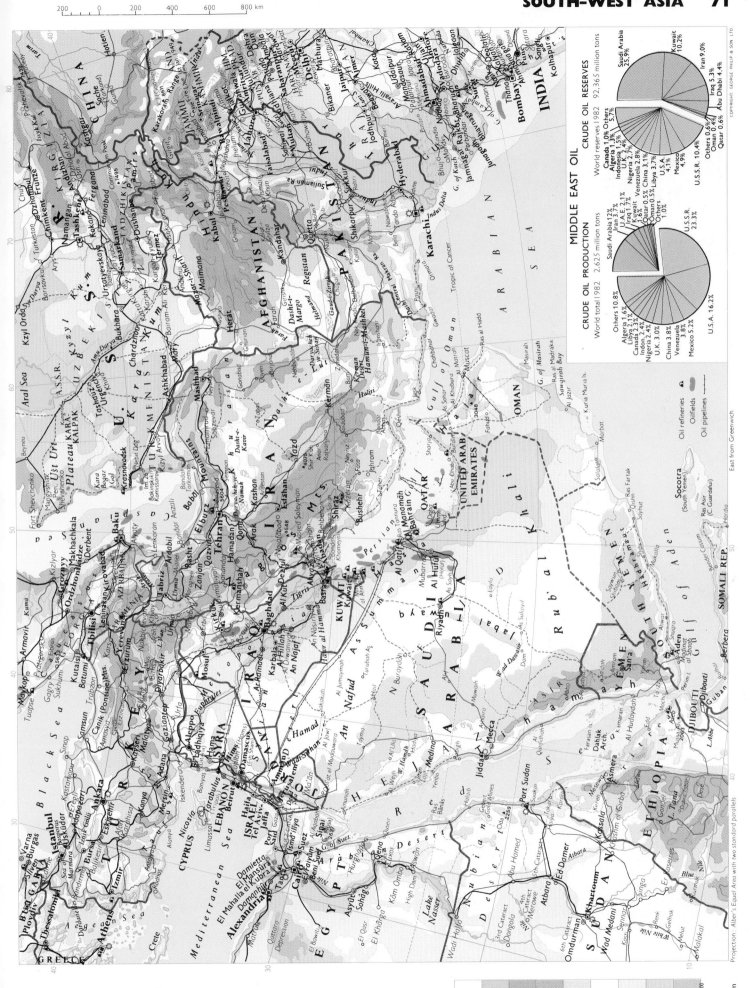

1:20 000 000

200   0   200   400   600   800 km

MIDDLE EAST OIL

CRUDE OIL RESERVES
World reserves 1982   92,365 million tons

Saudi Arabia 25.9%
Kuwait 10.2%
Iran 9.0%
Iraq 5.3%
Abu Dhabi 4.4%
U.S.S.R. 10.4%
Mexico 4.9%
U.S.A. 4.1%
Venezuela 2.8%
China 3.1%
Nigeria 2.1%
U.K. 2.4%
Indonesia 1.5%
Algeria 1.3%
Canada 1.0%   Others 5.7%
Qatar 0.6%
Others 0.6%
Libya 2.1%
Oman 0.5%

CRUDE OIL PRODUCTION
World total 1982   2,625 million tons

Saudi Arabia 12%
Iran 3.7%
U.A.E. 2.1%
Iraq 1.7%
Kuwait 1.6%
Qatar 0.5%
Oman 0.5%
U.K. 3.0%
Nigeria 2.4%
Indon 2.4%
Canada 2.1%
Libya 2.1%
Algeria 1.6%   Others 10.8%
U.S.S.R. 23.3%
U.S.A. 16.2%
Mexico 5.2%
Venezuela 3.8%
China 3.8%

Oil refineries
Oilfields
Oil pipelines

East from Greenwich

Projection: Alber's Equal Area with two standard parallels

m 6000 4000 3000 2000 1000 400 200 0 200 m

1:20 000 000

200 0 200 400 600 800 km

POPULATION
1:60 000 000

inhabitants per km²
over 600
200–600
100–200
50–100
10–50
1–10
under 1

Towns of over
1 million inhabitants

Hong Kong *Haiphong* *Hanoi* *Ho Chi Minh City* *Bangkok* *Rangoon* *Manila* *Jakarta* *Bandung* *Surabaya* *Singapore*

PACIFIC OCEAN

CERAM SEA SERAM BANDA SEA ARAFURA SEA TIMOR SEA

IRIAN JAYA Schouten Yapen Geelvink G. Vogelkop Wokam Kobroor Aru Is. Trangan Wessel Is. C. Arnhem Van Diemen Darwin AUSTRALIA Melville I. Bathurst I.

MOLUCCA SEA MOLUCCAS Halmahera Morotai Ternate Gebe Obi Is. Sula Is. Buru Ambon Banda Is. Namlea Tanimbar Is. Leti Wetar Alor Dili Kupang

SULAWESI (CELEBES) CELEBES SEA Manado Gorontalo G. of Tomini Banggai Arch. Peleng Taliabu Kendari Butung Muna Ujung Pandang (Makasar) Selayar Saleyer

FLORES SEA Flores Sumbawa Lombok Bali Sumba (Sandalwood) Sawu Nusa Tenggara (Lesser Sunda Islands) Sumba Sawu Sea

PHILIPPINE SEA LUZON Manila Quezon City Baguio Batan Is. Babuyan Is. Aparri Laoag Mindoro Masbate Samar Leyte Cebu Bacolod Iloilo Panay Negros Bohol MINDANAO Davao Davao Gulf Zamboanga Basilan Jolo Sulu Arch.

SULU SEA BALABAC STR. Palawan Spratly

SOUTH CHINA SEA Paracel Is. Hainan Haikow C. Bastion

CHINA TAIWAN (FORMOSA) Bashi Channel HONG KONG Kowloon Victoria Macau (Port.) Changkiang Kiungchow Str.

BURMA Rangoon Bassein Prome Moulmein Chiangmai Andaman Islands Nicobar Islands ANDAMAN SEA Mergui Arch.

THAILAND (SIAM) BANGKOK Ayutthaya Nakhon Ratchasima (Khorat) Isthmus of Kra Gulf of Thailand

LAOS Vientiane VIET-NAM Hanoi Haiphong Hue Da-Nang (Tourane) Nha Trang CAMBODIA PHNOM PENH Tonle Sap HO CHI MINH CITY (SAIGON) Con Son Is.

MALAYSIA PEN. MALAYA Kuala Lumpur George Town Penang Malacca Strait of Malacca SINGAPORE BRUNEI SARAWAK Kuching SABAH Kota Kinabalu (Jesselton) Labuan

BORNEO (KALIMANTAN) Pontianak Banjarmasin Balikpapan Samarinda Tarakan

SUMATRA Medan Padang Palembang Jambi Bengkulu Teluk Betung Nias Siberut Mentawai Is. Enggano

JAVA JAKARTA BANDUNG Bogor Cirebon SEMARANG SURABAYA Malang Madura Greater Sunda Islands

INDONESIA

INDIAN OCEAN Christmas I. (Austral.) Cocos or Keeling Is. (Austral.)

East from Greenwich

Equator

Projection: Bonne

COPYRIGHT. GEORGE PHILIP & SON. Ltd.

m 4000 2000 1000 400 200 0 200 m

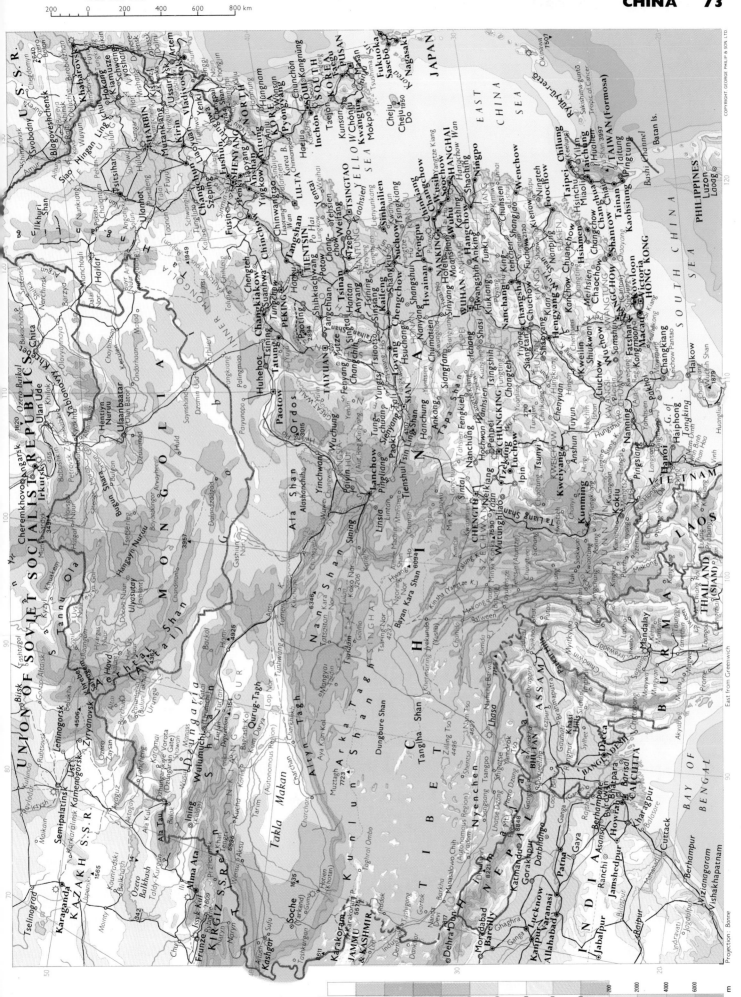

1:20 000 000

Projection: Bonne

1:35 000 000

200 0 200 400 600 800 1000 1200 1400 km

DENSITY OF POPULATION

POPULATION OF CITIES AND TOWNS

■ Over 2 million inhabitants
● 1-2 million inhabitants
● 250,000-1 million inhabitants
• 100,000-250,000 inhabitants

DENSITY OF POPULATION
inhabitants per km²

over 200
100-200
50-100
10-50
1-10
under 1
uninhabited

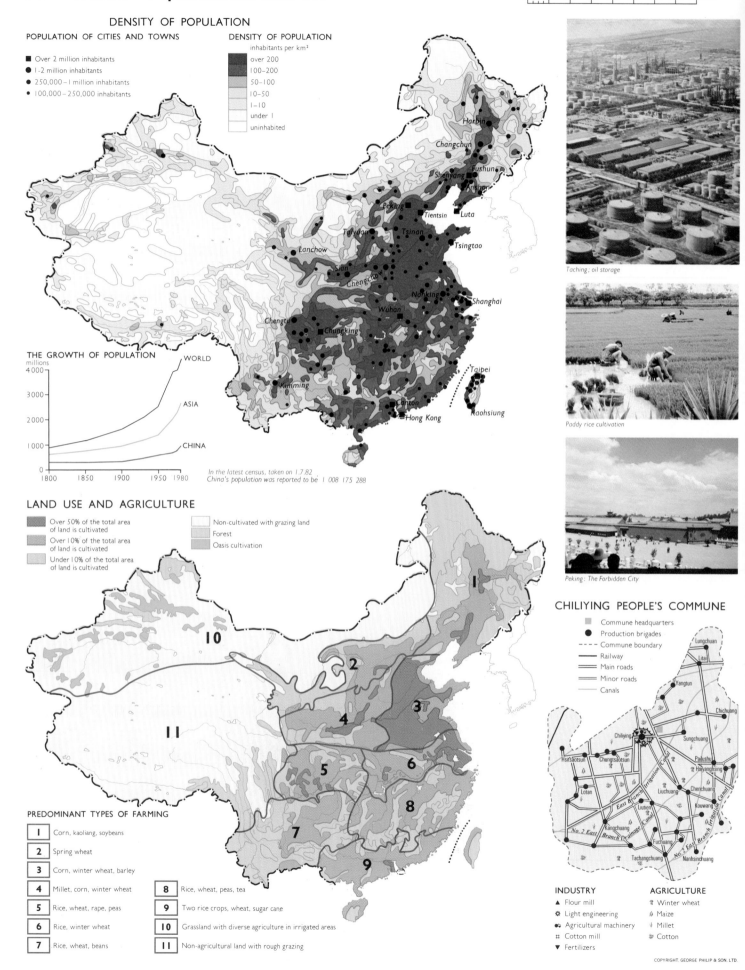

Harbin
Changchun
Fushun
Shenyang
Anshan
Peking
Tientsin
Luta
Taiyuan
Tsinan
Lanchow
Tsingtao
Sian
Chengchow
Nanking
Shanghai
Wuhan
Chengtu
Chungking
Kunming
Taipei
Canton
Hong Kong
Kaohsiung

THE GROWTH OF POPULATION
millions

WORLD
ASIA
CHINA

4000
3000
2000
1000
0

1800 1850 1900 1950 1980

In the latest census, taken on 1.7.82
China's population was reported to be 1 008 175 288

Taching; oil storage

Paddy rice cultivation

Peking: The Forbidden City

LAND USE AND AGRICULTURE

Over 50% of the total area of land is cultivated
Over 10% of the total area of land is cultivated
Under 10% of the total area of land is cultivated
Non-cultivated with grazing land
Forest
Oasis cultivation

CHILIYING PEOPLE'S COMMUNE

Commune headquarters
● Production brigades
- - - Commune boundary
Railway
Main roads
Minor roads
Canals

Lungchuan
Litai
Yangtun
Chichuang
Chiliying
Sungchuang
Hsitsaotsun
Chungtsaotsun
Pailushu
Haiyanghsing
Lotan
Liuchuang
Chenchuang
Liutien
Kouwang
Kangchuang
Fuchuang
Tachangchuang
Nanhsinchuang
East Branch Irrigation Canal
No. 2 East Branch Drainage Canal
No. 1 East Branch Irrigation Canal

PREDOMINANT TYPES OF FARMING

1	Corn, kaoliang, soybeans
2	Spring wheat
3	Corn, winter wheat, barley
4	Millet, corn, winter wheat
5	Rice, wheat, rape, peas
6	Rice, winter wheat
7	Rice, wheat, beans
8	Rice, wheat, peas, tea
9	Two rice crops, wheat, sugar cane
10	Grassland with diverse agriculture in irrigated areas
11	Non-agricultural land with rough grazing

INDUSTRY

▲ Flour mill
✿ Light engineering
⚙ Agricultural machinery
⊞ Cotton mill
▼ Fertilizers

AGRICULTURE

🌾 Winter wheat
🌾 Maize
⭒ Millet
❀ Cotton

1:50 000 000

500   0   500   1000   1500   2000 km

COAL

- ▬ Coalfields, near the surface
- ▬ Coalfields, deeply buried
- ★ Important production centres
- ✦ Other production centres

Hokang
Eusin Fushun
Tatung
Kailan
Hwainan

COAL PRODUCTION
million tons

600
500
400
300
200

1955 1960 1965 1970 1975 1980

IRON AND STEEL

- ▲ Iron and steel plants (major centres underlined)
- △ Iron plant
- ▲ Steel plant
- ■ Iron ore
- □ Coking coal
- ▬ Economic regions

Urumchi
Kiuchuan
Paotow
Suanhwa Fushun
Anshan Penki
Taiyuan Shihkiashan
Hantan Fengfeng
Pingtingshan
Hwaian Nanking
Maanshan Shanghai
Wuhan Twangshih
Chungking Siangtan
Tsunyi
Anning Shiukwan
Canton
Taipei

IRON AND STEEL PRODUCTION
million tons

40
30
20
10

Iron
Steel

1955 1960 1965 1970 1975 1980

MACHINERY

- ● Railway equipment
- ★ Mining machinery
- ▣ Textile machinery
- ▣ Agricultural machinery
- ◇ Diversified
- ✿ Machine tools
- ◣ Shipbuilding
- ◢ Motor vehicles

Tsitshar Harbin
Changchun
Shenyang Fushun
Changkiakow Shanhaikwan
Peking Luta
Tientsin Tangshan
Taiyuan Tsingtao
Yutze
Loyang Tsinan
Sian Chengchow
Lanchow
Chengtu Wuhan Nanking Shanghai
Chungking Changsha Nanchang
Siangtan Chuchow Kanchow Keelung
Hengyang
Kunming Taipei
Canton Kaohsiung

MACHINE TOOLS
thousand units

200
160
120
80
40

1955 1960 1965 1970 1975 1980

PETROLEUM

- ◭ Oilfields
- ⌂ Oil refineries
- ▬ Oil pipelines
- ◆ Gasfields
- ◆ Oil shale
- ⌂ Oil shale refinery
- ◆ Uranium

Karamai
Tushantze
Taching
Lenghu Yumen Fusin Fushun
Mangyai Luta
Lanchow Yanchang Shengli
Shengli
Nanking Shanghai
Tzekung Nanchung
Miaoli
Kaohsiung

CRUDE PETROLEUM
million tons

100
80
60
40
20

1955 1960 1965 1970 1975 1980

NON-FERROUS MINERALS

Sikwangshan
Fenghwang
Tungchwan Tayu
Kokiu

PRODUCTION '000 tons

	1949	1956	1965	1974	1980	% world production
+ Tungsten	7	11	10	11	15	28
▲ Antimony	3	13	15	12	10	18
● Tin	5	14	24	23	16	7
◉ Bauxite	—	150	400	600	1700	2
□ Manganese	51	158	300	300	1588	—
◠ Copper	5	12	90	150	165	2
● Mercury	—	0.6	0.9	1	0.6	9

	1949	1956	1965	1974	1980	% world production
◆ Lead	2	35	100	140	160	4
◆ Zinc	0	35	100	135	160	3
▣ Molybdenum	—	1.2	1.5	1.5	2	2
◆ Magnesite	—	—	1000	1000	2000	15

TEXTILES

- ▣ Cotton
- ▣ Linen
- ✳ Wool
- ◇ Silk

Harbin
Antung
Peking
Lanchow Chengchow
Sian Wusih Nantung
Nanking Shanghai
Chungking Hangchow
Canton
Shuntak Hong Kong
Khotan

COTTON CLOTH PRODUCTION
thousand million linear metres

16
12
8
4

1955 1960 1965 1970 1975 1980

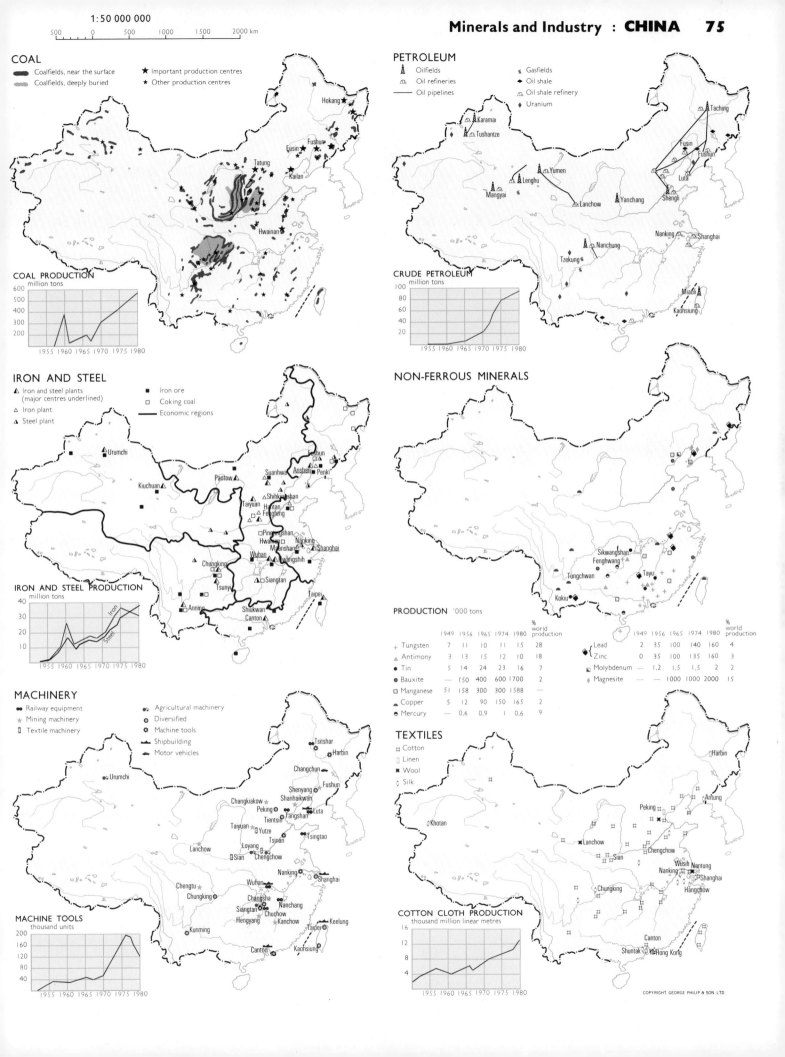

1 : 7 500 000

50 0 50 100 150 200 250 300 km

AGE STRUCTURE OF POPULATION

Total population (1980) 117 057 485

Age

MALES   FEMALES

80+
75-79
70-74
65-69
60-64
55-59
50-54
45-49
40-44
35-39
30-34
25-29
20-24
15-19
10-14
5-9
0-4

130 million persons

120

110

100

90

80

70

60

10   5   5   10

Percentage of total male population   Percentage of total female population

POPULATION GROWTH AND INDUSTRIAL GROWTH

Population growth

Amount of Gross Domestic Product derived from industry, indicating industrial growth

70 Billion Yen

60

50

40

30

20

10

0

Because of the high industrial growth rate and the resulting movement of the people to the towns, 72% of the population of Japan is concentrated in urban settlements.

1930 1935 1940 1945 1950 1955 1960 1965 1970 1975 1979

Sea of Okhotsk

HOKKAIDŌ

Rebun-Tō
Rishiri-Tō
Wakkanai
Teshio
Otoineppu
Embetsu
Mombetsu
Rumoi
Shibetsu
Kitami
Abashiri
Nemuro-Kaikyō
Asahikawa
2290
Daisetsu
Kushiro
Bibai
Iwamizawa
Obihiro
Nemuro
Sapporo
Yūbari
2052
Poroshiri Dake
Tomakomai
Muroran
Uchiura-Wan
Shiraoi
Okushiri-Tō
Esashi
Hakodate
Esan-Misaki

Tsugaru-Kaikyō

Matsumae
Mutsu
Aomori
Hirosaki
Ōdate
Hachinohe
Kuji
Oga-Hantō
Akita
Morioka
Miyako
Iwate-San
Honjō
Hanamaki
Yokote
Kamaishi
Ichinoseki
Sakata
Shinjō
TŌHOKU
Tsuruoka
Shiogama
Sendai
Yamagata
Ishinomaki
Iwanuma
Sado
Niigata
Shibata
Yonezawa
Fukushima
Bandai-San
1819
Nagaoka
Kōriyama
Kashiwazaki
Iwaki
Naoetsu
Takada
Nikkō
Hitachi
Nanao
Toyama-Wan
Nagano
Maebashi
Kiryū
Utsunomiya
Himi
Takaoka
Toyama
Matsumoto
Ueda
Takasaki
Mito
Kanazawa
CHŪBU
Takayama
Chichibu
Ōmiya
Tsuchiura
Fukui
Kōfu
Urawa
Ichikawa
Takefu
Tsuruga
3063
Ontake-San
Kiso
TOKYO
Chōshi
Gifu
Fuji-no-miya
Kawasaki
Yokohama
Yokosuka
Ichinomiya
Nagoya
Shizuoka
Fujisawa
Hikone
Ōtsu
Yokkaichi
Kōfu
3776
Numazu
Atami
Okayama
Kyoto
Amagasaki
Nara
Tsu
Hamamatsu
Toyohashi
Himeji
Kōbe
Osaka
Matsuzaka
Ise-Wan
 Shimada
Ito
Ō-Shima
Hōki
Akashi
Sakai
Kishiwada
Toba
Tateyama
Wakayama
Owase
Daiō-Misaki
KINKI
Shingū
Nii-Jima
Miyake-Jima
Mikura-Jima

KOREA

Kosŏng
Samchok
Ullung Do
Pusan

SEA OF JAPAN

Oki-Shotō

CHŪGOKU

Matsue
Tottori
Izumo
Yonago
Hi-no-Misaki
Tsuyama
Ayabe
Maizuru
Kyō-ga-Saki
Wakasa-Wan
Toyooka
Hamada
Masuda
Hiroshima
Fukuyama
Onomichi
Mihara
Kurashiki
Okayama
Yamaguchi
Hagi
Tokuyama
Iki
Shimonoseki
Ube
Kitakyūshū
Fukuoka
Karatsu
Nakatsu
Kurume
Sasebo
Saga
Ōmuta
Isahaya
Aso-zan
1592
Kumamoto
Nagasaki
Shimabara
Yatsushiro
Minamata
Sendai
Makurazaki
Kagoshima
Kanoya
Miyakonojō
Miyazaki
Kobayashi
KYŪSHŪ
Nobeoka
Nakamura
Ashizuri-zaki
SHIKOKU
Kōchi
Uwajima
Yawatahama
Matsuyama
Imabari
Niihama
Takamatsu
Marugame
Tokushima
Setonaikai
Kure
Takamatsu
Tsushima
Tsushima-Kaikyō
Korea Strait
Nakadori-Jima
Fukue-Shima
Shimo-Jima
Kuchinoerabu-Jima
Ōsumi-Shotō
Tane-ga-Shima
Yaku-Jima
Nishinoomote
Tokara-Kaikyō
Naka-no-Shima
Suwanose-Jima
Ōsumi-Kaikyō
Nishinoomote
Kagoshima-Wan
Satsuhi-Wan

PACIFIC OCEAN

Hachijo-Jima
Aoga-Shima

RYŪKYŪ ISLANDS

Continuation southwards on same scale

Ōsumi-Shotō
Kuchinoerabu-Jima
Tokara-Kaikyō
Yaku-Jima
Naka-no-Shima
Suwanose-Jima
Satsuna-Shotō
Nase
Kikai-Jima
Amami Ō Shima
Setouchi
Tokunoshima
Okinoerabu-Jima
Nansei-shotō (Ryūkyū Islands)
Okinawa-Jima
Ishikawa
Ginowan
Koza
Kerama-Shotō
Naha
Nansei-Shotō Trench
7507
Miyako-Jima
Hirara
Yaeyama-Shotō
Yonaguni-Jima
Iriomote-Jima
Ishigaki-Jima
Ishigaki
PACIFIC OCEAN

m
1500
1000
400
200
0
200
m

Projection: Bonne

East from Greenwich

COPYRIGHT. GEORGE PHILIP & SON. LTD.

1:18 750 000

100   0   100 200 300 400 500 600 700 km

Traditional methods of rice cultivation are still common despite increased mechanisation.

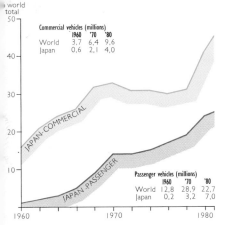
An oil tanker under construction in a shipyard near Yokohama

AGRICULTURE AND FISHING

- Rice
- Soft fruits
- Tea
- Orchards
- Other crops
- Forest

- - - Boundaries of fishing districts
- Warm currents
- Cool currents
- ● Major fishing ports

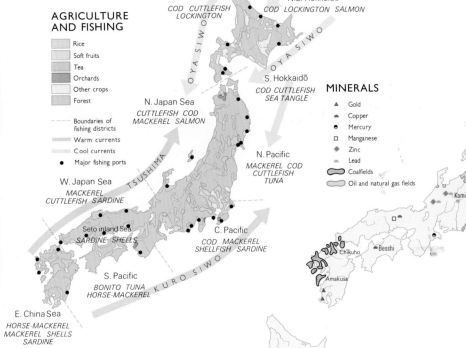

W. Hokkaidō — COD CUTTLEFISH LOCKINGTON
N.E. Hokkaidō — COD LOCKINGTON SALMON
S. Hokkaidō — COD CUTTLEFISH SEA TANGLE
N. Japan Sea — CUTTLEFISH COD MACKEREL SALMON
W. Japan Sea — MACKEREL CUTTLEFISH SARDINE
N. Pacific — MACKEREL COD CUTTLEFISH TUNA
Seto inland Sea — SARDINE SHELLS
C. Pacific — COD MACKEREL SHELLFISH SARDINE
S. Pacific — BONITO TUNA HORSE-MACKEREL
E. China Sea — HORSE-MACKEREL MACKEREL SHELLS SARDINE

OYA SIWO
TSUSHIMA
KURO SIWO

MINERALS
- ▲ Gold
- ▲ Copper
- ● Mercury
- □ Manganese
- ◆ Zinc
- ◢ Lead
- Coalfields
- Oil and natural gas fields

Kushiro, Toyoha, Kosaka, Sarukawa, Hosokura, Jōban, Kamioka, Besshi, Chikuho, Amakusa

MOTOR VEHICLES PRODUCTION SINCE 1960

% world total

Commercial vehicles (millions)	1960	'70	'80
World	3,7	6,4	9,6
Japan	0,6	2,1	4,0

Passenger vehicles (millions)	1960	'70	'80
World	12,8	28,9	22,7
Japan	0,2	3,2	7,0

JAPAN-COMMERCIAL
JAPAN-PASSENGER

1960   1970   1980

INDUSTRY
- ▲ Iron and steel
- Shipbuilding
- Cars
- ⊕ Electrical goods
- Major industrial areas
- Minor industrial areas

Sapporo, Tokyo, Yokohama, Nagoya, Kyoto, Osaka, Kinki, Kitakyushu

POWER AND ENERGY
- ⊙ Hydro-electric power stations
- ◆ Nuclear power stations
- ⊕ Thermal power stations
- — Major electricity transmission lines

JAPANESE TRADE, 1954-1980

IMPORTS 1954
Total $ US 2 394,2 million
- Food, animals and beverages 25,5%
- Raw materials and mineral fuels 45,5%
- Fuels 16%
- Chemicals 2,5%
- Basic manufactured goods 2,5%
- Machinery and transport equipment 7%
- Others 1%

IMPORTS 1980
Total $ US 140 520 million
- Food, animals and beverages 15%
- Raw materials and mineral fuels 20%
- Fuels 45%
- Chemicals 3%
- Basic manufactured goods 6%
- Machinery and transport equipment 7%
- Others 4%

EXPORTS 1954
Total $ US 1 629,5 million
- Food, raw materials and mineral fuels 14%
- Chemicals 5%
- Manufactured goods 48%
- Iron and steel 10%
- Machinery, cars and ships 13%
- Others 10%

EXPORTS 1980
Total $ US 129 248 million
- Food, raw materials and mineral fuels 3%
- Chemicals 7%
- Manufactured goods 14%
- Iron and steel 18%
- Machinery cars and ships 50%
- Others 8%

JAPANESE TRADING PARTNERS

COUNTRY OF ORIGIN OF JAPAN'S IMPORTS
figures give percentages of total imports

U.S.A., Saudi Arabia, Iran, Australia, Indonesia, Canada, Kuwait, South Korea, U.S.S.R., West Germany

COUNTRY OF DESTINATION OF JAPAN'S EXPORTS
figures give percentages of total exports

U.S.A., Liberia, China, South Korea, Indonesia, Australia, West Germany, United Kingdom, Hong Kong, Canada

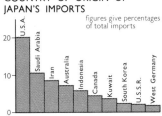

The Ghinza shopping district in Tokyo

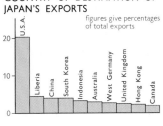

Industry and transport compete for land in Tokyo.

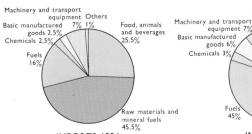
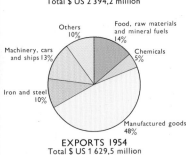

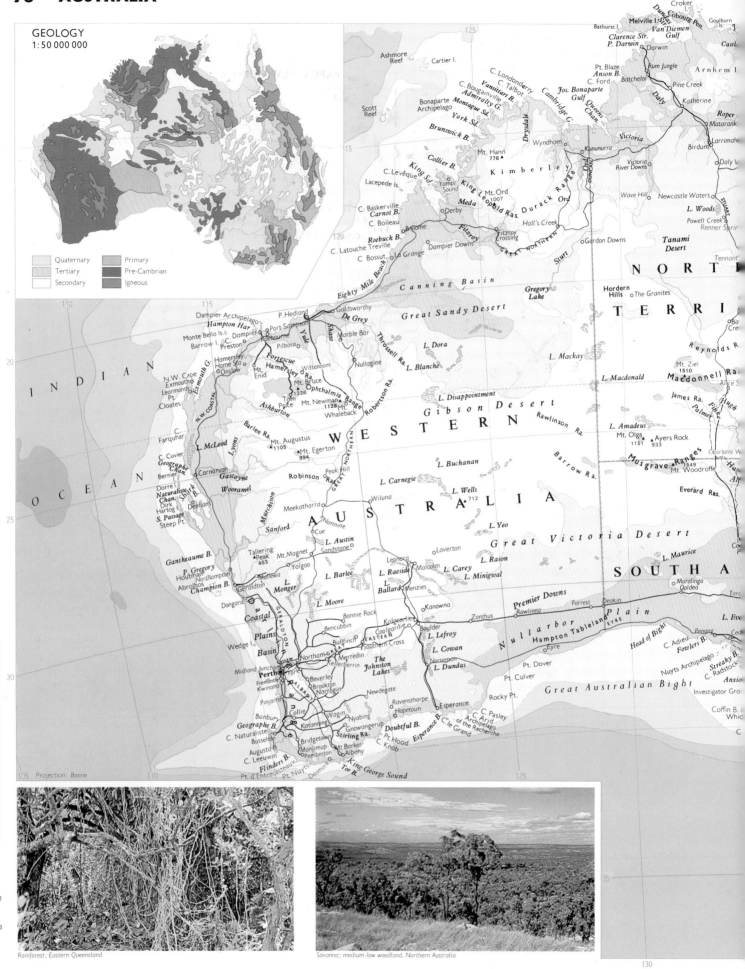

GEOLOGY
1:50 000 000

Quaternary   Primary
Tertiary   Pre-Cambrian
Secondary   Igneous

Rainforest; Eastern Queensland

Savanna; medium-low woodland, Northern Australia

Projection: Bonne

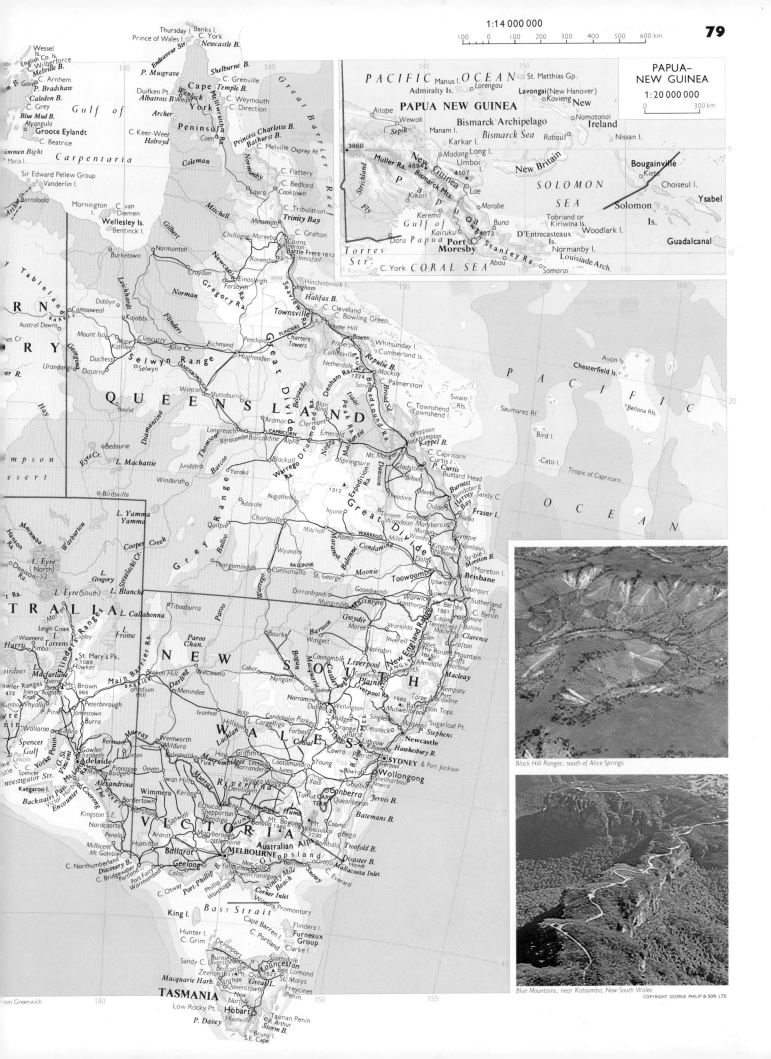

Black Hill Ranges; south of Alice Springs

Blue Mountains; near Katoomba, New South Wales

COPYRIGHT. GEORGE PHILIP & SON. LTD.

1:60 000 000

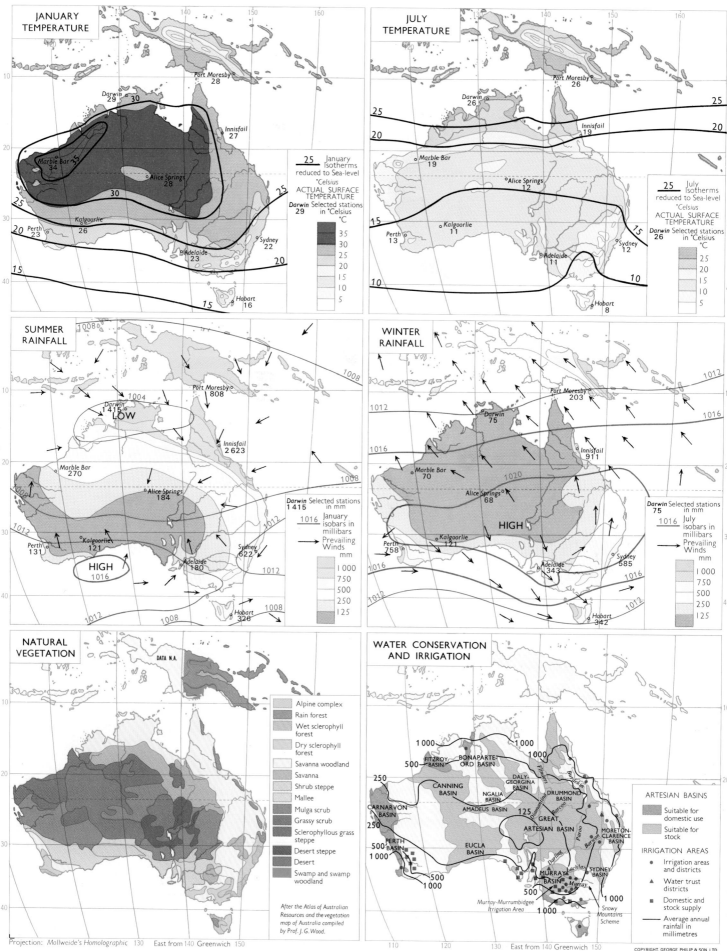

JANUARY TEMPERATURE

Port Moresby 28
Darwin 29 30
Innisfail 27
Marble Bar 35 34
Alice Springs 28
Kalgoorlie 26
Perth 23
Sydney 22
Adelaide 23
Hobart 16

25 January Isotherms reduced to Sea-level °Celsius
ACTUAL SURFACE TEMPERATURE
Darwin Selected stations in °Celsius
29 °C
35
30
25
20
15
10
5

JULY TEMPERATURE

Port Moresby 26
Darwin 26
Innisfail 19
Marble Bar 19
Alice Springs 12
Kalgoorlie 11
Perth 13
Sydney 12
Adelaide 11
Hobart 8

25 July Isotherms reduced to Sea-level °Celsius
ACTUAL SURFACE TEMPERATURE
Darwin Selected stations in °Celsius
26 °C
25
20
15
10
5

SUMMER RAINFALL

Darwin 1415 LOW
Port Moresby 808
Innisfail 2623
Marble Bar 270
Alice Springs 184
Perth 131
Kalgoorlie 121
Sydney 622
Adelaide 180
HIGH 1016
Hobart 326

Darwin Selected stations in mm 1415
1016 January isobars in millibars
→ Prevailing Winds
mm
1000
750
500
250
125

WINTER RAINFALL

Darwin 75
Port Moresby 203
Innisfail 911
Marble Bar 70
Alice Springs 68
HIGH
Perth 758
Kalgoorlie 121
Adelaide 343
Sydney 585
Hobart 342

Darwin Selected stations in mm 75
1016 July isobars in millibars
→ Prevailing Winds
mm
1000
750
500
250
125

NATURAL VEGETATION

DATA N.A.

Alpine complex
Rain forest
Wet sclerophyll forest
Dry sclerophyll forest
Savanna woodland
Savanna
Shrub steppe
Mallee
Mulga scrub
Grassy scrub
Sclerophyllous grass steppe
Desert steppe
Desert
Swamp and swamp woodland

After the Atlas of Australian Resources and the vegetation map of Australia compiled by Prof. J. G. Wood.

WATER CONSERVATION AND IRRIGATION

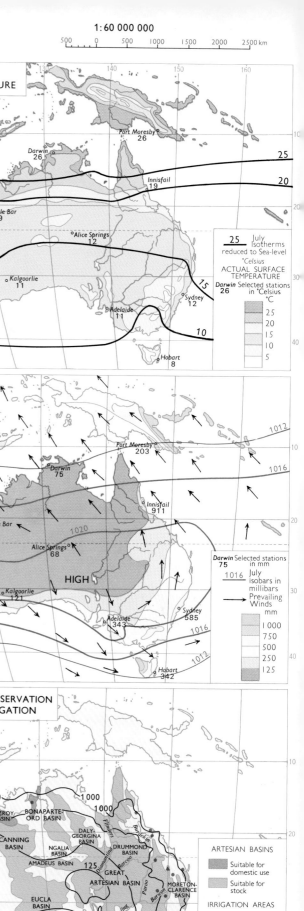

FITZROY BASIN
BONAPARTE-ORD BASIN
CANNING BASIN
DALY-GEORGINA BASIN
NGALIA BASIN
DRUMMOND BASIN
CARNARVON BASIN
AMADEUS BASIN
GREAT ARTESIAN BASIN
PERTH BASIN
EUCLA BASIN
MORETON-CLARENCE BASIN
MURRAY BASIN
SYDNEY BASIN
Murray-Murrumbidgee Irrigation Area
Snowy Mountains Scheme

Darling
Lachlan
Murray
Flinders
Burdekin
Barcoo
Diamantina
Warrego
Paroo

1000
500
250
125

ARTESIAN BASINS
Suitable for domestic use
Suitable for stock

IRRIGATION AREAS
● Irrigation areas and districts
▲ Water trust districts
■ Domestic and stock supply
— Average annual rainfall in millimetres

Projection: Mollweide's Homolographic   East from Greenwich

1:30 000 000

200 0 200 400 600 800 1000 1200 km

LAND USE

Tropic of Capricorn

Perth

Adelaide

Brisbane

Sydney

Melbourne

PAPUA NEW GUINEA
same scale

Wool

Wool and fat lamb production

Intensive beef cattle rearing

Extensive beef cattle rearing

Dairy farming

Grain production (principally wheat)

Cash crops (fruit, vegetables, cotton, sugar cane etc.)

Areas of scattered subsistence farming

Forests and timber reserves

Non-agricultural land

■ Major urban areas

MEAT PRODUCTION, 1960-1980

'000 tonnes

2000

1500

1000

500

0

1960   1965   1970   1975   1980

Beef

Mutton

AREA OF CROPS

Sunflowers
Sugar cane   Other cereals
Vegetables and   Legumes
other cash crops
Sorghum
Pastures for hay
Oats
Barley
Wheat

DIRECTION OF WOOL EXPORTS

Others
India
Taiwan
Yugoslavia
Poland
Belgium and
Luxembourg
U.S.S.R.
U.K.
West Germany
Italy
France
Japan

THE RIVER MURRAY SCHEME

Water conservation
■ Dams
▶ Weirs
➤ Locks and weirs
Reservoirs
– – Watershed of Murray Basin
Catchment area

Water consumption
Heavily irrigated areas
Irrigated areas, all uses
Irrigated areas, livestock and domestic areas

0   50   100   150 km

SOUTH
PIPELINE TO WHYALLA AND WOOMERA

Morgan

L. Victoria
Ana Branch
Darling

NEW SOUTH

L. Brewster

Renmark
Wentworth
Mildura

WALES

Lachlan

AUSTRALIA

Loxton

PROPOSED PIPELINE

Balranald

Hay   Murrumbidgee

Adelaide

Mannum

Gulf St. Vincent

Tailem Bend
Wellington
L. Alexandrina
L. Albert

MURRAY MOUTH BARRAGES

The Coorong

L. Tyrrell

L. Hindmarsh

Billabong Creek
Wakool
Edward
Yanko Creek

Deniliquin

Wagga Wagga
Tumut
Burrinjuck Res.
L. George

Canberra   **A.C.T.**

SNOWY MOUNTAINS SCHEME

VICTORIA

Avoca
Loddon

Yarrawonga
Echuca
Shepparton
Waranga Res.

L. Mulwala
Albury
Murray
Hume Res.
Ovens
Mitta Mitta

Geehi Dam

L. Eucumbene

Guthega Dam

PACIFIC OCEAN

L. Lonsdale Res.

Wimmera
Laanecoorie Res.
Tullaroop Res.

Carn Eppalock Res.
Curran Res.
Coliban Storages

Seymour
Goulburn

Eildon Res.

Bendigo

Ballarat

Snowy

SNOWY-MURRAY DEVELOPMENT

The Snowy-Murray Development diverts the flow of the Snowy River to the Upper Murray Basin. The water is used for electricity generation and irrigation.

■ Pumping stations
→ Direction of flow
■ Power stations

metres
2000
1500
1000
500

Great Dividing Range

Guthega Pondage

Geehi Res.

GUTHEGA 60 000 kW

Island Bend Pondage

SNOWY-GEEHI TUNNEL
14 km

EUCUMBENE-SNOWY TUNNEL
24 km

Lake Eucumbene

Lake Jindabyne

metres
2000
1500
1000
500

Murray 2 Pondage

MURRAY 1
950 000 kW

Swampy Plain River
Khancoban Pondage
MURRAY 2
550 000 kW

Intensive grazing and mixed farming near Orange, N.S.W.

Lake Eucumbene, N.S.W.

1:40 000 000

400 0 400 800 1200 1600 km

MINERALS, INDUSTRY AND POWER

Darwin
Mount Bundey
Gove
Rum Jungle
Frances Creek
Weipa
Groote Eylandt
McArthur River
Wolfram Camp
Yampi Sound
Pompey's Pillar
Mount Garnet
Tennant Creek
Mount Isa
Collinsville
Port Hedland
Dampier
Barrow I.
Pilbara
Mount Nicholas
Duchess
Mount Newman
Tropic of Capricorn
Rough Range
Mount Tom Price
Mereenie
Palm Valley
Mount Morgan
Rockhampton
Peak Hill
Warburton Range
Blackstone Range
Arcturus
Moura
Meekatharra
Gilmore
Mount Magnet
Coober Pedy
Roma
Brisbane
Gidgealpa-Moomba
Moonie
Dongara
Kalgoorlie
Broken Hill
Cobar
Grafton
Perth
Norseman
Whyalla
Kwinana
Ravensthorpe
Port Pirie
Wallerawang
Newcastle
Adelaide
Sydney
Port Kembla
Kangaroo I.
Snowy Mountains Scheme
Geelong
Melbourne
King I.
Gippsland Shelf
Bell Bay
Read-Rosebery
Rossarden
Hobart

50% of potential Australian H.E.P. is in Tasmania

FUEL AND POWER
Coal basins
Black (bituminous) coal
Lignite (brown coal)
Oil pipelines
Gas pipelines
★ Main mining centres
◆ Uranium
▲ Oilfields
⬠ Gasfields
⊙ Hydro-electric power stations
⊙ Thermal power stations

MAJOR METALS
● Bauxite
◆ Copper
■ Iron ore
● Lead
● Tin
◆ Zinc

OTHER METALS
▲ Antimony
▲ Gold
□ Manganese
● Nickel
▽ Silver
+ Tungsten

OTHER MINERALS
■ Asbestos
▽ Mineral sands (rutile, ilmenite and zircon)
○ Opals
▲ Salt
▲ Gypsum

EMPLOYMENT IN MANUFACTURING INDUSTRY
'000 people

	N.S.W.	Victoria	Queensland	South Australia	West Australia	Tasmania	Australia
Food, drink, tobacco	66,4	64,9	34,7	19,0	13,9	5,9	206,1
Textiles, clothing, leather	54,6	90,1	8,6	6,9	2,5	4,1	166,8
Wood products	70,1	56,8	22,7	15,6	13,7	10,5	191,1
Machinery, metal goods	186,9	119,1	24,9	41,3	18,7	6,2	398,8
Transport equipment	46,9	61,2	12,8	26,7	4,8	1,2	153,9
Others	83,1	69,6	13,2	13,1	9,5	2,9	192,0
Total manufacturing	508,0	461,7	116,9	122,6	63,1	30,8	1308,7

POPULATION

Darwin
Cairns
Mount Isa
Townsville
Mackay
Tropic of Capricorn
Rockhampton
Toowoomba
Ipswich
Kalgoorlie
Perth
Whyalla
Broken Hill
Orange
Newcastle
Gosford
Sydney
Adelaide
Wagga Wagga
Wollongong
Canberra
Bendigo
Albury
Ballarat
Melbourne
Moe
Geelong
Burnie
Launceston
Hobart

URBAN POPULATION
■ Over 1 million inhabitants
◉ 500 000–1 million inhabitants
◉ 100 000–500 000 inhabitants
◉ 20 000–100 000 inhabitants
— Aboriginal reserves

DENSITY OF POPULATION
inhabitants per km²
100–200
50–100
25–50
10–25
1–10
under 1

COMMUNICATIONS

AIRPORTS
Total passenger traffic (excluding international flights)
● Over 1 000 000
● 250 000–1 000 000
● 100 000–250 000
· under 100 000
Sydney International airport

PORTS
Volume of shipping entering ports '000 tonnes
■ Over 10 000
■ 2 000–10 000
■ 1 000–2 000
· under 1 000

Darwin
Weipa
Yampi Sound
Groote Eylandt
Port Hedland
Dampier
Cairns
Townsville
Bowen
Mount Isa
Mackay
Tropic of Capricorn
Alice Springs
Rockhampton
Gladstone
Geraldton
Brisbane
Coolangatta
Tamworth
Perth
Whyalla
Dubbo
Fremantle
Port Pirie
Newcastle
Bunbury
Port Lincoln
Wallaroo
Sydney
Albany
Adelaide
Wagga Wagga
Port Kembla
Kangaroo I.
Canberra
Geelong
Melbourne
Burnie
Port Latta
Devonport
Wynard
Launceston
Hobart

— Major roads
206 714 kilometres sealed roads
800 000 kilometres total roads
— Railways
- - - Railways under construction
40 474 route kilometres

In Australia 90% of passenger travel and 20% of freight transport is by road.

GROWTH OF POPULATION IN AUSTRALIA
million people
Total 1981 14,9 million
Total population of Australia
15
10
5
1881 91 1901 11 21 31 41 51 61 71
Rest of Australia
Victoria
New South Wales

COUNTRY OF ORIGIN OF FOREIGN BORN
'000 people
Other countries 252
Other European 340
U.K. and Ireland 1132
Malta 51
Poland 57
New Zealand 111
Netherlands 95
Germany 121
Greece 165
Italy 287

Immigration has been a major factor in the development of Australia. Over 2,5 million (or 20%) of Australia's population are immigrants.

Iron ore extraction at Mount Tom Price, Western Australia. The ore is taken to the coast by rail, from where it is exported by large ore-carriers.

Viticulture and citrus fruit cultivation near Mildura, New South Wales. Water from the River Murray Scheme allows large scale irrigation.

1:6 000 000

50 0 50 100 150 200 250 km

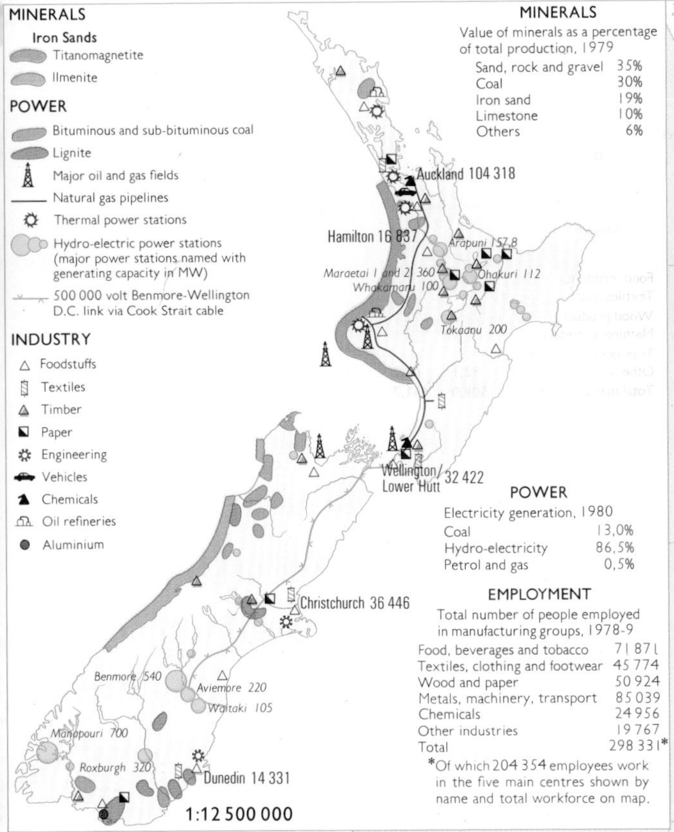

MINERALS

Iron Sands
Titanomagnetite
Ilmenite

POWER
Bituminous and sub-bituminous coal
Lignite
▲ Major oil and gas fields
— Natural gas pipelines
✿ Thermal power stations
⬭ Hydro-electric power stations (major power stations named with generating capacity in MW)
-- 500 000 volt Benmore-Wellington D.C. link via Cook Strait cable

INDUSTRY
△ Foodstuffs
▣ Textiles
▲ Timber
■ Paper
✿ Engineering
�car Vehicles
▲ Chemicals
⊡ Oil refineries
● Aluminium

MINERALS

Value of minerals as a percentage of total production, 1979

Sand, rock and gravel	35%
Coal	30%
Iron sand	19%
Limestone	10%
Others	6%

Auckland 104 318
Hamilton 16 837
Arapuni 157.8
Maraetai 1 and 2 360
Whakamaru 100
Ohakuri 112
Tokaanu 200
Wellington/Lower Hutt 32 422
Christchurch 36 446

Benmore 540
Aviemore 220
Waitaki 105
Manapouri 700
Roxburgh 320
Dunedin 14 331

POWER

Electricity generation, 1980

Coal	13,0%
Hydro-electricity	86,5%
Petrol and gas	0,5%

EMPLOYMENT

Total number of people employed in manufacturing groups, 1978-9

Food, beverages and tobacco	71 871
Textiles, clothing and footwear	45 774
Wood and paper	50 924
Metals, machinery, transport	85 039
Chemicals	24 956
Other industries	19 767
Total	298 331*

*Of which 204 354 employees work in the main centres shown by name and total workforce on map.

1:12 500 000

Wellington

Canterbury plains, near Methven

TRADE PATTERNS

figures give percentage of total trade

	EXPORTS			IMPORTS		
	U.K.	U.S.A.	Japan	U.K.	U.S.A.	Japan
1960	53	10	5	43	13	0
1970	36	13	10	30	15	8
1980	13	13	13	12	14	14

IMPORTS

Other goods
Machinery
Petroleum and mineral fuels
Chemicals
Basic manufactures

In 1940 88% of New Zealand's exports were to the United Kingdom: New Zealand has now moved away from this dependence with exports to North America and Japan.

EXPORTS

Other goods
Meat and meat products
Dairy produce
Wool

LAND USE

Extensive sheep farming, wool and store sheep production

Intensive sheep farming, fat lamb production

Dairy farming and fat lamb production

Dairy farming

Intensive sheep farming and cash crop production (wheat, oats, barley, potatoes, fruit and vegetables)

Non-agricultural land

1:12 500 000

m
4000
3000
2000
1000
400
200
0
200
m

Projection: Conical with two standard parallels

NORTH ISLAND

Three Kings Is.
C. Reinga
C. Maria van Diemen
North C.
Houhora
Rangaunu Bay
Doubtless Bay
Ahipara B.
Mangonui
Whangaroa Harb.
Kaitaia
Reef Pt.
Opua
B. of Islands
Rawene
C. Brett
Hokianga Harb.
Kaikohe
Hikurangi
NORTHLAND
Whangarei
Donnelly's Crossing
Whangarei Harb.
Bream Hd.
Dargaville
Waipu
Bream Bay
Lit. Barrier I.
C. Rodney
Gt. Barrier I.
Kaipara Harb.
Workworth
Helensville
C. Colville
Hauraki Gulf
Cuvier I.
Takapuna
Devonport
Coromandel
CENTRAL AUCKLAND
Onehunga
AUCKLAND
Manukau
Whitianga
Waiuku
Papakura
Thames
Waikato
Mercer
Paeroa
Waihi
Mayor I.
Huntly
Arapa
Tauranga Harb.
Raglan
Morrinsville
Mt. Maunganui
Te Puke
White I.
C. Runaway
Kawhia Harb.
Hamilton
Cambridge
SOUTH AUCKLAND
BAY OF PLENTY
Whakatane
Opotiki
Te Awamutu
Rotorua
Kawerau
Raukumara Ra.
Hikurangi 1753
Otorohanga
Te Kuiti
L. Tarawera
Tuneatua
Waipiro
Kinleith
KAINGAROA
Murupara
Moutohora
EAST COAST
Mokau
Mokai
Waiotapu
Tolaga
North Taranaki Bight
Ongarue
L.Taupo
Kaingaroa
Waikaremoana
Ormond
Gisborne
Waitara
New Plymouth
Taumarunui
Tarawera
Poverty Bay
Inglewood
Whangamomona
Waimarino
Kaimanawa Mts.
Nuhaka
TARANAKI
Mt. Egmont
Ruapehu 2796
Waiouru
Wairoa
Waikokopu
C. Egmont
Stratford
Raetihi
Waiouru
Mahia Peninsula
Opunake
Kapuni
Ohakune
Hawke Bay
South Taranaki Bight
Hawera
Waverley
Taihape
Mangaweka
Napier
C. Kidnappers
Patea
Wanganui
Marton
Hastings
Bulls
Hunterville
Waipawa
Feilding
Halcombe
Waipukurau
Palmerston N.
Foxton
Woodville
Danevirke
Shannon
Pahiatua
Levin
Eketahuna
C. Turnagain
Otaki
Te Horo
Masterton
Carterton
Greytown
WELLINGTON
Martinborough
Up. Hutt
Lr. Hutt
Petone
Eastbourne
WELLINGTON
Castle Pt.

SOUTH ISLAND

C. Farewell
Collingwood
Golden Bay
D'Urville I.
Takaka
NELSON
Tasman Bay
French Pass
Tasman Mts.
Motueka
Pelorus Sd.
Karamea Bight
Richmond
Havelock
Picton
Wakefield
Blenheim
MARLBOROUGH
Seddon
Seddonville
Wairau
Granity
Murchison
Awatere R.
Ward
Westport
Lyell
Inangahua Junction
L.Rotoroa
Spenser Mts.
Kaikoura
Reefton
Blackball
Runanga
Hanmer
Amuri P.
Clarence
Greymouth
Brunner
Kaikoura
Kumara
L. Brunner
Jacksons
Waiau
Hokitika
Otira Gorge
Culverden
Waiau
Ross
Arthurs Pass
Hurunui
Amberley
Abut Hd.
Bealey
Oxford
Waipara
Okarito
Springfield
Rangiora
Pegasus Bay
Coleridge
Kaiapoi
New Brighton
Whitecliffs
Christchurch
Mt. Cook 3764
Springburn
Riccarton
Lyttelton
Methven
Lincoln
Banks Peninsula
Hermitage
Fairlie
Rakaia
Akaroa
Mt. Aspiring 3035
Tekapo
L. Ellesmere
Little River
SOUTHERN ALPS
Rangitata
Ashburton Bight
Jacksan B.
Haast
Canterbury Plain
Southbridge
Mt. Earnslaw 2819
Temuka
WESTLAND
L. Pukaki
Timaru
St. Andrews
Milford Sd.
Wanaka
Fairlie
Canterbury Bight
Bligh Sd.
L. Wanaka
Hawea
George Sd.
Kurow
Waimate
Secretary I.
Queenstown
Arrowtown
Cromwell
Tokarahi
Ngapara
Doubtful Sd.
Wakatipu
Clyde
Oamaru
Breaksea Sd.
Te Anau
Alexandra
Kakanui Mts.
Maheno
Resolution I.
Manapouri
EYRE Mts.
Roxburgh
Hampden
Dusky Sd.
Mossburn
Ohai
Ediavale
Dunback
Palmerston
Chalky Inlet
SOUTHLAND
Lumsden
Waikouaiti
Preservation Inlet
Nightcaps
Lawrence
Dunedin
Port Chalmers
Te Waewae B.
Clifden
Tuatapere
Winton
Gore
Milton
Otago Harbour
Orepuki
Hedgehope
Clinton
Kelso
Balclutha
St. Kilda
Riverton
Mataura
Owaka
Kaitangata
C. Saunders
Wyndham
Nugget Pt.
Invercargill
Bluff
Ruapuke I.
Takaroa
Waikawa Harb.
S.W. Cape
Oban
Port Pegasus
Stewart I.

TASMAN SEA
T A S M A N   S E A

166   168   170   172   174
36   38   40   44   46

1 : 40 000 000

400   0   400   800   1200   1600 km

Spain

Mediterranean Sea

Madeira

Str. of Gibraltar

High Plateau Saharan Atlas
Middle Atlas
High Atlas
Anti Atlas Toubkal 4165
3718
Canary Is.
Tenerife

C. Bon Sicily Malta 5121 Crete Cyprus
G. of Gabes
Tripolitania G. of Sidra Cyrenaica

Levant Mesopotamia Tigris
Syrian Desert Euphrates
Sinai 2285 Arabian Desert
Bahrain I.
Tropic of Cancer

S a h a r a

Fezzan
Tuat
Tasili Plateau
Hoggar
Adrar
Air
Tibesti 3415
Bilma

Kufra Egypt
Libyan Desert El Kharga 1st Cat.
Nubian Desert
3rd Cat. 4th Cat. 5th Cat.
Nubia
6th Cat.

Red Sea Hejaz *Arabia*
Str. of Bab el Mandeb Gulf of Aden Perim
Rub' al Khali

Ras Nouadhibou (C. Blanc)

C. Vert
Senegambia
Gambia Senegal
Fouta Djalon

Niger (Joliba)
Volta
Benue
L. Chad Wadai Darfur Kordofan
Chari
White Nile Blue Nile
Atbara
Ras Dashen 4620
L. Tana Ethiopian Highlands

S u d a n

G u i n e a

Grain Coast Gold Coast Slave Coast
C. Palmas Ivory Coast Bight of Benin
Bioko Bight of Bonny
Adamawa Highlands Cameroon Peak 4070

Bahr el Ghazal Dar Banda
Uele
Zaire (Congo)
L. Mobutu Sese Seko (L. Albert) Ruwenzori 5109 Boyoma Falls
Elgon 4321 Kenya 5199
Somali Peninsula

Gulf of Guinea Principe São Tomé C. Lopez Annobón
Ogooué

A T L A N T I C

O C E A N

Congo
Basin
Cuango Zaire (Congo) Malebo Pool Kasai Sankuru Lualaba
L. Edward L. Kivu
L. Victoria Kilimanjaro 5895
INDIAN
Pemba Zanzibar
OCEAN

Projection: Lambert's Equivalent Azimuthal
West from Greenwich   East from Greenwich

L. Tanganyika
Kasai Cuanza Cuango Cubango
L. Mweru Rungwe 2961 L. Nyasa Ruvuma C. Delgado
Shaba L. Bangweulu Malawi Aldabra Is. Comoro Is.
Bié Plateau Lapula Luangwa
Mlanje 3000
Cunene Zambezi
Victoria Falls
C. Fria Cuando Limpopo Tropic of Capricorn
Walvis Bay *Kalahari* Delagoa Bay
Namib Desert Xai High Veld 3482 Drakensberg
Orange Compass B. 2505 Nuweveldberge Gt. Karoo Swartberg
C. of Good Hope Agulhas Bank Algoa Bay
C. Agulhas

Mozambique Channel *Madagascar* 2643

Pr. Edward Is.

m
4000
3000
2000
1500
400
200
0
200
1000
2000
4000
6000

AFRICA : POLITICAL
1 : 80 000 000

MOROCCO Rabat Algiers Tunis TUNISIA Tripoli
El Aaiun ALGERIA LIBYA Benghazi Cairo EGYPT
Dakhla WESTERN SAHARA
MAURITANIA Nouakchott
Dakar SENEGAL MALI NIGER CHAD Khartoum Tropic of Cancer
Banjul GAMBIA Bamako UPPER VOLTA Niamey N'Djamena SUDAN
GUINEA BISSAU Bissau Ouagadougou NIGERIA DJIBOUTI Djibouti
Conakry GUINEA Freetown IVORY GHANA Lagos Addis Ababa
SIERRA LEONE Monrovia LIBERIA COAST Accra Porto Novo CENTRAL AFRICA ETHIOPIA SOMALI REP.
Abidjan Lomé CAMEROON Bangui UGANDA KENYA Mogadishu
EQ. GUINEA Yaoundé Kampala Nairobi
Equator Libreville CONGO RWANDA
GABON Brazzaville ZAÏRE BURUNDI Zanzibar
Pointe-Noire Kinshasa TANZANIA Dodoma Dar-es-Salaam
Luanda ANGOLA ZAMBIA MALAWI
Lusaka Zomba
ZIMBABWE Harare MOZAMBIQUE Antananarivo MADAGASCAR
NAMIBIA BOTSWANA Tropic of Capricorn
Walvis Bay (Rep. of S.A.) Windhoek Gaborone Pretoria SWAZILAND Maputo
SOUTH AFRICA LESOTHO

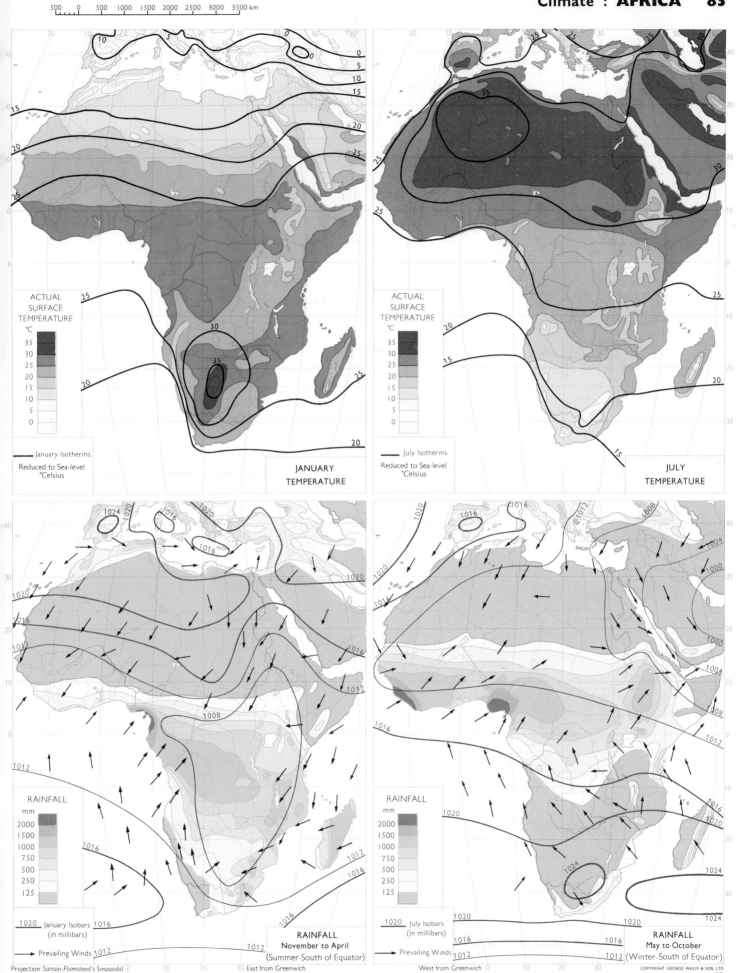

1:80 000 000

500   0   500 1000 1500 2000 2500 3000 3500 km

ACTUAL
SURFACE
TEMPERATURE
°C
35
30
25
20
15
10
5
0

January Isotherms
Reduced to Sea-level
°Celsius

JANUARY
TEMPERATURE

ACTUAL
SURFACE
TEMPERATURE
°C
35
30
25
20
15
10
5
0

July Isotherms
Reduced to Sea-level
°Celsius

JULY
TEMPERATURE

RAINFALL
mm
2000
1500
1000
750
500
250
125

1020 January Isobars
(in millibars)

Prevailing Winds

RAINFALL
November to April
(Summer-South of Equator)

RAINFALL
mm
2000
1500
1000
750
500
250
125

1020 July Isobars
(in millibars)

Prevailing Winds

RAINFALL
May to October
(Winter-South of Equator)

Projection: Sanson-Flamsteed's Sinusoidal   0   10   30 East from Greenwich

West from Greenwich

COPYRIGHT. GEORGE PHILIP & SON. LTD.
EID

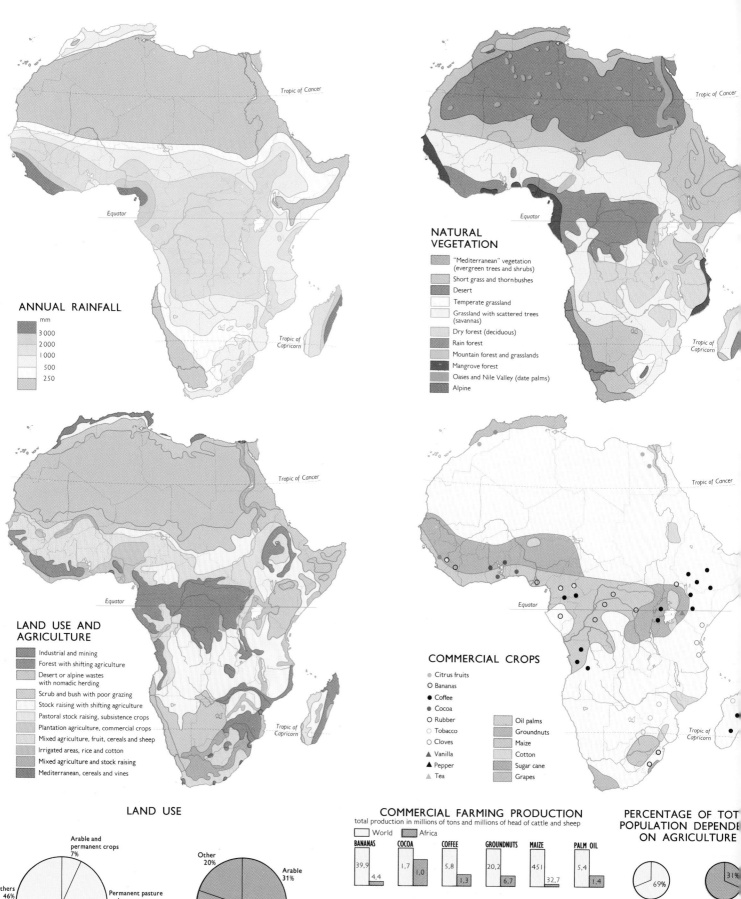

ANNUAL RAINFALL

mm
3 000
2 000
1 000
500
250

NATURAL VEGETATION

"Mediterranean" vegetation (evergreen trees and shrubs)
Short grass and thornbushes
Desert
Temperate grassland
Grassland with scattered trees (savannas)
Dry forest (deciduous)
Rain forest
Mountain forest and grasslands
Mangrove forest
Oases and Nile Valley (date palms)
Alpine

LAND USE AND AGRICULTURE

Industrial and mining
Forest with shifting agriculture
Desert or alpine wastes with nomadic herding
Scrub and bush with poor grazing
Stock raising with shifting agriculture
Pastoral stock raising, subsistence crops
Plantation agriculture, commercial crops
Mixed agriculture, fruit, cereals and sheep
Irrigated areas, rice and cotton
Mixed agriculture and stock raising
Mediterranean, cereals and vines

COMMERCIAL CROPS

Citrus fruits
Bananas
Coffee
Cocoa
Rubber
Tobacco
Cloves
Vanilla
Pepper
Tea

Oil palms
Groundnuts
Maize
Cotton
Sugar cane
Grapes

LAND USE

Arable and permanent crops 7%
Others 46%
Permanent pasture and crops 26%
Forest and woodland 21%

AFRICA

Other 20%
Arable 31%
Forest 21%
Permanent pasture 28%

E.E.C.

COMMERCIAL FARMING PRODUCTION
total production in millions of tons and millions of head of cattle and sheep

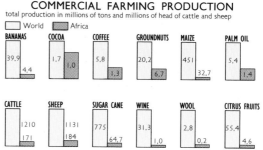

World Africa

BANANAS	COCOA	COFFEE	GROUNDNUTS	MAIZE	PALM OIL
39,9 / 4,4	1,7 / 1,0	5,8 / 1,3	20,2 / 6,7	451 / 32,7	5,4 / 1,4

CATTLE	SHEEP	SUGAR CANE	WINE	WOOL	CITRUS FRUITS
1210 / 171	1131 / 184	775 / 64,7	31,3 / 1,0	2,8 / 0,2	55,4 / 4,6

PERCENTAGE OF TOT POPULATION DEPENDE ON AGRICULTURE

69%
AFRICA

31%
SOUTH AFR

79%
ZAÏRE

60%
ALGERIA

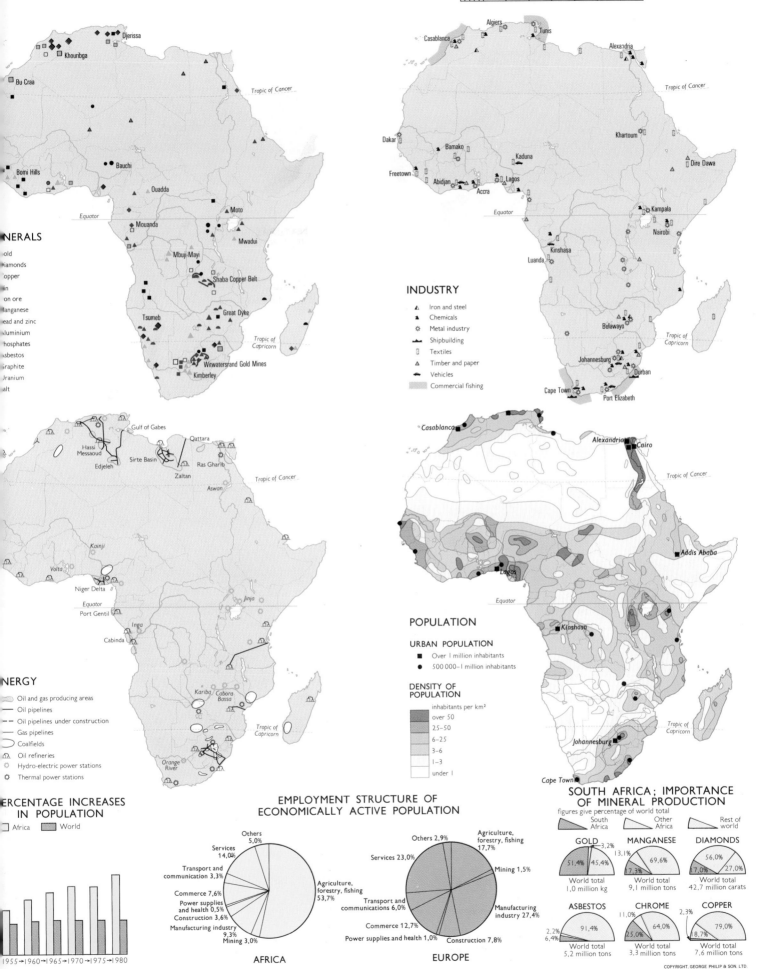

500 0 500 1000 1500 2000 2500 3000 3500 km

MINERALS

Djerissa
Khouribga
Bu Craa
Bomi Hills
Bauchi
Ouadda
Moto
Mouanda
Mwadui
Mbuji-Mayi
Shaba Copper Belt
Great Dyke
Tsumeb
Witwatersrand Gold Mines
Kimberley

Tropic of Cancer
Equator
Tropic of Capricorn

- Gold
- Diamonds
- Copper
- Tin
- Iron ore
- Manganese
- Lead and zinc
- Aluminium
- Phosphates
- Asbestos
- Graphite
- Uranium
- Salt

INDUSTRY

Algiers
Casablanca
Tunis
Alexandria
Dakar
Bamako
Kaduna
Khartoum
Freetown
Abidjan
Accra
Lagos
Dire Dawa
Kampala
Nairobi
Kinshasa
Luanda
Bulawayo
Johannesburg
Durban
Cape Town
Port Elizabeth

Tropic of Cancer
Equator
Tropic of Capricorn

- △ Iron and steel
- ▲ Chemicals
- ✿ Metal industry
- ⛴ Shipbuilding
- ▯ Textiles
- △ Timber and paper
- 🚗 Vehicles
- Commercial fishing

ENERGY

Gulf of Gabes
Qattara
Hassi Messaoud
Sirte Basin
Ras Gharib
Edjeleh
Zaltan
Aswan
Kainji
Volta
Niger Delta
Jinja
Port Gentil
Inga
Cabinda
Kariba
Cabora Bassa
Orange River

Tropic of Cancer
Equator
Tropic of Capricorn

- Oil and gas producing areas
- Oil pipelines
- Oil pipelines under construction
- Gas pipelines
- Coalfields
- Oil refineries
- Hydro-electric power stations
- Thermal power stations

POPULATION

Casablanca
Alexandria
Cairo
Addis Ababa
Lagos
Kinshasa
Johannesburg
Cape Town

Tropic of Cancer
Equator
Tropic of Capricorn

URBAN POPULATION

- ■ Over 1 million inhabitants
- ● 500 000–1 million inhabitants

DENSITY OF POPULATION

inhabitants per km²
- over 50
- 25–50
- 6–25
- 3–6
- 1–3
- under 1

PERCENTAGE INCREASES IN POPULATION

□ Africa ▨ World

1955→1960→1965→1970→1975→1980

EMPLOYMENT STRUCTURE OF ECONOMICALLY ACTIVE POPULATION

AFRICA

- Others 5,0%
- Services 14,0%
- Transport and communication 3,3%
- Commerce 7,6%
- Power supplies and health 0,5%
- Construction 3,6%
- Manufacturing industry 9,3%
- Mining 3,0%
- Agriculture, forestry, fishing 53,7%

EUROPE

- Others 2,9%
- Services 23,0%
- Transport and communications 6,0%
- Commerce 12,7%
- Power supplies and health 1,0%
- Construction 7,8%
- Manufacturing industry 27,4%
- Mining 1,5%
- Agriculture, forestry, fishing 17,7%

SOUTH AFRICA; IMPORTANCE OF MINERAL PRODUCTION

figures give percentage of world total

South Africa   Other Africa   Rest of world

GOLD
51,4% 45,4% 3,2%
World total 1,0 million kg

MANGANESE
13,1% 7,3% 69,6%
World total 9,1 million tons

DIAMONDS
56,0% 17,0% 27,0%
World total 42,7 million carats

ASBESTOS
91,4% 2,2% 6,4%
World total 5,2 million tons

CHROME
11,0% 25,0% 64,0%
World total 3,3 million tons

COPPER
2,3% 8,7% 79,0%
World total 7,6 million tons

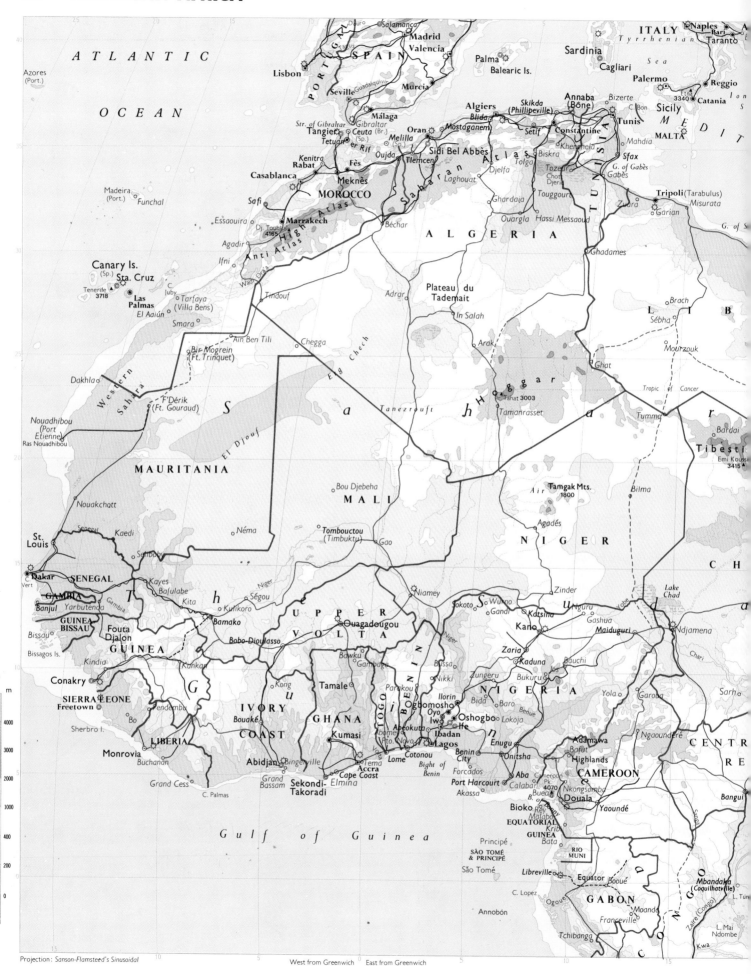

1:20 000 000

200 0 200 400 600 800 km

PALESTINE
Showing 1967 boundaries between the
Arab States and Israel

1:3 000 000
0 10 20 30 40 km

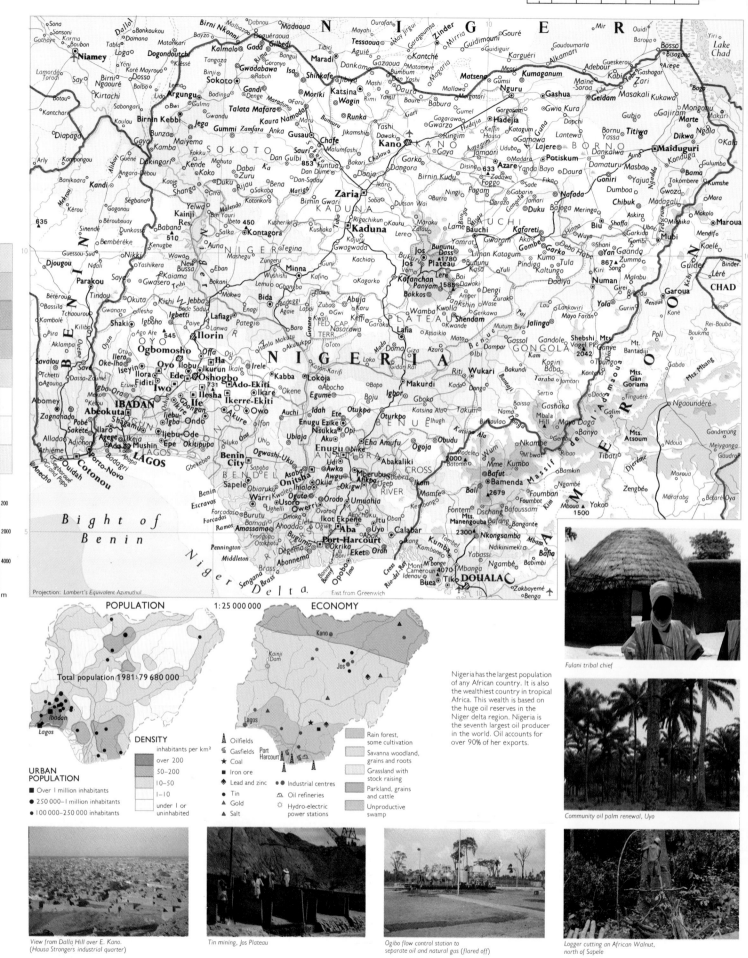

1:7 500 000

POPULATION

ECONOMY

Total population 1981: 79 680 000

Nigeria has the largest population of any African country. It is also the wealthiest country in tropical Africa. This wealth is based on the huge oil reserves in the Niger delta region. Nigeria is the seventh largest oil producer in the world. Oil accounts for over 90% of her exports.

DENSITY
inhabitants per km²
over 200
50–200
10–50
1–10
under 1 or uninhabited

URBAN POPULATION
■ Over 1 million inhabitants
● 250 000–1 million inhabitants
● 100 000–250 000 inhabitants

⚒ Oilfields
⚒ Gasfields
★ Coal
■ Iron ore
◆ Lead and zinc
● Tin
▲ Gold
▲ Salt

● Industrial centres
⚒ Oil refineries
⚙ Hydro-electric power stations

Rain forest, some cultivation
Savanna woodland, grains and roots
Grassland with stock raising
Parkland, grains and cattle
Unproductive swamp

Projection: Lambert's Equivalent Azimuthal.
East from Greenwich

Fulani tribal chief

Community oil palm renewal, Uyo

View from Dalla Hill over E. Kano. (Hausa Strongers industrial quarter)

Tin mining, Jos Plateau

Ogibo flow control station to separate oil and natural gas (flared off)

Logger cutting an African Walnut, north of Sapele

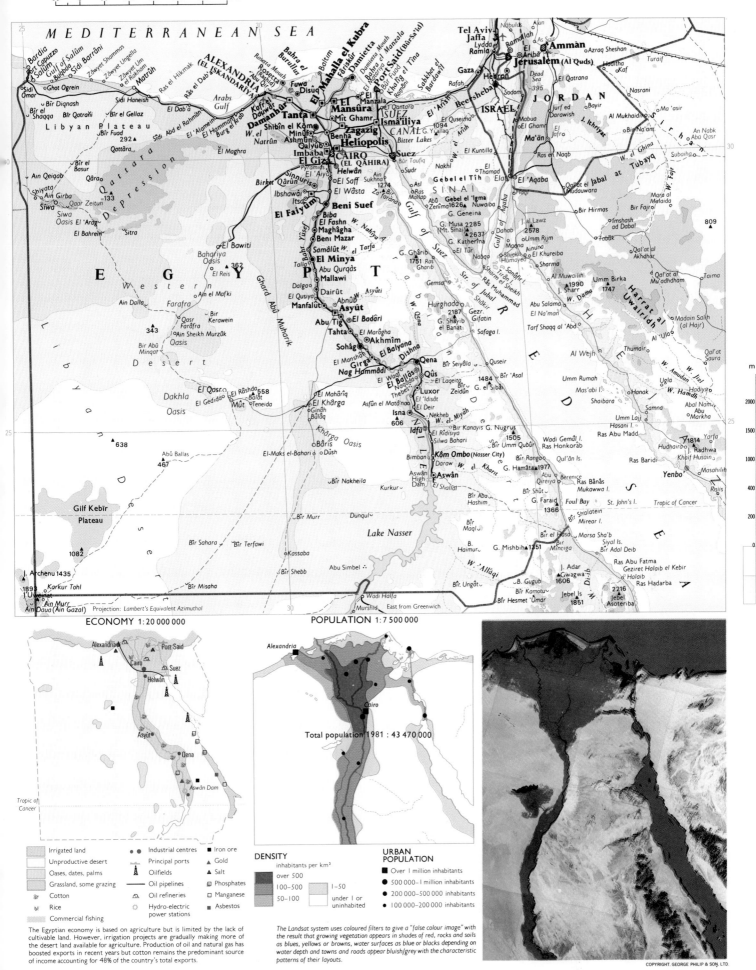

1:7 500 000

MEDITERRANEAN SEA

E G Y P T

Projection: Lambert's Equivalent Azimuthal

East from Greenwich

ECONOMY 1:20 000 000

Irrigated land
Unproductive desert
Oases, dates, palms
Grassland, some grazing
Cotton
Rice
Commercial fishing

Industrial centres
Principal ports
Oilfields
Oil pipelines
Oil refineries
Hydro-electric power stations

Iron ore
Gold
Salt
Phosphates
Manganese
Asbestos

The Egyptian economy is based on agriculture but is limited by the lack of cultivable land. However, irrigation projects are gradually making more of the desert land available for agriculture. Production of oil and natural gas has boosted exports in recent years but cotton remains the predominant source of income accounting for 48% of the country's total exports.

POPULATION 1:7 500 000

Total population 1981 : 43 470 000

DENSITY
inhabitants per km²
over 500
100–500
50–100
1–50
under 1 or uninhabited

URBAN POPULATION
Over 1 million inhabitants
500 000–1 million inhabitants
200 000–500 000 inhabitants
100 000–200 000 inhabitants

The Landsat system uses coloured filters to give a "false colour image" with the result that growing vegetation appears in shades of red, rocks and soils as blues, yellows or browns, water surfaces as blue or blacks depending on water depth and towns and roads appear bluish/grey with the characteristic patterns of their layouts.

1:20 000 000

200 0 200 400 600 800 km

NIGERIA
Cross
CAMEROON
Cameroon Pk. 4070
Bta
Douala
Yaoundé
Bf. of Biafra
Bioko
Bata
RIO MUNI
EQUATORIAL GUINEA
Libreville
C. Lopez
Ogowe
GABON
Franceville
Equator

CENTRAL AFRICAN REPUBLIC
Bangassou
M. Bomu
Ubangi
Bangui
Uele
Niangara
Lisala
Aketi
Buta
Aruwimi
Basoko
Kisangani (Stanleyville)
Ubundi
Mbandaka
Lomami
Zaïre (Congo)
CONGO
Kwa
Lualaba
L. Mai Ndombe
ZAÏRE (CONGO)
Brazzaville
Pool Malebo
Kinshasa (Léopoldville)
Pointe Noire
Boma
Cabinda
Muanda
Matadi
Ilebo
Sankuru
Kananga
Lusambo
Kongolo
Kindu (Costermansville)
Kabinda
Kabalo
Kasongo

SUDAN
Mongalla
Juba
Bahr-el-Jebel
Nile
Wadelai
Nimule
L. Mobutu Sese Seko
Irumu
Kabanega Falls
Butiaba
Semliki
UGANDA
L. Kioga
Kampala
Entebbe
Jinja
L. Edward
Ruwenzori
George
Lake Victoria
RWANDA
Kigali
Bukavu
Bukoba
BURUNDI
Bujumbura
Kasenga
Kigoma
Kasongo
Lukuga
Kalemie (Albertville)
Mpanda
Luvua
L. Mweru
Kamina
Shaba
Sandoa

ETHIOPIA
Omo
Chew Bahir (L. Stefanie)
L. Turkana
Marsabit
Mt. Elgon 4321
Kitale
Eldoret
Mt. Kenya 5199
Kisumu
Nakuru
KENYA
Naivasha
Nairobi
Kilimanjaro 5895
Moshi
Arusha
Voi
Tana
SOMALI REP.
Juba
Kismayu
Lamu
Malindi
Mombasa and Kilindini
Pemba
Zanzibar
Bagamoyo
Dar-es-Salaam
Mafia
Kilwa
Lindi
Mikindani
C. Delgado

L. Eyasi
L. Manyara
Mwanza
Tabora
TANZANIA
Dodoma
Kongwa
Mpwapwa
Morogoro
Iringa
Rufiji
L. Kasanga Rukwa
Mbeya
Tukuyu
Karonga
L. Mbala
Manda
Ruvuma

ANGOLA
Luanda
Cuanza
Malanje
Ambriz
Lobito
Benguela
Bié
Huambo
Plateau
Lubango
Namibe
Gt. Fish Bay
C. Frio
Cunene
Owambo
Cubango
Luena
Lualaba
Zambesi

ZAMBIA
Likasi
Lubumbashi (Elisabethville)
Kitwe
Ndola
Kafue
Kabwe
Lealui
Mongu
Barotseland
Lusaka
Kafue
Kariba
L. Kariba
Livingstone
Victoria Falls
Sesheke
L. Bangweulu
Chambeshi
Luangwa
Livingstonia
Salima
Chipata
Lilongwe
MALAWI
Shirwa
Zomba
Blantyre

MOZAMBIQUE
Zumbo
Zambesi
Cabora Bassa Dam
Tete
Sena
Nampula
Mozambique
Quelimane
Chinde
Zambesi
Beira
Sofala
Sabi
Inhambane

ZIMBABWE
Hwange
Harare (Salisbury)
Gweru
Mutare
Matabeleland
Bulawayo
Matopo Hills
Gwanda
West Nicholson
Masvingo
Zimbabwe

ATLANTIC OCEAN

NAMIBIA
Swakopmund
Walvis Bay
Windhoek
Damaraland
Otavi
Grootfontein
Etosha Pan
Namaland
Lüderitz
Possession I.
Keetmanshoop
Karas Mts.
Nossob
Hardap Dam

BOTSWANA
Makgadikgadi Salt pan
Serowe
Shoshong
Palapye
Tropic of Capricorn
Kalahari
Gaborone
Mafikeng
Molopo
Botletle
Limpopo
Messina

SOUTH AFRICA
Upington
Port Nolloth
Bushmanland
Orange
Kimberley
De Aar
Calvinia
St. Helena Bay
Nuweveldberge
Karoo
Swartberg
Oudtshoorn
Cape Town
Table Mountain
C. of Good Hope
C. Agulhas
Mosselbaai
Graaff-Reinet
Kommasberg 2504
Paarl
Algoa Bay
Pt. Elizabeth
Grahamstown
William's Town
East London
Umtata
TRANSKEI
Stormberg
CAPE PROVINCE
Bloemfontein
Maseru
LESOTHO
Mt. aux Sources 3298
ORANGE FREE STATE
Kroonstad
Vereeniging
Vryburg
Johannesburg
Germiston
Springs
Pretoria
TRANSVAAL
Lydenburg
Barberton
Krugersdorp
Klerksdorp
Pietersburg
Olifants
Messina
SWAZILAND
Maputo
Delagoa Bay
NATAL
Ladysmith
Newcastle
St. Lucia Bay
Pietermaritzburg
Durban
Mt. aux Sources 3482
Drakensberg
Kronstad

INDIAN OCEAN

Mozambique Channel

MADAGASCAR
C. Bobraomby
Antsiranana
Nossi-Be
Hell-Ville
Vohimarina
Sambava
2876
Tsaratanana
Andapa
Maroantsetra
Mahajanga
Marovoay
Besalampy
Maevatanana
L. Alaotra
Fenoarivo
Ambatondrazaka
Toamasina
Maintirano
2643
Antananarivo
Antsirabe
Mahanoro
Belo-Tsiribihina
Morondava
Mananjary
Morombé
Fianarantsoa
Mangoky
Ihosy
Manakara
Ankazoabo
Betroka
Farafangana
Toliara
Bekily
1956
Ambovombé
Faradofay
C. Vohimena
Tropic of Capricorn

On the same scale as the main map

m
3000
2000
1000
400
200
0
m
200

East from Greenwich

1:7 500 000

50   0   50   100   150   200   250   300 km

SUDAN   ETHIOPIA   SOMALI REP.   KENYA   UGANDA   ZAÏRE   RWANDA   BURUNDI   TANZANIA   ZAMBIA   MALAWI   MOZAMBIQUE

INDIAN OCEAN

LAKE VICTORIA   1134

Lake Turkana (Lake Rudolf)

Kampala   Entebbe   Jinja   Nairobi   Mombasa and Kilindini   Dar-es-Salaam   Zanzibar   Dodoma   Tabora   Kigali   Bujumbura (Usumbura)   Kigoma-Ujiji   Kalemie   Mbeya   Iringa   Morogoro   Tanga   Mtwara   Lindi   Moshi   Arusha

Kilimanjaro 5895   Mt. Kenya 5199

Projection: Modified Polyconic

East from Greenwich

COPYRIGHT. GEORGE PHILIP & SON. LTD

m   4000   3000   2000   1500   1000   400   200   0   200

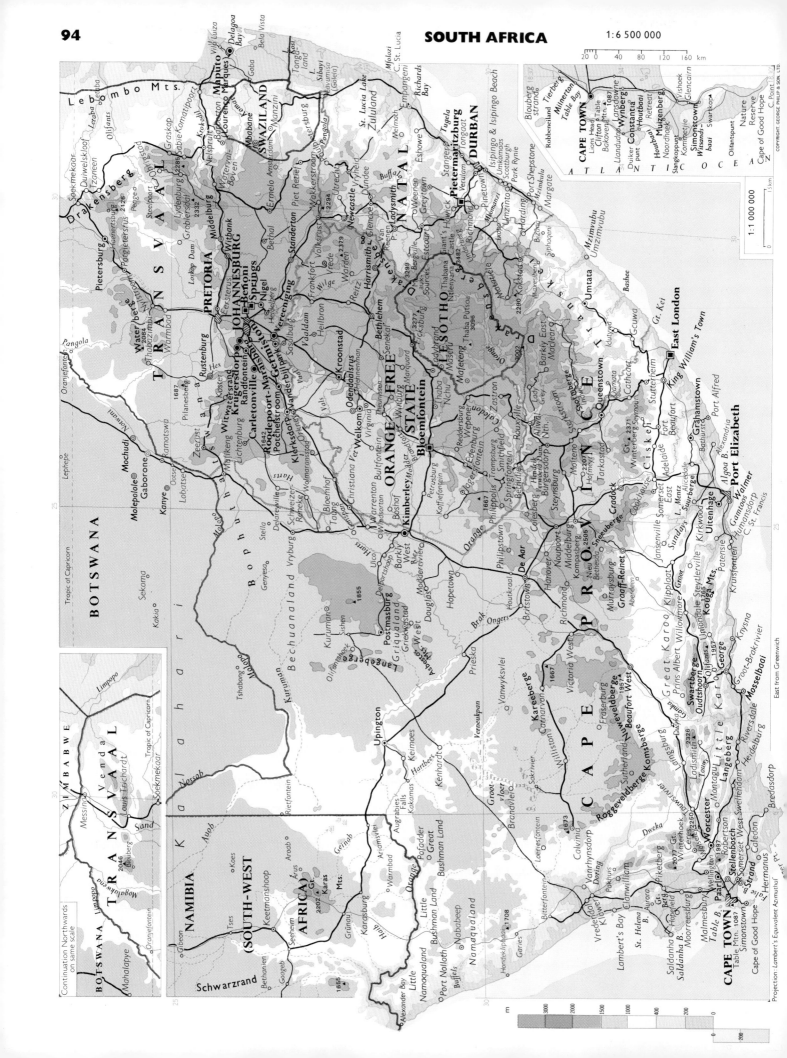

1:10 500 000

100   0   100   200   300   400 km

NAMIBIA
- East Caprivi
- Kavango
- Bushmanland
- Tswanaland
- Rehoboth Area
- Namaland
- Hereroland
- Owambo
- Kaokoland
- Damaraland

SOUTH AFRICA
- Transkei
- Bophuthatswana
- Lebowa
- Ciskei
- Gazankulu
- Venda
- South Ndebele
- Kwazulu
- Kangwane (Swazi)
- Qwa Qwa

Selected growth points
- ■ in border areas
- ◆ in homelands
- ○ ○ Major towns

Oshakati

Ohopoho

Rundu

Katima Mulilo

Tsumkwe

N A M I B I A

Khorixas

Okakarara

Okombahe

(S O U T H

Windhoek

Walvis Bay

Rehoboth

Tropic of Capricorn

W E S T

Tses

A F R I C A)

During the 1950's, the South African government gave recognition to the development of Black Homeland States.

Black people in South Africa were to be given automatic citizenship to one of these Homelands. This would be determined by exact tribal origin. Black people, resident or not, in a Homeland would therefore lose South African citizenship and take on that of their attached Homeland.

So far, nine Homelands have been given official recognition by the Republic of South Africa. Only three of these Homeland states, Transkei, Bophuthatswana and Venda, have been granted independence by South Africa. Neither these states, nor any of the other Homelands are recognized by any other nation.

VENDA

Makwarela

Sibasa   Giyani

Pietersburg

Lebowakgomo

Nyamazane

Mmabatho

Krugersdorp

Pretoria

Roodepoort-Maraisburg   Johannesburg   Benoni
Germiston   Springs
Vereeniging

BOPHUTHATSWANA

Mbabane

SWAZI-LAND

Welkom

Phuthaditjhaba

Ulundi

Kimberley

Ladysmith

Richards Bay

Bloemfontein

Maseru

LESOTHO

Pietermaritzburg

Durban

S O U T H   A F R I C A

Port Nolloth

Umtata

TRANSKEI

VALUE OF AGRICULTURAL PRODUCTION

CISKEI

Zwelitsha   East London

R '000
- 40 000
- 30 000
- 20 000
- 10 000
- 5 000
- 0

Port Elizabeth

Cape Town

Plant produce
Animal produce

Venda Gazankulu Ciskei Bophuthatswana Lebowa Kwazulu Transkei

RESIDENCE PATTERN OF BANTU GROUPS

percentage living outside homeland

percentage living within homeland

100 75 50 25 0

Others
Venda
Ndebele and others
Swazi
Shangaan
South Sotho
North Sotho
Tswana
Xhosa
Zulu

POPULATION

'000 people

2 250
2 000
1 750
1 500
1 250
1 000
750
500
250

Urban
Rural
Population density

inhabitants per km²
80
70
60
50
40
30
20
10
0

Kwazulu Transkei Lebowa Bophuthatswana Ciskei Venda Gazankulu Kangwane Qwa Qwa

GROSS DOMESTIC PRODUCT

R '000
150 000
125 000
100 000
75 000
50 000
25 000
12 500

Agriculture, forestry, hunting, fishing
Mining, quarrying
Manufacturing, industry, services, finance, trade, transport, health, education

Qwa Qwa Kangwane Venda Gazankulu Ciskei Lebowa Bophuthatswana Kwazulu Transkei

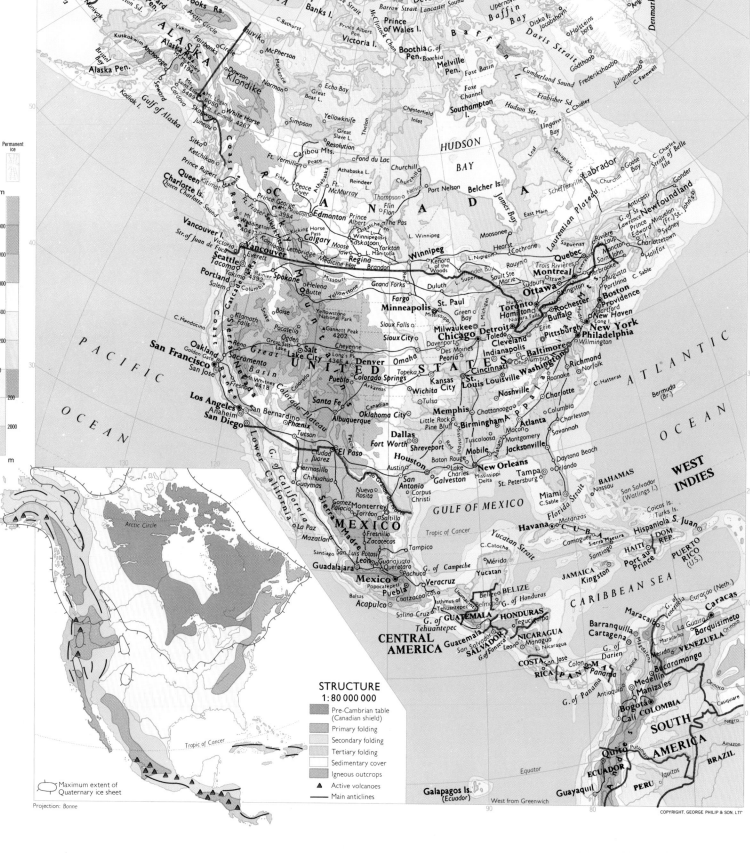

1:40 000 000

400   0   400   800   1200   1600 km

Permanent
ice

m
3000
2000
1000
400
200
0
200
2000
m

PACIFIC

OCEAN

ARCTIC OCEAN

ASIA
U.S.S.R.

ALASKA

CANADA

UNITED STATES

MEXICO

GREENLAND
(to Denmark)

ICELAND

ATLANTIC

OCEAN

**WEST
INDIES**

GULF OF MEXICO

CARIBBEAN SEA

**CENTRAL
AMERICA**

**SOUTH
AMERICA**

COLOMBIA

VENEZUELA

BRAZIL

PERU

ECUADOR

Galapagos Is.
(Ecuador)

STRUCTURE
1:80 000 000

- Pre-Cambrian table (Canadian shield)
- Primary folding
- Secondary folding
- Tertiary folding
- Sedimentary cover
- Igneous outcrops
▲ Active volcanoes
— Main anticlines

Maximum extent of
Quaternary ice sheet

Arctic Circle

Tropic of Cancer

Projection: Bonne

COPYRIGHT. GEORGE PHILIP & SON, LTD

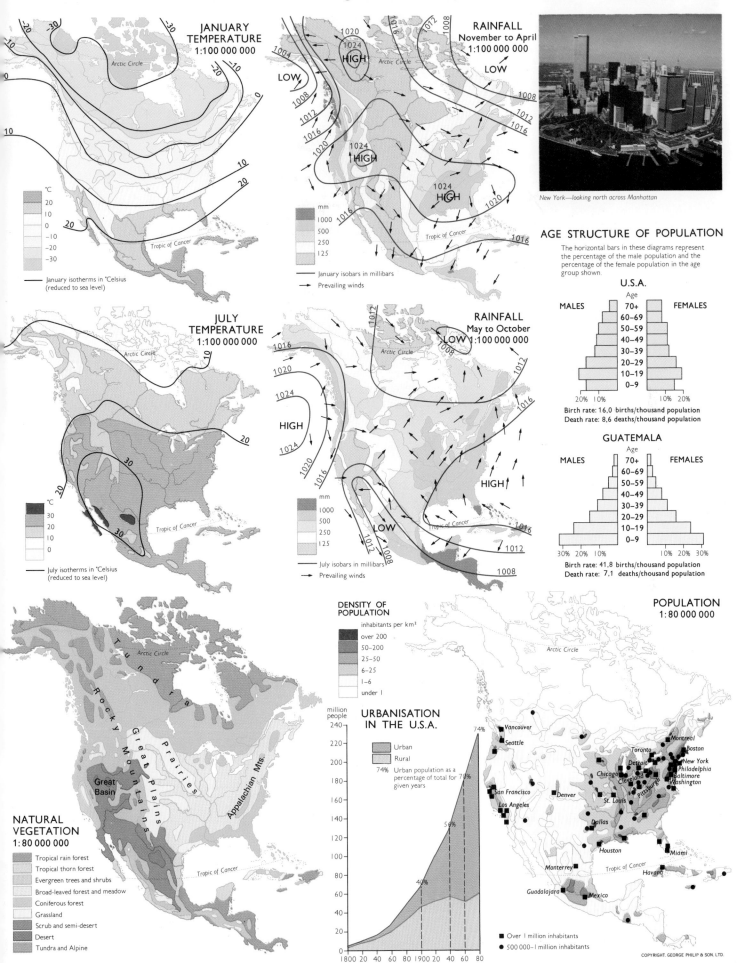

JANUARY TEMPERATURE
1:100 000 000

Arctic Circle

Tropic of Cancer

°C
20
10
0
-10
-20
-30

— January isotherms in °Celsius (reduced to sea level)

RAINFALL
November to April
1:100 000 000

LOW

HIGH

Arctic Circle

LOW

HIGH

HIGH

Tropic of Cancer

mm
1000
500
250
125

— January isobars in millibars
→ Prevailing winds

New York—looking north across Manhattan

AGE STRUCTURE OF POPULATION

The horizontal bars in these diagrams represent the percentage of the male population and the percentage of the female population in the age group shown.

U.S.A.

MALES | Age | FEMALES
70+
60-69
50-59
40-49
30-39
20-29
10-19
0-9

20% 10% | 10% 20%

Birth rate: 16,0 births/thousand population
Death rate: 8,6 deaths/thousand population

GUATEMALA

MALES | Age | FEMALES
70+
60-69
50-59
40-49
30-39
20-29
10-19
0-9

30% 20% 10% | 10% 20% 30%

Birth rate: 41,8 births/thousand population
Death rate: 7,1 deaths/thousand population

JULY TEMPERATURE
1:100 000 000

Arctic Circle

Tropic of Cancer

°C
30
20
10
0

— July isotherms in °Celsius (reduced to sea level)

RAINFALL
May to October
1:100 000 000

LOW

HIGH

Arctic Circle

HIGH

LOW

Tropic of Cancer

mm
1000
500
250
125

— July isobars in millibars
→ Prevailing winds

NATURAL VEGETATION
1:80 000 000

Tundra
Rocky Mountains
Great Plains
Prairies
Great Basin
Appalachian Mts.

Arctic Circle

Tropic of Cancer

Tropical rain forest
Tropical thorn forest
Evergreen trees and shrubs
Broad-leaved forest and meadow
Coniferous forest
Grassland
Scrub and semi-desert
Desert
Tundra and Alpine

DENSITY OF POPULATION

inhabitants per km²
over 200
50-200
25-50
6-25
1-6
under 1

URBANISATION IN THE U.S.A.

million people

Urban
Rural

74% Urban population as a percentage of total for given years

74%
59%
40%

240
220
200
180
160
140
120
100
80
60
40
20
0
1800 20 40 60 80 1900 20 40 60 80

POPULATION
1:80 000 000

Arctic Circle

Vancouver
Seattle
Montreal
Toronto
Boston
Detroit
New York
Chicago
Cleveland
Philadelphia
Baltimore
Washington
Pittsburgh
San Francisco
Denver
St. Louis
Los Angeles
Dallas
Houston
Miami
Monterrey
Havana
Tropic of Cancer
Guadalajara
Mexico

■ Over 1 million inhabitants
● 500 000-1 million inhabitants

COPYRIGHT. GEORGE PHILIP & SON. LTD.

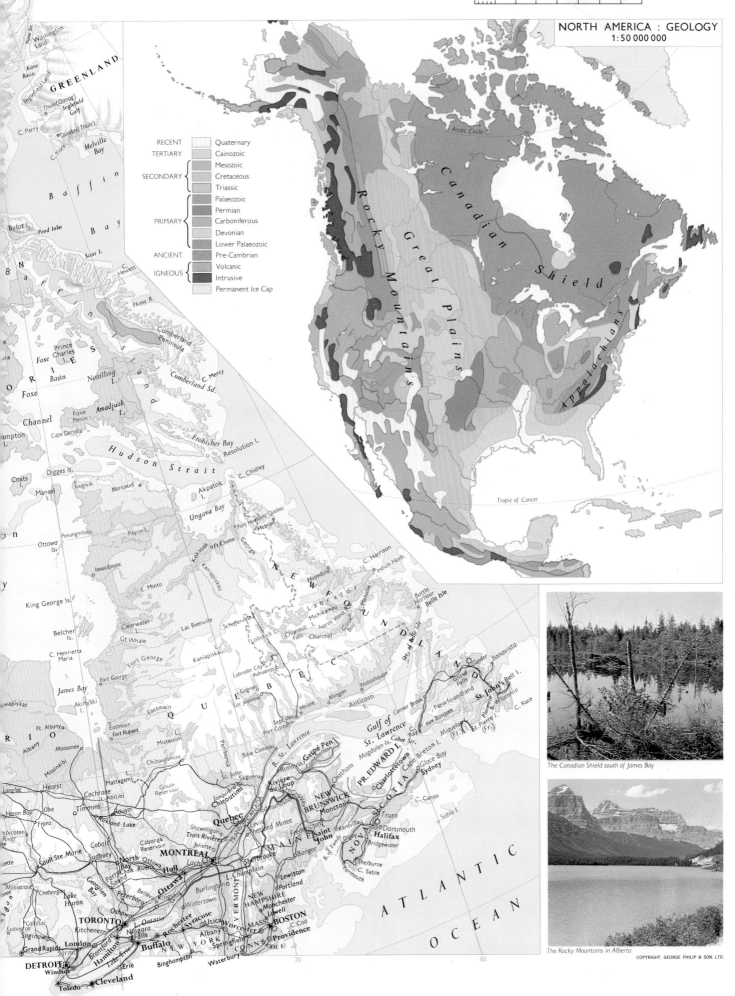

NORTH AMERICA : GEOLOGY
1:50 000 000

The Canadian Shield south of James Bay

The Rocky Mountains in Alberta

COPYRIGHT. GEORGE PHILIP & SON. LTD.

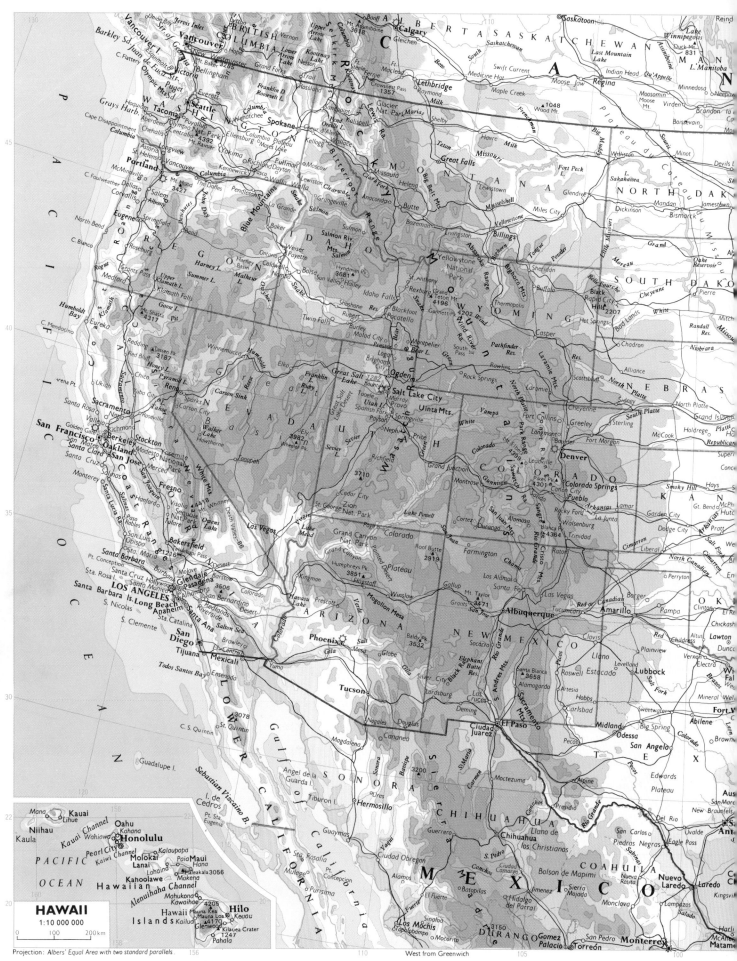

HAWAII
1:10 000 000

0   100   200km

Projection: Albers' Equal Area with two standard parallels

West from Greenwich

1:12 000 000

100 0 100 200 300 400 500 km

GULF OF MEXICO

ATLANTIC OCEAN

BAHAMAS

CANADA

MINNESOTA · WISCONSIN · MICHIGAN · IOWA · ILLINOIS · INDIANA · OHIO · PENNSYLVANIA · NEW YORK · MISSOURI · KENTUCKY · WEST VIRGINIA · VIRGINIA · TENNESSEE · NORTH CAROLINA · SOUTH CAROLINA · ARKANSAS · MISSISSIPPI · ALABAMA · GEORGIA · LOUISIANA · FLORIDA · MAINE · NEW BRUNSWICK

Minneapolis · St. Paul · Duluth · Milwaukee · Chicago · Detroit · Cleveland · Pittsburgh · Buffalo · Toronto · Montreal · Quebec · Ottawa · Boston · New York · Philadelphia · Baltimore · Washington D.C. · Richmond · Des Moines · Kansas City · St. Louis · Memphis · Nashville · Atlanta · Birmingham · Montgomery · New Orleans · Baton Rouge · Houston · Dallas · Shreveport · Jacksonville · Tampa · Miami · Orlando · Charlotte · Columbia · Savannah · Raleigh · Norfolk · Cincinnati · Indianapolis · Louisville · Knoxville · Chattanooga

Lake Superior · Lake Michigan · Lake Huron · Lake Erie · Lake Ontario · Georgian Bay · Lake Winnipeg · Lake of the Woods

Mississippi · Ohio · Missouri · Tennessee · Red River

Delta of the Mississippi · Florida Keys · Key West · Charlotte Harb. · C. Hatteras · C. Canaveral · Penobscot Bay · Cape Cod

1:60 000 000

500   0   500   1000   1500   2000   2500 km

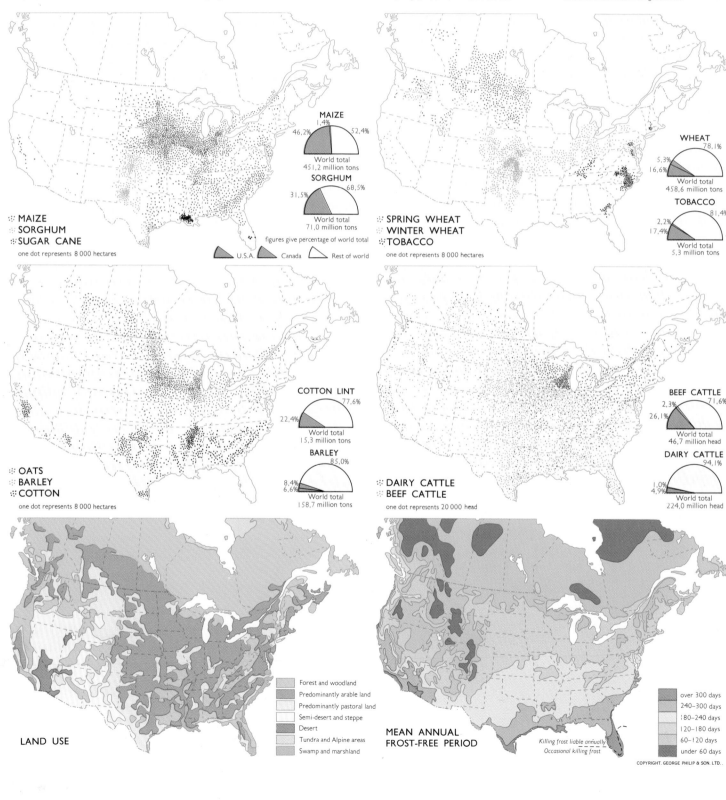

Stockyard, Phoenix

The spring wheat harvest

Aerial photograph of field patterns, Saskatchewan

Land Use; lumber mill, Washington, Seattle

MAIZE
1,4%
46,2%   52,4%
World total
451,2 million tons

SORGHUM
31,5%   68,5%
World total
71,0 million tons

figures give percentage of world total

U.S.A.   Canada   Rest of world

:: MAIZE
:: SORGHUM
:: SUGAR CANE
one dot represents 8 000 hectares

WHEAT
78,1%
5,3%
16,6%
World total
458,6 million tons

TOBACCO
81,4%
2,2%
17,4%
World total
5,3 million tons

:: SPRING WHEAT
:: WINTER WHEAT
:: TOBACCO
one dot represents 8 000 hectares

COTTON LINT
77,6%
22,4%
World total
15,3 million tons

BARLEY
85,0%
8,4%
6,6%
World total
158,7 million tons

:: OATS
:: BARLEY
:: COTTON
one dot represents 8 000 hectares

BEEF CATTLE
71,6%
2,3%
26,1%
World total
46,7 million head

DAIRY CATTLE
94,1%
1,0%
4,9%
World total
224,0 million head

:: DAIRY CATTLE
:: BEEF CATTLE
one dot represents 20 000 head

LAND USE

Forest and woodland
Predominantly arable land
Predominantly pastoral land
Semi-desert and steppe
Desert
Tundra and Alpine areas
Swamp and marshland

**MEAN ANNUAL
FROST-FREE PERIOD**

Killing frost liable annually
Occasional killing frost

over 300 days
240–300 days
180–240 days
120–180 days
60–120 days
under 60 days

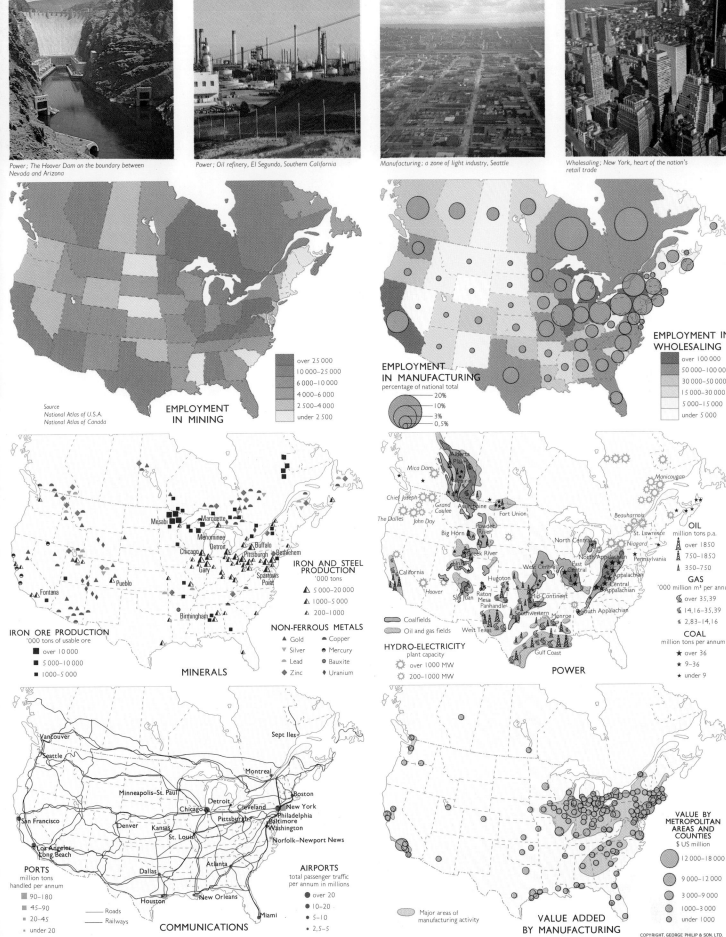

Power; The Hoover Dam on the boundary between Nevada and Arizona

Power; Oil refinery, El Segundo, Southern California

Manufacturing; a zone of light industry, Seattle

Wholesaling; New York, heart of the nation's retail trade

EMPLOYMENT IN MINING

Source
National Atlas of U.S.A.
National Atlas of Canada

	over 25 000
	10 000–25 000
	6 000–10 000
	4 000–6 000
	2 500–4 000
	under 2 500

EMPLOYMENT IN MANUFACTURING
percentage of national total
- 20%
- 10%
- 3%
- 0,5%

EMPLOYMENT IN WHOLESALING

	over 100 000
	50 000–100 000
	30 000–50 000
	15 000–30 000
	5 000–15 000
	under 5 000

MINERALS

IRON AND STEEL PRODUCTION
'000 tons
- 5 000–20 000
- 1 000–5 000
- 200–1 000

NON-FERROUS METALS
- Gold
- Silver
- Lead
- Zinc
- Copper
- Mercury
- Bauxite
- Uranium

IRON ORE PRODUCTION
'000 tons of usable ore
- over 10 000
- 5 000–10 000
- 1 000–5 000

Mesabi, Marquette, Menominee, Detroit, Chicago, Gary, Buffalo, Pittsburgh, Bethlehem, Sparrows Point, Fontana, Pueblo, Birmingham

POWER

Mica Dam, Alberta Plains, Prairie, Chief Joseph, Grand Coulee, Assiniboine, Fort Union, The Dalles, John Day, Big Horn, Powder River, Creek River, Uinta, Hoover, San Juan, Raton Mesa, Panhandle, Hugoton, West Central, East Central, Mid Continent, Southwestern, Monroe, South Appalachian, West Texas, Gulf Coast, California, Manicouagan, Beauharnois, St. Lawrence, Niagara, North Central, North Appalachian, Pennsylvania, Appalachian, Central Appalachian

HYDRO-ELECTRICITY
plant capacity
- over 1000 MW
- 200–1000 MW

Coalfields
Oil and gas fields

OIL
million tons p.a.
- over 1850
- 750–1850
- 350–750

GAS
'000 million m³ per annum
- over 35,39
- 14,16–35,39
- 2,83–14,16

COAL
million tons per annum
- over 36
- 9–36
- under 9

COMMUNICATIONS

Vancouver, Seattle, San Francisco, Los Angeles–Long Beach, Denver, Kansas, St. Louis, Dallas, Houston, New Orleans, Minneapolis–St. Paul, Chicago, Detroit, Cleveland, Pittsburgh, Atlanta, Montreal, Boston, New York, Philadelphia, Baltimore, Washington, Norfolk–Newport News, Miami, Sept Iles

PORTS
million tons handled per annum
- 90–180
- 45–90
- 20–45
- under 20

— Roads
— Railways

AIRPORTS
total passenger traffic per annum in millions
- over 20
- 10–20
- 5–10
- 2,5–5

VALUE ADDED BY MANUFACTURING

VALUE BY METROPOLITAN AREAS AND COUNTIES
$ US million
- 12 000–18 000
- 9 000–12 000
- 3 000–9 000
- 1 000–3 000
- under 1000

Major areas of manufacturing activity

1:6 000 000

50 0 50 100 150 200 250 km

THE ST. LAWRENCE SEAWAY

The St. Lawrence Seaway was opened in 1959 enabling 80% of ocean-going vessels to reach Lake Superior. The Seaway is frozen for over 90 days each year from late December to early April.

QUEBEC
Cargo loaded
(million tons)
Wheat 0.6
Barley 0.5
Zinc ore 0.4
Newsprint 0.2
Others 1.2
Fuel oil 1.4

MONTREAL
Cargo loaded
(million tons)
Fuel oil 0.9
Barley 0.4
Cement 0.2
Others 1.8
Wheat 1.5

HAMILTON
Cargo unloaded
(million tons)
Iron ore 3.9
Fuel oil 0.1
Others 2.6
Coal 5.1

Quebec to Atlantic Ocean 7 m
Montreal 20 m
L. St. Louis
L. St. Francis 46 m
L. St. Laurent 73 m
Lake Ontario 75 m
Hamilton
Welland Canal
Lake Erie 174 m
Windsor
Lake Michigan / Lake Huron 177 m

ST. LAWRENCE SEAWAY TRAFFIC
Total cargo carried (million tons)

OTHER GOODS 13.0
MANUFACTURES 1.6
AGRICULTURAL PRODUCTS 22.5
Wheat 10.9
Others 11.6
Iron ore 18.1
Coal 7.3
Others 5.6
MINERALS 31.0

LAND USE
Forest and woodland, mostly ungrazed
Woodland and forest, with some arable and pasture
Arable
Arable and pasture, with some woodland and forest
Pasture with some woodland and forest
Swamp
Urban and industrial areas

POWER AND MINERALS
Oilfields
Gasfields
Oil pipelines
Gas pipelines
Coalfields
Coal production
Oil refineries
Hydro-electric power stations
Railways

Iron
Cobalt
Nickel
Vanadium
Copper
Lead
Zinc
Silver
Titanium
Uranium
Asbestos
Mica
Potash
Salt

Projection: Alber's Equal area with two standard parallels

COPYRIGHT GEORGE PHILIP & SON LTD

Map labels (selected): LAKE SUPERIOR, Isle Royale, Hancock, Marquette, Negaunee, Ishpeming, Iron Mt., Escanaba, Green Bay, Manistique, Menominee, Marinette, Appleton, Sheboygan, MILWAUKEE, Racine, Kenosha, Waukegan, CHICAGO, Gary, Hammond, Joliet, Kankakee, La Fayette, Logansport, Kokomo, Marion, Fort Wayne, South Bend, Michigan City, INDIANA, MICHIGAN, Grand Rapids, Muskegon, Kalamazoo, Battle Creek, Lansing, Jackson, Cadillac, Traverse City, Cheboygan, Bay City, Saginaw, Flint, Pontiac, Ann Arbor, DETROIT, Windsor, Monroe, Toledo, Findlay, Lima, OHIO, Columbus, Springfield, Dayton, Middletown, CINCINNATI, Mansfield, Sandusky, Zanesville, Marion, CLEVELAND, Akron, Canton, Youngstown, New Castle, Lakewood, Lorain, Lima, LAKE ERIE, LAKE HURON, Georgian Bay, Manitoulin I., North Bay, L. Nipissing, Sudbury, Copper Cliff, Sault Ste. Marie, ONTARIO, TORONTO, Hamilton, Guelph, Kitchener, London, Brantford, Chatham, St. Clair, Sarnia, Port Huron, St. Catharines, Niagara Falls, BUFFALO, Rochester, Oshawa, Peterborough, Barrie, Belleville, Kingston, Watertown, Oswego, Auburn, Syracuse, Utica, Rome, Ithaca, Elmira, Binghamton, Williamsport, NEW YORK, PENNSYLVANIA, Scranton, Wilkes Barre, Allentown, Bethlehem, Reading, Lancaster, Harrisburg, York, Hagerstown, PITTSBURGH, McKeesport, Johnstown, Altoona, Wheeling, Bellaire, Clarksburg, Parkersburg, Cumberland, WEST VIRGINIA, MARYLAND, BALTIMORE, WASHINGTON D.C., DELAWARE, Dover, Wilmington, PHILADELPHIA, Camden, Trenton, NEW JERSEY, Atlantic City, NEW YORK, Jersey City, Newark, Elizabeth, Paterson, Bridgeport, New Haven, Waterbury, New Britain, Hartford, CONN., Springfield, Holyoke, New London, Providence, R.I., Pawtucket, Woonsocket, Fall River, New Bedford, BOSTON, Cambridge, Quincy, Brockton, Worcester, Lowell, Lawrence, Lynn, MASS., Manchester, Concord, NEW HAMPSHIRE, Portland, VERMONT, Montpelier, Burlington, L. Champlain, Saratoga Sps., Albany, Troy, Schenectady, Amsterdam, Glen Falls, Adirondack Mts., Hudson, Kingston, Catskill Mts., Delaware, Susquehanna, Allegheny, Ohio, Potomac, Connecticut, QUEBEC, Quebec, Trois Rivières, Thetford Mines, Drummondville, St. Hyacinthe, Sherbrooke, Shawinigan, Grand'Mère, St. Jérome, MONTREAL, St. Jean, Ottawa, Hull, Renfrew, Pembroke, Bancroft, St. Laurent

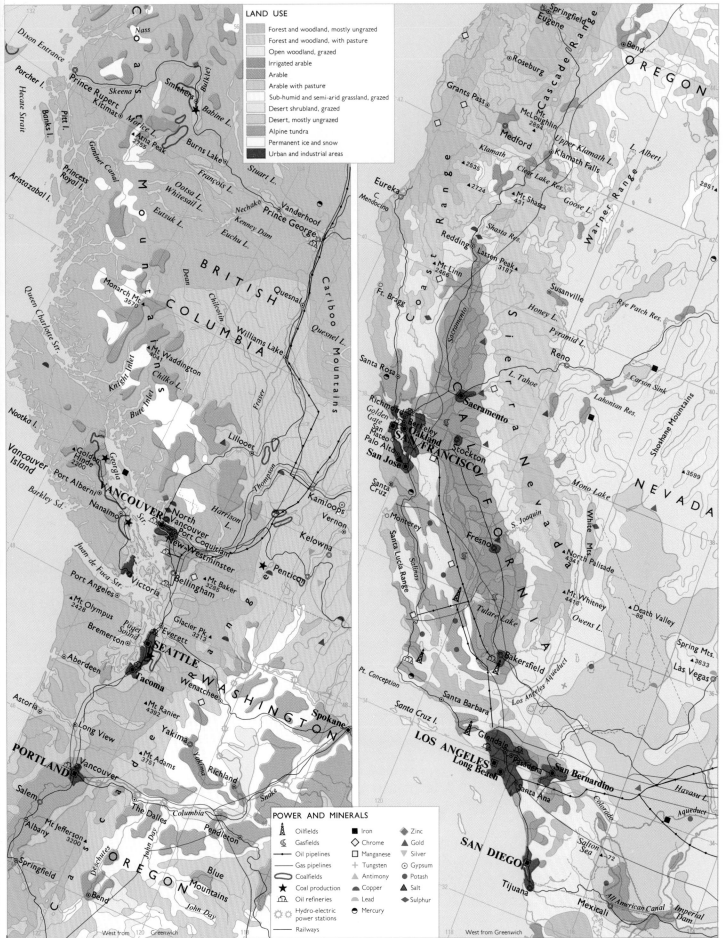

1:6 000 000

50   0   50   100   150   200   250 km

LAND USE

- Forest and woodland, mostly ungrazed
- Forest and woodland, with pasture
- Open woodland, grazed
- Irrigated arable
- Arable
- Arable with pasture
- Sub-humid and semi-arid grassland, grazed
- Desert shrubland, grazed
- Desert, mostly ungrazed
- Alpine tundra
- Permanent ice and snow
- Urban and industrial areas

POWER AND MINERALS

Oilfields	■ Iron	◆ Zinc
Gasfields	◇ Chrome	▲ Gold
Oil pipelines	□ Manganese	▽ Silver
Gas pipelines	+ Tungsten	◉ Gypsum
Coalfields	▲ Antimony	● Potash
★ Coal production	◖ Copper	▲ Salt
Oil refineries	◐ Lead	◆ Sulphur
Hydro-electric power stations	◑ Mercury	
Railways		

Projection: *Lambert's Equivalent Azimuthal*

Projection: *Alber's Equal Area with two standard parallels*

COPYRIGHT. GEORGE PHILIP & SON. LTD.

ECONOMY
1:30 000 000

EXPORTS
(Latest figures available)

Jamaica	
Cuba	
Mexico	

0   0,5   1   1,5   2   2,5   3   3,5 $ US million

- Minerals
- Chemicals
- Metals
- Food, beverages and tobacco
- Agricultural produce
- Textiles
- Other

MEXICO: OIL PRODUCTION

New discoveries of oil in the Chiapas-Tabasco region have dramatically increased production since 1974.

million tons
100
80
60
40
20
0
1950 55 60 65 70 75 80

LAND USE

- Arable land and plantations
- Permanent pasture
- Woods and forests
- Rough grazing
- Non-productive land

CROPS

- Cotton
- Wheat
- Sugar cane
- Maize
- Tobacco
- Coffee
- Sisal
- Bananas
- Rice

INDUSTRY AND POWER

- Industrial centres
- Oil refineries
- Oil pipelines
- Gas pipelines
- Oilfields
- Gasfields

VERACRUZ FIELDS

CHIAPAS-TABASCO FIELDS

MINERALS

- Copper
- Silver, lead and zinc
- Mercury
- Sulphur
- Manganese
- Iron
- Uranium
- Coal
- Gold
- Bauxite
- Nickel

WEST INDIES: SUGAR CANE PRODUCTION, 1979
figures in million tons

- Others 5,0
- P. Rico 2,1
- Haiti 2,9
- Jamaica 3,0
- Dom. Rep. 11,4
- Cuba 70,0

Total 94 367 000 tons

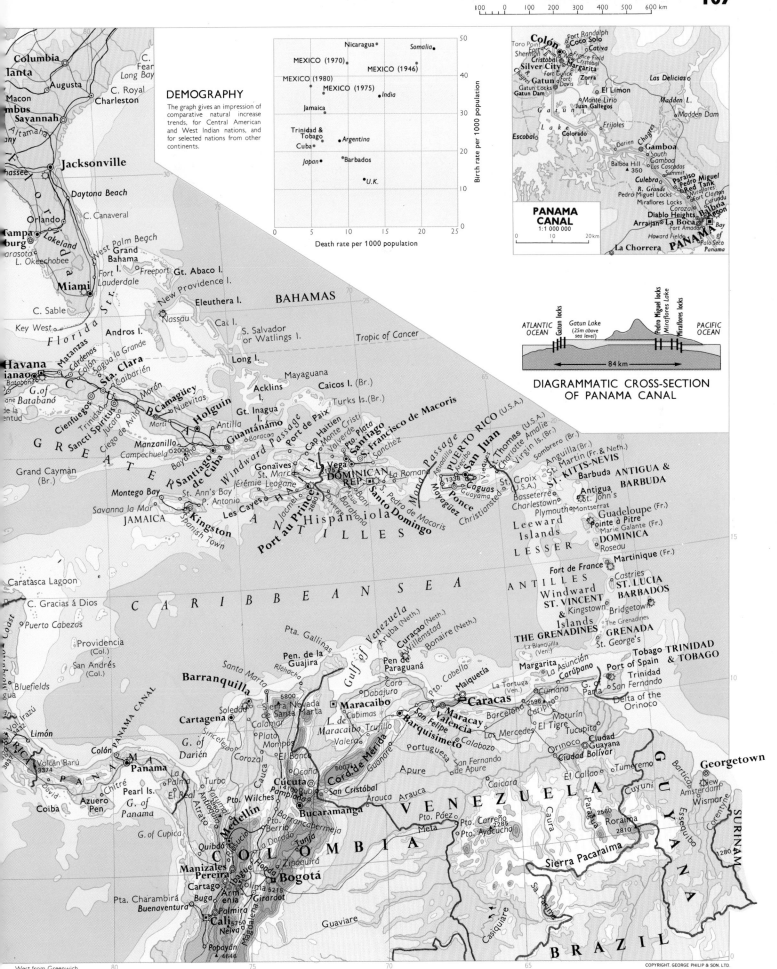

1:40 000 000

400 0 400 800 1200 1600 km

The Trans-Amazonian Highway, linking Recife with Peru

Map labels

G. of Campeche
C. Catoche
Yucatan Str.
CUBA
Turks Is.
Hispaniola
HAITI
DOM. REP.
S. Juan
PUERTO RICO (U.S.)
BELIZE
G. of Honduras
JAMAICA
Kingston
Port au Prince
Leeward Is.
Guadeloupe
GUATEMALA
Guatemala
HONDURAS
Tegucigalpa
San Salvador
SALVADOR
G. of Fonseca
NICARAGUA
Managua
L. Nicaragua
COSTA RICA
San Jose
CENTRAL AMERICA
PANAMA
Panamá
G. of Panama
G. of Darien
CARIBBEAN SEA
Martinique
Windward Is.
BARBADOS
Curaçao (Neth.)
G. of Venezuela
Maracaibo
Barranquilla
Cartagena
Bucra
Mérida
Sa. de Mérida
Medellín
Manizales
Bogotá
Cali
COLOMBIA
Port of Spain
TRINIDAD & TOBAGO
Caracas
Barquisimeto
Orinoco
VENEZUELA
Llanos
Roraima Falls 2810
Sa. Pacaraima
Orinoco
Casiquiare
GUYANA
Demerara
Georgetown
SURINAM
Paramaribo
FR. GUIANA
Cayenne
Sa. de Yumucumaque
Equator
Fernando Noronha
ECUADOR
Quito
Chimborazo 6267
Cotopaxi 5897
Guayaquil
Cuenca
C. Pariña
Marañon
Iquitos
Putumayo
Japurá
Negro
Amazon
Manaus
Santarém
Belém
Pará
Marajó I.
Amazon
São Luis (Maranhão)
Fortaleza (Ceará)
Teresina
Parnaiba
Natal
C. de São Roque
João Pessoa
Recife (Pernambuco)
C. Branco
Maceió
Chiclayo
Trujillo
PERU
Selvas
Purus
Ucayali
Madeira
S. Antonio Falls
Roosevelt
Juruá
Tapajós
Xingu
Tocantins
Araguaya
São Francisco
BRAZIL
Brazilian Highlands
Salvador (Bahia)
Aracajú
Callão
Lima
Cuzco
Ilampú 6560
Guaporé
Plateau of Mato Grosso
Cuiabá
Brasília
Goiânia
Montes Claros
Belo Horizonte
Ribeirão Prêto
BOLIVIA
La Paz
Cochabamba
Oruro
Sucre
Corumbá
Arequipa
Mollendo
Tacna
Arica
Iquique
Antofagasta
Atacama Desert
Bolivian Plateau
Salta
Ojos del Salado 6863
Tucumán
Campo Grande
Paraguay
PARAGUAY
Asunción
Paraná
Campinas
São Paulo
Santos
Sa. da Mantiqueira
Niteroi
Rio de Janeiro
C. Frio
Tropic of Capricorn
PACIFIC OCEAN
Juan Fernández (Chile)
Aconcagua
Córdoba
Mendoza
Rosario
Santa Fé
Paraná
Curitiba
Iguaçu Falls
Sa. do Mar
Pôrto Alegre
Lagoa dos Patos
Rio Grande do Sul
Viña del Mar
Valparaiso
Santiago
ARGENTINA
Entre Rios
URUGUAY
Montevideo
Buenos Aires
La Plata
Rio de la Plata
Talca
Concepción
Colorado
Negro
Bahia Blanca
Mar del Plata
Pta. Mogotes
Valdivia
Temuco
Puerto Montt
Chiloé
Chubut
Comodoro Rivadavia
G. of San Jorge
Chonos Arch.
Patagonia
G. of San Matias
ATLANTIC OCEAN
Falkland Is. (Br.) Stanley
Punta Arenas
Magellan's Str.
Tierra del Fuego
Staten I.
C. Froward
C. Horn
West from Greenwich
Galapagos Is. (Ecuador)

Elevation legend (m)
4000
2000
1000
400
200
0
200
2000

The High Andes, east of Antofagasta, Chile

Cross section from Australia to South America

AUSTRALIA
NEW ZEALAND
SOUTH AMERICA
metres
5000
sea level
-5000
-10 000
Lake Eyre
Great Divide
Tasman Sea
Kermadec Trench
PACIFIC OCEAN
East Pacific Ridge
Chile Trench
Andes
Brazilian Highlands

CROSS SECTION FROM AUSTRALIA TO SOUTH AMERICA

Pre-Cambrian tables | Hercynian folding | Tertiary folding | Movements in the earth's mantle

Projection: Lambert's Equivalent Azimuthal

STRUCTURE
1:80 000 000

Equator
Tropic of Capricorn

PRE-CAMBRIAN TABLES
Outcrops
Sedimentary cover
HERCYNIAN FOLDING
Outcrops
Sedimentary cover
TERTIARY FOLDING
Outcrops
Sedimentary cover
▲ Active volcanoes
— Main anticlines

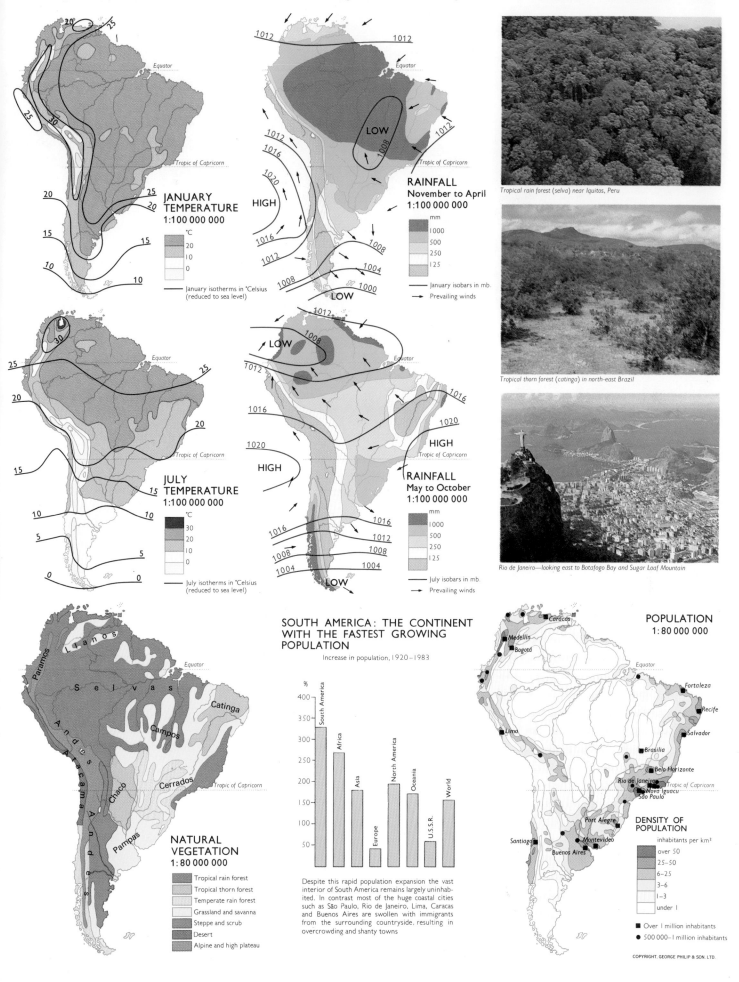

JANUARY TEMPERATURE
1:100 000 000

°C
20
10
0

January isotherms in °Celsius
(reduced to sea level)

RAINFALL
November to April
1:100 000 000

mm
1000
500
250
125

January isobars in mb.
Prevailing winds

Tropical rain forest (selva) near Iquitos, Peru

JULY TEMPERATURE
1:100 000 000

°C
30
20
10
0

July isotherms in °Celsius
(reduced to sea level)

RAINFALL
May to October
1:100 000 000

mm
1000
500
250
125

July isobars in mb.
Prevailing winds

Tropical thorn forest (catinga) in north-east Brazil

Rio de Janeiro—looking east to Botafogo Bay and Sugar Loaf Mountain

NATURAL VEGETATION
1:80 000 000

Tropical rain forest
Tropical thorn forest
Temperate rain forest
Grassland and savanna
Steppe and scrub
Desert
Alpine and high plateau

Paramos
Llanos
Selvas
Catinga
Campos
Andes
Cerrados
Atacama
Chaco
Andes
Pampas

SOUTH AMERICA: THE CONTINENT WITH THE FASTEST GROWING POPULATION

Increase in population, 1920–1983

%
400
350
300
250
200
150
100
50

South America
Africa
Asia
Europe
North America
Oceania
U.S.S.R.
World

Despite this rapid population expansion the vast interior of South America remains largely uninhabited. In contrast most of the huge coastal cities such as São Paulo, Rio de Janeiro, Lima, Caracas and Buenos Aires are swollen with immigrants from the surrounding countryside, resulting in overcrowding and shanty towns

POPULATION
1:80 000 000

Caracas
Medellín
Bogotá
Fortaleza
Recife
Lima
Salvador
Brasilia
Belo Horizonte
Rio de Janeiro
Nova Iguaçu
São Paulo
Port Alegre
Santiago
Montevideo
Buenos Aires

DENSITY OF POPULATION

inhabitants per km²
over 50
25–50
6–25
3–6
1–3
under 1

■ Over 1 million inhabitants
● 500 000–1 million inhabitants

COPYRIGHT. GEORGE PHILIP & SON. LTD.

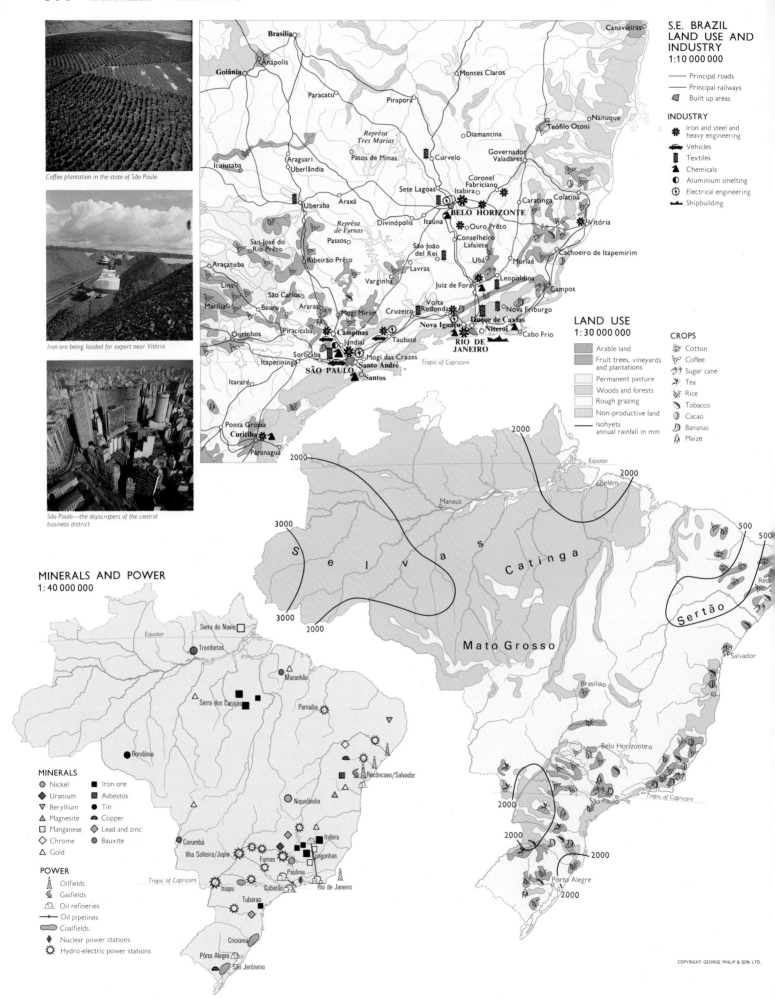

Coffee plantation in the state of São Paulo

Iron ore being loaded for export near Vitória

São Paulo—the skyscrapers of the central business district

S.E. BRAZIL LAND USE AND INDUSTRY
1:10 000 000

— Principal roads
— Principal railways
⬡ Built up areas

INDUSTRY

✳ Iron and steel and heavy engineering
✳ Vehicles
▮ Textiles
▲ Chemicals
◖ Aluminium smelting
✪ Electrical engineering
⚓ Shipbuilding

LAND USE
1:30 000 000

Arable land
Fruit trees, vineyards and plantations
Permanent pasture
Woods and forests
Rough grazing
Non-productive land
— Isohyets annual rainfall in mm

CROPS

🌿 Cotton
☕ Coffee
Sugar cane
Tea
Rice
Tobacco
Cacao
Bananas
Maize

MINERALS AND POWER
1:40 000 000

MINERALS

◉ Nickel
◆ Uranium
▽ Beryllium
△ Magnesite
▢ Manganese
◇ Chrome
△ Gold
■ Iron ore
▣ Asbestos
◣ Tin
◆ Copper
◇ Lead and zinc
◉ Bauxite

POWER

⛏ Oilfields
⛏ Gasfields
⛫ Oil refineries
— Oil pipelines
Coalfields
◆ Nuclear power stations
✸ Hydro-electric power stations

COPYRIGHT. GEORGE PHILIP & SON. LTD.

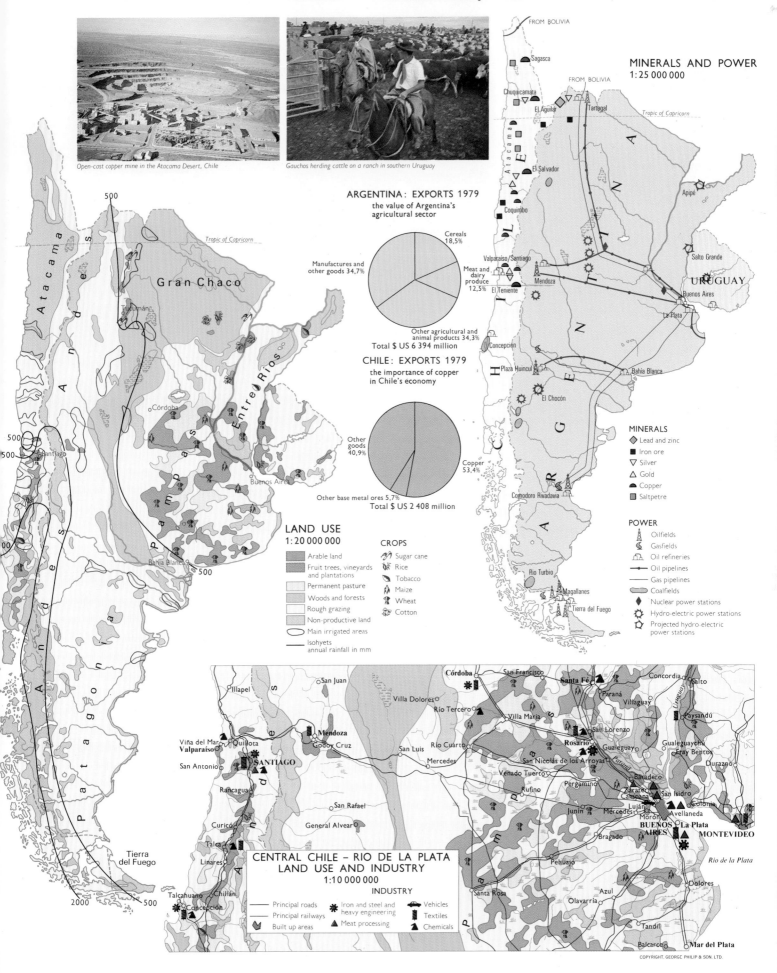

Open-cast copper mine in the Atacama Desert, Chile

Gauchos herding cattle on a ranch in southern Uruguay

MINERALS AND POWER
1:25 000 000

FROM BOLIVIA

Sagasca
Chuquicamata
El Aguilar
Tartagal
FROM BOLIVIA
Tropic of Capricorn
El Salvador
Apipé
Coquimbo
Salto Grande
Valparaiso/Santiago
Mendoza
URUGUAY
El Teniente
Buenos Aires
Concepción
La Plata
Plaza Huincul
Bahía Blanca
El Chocón
Comodoro Rivadavia
Río Turbio
Magallanes
Tierra del Fuego

MINERALS
- ◆ Lead and zinc
- ■ Iron ore
- ▽ Silver
- △ Gold
- ◓ Copper
- ▣ Saltpetre

POWER
- Oilfields
- Gasfields
- Oil refineries
- Oil pipelines
- Gas pipelines
- Coalfields
- ◆ Nuclear power stations
- ✸ Hydro-electric power stations
- ◇ Projected hydro-electric power stations

ARGENTINA : EXPORTS 1979
the value of Argentina's agricultural sector

- Cereals 18,5%
- Manufactures and other goods 34,7%
- Meat and dairy produce 12,5%
- Other agricultural and animal products 34,3%

Total $ US 6 394 million

CHILE : EXPORTS 1979
the importance of copper in Chile's economy

- Other goods 40,9%
- Copper 53,4%
- Other base metal ores 5,7%

Total $ US 2 408 million

LAND USE
1:20 000 000

- Arable land
- Fruit trees, vineyards and plantations
- Permanent pasture
- Woods and forests
- Rough grazing
- Non-productive land
- Main irrigated areas
- Isohyets annual rainfall in mm

CROPS
- Sugar cane
- Rice
- Tobacco
- Maize
- Wheat
- Cotton

(main map labels)
Atacama
Andes
Gran Chaco
Tropic of Capricorn
Tucumán
Entre Ríos
Córdoba
Pampas
Santiago
Buenos Aires
Bahía Blanca
Patagonia
Andes
Tierra del Fuego
500
2000
500

CENTRAL CHILE - RIO DE LA PLATA
LAND USE AND INDUSTRY
1:10 000 000
INDUSTRY

- Principal roads
- Principal railways
- Built up areas
- ✸ Iron and steel and heavy engineering
- ▲ Meat processing
- Vehicles
- Textiles
- Chemicals

Illapel
San Juan
San Francisco
Córdoba
Santa Fé
Concordia
Salto
Villa Dolores
Paraná
Villaguay
Río Tercero
Paysandú
Villa María
Viña del Mar
Quilota
Mendoza
Valparaíso
Godoy Cruz
San Lorenzo
San Antonio
Santiago
Rosario
Gualeguay
Gualeguaychú
Rancagua
Río Cuarto
San Luis
San Nicolás de los Arroyas
Fray Bentos
Durazno
Mercedes
Venado Tuerto
Baradero
Pergamino
Curicó
San Rafael
Rufino
Zárate
San Isidro
Colonia
General Alvear
Junín
Mercedes
Luján
Morón
Avellaneda
Talca
BUENOS AIRES
La Plata
MONTEVIDEO
Linares
Bragado
Río de la Plata
Pehuajó
Talcahuano
Chillán
Concepción
Santa Rosa
Azul
Dolores
Olavarría
Tandil
Balcarce
Mar del Plata

1:50 000 000

500   0   500   1000   1500   2000 km

Arctic (top map)

West from Greenwich   East from Greenwich

PACIFIC OCEAN

Qn. Charlotte Is.
G. of Alaska
Vancouver I.
Fraser
Pt. Robert
Rocky Mountains
Athabaska
Edmonton
N. Saskatchewan
S. Saskatchewan
NORTH AMERICA
Regina
Winnipeg
Nelson
Churchill
Hudson Bay
Mississippi
L. Michigan
Chicago
L. Superior
L. Huron
Moosonee
L. Erie
Toronto
Labrador

St. Lawrence I.
Bering Strait
Pt. Barrow
Beaufort Sea
Alaska
Yukon
Kuskokwim
Mackenzie
Gt. Bear L.
Gt. Slave L.
Banks I.
Dolphin & Union Str.
M'Clure Str.
Victoria I.
Pr. Patrick I.
Queen Elizabeth Is.
Sverdrup Is.
Bathurst I.
Pr. of Magnetic N.
Wales Pole
Somerset I.
G. of Boothia
Devon I.
Ellesmere I.
Lancaster Sound
Smith Sd.
Thule
Baffin Bay
Baffin I.
Southampton I.
Hudson Str.
Davis Str.

Wrangel I.
New Siberian Is.
ARCTIC OCEAN
C. Chelyuskin
Severnaya Zemlya
ARCTICA
North Pole
Franz Josef Land
Parry Is.
Kara Sea
Taimyr Peninsula
Yenisei
Ob
Tobol
Syr Darya
L. Aral
Novaya Zemlya
Barents Sea
Bear I.
N. Cape
Kola
White Sea
Dvina
Moscow
Leningrad
Volga
Don
Dnepr
Caspian Sea
Caucasus
Black Sea
Ankara
Istanbul
Danube
Belgrade
Vienna
Berlin
Hamburg
EUROPE
Baltic Sea
G. of Bothnia
Scandinavia
Svalbard
Greenland Sea
Jan Mayen I.
Arctic Circle
Faroe Is.
North Sea
Edinburgh
British Isles
Iceland
Denmark Str.
C. Farewell
GREENLAND
Petermann's Pk. 2940
Mt. Forel 3360

SIBERIA
U.S.S.R.
ASIA
Kolyma
Lena

Glaciers; Greenland

150   120   90   60   30

Antarctic (bottom map)

South Sandwich Is.
Is. Dependencies
Scotia Arc
South Georgia
South Orkney Is.
Falkland Is.
Elephant I.
Shetland Is.
S. Shetland Is.
Graham Land
Drake Passage
Magellan Str.
Horn
Tierra del Fuego
SOUTH AMERICA
Bellingshausen Sea
Alexander I.
Charcot I.
Antarctic Peninsula
British Antarctic Territory
Weddell Sea
Halley Bay
Coats Land
Shackleton
Ellsworth
General Belgrano
Berkner I.
Pensacola Mts.
South Ice
Eights
Byrd Sub-Glacial Basin
Byrd
Byrd Land
Little Rockford
Little America
Amundsen Sea

Molodezhnaya
Showa
Novolazarevskaya
Sanae
Antarctic Circle
Princess Martha Coast
Dronning Maud Land
1000
2800
ANTARCTICA
South Pole
Polar Sub-Glacial Basin
Beardmore Glacier
Mt. Markham 4349
Beardmore
Ross Ice Shelf
Roosevelt I.
Mt. Scott
Mt. Erebus
Bay of Whales
McMurdo Sound
Ross Sea
Mt. Hallett
C. Adare
Ross Dependency
Scott I.
Antarctic Circle

Enderby Land
Kemp Land
Mawson
C. Darnley
Charles Mts.
American Highland
Davis
Princess Elizabeth Land
Wilhelm II Land
Queen Mary Land
Mirny
Drygalski I.
Pionerskaya
Oasis
Vostok
Komsomolskaya
Wilkes
Australian Dependency
Wilkes Land
Wilkes Sub-Glacial Basin
Adélie Land
Charcot
Magnetic S. Pole
Dumont d'Urville
George V Land
George V Coast
Clarie Coast
Victoria Land
Balleny Is.
Macquarie I.
Campbell I.
Auckland Is.
Hobart
Tasmania

SOUTHERN OCEAN

Legend
- - - - Average minimum limit of pack ice (Autumn)
—— Average maximum limit of pack ice (Spring)
······ Average extreme limit of drift ice
Ice caps
100 Ice contours (in metres)

Position of Magnetic Poles, January 1980
North Pole 77° 18'N 101° 48'W   South Pole 65° 36'S 139° 24'E

m
4000
2000
1000
400
200
0

Icebergs in the Bay of Whales, Ross Sea

30   120

120

150

Projection: Zenithal Equidistant   150   West from Greenwich 180 East from Greenwich   COPYRIGHT. GEORGE PHILIP & SON. LTD.

Country or Dependency	Total G.D.P. million $	G.D.P per capita $	Annual average change %	Origin of G.D.P. % Agricultural	Origin of G.D.P. % Mining and Mf'g
Afghanistan	2 809	200	4.1	63	20
Algeria	31 359	1 724	—	7	40
Angola	2 701	432	—	—	—
Argentina	36 749	1 448	2.5	9	27
Australia	148 064	10 127	3.4	6	27
Austria	76 975	10 250	3.7	4	27
Bangladesh	12 683	145	6.2	48	8
Belgium	119 105	12 080	3.2	2	26
Belize	116	757	3.3	21	13
Benin	747	221	2.2	44	6
Bhutan	104	90	—	—	—
Bolivia	5 507	983	5.2	16	24
Botswana	608	800	12.5	12	31
Brazil	248 592	2 021	9.2	10	27
Brunei	4 864	21 148	—	1	83
Bulgaria	34 000*	3 820*	4.7	19	48
Burma	4 299	133	3.0	47	11
Burundi	899	212	3.7	51	9
Cambodia	1 192	147	2.2	41	17
Cameroon	4 934	612	—	31	12
Canada	253 379	10 584	4.2	4	23
Central African Rep.	397	193	1.3	32	15
Chad	693	172	—	41.4	16.4
Chile	4 952	485	0.8	7	27
China	328 000	320	5.6	—	—
Colombia	33 509	1 237	5.8	23	23
Congo	879	602	—	8	46
Costa Rica	4 036	1 860	6.1	23	20
Cuba	9 097	990	2.5	4	43
Cyprus	2 103	3 338	1.5	9	18
Czechoslovakia	137 200*	8 970*	4.9	7	61
Denmark	66 377	12 964	2.9	5	17
Djibouti	105	493	—	5.2	7.6
Dominican Republic	5 496	1 041	7.8	18	19
Ecuador	11 368	1 361	8.0	12	29
Egypt	17 821	435	8.0	22	27
El Salvador	3 388	715	4.8	23	15
Equatorial Guinea	82	257	—	—	—
Ethiopia	2 669	97	2.5	45	10
Fiji	997	1 609	5.2	21	12
Finland	49 893	10 438	2.9	8	25
France	651 893	12 137	3.7	4	27
Gabon	2 925	5 417	—	6	49
Gambia	146	256	—	56	3
Germany, East	162 900*	9 750*	4.5	9	74
Germany, West	818 977	13 304	2.6	2	40
Ghana	4 594	465	-0.7	61	9
Greece	40 148	4 182	4.7	16	19
Guatemala	7 853	1 082	5.9	25	16
Guinea	573	130	—	43	8
Guinea-Bissau	110	208	—	—	—
Guyana	504	647	3.9	21	25
Haiti	1 419	283	4.1	31	19
Honduras	2 554	692	4.1	25	16
Hong Kong	21 618	4 264	7.4	1	26
Hungary	63 700*	5 950*	5.8	14	49
Iceland	2 855	12 413	4.8	—	—
India	159 837	241	3.6	32	17
Indonesia	69 802	472	7.6	25	36
Iran	52 649	1 577	8.8	17	21
Iraq	19 293	1 620	8.7	7	60
Irish Republic	17 825	5 243	4.6	6	35
Israel	21 019	5 431	6.7	6	27
Italy	393 954	6 907	2.9	6	33
Ivory Coast	7 714	1 014	8.6	27	11
Jamaica	3 262	1 554	1.7	8	29
Japan	1 036 159	8 873	4.6	3	32
Jordan	2 906	897	—	6	16
Kenya	6 992	426	4.7	28	12
Korea, South	60 655	1 616	10.3	17	30
Kuwait	23 330	18 086	2.5	0	67
Laos	300	91	—	—	—
Lebanon	3 438	1 293	—	9	13
Lesotho	148	124	—	26	12
Liberia	945	505	2.3	16	24
Libya	19 971	7 289	10.8	2	53
Luxembourg	3 509	9 723	2.6	2	31
Madagascar	2 095	253	—	32	19
Malawi	1 011	178	12.3	38	13
Malaysia	15 472	1 194	9.2	24	22
Mali	507	87	—	27	4
Malta	1 136	3 156	3.5	3	32
Mauritania	544	353	0.7	25	18
Mauritius	1 082	1 127	5.2	12	13
Mexico	121 333	1 749	5.2	8	28
Morocco	12 426	657	6.4	14	23
Mozambique	3 272	356	—	—	—
Nepal	1 763	129	2.7	63	4
Netherlands	167 656	11 857	3.1	4	26
New Zealand	21 378	6 896	—	11	24
Nicaragua	2 133	889	4.9	25	21
Niger	736	160	—	50	14
Nigeria	50 170	717	7.7	23	29
Norway	57 400	14 034	4.6	4	31
Oman	5 285	5 938	—	2	64
Pakistan	27 960	339	4.8	26	16
Panama	3 391	1 843	3.4	10	10
Papua New Guinea	2 594	823	7.8	36	18
Paraguay	4 448	1 449	8.3	28	17
Peru	19 239	1 085	3.1	9	37
Philippines	35 481	733	6.3	23	28
Poland	178 000*	4 960*	7.2	30	42
Portugal	17 795	1 816	4.5	9	30
Puerto Rico	14 653	4 260	3.7	2	37
Romania	94 700*	4 230*	10.2	15	58
Rwanda	1 163	230	1.5	46	17
Saudi Arabia	73 062	8 845	10.4	1	58
Senegal	2 403	513	1.8	18	28
Sierra Leone	932	283	1.5	30	11
Singapore	10 982	4 595	8.4	1	30
Somali Republic	492	157	—	—	—
South Africa	79 970	2 639	2.6	7	41
Spain	197 044	5 300	4.2	7	24
Sri Lanka	4 176	283	5.8	27	18
Sudan	5 310	338	3.9	37	8
Suriname	739	1 999	—	10	27
Swaziland	356	699	—	20	18
Sweden	123 664	14 881	2	3	22
Switzerland	101 493	15 933	0.3	6	40
Syria	12 905	1 437	10.4	18	23
Tanzania	4 354	263	5.0	46	9
Thailand	32 902	698	7.1	24	22
Togo	1 002	406	—	27	15
Trinidad & Tobago	4 921	4 279	4.6	2	42
Tunisia	8 728	1 370	7.9	14	25
Turkey	50 076	1 161	6.9	21	26
Uganda	2 567	222	-0.1	73	6
U.S.S.R.	1 587 000*	5 930*	3.7	15	51
United Kingdom	523 256	9 352	2.1	2	26
United States	2 587 000	11 363	3.2	3	27
Upper Volta	826	126	—	37	11
Uruguay	9 864	3 401	3.1	7	22
Venezuela	60 028	4 315	5.5	6	39
Vietnam	—	—	2.8	29	7
Western Samoa	50*	320*	—	—	—
Yemen (North)	1 135	215	—	61	3
Yemen (South)	290	176	4.6	19	27
Yugoslavia	51 800*	2 300*	5.9	13	41
Zaire	3 785	168	0.3	26	16
Zambia	3 837	658	1.0	16	26
Zimbabwe	3 833	538	8.0	16	29

The Gross Domestic Product (G.D.P.) is a measure of a country's total production of goods and services. For comparison national currencies have been converted to U.S. dollars. Owing to difficulties in the use of exchange rates and individual national methods of calculation of G.D.P., the figures must be used cautiously. For countries where the G.D.P. figure was not available, Gross National Product (G.N.P.) figures are given which are a measure of the total value of goods and services produced in a given country together with its imports from abroad. For communist countries the Net Material Product (N.M.P.) is given. This is not strictly comparable with the G.D.P., it is the total value of goods and services but excludes many of the latter, for example, public administration, defense costs and professional services. The figures quoted are usually for 1980 or at least for a year in the period 1975-80 and the annual rate of change is from 1970-79.

*Gross National Product Figures

INTERNATIONAL TRADE

Country I = Imports E = Exports		Total trade (million U.S. $)	Primary Comms. as a % of total trade	Manuf'd Goods as a % of total trade	Fuels as a % of total trade	Growth rate % 1970-1980
Afghanistan	I	839	17	82	23	17.3
	E	705	79	15	18	23.4
Algeria	I	10 891	27	73	3	24.0
	E	9 164	100	1	2	29.8
Angola	I	680	22	78	1	8.4
	E	666	91	9	1	5.2
Argentina	I	5 081	28	72	13	16.9
	E	7 518	76	24	18	16.1
Australia*	I	24 187	22	77	14	16.3
	E	22 002	70	27	15	15.1
Austria	I	19 559	32	68	19	17.6
	E	15 690	14	86	25	16.9
Bahamas	I	7 014	94	6	91	35.5
	E	6 546	96	4	98	53.5
Bahrain	I	3 730	67	33	62	29.2
	E	3 789	90	11	58	28.6
Bangladesh	I	2 300	68	31	19	19.9
	E	769	32	68	65	17.4
Barbados	I	550	37	63	17	15.2
	E	257	36	63	49	16.8
Belgium-Lux.	I	58 007	39	58	21	16.7
	E	52 392	23	73	23	15.3
Benin	I	312	29	71	10	19.5
	E	27	88	8	40	-2.9
Bolivia	I	496	21	80	2	16.1
	E	832	62	39	2	15.3
Brazil	I	21 884	62	48	37	21.4
	E	19 551	59	38	48	21.5
Brunei	I	599	20	78	1	19.5
	E	4 068	100	0	0	41.0
Bulgaria*	I	10 600	—	—	16	17.5
	E	10 500	33	66	19	16.4
Burma	I	408	17	83	8	7.5
	E	380	94	6	12	14.0
Burundi	I	214	29	70	26	20.2
	E	88	97	3	11	10.4
Cameroon	I	1 205	22	78	10	17.5
	E	998	82	18	14	15.2
Canada*	I	55 064	24	75	12	15.6
	E	68 498	43	56	12	14.3
Chad	I	46	31	69	14	-4.0
	E	10	92	8	39	-1.0
Chile	I	3 529	42	57	20	19.1
	E	3 822	28	72	18	11.1
China	I	18 625	42	52	2	800
	E	22 380	47	42	23	950
Colombia	I	5 478	28	71	14	17.9
	I	3 095	72	27	25	14.3
Congo	I	431	35	65	7	18.7
	E	955	92	8	3	36.5
Costa Rica	I	887	26	70	15	17.5
	E	872	66	28	24	16.2
Cuba	I	6 293	33	48	10	13.1
	E	5 536	94	0	11	18.1
Cyprus	I	1 249	40	60	22	15.1
	E	565	44	55	43	16.1
Czechoslovakia*	I	15 499	43	56	23	13.6
	E	15,734	13	87	23	13.1
Denmark	I	17 162	41	57	24	13.4
	E	15 527	43	58	27	15.1
Dominican Rep.*	I	1 248	53	48	33	16.2
	E	768	81	19	48	15.0
Ecuador	I	2 130	12	87	2	21.1
	E	60	97	3	2	26.6
Egypt	I	9 078	43	57	3	24.6
	E	3 120	87	13	8	14.0
El Salvador	I	883	23	77	8	14.9
	E	646	72	28	10	12.0

Country I = Imports E = Exports		Total trade (million U.S. $)	Primary Comms. as a % of total trade	Manuf'd Goods as a % of total trade	Fuels as a % of total trade	Growth rate % 1970-1980
Ethiopia	I	787	27	73	17	14.2
	E	404	98	2	24	10.7
Fiji	I	515	40	56	22	17.8
	E	285	96	3	61	14.8
Finland	I	13 387	42	57	31	16.5
	E	13 132	25	75	31	17.8
France	I	115 405	44	56	29	18.2
	E	92 268	25	75	34	17.1
Gabon	I	674	22	78	2	23.2
	E	821	98	2	1	32.0
Germany, East*	I	21 743	—	—	—	13.8
	E	20 196	8	91	—	14.3
Germany, West	I	155 856	43	55	25	16.8
	E	176 428	12	86	23	16.1
Ghana	I	1 106	33	65	17	10.1
	E	1 063	95	6	18	9.7
Greece	I	10 023	39	61	22	14.7
	E	4 297	42	57	46	18.7
Guatemala	I	1 362	46	54	38	18.1
	E	1173	71	29	68	14.1
Guyana	I	283	28	63	16	12.0
	E	256	78	22	16	11.3
Haiti	I	266	40	60	13	19.9
	E	226	49	51	15	15.3
Honduras	I	949	27	73	16	16.5
	E	760	88	13	20	16.2
Hong Kong	I	23 554	25	74	8	19.0
	E	20 985	7	92	9	19.3
Hungary	I	8 825	34	66	17	12.5
	E	8 795	34	65	17	12.8
Iceland	I	942	30	70	17	18.7
	E	685	83	17	19	17.8
India	I	13 941	50	51	33	19.0
	E	7 960	41	59	43	16.2
Indonesia	I	16 858	29	71	13	26.0
	E	22 293	95	5	9	31.5
Iran	I	12 250	20	80	0	22.1
	E	17 610	99	1	0	18.5
Iraq	I	4 213	15	85	0	30.2
	E	10 878	100	1	0	33.4
Ireland	I	9 699	31	67	15	18.98
	E	8 064	38	58	20	20.1
Israel	I	7 848	42	58	26	16.7
	E	4 901	18	82	36	19.9
Italy	I	86 213	56	44	35	17.6
	E	73 490	16	84	41	17.1
Ivory Coast	I	2 184	44	55	22	18.0
	E	2 288	90	10	21	16.6
Jamaica	I	1 470	54	46	33	9.8
	E	820	94	6	51	10.0
Japan	I	131 932	77	22	52	20.2
	E	138 911	3	97	48	20.6
Jordan	I	3 241	40	63	17	29.6
	E	737	61	39	61	27.9
Kenya	I	1 585	36	64	28	15.1
	E	954	87	13	56	13.0
Korea, South	I	24 251	55	45	30	26.4
	E	21 853	9	91	37	34.2
Kuwait	I	6 969	17	82	1	26.5
	E	10 890	90	10	0	26.4
Lebanon	I	1 701	40	60	8	17.0
	E	436	21	79	33	11.9
Liberia	I	477	51	49	27	11.1
	E	531	98	1	25	8.5
Libya	I	8 382	22	78	1	23.8
	E	13 951	100	0	0	29.0
Madagascar	I	600	26	74	15	14.8
	E	402	94	6	26	10.3

Country I = Imports E = Exports		Total trade (million U.S. $)	Primary Comms. as a % of total trade	Manuf'd Goods as a % of total trade	Fuels as a % of total trade	Growth rate % 1970-1980
Malawi	I	314	21	79	10	13.9
	E	259	94	4	16	15.2
Malaysia	I	13 132	34	65	17	21.9
	E	12 884	75	24	18	19.8
Mali	I	365	41	54	11	25.3
	E	155	87	12	54	18.2
Malta	I	938	34	66	14	16.4
	E	497	7	93	29	24.8
Mauritania	I	273	41	58	8	15.2
	E	179	99	1	8	10.2
Mauritius	I	463	39	61	10	19.8
	E	362	88	11	11	16.0
Mexico	I	15 042	25	75	6	23.7
	E	21 006	59	41	12	28.1
Morocco	I	4 315	47	54	25	18.3
	E	2 062	70	30	47	14.9
Mozambique	I	278	24	77	8	-2.2
	E	129	97	2	17	-2.7
Netherlands	I	62 583	46	53	26	15.6
	E	66 322	49	50	25	17.4
Neths. Antilles	I	6771	88	12	83	21.5
	E	6054	98	2	98	21.5
New Caledonia	I	367	50	50	28	5.3
	E	265	20	78	33	5.4
New Zealand	I	5 752	29	71	20	14.8
	E	5 524	76	24	21	14.7
Nicaragua	I	883	37	63	21	17.2
	E	448	86	14	43	10.2
Niger	I	462	42	58	15	21.9
	E	448	98	2	17	27.3
Nigeria	I	20 821	21	78	2	29.3
	E	16 667	99	1	1	34.0
Norway	I	15 479	27	73	14	14.0
	E	17 595	61	38	13	19.8
Pakistan	I	5 381	49	51	28	18.6
	E	2 552	47	51	55	13.5
Panama	I	1 569	39	61	29	14.2
	E	309	90	10	91	10.4
Papua New Guinea*	I	1 017	33	63	11	13.8
	E	753	93	2	9	21.2
Paraguay*	I	631	37	63	21	20.7
	E	375	89	10	26	14.9
Peru	I	3 803	26	74	2	15.3
	E	3 255	59	41	2	12.0
Philippines	I	7 946	41	46	30	18.0
	E	4 852	53	25	45	15.8
Poland*	I	10 248	47	53	20	14.2
	E	11 208	21	79	23	12.7
Portugal	I	9 313	47	53	24	16.4
	E	4 111	29	70	58	14.3
Reunion	I	804	38	60	10	15.5
	E	69	88	11	72	6.9
Romania*	I	12 458	25	72	7	18.3
	E	12 610	29	69	6	19.1
Rwanda	I	243	36	65	8	23.7
	E	76	98	0	19	11.8
Saudi Arabia	I	40 654	17	83	1	42.9
	E	79 123	99	1	0	42.6
Senegal	I	861	48	51	19	14.6
	E	442	77	23	37	9.6

Country I = Imports E = Exports		Total trade (million U.S. $)	Primary Comms. as a % of total trade	Manuf'd Goods as a % of total trade	Fuels as a % of total trade	Growth rate % 1970-1980
Sierra Leone	I	311	39	61	14	13.9
	E	153	45	55	28	6.0
Singapore	I	28 167	46	53	34	24.6
	E	20 788	43	50	44	26.7
Somalia	I	144	36	64	6	19.8
	E	317	96	3	11	16.4
South Africa*	I	21 006	11	88	1	9.9
	E	12 502	41	49	1	18.2
Spain	I	31 535	62	38	43	19.1
	E	20 522	27	73	67	21.7
Sri Lanka	I	1 771	46	53	25	15.0
	E	1 015	78	22	45	10.6
Sudan	I	1 285	41	59	19	16.9
	E	499	99	1	58	7.6
Sweden	I	27 570	36	64	25	13.7
	E	26 803	18	81	25	14.0
Switzerland	I	28 670	24	76	12	13.1
	E	26 024	5	95	13	14.3
Syria	I	4 028	31	69	7	27.2
	E	2 026	92	8	12	23.6
Tanzania	I	1 140	36	64	21	14.3
	E	566	86	14	48	7.3
Thailand	I	8 573	40	56	30	20.3
	E	6 490	66	32	44	23.1
Togo	I	435	36	64	8	18.9
	E	208	85	16	18	12.8
Trinidad & Tobago	I	3 697	52	48	37	17.2
	E	3 072	92	8	30	20.5
Tunisia	I	3 287	42	58	21	24.7
	E	1 959	66	34	31	25.4
Turkey	I	8 753	52	48	44	23.1
	E	5 701	62	38	83	20.8
Uganda	I	293	10	90	2	-0.3
	E	345	96	4	1	1.0
U.S.S.R.*	I	77 793	31	65	4	18.1
	E	86 949	50	37	4	18.0
United Kingdom	I	99 656	35	64	14	15.1
	E	96 994	14	83	14	16.4
United States	I	254 884	43	55	31	19.1
	E	212 275	29	67	37	16.4
Upper Volta	I	338	43	57	16	19.2
	E	75	85	15	70	13.9
Uruguay	I	1 042	49	51	31	21.4
	E	1 023	70	30	42	16.2
Venezuela*	I	12 823	21	79	1	18.5
	E	16 512	96	4	1	18.6
Yemen, North	I	1 853	36	64	7	50.0
	E	23	49	47	—	22.6
Yemen, South	I	1 527	—	—	—	15.3
	E	779	—	—	—	3.1
Yugoslavia	I	14 057	40	60	24	16.7
	E	10 713	18	82	35	18.6
Zaire	I	480	28	71	10	2.1
	E	569	29	70	11	-1.6
Zambia*	I	831	23	77	14	8.6
	E	1 059	3	97	16	3.4
Zimbabwe	I	1 204	8	68	24	8.0
	E	1 129	53	45	2	11.0

Source: U.N. Monthly Bulletin of Statistics and U.N. Yearbook of International Trade Statistics, 1981

Primary Commodities refer to sections 0-4 of the Standard International Trade Classification (Revised) and Manufactured Goods include sections 5-8. These, together with a nominal amount of miscellaneous products make up the total trade. Fuels are included in the Primary Commodities and Manufactured Goods categories, but have also been separated out. All the trade values used in the compilation of this table are at current prices. Unless otherwise stated imports are in terms of c.i.f. transaction values and exports f.o.b. transaction values. The latest figures available have been used and these are usually for 1982, or at least for a year in the period 1975-1981.
* = Imports f.o.b.

CLIMATIC STATISTICS

These four pages give temperature and precipitation statistics for over 80 stations, which are arranged by listing the continents and the places within each continent in alphabetical order. The elevation of each station, in metres above mean sea level, is stated beneath its name. The average monthly temperature, in degrees Celsius, and the average monthly precipitation, in millimetres, are given. To the right, the average yearly rainfall, the average yearly temperature, and the annual range of temperature (the difference between the warmest and the coldest months) are also stated.

AFRICA

		Jan.	Feb.	Mar.	Apr.	May	June	July	Aug.	Sept.	Oct.	Nov.	Dec.	Year	Annual Range
Addis Ababa, Ethiopia															
	Precipitation	201	206	239	102	28	<3	0	<3	3	25	135	213	1 151	
2 450 m	Temperature	19	20	20	20	19	18	18	19	21	22	21	20	20	4
Cairo, Egypt															
	Precipitation	5	5	5	3	3	<3	0	0	<3	<3	3	5	28	
116 m	Temperature	13	15	18	21	25	28	28	28	26	24	20	15	22	15
Cape Town, South Africa															
	Precipitation	15	8	18	48	79	84	89	66	43	31	18	10	508	
17 m	Temperature	21	21	20	17	14	13	12	13	14	16	18	19	17	9
Casablanca, Morocco															
	Precipitation	53	48	56	36	23	5	0	<3	8	38	66	71	404	
50 m	Temperature	13	13	14	16	18	20	22	23	22	19	16	13	18	10
Johannesburg, South Africa															
	Precipitation	114	109	89	38	25	8	8	8	23	56	107	125	709	
1 665 m	Temperature	20	20	18	16	13	10	11	13	16	18	19	20	16	10
Khartoum, Sudan															
	Precipitation	<3	<3	<3	<3	3	8	53	71	18	5	<3	0	158	
390 m	Temperature	24	25	28	31	33	34	32	31	32	32	28	25	29	9
Kinshasa, Zaire															
	Precipitation	135	145	196	196	158	8	3	3	31	119	221	142	1 354	
325 m	Temperature	26	26	27	27	26	24	23	24	25	26	26	26	25	4
Lagos, Nigeria															
	Precipitation	28	46	102	150	269	460	279	64	140	206	69	25	1 836	
3 m	Temperature	27	28	29	28	28	26	26	25	26	26	28	28	27	4
Lusaka, Zambia															
	Precipitation	231	191	142	18	3	<3	<3	0	<3	10	91	150	836	
1 277 m	Temperature	21	22	21	21	19	16	16	18	22	24	23	22	21	8
Monrovia, Liberia															
	Precipitation	31	56	97	216	516	973	996	373	744	772	236	130	5 138	
23 m	Temperature	26	26	27	27	26	25	24	25	25	25	26	26	26	3
Nairobi, Kenya															
	Precipitation	38	64	125	211	158	46	15	23	31	53	109	86	958	
1 820 m	Temperature	19	19	19	19	18	16	16	16	18	19	18	18	18	3
Antananarivo, Madagascar															
	Precipitation	300	279	178	53	18	8	8	10	18	61	135	287	1 356	
1 372 m	Temperature	21	21	21	19	18	15	14	15	17	19	21	21	19	7
Timbuktu, Mali															
	Precipitation	<3	<3	3	<3	5	23	79	81	38	3	<3	<3	231	
301 m	Temperature	22	24	28	32	34	35	32	30	32	31	28	23	29	13
Tunis, Tunisia															
	Precipitation	64	51	41	36	18	8	3	8	33	51	48	61	419	
66 m	Temperature	10	11	13	16	19	23	26	27	25	20	16	11	18	17
Walvis Bay, South Africa															
	Precipitation	<3	5	8	3	3	<3	<3	3	<3	<3	<3	<3	23	
7 m	Temperature	19	19	19	18	17	16	15	14	14	15	17	18	18	5

AMERICA, NORTH

Anchorage, Alaska, U.S.A.															
	Precipitation	20	18	15	10	13	18	41	66	66	56	25	23	371	
40 m	Temperature	−11	−8	−5	2	7	12	14	13	9	2	−5	−11	2	25
Cheyenne, Wyo., U.S.A.															
	Precipitation	10	15	25	48	61	41	53	41	31	25	13	13	376	
1 871 m	Temperature	−4	−3	1	5	10	16	19	19	14	7	1	−2	7	23
Chicago, Ill., U.S.A.															
	Precipitation	51	51	66	71	86	89	84	81	79	66	61	51	836	
251 m	Temperature	−4	−3	2	9	14	20	23	22	19	12	5	−1	10	27
Churchill, Man., Canada															
	Precipitation	13	15	23	23	23	48	56	69	58	36	28	18	406	
13 m	Temperature	−28	−27	−21	−10	−1	6	12	11	5	−3	−15	−24	−8	40

		Jan.	Feb.	Mar.	Apr.	May	June	July	Aug.	Sept.	Oct.	Nov.	Dec.	Year	Annual range
Edmonton, Alta., Canada															
	Precipitation	23	15	20	23	46	78	84	58	33	18	18	20	439	
676 m	Temperature	−15	−11	−5	4	11	14	16	15	10	5	−4	−11	3	31
Honolulu, Hawaii, U.S.A.															
	Precipitation	104	66	79	48	25	18	23	28	36	48	64	104	643	
12 m	Temperature	23	18	19	20	22	24	25	26	26	24	22	19	22	8
Houston, Tex., U.S.A.															
	Precipitation	89	76	84	91	119	117	99	99	104	94	89	109	1 171	
12 m	Temperature	12	13	17	21	24	27	28	29	26	22	16	12	21	17
Kingston, Jamaica															
	Precipitation	23	15	23	31	102	89	38	91	99	180	74	36	800	
34 m	Temperature	25	25	25	26	26	28	28	28	27	27	26	26	26	3
Los Angeles, Calif., U.S.A.															
	Precipitation	79	76	71	25	10	3	<3	<3	5	15	31	66	381	
95 m	Temperature	13	14	14	16	17	19	21	22	21	18	16	14	17	9
Mexico City, Mexico															
	Precipitation	13	5	10	20	53	119	170	152	130	51	18	8	747	
2 309 m	Temperature	12	13	16	18	19	19	17	18	18	16	14	13	16	7
Miami, Fla., U.S.A.															
	Precipitation	71	53	64	81	173	178	155	160	203	234	71	51	1 516	
8 m	Temperature	20	20	22	23	25	27	28	28	27	25	22	21	24	8
Montreal, Que., Canada															
	Precipitation	97	76	89	66	79	86	94	89	94	86	89	91	1 036	
57 m	Temperature	−10	−9	−3	5	13	19	21	19	15	8	1	−7	6	31
New York, N.Y., U.S.A.															
	Precipitation	94	97	91	81	81	84	107	109	86	89	76	91	1 092	
96 m	Temperature	−1	−1	3	10	16	20	23	23	21	15	7	2	8	24
St. Louis, Mo., U.S.A.															
	Precipitation	58	64	89	97	114	114	89	86	81	74	71	64	1 001	
173 m	Temperature	0	1	7	13	19	24	26	26	22	15	8	2	14	26
San Francisco, Calif., U.S.A.															
	Precipitation	119	97	79	38	18	3	<3	<3	8	25	64	112	561	
16 m	Temperature	10	12	13	13	14	15	15	15	17	16	14	11	14	7
San José, Costa Rica															
	Precipitation	15	5	20	46	229	241	211	241	305	300	145	41	1 798	
1 146 m	Temperature	19	19	21	21	22	21	21	21	21	20	20	19	20	2
Vancouver, B.C., Canada															
	Precipitation	218	147	127	84	71	64	31	43	91	147	211	224	1 458	
14 m	Temperature	3	4	6	9	13	16	18	18	14	10	6	4	10	15
Washington, D.C., U.S.A.															
	Precipitation	86	76	91	84	94	99	112	109	94	74	66	79	1 064	
22 m	Temperature	1	2	7	12	18	23	25	24	20	14	8	3	13	24

AMERICA, SOUTH

		Jan.	Feb.	Mar.	Apr.	May	June	July	Aug.	Sept.	Oct.	Nov.	Dec.	Year	Annual range
Antofagasta, Chile															
	Precipitation	0	0	0	<3	<3	3	5	3	<3	3	<3	0	13	
94 m	Temperature	21	21	20	18	16	15	14	14	15	16	18	19	17	7
Buenos Aires, Argentina															
	Precipitation	79	71	109	89	76	61	56	61	79	86	84	99	950	
27 m	Temperature	23	23	21	17	13	9	10	11	13	15	19	22	16	14
Caracas, Venezuela															
	Precipitation	23	10	15	33	79	102	109	109	107	109	94	46	836	
1 042 m	Temperature	19	19	20	21	22	21	21	21	21	21	20	20	21	3
Lima, Peru															
	Precipitation	3	<3	<3	<3	5	5	8	8	8	3	3	<3	41	
120 m	Temperature	23	24	24	22	19	17	17	16	17	18	19	21	20	8
Manaus, Brazil															
	Precipitation	249	231	262	221	170	84	58	38	46	107	142	203	1 811	
44 m	Temperature	28	28	28	27	28	28	28	28	29	29	29	28	28	2
Paraná, Brazil															
	Precipitation	287	236	239	102	13	<3	3	5	28	127	231	310	1 582	
260 m	Temperature	23	23	23	23	23	21	21	22	24	24	24	23	23	3
Quito, Ecuador															
	Precipitation	99	112	142	175	137	43	20	31	69	112	97	79	1 115	
2 879 m	Temperature	15	15	15	15	15	14	14	15	15	15	15	15	15	1
Rio de Janeiro, Brazil															
	Precipitation	125	122	130	107	79	53	41	43	66	79	104	137	1 082	
61 m	Temperature	26	26	25	24	22	21	21	21	21	22	23	25	23	5
Santiago, Chile															
	Precipitation	3	3	5	13	64	84	76	56	31	15	8	5	358	
520 m	Temperature	21	20	18	15	12	9	9	10	12	15	17	19	15	12

ASIA

		Jan.	Feb.	Mar.	Apr.	May	June	July	Aug.	Sept.	Oct.	Nov.	Dec.	Year	Annual range
Bahrain															
	Precipitation	8	18	13	8	<3	0	0	0	0	0	18	18	81	
5 m	Temperature	17	18	21	25	29	32	33	34	31	28	24	19	26	16
Bangkok, Thailand															
	Precipitation	8	20	36	58	198	160	160	175	305	206	66	5	1 397	
2 m	Temperature	26	28	29	30	29	29	28	28	28	28	26	25	28	5
Beirut, Lebanon															
	Precipitation	191	158	94	53	18	3	<3	<3	5	51	132	185	892	
34 m	Temperature	14	14	16	18	22	24	27	28	26	24	19	16	21	14
Bombay, India															
	Precipitation	3	3	3	<3	18	485	617	340	264	64	13	3	1 809	
11 m	Temperature	24	24	26	28	30	29	27	27	27	28	27	26	27	6
Calcutta, India															
	Precipitation	10	31	36	43	140	297	325	328	252	114	20	5	1 600	
6 m	Temperature	20	22	27	30	30	30	29	29	29	28	23	19	26	11
Colombo, Sri Lanka															
	Precipitation	89	69	147	231	371	224	135	109	160	348	315	147	2 365	
7 m	Temperature	26	26	27	28	28	27	27	27	27	27	26	26	27	2
Jakarta, Indonesia															
	Precipitation	300	300	211	147	114	97	64	43	66	112	142	203	1 798	
8 m	Temperature	26	26	27	27	27	27	27	27	27	27	27	26	27	1
Harbin, China															
	Precipitation	5	5	10	23	43	94	112	104	46	33	8	5	488	
160 m	Temperature	−18	−15	−5	6	13	19	22	21	14	4	−6	−16	3	40
Hong Kong															
	Precipitation	33	46	74	137	292	394	381	361	257	114	43	31	2 162	
33 m	Temperature	16	15	18	22	26	28	28	28	27	25	21	18	23	13
Kabul, Afghanistan															
	Precipitation	31	36	94	102	20	5	3	3	<3	15	20	10	338	
1 815 m	Temperature	−3	−1	6	13	18	22	25	24	20	14	7	3	12	28
Karachi, Pakistan															
	Precipitation	13	10	8	3	3	18	81	41	13	<3	3	5	196	
4 m	Temperature	19	20	24	28	30	31	30	29	28	28	24	20	26	12
Delhi, India															
	Precipitation	23	18	13	8	13	74	180	172	117	10	3	10	640	
218 m	Temperature	14	17	23	28	33	34	31	30	29	26	20	15	25	20
Ho Chi Minh City, Vietnam															
	Precipitation	15	3	13	43	221	330	315	269	335	269	114	56	1 984	
9 m	Temperature	26	27	29	30	29	28	28	28	27	27	27	26	28	4
Shanghai, China															
	Precipitation	48	58	84	94	94	180	147	142	130	71	51	36	1 135	
7 m	Temperature	4	5	9	14	20	24	28	28	23	19	12	7	16	24
Singapore															
	Precipitation	252	173	193	188	173	173	170	196	178	208	254	257	2 413	
10 m	Temperature	26	27	28	28	28	28	28	27	27	27	27	27	27	2
Tehran, Iran															
	Precipitation	46	38	46	36	13	3	3	3	3	8	20	31	246	
1 220 m	Temperature	2	5	9	16	21	26	30	29	25	18	12	6	17	28
Tokyo, Japan															
	Precipitation	48	74	107	135	147	165	142	152	234	208	97	56	1 565	
6 m	Temperature	3	4	7	13	17	21	25	26	23	17	11	6	14	23
Ulaanbaatar, Mongolia															
	Precipitation	<3	<3	3	5	10	28	76	51	23	5	5	3	208	
1 325 m	Temperature	−26	−21	−13	−1	6	14	16	14	8	−1	−13	−22	−3	42

AUSTRALIA, NEW ZEALAND and ANTARCTICA

		Jan.	Feb.	Mar.	Apr.	May	June	July	Aug.	Sept.	Oct.	Nov.	Dec.	Year	Annual range
Alice Springs, Australia															
	Precipitation	43	33	28	10	15	13	8	8	8	18	31	38	252	
579 m	Temperature	29	28	25	20	15	12	12	14	18	23	26	28	21	17
Christchurch, New Zealand															
	Precipitation	56	43	48	48	66	66	69	48	46	43	48	56	638	
10 m	Temperature	16	16	14	12	9	6	6	7	9	12	14	16	11	10
Darwin, Australia															
	Precipitation	386	312	254	97	15	3	<3	3	13	51	119	239	1 491	
30 m	Temperature	29	29	29	29	28	26	25	26	28	29	30	29	28	5
Mawson, Antarctica															
	Precipitation	11	30	20	10	44	180	4	40	3	20	0	0	362	
14 m	Temperature	0	−5	−10	−14	−15	−16	−18	−18	−19	−13	−5	−1	−11	18

		Jan.	Feb.	Mar.	Apr.	May	June	July	Aug.	Sept.	Oct.	Nov.	Dec.	Year	Annual Range
Melbourne, Australia															
	Precipitation	48	46	56	58	53	53	48	48	58	66	58	58	653	
35 m	Temperature	20	20	18	15	13	10	9	11	13	14	16	18	15	11
Perth, Australia															
	Precipitation	8	10	20	43	130	180	170	149	86	56	20	13	881	
60 m	Temperature	23	23	22	19	16	14	13	13	15	16	19	22	18	10
Sydney, Australia															
	Precipitation	89	102	127	135	127	117	117	76	73	71	73	73	1 181	
42 m	Temperature	22	22	21	18	15	13	12	13	15	18	19	21	17	10

EUROPE and U.S.S.R.

		Jan.	Feb.	Mar.	Apr.	May	June	July	Aug.	Sept.	Oct.	Nov.	Dec.	Year	Annual Range
Arkhangelsk, U.S.S.R.															
	Precipitation	31	19	25	29	42	52	62	56	63	63	47	41	530	
13 m	Temperature	−16	−14	−9	0	7	12	15	14	8	2	−4	−11	0	31
Athens, Greece															
	Precipitation	62	37	37	23	23	14	6	7	15	51	56	71	402	
107 m	Temperature	10	10	12	16	20	25	28	28	24	20	15	11	18	18
Berlin, Germany															
	Precipitation	46	40	33	42	49	65	73	69	48	49	46	43	603	
55 m	Temperature	−1	0	4	9	14	17	19	18	15	9	5	1	9	20
Istanbul, Turkey															
	Precipitation	109	92	72	46	38	34	34	30	58	81	103	119	816	
114 m	Temperature	5	6	7	11	16	20	23	23	20	16	12	8	14	18
Aralsk, U.S.S.R.															
	Precipitation	10	10	13	13	15	5	5	8	8	10	13	15	125	
63 m	Temperature	−12	−11	−3	6	18	23	25	23	16	8	−1	−7	7	37
Lisbon, Portugal															
	Precipitation	111	76	109	54	44	16	3	4	33	62	93	103	708	
77 m	Temperature	11	12	14	16	17	20	22	23	21	18	14	12	17	12
London, U.K.															
	Precipitation	54	40	37	37	46	45	57	59	49	57	64	48	593	
5 m	Temperature	4	5	7	9	12	16	18	17	15	11	8	5	11	14
Málaga, Spain															
	Precipitation	61	51	62	46	26	5	1	3	29	64	64	62	474	
33 m	Temperature	12	13	15	17	19	29	25	26	23	20	16	13	18	17
Moscow, U.S.S.R.															
	Precipitation	39	38	36	37	53	58	88	71	58	45	47	54	624	
156 m	Temperature	−13	−10	−4	6	13	16	18	17	12	6	−1	−7	4	31
Odessa, U.S.S.R.															
	Precipitation	57	62	30	21	34	34	42	37	37	13	35	71	473	
64 m	Temperature	−3	−1	2	9	15	20	22	22	18	12	9	1	10	25
Omsk, U.S.S.R.															
	Precipitation	15	8	8	13	31	51	51	51	28	25	18	20	318	
85 m	Temperature	−22	−19	−12	−1	10	16	18	16	10	1	−11	−18	−1	40
Palma de Mallorca, Spain															
	Precipitation	39	34	51	32	29	17	3	25	55	77	47	40	449	
10 m	Temperature	10	11	12	15	17	21	24	25	23	18	14	11	17	15
Paris, France															
	Precipitation	56	46	35	42	57	54	59	64	55	50	51	50	619	
75 m	Temperature	3	4	8	11	15	18	20	19	17	12	7	4	12	17
Rome, Italy															
	Precipitation	71	62	57	51	46	37	15	21	63	99	129	93	744	
17 m	Temperature	8	9	11	14	18	22	25	25	22	17	13	10	16	17
Shannon, Irish Republic															
	Precipitation	94	67	56	53	61	57	77	79	86	86	96	117	929	
2 m	Temperature	5	5	7	9	12	14	16	16	14	11	8	6	10	11
Stavanger, Norway															
	Precipitation	93	56	45	70	49	84	93	118	142	129	125	126	1 130	
85 m	Temperature	1	1	3	6	10	13	15	15	13	9	6	3	8	14
Stockholm, Sweden															
	Precipitation	43	30	25	31	34	45	61	76	60	48	53	48	554	
44 m	Temperature	−3	−3	−1	5	10	15	18	17	12	7	3	0	7	21
Verkhoyansk, U.S.S.R.															
	Precipitation	5	5	3	5	8	23	28	25	13	8	8	5	134	
100 m	Temperature	−50	−45	−32	−15	0	12	14	9	2	−15	−38	−48	−17	64
Warsaw, Poland															
	Precipitation	27	32	27	37	46	69	96	65	43	38	31	44	555	
110 m	Temperature	−3	−3	2	7	14	17	19	18	14	9	3	0	8	22

INDEX

The number printed in bold type against each index entry indicates the map page where the feature will be found. The geographical coordinates which follow the name are sometimes only approximate but are close enough for the place name to be located.

An open square □ signifies that the name refers to an administrative subdivision of a country while a solid square ■ follows the name of a country.

The alphabetical order of names composed of two or more words is governed primarily by the first word and then by the second. This rule applies even if the second word is a description or its abbreviation, R.,L.,I. for example. Names composed of a proper name (Gibraltar) and a description (Strait of) are positioned alphabetically by the proper name. If the same place name occurs twice or more times in the index and all are in the same country, each is followed by the name of the administrative subdivision in which it is located. The names are placed in the alphabetical order of the subdivisions. If the same place name occurs twice or more in the index and the places are in different countries they will be followed by their country names, the latter governing the alphabetical order. In a mixture of these situations the primary order is fixed by the alphabetical sequence of the countries and the secondary order by that of the country subdivisions.

A. R. – Autonomous Region
A. S. S. R. – Autonomous Soviet Socialist Republic
Afr. – Africa
Ala. – Alabama
Alas. – Alaska
Alta. – Alberta
Amer. – America
Arch. – Archipelago
Ariz. – Arizona
Ark. – Arkansas
Atl. Oc. – Atlantic Ocean
Austral. – Australia
B. – Bay, Bight
B.C. – British Columbia
Belg. – Belgium
Berks. – Berkshire
Br. – British
Bucks. – Buckinghamshire
C. – Cabo, Cape
C. Prov. – Cape Province
Calif. – California
Cambs. – Cambridgeshire
Can. – Canada
Cent. – Central
Chan. – Channel
Ches. – Cheshire
Co. – Country
Colo. – Colorado
Conn. – Connecticut
Cord. – Cordillera
Corn. – Cornwall
Cumb. – Cumbria
D.C. – District of Columbia
Del. – Delaware
Dep. – Dependency
Derby. – Derbyshire
Des. – Desert
Dist. – District
Dumf. & Gall. – Dumfries and Galloway
E. – East
Eng. – England
Fed. – Federal, Federation
Fla. – Florida
Fr. – France, French
Fs. – Falls
Ft. – Fort
G. – Golf, Golfo, Gulf
Ga. – Georgia
Germ. – Germany
Glam. – Glamorgan
Glos. – Gloucestershire
Gr. – Grande, Great, Greater, Group
Hants. – Hampshire
Harb. – Harbour
Hd. – Head
Here. & Worcs. – Hereford and Worcester
Herts. – Hertfordshire
I.o.M. – Isle of Man
I. of W. – Isle of Wight
I.(s). – Île, Island, Isle
Id. – Idaho
Ill. – Illinois
Ind. – Indiana

Ind. Oc. – Indian Ocean
J. – Jabal, Jabel, Jazira
Junc. – Junction
Kans. – Kansas
Ky. – Kentucky
L. – Lac, Lago, Lake, Loch, Lough
La. – Lousiana
Lancs. – Lancashire
Leics. – Leicestershire
Lim. – Limerick
Lincs. – Lincolnshire
Lr. – Lower
Malay. – Malaysia
Man. – Manitoba
Manch. – Manchester
Mass. – Massachusetts
Md. – Maryland
Me. – Maine
Mich. – Michigan
Mid. – Middle
Minn. – Minnesota
Miss. – Mississippi
Mo. – Missouri
Mont. – Montana
Mt.(e). – Mont, Monte, Monti, Montaña, Mountain
N. – North, Northern, Nouveau
N.B. – New Brunswick
N.C. – North Carolina
N.D. – North Dakota
N.H. – New Hampshire
N.I. – Northern Ireland
N.J. – New Jersey
N. Mex. – New Mexico
N.S. – Nova Scotia
N.S.W. – New South Wales
N.T. – Northern Territory
N.W.T. – North West Territory
N.Y. – New York
N.Z. – New Zealand
Nat. – National
Nat Park. – National Park
Nebr. – Nebraska
Neth. – Netherlands
Nev. – Nevada
Newf. – Newfoundland
Nic. – Nicaragua
Norf. – Norfolk
Northants. – Northamptonshire
Northumb. – Northumberland
Notts. – Nottinghamshire
Okla. – Oklahoma
Ont. – Ontario
Or. – Orientale
Oreg. – Oregon
Oxon. – Oxfordshire
Oz. – Ozero
P. – Pass
Pa. – Pennsylvania
Pac. Oc. – Pacific Ocean
Pak. – Pakistan
Pass. – Passage
Pen. – Peninsula
Pk. – Peak
Plat. – Plateau
P-ov. – Poluostrov

Port. – Portugal, Portuguese
Prov. – Province, Provincial
Pt. – Point
Pta. – Punta
Pte. – Pointe
Qué. – Québec
Queens. – Queensland
R. – Rio, River
R.I. – Rhode Island
R.S.F.S.R. – Russian Soviet Federative Socialist Republic
Ra.(s). – Range(s)
Raj. – Rajasthan
Reg. – Region
Rep. – Republic
Res. – Reserve, Reservoir
Rhld. – Pfz. – Rheinland – Pfalz
Rosc. – Roscommon
S. – San, South
S. Afr. – South Africa
S. Austral. – South Australia
S.C.. – South Carolina
S.D. – South Dakota
S.-Holst. – Schleswig-Holstein
S.S.R. – Soviet Socialist Republic
S.-U. – Sinkiang-Uighur
Sa. – Serra, Sierra
Sask. – Saskatchewan
Scot. – Scotland
Sd. – Sound
Som. – Somerset
St. – Saint
Sta. – Santa
Staffs. – Staffordshire
Sto. – Santo
Str. – Strait
Suff. – Suffolk
Switz. – Switzerland
Tas. – Tasmania
Tenn. – Tennessee
Terr. – Territory
Tex. – Texas
Tipp. – Tipperary
Trans. – Transvaal
U.K. – United Kingdom
U.S.A. – United States of America
U.S.S.R. – Union of Soviet Socialist Republics
Ukr. – Ukraine
Va. – Virginia
Vic. – Victoria
Viet. – Vietnam
Vol. – Volcano
Vt. – Vermont
W. – Wadi, West
W.A. – Western Australia
W. Isles – Western Isles
War. – Warwickshire
Wash. – Washington
Wilts. – Wiltshire
Wis. – Wisconsin
Wyo. – Wyoming
Yorks. – Yorkshire
Yug. – Yugoslavia
Zimb. – Zimbabwe

Aachen As Salt

A

Aachen 52 50 47N 6 4E
Aalsmeer 52 52 17N 4 43E
Aalst 52 50 56N 4 2E
Aare, R. 54 47 33N 8 14E
Aba 90 5 10N 7 19E
Abadan 71 30 22N 48 20E
Abakaliki 90 6 22N 8 2E
Abashiri 76 44 0N 144 15E
Abau 79 10 11S 148 46E
Abaya L. 89 6 30N 37 50E
Abbeville 56 50 6N 1 49E
Abbey Town 44 54 50N 3 18W
Abbeyfeale 51 52 23N 9 20W
Abbeyleix 51 52 55N 7 20W
Abbots Langley 41 51 43N 0 25W
Abbotsbury 43 50 40N 2 36W
Abeokuta 90 7 3N 3 19E
Aberaeron 42 52 15N 4 16W
Abercarn 43 51 39N 3 9W
Aberchirder 48 57 34N 2 40W
Aberdare 43 51 43N 3 27W
Aberdaron 42 52 48N 4 41W
Aberdeen, S. Afr. 94 32 28S 24 2E
Aberdeen, U.K. 48 57 9N 2 6W
Aberdeen, S.D., U.S.A. 100 45 30N 98 30W
Aberdeen, Wash., U.S.A. 105 47 0N 123 50W
Aberdour 47 56 2N 3 18W
Aberdyfi 42 52 33N 4 3W
Aberfeldy 48 56 37N 3 50W
Aberfoyle 46 56 10N 4 23W
Abergele 42 53 17N 3 35W
Abernethy 47 56 19N 3 18W
Abersoch 42 52 50N 4 30W
Abersychan 43 51 44N 3 3W
Abertillery 43 51 44N 3 9W
Aberystwyth 42 52 25N 4 6W
Abidjan 88 5 26N 3 58W
Abilene 100 32 22N 99 40W
Abington 46 55 30N 3 42W
Abnûb 91 27 18N 31 4E
Abocho 90 7 35N 6 56E
Abomey 88 7 10N 2 5E
Abonnema 90 4 41N 6 49E
Aboyne 48 57 4N 2 48W
Abram 45 53 30N 2 40W
Abrantes 60 39 24N 8 7W
Abrud 55 46 19N 23 5E
Abruzzi □ 58 42 15N 14 0E
Absaroka Ra. 100 44 40N 110 0W
Abū Dhabī 71 24 28N 54 36E
Abu Hamed 89 19 32N 33 13E
Abu Qurqâs 91 28 1N 30 44E
Abu Tig 91 27 4N 31 15E
Abuja 90 9 16N 7 2E
Acaponeta 106 22 30N 105 20W
Acapulco de Juárez 106 16 51N 99 56W
Accra 88 5 35N 0 6W
Accrington 45 53 46N 2 22W
Achalpur 70 21 22N 77 32E
Achill Hd. 50 53 59N 10 15W
Achill I. 50 53 58N 10 5W
Achnasheen 48 57 35N 5 5W
Ackworth 45 53 39N 1 20W
Acle 40 52 38N 1 32E
Aconcagua 108 32 50S 70 0W
Acre 89 32 35N 35 4E
Adana 71 37 0N 35 16E
Adapazari 71 40 48N 30 25E
Adare, C. 112 71 0S 171 0E
Adda, R. 58 45 8N 9 53E
Addis Ababa 89 9 2N 38 42E
Addlestone 41 51 22N 0 30W
Adelaide, Austral. 79 34 52S 138 30E
Adelaide, S. Afr. 94 32 42S 26 20E
Adelaide Pen. 98 68 15N 97 30W
Adélie, Ld. 112 67 0S 140 0E
Aden, G. of 71 13 0N 50 0E
Aden 71 12 50N 45 0E
Adige, R. 58 45 9N 12 20E
Adirondack Mts. 104 44 0N 74 15W
Adjohon 90 6 41N 2 32E
Adlington 45 53 36N 2 36W
Admiralty Is. 79 2 0S 147 0E
Ado 90 6 36N 2 56E
Ado Ekiti 90 7 38N 5 12E
Adour, R. 56 43 32N 1 32W
Adra 60 36 43N 3 3W
Adrano 58 37 40N 14 49E
Adriatic Sea 58 43 0N 16 0E
Aegean Sea 71 37 0N 25 0E
Aerht'ai Shan 73 46 40N 92 45E
Afghanistan ■ 71 33 0N 65 0E
Afif 71 23 53N 42 56E
Afikpo 90 5 53N 7 54E
Africa 92 10 0N 20 0E
Afula 89 32 37N 35 17E
Afyon Karahisar 71 38 45N 30 33E
Agadès 90 16 58N 7 59E
Agadir 88 30 28N 9 35W
Agano, R. 76 37 50N 139 30E
Agege 90 6 35N 3 9E
Agen 56 44 12N 0 38E
Agra 70 27 17N 77 58E
Agrigento 58 37 19N 13 33E
Agua Prieta 106 31 20N 109 32W
Aguascalientes 106 22 0N 102 12W
Aguilas 60 37 23N 1 35W
Agulhas, C. 94 34 52S 20 0E
Ahlen 52 51 45N 7 52E
Ahmadabad 70 23 0N 72 40E
Ahoada 90 5 8N 6 36E
Ahvāz 71 31 20N 48 40E
Ahvenanmaa 61 60 15N 20 0E
Ain el Mafki 91 27 30N 28 15E
Ainsdale 45 53 37N 3 2W
Aintree 45 53 28N 2 56W
Aïr 88 18 30N 8 0E
Airdrie 47 55 53N 3 57W
Aire, R. 44 53 42N 1 30W
Aisne, R. 56 49 26N 2 50E
Aitape 79 3 11S 142 22E
Aiud 55 46 19N 23 44E
Aix-en-Provence 56 43 32N 5 27E
Aix-les-Bains 56 45 41N 5 53E
Aizuwakamatsu 76 37 30N 139 56E
Ajaccio 56 41 55N 8 40E
Ajmer 70 26 28N 74 37E
Akaroa 83 43 49S 172 59E
Akashi 76 34 45N 135 0E
Aketi 92 2 38N 23 47E
Akhmîm 91 26 31N 31 47E
Akita 76 39 45N 140 0E
Akola 70 20 42N 77 2E
Akpatok I. 99 60 25N 68 8W
Akron 104 40 13N 103 15W
Aktogay 73 44 25N 76 44E
Aku 90 6 40N 7 18E
Akure 90 7 15N 5 5E
Akyab 70 20 18N 92 45E
Al Dīwaniyah 71 32 0N 45 0E
Al Hillah 71 32 30N 44 25E
Al Hūfuf 71 25 25N 49 45E
Al Jawf, Libya 89 24 10N 23 24E
Al Jawf, Si Arab. 71 29 55N 39 40E
Al Jazir 71 18 30N 56 31E
Al Khalih 89 31 32N 35 6E
Al Kūt 71 32 30N 46 0E
Al Manamāh 71 26 10N 50 30E
Al Marj 89 32 25N 20 30E
Al Matrah 71 23 37N 58 30E
Al Qatif 71 26 35N 50 0E
Al Qunfidha 71 19 3N 41 4E
Al Wajh 91 26 10N 36 30E
Ala Shan 73 40 0N 104 0E
Alabama □ 101 33 0N 87 0W
Alabama, R. 101 31 8N 87 57W
Alamogordo 100 32 59N 106 0W
Alamosa 100 37 30N 106 0W
Alashanchih 73 38 58N 105 14E
Alaska □ 98 65 0N 150 0W
Alaska, G. of 96 58 0N 145 0W
Alaska Pen. 96 56 0N 160 0W
Alaska Range 98 62 50N 151 0W
Alba 58 44 41N 8 1E
Alba de Tormes 60 40 50N 5 30W
Alba-Iulia 55 46 8N 23 39E
Albacete 60 39 0N 1 50W
Albania ■ 23 41 0N 20 0E
Albany, Austral. 78 35 1S 117 58E
Albany, Ga., U.S.A. 101 31 40N 84 10W
Albany, N.Y., U.S.A. 104 42 35N 73 47W
Albany, Oreg., U.S.A. 105 44 41N 123 0W
Alberche, R. 60 40 10N 4 30W
Albert, L. = Mobutu Sese Seko, L. 92 1 30N 31 0E
Alberta □ 98 54 40N 115 0W
Albi 56 43 56N 2 9E
Ålborg 61 57 2N 9 54E
Albrighton 41 52 38N 2 17W
Albuquerque 100 35 5N 106 47W
Alburquerque 60 39 15N 6 59W
Albury 79 36 3S 146 56E
Alcaniz 60 41 2N 0 8W
Alcántara 60 39 41N 6 57W
Alcaraz, Sierra de 60 38 40N 2 20W
Alcázar de San Juan 60 39 24N 3 12W
Alcester 42 52 13N 1 52W
Alcira 60 39 9N 0 30W
Alcoy 60 38 43N 0 30W
Aldeburgh 40 52 9N 1 35E
Alderley Edge 45 53 18N 2 15W
Alderney, I. 43 49 42N 2 12W
Aldershot 41 51 15N 0 43W
Aldridge 41 52 36N 1 55W
Alençon 56 48 27N 0 4E
Aleppo 71 36 10N 37 15E
Alès 56 44 9N 4 5E
Alessándria 58 44 54N 8 37E
Ålesund 61 62 28N 6 12E
Alexander I. 112 69 0S 70 0W
Alexandra 83 45 14S 169 25E
Alexandria, Can. 98 52 35N 122 27W
Alexandria, Egypt 91 31 0N 30 0E
Alexandria, U.K. 47 55 59N 4 40W
Alexandria, U.S.A. 101 31 20N 92 30W
Alexandrina, L. 79 35 25S 139 10E
Alford, Grampian, U.K. 48 57 13N 2 42W
Alford, Lincs., U.K. 44 53 16N 0 10E
Alfreton 44 53 6N 1 22W
Algarve 60 37 15N 8 10W
Algeciras 60 36 9N 5 28W
Algemesí 60 39 11N 0 27W
Algeria ■ 88 35 10N 3 11E
Alghero 58 40 34N 8 20E
Algiers 88 36 42N 3 8E
Algoa B. 94 33 50S 25 45E
Alhambra 100 34 2N 118 10W
Alicante 60 38 23N 0 30W
Alice Springs 78 23 40S 135 50E
Aligarh 70 25 55N 76 15E
Aliwal North 94 30 45S 26 45E
Alkmaar 52 52 37N 4 45E
Allahabad 70 25 25N 81 58E
Allaqi, Wadi 91 22 15N 34 55E
Allegheny Mts. 101 38 0N 80 0W
Allen, Bog of 51 53 15N 7 0W
Allen, L. 50 54 12N 8 5W
Allentown 104 40 36N 75 30W
Alliance 100 42 10N 102 50W
Allier, R. 56 46 57N 3 4E
Alloa 47 56 7N 3 49W
Alma Ata 73 43 15N 76 57E
Almada 60 38 40N 9 9W
Almadén 60 38 49N 4 52W
Almansa 60 38 51N 1 5W
Almanzor, Pico de 60 40 15N 5 18W
Almazán 60 41 30N 2 30W
Almelo 52 52 22N 6 42E
Almeria 60 36 52N 2 32W
Almora 70 29 38N 79 4E
Alnwick 46 55 25N 1 42W
Alor, I. 72 8 15S 124 30E
Alpine 100 30 25N 103 35W
Alps 24 47 0N 8 0E
Alsace 56 48 15N 7 25E
Alsask 98 51 21N 109 59W
Alsásua 60 42 54N 2 10W
Alsdorf 52 50 53N 6 10E
Alston 44 54 48N 2 26W
Altai Mts. 62 46 40N 92 45E
Altea 60 38 38N 0 2W
Altofts 45 53 42N 1 26W
Alton 40 51 8N 0 59W
Altona 54 53 32N 9 56E
Altoona 104 40 32N 78 24W
Altrincham 45 53 25N 2 21W
Altus 100 34 30N 99 25W
Altyn Tagh 73 39 0N 90 0E
Alva 47 56 9N 3 49W
Alvarado 106 18 40N 95 50W
Alwar 70 27 38N 76 34E
Amadeus, L. 78 24 54S 131 0E
Amadjuak L. 99 65 0N 71 8W
Amagasaki 76 34 42N 135 20E
Amami-O-Shima 76 28 0N 129 0E
Amarillo 100 35 14N 101 46W
Amassama 90 5 1N 6 2E
Amasya 71 40 40N 35 50E
Amazon, R. 108 2 0S 53 30W
Ambala 70 30 23N 76 56E
Amberg 54 49 25N 11 52E
Amberley 83 43 9S 172 44E
Amble 46 55 20N 1 36W
Ambleside 44 54 26N 2 58W
Ambon 72 3 35S 128 20E
Ambriz 92 7 48S 13 8E
Ameca 106 20 30N 104 0W
Ameland 52 53 27N 5 45E
Amersfoort 52 52 9N 5 23E
Amersham 41 51 40N 0 38W
Ames 101 42 0N 93 40W
Amesbury 42 51 10N 1 46W
Amiens 56 49 54N 2 16E
Amirante Is. 23 6 0S 53 0E
Amlwch 42 53 24N 4 21W
'Ammān 89 32 0N 35 52E
Ampthill 40 52 3N 0 30W
Amran 71 15 43N 43 57E
Amraoti 70 20 55N 77 45E
Amritsar 70 31 35N 74 57E
Amsterdam, Neth. 52 52 23N 4 54E
Amsterdam, U.S.A. 104 42 58N 74 10W
Amudarya, R. 71 37 50N 65 0E
Amundsen Gulf 98 71 0N 124 0W
Amundsen Sea 112 72 0S 115 0W
Amur, R. 62 53 30N 122 30E
Amuri Pass 83 42 31S 172 11E
An Nafūd 71 28 15N 41 0E
An Najaf 71 32 3N 44 15E
An Nasiriyah 71 31 0N 46 15E
Anaconda 100 46 7N 113 0W
Anadyr 62 64 35N 177 20E
Anadyr, G. of 62 64 0N 180 0E
Anaheim 100 33 50N 118 0W
Anaimalai Hills 70 10 20N 76 40E
Anambas Is. 72 3 20N 106 30E
Anchorage 98 61 10N 149 50W
Ancona 58 43 37N 13 30E
Andalucía = Andalusia, Reg. 60 37 35N 5 0W
Andaman Is. 72 12 30N 92 30E
Andaman Sea 72 13 0N 96 0E
Anderlues 52 50 25N 4 16E
Andernach 52 50 24N 7 25E
Anderson 101 34 32N 82 40W
Andes, mts. 108 20 0S 68 0W
Andhra Pradesh □ 70 15 0N 80 0E
Andizhan 71 41 10N 72 0E
Andkhui 71 36 52N 65 8E
Andorra ■ 60 42 30N 1 30E
Ándria 58 41 13N 16 17E
Andros I. 107 24 30N 78 0W
Andújar 60 38 3N 4 5W
Aneto, Pico de 56 42 37N 0 40E
Angangki 73 47 9N 123 48E
Angara, R. 62 58 30N 97 0E
Angarsk 73 52 30N 104 0E
Ånge 61 62 31N 15 35E
Ångerman R. 61 64 0N 17 20E
Angers 56 47 30N 0 35W
Anglesey, I. 42 53 17N 4 20W
Angmagssalik 96 65 40N 37 20W
Angola ■ 92 12 0S 18 0E
Angoulême 56 45 39N 0 10E
Angoumois 56 45 50N 0 25E
Anguilla, I. 107 18 14N 63 5W
Angus, Braes of 48 56 51N 3 0W
Anhwei □ 73 33 15N 116 50E
Anjou 56 47 20N 0 15W
Anju 73 39 36N 125 40E
Anka 90 12 13N 5 58E
Ankang 73 32 38N 109 5E
Ankara 71 40 0N 32 54E
Ankazoabo 92 22 18S 44 31E
Anking 73 30 34N 117 1E
Annaba 88 36 50N 7 46E
Annan 46 55 0N 3 17W
Annan, R. 46 54 58N 3 18W
Annandale 46 55 10N 3 25W
Annecy 56 45 55N 6 8E
Annfield Plain 44 54 52N 1 45W
Ansbach 54 49 17N 10 34E
Anshun 73 26 2N 105 57E
Ansi 73 40 21N 96 10E
Anstey 41 52 41N 1 14W
Anstruther 46 56 14N 2 40W
Antalya 71 36 52N 30 45E
Antananarivo 92 18 55S 47 35E
Antarctic Pen. 112 67 0S 60 0W
Antarctica 112 90 0S 0 0
Anti Atlas, Mts. 88 30 30N 6 30W
Antibes 56 43 34N 7 6E
Anticosti, I. 99 49 30N 63 0W
Antigua & Barbuda ■ 107 17 0N 61 50W
Antipodes Is. 23 49 45S 178 40E
Antofagasta 108 23 50S 70 30W
Antrim □ 50 54 42N 6 20W
Antrim 50 54 58N 6 20W
Antrim, Mts. of 50 54 57N 6 8W
Antsirabé 92 19 55S 47 2E
Antung 73 40 10N 124 18E
Antwerp 52 51 13N 4 25E
Antwerp □ 52 51 15N 4 40E
Anuradhapura 70 8 22N 80 28E
Anyang 73 36 7N 114 26E
Anzio 58 41 28N 12 37E
Aomori 76 40 45N 140 45E
Aosta 58 45 43N 7 20E
Aparri 72 18 22N 121 38E
Apeldoorn 52 52 13N 5 57E
Apennines 58 44 20N 10 20E
Apostle Is. 101 47 0N 90 30W
Appalachian Mts. 101 38 0N 80 0W
Appingedam 52 53 19N 6 51E
Appleby 44 54 35N 2 29W
Appleton 101 44 17N 88 25W
Apulia 58 41 0N 16 30E
Apure, R. 107 8 0N 69 20W
Aqaba 91 29 37N 35 0E
Aqaba, G. of 91 28 15N 33 20E
Ar Rab 'al Khāli 71 21 0N 51 0E
Ar Ramadi 71 33 25N 43 20E
Arabian Desert 91 28 0N 32 20E
Arabian Sea 71 16 0N 65 0E
Arabs Gulf 91 30 55N 29 0E
Aracajú 108 10 55S 37 4W
Arad 55 46 10N 21 20E
Arafura Sea 72 10 0S 135 0E
Aragón 60 41 25N 1 0W
Aragón, R. 60 42 35N 0 50W
Araguaia, R. 108 7 0S 49 15W
Arāk 71 34 0N 49 40E
Arakan Yoma 70 20 0N 94 30E
Araks, R. 71 39 10N 47 10E
Aral Sea 62 44 30N 60 0E
Aralsk 62 46 50N 61 20E
Aramac 79 22 58S 145 14E
Aran Fawddwy 42 52 48N 3 40W
Aran, I. 50 55 0N 8 30W
Aran Is. 51 53 5N 9 42W
Aranjuez 60 40 1N 3 40W
Ararat 79 37 16S 143 0E
Arauca 107 7 0N 70 40W
Arauca, R. 107 7 30N 69 0W
Arbatax 58 39 57N 9 42E
Arbroath 48 56 34N 2 35W
Arcachon 56 44 40N 1 10W
Arctic Ocean 112 78 0N 160 0W
Arctic Village 98 68 5N 145 45W
Ardabrīl 71 38 15N 48 18E
Ardara 50 54 47N 8 25W
Ardee 50 53 51N 6 32W
Ardennes 52 49 30N 5 10E
Ardgour 48 56 45N 5 25W
Ardnamurchan, Pt. of 48 56 44N 6 14W
Ardrahan 51 53 10N 8 48W
Ardrossan 47 55 39N 4 50W
Ards □ 50 54 35N 5 30W
Ards Pen. 50 54 30N 5 25W
Arendal 61 58 28N 8 46E
Arequipa 108 16 20S 71 30W
Arévalo 60 41 3N 4 43W
Arezzo 58 43 28N 11 50E
Argentan 56 48 45N 0 1W
Argentina ■ 108 35 0S 66 0W
Argun, R. 73 53 20N 121 28E
Argungu 90 12 40N 4 31E
Århus 61 56 8N 10 11E
Ariamsvlei 94 28 9S 19 51E
Arica 108 18 32S 70 20W
Arinagour 48 56 38N 6 31W
Arisaig 48 56 55N 5 50W
Arish, W. el 91 31 9N 33 49E
Aristazabal, I. 105 52 40N 129 10W
Arizona □ 100 34 20N 111 30W
Arka Tagh 73 36 30N 90 0E
Arkaig, L. 48 56 58N 5 10W
Arkansas □ 101 35 0N 92 30W
Arkansas City 101 37 4N 97 3W
Arkansas, R. 100 33 48N 91 4W
Arkhangelsk 61 64 40N 41 0E
Arklow 51 52 48N 6 10W
Arlanza, R. 60 42 6N 4 0W
Arlberg Pass 54 49 9N 10 12E
Arles 56 43 41N 4 40E
Arlon 52 49 42N 5 49E
Armadale, Lothian, U.K. 47 55 54N 3 42W
Armadale, Skye, U.K. 48 57 4N 5 54W
Armagh 50 54 22N 6 40W
Armagh □ 50 54 18N 6 37W
Armançon, R. 56 47 59N 3 30E
Armavir 71 45 2N 41 7E
Armenia 107 4 35N 75 45W
Armenia S.S.R. □ 71 40 0N 41 0E
Armidale 79 30 30S 151 40E
Arnhem 52 51 58N 5 55E
Arnhem Ld. 78 13 10S 135 0E
Arno, R. 58 43 41N 10 17E
Arnold 44 53 0N 1 8W
Aroab 94 26 41S 19 39E
Arran, I. 46 55 34N 5 12W
Arras 56 50 17N 2 46E
Arrow, L. 50 54 3N 8 20W
Arrowtown 83 44 57S 168 50E
Artem 73 43 5N 132 0E
Artesia 100 32 55N 104 25W
Arthurstown 51 52 15N 6 58W
Artois 56 50 20N 2 30E
Aru Is. 72 6 0S 134 30E
Arua 93 3 1N 30 58E
Aruba I. 107 12 30N 70 0W
Arun R. 40 50 48N 0 33W
Arundel 40 50 52N 0 32W
Arusha 93 3 20S 36 40E
Aruwimi, R. 92 1 30N 25 0E
Arys 71 42 26N 68 48E
As Salt 89 32 2N 35 43E

As Sohar Belomorsk

As Sohar 71 24 20N 56 40E
Asaba 90 6 12N 6 38E
Asahikawa 76 43 45N 142 30E
Asansol 70 23 40N 87 1E
Asbestos Mts. 94 29 0S 23 0E
Ascension, I. 22 8 0S 14 15W
Ascoli Piceno 58 42 51N 13 34E
Aseb 89 13 0N 42 40E
Ash 40 51 14N 0 43W
Ashaira 71 21 40N 40 40E
Ashan 73 41 3N 122 58E
Ashbourne 44 53 2N 1 44W
Ashburton, N.Z. 83 43 53S 171 48E
Ashburton, U.K. 43 50 31N 3 45W
Ashburton, R. 78 21 40S 114 56E
Ashby-de-la-Zouch 45 52 45N 1 29W
Asheville 101 35 39N 82 30W
Ashford 40 51 8N 0 53E
Ashington 44 55 12N 1 35W
Ashkhabad 71 38 0N 57 50E
Ashland 101 38 25N 82 40W
Ashmûn 91 30 18N 30 55E
Ashq'elon 89 31 42N 34 55E
Ashton-in-Makerfield 45 53 29N 2 39W
Ashton-u.-Lyne 45 53 30N 2 8E
Asia 66 45 0N 75 0E
Asinara, G. of 58 41 0N 8 30E
Asinara I. 58 41 5N 8 15E
Asir □ 89 18 40N 42 30E
Askeaton 51 52 37N 8 58W
Asmera 89 15 19N 38 55E
Aspiring, Mt. 83 44 23S 168 46E
Aspull 45 53 33N 2 36W
Assam □ 70 25 45N 92 30E
Assen 52 53 0N 6 35E
Assisi 58 43 4N 12 36E
Asti 58 44 54N 8 11E
Astorga 60 42 29N 6 8W
Astoria 105 46 16N 123 50W
Astrakhan 62 46 25N 48 5E
Asturias 60 43 15N 6 0W
Asunción 108 25 21S 57 30W
Asunción, La 107 11 2N 63 53W
Aswân 91 24 4N 32 57E
Aswan High Dam 91 24 5N 32 54E
Asyût 91 27 11N 31 4E
Asyûti, Wadi 91 27 18N 31 20E
Atacama Desert 108 24 0S 69 20W
Atami 76 35 0N 139 55E
Atbara 89 17 42N 33 59E
'Atbara, R. 89 17 40N 33 56E
Ath 52 50 38N 3 47E
Athabasca 98 54 45N 113 20W
Athabasca, L. 98 59 15N 109 15W
Athabasca, R. 98 58 40N 110 50W
Athenry 51 53 18N 8 45W
Athens, Greece 89 37 58N 23 46E
Athens, U.S.A. 101 33 56N 83 24W
Atherstone 41 52 35N 1 32W
Atherton, Austral. 79 17 17S 145 30E
Atherton, U.K. 45 53 32N 2 30W
Athlone 51 53 26N 7 57W
Atholl, Forest of 48 56 51N 3 50W
Athy 51 53 0N 7 0W
Atlanta 101 33 50N 84 24W
Atlantic City 104 39 25N 74 25W
Atlantic Ocean 22 0 0 20 0W
Atsoum, mts. 90 7 0N 12 30E
Attleborough 40 52 32N 1 1E
Aube, R. 56 48 34N 3 17E
Auburn 104 42 57N 76 39W
Auchi 90 7 6N 6 13E
Auchterarder 47 56 18N 3 43W
Auchterderran 47 56 8N 3 16W
Auchtermuchty 47 56 18N 3 15W
Auckland 83 36 52S 174 46E
Auckland Is. 23 51 0S 166 0E
Aude, R. 56 44 13N 3 15E
Audenshaw 45 53 29N 2 06W
Augathella 79 25 48S 146 35E
Aughnacloy 50 54 25N 7 0W
Aughrim 51 52 52N 6 20W
Augsburg 54 48 22N 10 54E
Augusta, Italy 58 37 14N 15 12E
Augusta, Ga., U.S.A. 101 33 29N 81 59W
Augusta, Me., U.S.A. 101 44 20N 69 46W
Augustus, Mt. 78 24 20S 116 50E
Aunis 56 46 0N 0 50W
Auob, R. 94 25 0S 18 50E
Aurangabad 70 19 50N 75 23E
Aurich 52 53 28N 7 30E
Aurora 101 41 42N 88 12W
Austerlitz 54 49 10N 16 52E
Austin 100 30 20N 97 45W
Austral Downs 79 20 30S 137 45E
Australia ■ 78 23 0S 135 0E
Australian Alps 79 36 30S 148 8E
Australian Cap. Terr. □ 79 35 15S 149 8E
Austria ■ 54 47 0N 14 0E
Auvergne 56 45 20N 3 0E
Auxerre 56 47 48N 3 32E
Aveiro 60 40 37N 8 38W
Avellino 58 40 54N 14 46E
Aversa 58 40 58N 14 11E
Aveyron, R. 56 44 5N 1 16E
Aviemore 48 57 11N 3 50W
Avignon 56 43 57N 4 50E
Avila 60 40 39N 4 43W
Avilés 60 43 35N 5 57W
Avon □ 42 51 30N 2 40W
Avon, R., Avon, U.K. 42 51 30N 2 43W
Avon, R., Warwick, U.K. 42 52 0N 2 9W
Avonmouth 43 51 30N 2 42W
Avranches 56 48 40N 1 20W
Awe, L. 46 56 15N 5 15W
Ax-les-Thermes 56 42 44N 1 50E
Axbridge 42 51 17N 2 50W
Axe Edge 44 53 14N 2 2W
Axel Heiberg I. 98 80 0N 90 0W
Axminster 43 50 47N 3 1W
Ayabe 76 35 20N 135 20E
Ayaguz 73 48 10N 80 0E
Ayamonte 60 37 12N 7 24W
Ayers Rock 78 25 23S 131 5E
Aylesbury 40 51 48N 0 49W
Aylsham 40 52 48N 1 16E
Ayr, Austral. 79 19 35S 147 25E
Ayr, U.K. 46 55 28N 4 37W
Ayr, R. 46 55 29N 4 40W
Ayre, Pt. of 42 54 27N 4 21W
Ayutla 106 16 58N 99 17W
Azare 90 11 55N 10 10E
Azerbaijan S.S.R. □ 71 40 20N 48 0E
Azores, Is. 22 38 44N 29 0W
Azov, Sea of 62 46 0N 36 30E
Azuaga 60 38 16N 5 39W

B

Baarle Nassau 52 51 27N 4 56E
Baarn 52 52 12N 5 17E
Bāb el Māndeb 89 12 35N 43 25E
Babine L. 105 54 48N 126 0W
Babura 90 12 51N 8 59E
Babuyan Chan. 72 18 40N 121 30E
Babuyan Is. 72 19 10N 121 40E
Bacău 55 46 35N 26 55E
Bacolod 72 10 40N 122 57E
Bacup 45 53 42N 2 12W
Bad Godesberg 52 50 41N 7 4E
Bad Honnef 52 50 39N 7 13E
Bad Ischl 54 47 44N 13 38E
Bad Kreuznach 52 49 47N 7 47E
Bad Lands 100 43 40N 102 10W
Bad Zwischenahn 52 53 15N 8 0E
Badagri 90 6 25N 2 55E
Badajoz 60 38 50N 6 59W
Badalona 60 41 26N 2 15E
Baden 54 48 1N 16 13E
Baden-Baden 54 48 45N 8 15E
Baden-Württemberg □ 54 48 40N 9 0E
Badgastein 54 47 7N 13 9E
Baffin Bay 99 72 0N 64 0W
Baffin I. 99 68 0N 75 0W
Bafia 90 4 40N 11 10E
Bafoulabé 88 13 50N 10 55W
Bafut 90 6 6N 10 2E
Bagamoyo 93 6 28S 38 55E
Bagan Siapiapi 72 2 12N 100 50E
Baghdād 71 33 20N 44 30E
Bagshot 41 51 22N 0 41W
Baguio 72 16 26N 120 34E
Bahamas, Is. 107 24 40N 74 0W
Bahamas ■ 107 24 0N 74 0W
Bahawalpur □ 71 29 5N 71 3E
Bahia = Salvador 108 13 0S 38 30W
Bahia Blanca 108 38 35S 62 13W
Bahr el 'Arab, R. 89 10 0N 26 0E
Bahr el Jebel 89 7 30N 30 30E
Bahr Yûsef 91 28 25N 30 35E
Bahra el Burullus 91 31 28N 30 48E
Bahra el Manzala 91 31 28N 32 01E
Bahrain ■ 71 26 0N 50 35E
Bai Bung Pt. 72 8 35N 104 42E
Baie Comeau 99 49 12N 68 10W
Baikal, L. = Baykal, Oz. 62 53 0N 108 0E
Baildon 45 53 52N 1 46W
Baile Atha Cliath = Dublin 51 53 20N 6 18W
Baillieborough 50 53 55N 7 0W
Baillieston 47 55 51N 4 08W
Baird Inlet 98 64 49N 164 18W
Bairnsdale 79 37 48S 147 36E
Baja 55 46 12N 18 59E
Baja, Pte. 106 29 50N 116 0W
Baker 100 44 50N 117 55W
Baker Is. 22 0 10N 176 35E
Baker Mt. 105 48 50N 121 49W
Bakersfield 105 35 25N 119 0W
Bakewell 44 53 13N 1 40W
Bakony Forest 55 47 10N 17 30E
Baku 71 40 25N 49 45E
Bala 42 52 54N 3 36W
Balaguer 60 41 50N 0 50E
Balasore 70 21 35N 87 3E
Balaton 55 46 50N 17 40E
Balbriggan 51 53 35N 6 10W
Balclutha 83 46 15S 169 45E
Baldoyle 51 53 24N 6 10W
Baldy Peak 100 33 50N 109 30W
Balearic Is. 60 39 30N 3 0E
Balerno 47 55 53N 3 20W
Bali 90 5 54N 10 0E
Bali, I. 72 8 20S 115 0E
Balikesir 71 39 35N 27 58E
Balikpapan 72 1 10S 116 55E
Balkan Pen. 24 42 0N 22 0E
Balkhash 62 46 50N 74 50E
Balkhash, L. 62 46 0N 74 50E
Ballaghaderreen 50 53 55N 8 35W
Ballantrae 46 55 6N 5 0W
Ballarat 79 37 33S 143 50E
Ballater 48 57 2N 3 2W
Balleny Is. 112 66 30S 163 0E
Ballina 50 54 7N 9 10W
Ballinamore 50 54 3N 7 48W
Ballinasloe 51 53 20N 8 12W
Ballingeary 51 51 51N 9 13W
Ballingry 47 56 10N 3 20W
Ballinrobe 51 53 36N 9 13W
Balloch 46 56 0N 4 35W
Ballybay 50 54 8N 6 52W
Ballybofey 50 54 48N 7 47W
Ballybunion 51 52 30N 9 40W
Ballycastle, Ireland 50 54 17N 9 24W
Ballycastle, U.K. 50 55 12N 6 15W
Ballyclare 50 54 46N 6 0W
Ballycotton 51 51 50N 8 0W
Ballygawley 50 54 27N 7 2W
Ballyhaunis 50 53 47N 8 47W
Ballyheige I. 51 52 22N 9 51W
Ballylongford 51 52 34N 9 30W
Ballymahon 51 53 35N 7 45W
Ballymena 50 54 53N 6 18W
Ballymena □ 50 54 53N 6 18W
Ballymoney 50 55 5N 6 30W
Ballymoney □ 50 55 5N 6 23W
Ballymote 50 54 5N 8 30W
Ballynahinch 50 54 24N 5 55W
Ballyragget 51 52 47N 7 20W
Ballysadare 50 54 12N 8 30W
Ballyshannon 50 54 30N 8 10W
Balmoral 48 57 3N 3 13W
Balranald 79 34 38S 143 33E
Balsas, R. 106 18 30N 101 20W
Baltic Sea 61 56 0N 20 0E
Baltim 91 31 35N 31 10E
Baltimore, Ireland 51 51 29N 9 22W
Baltimore, U.S.A. 104 39 18N 76 37W
Baltinglass 51 52 57N 6 42W
Bam 71 29 7N 58 14E
Bama 90 11 33N 13 33E
Bamako 88 12 34N 7 55W
Bamberg 54 49 54N 10 53E
Bamburgh 46 55 37N 1 43W
Bampton 43 50 59N 3 29W
Banbridge 50 54 21N 6 17W
Banbridge □ 50 54 21N 6 16W
Banchory 48 57 3N 2 30W
Banda Aceh 72 5 35N 95 20E
Banda Is. 72 4 37S 129 50E
Banda Sea 72 6 0S 130 0E
Bandar-e Anzalī 71 37 30N 49 30E
Bandar-e Torkeman 71 37 0N 54 10E
Bandirma 71 40 20N 28 0E
Bandon 51 51 44N 8 45W
Bandon, R. 51 51 40N 8 11W
Bandung 72 6 36S 107 48E
Banff, Can. 98 51 10N 115 34W
Banff, U.K. 48 57 40N 2 32W
Bangalore 70 12 59N 77 40E
Bangassou 89 4 55N 23 55E
Banggai 72 1 40S 123 30E
Banggai Arch. 72 2 0S 123 15E
Bangka Str. 72 3 30S 105 30E
Bangkok 72 13 45N 100 35E
Bangladesh ■ 70 24 0N 90 0E
Bangor, Ireland 50 54 09N 9 44W
Bangor, N.I., U.K. 50 54 40N 5 40W
Bangor, Wales, U.K. 42 53 13N 4 9W
Bangor, U.S.A. 101 44 48N 68 42W
Bangui 88 4 23N 18 35E
Bangweulu, L. 92 11 0S 30 0E
Bani 107 18 16N 70 22W
Banja Luka 58 44 49N 17 26E
Banjul 88 13 28N 16 40W
Banks I. 105 53 20N 130 0W
Banks Peninsula 83 43 45S 173 15E
Bann R. 50 54 30N 6 31W
Bannockburn 47 56 5N 3 55W
Banstead 41 51 19N 0 10W
Bantry 51 51 40N 9 28W
Bantry, B. 51 51 35N 9 50W
Baqūbah 71 33 45N 44 50E
Bar Harbor 101 44 15N 68 20W
Bar-le-Duc 56 48 47N 5 10E
Barahona 107 18 13N 71 7W
Barbados ■ 107 13 0N 59 30W
Barberton 94 25 42S 31 2E
Barbuda I. 107 17 30N 61 40W
Barcaldine 79 23 33S 145 13E
Barcelona, Spain 60 41 21N 2 10E
Barcelona, Venez. 107 10 10N 64 40W
Bardiyah 91 31 45N 25 0E
Bardsey 45 53 53N 1 26W
Bardsey, I. 42 52 46N 4 47W
Bareilly 70 28 22N 79 27E
Barents Sea 62 73 0N 39 0E
Bargoed 43 51 42N 3 22W
Bari 58 41 6N 16 52E
Bârîs 91 24 42N 30 31E
Barisal 70 22 30N 90 20E
Barito, R. 72 2 50S 114 50E
Barking 41 51 31N 0 10E
Barkley Sound 105 48 50N 125 10W
Barkly East 94 30 58S 27 33E
Barkly Tableland 78 19 50S 138 40E
Barkly West 94 28 5S 24 31E
Barkol 73 43 37N 93 2E
Bârlad 55 46 15N 27 38E
Barlee, L. 78 29 15S 119 30E
Barlee Ra. 78 23 30S 116 0E
Barletta 58 41 20N 16 17E
Barmer 70 25 45N 71 20E
Barmouth 42 52 44N 4 3W
Barnard Castle 44 54 33N 1 55W
Barnaul 62 53 20N 83 40E
Barnet 41 51 37N 0 15W
Barnoldswick 45 53 55N 2 11W
Barnsley 45 53 33N 1 29W
Barnstaple 42 51 5N 4 3W
Barquisimeto 107 9 58N 69 13W
Barra Hd. 49 56 47N 7 40W
Barra, I. 49 57 0N 7 30W
Barrancos 60 38 10N 6 58W
Barranquilla 107 11 0N 74 50W
Barre 101 42 26N 72 6W
Barreiro 60 38 40N 9 6W
Barrhead 47 55 48N 4 23W
Barrow, C. 98 71 10N 156 20W
Barrow Creek T.O. 78 21 30S 133 55E
Barrow-in-Furness 44 54 8N 3 15W
Barrow, Pt. 98 71 22N 156 30W
Barrow Ra. 78 26 0S 127 40E
Barrowford 45 53 51N 2 14W
Barry 43 51 23N 3 19W
Bartica 107 6 25N 58 40W
Bartle Frere, Mt. 79 17 27S 145 50E
Barton-upon-Humber 44 53 41N 0 27W
Barvas 48 58 21N 6 31W
Barwell 41 52 35N 1 22W
Bashi Channel 73 21 15N 122 0E
Basilan, I. 72 6 35N 122 0E
Basildon 41 51 34N 0 29E
Basilicata □ 58 40 30N 16 0E
Basle 54 47 35N 7 35E
Basoka 92 1 16N 23 40E
Basque Provinces 60 42 50N 2 45W
Basra 71 30 30N 47 50E
Bass Strait 79 39 15S 146 30E
Bassano 58 50 48N 112 20W
Bassein 70 16 30N 94 30E
Bastia 56 42 40N 9 30E
Batabanó 107 22 40N 82 20W
Batan I. 72 20 58N 122 5E
Batanes Is. 72 20 30N 122 0E
Bataszék 55 46 10N 18 44E
Batchelor 78 13 4S 131 1E
Bath 101 43 50N 69 49W
Bathgate 47 55 54N 3 38W
Bathurst 79 33 25S 149 31E
Bathurst, C. 98 70 34N 128 0W
Bathurst I. 98 76 0N 100 30W
Bathurst Inlet 98 66 50N 108 1W
Batley 45 53 43N 1 38W
Baton Rouge 101 30 30N 91 5W
Battambang 72 13 7N 103 12E
Battle 40 50 55N 0 30E
Battle Creek 104 42 20N 85 6W
Battle Harbour 99 52 16N 55 35W
Battleford 98 52 45N 108 15W
Batu Is. 72 0 30S 98 25E
Batu Pahat 72 1 50N 102 56E
Batumi 71 41 30N 41 30E
Bauchi 90 10 22N 9 48E
Bautzen 54 51 11N 14 25E
Bavaria 54 49 7N 11 30E
Bawean 72 5 46S 112 35E
Bawtry 44 53 25N 1 1W
Bay City 104 43 35N 83 51W
Bay View 83 39 25S 176 50E
Bayan Kara Shan 73 34 0N 98 0E
Bayeux 56 49 17N 0 42W
Bayonne 56 43 30N 1 28W
Bayreuth 54 49 56N 11 35E
Bayrut = Beirut 89 33 53N 35 31E
Baza 60 37 30N 2 47W
Beachy Head 40 50 44N 0 16E
Beaconsfield, Austral. 79 41 11S 146 48E
Beaconsfield, U.K. 41 51 36N 0 39W
Bealey 83 43 2S 171 36E
Beaminster 43 50 48N 2 44W
Bear I. 51 51 38N 9 50W
Bear L. 100 42 0N 111 20W
Beardmore Glacier 112 84 30S 170 0E
Béarn 56 43 28N 0 36W
Bearsden 47 55 55N 4 21W
Bearsted 41 51 15N 0 35E
Beauce, Plaines de 56 48 10N 1 45E
Beaufort Sea 98 72 0N 140 0W
Beaufort-West 94 32 18S 22 36E
Beaulieu 40 50 49N 1 27W
Beauly 48 57 29N 4 27W
Beauly Firth 48 57 30N 4 20W
Beauly, R. 48 57 26N 4 28W
Beaumaris 42 53 16N 4 7W
Beaumont 101 30 5N 94 8W
Beaune 56 47 2N 4 50E
Beauvais 56 49 25N 2 8E
Beawar 70 26 3N 74 18E
Bebington 45 53 23N 3 1W
Beccles 40 52 27N 1 33E
Béchar 88 31 38N 2 18W
Bechuanaland, reg. 94 26 30S 22 30E
Beddau 43 51 33N 3 23W
Bedford 40 52 8N 0 29W
Bedford □ 40 52 4N 0 28W
Bedford Level 40 52 25N 0 5E
Bedlington 44 55 8N 1 35W
Bedourie 79 24 30S 139 30E
Bedwas 43 51 36N 3 10W
Bedworth 41 52 28N 1 29W
Beersheba 89 31 15N 34 48E
Beeston, Ches. 45 53 07N 2 41W
Bega 79 36 41S 149 51E
Behbehan 71 30 30N 50 15E
Beighton 45 53 21N 1 21W
Beira 92 19 50S 34 52E
Beira-Alta 60 40 35N 7 35W
Beira-Baixa 60 40 2N 7 30W
Beira-Litoral 60 40 5N 8 30W
Beirut 89 33 53N 35 31E
Beit Shean 89 32 30N 35 30E
Beith 47 55 45N 4 38W
Beja □ 60 37 55N 7 55W
Békéscsaba 55 46 40N 21 10E
Bekily 92 24 13S 45 19E
Bela Crkva 55 44 55N 21 27E
Belaya Tserkov 55 49 45N 30 10E
Belbroughton 41 52 23N 2 5W
Belcoo 50 54 18N 7 52W
Belem 108 1 20S 48 30W
Belfast 50 54 35N 5 56W
Belfast □ 50 54 35N 5 56W
Belfast, L. 50 54 40N 5 50W
Belford 46 55 36N 1 50W
Belfort 56 47 38N 6 50E
Belgium ■ 52 51 30N 5 0E
Belgorod Dnestrovskiy 55 46 11N 30 23E
Belgrade 55 44 50N 20 37E
Belize ■ 106 17 0N 88 30W
Belize City 106 17 25N 88 0W
Bell I. 99 50 46N 55 35W
Bella Coola 98 52 25N 126 40W
Bellananagh 50 53 55N 7 25W
Bellary 70 15 10N 76 56E
Belle-Ile 56 47 20N 3 10W
Belle Isle 99 51 57N 55 25W
Belle Isle, Str. of 99 51 30N 56 30W
Belleville 104 44 10N 77 23W
Bellingham, U.K. 44 55 09N 2 16W
Bellingham, U.S.A. 105 48 45N 122 27W
Bellingshausen Sea 112 66 0S 80 0W
Bellinzona 54 46 11N 9 1E
Belluno 58 46 8N 12 6E
Belmont 45 53 38N 2 30W
Belmullet 50 54 13N 9 58W
Belo Horizonte 108 19 55S 43 56W
Belomorsk 61 64 35N 34 30E

Beloye L **Brunswick**

Beloye L. 61 60 10N 37 35E
Belper 44 53 2N 1 29W
Belshill 47 55 49N 4 01W
Belton 100 31 4N 97 30W
Beltsy 55 47 48N 28 0E
Belturbet 50 54 6N 7 28W
Bemidji 101 47 30N 94 50W
Ben Alder 48 56 50N 4 30W
Ben Cruachan 48 56 26N 5 8W
Ben Dearg 48 57 47N 4 58W
Ben Hope 48 58 24N 4 36W
Ben Klibreck 48 58 14N 4 25W
Ben Lawers 48 56 33N 4 13W
Ben Macdhui 48 57 4N 3 40W
Ben More, Mull, U.K. 48 56 26N 6 2W
Ben More, Perth, U.K. 48 56 23N 4 31W
Ben More Assynt 48 58 7N 4 51W
Ben Nevis 48 56 48N 5 0W
Ben Vorlich 46 56 22N 4 15W
Bena 90 11 20N 5 50E
Benalla 79 36 30S 146 0E
Bencubbin 78 30 48S 117 52E
Bend 105 44 2N 121 15W
Bendery 55 46 50N 29 50E
Bendigo 79 36 40S 144 15E
Benevento 58 41 7N 14 45E
Bengal, Bay of 70 18 0N 90 0E
Benghazi 89 32 11N 20 3E
Benguela 92 12 37S 13 25E
Benha 91 30 26N 31 8E
Beni 93 0 30N 29 27E
Benî Mazâr 91 28 32N 30 44E
Benî Suêf 91 29 5N 31 6E
Benin ■ 90 10 0N 2 0E
Benin City 90 6 20N 5 31E
Benoni 94 26 11S 28 18E
Bentley 44 53 33N 1 9W
Benue □ 90 7 30N 7 30E
Benue, R. 90 7 50N 6 30E
Benwee Hd. 50 54 20N 9 50W
Beograd = Belgrade 55 44 50N 20 37E
Beppu 76 33 15N 131 30E
Beragh 50 54 34N 7 10W
Berbera 89 10 30N 45 2E
Berdichev 55 49 57N 28 30E
Beregovo 55 48 15N 22 45E
Bérgamo 58 45 42N 9 40E
Bergen 61 60 23N 5 20E
Bergen-op-Zoom 52 51 30N 4 18E
Bergerac 56 44 51N 0 30E
Bergisch-Gladbach 52 50 59N 7 9E
Berhampore 70 24 2N 88 27E
Berhampur 70 19 15N 84 54E
Bering Sea 62 58 0N 167 0E
Bering Str. 96 66 0N 170 0W
Berkel, R. 52 52 8N 6 12E
Berkhamsted 41 51 45N 0 33W
Berkner I. 112 79 30S 50 0W
Berlin 54 52 32N 13 24E
Bermuda, I. 96 32 45N 65 0W
Bern 54 46 57N 7 28E
Bernay 56 49 5N 0 35E
Bernburg 54 51 40N 11 42E
Berneray I. 49 56 47N 7 40W
Bernina Pass 54 46 22N 9 54E
Berry 56 47 0N 2 0E
Berwick-upon-Tweed 46 55 47N 2 0W
Berwyn Mts. 42 52 54N 3 26W
Besalampy 92 16 43S 44 29E
Besançon 56 47 9N 6 0E
Bessarabiya 55 46 20N 29 0E
Bessemer 101 46 27N 90 0W
Bethal 94 26 27S 29 28E
Bethesda 42 53 11N 4 3W
Bethlehem, Jordan 89 31 43N 35 12E
Bethlehem, S. Afr. 94 28 14S 28 18E
Bethlehem, U.S.A. 104 40 39N 75 24W
Bethulie 94 30 30S 25 59E
Béthune 56 50 30N 2 38E
Betroka 92 23 16S 46 0E
Bettiah 70 26 48N 84 33E
Bettyhill 48 58 31N 4 12W
Betws-y-Coed 42 53 4N 3 49W
Beverley, Austral. 78 32 9S 116 56E
Beverley, U.K. 44 53 52N 0 26W
Beverwijk 52 52 28N 4 38E
Bewdley 41 52 23N 2 19W
Bexhill 40 50 51N 0 29E
Bexley 41 51 26N 0 10E
Beyneu 71 45 10N 55 3E
Béziers 56 43 20N 3 12E
Bhagalpur 70 25 10N 87 0E
Bhamo 70 24 15N 97 15E
Bharatpur 70 27 15N 77 30E
Bhaunagar 70 21 45N 72 10E
Bhilwara 70 25 25N 74 38E
Bhopal 70 23 20N 77 53E
Bhubaneswar 70 20 15N 85 50E
Bhutan ■ 70 27 25N 89 50E
Biała Podlaska 55 52 4N 23 6E
Białystok 55 53 10N 23 10E
Biarritz 56 43 29N 1 33W
Biba 91 28 55N 31 0E
Bibaï 76 43 19N 141 52E
Bida 90 9 3N 5 58E
Biddulph 44 53 8N 2 11W
Bideford 43 51 1N 4 13W
Bideford Bay 42 51 5N 4 20W
Bié 92 12 22S 16 55E
Bié Plateau 92 12 0S 16 0E
Biel 54 47 8N 7 14E
Bielefeld 54 52 2N 8 31E
Biella 58 45 33N 8 3E
Bielsko-Biała 55 49 50N 19 8E
Bien Hoa 72 10 57N 106 49E
Big Belt Mts. 100 46 50N 111 30W
Big Delta 98 64 15N 145 0W
Big Sioux, R. 101 42 30N 96 25W
Big Spring 100 32 10N 101 25W
Biggar 47 55 37N 3 31W
Biggleswade 40 52 6N 0 16W
Bighorn Mts. 100 44 30N 107 30W
Bihar □ 70 25 0N 86 0E
Bijapur 70 16 50N 75 55E
Bikaner 70 28 2N 73 18E
Bilbao 60 43 16N 2 56W
Billericay 41 51 38N 0 25E
Billingham 44 54 36N 1 18W
Billings 100 45 43N 108 29W
Billiton Is. 72 3 10S 107 50E
Biloela 79 24 24S 150 31E
Biloxi 101 30 30N 89 0W
Bilston 41 52 34N 2 5W
Binche 52 50 26N 4 10E
Bingen 52 49 57N 7 53E
Bingerville 88 5 18N 3 49W
Bingley 45 53 51N 1 50W
Bir Hirmas 91 28 57N 36 25E
Birdsville 79 25 51S 139 20E
Birdum 78 15 39S 133 13E
Birkdale 45 53 38N 3 2W
Birkenhead 45 53 24N 3 1W
Birkenshaw 45 53 45N 1 41W
Birket Qârûn 91 29 30N 30 40E
Birmingham, U.K. 41 52 30N 1 55W
Birmingham, U.S.A. 101 33 31N 86 50W
Birni Nkonni 90 13 55N 5 15E
Birnin Kebbi 90 12 32N 4 12E
Birnin Kudu 90 11 30N 9 29E
Birobidzhan 73 48 50N 132 50E
Birr 51 53 7N 7 55W
Birtley 44 54 53N 1 34W
Biscay, B. of 56 45 0N 2 0W
Bishop Auckland 44 54 40N 1 40W
Bishopbriggs 47 55 54N 4 14W
Bishop's Castle 45 52 29N 3 0W
Bishop's Stortford 40 51 52N 0 11E
Bishop's Waltham 40 50 57N 1 13W
Bishopton 47 55 54N 4 30W
Biskra 88 34 50N 5 44E
Bismarck 100 46 49N 100 49W
Bismarck Arch. 79 2 30S 150 0E
Bismarck Ra. 79 5 35S 145 0E
Bismarck Sea 79 4 10S 146 50E
Bissau 88 11 45N 15 45W
Bistrița 55 47 9N 24 35E
Bitlis 71 38 20N 42 3E
Bitter Lakes 91 30 15N 32 40E
Bitterroot Range 100 46 0N 114 20W
Biu 90 10 40N 12 3E
Biwa-Ko 76 35 15N 135 45E
Biysk 62 52 40N 85 0E
Bjelovar 58 45 56N 16 49E
Blaby 41 52 34N 1 10W
Black Hills 100 44 0N 103 50W
Black Isle, dist. 48 57 35N 4 10W
Black Mts. 42 51 52N 3 5W
Black Range, Mts. 100 33 30N 107 55W
Black Sea 71 43 30N 35 0E
Blackall 79 24 25S 145 45E
Blackball 83 42 22S 171 26E
Blackburn, Lancs., U.K. 45 53 44N 2 30W
Blackburn, Lothian, U.K. 47 55 52N 3 38W
Blackdown Hills 43 50 57N 3 15W
Blackfoot 100 43 13N 112 12W
Blackford 47 56 15N 3 48W
Blackpool 45 53 48N 3 3W
Blackrock 51 53 18N 6 11W
Blackrod 45 53 35N 2 35W
Blacksod B. 50 54 6N 10 0W
Blackwater 51 52 26N 6 20W
Blackwater, R., Meath, Ireland 50 53 46N 7 0W
Blackwater, R., Munster, Ireland 51 51 55N 7 50W
Blackwater, R., Essex, U.K. 40 51 44N 0 53E
Blackwater, R., Ulster, U.K. 50 54 31N 6 35W
Blackwell 100 36 55N 97 20W
Blackwood 43 51 40N 3 13W
Blaenau Ffestiniog 42 53 0N 3 57W
Blaenavon 43 51 46N 3 5W
Blaengawr 43 51 37N 3 35W
Blagoveshchensk 62 55 1N 55 59E
Blaina 43 51 46N 3 10W
Blair Athol 79 22 42S 147 31E
Blair Atholl 48 56 46N 3 50W
Blairgowrie 48 56 36N 3 20W
Blakeney 43 51 45N 2 29W
Blanc, Mt. 54 45 48N 6 50E
Blanca Peak 100 37 35N 105 29W
Blanchland 44 54 50N 2 03W
Blanco, C. 100 42 50N 124 40W
Blandford Forum 43 50 25N 2 10W
Blankenberge 52 51 20N 3 9E
Blantyre 92 15 45S 35 0E
Blarney 51 51 57N 8 35W
Blaydon 44 54 56N 1 47W
Bleiburg 54 46 35N 14 49E
Blenheim 83 41 38S 174 5E
Blessington 51 53 10N 6 32W
Blewbury 40 51 33N 1 14W
Blida 88 36 30N 2 49E
Blitar 72 8 5S 112 11E
Bloemfontein 94 29 6S 26 14E
Bloemhof 94 27 38S 25 32E
Blois 56 47 35N 1 20E
Bloody Foreland 50 55 10N 8 18W
Bloubergstrand 94 33 48S 18 28E
Blue Mts., Austral. 79 33 40S 150 0E
Blue Mts., U.S.A. 100 45 15N 119 0W
Blue Nile, R. 89 12 30N 34 30E
Blue Ridge, Mts. 101 36 30N 80 15W
Blue Stack Mts. 50 54 46N 8 5W
Bluefield 101 37 18N 81 14W
Bluefields 107 12 0N 83 50W
Bluff 83 46 37S 168 20E
Blyth, Northumberland, U.K. 44 55 8N 1 32W
Blyth, Notts., U.K. 43 53 22N 1 2W
Bobo-Dioulasso 88 11 8N 4 13W
Bocholt 52 51 50N 6 35E
Bochum 52 51 28N 7 12E
Boddam 48 57 28N 1 46W
Boden 61 65 50N 21 42E
Bodmin 43 50 28N 4 44W
Bodmin Moor 43 50 33N 4 36W
Bodø 61 67 17N 14 24E
Boggeragh Mts. 51 52 2N 8 55W
Bognor Regis 40 50 47N 0 40W
Bogong, Mt. 79 36 47S 147 17E
Bogor 72 6 36S 106 48E
Bogotá 107 4 34N 74 0W
Bohemia 54 50 0N 14 0E
Bohemian Forest 54 49 20N 13 0E
Boholl, I. 72 9 50N 124 10E
Boise 100 43 43N 116 9W
Boju 90 7 22N 7 55E
Bokkos 90 9 17N 9 1E
Bokpyin 70 11 18N 98 42E
Bolbec 56 49 30N 0 30E
Boldon 44 54 57N 1 28W
Bolivia ■ 108 17 6S 64 0W
Bolivian Plateau 108 20 0S 67 30W
Bollington 45 53 18N 2 05W
Bologna 58 44 30N 11 20E
Bologoye 61 57 55N 34 0E
Bolsena 58 42 40N 11 58E
Bolshevik I. 62 78 30N 102 0E
Bolsover 45 53 14N 1 18W
Bolton 45 53 35N 2 26W
Bolton-on-Dearne 45 53 31N 1 19W
Bolus Hd. 51 51 48N 10 20W
Bolzano 58 46 30N 11 20E
Boma 92 5 50S 13 4E
Bombala 79 36 56S 149 15E
Bombay 70 18 55N 72 50E
Bona Mt. 98 61 20N 140 0W
Bonaire, I. 107 12 10N 68 15W
Bonarbridge 48 57 53N 4 20W
Bonavista 99 48 40N 53 5W
Bo'ness 47 56 0N 3 38W
Bonhill 47 55 59N 4 34W
Bonifacio, Str. of 58 41 12N 9 15E
Bonin Is. 23 27 0N 142 0E
Bonn 52 50 43N 7 6E
Bonnie Rock 78 30 29S 118 22E
Bonnybridge 47 56 00N 3 53W
Bonnyrigg 47 55 52N 3 8W
Boom 52 51 6N 4 20E
Boothia, Gulf of 98 71 0N 91 0W
Boothia Pen. 98 71 0N 94 0W
Bootle 45 53 28N 3 1W
Borås 61 57 43N 12 56E
Bordeaux 56 44 50N 0 36W
Borders □ 46 55 45N 2 50W
Borehamwood 41 51 40N 0 15W
Borger 100 35 40N 101 20W
Borisovka 71 43 15N 68 10E
Borneo, I. 72 1 0N 115 0E
Bornholm, I. 61 55 10N 15 0E
Borno □ 90 12 30N 12 30E
Borough Green 41 51 17N 0 18E
Borovichi 61 58 25N 33 55E
Borrisokane 51 53 0N 8 8W
Borroloola 79 16 4S 136 17E
Borrowdale 44 54 31N 3 10W
Borzya 73 50 24N 116 31E
Bosa 58 40 17N 8 32E
Boshof 94 28 31S 25 13E
Bosna, R. 58 45 4N 18 29E
Bosnia 58 44 0N 18 0E
Boston, U.K. 44 52 59N 0 2W
Boston, U.S.A. 104 42 20N 71 0W
Bothnia, G. of 61 63 0N 21 0E
Bothwell 47 55 48N 4 04W
Botoşani 55 47 42N 26 41E
Botswana ■ 92 22 0S 24 0E
Bottesford 44 52 57N 0 48W
Bottrop 52 51 34N 6 59E
Bouaké 88 7 40N 5 2W
Bougainville I. 79 6 0S 155 0E
Boulder, Austral. 78 30 46S 121 30E
Boulder, U.S.A. 100 40 3N 105 10W
Boulia 79 22 52S 139 51E
Boulogne-sur-Mer 56 50 42N 1 36E
Bountiful 100 40 57N 111 58W
Bourbonnais 56 46 28N 3 0E
Bourg-en-Bresse 56 46 13N 5 12E
Bourges 56 47 9N 2 25E
Bourke 79 30 8S 145 55E
Bourne 45 52 46N 0 22W
Bourton-on-the-Water 42 51 53N 1 45W
Boussu 52 50 26N 3 48E
Bovey Tracey 43 50 36N 3 40W
Bovingdon 41 51 43N 0 32W
Bowen 79 20 0S 148 16E
Bowes 44 54 31N 1 59W
Bowland, Forest of 44 54 0N 2 30W
Bowling Green 101 37 0N 86 25W
Bowmore 46 55 45N 6 18W
Bowness 44 54 57N 3 13W
Boyle 50 53 58N 8 19W
Boyne, R. 50 53 40N 6 34W
Boyoma Falls 92 0 12N 25 25E
Brabant □ 52 50 46N 4 30E
Brač 58 43 20N 16 40E
Bracciano, L. 58 42 8N 12 11E
Bräcke 61 62 45N 15 26E
Brackley 40 52 3N 1 9W
Bracknell 41 51 24N 0 45W
Brad 55 46 10N 22 50E
Bradford 45 53 47N 1 45W
Bradford-on-Avon 42 51 20N 2 15W
Bradworthy 43 50 54N 4 22W
Braemar 48 57 2N 3 20W
Braemar, dist. 48 57 2N 3 20W
Braga 60 41 35N 8 25W
Brahmaputra, R. 70 26 30N 93 30E
Braich-y-pwll 42 52 47N 4 46W
Brăila 55 45 19N 27 59E
Brainerd 101 46 20N 94 10W
Braintree 40 51 53N 0 34E
Bramhall 45 53 22N 2 10W
Bramhope 45 53 53N 1 37W
Bramley 45 53 25N 1 16W
Brampton 44 54 56N 2 43W
Branco, C. 108 7 9S 34 47W
Brandenburg 54 52 24N 12 33E
Brandon, Can. 98 49 50N 99 57W
Brandon, Durham, U.K. 44 54 46N 1 37W
Brandon, Suffolk, U.K. 40 52 27N 0 37E
Brandon, Mt. 51 52 15N 10 15W
Brandvlei 94 30 25S 20 30E
Brantford 104 43 10N 80 15W
Brasilia 108 15 47S 47 55E
Braşov 55 45 38N 25 35E
Brass, R. 90 4 15N 6 13E
Brasschaat 52 51 19N 4 27E
Bratislava 54 48 10N 17 7E
Braunstone 41 52 36N 1 10W
Bray 51 53 12N 6 6W
Brazil ■ 108 5 0N 20 0W
Brazilian Highlands 108 18 0S 46 30W
Brazzaville 92 4 9S 15 12E
Breadalbane 48 56 30N 4 15W
Bream 43 51 45N 2 34W
Brechin 48 56 44N 2 40W
Breckland 40 52 30N 0 40E
Brecon 42 51 57N 3 23W
Brecon Beacons 42 51 53N 3 27W
Breda 52 51 35N 4 45E
Bredasdorp 94 34 33S 20 2E
Bredbury 45 53 24N 2 08W
Bremen 54 53 4N 8 47E
Bremerhaven 54 53 34N 8 35E
Bremerton 105 47 30N 122 38W
Brendon Hills 42 51 6N 3 25W
Brenner Pass 54 47 0N 11 30E
Brent 41 51 33N 0 18W
Brentford 41 51 30N 0 19W
Breslau = Wrocław 54 51 5N 17 5E
Bressanone 58 46 43N 11 40E
Bressay 49 60 10N 1 6W
Brest, France 56 48 24N 4 31W
Brest, U.S.S.R. 55 52 10N 23 40E
Brett, C. 83 35 10S 174 20E
Brewood 41 52 41N 2 10W
Bricket Wood 41 51 42N 0 21W
Bridge of Allan 47 56 9N 3 57W
Bridge of Earn 47 56 20N 3 25W
Bridge of Orchy 48 56 29N 4 48W
Bridge of Weir 47 55 51N 4 35W
Bridgend 43 51 30N 3 35W
Bridgeport 104 41 12N 73 12W
Bridgetown, Austral. 78 33 58S 116 7E
Bridgetown, Barbados 107 13 0N 59 30W
Bridgetown, Can. 99 44 55N 65 18W
Bridgetown, Ireland 51 52 13N 6 33W
Bridgwater 42 51 7N 3 0W
Bridgwater B. 42 51 15N 3 15W
Bridlington 44 54 6N 0 11W
Bridport 43 50 43N 2 45W
Brierfield 45 53 49N 2 15W
Brierley Hill 41 52 29N 2 7W
Brig 54 46 18N 7 59E
Brigg 44 53 33N 0 30W
Brigham City 100 41 30N 112 1W
Brighouse 45 53 42N 1 47W
Brightlingsea 40 51 49N 1 1E
Brighton 40 50 50N 0 9W
Brindisi 58 40 39N 17 55E
Brisbane 79 27 25S 153 2E
Bristol 43 51 26N 2 35W
Bristol B. 96 58 0N 160 0W
Bristol Channel 42 51 18N 4 30W
British Columbia □ 98 55 0N 125 15W
British Isles 24 55 0N 4 0W
Britstown 94 30 37S 23 30E
Brittany, reg. 56 48 0N 3 0W
Brittas 51 53 14N 6 29W
Brive-la-Gaillarde 56 45 10N 1 32E
Brixham 43 50 24N 3 31W
Brno 54 49 10N 16 35E
Broad Law, Mt. 46 55 30N 3 22W
Broad Sd. 79 22 0S 149 45E
Broadford 48 57 14N 5 55W
Broads, The 40 52 45N 1 30E
Broadsound Ra. 79 22 50S 149 30E
Broadstairs 40 51 21N 1 28E
Broadstone 43 50 45N 1 59W
Broadway 42 52 2N 1 51W
Brockenhurst 40 50 49N 1 34W
Brockton 104 42 8N 71 2W
Brod 58 41 35N 21 17E
Brodick 46 55 34N 5 9W
Brody 55 50 5N 25 10E
Broken Hill 79 31 58S 141 29E
Bromley 41 51 20N 0 5E
Bromsgrove 42 52 20N 2 3W
Bromyard 42 52 12N 2 30W
Brookings 101 44 20N 96 45W
Brookmans Park 41 51 43N 0 11W
Brooks Ra. 98 68 40N 147 0W
Brookton 78 32 22S 116 57E
Broom, L. 48 57 55N 5 15W
Broome 78 18 0S 122 15E
Brosna, R. 51 53 8N 8 0W
Brough, Cumbria, U.K. 43 54 32N 2 19W
Brough, Humberside, U.K. 44 53 44N 0 35W
Broughton 45 53 33N 0 36W
Brown, Mt. 79 32 30S 138 0E
Brown Willy 43 50 35N 4 34W
Brownhills 41 52 38N 1 57W
Brownsville 101 35 35N 89 15W
Brownwood 100 31 45N 99 0W
Broxbourne 41 51 44N 0 00
Broxburn 47 55 56N 3 23W
Bruay-en-Artois 56 50 29N 2 33E
Bruce, Mt. 78 22 37S 118 8E
Bruck a.d. Mur 54 47 24N 15 16E
Brue, R. 42 51 10N 2 59W
Bruges = Brugge 52 51 13N 3 13E
Brugge 52 51 13N 3 13E
Brühl 52 50 49N 6 51E
Brunei ■ 72 4 50N 115 0E
Brunner 83 42 27S 171 20E
Brunswick, Ger. 54 52 17N 10 28E
Brunswick, U.S.A. 101 31 10N 81 30W

Brussels	52	50 51N	4 21E
Bruton	42	51 6N	2 28W
Bruxelles = Brussels	52	50 51N	4 21E
Bryan	101	30 40N	96 27W
Brynamman	42	51 49N	3 52W
Brynmawr	43	51 48N	3 11W
Buabuq	91	31 29N	25 29E
Bucaramanga	107	7 0N	73 0W
Buchan	48	57 32N	2 8W
Buchanan	88	5 57N	10 2W
Bucharest	55	44 27N	26 10E
Buckfastleigh	43	50 28N	3 47W
Buckhaven	47	56 10N	3 02W
Buckie	48	57 40N	2 58W
Buckingham	40	52 0N	0 59W
Buckingham □	40	51 50N	0 55W
Bucureşti = Bucharest	55	44 27N	26 10E
Budapest	55	47 29N	19 5E
Bude	43	50 49N	4 33W
Bude Bay	43	50 50N	4 40W
Budleigh Salterton	43	50 37N	3 19W
Buea	90	4 10N	9 9E
Buenaventura	107	3 53N	77 4W
Buenos Aires	108	34 30S	58 20W
Buffalo, N.Y., U.S.A.	104	42 55N	78 50W
Buffalo, Wyo., U.S.A.	100	44 25N	106 50W
Bug, R., Poland	55	52 31N	21 5E
Bug, R., U.S.S.R.	55	48 0N	31 0E
Buga	107	4 0N	77 0W
Buguma	90	4 42N	6 55E
Bugun Shara	73	49 0N	104 0E
Builth Wells	42	52 10N	3 26W
Bujumbura	93	3 16S	29 18E
Bukama	92	9 10S	25 50E
Bukavu	92	2 20S	28 52E
Bukhara	71	39 48N	64 25E
Bukoba	93	1 20S	31 49E
Bukombe	93	3 31S	32 4E
Bukuru	90	9 42N	8 48E
Bulawayo	92	20 7S	28 32E
Bulgaria ■	55	42 35N	25 30E
Bulkington	41	52 29N	1 25W
Bullfinch	78	30 58S	119 3E
Bulls	83	40 10S	175 24E
Bully-les-Mines	56	50 27N	2 44E
Bultfontein	94	28 18S	26 10E
Buna	79	8 42S	148 27E
Bunbeg	50	55 4N	8 18W
Bunbury	78	33 20S	115 35E
Bunclody	51	52 40N	6 40W
Buncrana	50	55 8N	7 28W
Bundaberg	79	24 54S	152 22E
Bundoran	50	54 24N	8 17W
Bungay	40	52 27N	1 26E
Bungo Channel	76	33 0N	132 15E
Bunia	93	1 35N	30 20E
Bununu Doss	90	10 6N	9 25E
Bunza	90	12 8N	4 0E
Bûr Fuad	91	31 15N	32 20E
Bûr Said = Port Said	91	31 16N	32 18E
Bura	93	1 4S	39 58E
Burbage	41	52 31N	1 20W
Burbank	100	34 9N	118 23W
Bure, R.	40	52 38N	1 45E
Bureya	73	50 35N	132 0E
Bureya, R.	73	51 30N	133 0E
Burford	40	51 48N	1 38W
Burg el Arab	91	30 54N	29 32E
Burgenland □	54	47 20N	16 20E
Burgersdorp	94	31 0S	26 20E
Burgess Hill	40	50 57N	0 7W
Burghead	48	57 42N	3 30W
Burgos	60	42 21N	3 41W
Burgsteinfurt	52	52 9N	7 23E
Burgundy, reg.	56	47 0N	4 30E
Burketown	79	17 45S	139 33E
Burley	100	42 37N	113 55W
Burlington	104	42 41N	88 18W
Burlyu-Tyube	62	46 30N	79 10E
Burma ■	70	21 0N	96 30E
Burnham, Essex, U.K.	41	51 37N	0 50E
Burnham, Somerset, U.K.	42	51 14N	3 0W
Burnham Market	40	52 57N	0 43E
Burnie	79	41 4S	145 56E
Burnley	45	53 47N	2 15W
Burns Lake	105	54 20N	125 45W
Burnsall	44	54 03N	1 57W
Burntisland	46	56 4N	3 14W
Burra	79	33 40S	138 55E
Bursa	71	40 15N	29 5E
Burscough	45	53 36N	2 52W
Burton	45	53 15N	3 02W
Burton Latimer	40	52 23N	0 41W
Burton-upon-Trent	45	52 48N	1 39W
Buru, I.	72	3 30S	126 30E
Burundi ■	93	3 15S	30 0E
Burutu	90	5 20N	5 29E
Bury	45	53 36N	2 19W
Bury St. Edmunds	40	52 15N	0 42E
Bushehr	71	28 55N	50 55E
Bushey	41	51 38N	0 20W
Bushmills	50	55 14N	6 32W
Busselton	78	33 42S	115 15E
Bussum	52	52 16N	5 10E
Buta	92	2 50N	24 53E
Bute, I.	46	55 48N	5 2W
Butte	100	46 0N	112 31W
Butterworth	72	5 24N	100 23E
Buttevant	51	52 14N	8 40E
Butung, I.	72	5 0S	122 45E
Buxton	44	53 16N	1 54W
Buzău, Pasul	55	45 35N	26 12E
Bydgoszcz	55	53 10N	18 0E
Byfleet	41	51 20N	0 28W
Bylot I.	99	73 13N	78 34W
Byrd Ld.	112	79 30S	125 0W
Byron, C.	79	28 38S	153 40E
Bytom	55	50 25N	19 0E

C

Cabinda	92	5 40S	12 11E
Cabonga Réservoir	99	47 20N	76 40W
Cabot Strait	99	47 15N	59 40W
Cabrera, I.	60	39 6N	2 59E
Cacak	55	43 54N	20 20E
Cáceres	60	39 26N	6 23W
Cader Idris	42	52 43N	3 56W
Cadillac	104	44 16N	85 25W
Cadishead	45	53 25N	2 25W
Cádiz	60	36 30N	6 20W
Cadiz, G. of	60	36 40N	7 0W
Caen	56	49 10N	0 22W
Caerleon	43	51 37N	2 57W
Caernarfon	42	53 8N	4 17W
Caernarfon B.	42	53 4N	4 40W
Caersws	42	52 32N	3 27W
Cagayan, I.	72	9 37N	121 12E
Cágliari	58	39 15N	9 6E
Cagliari, G. of	58	39 8N	9 10E
Caguas	107	18 14N	66 4W
Caha Mts.	51	51 45N	9 40W
Caher	51	52 23N	7 56W
Caher I.	51	53 44N	10 1W
Cahersiveen	51	51 57N	10 13W
Cahore Pt.	51	52 34N	6 11W
Cahors	56	44 27N	1 27E
Caicos Is.	107	21 40N	71 40W
Cairngorm Mts.	48	57 6N	3 42W
Cairnryan	46	54 59N	5 0W
Cairns	79	16 57S	145 45E
Cairo	91	30 1N	31 14E
Caister-on-Sea	40	52 38N	1 43E
Caistor	44	53 29N	0 20W
Caithness	48	58 25N	3 25W
Calabar	90	4 57N	8 20E
Calabozo	107	9 0N	67 20W
Calábria □	58	39 24N	16 30E
Calais	56	50 57N	1 56E
Calamian Group	72	11 50N	119 55E
Calamocha	60	40 50N	1 17W
Calapan	72	13 25N	121 7E
Calatayud	60	41 20N	1 40W
Calcutta	70	22 36N	88 24E
Calder, R.	45	53 44N	1 21W
Calderbrook	45	53 39N	2 08W
Caldercruix	47	55 53N	3 53W
Caldicot	43	51 36N	2 45W
Caldwell	100	43 45N	116 42W
Caldy	45	53 21N	3 10W
Caldy I.	42	51 38N	4 42W
Caledon	94	34 14S	19 26E
Caledon, R.	94	30 0S	26 46E
Calgary	98	51 0N	114 10W
Cali	107	3 25N	76 35W
California □	100	37 25N	120 0W
California, G. of	106	27 0N	111 0W
Callan	51	52 33N	7 25W
Callander	46	56 15N	4 14W
Callao	108	12 0S	77 0W
Callington	43	50 30N	4 18W
Calne	42	51 26N	2 0W
Caltagirone	58	37 13N	14 30E
Caltanissetta	58	37 30N	14 3E
Calvinia	94	31 28S	19 45E
Cam, R.	40	52 21N	0 16E
Camagüey	107	21 20N	78 0W
Camargue	56	43 34N	4 34E
Cambay, G. of	70	20 45N	72 30E
Camberley	41	51 20N	0 44W
Camberwell	41	51 28N	0 04W
Cambodia ■	72	12 15N	105 0E
Camborne	43	50 13N	5 18W
Cambrai	56	50 11N	3 14E
Cambrian Mts.	42	52 25N	3 52W
Cambridge, N.Z.	83	37 54S	175 29E
Cambridge, U.K.	40	52 13N	0 8E
Cambridge, U.S.A.	104	42 20N	71 8W
Cambridge Gulf	78	14 45S	128 0E
Cambridgeshire □	40	52 12N	0 7E
Cambusbarron	47	56 06N	3 58W
Cambuslang	47	55 49N	4 11W
Camden, U.K.	41	51 33N	0 10W
Camden, U.S.A.	104	39 57N	75 1W
Camelford	43	50 37N	4 41W
Cameroon ■	90	3 30N	12 30E
Caminha	60	41 50N	8 50W
Camooweal	79	19 56S	138 7E
Campania □	58	40 50N	14 45E
Campbell I.	23	52 30S	169 0E
Campbellton	99	47 57N	66 43W
Campbeltown	46	55 25N	5 36W
Campeche	106	19 50N	90 32W
Campeche, G. of	106	19 30N	93 0W
Campinas	108	22 50S	47 0W
Campo Grande	108	20 25S	54 40W
Campobasso	58	41 34N	14 40E
Campsie Fells	47	56 2N	4 20W
Camrose	98	53 0N	112 50W
Canada ■	96	60 0N	100 0W
Canadian, R.	101	35 27N	95 3W
Canary Is.	88	29 30N	17 0W
Canaveral, C.	101	28 28N	80 31W
Canberra	79	35 15S	149 8E
Canfranc	60	42 42N	0 31W
Canik Mts.	71	40 30N	38 0E
Canna I.	48	57 3N	6 33W
Cannes	56	43 32N	7 0E
Canning Basin	78	19 50S	124 0E
Cannock	45	52 42N	2 2W
Cannock Chase, hills	45	52 43N	2 0W
Canon City	100	39 30N	105 20W
Canora	98	51 40N	102 30W
Canso	99	45 20N	61 0W
Cantabrian Mts.	60	43 0N	5 10W
Canterbury	40	51 17N	1 5E
Canterbury □	83	43 45S	171 19E
Canterbury Bight	83	44 16S	171 55E
Canterbury Plains	83	43 55S	171 22E
Canton	104	40 32N	90 0W
Canton I.	22	2 30S	172 0W
Canvey	41	51 32N	0 35E
Cap Haïtien	107	19 40N	72 20W
Cape Breton I.	99	46 0N	60 30W
Cape Coast	88	5 5N	1 15W
Cape Dorset	99	64 14N	76 32W
Cape Province □	94	32 0S	23 0E
Cape Town	94	33 55S	18 22E
Cape Verde Is.	22	17 10N	25 20W
Cape York Peninsula	79	33 34S	115 33E
Cappoquin	51	52 9N	7 46W
Capri, I.	58	40 34N	14 15E
Caracal	55	44 8N	24 22E
Caracas	107	10 30N	66 55W
Caransebeş	55	45 28N	22 18E
Carbonara, C.	58	39 8N	9 30E
Carcassonne	56	43 13N	2 20E
Cardamom Hills	70	9 30N	77 15E
Cárdenas	107	23 0N	81 30W
Cardenden	47	56 08N	3 15W
Cardiff	43	51 28N	3 11W
Cardigan	42	52 6N	4 41W
Cardigan B.	42	52 30N	4 30W
Cardona	60	41 56N	1 40E
Cardross	47	55 58N	4 38W
Carei	55	47 40N	22 29E
Cargelligo, L.	79	33 17S	146 24E
Caribbean Sea	107	15 0N	75 0W
Cariboo Mts.	105	53 0N	121 0W
Caribou	101	46 55N	68 0W
Caribou Mts.	98	59 12N	115 40W
Carinthia □	54	46 52N	13 30E
Caripito	107	10 8N	63 6W
Carletonville	94	26 23S	27 22E
Carlingford	50	54 3N	6 10W
Carlingford, L.	50	54 0N	6 5W
Carlisle	44	54 54N	2 55W
Carlow	51	52 50N	6 58W
Carlow □	51	52 43N	6 50W
Carloway	48	58 17N	6 48W
Carlsbad	100	32 20N	104 7W
Carlton	45	53 35N	1 27W
Carluke	47	55 44N	3 50W
Carmarthen	42	51 52N	4 20W
Carmarthen B.	42	51 40N	4 30W
Carmel Hd.	42	53 24N	4 34W
Carmel Mt.	89	32 45N	35 3E
Carmona	60	37 28N	5 42W
Carmunnock	47	55 47N	4 16W
Carmyle	47	55 50N	4 11W
Carn Eige	48	57 17N	5 9W
Carnarvon, Austral.	78	24 51S	113 42E
Carnarvon, S. Afr.	94	30 56S	22 8E
Carndonagh	50	55 15N	7 16W
Carnegie, L.	78	26 5S	122 30E
Carnforth	44	54 8N	2 47W
Carnic Alps	54	46 34N	12 50E
Carnoustie	48	56 30N	2 41W
Carnsore Pt.	51	52 10N	6 20W
Carnwath	47	55 42N	3 38W
Caroline Is.	23	8 0N	150 0E
Carpathians, Mts.	55	46 20N	26 0E
Carpentaria, G. of	79	14 0S	139 0E
Carra, L.	51	53 41N	9 12W
Carrara	58	44 5N	10 7E
Carrbridge	48	57 17N	3 50W
Carrick	46	55 12N	4 38W
Carrick-on-Shannon	50	53 57N	8 7W
Carrick-on-Suir	51	52 22N	7 30W
Carrickfergus	50	54 43N	5 50W
Carrickfergus □	50	54 43N	5 49W
Carrickmacross	50	54 0N	6 43W
Carron, R.	47	56 02N	3 44W
Carshalton	41	51 21N	0 09W
Carson City	100	39 12N	119 46W
Carson Sink	105	39 50N	118 40W
Carstairs	47	55 42N	3 41W
Cartagena, Colomb.	107	10 25N	75 33W
Cartagena, Spain	60	37 38N	0 59W
Cartago	107	4 45N	75 55W
Carterton	83	41 2S	175 31E
Carthage	101	37 10N	94 20W
Carúpano	107	10 45N	63 15W
Casablanca	88	33 36N	7 36W
Casale Monferrato	58	45 8N	8 28E
Cascade Ra.	100	45 0N	121 30W
Cascais	60	38 41N	9 25W
Caserta	58	41 5N	14 20E
Cashel	51	52 31N	7 53W
Casino	79	28 52S	153 3E
Casiquiare, R.	107	2 45N	66 20W
Caspe	60	41 14N	0 1W
Casper	100	42 52N	106 27W
Caspian Sea	62	43 0N	50 0E
Cassiar Mts.	98	59 30N	130 30W
Castellammare, G.	58	38 5N	12 55E
Castellón □	60	40 15N	0 5W
Castelnaudary	56	43 20N	1 58E
Castelo Branco	60	39 50N	7 31W
Castelvetrano	58	37 40N	12 46E
Castle Bromwich	41	52 30N	1 47W
Castle Cary	42	51 5N	2 32W
Castle Douglas	46	54 57N	3 57W
Castlebar	50	53 52N	9 17W
Castlebay	49	56 57N	7 30W
Castleblaney	50	54 7N	6 44W
Castlecomer	51	52 49N	7 13W
Castlederg	50	54 43N	7 35W
Castleford	45	53 43N	1 21W
Castleisland	51	52 14N	9 28W
Castlemaine	79	37 2S	144 12E
Castlepollard	51	53 40N	7 20W
Castlerea	50	53 46N	8 29W
Castlereagh	50	53 47N	8 30W
Castlereagh □	50	54 33N	5 33W
Castlerock	50	55 09N	6 47W
Castleton, Gwent, U.K.	42	51 33N	3 05W
Castleton, Manch., U.K.	45	53 35N	2 11W
Castletown	48	58 35N	3 22W
Castletown Bearhaven	51	51 40N	9 54W
Castres	56	43 37N	2 13E
Catalonia □	60	41 40N	1 15E
Catanduanas, Is.	72	13 50N	124 20E
Catánia	58	37 31N	15 4E
Caterham	41	51 16N	0 4W
Cathcart, S. Afr.	94	32 18S	27 10E
Cathcart, U.K.	47	55 48N	4 15W
Catoche, C.	106	21 40N	87 0W
Catorce	106	23 50N	100 55W
Catskill Mts.	104	42 15N	74 15W
Catterick	44	54 23N	1 38W
Caucasus Ra.	71	43 0N	44 0E
Caura, R.	107	6 20N	64 30W
Cavan	50	54 0N	7 22W
Cavan □	50	53 58N	7 10W
Cayenne	108	5 0N	52 18W
Cayes, Les	107	18 15N	73 46W
Ceanannus Mor	50	53 42N	6 53W
Ceará = Fortaleza	108	3 35S	38 35W
Cebú	72	10 18N	123 54E
Cedar City	100	37 41N	113 3W
Cedar Falls	101	42 39N	92 29W
Cedar L.	98	53 20N	100 10W
Cedar Rapids	101	42 0N	91 38W
Ceduna	78	32 7S	133 46E
Cefalù	58	38 3N	14 1E
Cegléd	55	47 11N	19 47E
Ceiba, La	106	15 40N	86 50W
Celaya	106	20 31N	100 37W
Celbridge	51	53 20N	6 33W
Celebes Sea	72	3 0N	123 0E
Celje	58	46 16N	15 18E
Celle	54	52 37N	10 4E
Cemmaes Road	42	52 39N	3 41W
Central □, Scotland	46	56 0N	4 30W
Central African Republic ■	89	7 0N	20 0E
Central America	96	10 0N	83 0W
Central Auckland □	83	37 30S	175 30E
Central Makran Range	71	26 30N	64 15E
Central Russian Uplands	24	54 0N	36 0E
Central Siberian Plateau	62	65 0N	105 0E
Centralia	100	46 46N	122 59W
Ceram Sea	72	2 30S	128 30E
Ceres, S. Afr.	94	33 21S	19 18E
Ceres, U.K.	47	56 18N	2 57W
Cerignola	58	41 17N	15 53E
Cerne Abbas	43	50 49N	2 29W
Cervera	60	41 40N	1 16E
Cesena	58	44 9N	12 14E
České Budějovice	54	48 55N	14 25E
Český Těšín	55	49 45N	18 39E
Cessnock	79	32 50S	151 21E
Ceuta	88	35 52N	5 18W
Cévennes, mts.	56	44 10N	3 50E
Chad ■	88	12 30N	17 15E
Chad, L.	88	13 30N	14 30E
Chadderton	45	53 27N	2 08W
Chadron	100	42 50N	103 0W
Chadwell St. Mary	41	51 28N	0 22E
Chafe	90	11 59N	6 50E
Chagos Arch.	23	6 0S	72 0E
Chake Chake	93	5 15S	39 45E
Chalatun	73	48 0N	122 40E
Chalfont St. Peter	41	51 36N	0 33W
Chalfont St. Giles	41	51 37N	0 34W
Chalon-sur-Saône	56	46 48N	4 50E
Châlons-sur-Marne	56	48 58N	4 20E
Chama, R.	100	36 57N	106 37W
Chambéry	56	45 34N	5 55E
Champagne	56	49 0N	4 40E
Chandernagore	70	22 52N	88 24E
Changchih	73	36 11N	113 6E
Changchow, Fukien, China	73	24 32N	117 44E
Changchow, Shantung, China	73	36 55N	118 3E
Changchun	73	43 58N	125 19E
Changhua	73	30 10N	119 15E
Changkiakow	73	40 52N	114 45E
Changkiang (Shihlu)	73	19 25N	108 57E
Changpai Shan	73	42 25N	129 0E
Changsha	73	28 5N	113 1E
Changteh	73	29 12N	111 43E
Channel Is.	43	49 30N	2 40W
Chanthaburi	72	12 38N	102 12E
Chantilly	56	49 12N	2 29E
Chaochow	73	23 45N	116 32E
Chaotung	73	27 19N	103 42E
Chapel-en-le-Frith	45	53 19N	1 54W
Chapelhall	47	55 50N	3 56W
Chapeltown	45	53 27N	1 28W
Charambirá, Punta	107	4 16N	77 32W
Charcas	106	23 10N	101 20W
Charchan	73	38 4N	85 16E
Charchan, R.	73	39 0N	86 0E
Charcot I.	112	70 0S	75 0W
Chard	43	50 52N	2 59W
Chardzhou	71	39 6N	63 34E
Chârib, G.	91	28 6N	32 54E
Charing	40	51 12N	0 49E
Charleroi	52	50 24N	4 27E
Charles, C.	101	37 10N	75 52W
Charleston	101	32 47N	79 56W
Charlestown	50	53 58N	8 48W
Charlestown of Aberlour	48	57 27N	3 13W
Charleville, Austral.	79	26 24S	146 15E
Charleville, Ireland	51	52 21N	8 40W
Charleville-Mézières	56	49 44N	4 40E
Charlotte	101	35 16N	80 46W
Charlotte Waters	78	25 56S	134 54E
Charlottenburg	54	52 31N	13 15E
Charlottesville	101	38 1N	78 30W
Charlottetown	99	46 14N	63 8W
Charnwood Forest	45	52 43N	1 18W
Charters Towers	79	20 5S	146 13E
Chartres	56	48 29N	1 30E
Chasetown	41	52 40N	1 55W
Châteaubriant	56	47 43N	1 23W
Châteauroux	56	46 50N	1 40E
Châtellerault	56	46 50N	0 30E
Chatham, N.B., Can.	99	47 2N	65 28W
Chatham, Ont., Can.	104	42 24N	82 11W
Chatham, U.K.	41	51 22N	0 32E
Chatham Is.	22	44 0S	176 40W

Chattanooga Cullen

Chattanooga 101 35 2N 85 17W
Chatteris 40 52 27N 0 3E
Chaumont 56 48 7N 5 8E
Chaux de Fonds, La 54 47 7N 6 50E
Cheadle 45 53 23N 2 14W
Cheadle Hulme 45 53 22N 2 12W
Cheb 54 50 9N 12 20E
Cheboygan 101 45 38N 84 29W
Cheddar 42 51 16N 2 47W
Chehalis 100 46 44N 122 59W
Cheju 73 33 28N 126 30E
Cheju Do 73 33 29N 126 34E
Chekiang □ 73 29 30N 120 0E
Chełm 55 51 8N 23 30E
Chelmer, R. 41 51 45N 0 42E
Chelmsford 41 51 44N 0 29E
Chelmża 55 53 10N 18 39E
Cheltenham 42 51 55N 2 5W
Chelyabinsk 62 55 10N 61 24E
Chengchow 73 34 47N 113 46E
Chengteh 73 41 0N 117 55E
Chengtu 73 30 45N 104 0E
Chenyüan 73 27 0N 108 20E
Chepstow 43 51 38N 2 40W
Cher, R. 56 47 10N 2 10E
Cherbourg 56 49 39N 1 40W
Cheremkhovo 62 53 32N 102 40E
Cherepovets 61 59 5N 37 55E
Chernovtsy 55 48 0N 26 0E
Cherskiy Ra. 62 65 0N 143 0E
Chertsey 41 51 23N 0 30W
Chesapeake Bay 101 38 0N 76 12W
Chesham 41 51 42N 0 36W
Cheshire □ 44 53 14N 2 30W
Cheshunt 41 51 42N 0 1W
Chesil Beach 43 50 37N 2 33W
Cheslyn Hay 41 52 41N 2 01W
Chester, U.K. 44 53 12N 2 53W
Chester, U.S.A. 101 39 54N 75 20W
Chester-le-Street 44 54 53N 1 34W
Chesterfield 44 53 14N 1 26W
Chesterfield Inlet 98 63 30N 90 45W
Chesterfield, Is. 79 19 52S 158 15E
Cheviot Hills 46 55 20N 2 30W
Chew Bahir 89 4 40N 30 50E
Cheyenne 100 41 9N 104 49W
Chiai 73 23 29N 120 25E
Chiang Mai 72 18 47N 98 59E
Chiapa, R. 106 16 42N 93 0W
Chiávari 58 44 20N 9 20E
Chiba 76 35 30N 140 7E
Chibougamau 99 49 56N 74 24W
Chibuk 90 10 52N 12 50E
Chicago 104 41 53N 87 40W
Chichagof I. 98 58 10N 136 0W
Chichester 40 50 50N 0 47W
Chichibu 76 36 5N 139 10E
Chickasha 100 35 0N 98 0W
Chiclayo 108 6 42S 79 50W
Chico 100 39 45N 121 54W
Chicoutimi 99 48 28N 71 5W
Chidley C. 99 60 23N 64 26W
Chigwell 41 51 37N 0 05E
Chihuahua 106 28 40N 106 3W
Chilapa 106 17 40N 99 20W
Childress 100 34 30N 100 15W
Chile ■ 108 35 0S 71 15W
Chillagoe 79 17 14S 144 33E
Chillicothe 101 40 55N 89 32W
Chiloé I. 108 42 50S 73 45W
Chilpancingo 106 17 30N 99 40W
Chiltern Hills 40 51 44N 0 42W
Chilumba 93 10 28S 34 12E
Chilung 73 25 3N 121 45E
Chimborazo 108 1 20S 78 55W
Chimkent 71 42 18N 69 36E
China ■ 73 30 0N 110 0E
Chinchow 73 41 10N 121 2E
Chinde 92 18 45S 36 30E
Chindwin, R. 70 21 26N 95 15E
Chinju 73 35 12N 128 2E
Chinkiang 73 32 2N 119 29E
Chins Division □ 70 22 30N 93 30E
Chinteche 93 11 50S 34 5E
Chinwangtao 73 40 0N 119 31E
Chióggia 58 45 13N 12 15E
Chipata 92 13 38S 32 28E
Chippenham 42 51 27N 2 7W
Chipping Campden 42 52 4N 1 48W
Chipping Norton 40 51 56N 1 32W
Chipping Ongar 41 51 42N 0 11E
Chipping Sodbury 43 51 31N 2 23W
Chita 62 52 0N 113 25E
Chittagong 70 22 19N 91 55E
Chiusi 58 43 1N 11 58E
Chivasso 58 45 10N 7 52E
Chobham 41 51 20N 0 36W
Choctawhatchee B. 101 30 15N 86 30W
Choiseul I. 79 7 0S 156 40E
Chojnice 55 53 42N 17 40E
Cholet 56 47 4N 0 52W
Chomutov 54 50 28N 13 23E
Chŏnju 73 35 50N 127 4E
Chonos Arch. 108 45 0S 75 0W
Chorley 45 53 39N 2 39W
Chorleywood 41 51 39N 0 29W
Chortkov 55 49 2N 25 46E
Chorzów 55 50 18N 19 0E
Choshi 76 35 45N 140 45E
Choszczno 54 53 7N 15 25E
Chott Djerid, L. 88 33 30N 8 30E
Choybalsan 73 48 4N 114 30E
Christchurch 83 43 33S 172 47E
Christiana 94 27 52S 25 8E
Christmas I., Ind. Oc. 72 10 0S 105 40E
Christmas I., Pac. Oc. 22 1 58N 157 27W
Chu 73 43 36N 73 42E
Chuanchow 73 24 57N 118 31E
Chubut, R. 108 43 0S 70 0W
Chuchou 73 27 50N 113 10E
Chudskoye, L. 61 58 13N 27 30E
Chühsien 73 35 35N 118 49E
Chuka 93 0 23S 37 38E
Chukot Ra. 62 68 0N 175 0E
Chulmleigh 43 50 55N 3 52W
Chumatien 73 33 0N 114 4E
Chumphon 72 10 35N 99 14E
Chunchŏn 73 37 58N 127 44E
Chungking 73 29 30N 106 30E
Chunya 93 8 30S 33 27E
Chur 54 46 52N 9 32E
Church Stretton 45 52 32N 2 49W
Churchill Falls 99 53 36N 64 19W
Churchill Pk. 98 58 10N 125 10W
Churchill, R. 98 53 19N 60 10W
Cienfuegos 107 22 10N 80 30W
Cieza 60 38 17N 1 23W
Cimone, Mte. 58 44 10N 10 40E
Cîmpina 55 45 10N 25 45E
Cincinnati 104 39 10N 84 26W
Cinderford 43 51 49N 2 30W
Cinto, Mt. 56 42 24N 8 54E
Cirebon 72 6 45S 108 32E
Cirencester 42 51 43N 1 59W
Ciudad del Carmen 106 18 20N 97 50W
Ciudad Guayana 107 8 22N 62 40W
Ciudad Juárez 106 31 40N 106 28W
Ciudad Madero 106 22 19N 97 50W
Ciudad Mante 106 22 50N 99 0W
Ciudad Obregón 106 27 28N 109 59W
Ciudad Real 60 38 59N 3 55W
Ciudad Rodrigo 60 40 35N 6 32W
Ciudad Victoria 106 23 41N 99 9W
Civitanova Marche 58 43 18N 13 41E
Civitavécchia 58 42 6N 11 46E
Clackmannan 47 56 10N 3 50W
Clacton-on-Sea 40 51 47N 1 10E
Clanwilliam 94 32 11S 18 52E
Claonaig 46 55 45N 5 24W
Clare □ 51 52 20N 7 38W
Clare I. 50 53 48N 10 0W
Clare, R. 51 53 20N 9 0W
Claremorris 50 53 45N 9 0W
Clarence 83 42 9S 173 56E
Clarksburg 104 39 18N 80 21W
Clarkston 47 55 47N 4 17W
Clarksville 101 36 32N 87 20W
Claunie, L. 48 57 8N 5 6W
Clay Cross 44 53 11N 1 26W
Clayton-le-Moors 45 53 46N 2 23W
Clear, C. 51 51 26N 9 30W
Clear Lake Res. 105 41 55N 121 10W
Clearwater 101 27 58N 82 45W
Cleator Moor 44 54 30N 3 32W
Cleckheaton 45 53 43N 1 43W
Clee Hills 45 52 26N 2 35W
Cleethorpes 44 53 33N 0 2W
Cleeve Cloud 42 51 56N 2 0W
Clermont 79 22 49S 147 39E
Clermont-Ferrand 56 45 46N 3 4E
Clevedon 43 51 26N 2 52W
Cleveland, U.K. 44 54 29N 1 0W
Cleveland, U.S.A. 104 41 28N 81 43W
Cleveland Hills 44 54 25N 1 11W
Cleveleys 45 53 52N 3 03W
Clew Bay 50 53 54N 9 50W
Clifden, Ireland 51 53 30N 10 2W
Clifden, N.Z. 83 46 1S 167 42E
Clifton 43 51 28N 2 38W
Clinch Mts. 101 36 30N 83 0W
Clinton, N.Z. 83 46 12S 169 23E
Clinton, Iowa, U.S.A. 101 41 50N 90 12W
Clinton, Okla., U.S.A. 100 35 30N 99 0W
Clisham, Mt. 48 57 57N 6 49W
Clitheroe 45 53 52N 2 23W
Cloghan 51 53 13N 7 53W
Clogher Hd. 50 53 48N 6 15W
Cloghran 51 53 26N 6 14W
Clonakilty 51 51 37N 8 53W
Cloncurry 79 20 40S 140 28E
Clondalkin 51 53 20N 6 25W
Clonee 51 53 25N 6 28W
Clones 50 54 10N 7 13W
Clonmel 51 52 22N 7 42W
Clonroche 51 52 27N 6 42W
Clontarf 51 53 22N 6 10W
Cloppenburg 52 52 50N 8 3E
Clovelly 43 51 0N 4 25W
Clovis 100 36 54N 119 45W
Cloyne 51 51 52N 8 7W
Cluj 55 46 47N 23 38E
Clutha, R. 83 46 20S 169 49E
Clwyd □ 42 53 5N 3 20W
Clwyd, R. 42 53 12N 3 30W
Clwydian Range 42 53 10N 3 15W
Clydach 43 51 42N 3 54W
Clyde 83 45 12S 169 20E
Clyde, Firth of 46 55 20N 5 0W
Clyde, R. 46 55 46N 4 58W
Clydebank 47 55 54N 4 25W
Coalisland 50 54 33N 6 42W
Coalville 45 52 43N 1 21W
Coast Mts. 98 52 0N 126 0W
Coast Range 100 40 0N 124 0W
Coastal Plains Basin 78 30 10S 115 30E
Coatbridge 47 55 52N 4 2W
Coats I. 99 62 30N 83 0W
Coats Land 112 77 0S 25 0W
Coatzacoalcos 106 18 7N 94 35W
Cobalt 99 47 25N 79 42W
Cobar 79 31 27S 145 48E
Cobh 51 51 50N 8 18W
Cobham 41 51 19N 0 25W
Coburg 54 50 15N 10 58E
Cochabamba 108 17 15S 66 20W
Cochin 70 9 55N 76 22E
Cochrane 99 49 0N 81 0W
Cockenzie 47 55 58N 2 59W
Cockermouth 44 54 40N 3 22W
Cocos, Is. 70 12 10S 96 50E
Cocos (Keeling) Is. 72 12 12S 96 54E
Codsall 41 52 38N 2 12W
Coen 79 13 52S 143 12E
Coeur d'Alene 100 47 45N 116 51W
Coffs Harbour 79 30 16S 153 5E
Coggeshall 40 51 53N 0 41E
Coiba I. 107 7 30N 81 40W
Coimbatore 70 11 2N 76 59E
Coimbra 60 40 15N 8 27W
Colac 79 38 21S 143 35E
Colchester 40 51 54N 0 55E
Coldstream 46 55 39N 2 14W
Coleford 42 51 46N 2 38W
Coleraine 50 55 8N 6 40E
Coleraine □ 50 55 8N 6 40E
Colesberg 94 30 45S 25 5E
Coleshill 41 52 30N 1 42W
Colima 106 19 10N 103 40W
Colinton 47 55 54N 3 15W
Colintraive 46 55 55N 5 09W
Coll, I. 48 56 40N 6 35W
Collie 78 33 22S 116 8E
Collier B. 78 16 10S 124 15E
Collingwood 83 40 25S 172 40E
Collinsville 79 20 30S 147 56E
Collon 50 53 46N 6 29W
Collooney 50 54 11N 8 28W
Colmar 56 48 5N 7 20E
Colne 45 53 51N 2 11W
Colne, R. 41 51 36N 0 30W
Cologne 52 50 56N 9 58E
Colombia ■ 107 3 45N 73 0W
Colombo 70 6 56N 79 58E
Colón 107 9 20N 80 0W
Colonsay, I. 46 56 4N 6 12W
Colorado □ 100 37 40N 106 0W
Colorado Desert 100 34 20N 116 0W
Colorado Plateau 100 36 40N 110 30W
Colorado, R. 108 37 30S 69 0W
Colorado Springs 100 38 55N 104 50W
Coltishall 40 52 44N 1 21E
Columbia, Mo., U.S.A. 101 38 58N 92 20W
Columbia, S.C., U.S.A. 101 34 0N 81 0W
Columbia, Tenn., U.S.A. 101 35 40N 87 0W
Columbia Plateau 100 47 30N 118 30W
Columbia, R. 100 46 15N 124 5W
Columbretes, Is. 60 39 50N 0 50E
Columbus, Ga., U.S.A. 101 32 30N 84 58W
Columbus, Miss., U.S.A. 101 33 30N 88 26W
Colwyn Bay 42 53 17N 3 44W
Comácchio 58 44 41N 12 10E
Comayagua 106 14 25N 87 37W
Combe Martin 42 51 12N 4 2W
Comber 50 54 33N 5 45W
Comeragh Mts. 51 52 17N 7 35W
Communism Pk. 71 38 40N 72 20E
Como 58 45 48N 9 5E
Como, L. 58 46 5N 9 17E
Comodoro Rivadavia 108 45 50S 67 40W
Comorin, C. 70 8 3N 77 40E
Comoro Is. 23 12 10S 44 15E
Compiègne 56 49 24N 2 50E
Comrie 46 56 22N 4 0W
Con Son, Is. 72 8 41N 106 37E
Conakry 88 9 29N 13 49W
Concepción 108 36 50S 73 0W
Concepción del Oro 106 24 40N 101 30W
Conception, Pt. 105 34 27N 120 28W
Conchos, R. 106 29 20N 105 0W
Concord 104 43 12N 71 30W
Concordia 100 39 35N 97 40W
Condobolin 79 33 4S 147 6E
Congleton 44 53 10N 2 12W
Congo ■ 92 1 0S 16 0E
Congo, R. = Zaïre, R. 92 1 30N 28 0E
Congresbury 42 51 20N 2 49W
Coniston 44 54 22N 3 6W
Coniston Water 44 54 20N 3 5W
Conn, L. 50 54 3N 9 15W
Connacht 50 53 23N 8 40W
Connah's Quay 45 53 13N 3 6W
Connecticut □ 101 41 40N 72 40W
Connecticut, R. 101 41 17N 72 21W
Connemara 51 53 29N 9 45W
Connersville 101 39 40N 85 10W
Consett 44 54 52N 1 50W
Constanţa 55 44 14N 28 38E
Constantia 94 34 2S 18 26E
Constantine 88 36 25N 6 42E
Conwy 42 53 17N 3 50W
Conwy, R. 42 53 18N 3 50W
Cook Is. 22 20 0S 160 0W
Cook, Mt. 83 43 36S 170 9E
Cook Strait 83 41 15S 174 29E
Cookhouse 94 32 44S 25 47E
Cookstown 50 54 40N 6 43W
Cookstown □ 50 54 40N 6 43W
Cooktown 79 15 30S 145 16E
Coolgardie 78 30 55S 121 8E
Cooma 79 36 12S 149 8E
Coonamble 79 30 56S 148 27E
Coopers Creek, R. 79 28 0S 141 0E
Cootamundra 79 34 36S 148 1E
Cootehill 50 54 5N 7 5W
Copenhagen 61 55 41N 12 34E
Copley 79 30 24S 138 26E
Coppermine 98 67 50N 115 5W
Coppull 45 53 37N 2 39W
Coquet, R. 46 55 18N 1 45W
Corabia 55 43 48N 24 30E
Coral Gables 101 25 46N 80 16W
Coral Sea 79 15 0S 150 0E
Corbeil-Essonnes 56 48 36N 2 26E
Corbridge 44 54 58N 2 0W
Corby 45 52 49N 0 31W
Córdoba, Argent. 108 31 20S 64 10W
Córdoba, Spain 60 37 50N 4 50W
Cordova 98 60 36N 145 45W
Corfe Castle 43 50 37N 2 3W
Corigliano 58 39 37N 16 32E
Cork 51 51 54N 8 30W
Cork □ 51 51 50N 8 50W
Cork Harbour 51 51 46N 8 16W
Corner Brook 99 48 57N 57 58W
Cornforth 44 54 42N 1 28W
Cornwall □ 43 50 26N 4 40W
Coromandel 83 36 45S 175 31E
Coromandel Coast 70 12 30N 81 0E
Coronation Gulf 98 68 25N 112 0W
Corozal, Belize 106 18 30N 88 30W
Corozal, Colomb. 107 9 19N 75 18W
Corpus Christi 100 27 50N 97 28W
Corran 48 56 44N 5 14W
Corrib, L. 51 53 25N 9 10W
Corrientes, C. 106 20 25N 105 42W
Corringham 41 51 30N 0 26E
Corse, C. 56 43 1N 9 25E
Corsham 42 51 25N 2 11W
Corsica, I. 56 42 0N 9 0E
Corsicana 101 32 5N 96 30W
Corté 56 42 19N 9 11E
Corumbá 108 19 0S 57 30W
Coruña, La 60 43 20N 8 25W
Corvallis 100 44 36N 123 15W
Corwen 42 52 59N 3 23W
Coseley 41 52 33N 2 6W
Cosenza 58 39 17N 16 14E
Costa Rica ■ 107 10 0N 84 0W
Côte d'Or □ 56 47 30N 4 50E
Coteau du Missouri, Plat. du 100 47 0N 101 0W
Cotonou 90 6 20N 2 25E
Cotopaxi, Vol. 108 0 30S 78 30W
Cotswold Hills 42 51 42N 2 10W
Cottbus 54 51 44N 14 20E
Council Bluffs 101 41 20N 95 50W
Coundon 44 54 40N 1 39W
Coupar Angus 48 56 33N 3 17W
Courtenay 98 49 45N 125 0W
Courtmacsherry 51 51 38N 8 43W
Courtown 51 52 39N 6 14W
Coventry 41 52 25N 1 31W
Covington 101 39 5N 84 30W
Cowal. 46 56 5N 5 8W
Cowan, L. 78 31 45S 121 45E
Cowbridge 43 51 28N 3 28W
Cowdenbeath 47 56 7N 3 20W
Cowie 47 56 04N 3 52W
Cowra 79 33 49S 148 42E
Coxhoe 44 54 43N 1 30W
Cradock 94 32 8S 25 36E
Craig-y-nos 42 51 49N 3 41W
Craigavon □ 50 54 30N 6 25W
Craigellachie 48 57 29N 3 9W
Craignure 48 56 28N 5 43W
Crail 46 56 16N 2 38W
Craiova 55 44 21N 23 48E
Cramlington 44 55 5N 1 36W
Cranbrook 40 51 6N 0 33E
Cranleigh 40 51 8N 0 29W
Crathie 48 57 3N 3 12W
Craven Arms 45 52 27N 2 49W
Crawcrook 44 54 57N 1 50W
Crawford 46 55 28N 3 40W
Crawley 40 51 7N 0 10W
Crediton 43 50 47N 3 39W
Creil 56 49 15N 2 34E
Cremona 58 45 8N 10 2E
Cres 58 44 58N 14 25E
Crete, I. 89 35 15N 25 0E
Creus, C. 60 42 20N 3 19E
Creuse, R. 56 47 0N 0 34E
Creusot, Le 56 46 48N 4 26E
Crewe 44 53 6N 2 28W
Crewkerne 43 50 53N 2 48W
Crianlarich 46 56 24N 4 37W
Criccieth 42 52 55N 4 15W
Crickhowell 42 51 52N 3 8W
Cricklade 42 51 38N 1 50W
Crieff 46 56 22N 3 50W
Criffell 44 54 56N 3 38W
Crigglestone 45 53 38N 1 32W
Crimea 62 45 0N 34 0E
Crinan 46 56 6N 5 34W
Croatia 58 45 20N 16 0E
Crofton 45 53 39N 1 25W
Cromarty 48 57 40N 4 2W
Cromarty Firth 48 57 40N 4 15W
Cromer 40 52 56N 1 18E
Cromwell 83 45 3S 169 14E
Crook 43 54 43N 1 45W
Crookhaven 51 51 28N 9 43W
Croom 51 52 32N 8 43W
Crosby 45 53 30N 3 2W
Cross Fell 44 54 44N 2 29W
Cross Hands 42 51 48N 4 04W
Crosse, La 101 43 48N 91 13W
Crosshaven 51 51 48N 8 19W
Crosskeys 43 51 37N 3 07W
Crossmaglen 50 54 5N 6 37W
Crossmolina 50 54 6N 9 21W
Crotone 58 39 5N 17 6E
Crouch, R. 40 51 37N 0 53E
Crowborough 40 51 3N 0 9E
Crowsnest Pass 98 49 40N 114 40W
Crowthorne 41 51 22N 0 45W
Croyde 42 51 7N 4 13W
Croydon, Austral. 79 18 13S 142 14E
Croydon, U.K. 41 51 18N 0 5W
Crozet, I. 23 46 27S 52 0E
Cuando, R. 92 14 0S 19 30E
Cuanza R. 92 9 2S 13 30E
Cuba ■ 107 22 0N 79 0W
Cubango, R. 92 16 15S 17 45E
Cuckfield 40 51 0N 0 8W
Cúcuta 107 7 54N 72 31W
Cudworth 45 53 35N 1 25W
Cue 78 27 25S 117 54E
Cuenca, Ecuador 108 2 50S 79 9W
Cuenca, Spain 60 40 5N 2 10W
Cuenca, Serrania de 60 39 55N 1 50W
Cuernavaca 106 18 50N 99 20W
Cuevas del Almanzora 60 37 18N 1 58W
Cuffley 41 51 43N 0 09W
Cuiabá, R. 108 16 50S 56 30W
Cuidad Bolivar 107 8 21N 70 34W
Cuillin Hills 48 57 14N 6 15W
Cuillin Sd. 48 57 4N 6 20W
Cŭlaraşi 55 44 14N 27 23E
Culcheth 45 53 28N 2 30W
Culiacán 106 24 50N 107 40W
Cullen 48 57 45N 2 50W

Cullera Eday, I

Cullera 60 39 9N 0 17W
Cullercoats 44 55 02N 1 26W
Cullompton 43 50 52N 3 23W
Culross 47 56 4N 3 38W
Culverden 83 42 47S 172 49E
Cumaná 107 10 30N 64 5W
Cumberland 104 39 40N 78 43W
Cumberland Pen. 99 67 0N 64 0W
Cumberland Plat. 101 36 0N 84 30W
Cumberland Sd. 99 65 30N 66 0W
Cumbria □ 44 54 35N 2 55W
Cumbrian Mts. 44 54 30N 3 0W
Cunene, R. 92 17 0S 15 0E
Cúneo 58 44 23N 7 31E
Cunnamulla 79 28 2S 145 38E
Cunninghame 46 55 38N 4 35W
Cupar 47 56 20N 3 0W
Curaçao, I. 107 12 10N 69 0W
Curitiba 108 25 20S 49 10W
Currie 47 55 53N 3 17W
Cushendall 50 55 5N 6 3W
Cuttack 70 20 25N 85 57E
Cuxhaven 54 53 51N 8 41E
Cuyuni, R. 107 7 0N 59 30W
Cuzco 108 13 32S 72 0W
Cwm 43 51 44N 3 11W
Cymmer 43 51 37N 3 38W
Cyprus ■ 71 35 0N 33 0E
Czechoslovakia ■ 55 49 0N 17 0E
Czeremcha 55 52 32N 23 20E
Częstochowa 55 50 49N 19 7E

D

Da Nang 72 16 4N 108 13E
Dab'a, Râs el 91 31 3N 28 31E
Dabai 90 11 25N 5 15E
Dąbie 54 53 27N 14 45E
Dacca 70 23 43N 90 26E
Dadiya 90 9 35N 11 24E
Dagenham 41 51 33N 0 10E
Dagupan 72 16 3N 120 20E
Dahlak Arch 71 15 40N 40 5E
Daingean 51 53 18N 7 15W
Dairût 91 27 34N 30 43E
Dajarra 79 21 42S 139 30E
Dakar 88 14 34N 17 29W
Dakhla Oasis 91 25 30N 28 50E
Dakingari 90 11 37N 4 1E
Dal, R. 61 60 12N 16 40E
Dalbandin 71 29 0N 64 23E
Dalbeattie 46 54 55N 3 50W
Dalby 79 27 10S 151 17E
Dalga 91 27 39N 30 41E
Dalkeith 47 55 54N 3 5W
Dalkey 51 53 16N 6 7W
Dallas, Oregon, U.S.A. 100 45 0N 123 15W
Dallas, Texas, U.S.A. 101 32 50N 96 50W
Dalmally 46 56 25N 5 0W
Dalmatia, dist. 58 43 20N 17 0E
Dalneretchensk 73 45 50N 133 40E
Dalry 47 55 44N 4 42W
Dalton 45 54 09N 3 10W
Dalwhinnie 48 56 56N 4 14W
Daly, R. 78 13 21S 130 18E
Daly Waters 78 16 15S 133 24E
Dam 71 20 30N 44 35E
Daman 70 20 25N 72 57E
Damanhûr 91 31 0N 30 30E
Damaraland 92 21 0S 17 0E
Damascus 71 33 30N 36 18E
Dâmbovița, R. 55 44 40N 26 0E
Damietta 91 31 24N 31 48E
Damme 52 52 32N 8 12E
Dampier 78 20 41S 116 42E
Dampier Downs 78 18 24S 123 5E
Dan Gulbi 90 11 40N 6 15E
Danger Pt. 94 34 40S 19 17E
Dangora 90 11 30N 8 7E
Danja 90 11 29N 7 30E
Dankama 90 13 20N 7 44E
Dannemora 61 60 12N 17 51E
Dannevirke 83 40 12S 176 8E
Danube, R. 55 45 0N 28 20W
Danville, Ill., U.S.A. 101 40 10N 87 40W
Danville, Ky., U.S.A. 101 37 40N 84 45W
Dar-es-Salaam 93 6 50S 39 12E
Darbhanga 70 26 15N 86 8E
Dardanelles 71 40 0N 26 20E
Darent, R. 41 51 22N 0 12E
Darfield 45 53 32N 1 23W
Dargaville 83 35 57S 173 52E
Darien, G. of 96 9 0N 77 0W
Darjeeling 70 27 3N 88 18E
Darlaston 41 52 35N 2 1W
Darling, R. 79 34 4S 141 54E
Darling Ra. 78 32 30S 116 0E
Darlington 44 54 33N 1 33W
Darmstadt 54 49 51N 8 40E
Darnley, C. 112 68 0S 69 0E
Dart, R. 43 50 24N 3 36W
Dartford 41 51 26N 0 15E
Dartmoor 43 50 36N 4 0W
Dartmouth, Can. 99 44 40N 63 30W
Dartmouth, U.K. 43 50 21N 3 35W
Darton 45 53 36N 1 32W
Daru 79 9 3S 143 13E
Darvel 47 55 37N 4 20W
Darwen 45 53 42N 2 29W
Darwin 78 12 25S 130 51E
Dasht-e Lūt 71 31 30N 58 0E
Dasht-i-Margo 71 30 40N 62 30E
Dasht, R. 71 25 40N 62 20E
Datchet 41 51 28N 0 34W
Datteln 52 51 39N 7 23E
Daugavpils 61 55 53N 26 32E
Dauphin 98 51 9N 100 5W
Dauphiné 56 45 15N 5 25E
Daura 90 11 31N 11 24E
Davangere 70 14 25N 75 50E
Davao 72 7 0N 125 40E
Davao, G. of 72 6 30N 125 48E
Davenport 101 41 30N 90 40W
Davis Str. 96 65 0N 58 0W
Dawlish 43 50 34N 3 28W
Dawson 98 64 10N 139 30W
Dawson Creek 98 55 45N 120 15W
Dax 56 43 43N 1 3W
Dayton, Ohio, U.S.A. 104 39 45N 84 10W
Dayton, Wash., U.S.A. 100 46 20N 118 10W
Daytona Beach 101 29 14N 81 0W
De Aar 94 30 39S 24 0E
De Grey 78 20 12S 119 12E
Dead Sea 89 31 30N 35 30E
Deakin 78 30 46S 129 58E
Deal 40 51 13N 1 25E
Dean, Forest of 42 51 50N 2 35W
Death Valley 100 36 27N 116 52W
Debre Tabor 89 11 50N 38 26E
Debrecen 55 47 33N 21 42E
Decatur, Ala., U.S.A. 101 34 35N 87 0W
Decatur, Ga., U.S.A. 101 33 47N 84 17W
Decatur, Ill., U.S.A. 101 39 50N 89 0W
Decazeville 56 44 34N 2 15E
Deccan 70 14 0N 77 0E
Dee, R., Scot., U.K. 48 57 4N 2 7W
Dee, R., Wales, U.K. 44 53 15N 3 7W
Deggendorf 54 48 49N 12 59E
Dehiwala 70 6 50N 79 51E
Dej 55 47 10N 23 52E
Del Rio 100 29 15N 100 50W
Delagoa B. 92 25 50S 32 45E
Delareyville 94 26 41S 25 26E
Delaware □ 101 39 0N 75 40W
Delaware B. 101 38 50N 75 0W
Delft 52 52 1N 4 22E
Delfzijl 52 53 20N 6 55E
Delhi 70 28 38N 77 17E
Demanda, Sierra de la 60 42 15N 3 0W
Deming 100 32 10N 107 50W
Den Helder 52 52 57N 4 45E
Denain 56 50 20N 3 22E
Denbigh 42 53 12N 3 26W
Denby Dale 45 53 35N 1 40W
Dengi 90 9 25N 9 55E
Denham 78 25 56S 113 31E
Denholme 45 53 47N 1 54W
Deniliquin 79 35 30S 144 58E
Denmark 78 34 59S 117 18E
Denmark ■ 61 55 30N 9 0E
Denmark Str. 96 66 0N 30 0W
Denny 47 56 1N 3 55W
Denpasar 72 8 45S 115 5E
Denton, U.K. 45 53 26N 2 10W
Denton, U.S.A. 101 33 12N 97 10W
Denver 100 39 45N 105 0W
Der'a 89 32 36N 36 7E
Dera Ismail Khan 71 31 50N 70 50E
Derbent 71 42 5N 48 15E
Derby 45 52 55N 1 28W
Derby □ 45 52 55N 1 28W
Derg, L., Ireland 51 53 0N 8 20W
Derg, L., Donegal, Ireland 50 54 37N 7 53W
Derna 89 32 40N 22 35E
Derry = Londonderry 50 55 0N 7 19W
Derrynsaggart Mts. 51 51 58N 9 15W
Derryveagh Mts. 50 55 0N 8 40W
Dersingham 40 52 51N 0 30E
Derwent, R., N. Yorks., U.K. 44 53 45N 0 57W
Derwent, R., Tyne & Wear, U.K. 44 54 58N 1 40W
Derwentwater, L. 44 54 34N 3 9W
Des Moines 101 41 35N 93 37W
Desborough 45 52 27N 0 50W
Deschutes, R. 105 45 30N 121 0W
Desford 41 52 38N 1 19W
Desna, R. 55 52 0N 33 15E
Dessau 54 51 49N 12 15E
Detroit 104 42 13N 83 22W
Deurne 52 51 27N 5 49E
Deventer 52 52 15N 6 10E
Deveron, R. 48 57 40N 2 31W
Devil's Bridge 42 52 23N 3 50W
Devils Lake 100 48 5N 98 50W
Devizes 42 51 21N 2 0W
Devon I. 98 75 47N 88 0W
Devon, R. 47 56 07N 3 51W
Devonport, Austral. 79 41 10S 146 22E
Devonport, N.Z. 83 36 49S 174 49E
Devonshire □ 43 50 50N 3 40W
Dewsbury 45 53 42N 1 38W
Dezfūl 71 32 20N 48 30E
Dhaulagiri Mt. 70 28 45N 83 45E
Diapaga 90 12 5N 1 46E
Dickinson 100 46 50N 102 40W
Didcot 40 51 36N 1 14W
*Diégo Suarez 92 12 25S 49 20E
Dieppe 56 49 54N 1 4E
Dieren 52 52 3N 6 6E
Differdange 52 49 81N 5 54E
Digby 99 44 38N 65 50W
Digges Is. 99 62 40N 77 50W
Dijon 56 47 20N 5 0E
Dikwa 90 12 4N 13 30E
Dila 89 6 14N 38 22E
Dili 72 8 39S 125 34E
Dillingen 52 49 22N 6 42E
Dinan 56 48 28N 2 2W
Dinaric Alps 58 44 0N 17 30E
Dinas Mawddwy 42 52 44N 3 41W
Dingle 51 52 9N 10 17W
Dingle B. 51 52 3N 10 20W
Dingwall 48 57 36N 4 26W
Dire Dawa 89 9 35N 41 45E
Dirranbandi 79 28 33S 148 17E
Disappointment, C. 100 46 20N 124 0W
Disappointment L. 78 23 20S 122 40E
Dishna 91 26 9N 32 32E
Disko 96 69 45N 53 30W
Diss 40 52 23N 1 6E
Disûq 91 31 8N 30 35E
Diu, I. 70 20 45N 70 58E

* Renamed Antsiranana

Diyarbakir 71 37 55N 40 18E
Djelfa 88 34 40N 3 15E
Djibouti 89 11 30N 43 5E
Djibouti ■ 89 11 30N 42 15E
Djougou 90 9 40N 1 45E
Dnepropetrovsk 62 48 30N 35 0E
Dnestr, R. 55 48 30N 26 30E
Dniepr, R. 62 52 29N 35 10E
Dobbyn 79 19 44S 139 59E
Dobrogea 55 44 30N 28 15E
Docking 40 52 55N 0 39E
Dodge City 100 37 42N 100 0W
Dodoma 93 6 8S 35 45E
Dodworth 45 53 32N 1 32W
Doetinchem 52 51 59N 6 18E
Dogondoutchi 90 13 38N 4 2E
Doha 71 25 15N 51 32E
Dole 56 47 7N 5 31E
Dolgellau 42 52 44N 3 53W
Dollar 47 56 9N 3 41W
Dolomites 58 46 30N 11 40E
Doma 90 8 25N 8 18E
Dominica ■ 107 15 20N 61 20W
Dominican Rep. ■ 107 19 0N 70 30W
Domodóssola 58 46 6N 8 19E
Don, R., Eng., U.K. 44 53 41N 0 51W
Don, R., Scot., U.K. 48 57 14N 2 5W
Don, R., U.S.S.R. 62 49 35N 41 40E
Donaghadee 50 54 38N 5 32W
Doncaster 44 53 31N 1 9W
Dondra Head 70 5 55N 80 40E
Donegal 50 54 39N 8 8W
Donegal □ 50 54 53N 8 0W
Donegal B. 50 54 30N 8 35W
Donetsk 62 48 0N 37 45E
Dongara 78 29 14S 114 57E
Donington 45 52 54N 0 12W
Donnelly's Crossing 83 35 42S 173 38E
Dooagh 50 53 59N 10 7W
Doon, R. 46 55 26N 4 41W
Dora Báltea, R. 58 45 11N 8 5E
Dorchester, Dorset, U.K. 43 50 42N 2 28W
Dorchester, Oxon., U.K. 40 51 38N 1 10W
Dordogne, R. 56 45 2N 0 36W
Dordon 41 52 36N 1 39W
Dordrecht 52 51 48N 4 39E
Dorking 40 51 14N 0 20W
Dornoch 48 57 52N 4 0W
Dornoch Firth 48 57 52N 4 0W
Dorridge 41 52 22N 1 45W
Dorset □ 43 50 48N 2 25W
Dortmund 52 51 32N 7 28E
Dothan 101 31 10N 85 25W
Douai 56 50 21N 3 4E
Douala 90 4 0N 9 45E
Doubtful B. 78 34 15S 119 28E
Douglas, S. Afr. 94 29 4S 23 46E
Douglas, U.K. 42 54 9N 4 29W
Douglas, U.S.A. 100 31 21N 109 30W
Doune 46 56 12N 4 3W
Dounreay 48 58 40N 3 28W
Douro Litoral □ 60 41 10N 8 20W
Douro, R. 60 41 1N 8 16W
Dove, R. 44 52 51N 1 36W
Dover, U.K. 40 51 7N 1 19E
Dover, U.S.A. 104 39 10N 75 31W
Dover, Str. of 40 51 0N 1 30E
Dovey, R. 42 52 32N 4 0W
Dovrefjell 61 62 15N 9 33E
Downham Market 40 52 36N 0 22E
Downpatrick 50 54 20N 5 43W
Drake Passage 112 58 0S 68 0W
Drakensberg 94 31 0S 25 0E
Drammen 61 59 42N 10 12E
Draperstown 50 54 48N 6 47W
Drava, R. 55 45 33N 18 55E
Drenthe □ 52 52 52N 6 40E
Dresden 54 51 2N 13 45E
Dreux 56 48 44N 1 23E
† Driffield 44 54 0N 0 25W
Drighlington 45 53 45N 1 40W
Drina, R. 55 44 53N 19 21E
Drogheda 50 53 45N 6 20W
Droichead Nua 51 53 11N 6 50W
Droitwich 42 52 16N 2 10W
Dromore, Down, U.K. 50 54 24N 6 10W
Dromore, Tyrone, U.K. 50 54 31N 7 28W
Dronfield 45 53 18N 1 29W
Dronne, R. 56 45 2N 0 12W
Drumcondra 51 53 50N 6 40W
Drumheller 98 51 25N 112 40W
Drummond Ra. 79 23 45S 147 10E
Drummondville 104 45 55N 72 25W
Drummore 46 54 41N 4 53W
Drumshanbo 50 54 2N 8 4W
Drybrook 43 51 51N 2 30W
Drygalski I. 112 66 0S 92 0E
Dschang 90 5 32N 10 3E
Dubawnt, R. 98 64 33N 100 6W
Dubbo 79 32 11S 148 35E
Dublin 51 53 20N 6 18W
Dublin □ 51 53 24N 6 20W
Dublin, B. 51 53 24N 6 20W
Dubrovnik 58 42 39N 18 6E
Duchess 79 21 20S 139 50E
Ducie I. 22 24 47S 124 40W
Duddon, R. 44 54 12N 3 15W
Dudley 41 52 30N 2 5W
Duero, R. 60 41 37N 4 25W
Duffel 52 51 6N 4 30E
Dugi Otok 58 44 0N 15 0E
Duisburg 52 51 27N 6 42E
Duiwelskloof 94 23 42S 30 10E
Dukana 93 3 59N 37 20E
Dukinfield 45 53 29N 2 05W
Duku 90 11 11N 4 55E
Dülmen 52 51 49N 7 18E
Duluth 101 46 48N 92 10W
Dulverton 43 51 2N 3 33W
Dumbarton 47 55 58N 4 35W
Dumfries 46 55 4N 3 37W
Dumfries & Galloway □ 46 55 0N 4 0W

† Renamed Great Driffield

Dun Laoghaire 51 53 17N 6 9W
Dunback 83 45 23S 170 36E
Dunbar 46 56 0N 2 32W
Dunbeath 48 58 15N 3 25W
Dunblane 47 56 10N 3 58W
Dunboyne 51 53 25N 6 30W
Duncan 100 34 25N 98 0W
Duncansby 48 58 37N 3 3W
Dundalk 50 54 1N 6 45W
Dundalk B. 50 53 55N 6 15W
Dundas 99 43 17N 79 59W
Dundas, L. 78 32 35S 121 50E
Dundee, S. Afr. 94 28 11S 30 15E
Dundee, U.K. 47 56 29N 3 0W
Dundrum, Ireland 51 53 17N 6 15W
Dundrum, U.K. 50 54 17N 5 50W
Dunedin 83 45 50S 170 33E
Dunfermline 47 56 5N 3 28W
Dungannon 50 54 30N 6 47W
Dungannon □ 50 54 30N 6 55W
Dungarvan 51 52 6N 7 40W
Dungbure Shan 73 35 0N 90 0E
Dungeness 40 50 54N 0 59E
Dungiven 50 54 55N 6 56W
Dunglow 50 54 57N 8 20W
Dunipace 47 56 01N 3 55W
Dunkeld 48 56 34N 3 36W
Dunkery Beacon 42 51 15N 3 37W
Dunleary = Dun Laoghaire 51 53 17N 6 8W
Dunleer 50 53 50N 6 23W
Dunlop 47 55 43N 4 32W
Dunmanus B. 51 51 31N 9 50W
Dunmanway 51 51 43N 9 8W
Dunnet Hd. 48 58 38N 3 22W
Dunoon 47 55 57N 4 56W
Duns 46 55 47N 2 20W
Dunshaughlin 51 53 31N 6 32W
Dunstable 40 51 53N 0 31W
Dunstan Mts. 83 44 53S 169 35E
Dunster 42 51 11N 3 28W
Dunvegan 48 57 26N 6 35W
Durack Ra. 78 16 50S 127 40E
Durance, R. 56 43 55N 4 45E
Durango, Mexico 106 24 3N 104 39W
Durango, Spain 60 43 13N 2 40W
Durango, U.S.A. 100 37 10N 107 50W
Durban 94 29 49S 31 1E
Düren 52 50 48N 6 30E
Durham, U.K. 44 54 47N 1 34W
Durham, U.S.A. 101 36 0N 78 55W
Durham □ 43 54 42N 1 45W
Durrow, Ireland 51 52 51N 7 23W
Durrow, Offaly, Ireland 51 53 20N 7 31W
Dursey I. 51 51 36N 10 12W
Dursley 43 51 41N 2 21W
D'Urville Island 83 40 50S 173 55E
Dushanbe 71 38 33N 68 48E
Düsseldorf 52 51 15N 6 46E
Dvina, N., R. 62 61 40N 45 30E
Dyce 48 57 12N 2 11W
Dyfed □ 42 52 0N 4 30W
Dymchurch 40 51 2N 1 0E
Dysart 47 56 8N 3 8W
Dzamin Und 73 44 0N 111 0E
Dzhalal-Abad 71 40 56N 73 0E
Dzhambul 71 42 54N 71 22E
Dzhungarskiye Vorota 73 45 0N 82 0E
Dzungaria 73 44 10N 88 0E
Dzuunmod 73 47 45N 106 58E

E

Eagle Pass 100 28 45N 100 35W
Eaglescliffe 44 54 32N 1 21W
Eagleshan 47 55 44N 4 18W
Ealing 41 51 30N 0 19W
Earby 45 53 55N 2 8W
Earl Shilton 41 52 35N 1 20W
Earn, L. 46 56 23N 4 14W
Earn, R. 46 56 20N 3 19W
Earnslaw, Mt. 83 44 32S 168 27E
Easington 44 54 50N 1 24W
Easington Lane 44 54 47N 1 21W
Easingwold 44 54 8N 1 11W
East Beskids, mts. 55 49 30N 18 45E
East C. 83 37 42S 178 35E
East China Sea 73 30 5N 126 0E
East Dereham 40 52 40N 0 57E
East Grinstead 40 51 8N 0 1W
East Horsley 41 51 15N 0 26W
East Keswick 45 53 54N 1 26W
East Linton 46 56 0N 2 40W
East London 94 33 0S 27 55E
East Point 101 33 40N 84 28W
East Retford 44 53 19N 0 55W
East Schelde, R. 52 51 38N 3 40E
E. Siberian Sea 62 73 0N 160 0E
East Sussex □ 40 51 0N 0 20E
East Wemyss 47 56 8N 3 5W
East Wittering 40 50 46N 0 53W
Eastbourne, N.Z. 83 41 19S 174 55E
Eastbourne, U.K. 40 50 46N 0 18E
Eastern Ghats 70 15 0N 80 0E
Eastmain, R. 99 52 27N 72 26W
Eau Claire 101 44 46N 91 30W
Ebbw Vale 43 51 47N 3 12W
Eboli 58 40 39N 15 2E
Ebro, R. 60 41 49N 1 5W
Ecclefechan 46 55 3N 3 18W
Eccles 45 53 29N 2 20W
Ecclesfield 45 53 26N 1 28W
Eccleshall 45 52 52N 2 14W
Eccleston 45 53 38N 2 43W
Echo Bay 98 66 10N 117 40W
Echuca 79 36 3S 144 46E
Ecija 60 37 30N 5 10W
Eckington 45 53 19N 1 21W
Ecuador ■ 108 2 0S 78 0W
Ed Dâmer 89 17 27N 34 0E
Eday, I. 49 59 11N 2 47W

Eddrachillis B **Fremont**

Eddrachillis B.	**48**	58 16N	5 10W
Ede, Neth.	**52**	52 4N	5 40E
Ede, Nigeria	**90**	7 45N	4 29E
Eden, R.	**44**	54 57N	3 2W
Edenbridge	**40**	51 12N	0 4E
Edenburg	**94**	29 43S	25 58E
Edenderry	**51**	53 21N	7 3W
Edgerston Tofts	**46**	55 24N	2 29W
Edgworth	**45**	53 38N	2 23W
Edievale	**83**	45 49S	169 22E
Edinburgh	**47**	55 57N	3 12W
Edmonton	**98**	53 30N	113 30W
Edmundston	**99**	47 23N	68 20W
Edward, L. = Idi Amin Dada, L.	**93**	0 25S	29 40E
Edwards Plat.	**100**	30 30N	101 5W
Eekloo	**52**	51 11N	3 33E
Eersterus	**94**	25 44S	28 21E
Egadi Is.	**58**	37 55N	12 10E
Egersund, Norway	**61**	58 26N	6 1E
Egerton, Mt.	**78**	24 42S	117 44E
Egglescliffe	**44**	54 31N	1 21W
Egham	**41**	51 25N	0 33W
Egmont, C.	**83**	39 16S	173 45E
Egmont, Mt.	**83**	39 17S	174 5E
Egremont	**44**	54 28N	3 33W
Egume	**90**	7 30N	7 14E
Egypt ■	**91**	28 0N	31 0E
Eha Amufu	**90**	6 30N	7 40E
Eifel	**52**	50 10N	6 45E
Eigg, I.	**48**	56 54N	6 10W
Eil	**89**	8 0N	49 50E
Eindhoven	**52**	51 26N	5 30E
Eitorf	**52**	50 46N	7 28E
Eket	**90**	4 38N	7 56W
Eketahuna	**83**	40 38S	175 43E
El 'Aiyat	**91**	29 36N	31 15E
El Alamein	**91**	30 48N	28 58E
El 'Arîsh	**91**	31 8N	33 50E
El Badâri	**91**	27 4N	31 25E
El Ballâs	**91**	26 2N	32 43E
El Balyana	**91**	26 10N	32 3E
El Bawiti	**91**	28 25N	28 45E
El Blanco	**107**	10 28N	74 52W
El Callao	**107**	7 25N	61 50W
El Centro	**100**	32 50N	115 40W
El Dab'a	**91**	31 0N	28 27E
El Djouf	**88**	20 0N	11 30E
El Dorado, Ark., U.S.A.	**101**	33 10N	92 40W
El Dorado, Kans., U.S.A.	**101**	37 55N	96 56W
El Escorial	**60**	40 35N	4 7W
El Faiyûm	**91**	29 19N	30 50E
El Fâsher	**89**	13 33N	25 26E
El Fashn	**91**	28 50N	30 54E
El Fuerte	**106**	26 30N	108 40W
El Gedida	**91**	25 40N	28 30E
El Geneina	**89**	13 27N	22 45E
El Gîza	**91**	30 0N	31 10E
El Hammam	**91**	30 52N	29 25E
El Iskandarîya = Alexandria	**91**	31 0N	30 0E
El Khârga	**91**	25 30N	30 33E
El Kuntilla	**91**	30 1N	34 45E
El Mahalla el Kubra	**91**	31 0N	31 0E
El Mahârîq	**91**	25 35N	30 35E
El Mansûra	**91**	31 0N	31 19E
El Manzala	**91**	31 10N	31 50E
El Matariya	**91**	31 15N	32 0E
El Minyâ	**91**	28 7N	30 33E
El Obeid	**89**	13 8N	30 10E
El Paso	**100**	31 50N	106 30W
El Qâhira = Cairo	**91**	30 1N	31 14E
El Qantara	**91**	30 51N	32 20E
El Qasr	**91**	25 44N	28 42E
El Quseima	**91**	30 40N	34 15E
El Qusîya	**91**	27 29N	30 44E
El Râshda	**91**	25 36N	28 57E
El Real	**107**	8 0N	77 40W
El Reis	**91**	27 50N	28 40E
El Reno	**100**	35 30N	98 0W
El Saff	**91**	29 34N	31 16E
El Thamad	**91**	29 40N	34 28E
El Tigre	**107**	8 55N	64 15W
El Wak	**93**	2 49N	40 56E
El Waqf	**91**	25 45N	32 15E
El Wâsta	**91**	29 19N	31 12E
Elat	**91**	29 30N	34 56E
Elâziğ	**71**	38 37N	39 22E
Elba.	**58**	42 48N	10 15E
Elbe, R.	**54**	53 50N	9 0E
Elbert, Mt.	**100**	39 12N	106 36W
Elbeuf	**56**	49 17N	1 2E
Elblag	**55**	54 10N	19 25E
Elbrus, Mt.	**62**	43 30N	42 30E
Elburz Mts.	**71**	36 0N	52 0E
Elche	**60**	38 15N	0 42W
Eldoret	**93**	0 30N	35 25E
Electra	**100**	34 0N	99 0W
Elephant I.	**112**	61 0S	55 0W
Eleuthera I.	**107**	25 0N	76 20W
Elgin, U.K.	**48**	57 39N	3 20W
Elgin, U.S.A.	**101**	42 0N	88 20W
Elgol	**48**	57 9N	6 6W
Elgon, Mt.	**93**	1 10N	34 30E
Elizabeth, Austral.	**79**	34 42S	138 41E
Elizabeth, U.S.A.	**104**	40 37N	74 12W
Elkhart	**101**	41 42N	85 55W
Elkins	**101**	38 53N	79 53W
Elko	**100**	40 50N	115 50W
Elland	**45**	53 41N	1 49W
Ellensburg	**100**	47 0N	120 30W
Ellesmere	**45**	52 55N	2 53W
Ellesmere I.	**99**	79 30N	80 0W
Ellesmere Port	**45**	53 17N	2 55W
Ellesworth Land	**22**	74 0S	85 0W
Ellon	**48**	57 21N	2 5W
Ellsworth Land	**112**	76 0S	89 0W
Elmenteita	**93**	0 32S	36 14E
Elmina	**88**	5 5N	1 21W
Elmira	**104**	42 8N	76 49W
Eltham	**83**	39 26S	174 19E

Eluru	**70**	16 48N	81 8E
Elvas	**60**	38 50N	7 17W
Ely, Cambs., U.K.	**40**	52 24N	0 16E
Ely, S. Glam., U.K.	**43**	51 28N	3 12W
Ely, U.S.A.	**100**	39 10N	114 50W
Elyria	**101**	41 22N	82 8W
Embu	**93**	0 32S	37 38E
Emden	**52**	53 22N	7 12E
Emerald	**79**	23 32S	148 10E
Emilia-Romagna □	**58**	44 33N	10 40E
Emmen	**52**	52 48N	6 57E
Emmerich	**52**	51 50N	6 12E
Empangeni	**94**	28 50S	31 52E
Ems, R.	**52**	53 25N	7 0E
Emsdetten	**52**	52 11N	7 31E
Enard B.	**48**	58 5N	5 20W
Endeavour Str.	**79**	10 45S	142 0E
Enderby	**41**	52 35N	1 15W
Enderby Land	**112**	66 0S	53 0E
Endicott Mts.	**98**	68 0N	152 30W
Enfield	**41**	51 39N	0 4W
Enggano, I.	**72**	5 20S	102 40E
England □	**44**	53 0N	2 0W
Englefield Green	**41**	51 26N	1 06W
English Channel	**24**	50 0N	2 0W
Enid	**100**	36 26N	97 52W
Enid, Mt.	**78**	21 43S	116 25E
Enna	**58**	37 34N	14 15E
Ennell, L.	**51**	53 29N	7 25W
Ennis	**51**	52 51N	8 59W
Enniscorthy	**51**	52 30N	6 35W
Enniskillen	**50**	54 20N	7 40W
Ennistimon	**51**	52 56N	9 18W
Enschede	**52**	52 13N	6 53E
Ensenada	**106**	31 50N	116 50W
Entebbe	**93**	0 4N	32 28E
Entre Rios □	**108**	30 30S	58 30W
Entrecasteaux, Pt. d'	**79**	34 50S	115 56E
Enugu	**90**	6 30N	7 30E
Enugu Ezike	**90**	7 0N	7 29E
Epe	**90**	6 36N	3 59E
Épernay	**56**	49 3N	3 56E
Épinal	**56**	48 19N	6 27E
Epping	**41**	51 42N	0 8E
Eppynt, Mynydd	**42**	52 07N	3 30W
Epsom	**41**	51 19N	0 16W
Epworth	**44**	53 30N	0 50W
Equatorial Guinea ■	**88**	2 0S	8 0E
Erebus, Mt.	**112**	77 35S	167 0E
Ereğli	**71**	41 15N	31 30E
Erfurt	**54**	50 58N	11 2E
Erg Chech, dist.	**88**	50 59N	11 0E
Eriboll, L.	**48**	58 28N	4 41W
Ericht, L.	**48**	56 50N	4 25W
Erie	**104**	42 10N	80 7W
Erie, L.	**104**	42 15N	81 0W
Eriskay, I.	**49**	57 4N	7 18W
Eritrea □	**89**	14 0N	41 0E
Ermelo	**94**	26 31S	29 59E
Erne, Lough	**50**	54 26N	7 46W
Errigal, Mt.	**50**	55 2N	8 8W
Errol	**47**	56 24N	3 13W
Erz Gebirge, mts.	**54**	50 25N	13 0E
Erzincan	**71**	39 46N	39 30E
Erzurum	**71**	39 57N	41 15E
Esbjerg	**61**	55 29N	8 29E
Esch	**52**	51 37N	5 17E
Eschweiler	**52**	50 49N	6 14E
Escravos, R.	**90**	5 30N	5 10E
Escuinapa	**106**	22 50N	105 50W
Esfahān □	**71**	33 0N	53 0E
Esh Winning	**44**	54 47N	1 42W
Esher	**41**	51 21N	0 22W
Eshowe	**94**	28 50S	31 30E
Esk, R., Dumfries, U.K.	**48**	54 58N	3 4W
Esk, R., N. Yorks., U.K.	**44**	54 27N	0 36W
Eskbank	**47**	55 52N	3 04W
Eskilstuna	**61**	59 22N	16 32E
Eskişehir	**71**	39 50N	30 35E
Esperance	**78**	33 45S	121 55E
Essen	**52**	51 28N	6 59E
Essequibo, R.	**107**	5 45N	58 50W
Essex □	**40**	51 48N	0 30E
Estcourt	**94**	28 58S	29 53E
Eston	**44**	54 33N	1 6W
Estonian S.S.R. □	**61**	48 30N	25 30E
Estrêla, Serra da	**60**	40 10N	7 45W
Estremadura	**60**	39 0N	9 0W
Étampes	**56**	48 26N	2 10E
Eteh	**90**	7 2N	7 28E
Ethiopia ■	**89**	8 0N	40 0E
Ethiopian Highlands	**89**	10 0N	37 0E
Etive, L.	**48**	56 30N	5 12W
Etna, Mt.	**58**	37 45N	15 0E
Etoshapan	**92**	18 40S	16 30E
Ettrick	**46**	55 31N	2 55W
Euclid	**101**	41 32N	81 31W
Eugene	**105**	44 0N	123 8W
Eupen	**52**	50 37N	6 3E
Euphrates, R.	**71**	31 0N	47 25E
Eureka	**105**	40 50N	124 0W
Europa Pt.	**60**	36 2N	6 32W
Europe	**24**	20 0N	20 0E
Euskirchen	**52**	50 40N	6 45E
Euxton	**45**	53 41N	2 42W
Evanston	**104**	42 0N	87 40W
Evansville	**101**	38 0N	87 35W
Evanton	**48**	57 40N	4 20W
Everard Ras.	**78**	27 5S	132 28E
Everest, Mt.	**70**	28 5N	86 58E
Everett	**105**	48 0N	122 10W
Everglades	**101**	26 0N	80 30W
Évora	**60**	38 33N	7 57W
Évreux	**56**	49 0N	1 8E
Ewe, L.	**48**	57 49N	5 38W
Ewell	**41**	51 20N	0 15W
Exe, R.	**43**	50 38N	3 27W
Exeter	**43**	50 43N	3 31W
Exmoor	**42**	51 10N	3 59W
Exmouth, Austral.	**78**	22 6S	114 0E
Exmouth, U.K.	**43**	50 37N	3 26W
Exmouth G.	**78**	22 15S	114 15E
Expedition Range	**79**	24 30S	149 12E

Eyam	**45**	53 17N	1 40W
Eye, Camb., U.K.	**40**	52 36N	0 11W
Eye, Suff., U.K.	**40**	52 19N	1 09E
Eye Pen.	**48**	58 13N	6 10W
Eyemouth	**46**	55 53N	2 5W
Eyre	**78**	32 15S	126 18E
Eyre, L.	**79**	29 30S	137 26E
Eyre Mts.	**83**	45 25S	168 25E
Eyre Pen.	**79**	33 30S	137 17E

F

Fabriano	**58**	43 20N	12 52E
Faenza	**58**	44 17N	11 53E
Fagam	**90**	11 1N	10 1E
Fahūd	**71**	22 18N	56 28E
Failsworth	**45**	53 31N	2 08W
Fairbanks	**98**	64 59N	147 40W
Fairlie, N.Z.	**83**	44 5S	170 49E
Fairlie, U.K.	**47**	55 44N	4 52W
Fairmont	**101**	39 29N	80 10W
Faizabad, Afghan.	**71**	37 7N	70 33E
Faizabad, India	**70**	26 45N	82 10E
Fakenham	**40**	52 50N	0 51E
Falkirk	**47**	56 0N	3 47W
Falkland	**47**	56 15N	3 13W
Falkland Is.	**108**	51 30S	59 0W
Falkland Is. Dep.	**112**	57 0S	40 0W
Fall River	**104**	41 45N	71 5W
Falmouth	**43**	50 9N	5 5W
False B.	**94**	34 15S	18 40E
Falun	**61**	60 37N	15 37E
Fannich, L.	**48**	57 40N	5 0W
Fanning I.	**22**	3 51N	159 22W
Fano	**58**	43 50N	13 0E
Farâfra Oasis	**91**	27 15N	28 20E
Farah	**71**	32 20N	62 7E
Faraid, Gebel	**91**	23 33N	35 19E
Farasan Is.	**71**	16 45N	41 55E
Fareham	**40**	50 52N	1 11W
Farewell, C., Greenl.	**96**	59 48N	43 55W
Farewell, C., N.Z.	**83**	40 29S	172 43E
Fargo	**101**	47 0N	97 0W
Faribault	**101**	44 15N	93 19W
Faringdon	**40**	51 39N	1 34W
Farmington	**100**	36 45N	108 28W
Farnborough	**41**	51 17N	0 46W
Farnham	**40**	51 13N	0 49W
Farnworth	**45**	53 33N	2 24W
Faro	**60**	37 2N	7 55W
Faroe Is.	**22**	62 0N	7 0W
Fasā	**71**	29 0N	53 32E
Fastov	**55**	50 7N	29 57E
Fatshan	**73**	23 0N	113 4E
Fauldhouse	**47**	55 50N	3 44W
Faversham	**40**	51 18N	0 54E
Fawley	**40**	50 49N	1 20W
Fayetteville	**101**	36 0N	94 5W
Fazeley	**41**	52 36N	1 42W
Featherston	**83**	41 6S	175 20E
Featherstone	**45**	53 42N	1 22W
Fehmarn	**54**	54 26N	11 10E
Fehmarn Belt	**54**	54 35N	11 20E
Feilding	**83**	40 13S	175 35E
Feldkirch	**54**	47 15N	9 37E
Felixstowe	**40**	51 58N	1 22E
Felling	**44**	54 57N	1 33W
Feltham	**41**	51 27N	0 25W
*Fénérive	**92**	17 22S	49 25E
Fengkieh (Kweichow)	**73**	31 0N	109 33E
Fens, The	**40**	52 45N	0 2E
Fenyang	**73**	37 19N	111 46E
Feolin Ferry	**46**	55 50N	6 05W
Ferbane	**51**	53 17N	7 50W
Fergana	**71**	40 23N	71 46E
Fergus, R.	**51**	52 45N	9 0W
Fermanagh □	**50**	54 21N	7 40W
Fermoy	**51**	52 4N	8 18W
Fernando de Noronha, I.	**108**	4 0S	33 10W
Ferndale	**43**	51 40N	3 27W
Ferns	**51**	52 35N	6 30W
Ferozepore	**71**	30 55N	74 40E
Ferrara	**58**	44 50N	11 36E
Ferret, C.	**56**	44 38N	1 15W
Ferrol	**60**	43 29N	8 15W
Ferrybridge	**45**	53 42N	1 16W
Ferryhill	**44**	54 42N	1 32W
Fès	**88**	34 0N	5 0W
Fethard	**51**	52 29N	7 42W
Fetlar, I.	**49**	60 36N	0 52W
Fettercairn	**48**	56 50N	2 33W
Ffestiniog	**42**	52 58N	3 56W
Fianarantsoa	**92**	21 20S	46 45E
Fichtelgebirge	**54**	50 10N	12 0E
Fiditi	**90**	7 45N	3 53E
Fife □	**46**	56 13N	3 2W
Fife Ness	**46**	56 17N	2 35W
Figueras	**60**	42 18N	2 58E
Fiji ■	**23**	17 20S	179 0E
Filey	**44**	54 13N	0 18W
Findhorn	**48**	57 39N	3 36W
Findhorn, R.	**48**	57 38N	3 38W
Finglas	**51**	53 22N	6 18W
Finisterre, C.	**60**	42 50N	9 19W
Finland ■	**61**	64 0N	27 0E
Finland, G. of	**61**	60 0N	26 0E
Finlay, R.	**98**	56 50N	125 10W
Fintona	**50**	54 30N	7 20W
Fionnphort	**46**	56 19N	6 23W
Fishguard	**42**	51 59N	4 59W
Fitzroy Crossing	**78**	18 9S	125 38E
Fitzroy, R.	**78**	17 25S	124 0E
Flagstaff	**100**	35 10N	111 40W
Flamborough Hd.	**44**	54 8N	0 4W
Flanders	**56**	51 10N	3 15E
Flandre Occidental □	**52**	51 0N	3 0E
Flandre Orientale □	**52**	51 0N	4 0E
Flattery, C.	**100**	48 21N	124 43W
Flèche, La	**56**	47 42N	0 4W
Fleet	**41**	51 16N	0 50W
Fleetwood	**45**	53 55N	3 00W

* *Renamed Fenoarivo*

Flensburg	**54**	54 46N	9 28E
Flers	**56**	48 47N	0 33W
Flin Flon	**98**	54 46N	101 53W
Flinders B.	**78**	34 19S	115 9E
Flinders I.	**79**	40 0S	148 0E
Flinders, R.	**79**	17 36S	140 36E
Flinders Ranges	**79**	31 30S	138 30E
Flint	**104**	43 5N	83 40W
Flint □	**45**	53 15N	3 12W
Florence, Italy	**58**	43 47N	11 15E
Florence, Ala., U.S.A.	**101**	34 50N	87 50W
Florence, S.C., U.S.A.	**101**	34 5N	79 50W
Flores, I.	**72**	8 35S	121 0E
Flores Sea	**72**	6 30S	124 0E
Florida □	**101**	28 30N	82 0W
Florida B.	**101**	25 0N	81 20W
Florida, Strait of	**107**	25 0N	80 0W
Flushing = Vlissingen	**52**	51 26N	3 34E
Fochabers	**48**	57 37N	3 7W
Focşani	**55**	45 41N	27 15E
Fóggia	**58**	41 28N	15 31E
Foggo	**90**	11 21N	9 57E
Foligno	**58**	42 58N	12 40E
Folkestone	**40**	51 5N	1 11E
Fond du lac	**101**	43 46N	88 26W
Fonesca, G. of	**106**	13 10N	87 40W
Fontainebleau	**56**	48 24N	2 40E
Fontem	**90**	5 32N	9 52E
Foochow (Minhow)	**73**	26 2N	119 25E
Forbach	**56**	49 10N	6 52E
Forbes	**79**	33 22S	148 0E
Forcados	**90**	5 26N	5 26E
Fordingbridge	**40**	50 56N	1 48W
Forfar	**48**	56 40N	2 53W
Forli	**58**	44 14N	12 2E
Formartine, dist.	**48**	57 20N	2 15W
Formby	**45**	53 33N	3 03W
Formentera, I.	**60**	38 40N	1 30E
Formosa = Taiwan ■	**73**	24 0N	121 0E
Forres	**48**	57 37N	3 38W
Forrest	**78**	30 51S	128 6E
Forsayth	**79**	18 33S	143 34E
Forst	**54**	51 43N	14 37E
Fort Albany	**99**	52 15N	81 35W
Fort Augustus	**48**	57 9N	4 40W
Fort Beaufort	**94**	32 46S	26 40E
Fort Bragg	**105**	39 28N	123 50W
Fort Chimo	**99**	58 6N	68 25W
Fort Collins	**100**	40 30N	105 4W
*Fort-Dauphin	**92**	25 2S	47 0E
Fort-de-France	**107**	14 36N	61 2W
Fort Dodge	**101**	42 29N	94 10W
Fort George	**99**	53 50N	79 0W
Fort Good-Hope	**98**	66 14N	128 40W
Fort Gouraud	**88**	22 40N	12 45W
Fort Lauderdale	**101**	26 10N	80 5W
Fort Liard	**98**	60 20N	123 30W
Fort McMurray	**98**	56 44N	111 23W
Fort McPherson	**98**	67 30N	134 55W
Fort Morgan	**100**	40 10N	103 50W
Fort Myers	**101**	26 30N	81 50W
Fort Norman	**98**	64 57N	125 30W
Fort Portal	**93**	0 40N	30 20E
Fort Providence	**98**	61 21N	117 40W
Fort Resolution	**98**	61 10N	113 40W
Fort Rupert	**99**	51 30N	78 40W
Fort Shevchenko	**71**	44 30N	50 10E
Fort Simpson	**98**	61 45N	121 23W
Fort Smith	**101**	35 25N	94 25W
Fort Trinquet	**88**	25 10N	11 25W
Fort Vermilion	**96**	58 24N	116 0W
†Fort Victoria	**92**	20 8S	30 55E
Fort Wayne	**104**	41 5N	85 10W
Fort William	**48**	56 48N	5 8W
Fort Worth	**100**	32 45N	97 25W
Fortaleza	**108**	3 35S	38 35W
Forth	**47**	55 45N	3 41W
Forth, Firth of	**47**	56 5N	2 55W
Fortrose	**48**	57 35N	4 10W
Fougères	**56**	48 21N	1 14W
Foulness I.	**40**	51 36N	0 55E
Foulridge	**45**	53 52N	2 10W
Foumban	**90**	5 45N	10 50E
Fouta Djalon	**88**	11 20N	12 10W
Foveaux Str.	**83**	46 42S	168 10E
Fowey	**43**	50 20N	4 39W
Foxe Basin	**99**	68 30N	77 0W
Foxe Channel	**99**	66 0N	80 0W
Foxford	**50**	54 0N	9 7W
Foxton	**83**	40 29S	175 18E
Foyers	**48**	57 15N	4 30W
Foyle, Lough	**50**	55 6N	7 8W
Foynes	**51**	52 30N	9 5W
Frampton on Severn	**43**	51 46N	2 22W
Framwellgate Moor	**44**	54 47N	1 34W
Francavilla Fontana	**58**	40 32N	17 35E
France ■	**56**	47 0N	3 0E
Franceville	**92**	1 40S	13 32E
Franche Comté	**56**	46 30N	5 50E
François L.	**105**	54 0N	125 30W
Franeker	**52**	53 12N	5 33E
Frankford	**51**	53 10N	7 43W
Frankfort	**94**	27 17S	28 29E
Frankfurt □	**54**	52 30N	14 0E
Frankfurt am Main	**54**	50 7N	8 40E
Franklin □	**98**	71 0N	99 0W
Franklin Mts.	**98**	65 0N	125 0W
Franz	**99**	48 25N	84 30W
Franz Josef Land	**112**	81 0N	60 0E
Fraser I.	**79**	25 15S	153 10E
Fraser, R.	**105**	49 7N	123 11W
Fraserburg	**94**	31 55S	21 30E
Fraserburgh	**48**	57 41N	2 0W
Freckleton	**45**	53 45N	2 52W
Fredericksburg	**101**	38 16N	77 29W
Fredericton	**99**	45 57N	66 40W
Frederikshåb	**96**	62 0N	49 30W
Fredrikstad	**61**	59 13N	10 57E
Freeport	**107**	25 45N	88 30E
Freetown	**88**	8 30N	13 10W
Freiberg	**54**	50 55N	13 20E
Fremantle	**78**	32 1S	115 47E
Fremont	**101**	41 30N	96 30W

* *Renamed Faradofay*

† *Renamed Nyanda*

French Guiana ■ Gujarat □

French Guiana ■ **108** 4 0N 53 0W
Frenchpark **50** 53 53N 8 25W
Fresnillo **106** 23 10N 103 0W
Fresno **105** 36 47N 119 50W
Freuchie **47** 56 14N 3 8W
Fribourg **54** 46 49N 7 9E
Friedrichshafen **54** 47 39N 9 29E
Friendly, Is. = Tonga **22** 19 50S 174 30W
Friesland □ **52** 53 5N 5 50E
Frimley **41** 51 18N 0 43W
Frinton-on-Sea **40** 51 50N 1 16E
Frio, C., Brazil **108** 22 50S 41 50W
Frio, C., Namibia **92** 18 0S 12 0E
Frisian Is. **54** 53 30N 6 0E
Friuli-Venezia Giulia □ **58** 46 0N 13 0E
Frobisher B. **99** 63 0N 67 0W
Frodsham **45** 53 18N 2 44W
Frome **42** 51 16N 2 17W
Frome, R. **43** 50 44N 2 5W
Front Range **100** 40 0N 105 40W
Frosinone **58** 41 38N 13 20E
Froward C. **108** 55 0S 71 0W
Frunze **71** 42 54N 74 36E
Fuchow **73** 27 50N 116 14E
Fuente Ovejuna **60** 38 15N 5 25W
Fuerte, R. **106** 26 0N 109 0W
Fuji-no-miya **76** 35 20N 138 40E
Fuji-San **76** 35 22N 138 44E
Fujisawa **76** 35 22N 139 29E
Fukien □ **73** 26 0N 117 30E
Fukui **76** 36 0N 136 10E
Fukuoka **76** 33 30N 130 30E
Fukushima **76** 37 30N 140 15E
Fukuyama **76** 34 35N 133 20E
Fulda **54** 50 32N 9 41E
Fulda, R. **54** 50 37N 9 40E
Fulwood **45** 53 21N 1 33W
Fundy, B. of **99** 45 0N 66 0W
Furneaux Group **79** 40 10S 147 50E
Fürth **54** 49 29N 11 0E
Fushun **73** 41 50N 123 55E
Fusin **73** 42 12N 121 33E
Fuwa **91** 31 12N 30 33E
Fuyü **73** 45 10N 124 50E
Fuyuan **73** 48 9N 134 3E
Fylde **44** 53 50N 2 58W
Fyn **61** 55 20N 10 30E
Fyne, L. **46** 56 0N 5 20W
Fyvie **48** 57 26N 2 24W

G

Gaanda **90** 10 10N 12 27E
Gabès **88** 33 53N 10 2E
Gabon ■ **88** 0 10S 10 0E
Gaborone **94** 24 37S 25 57E
Gada **90** 13 38N 5 36E
Gadsden **101** 34 1N 86 0W
Gaeta **58** 41 12N 13 35E
Gagnon **99** 51 50N 68 5W
Gainesville **101** 29 38N 82 20W
Gainsborough **44** 53 23N 0 46W
Gairdner L. **79** 31 30S 136 0E
Gairloch **48** 57 42N 5 40W
Galapagos Is. **108** 0 0 89 0W
Galashiels **46** 55 37N 2 50W
Galaţi **55** 45 27N 28 2E
Galatina **58** 40 10N 18 10E
Galdhøpiggen **61** 61 38N 8 18E
Galeana **106** 24 50N 100 4W
Galesburg **101** 40 57N 90 23W
Galicia, Poland **55** 49 30N 23 0E
Galicia, Spain **60** 42 43N 8 0W
Galilee, Sea of **89** 32 53N 35 18E
Galle **70** 6 5N 80 10E
Galley Hd. **51** 51 32N 8 56W
Gallinas, Pta. **107** 12 28N 71 40W
Gallipoli **58** 40 8N 18 0E
Gällivare **61** 67 9N 20 40E
Galloway **46** 55 0N 4 25W
Galloway, Mull of **46** 54 38N 4 50W
Gallup **100** 35 30N 108 54W
Galty Mts. **51** 52 22N 8 10W
Galtymore **51** 52 22N 8 12W
Galula **93** 8 40S 33 0E
Galveston **101** 29 15N 94 48W
Galway **51** 53 16N 9 4W
Galway □ **51** 53 16N 9 3W
Galway B. **51** 53 10N 9 20W
Gamawa **90** 12 10N 10 31E
Gambia ■ **88** 13 25N 16 0W
Gamtoos **94** 33 52S 24 55E
Gander **99** 48 58N 54 35W
Gandi **90** 12 55N 5 49E
Ganga, R. **70** 25 0N 88 0E
Ganganagar **70** 29 56N 73 56E
Ganges = Ganga, R. **70** 25 0N 88 0E
Gangtok **70** 27 20N 88 37E
Gannett Pk. **100** 43 15N 109 47W
Gara, L. **50** 53 57N 8 26W
Garda, L. **58** 45 40N 10 40E
Garden City **100** 38 0N 100 45W
Gare, L. **47** 56 1N 4 50W
Garelochhead **46** 56 7N 4 50W
Garforth **45** 53 48N 1 22W
Gargans, Mt. **58** 45 37N 1 39E
Garies **94** 30 32S 17 59E
Garissa **93** 0 25S 39 40E
Garko **90** 11 45N 8 53E
Garnock, R. **47** 55 36N 4 42W
Garonne, R. **56** 45 2N 0 36W
Garoua **90** 9 19N 13 21E
Garry, L. **48** 57 5N 4 52W
Garstang **45** 53 53N 2 47W
Garston **45** 53 21N 2 55W
Garvagh **50** 55 0N 6 41W
Garvie Mts. **83** 45 30S 168 50E
Gary **104** 41 35N 87 20W
Gascony **56** 43 45N 0 20E
Gascoyne, R. **78** 24 52S 113 37E
Gashaka **90** 7 20N 11 29E
Gashua **90** 12 54N 11 0E
Gaspé Pen. **99** 48 45N 65 40W
Gata, C. de **60** 36 41N 2 13W
Gata, Sierra de **60** 40 20N 6 20W
Gatehouse of Fleet **46** 54 53N 4 10W
Gateshead **44** 54 57N 1 37W
Gatley **45** 53 25N 2 15W
Gävle **61** 60 40N 17 9E
Gawler **79** 34 30S 138 42E
Gaya **70** 24 47N 85 4E
Gayndah **79** 25 35S 151 39E
Gaza **89** 31 30N 34 28E
Gaziantep **71** 37 6N 37 23E
Gboko **90** 7 17N 9 4E
Gbongan **90** 7 28N 4 20E
Gdańsk **55** 54 22N 18 40E
Gdańsk □ **55** 54 10N 18 30E
Gdynia **55** 54 35N 18 33E
Gebe, I. **72** 0 5N 129 25E
Gedser **61** 54 35N 11 55E
Geel **52** 51 10N 4 59E
Geelong **79** 38 10S 144 22E
Geelvink B. **72** 3 0S 135 20E
Gela **58** 37 6N 14 18E
Gelderland □ **52** 52 5N 6 10E
Geleen **52** 50 57N 5 49E
Gelligaer **43** 51 40N 3 15W
Gelsenkirchen **52** 51 30N 7 5E
Gembloux **52** 50 34N 4 43E
Geneina, Gebel **91** 29 2N 33 55E
Geneva **54** 46 12N 6 9E
Geneva, L. **54** 46 26N 6 30E
Genk **52** 50 58N 5 32E
Genoa **58** 44 24N 8 57E
Genoa, G. of **58** 44 0N 9 0E
Gent **52** 51 2N 3 37E
Geographe Chan. **78** 24 30S 113 0E
George **94** 33 58S 22 29E
George Town **72** 5 25N 100 19E
George V Coast **112** 67 0S 148 0E
Georgetown **107** 6 50N 58 12W
Georgia, Str. of **105** 49 25N 124 0W
Georgian B. **99** 45 15N 81 0W
Georgian S.S.R. □ **71** 41 0N 45 0E
Gera **54** 50 53N 12 5E
Geraldton **78** 28 48S 114 32E
Germany, East ■ **54** 52 0N 12 0E
Germiston **94** 26 11S 28 10E
Gerona **60** 41 58N 2 46E
Gerrards Cross **41** 51 35N 0 32W
Gevelsberg **52** 51 21N 7 7E
Ghadames **88** 30 11N 9 29E
Ghana ■ **88** 6 0N 1 0W
Ghard Abû Muharik **91** 26 50N 30 0E
Ghot Ogrein **91** 31 10N 25 20E
Giant's Causeway **50** 55 15N 6 30W
Giarre **58** 37 44N 15 10E
Gibeon **94** 25 7S 17 45E
Gibraltar **60** 36 7N 5 22W
Gibraltar, Str. of **60** 35 55N 5 40W
Gibson Des. **78** 24 0S 126 0E
Gien **56** 47 40N 2 36E
Giessen **54** 50 34N 8 40E
Gifatin, Geziret **91** 27 10N 33 50E
Gifu **76** 35 30N 136 45E
Gigha, I. **46** 55 42N 5 45W
Gijón **60** 43 32N 5 42W
Gila, R. **100** 32 43N 114 33W
Gilbedi **90** 13 40N 5 45E
Gilbert Is. **23** 1 0S 176 0E
Gilbert, R. **79** 16 35S 141 15E
Gilf Kebir Plat. **91** 23 0N 26 0E
Gilfach Goch **43** 51 36N 3 29W
Gilford **50** 54 23N 6 20W
Gilgandra **79** 31 43S 148 39E
Gilgil **93** 0 30S 36 20E
Gill, L. **50** 54 15N 8 25W
Gillingham **41** 51 23N 0 34E
Gilly **52** 50 25N 4 30E
Ginowan **76** 26 15N 127 47E
Gippsland **79** 37 45S 147 15E
Girardot **107** 4 18N 74 48W
Girga **91** 26 17N 31 55E
Gironde, R. **56** 45 27N 0 53W
Girvan **46** 55 15N 4 50W
Gisborne **83** 38 39S 178 5E
Gitega (Kitega) **93** 3 26S 29 56E
Giurgiu **55** 43 52N 25 57E
Gizhiga **62** 62 0N 150 27E
Giżycko **55** 54 2N 21 48E
Glace Bay **99** 46 11N 59 58W
Glacier National Park **100** 48 35N 113 40W
Glacier Peak **105** 48 7N 121 7W
Glanaman **43** 51 48N 3 56W
Glas Maol **48** 56 52N 3 20W
Glasgow **47** 55 52N 4 14W
Glastonbury **42** 51 9N 2 42W
Glauchau **54** 50 50N 12 33E
Gleadless Townend **45** 53 20N 1 24W
Glen Affric **48** 57 15N 5 0W
Glen Innes **79** 29 40S 151 39E
Glen Parva **41** 52 34N 1 07W
Glen Shiel **48** 57 8N 5 20W
Glenarm **50** 54 58N 5 58W
Glencairn **94** 34 11S 18 26E
Glencoe **94** 28 11S 30 11E
Glendale **105** 34 7N 118 18W
Glendive **100** 47 7N 104 40W
Glenfarg **47** 56 16N 3 24W
Glenfield **41** 52 38N 1 12W
Glenfinnan **48** 56 52N 5 28W
Glenluce **46** 54 53N 4 50W
Glenorchy **79** 42 49S 147 18E
Glenridding **44** 54 32N 2 57W
Glenties **50** 54 48N 8 18W
Glin **51** 52 34N 9 17W
Gliwice **55** 50 22N 18 41E
Globe **100** 33 25N 110 53W
Głogów **54** 51 37N 16 5E
Glossop **45** 53 27N 1 56W
Gloucester **43** 51 52N 2 15W
Gloucestershire □ **42** 51 44N 2 10W
Glyncorrwg **43** 51 40N 3 39W
Gmünd **54** 48 45N 15 0E
Gmunden **54** 47 55N 13 48E
Gniezno **55** 52 30N 17 35E
Gnowangerup **78** 33 58S 117 59E
Goa **70** 15 33N 73 59E
Goat Fell **46** 55 37N 5 11W
Gobi, desert **73** 44 0N 111 0E
Goch **52** 51 40N 6 9E
Godalming **40** 51 12N 0 37W
Godavari, R. **70** 19 5N 79 0E
Godmanchester **40** 52 19N 0 11W
Godstone **41** 51 15N 0 3W
Godthåb **96** 64 10N 51 46W
Godwin Austen (K2) **70** 36 0N 77 0E
Goeree **52** 51 50N 4 0E
Goiânia **108** 16 35S 49 20W
Golborne **45** 53 28N 2 36W
Golden Bay **83** 40 40S 172 50E
Golden Gate **105** 37 54N 122 30W
Golden Hinde, mt. **105** 49 40N 125 44W
Golden Vale **51** 52 33N 8 17W
Goldsworthy **78** 20 21S 119 30E
Goldthorpe **45** 53 32N 1 19W
Golęniów **54** 53 35N 14 50E
Golspie **48** 57 58N 3 58W
Gombe **90** 10 19N 11 2E
Gomel **62** 52 28N 31 0E
Gomersal **45** 53 46N 1 49W
Gómez Palacio **106** 25 40N 104 40W
Gonaives, Gulf of **107** 19 29N 72 42W
Gongola □ **90** 8 0N 12 0E
Good Hope, C. of **94** 34 24S 18 30E
Goole **44** 53 42N 0 52W
Goondiwindi **79** 28 30S 150 21E
Goose Bay **99** 53 15N 60 20W
Goose L. **105** 42 0N 120 30W
Gorakhpur **70** 26 47N 83 32E
Gordon Downs **78** 18 48S 128 40E
Gore **83** 46 5S 168 58E
Gorebridge **47** 55 51N 3 2W
Gorey **51** 52 41N 6 18W
Goring, Oxon, U.K. **40** 51 31N 1 8W
Goring, W. Sussex, U.K. **40** 50 49N 0 26W
Gorízia **58** 45 56N 13 37E
Gorki **62** 56 20N 44 0E
Gorodok **55** 49 46N 23 32E
Gorseinon **43** 51 40N 4 2W
Gort **51** 53 4N 8 50W
Gorumna I. **51** 53 15N 9 44W
Gosforth **44** 55 00N 1 37W
Gospič **58** 44 35N 15 23E
Gota Canal **61** 58 35N 14 15E
Göteborg **61** 57 43N 11 59E
Gotha **54** 50 56N 10 42E
Gotland **61** 57 30N 18 30E
Göttingen **54** 51 31N 9 55E
Gottwaldov (Zlin) **55** 49 14N 17 40E
Gouda **52** 52 1N 4 42E
Gouin Rés. **99** 48 35N 74 40W
Goulburn **79** 34 44S 149 44E
Gourock **47** 55 58N 4 49W
Govan **47** 55 51N 4 19W
Gower, The **42** 51 35N 4 10W
Gowrie, Carse of **47** 57 30N 4 35W
Gozo, I. **58** 36 0N 14 13E
Gračac **58** 44 18N 15 57E
Grado **60** 43 23N 6 4W
Graff-Reinet **94** 32 15S 24 30E
Grafton **79** 29 38S 152 58E
Graham Land **112** 65 0S 64 0W
Grahamstown **94** 33 19S 26 31E
Graiguenamanagh **51** 52 32N 6 58W
Grampian □ **48** 57 0N 3 0W
Grampian Mts. **48** 56 50N 4 0W
Gran Chaco **108** 25 0S 61 0W
Gran Paradiso **58** 45 33N 7 17E
Gran Sasso d'Italia, Mt. **58** 42 25N 13 30E
Granada **60** 37 10N 3 35W
Granard **50** 53 47N 7 30W
Grand Bahama I. **107** 26 40N 78 30W
Grand Canyon National Park **100** 36 15N 112 20W
Grand Cayman **107** 19 20N 81 20W
Grand Cess **88** 4 40N 8 12W
Grand Falls **99** 48 56N 55 40W
Grand Forks **101** 48 0N 97 3W
Grand Island **100** 40 59N 98 25W
Grand Junction **100** 39 0N 108 30W
Grand Rapids, Can. **98** 53 12N 99 19W
Grand Rapids, U.S.A. **104** 42 57N 85 40W
Grand Teton **100** 43 54N 111 57W
Grande Prairie **98** 55 10N 118 50W
Grange, La, Austral. **78** 18 45S 121 43E
Grange, La, U.S.A. **101** 33 4N 85 0W
Grange-over-Sands **44** 54 12N 2 55W
Grangemouth **47** 56 1N 3 43W
Grangeville **100** 45 57N 116 4W
Granity **83** 41 39S 171 51E
Granollers **60** 41 39N 2 18E
Grantham **45** 52 55N 0 39W
Grantown-on-Spey **48** 57 19N 3 36W
Grants **100** 35 14N 107 57W
Grants Pass **105** 42 30N 123 22W
Grappenhall **45** 53 22N 2 34W
Graskop **94** 24 56S 30 49E
Grasmere **44** 54 28N 3 2W
Grasse **56** 43 38N 6 56E
Grassington **44** 54 5N 2 0W
Gravesend **41** 51 25N 0 22E
Grays Harbor **100** 46 55N 124 8W
Grays-Thurrock **41** 51 28N 0 23E
Graz **54** 47 4N 15 27E
Greasbrough **45** 53 27N 1 22W
Greasby **45** 53 24N 3 04W
Great Abaco I. **107** 26 15N 77 10W
Great Australian Bight **78** 33 30S 130 0E
Great Baddow **41** 51 43N 0 31E
Great Barrier I. **83** 36 11S 175 25E
Great Barrier Reef **79** 19 0S 149 0E
Great Basin **100** 40 0N 116 30W
Great Bear L. **98** 65 30N 120 0W
Great Belt **61** 55 20N 11 0E
Great Bend **100** 38 25N 98 55W
Great Bernera, I. **48** 58 15N 6 50W
Great Britain **24** 54 0N 2 15W
Great Bushman Land **94** 29 20S 19 20E
Great Chesterford **40** 52 4N 0 11E
Great Cumbrae I. **47** 55 46N 4 57W
Great Divide **79** 23 0S 146 0E
Great Dunmow **40** 51 52N 0 22E
Great Falls **100** 47 27N 111 12W
Great Fish R. **92** 33 28S 27 5E
Great Harwood **45** 53 47N 2 25W
Gt. Karas Mts. **94** 27 10S 18 45E
Gt. Karoo, reg. **94** 32 30S 23 0E
Great Kei, R. **94** 32 15S 27 45E
Great Malvern **42** 52 7N 2 19W
Great Missenden **41** 51 42N 0 42W
Great Ouse, R. **40** 52 20N 0 8E
Gt. St. Bernard P. **58** 45 50N 7 10E
Great Salt Lake **100** 41 0N 112 30W
Great Salt Lake Desert **100** 40 20N 113 50W
Great Sandy Desert **78** 21 0S 124 0E
Great Sankey **45** 53 23N 2 37W
Great Shelford **40** 52 9N 0 9E
Great Slave L. **98** 61 23N 115 38W
Great Torrington **43** 50 57N 4 9W
Gt. Victoria Des. **78** 29 30S 126 30E
Great Wall **73** 38 30N 109 30E
Gt. Winterberg, mt. **94** 32 20S 26 20E
Great Winterhoek, mt. **94** 33 07S 19 10E
Great Wyrley **41** 52 40N 2 1W
Great Yarmouth **40** 52 40N 1 45E
Greater Antilles **107** 17 40N 74 0W
Greater London □ **40** 51 31N 0 6W
Greater Manchester □ **44** 53 30N 2 15W
Greater Sunda Is. **72** 2 30S 110 0E
Greatham **44** 54 38N 1 14W
Gredos, Sierra de **60** 40 20N 5 0W
Greece ■ **23** 40 0N 23 0E
Greeley **100** 40 30N 104 40W
Green Bay **104** 44 30N 88 0W
Green Island **83** 45 55S 170 26E
Greenfield **45** 53 32N 2 01W
Greenland **96** 66 0N 45 0W
Greenland Sea **96** 73 0N 10 0W
Greenlaw **46** 55 42N 2 28W
Greenock **47** 55 57N 4 46W
Greenore **50** 54 2N 6 8W
Greensboro **101** 36 7N 79 46W
Greenville, Miss., U.S.A. **101** 33 25N 91 0W
Greenville, S.C., U.S.A. **101** 34 54N 82 24W
Greenville, Tex., U.S.A. **101** 33 5N 96 5W
Greenwich **41** 51 28N 0 0
Greenwood **101** 33 30N 90 4W
Gregory, L. **78** 28 55S 139 0E
Gregory Ra. **79** 19 30S 143 40E
Grenada ■ **107** 12 10N 61 40W
Grenoble **56** 45 12N 5 42E
Gretna **46** 54 59N 3 4W
Grevenbroich **52** 51 6N 6 32E
Grey, R. **83** 42 27S 171 12E
Grey Range **79** 27 0S 143 30E
Greyabbey **50** 54 32N 5 35W
Greymouth **83** 42 29S 171 13E
Greystones **51** 53 9N 6 4W
Greytown, N.Z. **83** 41 5S 175 29E
Greytown, S. Afr. **94** 29 1S 30 36E
Griekwastad **94** 28 49S 23 15E
Griffith **79** 34 18S 146 2E
Griffithstown **43** 51 41N 3 01W
Grimethorpe **45** 53 34N 1 24W
Grimsby **44** 53 35N 0 5W
Griqualand East **94** 30 30S 29 0E
Griqualand West **94** 28 40S 23 30E
Gris Nez, C. **56** 50 52N 1 35E
Groblersdal **94** 25 15S 29 25E
Grodno **55** 53 42N 23 52E
Gronau **52** 52 13N 7 2E
Groningen **52** 53 15N 6 35E
Groningen □ **52** 53 16N 6 40E
Groot-Brakrivier **94** 34 2S 22 18E
Groot-Vloer **94** 30 0S 20 40E
Groote Eylandt **79** 14 0S 136 50E
Grootfontein **92** 19 31S 18 6E
Gross Glockner **54** 47 5N 12 40E
Grossenbrode **54** 54 21N 11 4E
Grossenhain **54** 51 17N 13 32E
Groznyy **71** 43 20N 45 45E
Grudziądz **55** 53 30N 18 47E
Gruinard B. **48** 57 56N 5 35W
Grünau **94** 27 45S 18 26E
Grutness **49** 59 53N 1 17W
Guadalajara **106** 20 40N 103 20W
Guadalcanal, I. **79** 9 32S 160 12E
Guadalhorce, R. **60** 36 50N 4 42W
Guadalquivir, R. **60** 38 0N 4 0W
Guadalupe **60** 39 27N 5 17W
Guadarrama, Sierra de **60** 41 0N 4 0W
Guadeloupe, I. **107** 16 20N 61 40W
Guadiana, R. **60** 37 45N 7 35W
Guadix **60** 37 18N 3 11W
Guam I. **23** 13 27N 144 45E
Guamuchil **106** 25 25N 108 3W
Guanajuato **106** 21 0N 101 20W
Guanare **107** 8 42N 69 12W
Guantánamo **107** 20 10N 75 20W
Guaporé, R. **108** 13 0S 63 0W
Guarda **60** 40 32N 7 20W
Guardafui, C. **89** 11 55N 51 10E
Guatemala **106** 14 40N 90 30W
Guatemala ■ **106** 15 40N 90 30W
Guaviare, R. **107** 3 30N 71 0W
Guayaquil **108** 2 15S 79 52W
Guaymas **106** 27 50N 111 0W
Guecho **60** 43 21N 2 59W
Guernsey I. **43** 49 30N 2 35W
Guider **90** 9 55N 13 59E
Guildford **41** 51 14N 0 34W
Guinea ■ **88** 10 20N 10 0W
Guinea Bissau ■ **88** 12 0N 15 0W
Guinea, Gulf of **88** 3 0N 2 30E
Guinea, Port. **88** 12 0N 15 0W
Guiseley **45** 53 52N 1 43W
Gujarat □ **70** 23 20N 71 0E

Gujranwala Hythe

Gujranwala	71	32 10N	74 12E
Gulbargâ	70	17 20N	76 50E
Gulfport	101	30 28N	89 3W
Gulu	93	2 48N	32 17E
Gummersbach	52	51 2N	7 32E
Gummi	90	12 4N	5 9E
Gunnedah	79	30 59S	150 15E
Gunnislake	43	50 32N	4 12W
Guryev	62	47 5N	52 0E
Gusau	90	12 18N	6 31E
Güstrow	54	53 47N	12 12E
Guthrie	100	35 55N	97 30W
Guyana ■	107	5 0N	59 0W
Guyenne	56	44 30N	0 40E
Gwadabawa	90	13 20N	5 15E
Gwalior	70	26 12N	78 10E
Gwanda	92	20 55S	29 0E
Gwaram	90	11 15N	9 51E
Gwarzo	90	12 20N	8 55E
Gwasero	90	9 30N	8 30E
Gweebarra B.	50	54 52N	8 21W
Gwelo	92	19 28S	29 45E
Gwent □	42	51 45N	2 55W
Gwynedd □	42	53 0N	4 0W
Gympie	79	26 11S	152 38E
Gyoda	76	36 10N	139 30E
Györ	55	47 41N	17 40E
Gypsumville	98	51 45N	98 40W
Gyula	55	46 38N	21 17E
H			
Ha Tinh	72	18 20N	105 54E
Haarlem	52	52 23N	4 39E
Hachinohe	76	40 30N	141 29E
Hackney	41	51 33N	0 2W
Hadarba, Ras	91	22 4N	36 51E
Haddenham	41	51 46N	0 56W
Haddington	46	55 57N	2 48W
Hadeija	90	12 30N	10 5E
Hadfield	45	53 28N	1 58W
Hadhramaut	71	15 30N	49 30E
Hadiya	71	25 30N	36 56E
Hadleigh	41	52 3N	0 58E
Haeju	73	38 3N	125 45E
Hagen	52	51 21N	7 29E
Hagi	76	34 30N	131 30E
Hague, C. de la	56	49 44N	1 56W
Hague, The	52	52 7N	4 17E
Haifa	89	32 46N	35 0E
Haikow	73	20 0N	110 20E
Hā'il	71	27 28N	42 2E
Hailar	73	49 12N	119 37E
Hailey	100	43 30N	114 15W
Hailsham	40	50 52N	0 17E
Hailun	73	47 24N	127 0E
Hailung	73	42 30N	125 40E
Hainan, I.	72	19 0N	110 0E
Hainaut □	52	50 30N	4 0E
Haiphong	72	20 47N	106 35E
Haiti ■	107	19 0N	72 30W
Hakodate	76	41 45N	140 44E
Halberstadt	54	51 53N	11 2E
Halcombe	83	40 8S	175 30E
Hale	45	53 24N	2 21W
Halesowen	41	52 27N	2 2W
Halesworth	40	52 21N	1 30E
Halewood	45	53 22N	2 49W
Halifax, Can.	99	44 38N	63 35W
Halifax, U.K.	45	53 43N	1 51W
Halifax B.	79	18 50S	147 0E
Halkirk	48	58 30N	3 30W
Halle, Belg.	52	50 44N	4 13E
Halle, Ger.	54	51 29N	12 0E
Halley Bay	112	75 31S	26 36W
Hall's Creek	78	18 16S	127 46E
Halmahera, I.	72	0 40N	128 0E
Halmstad	61	56 41N	12 52E
Halstead	40	51 59N	0 39E
Haltern	52	51 44N	7 10E
Haltwhistle	44	54 58N	2 27W
Hamada	76	34 50N	132 10E
Hamadān	71	34 52N	48 32E
Hamamatsu	76	34 45N	137 45E
Hamar	61	60 48N	11 7E
Hamâta, Gebel	91	24 17N	35 0E
Hambantota	70	6 10N	81 10E
Hambleton Hills	44	54 17N	1 12W
Hamburg	54	53 32N	9 59E
Hämeenlinna	61	61 0N	24 28E
Hameln	54	52 7N	9 24E
Hamersley Ra.	78	22 0S	117 45E
Hamhung	73	40 0N	127 30E
Hami	73	42 47N	93 32E
Hamilton, Austral.	79	37 45S	142 2E
Hamilton, Can.	104	43 15N	79 50W
Hamilton, N.Z.	83	37 47S	175 19E
Hamilton, U.K.	47	55 47N	4 2W
Hamm	52	51 40N	7 58E
Hammerfest	61	70 39N	23 41E
Hammersmith	41	51 30N	0 15W
Hammond	104	41 40N	87 30W
Hampden	83	45 18S	170 50E
Hamun-i-Mashkel	71	28 30N	63 0E
Hanamaki	76	39 23N	141 7E
Hanchung	73	33 10N	107 2E
Handeni	93	5 25S	38 2E
Hanford	100	36 25N	119 39W
Hangayn Nuruu	73	47 30N	100 0E
Hangchow	73	30 12N	120 1E
Hangchow Wan	73	30 30N	121 30E
Hanko	61	59 59N	22 57E
Hanku	73	39 16N	117 50E
Hanmer	83	42 32S	172 50E
Hannibal	101	39 42N	91 22W
Hanoi	72	21 5N	105 55E
Hanover, Ger.	54	52 23N	9 43E
Hanover, S. Afr.	94	31 4S	24 29E
Hantan	73	36 42N	114 30E
Haparanda	61	65 52N	24 8E
Harbin	73	45 46N	126 51E
Harburg	54	53 27N	9 58E
Hardanger Fjord, Norway	61	60 15N	6 0E
Hardanger Fjord, Norway	61	60 15N	6 0E
Hardap Dam	92	24 32S	17 50E
Harding	94	30 22S	29 55E
Harelbeke	52	50 52N	3 20E
Hari, R.	72	1 10S	101 50E
Haringey	41	51 35N	0 7W
Harlech	42	52 52N	4 7W
Harleston	40	52 25N	1 18E
Harlingen, Neth.	52	53 11N	5 25E
Harlingen, U.S.A.	100	26 20N	97 50W
Harlow	41	51 47N	0 9E
Harpenden	40	51 48N	0 20W
Harrat al Uwairidh	91	26 50N	38 0E
Harris	48	57 50N	6 55W
Harris, Sd. of	48	57 44N	7 6W
Harrisburg	104	40 18N	76 52W
Harrismith	94	28 15S	29 8E
Harrison, C.	99	54 55N	57 55W
Harrogate	44	53 59N	1 32W
Harrow	41	51 35N	0 15W
Hartford	104	41 47N	72 41W
Harthill, U.K.	47	55 52N	3 45W
Harthill, Ches., U.K.	45	53 05N	2 45W
Hartland	43	50 59N	4 29W
Hartland Pt.	43	51 2N	4 32W
Hartlepool	44	54 42N	1 11W
Harts R.	94	27 15S	25 12E
Hartshill	41	51 32N	1 31W
Harwich	40	51 56N	1 18E
Haryana □	70	29 0N	76 10E
Harz	54	51 40N	10 40E
Hasa	71	26 0N	49 0E
Haslemere	40	51 5N	0 41W
Haslingden	45	53 43N	2 20W
Hasselt	52	50 56N	5 21E
Hastings, N.Z.	83	39 39S	176 52E
Hastings, U.K.	40	50 51N	0 36E
Hastings, U.S.A.	100	40 34N	98 22W
Hatfield	41	51 46N	0 11W
Hatherleigh	43	50 49N	4 4W
Hathersage	45	53 20N	1 39W
Hatteras, C.	101	35 10N	75 30W
Hattiesburg	101	31 20N	89 20W
Hatvan	55	47 40N	19 45E
Haugesund	61	59 23N	5 13E
Hauraki Gulf	83	36 35S	175 5E
Havana	107	23 8N	82 22W
Havant	40	50 51N	0 59W
Havasu, L.	100	34 18N	114 28W
Havel, R.	54	52 40N	12 15E
Havelock	83	41 17S	173 48E
Haverfordwest	42	51 48N	4 59W
Haverhill	40	52 6N	0 27E
Havering	41	51 33N	0 20E
Havre	100	48 40N	109 34W
Havre, Le	56	49 30N	0 5E
Hawaii I.	22	20 0N	155 0W
Hawaiian Is.	22	20 30N	156 0W
Hawarden	45	53 11N	3 2W
Hawea Lake	83	44 28S	169 19E
Hawera	83	39 35S	174 19E
Hawes	44	54 18N	2 12W
Haweswater	44	54 32N	2 48W
Hawick	46	55 25N	2 48W
Hawke B.	83	39 25S	177 20E
Hawke's Bay □	83	39 45S	176 35E
Hawkhurst	40	51 2N	0 31E
Hawkshead	44	54 23N	3 0W
Hawkwell	41	51 35N	0 40E
Haworth	45	53 50N	1 57W
Hay	79	34 30S	144 51E
Hay-on-Wye	42	52 4N	3 9W
Hay River	98	60 51N	115 44W
Hayange	56	49 20N	6 2E
Haydock	45	53 27N	2 42W
Hayle	43	50 12N	5 25W
Hays	100	38 55N	99 25W
Hayward's Heath	40	51 0N	0 5W
Hazel Grove	45	53 23N	2 07W
Hazelton	98	55 20N	127 42W
Headcorn	40	51 10N	0 39E
Headford	51	53 28N	9 6W
Heald Green	45	53 23N	2 12W
Heanor	44	53 1N	1 20W
Heard I.	23	53 0S	74 0E
Hearst	99	49 40N	83 41W
Heathfield	40	50 58N	0 18E
Hebburn	44	54 59N	1 30W
Hebden Bridge	45	53 45N	2 0W
Hebrides, Inner Is.	48	57 20N	6 40W
Hebron	99	58 12N	62 38W
Heckmondwike	45	53 42N	1 40W
Hedgehope	83	46 12S	168 34E
Heemstede	52	52 22N	4 37E
Heerenveen	52	52 57N	5 55E
Heerlen	52	50 55N	6 0E
Heidelberg, Ger.	54	49 23N	8 41E
Heidelberg, C. Prov., S. Afr.	94	34 6S	20 59E
Heidelberg, Trans., S. Afr.	94	26 30S	28 23E
Heilbron	94	27 16S	27 59E
Heilbronn	54	49 8N	9 13E
Heilungkiang □	73	47 30N	129 0E
Hejaz	71	26 0N	37 30E
Helena	100	46 40N	112 0W
Helensburgh	47	56 0N	4 44W
Helensville	83	36 41S	174 29E
Heligoland	54	54 10N	7 51E
Heliopolis	91	30 6N	31 17E
Hell-Ville	92	13 25S	48 16E
Hellin	60	38 31N	1 40W
Helmand, R.	71	34 0N	67 0E
Helmond	52	51 29N	5 41E
Helmsdale	48	58 7N	3 40W
Helmsley	44	54 15N	1 2W
Helsby	45	53 16N	2 47W
Helsingborg	61	56 3N	12 42E
Helsinki	61	60 15N	25 3E
Helvellyn	44	54 31N	3 1W
Helwân	91	29 50N	31 20E
Hemel Hempstead	41	51 45N	0 28W
Hemsworth	45	53 37N	1 21W
Henares, R.	60	40 55N	3 0W
Henfield	40	50 56N	0 17W
Hengelo	52	52 16N	6 48E
Hengoed	43	51 39N	3 14W
Hengyang	73	26 51N	112 30E
Henley	40	51 32N	0 53W
Hentiyn Nuruu	73	48 30N	108 30E
Henzada	70	17 38N	95 35E
Heptonstall	45	53 45N	2 01W
Herāt	71	34 20N	62 7E
Hercegnovi	58	42 30N	18 33E
Hercegovina	58	43 20N	18 0E
Hereford	42	52 4N	2 42W
Hereford and Worcester □	42	52 10N	2 30W
Herentals	52	51 12N	4 51E
Herford	54	52 7N	8 40E
Herm I.	43	49 30N	2 28W
Herma Ness	49	60 50N	0 54W
Hermanus	94	34 27S	19 12E
Hermitage	83	43 44S	170 5E
Hermon, Mt.	89	33 20N	36 0E
Hermosillo	106	29 10N	111 0W
Herne	52	51 33N	7 12E
Herne Bay	40	51 22N	1 8E
Heron Bay	99	48 40N	86 25W
Herschel I.	98	69 35N	139 5W
Herstal	52	50 40N	5 38E
Hertford	41	51 47N	0 4W
Hertford □	40	51 51N	0 5W
's-Hertogenbosch	52	51 42N	5 17E
Hervey B.	79	25 0S	152 52E
Herzliyya	89	32 10N	34 50E
Hesketh Bank	45	53 42N	2 51W
Hessen □	54	50 40N	9 20E
Hessle	44	53 44N	0 28E
Heswall	45	53 19N	3 06W
Hetton-le-Hole	44	54 49N	1 26W
Hewett, C.	99	70 16N	67 45W
Hex River	94	33 30S	19 35E
Hexham	44	54 58N	2 7W
Heybridge	41	51 44N	0 42E
Heysham	44	54 5N	2 53W
Heywood	45	53 36N	2 13W
Hibbing	101	47 30N	93 0W
High Atlas, Mts.	88	32 30N	5 0W
High Blantyre	47	55 46N	4 06W
High Tatra	55	49 30N	20 00E
High Wycombe	41	51 37N	0 45W
Higham Ferrers	40	52 18N	0 36W
Highbridge	42	51 13N	2 59W
Higher Penwortham	45	53 45N	2 44W
Highland □	48	57 30N	5 0W
Highworth	42	51 38N	1 42W
Hiiumaa	61	58 50N	22 45E
Hildesheim	54	52 9N	9 55E
Hillegom	52	52 18N	4 35E
Hillingdon	41	51 33N	0 29W
Hillston	79	33 30S	145 31E
Hilversum	52	52 14N	5 10E
Himachal Pradesh □	70	31 30N	77 0E
Himalaya, mts.	70	29 0N	84 0E
Himeji	76	34 50N	134 40E
Hims	71	34 40N	36 45E
Hinckley	41	52 33N	1 21W
Hindhead	40	51 6N	0 42W
Hindley	45	53 32N	2 35W
Hindu Kush	71	36 0N	71 0E
Hindupur	70	13 49N	77 32E
Hines Creek	98	56 20N	118 40W
Hirara	76	24 48N	125 17E
Hirosaki	76	40 34N	140 28E
Hiroshima	76	34 30N	132 30E
Hirson	56	49 55N	4 4E
Hirwaun	43	51 43N	3 30W
Hispaniola, I.	107	19 0N	71 0W
Hitachi	76	36 36N	140 39E
Hitchin	40	51 57N	0 16W
Hjälmaren	61	59 18N	15 40E
Ho Chi Minh City	72	10 58N	106 40E
Hobart	79	42 50S	147 21E
Hobbs	100	32 40N	103 3W
Hoboken	52	51 11N	4 21E
Hoch'ih	73	24 43N	108 2E
Hochwan	73	30 0N	106 15E
Hockley	41	51 35N	0 39E
Hoddesdon	41	51 45N	0 1W
Hódmezövásárhely	55	46 28N	20 22E
Hodonín	54	48 50N	17 0E
Hoek van Holland	52	52 0N	4 7E
Hof	54	50 18N	11 55E
Hofei	73	31 52N	117 15E
Hofmeyr	94	31 39S	25 50E
Hoggar, Mts.	88	23 0N	6 30E
Hohenlimburg	52	51 21N	7 35E
Hokang	73	47 36N	130 28E
Hokitika	83	42 42S	171 0E
Hokkaidō □	76	43 30N	143 0E
Holbeach	45	52 48N	0 1E
Holderness	44	53 45N	0 5W
Holdrege	100	40 25N	99 30W
Holguin	107	20 50N	76 20W
Hollywood	100	34 7N	118 25W
Holme	45	53 34N	1 50W
Holmfirth	45	53 34N	1 48W
Holsteinsborg	96	66 40N	53 30W
Holt	40	52 55N	1 4E
Holy I., Scotland, U.K.	46	55 31N	5 4W
Holy I., Wales, U.K.	42	53 17N	4 37W
Holyhead	42	53 18N	4 38W
Holyoke	104	42 14N	72 37W
Holywell	42	53 16N	3 14W
Holywood	50	54 38N	5 50W
Homburg	52	49 19N	7 21E
Home Hill	79	19 43S	147 25E
Honan □	73	33 50N	113 15E
Honda	107	5 12N	74 45W
Honduras ■	106	14 40N	86 30W
Honduras, G. of	106	16 50N	87 0W
Honey L.	105	40 13N	120 14W
Hong Kong ■	73	22 11N	114 14E
Honiton	43	50 48N	3 11W
Honjo	76	39 23N	140 3E
Honkorâb, Ras	91	24 35N	35 10E
Honley	45	53 36N	1 48W
Honolulu	22	21 19N	157 52W
Honshū	76	36 0N	138 0E
Hood Mt.	100	45 30N	121 50W
Hoogeveen	52	52 44N	6 30E
Hook	41	51 17N	0 55W
Hook Hd.	51	52 8N	6 57W
Hoorn	52	52 38N	5 4E
Hopedale	99	55 28N	60 13W
Hopefield	94	33 3S	18 22E
Hopei □	73	39 25N	116 45E
Hopetoun	78	33 57S	120 7E
Hopetown	94	29 34S	24 3E
Hoquiam	100	46 50N	123 55W
Horbury	45	53 40N	1 33W
Horley	40	51 10N	0 10W
Horn, C.	108	55 50S	67 30W
Horncastle	44	53 13N	0 8W
Hornsea	44	53 55N	0 10W
Horsforth	45	53 50N	1 39W
Horsham, Austral.	79	36 44S	142 13E
Horsham, U.K.	40	51 4N	0 20W
Horwich	45	53 37N	2 33W
Hospital	51	52 30N	8 28W
Hospitalet de Llobregat	60	41 21N	2 6E
Hot Springs, Ark, U.S.A.	101	34 30N	93 0W
Hot Springs, S.D., U.S.A.	100	43 25N	103 30W
Hotien (Khotan)	73	37 6N	79 59E
Houghton-le-Spring	44	54 51N	1 28W
Houhora	83	34 49S	173 9E
Houma	101	29 35N	90 50W
Hounslow	41	51 29N	0 20W
Hourn, L.	48	57 7N	5 35W
Houston	101	29 50N	95 20W
Hovd (Jargalant)	73	48 2N	91 37E
Hove	40	50 50N	0 10W
Howden	44	53 45N	0 52W
Howick	94	29 28S	30 14E
Howrah	70	22 37N	88 27E
Howth	51	53 23N	6 3W
Hoy I.	49	58 50N	3 15W
Høyanger	61	61 25N	6 50E
Hoylake	45	53 24N	3 11W
Hoyland Nether	45	53 30N	1 27W
Hrádec Králové	54	50 15N	15 50E
Hsiamen	73	24 30N	118 7E
Hsinchu	73	24 48N	120 58E
Hsuchang	73	34 1N	113 53E
Hualien	73	24 0N	121 30E
Huatabampo	106	26 50N	109 50W
Hubli-Dharwar	70	15 22N	75 15E
Hucknall	44	53 3N	1 12W
Huddersfield	45	53 38N	1 49W
Hudiksvall	61	61 43N	17 10E
Hudson Bay	99	60 0N	86 0W
Hudson, R.	101	40 42N	74 2W
Hudson Str.	99	62 0N	70 0W
Huê	72	16 30N	107 35E
Huelva	60	37 18N	6 57W
Huesca	60	42 8N	0 25W
Hughenden	79	20 52S	144 10E
Huhehot	73	40 52N	111 36E
Huixtla	106	15 9N	92 28W
Hulan	73	46 0N	126 44E
Huld	73	45 5N	105 30E
Hull, Can.	104	45 25N	75 44W
Hull, U.K.	44	53 45N	0 20W
Hull, R.	44	53 55N	0 23W
Humansdorp	94	34 2S	24 46E
Humber, R.	44	53 40N	0 10W
Humberside □	44	53 50N	0 30W
Humboldt, R.	100	40 2N	118 31W
Humphreys Pk.	100	35 24N	111 38W
Hunan □	73	27 30N	111 30E
Hunedoara	55	45 40N	22 50E
Hungary ■	55	47 20N	19 20E
Hungerford	40	51 25N	1 30W
Hungkiang	73	27 0N	109 49E
Hungshui Ho, R.	73	23 24N	110 12E
Hungtse Hu	73	33 15N	118 45E
Hunsrück	52	49 30N	7 0E
Hunstanton	40	52 57N	0 30E
Hunterville	83	39 56S	175 35E
Huntingdon	40	52 20N	0 11W
Huntington, Ind., U.S.A.	101	40 52N	85 30W
Huntington, W. Va., U.S.A.	101	38 20N	82 30W
Huntly, N.Z.	83	37 34S	175 11E
Huntly, U.K.	48	57 27N	2 48W
Huonville	79	43 0S	147 5E
Hupei □	73	31 5N	113 5E
Hurghada	91	27 15N	33 50E
Huron	100	44 30N	98 20W
Huron, L.	104	45 0N	83 0W
Hursley	40	51 1N	1 23W
Hurstpierpoint	40	50 56N	0 11W
Hutchinson	100	38 3N	97 59W
Huy	52	50 31N	5 15E
Huyton-with-Roby	45	53 24N	2 51W
Hvar, I.	58	43 11N	16 28E
Hwai Ho	73	32 20N	114 30E
Hwainan	73	32 44N	117 1E
Hwang-ho, R.	73	40 50N	107 30E
Hwangshih	73	30 27N	115 0E
Hyde	45	53 26N	2 6W
Hyderabad, India	70	17 10N	78 29E
Hyderabad, Pak.	71	25 23N	68 36E
Hyères	56	43 8N	6 9E
Hyeres, Is.	56	43 0N	6 28E
Hythe	40	51 4N	1 5E

* Renamed Gweru

Ialomiţa, R
Kearsley

I

Ialomiţa, R.	55	44 45N	27 57 E
Iaşi	55	47 10N	27 40 E
Ibadan	90	7 22N	3 58 E
Ibagué	107	4 27N	73 14W
Ibbenbüren	52	52 16N	7 41 E
Iberian Peninsula	24	40 0N	5 0W
Ibiza	60	38 54N	1 26 E
Ibiza, I.	60	39 0N	1 30 E
Ibshawâi	91	29 21N	30 40 E
Iceland, I. ■	96	65 0N	19 0W
Ichang	73	30 48N	111 29 E
Ichikawa	76	35 44N	139 55 E
Ichinomiya	76	35 18N	136 48 E
Ichinoseki	76	38 55N	141 8 E
Ichun	73	47 42N	129 8 E
Idah	90	6 10N	6 40 E
Idaho □	100	44 10N	114 0W
Idaho Falls	100	43 30N	112 10W
Idar-Oberstein	52	49 43N	7 19 E
Idfû	91	25 0N	32 49 E
* Idi Amin Dada, L.	93	0 25 S	29 40 E
Idutywa	94	32 8 S	28 18 E
Ife	90	7 30N	4 31 E
Igbetti	90	8 44N	4 8 E
Igbo-Ora	90	7 10N	3 15 E
Igboho	90	8 40N	3 50 E
Iglésias	58	39 19N	8 27 E
Iguaçu Falls	108	25 41 S	54 26W
Iguala	106	18 20N	99 40W
Igualada	60	41 37N	1 37 E
Ihiala	90	5 40N	6 55 E
Iisalmi	61	63 32N	27 10 E
Ijebu-Igbo	90	6 56N	4 1 E
Ijebu-Ode	90	6 47N	3 52 E
IJmuiden	52	52 28N	4 35 E
IJsselmeer	52	52 45N	5 20 E
Ikare	90	7 18N	5 40 E
Ikeja	90	6 28N	3 45 E
Ikerre	90	7 25N	5 19 E
Ikire	90	7 10N	4 15 E
Ikot Ekpene	90	5 12N	7 40 E
Ila	90	8 0N	4 51 E
Ilaro Agege	90	6 53N	3 3 E
Ilchester	43	51 0N	2 41W
Île de France □	56	49 0N	2 20 E
Ilebo	92	4 17 S	20 47 E
Ilero	90	8 0N	3 20 E
Ilesha	90	7 37N	4 40 E
Ilfracombe	42	51 13N	4 8W
Ilkeston	45	52 59N	1 19W
Ilkhuri Shan	73	51 30N	124 0 E
Ilkley	45	53 56N	1 49W
Illinois □	101	40 15N	89 30W
Ilmen L.	61	58 15N	31 10 E
Ilminster	43	50 55N	2 56W
Ilobu	90	7 45N	4 25 E
Iloilo	72	10 45N	122 33 E
Ilora	90	7 45N	3 50 E
Ilorin	90	8 30N	4 35 E
Imatra	61	61 12N	28 48 E
Imbaba	91	30 5N	31 12 E
Immingham	44	53 37N	0 12W
Imo □	90	5 15N	7 20 E
Imola	58	44 20N	11 42 E
Impéria	58	43 52N	8 0 E
Imphal	70	24 48N	93 56 E
In Salah	88	27 10N	2 32 E
Ina	76	35 50N	138 0 E
Inangahua Junc.	83	41 52 S	171 59 E
Inari	61	68 54N	27 5 E
Inari, L.	61	69 0N	28 0 E
Inca	60	39 43N	2 54 E
Inch'ŏn	73	37 27N	126 40 E
Indal	61	62 35N	17 5 E
India ■	70	20 0N	80 0 E
Indian Harbour	99	54 27N	57 13W
Indian Ocean	23	5 0 S	75 0 E
Indiana □	101	40 0N	86 0W
Indianapolis	101	39 42N	86 10W
Indigirka, R.	62	69 0N	147 0 E
Indonesia ■	72	5 0 S	115 0 E
Indore	70	22 42N	75 53 E
Indre, R.	56	47 2N	1 8 E
Indus, R.	71	28 40N	70 10 E
Ingatestone	41	51 40N	0 23W
Inglefield Land	99	78 30N	70 0W
Inglewood	83	39 9 S	174 14 E
Ingolstadt	54	48 45N	11 26 E
Inhambane	92	23 54 S	35 30 E
Ining (Kuldja)	73	43 57N	81 20 E
Inishbofin I.	51	53 35N	10 12W
Inishcrone	50	54 13N	9 05W
Inishmore, I.	51	53 8N	9 45W
Inishowen, Pen.	50	55 14N	7 15W
Inishturk I.	50	53 42N	10 8W
Inistioge	51	52 30N	7 5W
Inn, R.	54	48 35N	13 28 E
Innellan	47	55 54N	4 58W
Inner Mongolia □	73	44 50N	117 40 E
Innisfail	79	17 33 S	146 5 E
Innsbruck	54	47 16N	11 23 E
Inoucdjouac	99	58 27N	78 6W
Inowrocław	55	52 50N	18 20 E
Interlaken	54	46 41N	7 50 E
Inuvik	98	68 16N	133 40W
Inveraray	46	56 13N	5 5W
Inverbervie	48	56 50N	2 17W
Invercargill	83	46 24 S	168 24 E
Inverell	79	29 45 S	151 8 E
Invergarry	48	57 5N	4 48W
Invergordon	48	57 41N	4 10W
Inverkeithing	47	56 2N	3 24W
Invermoriston	48	57 13N	4 38W
Inverness	48	57 29N	4 12W
Inverurie	48	57 15N	2 21W
Investigator Str.	79	35 30 S	137 0 E
Iona I.	46	56 20N	6 25W
Ionian Sea	58	37 30N	17 30 E
Iowa □	101	42 18N	93 30W
Ipin	73	28 48N	104 33 E
Ipoh	72	4 35N	101 5 E
Ipswich, Austral.	79	27 35 S	152 46 E
Ipswich, U.K.	40	52 4N	1 9 E
Iquique	108	20 19 S	70 5W
Iquitos	108	3 45 S	73 10W
Iran ■	71	33 0N	53 0 E
Iran Ra.	72	2 20N	114 50 E
Irapuato	106	20 40N	101 40W
Iraq ■	71	33 0N	44 0 E
Ireland ■	51	53 0N	8 0W
Ireland's Eye	51	53 25N	6 4W
Irele	90	7 40N	5 40 E
Irian Jaya □	72	4 0 S	137 0 E
Iringa	93	7 48 S	35 43 E
Iriomote-Jima	76	24 19N	123 48 E
Irish Sea	24	54 0N	5 0W
Irkutsk	62	52 10N	104 20 E
Irlam	45	53 26N	2 27W
Iron Knob	79	32 46 S	137 8 E
Ironbridge	45	52 38N	2 29W
Irrawaddy, R.	70	15 50N	95 6 E
Irthlingborough	40	52 20N	0 37W
Irtysh, R.	62	53 36N	75 30 E
Irún	60	43 20N	1 52W
Irvine	47	55 37N	4 40W
Irvinestown	50	54 28N	7 38W
Isahaya	76	32 52N	130 2 E
Isar, R.	54	48 40N	12 30 E
Isbister	49	60 22N	0 54W
Ischia, I.	58	40 45N	13 51 E
Isère, R.	56	45 15N	5 30 E
Iserlohn	52	51 22N	7 40 E
Iseyin	90	8 0N	3 36 E
Ishigaki	76	24 20N	124 10 E
Ishikari-Wan	76	43 20N	141 20 E
Ishikawa	76	26 25N	127 48 E
Ishinomaki	76	38 32N	141 20 E
Isiolo	93	0 24N	37 33 E
Isipingo	94	30 00 S	30 57 E
Isipingo Beach	94	30 00 S	30 57 E
Isiro	92	2 53N	27 58 E
Iskenderun	71	36 32N	36 10 E
Isla, R.	48	56 32N	3 20W
Islamabad	71	33 40N	73 0 E
Islay, I.	46	55 46N	6 10W
Islington	41	51 32N	0 06W
Ismâ'ilîya	91	30 37N	32 18 E
Isna	91	25 17N	32 30 E
Isoka	93	10 4 S	32 42 E
Ispica	58	36 47N	14 53 E
Israel ■	89	32 0N	34 50 E
Issoire	56	45 32N	3 15 E
Issyk-Kul, L.	62	42 25N	77 15 E
Istanbul	71	41 0N	29 0 E
Istra	58	45 10N	14 0 E
Ithaca	104	42 25N	76 30W
Itsa	91	29 15N	30 40 E
Itu	90	5 10N	7 58 E
Ivanhoe	79	32 56 S	144 20 E
Ivano-Frankovsk	55	49 0N	24 40 E
Ivanovo	62	57 5N	41 0 E
Ivory Coast ■	88	7 30N	5 0W
Ivrea	58	45 30N	7 52 E
Ivugivik	99	62 24N	77 55W
Ivybridge	43	50 24N	3 56W
Iwaki	76	37 3N	140 55 E
Iwamisawa	76	43 12N	141 46 E
Iwanai	76	42 58N	140 30 E
Iwanuma	76	38 7N	140 58 E
Iwate-San	76	39 51N	141 0 E
Iwo	90	7 39N	4 9 E
Izegem	52	50 55N	3 12 E
Izhevsk	62	56 51N	53 14 E
Izmail	55	45 22N	28 46 E
Izmir	71	38 25N	27 8 E
Izumo	76	35 20N	132 55 E

J

Jabalpur	70	23 9N	79 58 E
Jaca	60	42 35N	0 33W
Jackson, Mich., U.S.A.	104	42 18N	84 25W
Jackson, Miss., U.S.A.	101	32 20N	90 10W
Jackson, Tenn., U.S.A.	101	35 40N	88 50W
Jacksons	83	42 46 S	171 32 E
Jacksonville, Fla., U.S.A.	101	30 15N	81 38W
Jacksonville, Ill., U.S.A.	101	39 42N	90 15W
Jacobabad	71	28 20N	68 29 E
Jaén	60	37 44N	3 43W
Jaffna	70	9 45N	80 2 E
Jagdalpur	70	19 3N	82 6 E
Jagersfontein	94	29 44 S	25 27 E
Jahrom	71	28 30N	53 31 E
Jaipur	70	27 0N	76 10 E
Jakarta	72	6 9 S	106 49 E
Jalalabad	71	34 30N	70 29 E
Jalapa	106	19 30N	96 50W
Jalgaon	70	21 0N	75 42 E
Jalingo	90	8 55N	11 25 E
Jalón, R.	60	41 20N	1 40W
Jamaari	90	11 44N	9 53 E
Jamaica, I. ■	107	18 10N	77 30W
Jambi	72	1 38 S	103 30 E
Jamestown, Austral.	79	33 10 S	138 32 E
Jamestown, N.D., U.S.A.	100	47 0N	98 45W
Jamestown, N.Y., U.S.A.	104	42 5N	79 18W
Jammu	70	32 43N	74 54 E
Jammu & Kashmir □	70	34 25N	77 0 E
Jamnagar	70	22 30N	70 0 E
Jamshedpur	70	22 44N	86 20 E
Jan Mayen Is.	112	71 0N	11 0W
Jansenville	94	32 57 S	24 39 E
Japan ■	76	36 0N	136 0 E
Japan, Sea of	76	40 0N	135 0 E
Japurá, R.	108	3 8 S	64 46W
Jarosław	55	50 2N	22 42 E
Jarrow	44	54 58N	1 28W
Jarvis I.	22	0 15 S	159 55W
Jasło	55	49 45N	21 30 E
Játiva	60	39 0N	0 32W
Java, I.	72	7 0 S	110 0 E
Java Sea	72	4 35 S	107 15 E
Jebba	90	9 9N	4 48 E
Jedburgh	46	55 28N	2 33W
Jędrzejów	55	50 35N	20 15 E
Jefferson, Mt.	105	44 45N	121 50W
Jega	90	12 15N	4 23 E
Jelenia Góra	54	50 50N	15 45 E
Jelgava	61	56 41N	22 49 E
Jemappes	52	50 27N	3 54 E
Jemeppe	52	50 37N	5 30 E
Jena	54	50 56N	11 33 E
Jérez	60	36 41N	6 7W
Jersey City	104	40 41N	74 8W
Jersey, I.	43	49 13N	2 7W
Jerusalem	89	31 47N	35 10 E
Jervis Bay	79	35 8 S	150 43 E
Jhansi	70	25 30N	78 36 E
Jhelum	71	33 0N	73 45 E
Jiddah	71	21 29N	39 16 E
Jido	70	29 2N	94 58 E
Jihlava	54	49 28N	15 35 E
Jiloca, R.	60	41 0N	1 20W
Jinja	93	0 25N	33 12 E
Jiu, R.	55	44 50N	23 20 E
João Pessoa	108	7 10 S	34 52W
Jodhpur	70	26 23N	73 2 E
Joensuu	61	62 37N	29 49 E
Johannesburg	94	26 10 S	28 8 E
John Day, R.	105	45 44N	120 39W
John o' Groats	48	58 39N	3 3W
Johnston Lakes	78	32 20 S	120 45 E
Johnstone	47	55 50N	4 31W
Johnstown, Ireland	51	52 46N	7 34W
Johnstown, U.S.A.	104	40 19N	78 53W
Johor Baharu	72	1 28N	103 46 E
Joliet	104	41 30N	88 0W
Joliette	99	46 3N	73 24W
Jolo I.	72	6 0N	121 0 E
Jones Sound	99	76 0N	89 0W
Jönköping	61	57 45N	14 10 E
Jonquière	99	48 27N	71 14W
Joplin	101	37 0N	94 25W
Jordan ■	89	31 0N	36 0 E
Jordan, R.	89	31 48N	35 32 E
Jorhat	70	26 45N	94 20 E
Jos	90	9 53N	8 51 E
Joseph Bonaparte G.	78	14 35 S	128 50 E
Jotunheimen	61	61 35N	8 25 E
Juan de Fuca Str.	105	48 15N	124 0W
Juan Fernandez, Is.	108	33 50 S	80 0W
Juba	89	4 57N	31 35 E
Jubal, Str. of	91	27 30N	34 0 E
Júcar, R.	60	40 8N	2 13W
Júcaro	107	21 37N	78 51W
Judea	89	31 35N	34 57 E
Julia Cr.	79	20 0 S	141 11 E
Julianehåb	96	60 43N	46 0W
Jullundur	70	31 20N	75 40 E
Jumet	52	50 27N	4 25 E
Jumilla	60	38 28N	1 19W
Jumna, R.	70	27 0N	78 30 E
Junagadh	70	21 30N	70 30 E
Juneau	98	58 26N	134 30W
Junee	79	34 53 S	147 35 E
Junta, La	100	38 0N	103 30W
Jura	56	46 35N	6 5 E
Jura, I.	46	56 0N	5 50W
Jura, Mts.	54	46 40N	6 5 E
Jura, Paps of.	46	55 55N	6 0W
Jura, Sd. of	46	55 57N	5 45W
Jutland	61	56 0N	8 0 E
Jye-kundo	73	33 0N	96 50 E
Jyväskylä	61	62 14N	25 44 E

K

K2, Mt.	70	36 0N	77 0 E
Kabale	93	1 15 S	30 0 E
Kabalo	92	6 0 S	27 0 E
Kabarega Falls	93	2 15N	31 38 E
Kabarnet	93	0 31N	35 44 E
Kabba	90	7 57N	6 3 E
Kabinda	92	6 23 S	24 28 E
Kabul	71	34 28N	69 18 E
Kabwe	92	14 30 S	28 29 E
Kachin □	70	26 0N	97 0 E
Kadina	79	34 0 S	137 43 E
Kaduna	90	10 30N	7 21 E
Kafanchan	90	9 40N	8 20 E
Kafareti	90	10 25N	11 12 E
Kafr el Dauwâr	91	31 8N	30 8 E
Kafue	92	15 46 S	28 9 E
Kafue, R.	92	15 30 S	26 0 E
Kagadi	93	0 58N	30 48 E
Kagoshima	76	31 36N	130 40 E
Kahe	93	3 30 S	37 25 E
Kai Is.	72	5 55 S	132 45 E
Kaiapoi	83	42 24 S	172 40 E
Kaifeng	73	34 49N	114 30 E
Kaikohe	83	35 25 S	173 49 E
Kaikoura	83	42 25 S	173 43 E
Kaikoura Ra.	83	41 59 S	173 41 E
Kaimanawa Mts.	83	39 15 S	175 56 E
Kainji Res.	90	10 1N	4 40 E
Kairuku	79	8 51 S	146 35 E
Kaiserslautern	52	49 30N	7 43 E
Kaitaia	83	35 8 S	173 17 E
Kaitangata	83	46 17 S	169 51 E
Kajaani	61	64 17N	27 46 E
Kajabbi	79	20 0 S	140 1 E
Kakamas	94	28 45 S	20 33 E
Kakamega	93	0 20N	34 46 E
Kakanui Mts.	83	45 10 S	170 30 E
Kakia	94	24 48 S	23 22 E
Kakinada	70	16 50N	82 11 E
Kalahari, Des.	92	24 0 S	22 0 E
Kalamazoo	104	42 20N	85 35W
Kalemie	93	5 55 S	29 9 E
Kalgoorlie	78	30 40 S	121 22 E
Kalimantan Barat □	72	0 0	110 30 E
Kalinin	62	56 55N	35 55 E
Kaliningrad	61	54 42N	20 32 E
Kalispell	100	48 10N	114 22W
Kalisz	55	51 45N	18 8 E
Kaliua	93	5 5 S	31 48 E
Kalmar	61	56 40N	16 20 E
Kama, R.	62	60 0N	53 0 E
Kamaishi	76	39 20N	142 0 E
Kamba	90	11 50N	3 45 E
Kamchatka Pen.	62	57 0N	160 0 E
Kamenets-Podolskiy	55	48 45N	26 10 E
Kamenjak, C.	58	44 47N	13 55 E
Kamenka Bugskaya	55	50 8N	24 16 E
Kames	46	55 53N	5 15W
Kamina	92	8 45 S	25 0 E
Kamloops L.	98	50 45N	120 40W
Kamp-Lintfort	52	51 31N	6 32 E
Kampala	93	0 20N	32 30 E
Kampen	52	52 33N	5 53 E
Kananga	92	5 55 S	22 18 E
Kanazawa	76	36 30N	136 38 E
Kanchenjunga, Mt.	70	27 50N	88 10 E
Kanchow	73	25 58N	114 55 E
Kandahar	71	31 32N	65 30 E
Kandalaksha	61	67 9N	32 30 E
Kandi	90	11 7N	2 55 E
Kandy	70	7 18N	80 43 E
Kangaroo I.	79	35 45 S	137 0 E
Kangean Is.	72	6 55 S	115 23 E
Kangnŭng	73	37 45N	128 54 E
Kaniapiskau, R.	99	57 40N	69 30W
Kanin Pen.	62	68 0N	45 0 E
Kankakee	104	41 6N	87 50W
Kankan	88	10 30N	9 15W
Kanker	70	20 10N	81 40 E
Kano	90	12 2N	8 30 E
Kanowna	78	30 32 S	121 31 E
Kanoya	76	31 25N	130 50 E
Kanpur	70	26 35N	80 20 E
Kansas □	100	38 40N	98 0W
Kansas City	101	39 0N	94 40W
Kansas, R.	101	39 7N	94 36W
Kantché	90	13 31N	8 30 E
Kanturk	51	52 10N	8 55W
Kanye	94	25 0 S	25 28 E
Kaohsiung	73	22 35N	120 16 E
Kapela, Mts.	58	44 40N	15 40 E
Kapuas Hulu Ra.	72	1 30N	113 30 E
Kapuas, R.	72	0 20N	111 40 E
Kara Bogaz Gol, Zaliv	71	41 0N	53 30 E
Kara Kalpak A.S.S.R. □	71	43 0N	60 0 E
Kara Sea	62	75 0N	70 0 E
Karachi	71	24 53N	67 0 E
Karaganda	62	49 50N	73 0 E
Karakoram	70	35 20N	76 0 E
Karakum, Peski	71	39 30N	60 0 E
Karamai	73	45 57N	84 30 E
Karamea Bight	83	41 22 S	171 40 E
Karasburg	94	28 0 S	18 44 E
Karatsu	76	33 30N	130 0 E
Karawanken	58	46 30N	14 40 E
Karbalā	71	32 47N	44 3 E
Karcag	55	47 19N	21 1 E
Kareeberge	94	30 50 S	22 0 E
Karelian A.S.S.R. □	61	65 30N	32 30 E
Kariba Lake	92	16 40 S	28 25 E
Karikal	70	10 59N	79 50 E
Karimata I.	72	1 40 S	109 0 E
Karkaralinsk	73	49 27N	75 37 E
Karkur Tohl	91	22 5N	25 5 E
Karl-Marx-Stadt	54	50 50N	12 55 E
Karlovac	58	45 31N	15 36 E
Karlskrona	61	56 10N	15 35 E
Karlsruhe	54	49 3N	8 23 E
Karlstad	61	59 23N	13 30 E
Karnataka □	70	13 15N	77 0 E
Kars	71	40 40N	43 5 E
Karsakpay	62	47 55N	66 40 E
Karshi	71	38 53N	65 48 E
Karungu	93	0 50 S	34 10 E
Kasama	93	10 16 S	31 9 E
Kāshān	71	34 5N	51 30 E
Kashgar	73	39 46N	75 52 E
Kashima	76	33 7N	130 6 E
Kashing	73	30 45N	120 41 E
Kashiwazaki	76	37 22N	138 33 E
Kasongo	92	4 30 S	26 33 E
Kassaba	91	22 40N	29 55 E
Kassala	89	15 23N	36 26 E
Kassel	54	51 19N	9 32 E
Kastamonu	71	41 25N	33 43 E
Katanning	78	33 40 S	117 33 E
Katha	70	24 10N	96 30 E
Katherîna, Gebel	91	28 30N	33 57 E
Katherine	78	14 27 S	132 20 E
Katihar	70	25 34N	87 36 E
Katmandu	70	27 45N	85 12 E
Katoomba	79	33 41 S	150 19 E
Katowice	55	50 17N	19 5 E
Katrine, L.	46	56 15N	4 30W
Katsina	90	7 10N	9 20 E
Katsuura	76	35 15N	140 20 E
Kattakurgan	71	39 55N	66 15 E
Kattegat	61	57 0N	11 20 E
Katumba	93	7 40 S	25 17 E
Katwe	93	0 8 S	29 52 E
Katwijk-aan-Zee	52	52 12N	4 24 E
Kaunas	61	54 54N	23 54 E
Kawagoe	76	35 55N	139 29 E
Kawaguchi	76	35 52N	138 45 E
Kawambwa	93	9 48 S	29 3 E
Kawerau	83	38 7 S	176 42 E
Kawthoolei □	70	18 0N	97 30 E
Kayah □	70	19 15N	97 15 E
Kayseri	71	38 45N	35 30 E
Kazakhstan	62	51 11N	53 0 E
Kazan	62	55 48N	49 3 E
Kazatin	55	49 45N	28 50 E
Kāzerūn	71	29 38N	51 40 E
Keady	50	54 15N	6 42W
Kearsley	45	53 33N	2 23W

* Renamed Edward, L.

Kebnekaise, mt

Langholm

Kebnekaise, mt. 61 67 54N 18 33E
Kecskemét 55 46 57N 19 35E
Kediri 72 7 51S 112 1E
Keeper Hill 51 52 46N 8 17W
Keetmanshoop 94 26 35S 18 8E
Keewatin □ 98 63 20N 94 40W
Keffi 90 8 55N 7 43E
Keighley 45 53 52N 1 54W
Keimoes 94 28 41S 21 0E
Keith 48 57 33N 2 58W
Kelang 72 3 2N 101 26E
Kellerberrin 78 31 36S 117 38E
Kellogg 100 47 30N 116 5W
Kelowna 105 49 50N 119 25W
Kelso 46 55 36N 2 27W
Kelty 47 56 08N 3 23W
Kem 61 65 0N 34 38E
Kemerovo 62 55 20N 85 50E
Kemi 61 65 44N 24 34E
Kemi, R. 61 67 30N 28 30E
Kemp Coast 112 69 0S 55 0E
Kempsey 79 31 1S 152 50E
Kempten 54 47 42N 10 18E
Kemsing 41 51 18N 0 14E
Kendal 44 54 19N 2 44W
Kendari 72 3 50S 122 30E
Kende 90 11 30N 4 12E
Keng Tung 70 21 0N 99 30E
Kenhardt 94 29 19S 21 12E
Kenilworth 42 52 22N 1 35W
Kenitra 88 34 15N 6 40W
Kenmare 51 51 52N 9 35W
Kenmare, R. 51 51 40N 10 0W
Kennet, R. 40 51 24N 1 7W
Kennewick 100 46 11N 119 2W
Kenosha 104 42 33N 87 48W
Kent □ 40 51 12N 0 40E
Kentucky □ 101 37 20N 85 0W
Kentville 99 45 6N 64 29W
Kenya ■ 93 2 20N 38 0E
Kenya, Mt. 93 0 10S 37 18E
Kerala □ 70 11 0N 76 15E
Kerama-Shotō 76 26 12N 127 22E
Kerang 79 35 40S 143 55E
Kerch 62 45 20N 36 20E
Kerema 79 7 58S 145 50E
Kerguelen I. 23 48 15S 69 10E
Kericho 93 0 22S 35 15E
Kerinci 72 2 5S 101 0E
Kerki 71 37 50N 65 12E
Kermadec Is. 22 31 8S 175 16W
Kermān 71 30 15N 57 1E
Kermānshāh 71 34 23N 47 0E
Kerrera I. 46 56 24N 5 32W
Kerry □ 51 52 7N 9 35W
Kerulen, R. 73 48 48N 117 0E
Kesh 50 54 31N 7 43W
Keswick 44 54 35N 3 9W
Ketchikan 96 55 25N 131 40W
Kętrzyn 55 54 7N 21 22E
Kettering 45 52 24N 0 44W
Kexbrough 45 53 35N 1 32W
Key West 101 24 40N 82 0W
Keynsham 42 51 25N 2 30W
Khalig el Tina, B. 91 31 20N 32 42E
Kharagpur 70 22 20N 87 25E
Kharga, Oasis de 91 25 0N 30 0E
Kharit, Wadi el 91 24 5N 34 10E
Kharkov 62 49 58N 36 20E
Khartoum 89 15 31N 32 35E
Khashm el Girba 89 14 59N 35 58E
Khasi Hills 70 25 30N 91 30E
Khatanga 62 72 0N 102 20E
Kherson 62 46 35N 32 35E
Khetinsiring 73 32 54N 92 50E
Khilok 73 51 30N 110 45E
Khiva 71 41 30N 60 18E
Kholm 61 57 10N 31 15E
Khong, R. 72 15 0N 106 50E
Khorramshahr 71 30 29N 48 15E
Khotin 55 48 31N 26 27E
Khurasan, prov. 71 34 0N 57 0E
Khust 55 48 10N 23 18E
Khvoy 71 38 35N 45 0E
Khyber Pass 70 34 10N 71 8E
Kiambu 93 1 8S 36 50E
Kiamusze 73 46 45N 130 30E
Kian 73 27 1N 114 58E
Kiangsi □ 73 27 20N 115 40E
Kiangsu □ 73 33 0N 119 50E
Kiaohsien 73 36 20N 120 0E
Kibwezi 93 2 27S 37 57E
Kicking Horse Pass 98 51 28N 116 16W
Kidderminster 41 52 24N 2 13W
Kidsgrove 44 53 6N 2 15W
Kidwelly 42 51 44N 4 20W
Kiel 54 54 16N 10 8E
Kiel B. 54 54 20N 10 20E
Kielce 55 50 58N 20 42E
Kienow 73 27 0N 118 16E
Kienshui 73 23 57N 102 45E
Kiev 55 50 30N 30 28E
Kigali 93 1 5S 30 4E
Kigoma-Ujiji 93 5 30S 30 0E
Kii Chan. 76 33 40N 135 0E
Kikinda 55 45 50N 20 30E
Kikori 79 7 13S 144 15E
Kilbeggan 51 53 22N 7 30W
Kilbirnie 47 55 46N 4 42W
Kilcormac 51 53 11N 7 44W
Kilcreggan 47 55 59N 4 50W
Kilcullen 51 53 8N 6 45W
Kildare 51 53 10N 6 50W
Kildare □ 51 53 10N 6 50W
Kildonan 48 58 10N 3 50W
Kilgetty 42 51 43N 4 43W
Kilifi 93 3 40S 39 48E
Kilimanjaro, Mt. 93 3 7S 37 20E
Kilindini 93 4 4S 39 40E
Kiliya 55 45 28N 29 16E
Kilkee 51 52 41N 9 40W
Kilkeel 50 54 4N 6 0W
Kilkenny 51 52 40N 7 17W
Kilkenny □ 51 52 35N 7 15W
Kill 51 52 11N 7 20W
Killala B. 50 54 20N 9 12W
Killaloe 51 52 48N 8 28W
Killamarsh 45 53 19N 1 19W
Killarney 51 52 2N 9 30W
Killarney, L's. of 51 52 0N 9 30W
Killashandra 50 54 1N 7 32W
Killay 42 51 36N 4 02W
Killenaule 51 52 35N 7 40W
Killiecrankie, Pass of 48 56 44N 3 46W
Killimor 51 53 10N 8 17W
Killiney 51 53 15N 6 8W
Killorglin 51 52 6N 9 48W
Killybegs 50 54 38N 8 26W
Kilmacolm 47 55 54N 4 39W
Kilmacthomas 51 52 13N 7 27W
Kilmallock 51 52 22N 8 35W
Kilmarnock 47 55 36N 4 30W
Kilmaurs 47 55 37N 4 33W
Kilosa 93 6 48S 37 0E
Kilrea 50 54 58N 6 34W
Kilronan 51 53 8N 9 40W
Kilrush 51 52 39N 9 30W
Kilsyth 47 55 58N 4 3W
Kiltamagh 50 53 52N 9 0W
Kilwa Kisiwani 93 8 58S 39 32E
Kilwa Kivinje 93 8 45S 39 25E
Kilwinning 47 55 40N 4 41W
Kimba 79 33 8S 136 23E
Kimberley, Austral. 78 16 20S 127 0E
Kimberley, S. Afr. 94 28 43S 24 46E
Kinabalu, mt. 72 6 0N 116 0E
Kinbrace 48 58 16N 3 56W
Kincardine 47 56 4N 3 43W
Kindu 92 2 55S 25 50E
King George Is. 99 53 40N 80 30W
King I. 79 39 50S 144 0E
King Leopold Ranges 78 17 20S 124 20E
King Sd. 78 16 50S 123 20E
King William's Town 94 32 51S 27 22E
Kinghorn 47 56 4N 3 10W
Kingman 100 35 12N 114 2W
Kings Langley 41 51 42N 0 27W
King's Lynn 40 52 45N 0 25E
King's Worthy 40 51 6N 1 18W
Kingscourt 51 53 55N 6 48W
Kingsclere 40 51 19N 1 15W
Kingston, Can. 104 44 14N 76 30W
Kingston, Jamaica 107 18 0N 76 50W
Kingston, N.Z. 83 45 20S 168 43E
Kingston, U.S.A. 104 41 55N 74 0W
Kingston-upon-Thames 41 51 23N 0 20W
Kingstown 107 13 10N 61 10W
Kingsville 100 27 30N 97 53W
Kingswood, Glos., U.K. 43 51 26N 2 31W
Kingswood, War., U.K. 41 52 20N 1 43W
Kingtehchen (Fowliang) 73 29 8N 117 21E
Kington 42 52 12N 3 2W
Kingussie 48 57 5N 4 2W
Kinleith 83 38 20S 175 56E
Kinloch 83 44 51S 168 20E
Kinlochewe 48 57 37N 5 20W
Kinlochleven 48 56 42N 4 59W
Kinnairds Hd. 48 57 40N 2 0W
Kinnegad 51 53 28N 7 8W
Kinross 47 56 13N 3 25W
Kinsale 51 51 42N 8 31W
Kinsale, Old Hd. of 51 51 37N 8 32W
Kinshasa 92 4 20S 15 15E
Kinston 101 35 18N 77 35W
Kintore 48 57 14N 2 20W
Kintyre 46 55 30N 5 35W
Kintyre, Mull of 46 55 17N 5 4W
Kipini 93 2 30S 40 32E
Kippax 45 53 46N 1 22W
Kirby Muxloe 41 52 37N 1 13W
Kirensk 62 57 50N 107 55E
Kirgiz S.S.R. □ 71 42 0N 75 0E
Kirin 73 43 58N 126 31E
Kirin □ 73 43 50N 125 45E
Kirkburton 45 53 36N 1 42W
Kirkby 45 53 29N 2 54W
Kirkby Lonsdale 44 54 13N 2 36W
Kirkby Moorside 44 54 16N 0 56W
Kirkby Steven 44 54 27N 2 23W
Kirkcaldy 47 56 7N 3 10W
Kirkcolm 46 54 59N 5 4W
Kirkconnel 46 55 23N 4 0W
Kirkcudbright 46 54 50N 4 3W
Kirkham 45 53 47N 2 52W
Kirkheaton 45 53 39N 1 44W
Kirkintilloch 47 55 57N 4 10W
Kirkland Lake 99 48 9N 80 2W
Kirkliston 47 55 55N 3 27W
Kirkūk 71 35 30N 44 21E
Kirkwall 49 58 59N 2 59W
Kirkwood 94 33 22S 25 15E
Kirov 62 58 35N 49 40E
Kirovabad 71 40 45N 46 10E
Kirovsk 61 67 48N 33 50E
Kirtachi 90 12 52N 2 30E
Kiruna 61 67 52N 20 15E
Kiryū 76 36 24N 139 20E
Kisangani 92 0 35N 25 15E
Kishangarh 70 27 50N 70 30E
Kishinev 55 47 0N 28 50E
Kishiwada 76 34 28N 135 22E
Kisi 73 45 21N 131 0E
Kisii 93 0 40S 34 45E
Kiskörös 55 46 37N 19 20E
Kiskunfélegyháza 55 46 42N 19 53E
Kismayu 89 0 20S 42 30E
Kisumu 93 0 3S 34 45E
Kitakyūshū 76 33 50N 130 50E
Kitale 93 1 0N 35 12E
Kitami 76 43 48N 143 54E
Kitchener 99 43 30N 80 30W
Kitgum Matidi 93 3 17N 32 52E
Kitimat 98 54 3N 128 38W
Kitui 93 1 17S 38 0E
Kitwe 92 12 54S 28 7E
Kiukiang 73 29 37N 116 2E
Kizil Avvat 71 39 0N 56 25E
Kizlyar 71 43 51N 46 40E
Kladno 54 50 10N 14 7E
Klagenfurt 54 46 38N 14 20E
Klaipeda 61 55 43N 21 10E
Klamath Falls 105 42 20N 121 50W
Klamath, R. 105 41 40N 124 4W
Klatovy 54 49 23N 13 18E
Klawer 94 31 44S 18 36E
Klerksdorp 94 26 51S 26 38E
Kleve 52 51 46N 6 10E
Klipplaat 94 33 0S 24 22E
Klondike 98 64 0N 139 26W
Klyuchevsk, mt. 62 55 50N 160 30E
Knapdale 46 55 55N 5 30W
Knaresborough 44 54 1N 1 29W
Knighton 42 52 21N 3 2W
Knockmealdown Mts. 51 52 16N 8 0W
Knokke 52 51 20N 3 17E
Knottingley 44 53 42N 1 15W
Knowle 41 52 23N 1 43W
Knowsley 45 53 27N 2 51W
Knoxville 101 35 58N 83 57W
Knoydart, dist. 48 57 3N 5 33W
Knutsford 45 53 18N 2 22W
Knysna 94 34 2S 23 2E
Kobarid 58 46 15N 13 30E
Kobayashi 76 31 56N 130 59E
Kōbe 76 34 45N 135 10E
Koblenz 52 50 21N 7 36E
Kobroor, I. 72 6 10S 134 30E
Kočevje 58 45 39N 14 50E
Kōchi 76 33 30N 133 35E
Kōfu 76 35 40N 138 30E
Kogota 76 38 33N 141 3E
Kohlscheid 52 50 50N 6 6E
Kohtla-Järve 61 59 20N 27 20E
Kokand 71 40 30N 70 57E
Kokchetav 62 53 20N 69 10E
Kokiu 73 23 30N 103 0E
Koko 90 11 28N 4 29E
Koko-Nor 73 37 0N 100 0E
Kokomo 104 40 30N 86 6W
Kokstad 94 30 32S 29 29E
Kola Pen. 61 67 30N 38 0E
Kolar 70 13 12N 78 15E
Kolguyev, I. 62 69 20N 48 30E
Kolhapur 70 16 43N 74 15E
Kolin 54 50 2N 15 9E
Köln = Cologne 52 50 56N 9 58E
Kołobrzeg 54 54 10N 15 35E
Kolomyya 55 48 31N 25 2E
Kolyma, R. 62 64 40N 153 0E
Kolyma Ra. 62 63 0N 157 0E
Kôm Ombo 91 24 25N 32 52E
Komandorskiye, Is. 62 55 0N 167 0E
Komárno 55 47 49N 18 5E
Komatipoort 94 25 25S 31 57E
Kompong Som 72 10 38N 103 30E
Komsberge 94 32 40S 20 45E
Komsomolets I. 62 80 30N 95 0E
Komsomolsk 62 50 30N 137 0E
Kondoa 93 4 55S 35 50E
Kong 88 8 54N 4 36W
Kongmoon 73 22 35N 113 1E
Kongolo 92 5 22S 27 0E
Konjic 58 43 42N 17 58E
Konskie 55 51 15N 20 23E
Konstanz 54 47 39N 9 10E
Kontagora 90 10 23N 5 27E
Konya 71 37 52N 32 35E
Konza 93 1 45S 37 0E
Korčula, I. 58 42 57N 17 0E
Korea Bay 73 39 0N 124 0E
Korea, South ■ 73 36 0N 128 0E
Korea Strait 73 34 0N 129 30E
Korea, North ■ 73 40 0N 127 0E
Koreh Wells 93 0 3N 38 45E
Kōriyama 76 37 24N 140 23E
Korogwe 93 5 5S 38 25E
Körös, R. 55 46 45N 20 20E
Korosten 55 50 57N 28 25E
Kortrijk 52 50 50N 3 17E
Kościan 54 52 5N 16 40E
Kosciusko, Mt. 79 36 27S 148 16E
Kosi, L. 94 27 0S 32 50E
Košice 55 48 42N 21 15E
Koster 94 25 52S 26 54E
Kostrzyn 54 52 24N 17 14E
Koszalin 54 54 12N 16 8E
Kota 70 25 14N 75 49E
Kota Kinabalu 72 6 0N 116 12E
Kotka 61 60 28N 26 58E
Kotlas 62 61 15N 47 0E
Kotovsk 55 47 55N 29 35E
Kouga Mts. 94 33 40S 23 55E
Kounradski 62 47 20N 75 0E
Kovel 55 51 10N 24 20E
Kowloon 73 22 20N 114 15E
Koyuk 98 64 55N 161 20W
Koza 76 26 19N 127 46E
Kra, Isthmus of 72 10 15N 99 30E
Kragujevac 55 44 2N 20 56E
Kraków 55 50 4N 19 57E
Krasnodar 62 45 5N 38 50E
Krasnovodsk 71 40 0N 52 52E
Krasnoyarsk 62 56 8N 93 0E
Kratie 72 12 32N 106 10E
Krefeld 52 51 20N 6 22E
Krishna, R. 70 16 30N 77 0E
Kristiansand 61 58 9N 8 1E
Kristiansund 61 63 7N 7 45E
Krivoy Rog 62 47 51N 33 20E
Krk 58 45 8N 14 40E
Kronshtadt 61 60 5N 29 35E
Kroonstad 94 27 43S 27 19E
Krotoszyn 55 51 42N 17 23E
Krugersdorp 94 26 5S 27 46E
Kruidfontein 94 32 48S 21 59E
Kuala Lumpur 72 3 9N 101 41E
Kucha 73 41 50N 82 30E
Kuching 72 1 33N 110 25E
Kudat 72 6 55N 116 55E
Kufra Oasis 89 24 17N 23 15E
Kufstein 54 47 35N 12 11E
Kuji 76 40 11N 141 46E
Kulunda 73 52 45N 79 15E
Kum Darya 73 41 0N 89 0E
Kumamoto 76 32 45N 130 45E
Kumara 83 42 37S 171 12E
Kumasi 88 6 41N 1 38W
Kumba 90 4 36N 9 24E
Kumbo 90 6 15N 10 36E
Kunlun Shan 73 36 0N 86 30E
Kunming 73 25 11N 102 37E
Kunsan 73 35 59N 126 45E
Kununurra 78 15 40S 128 39E
Kuopio 61 62 53N 27 35E
Kupa, R. 58 45 30N 16 24E
Kupang 72 10 19S 123 39E
Kurashiki 76 34 40N 133 50E
Kure 76 34 14N 132 32E
Kurgan 62 55 26N 65 18E
Kuril Is. 62 45 0N 150 0E
Kurnool 70 15 45N 78 0E
Kurow 83 44 4S 170 29E
Kursk 62 51 42N 36 11E
Kuruman 94 27 28S 23 28E
Kuruman R. 94 27 5S 21 30E
Kurume 76 33 15N 130 30E
Kushiro 76 43 0N 144 25E
Kuskokwim Mts. 98 63 0N 156 0W
Kutaisi 71 42 19N 42 40E
Kutch, G. of 70 22 50N 69 15E
Kutno 55 52 15N 19 23E
Kuwait ■ 71 29 30N 47 30E
Kuwana 76 35 0N 136 43E
Kuybyshev 62 55 27N 78 19E
Kvarner 58 44 50N 14 10E
Kwangchow 73 23 10N 113 10E
Kwangju 73 35 9N 126 55E
Kwangsi-Chuang □ 73 23 30N 108 55E
Kwangtung □ 73 23 45N 114 0E
Kwara □ 90 8 0N 5 0E
Kweichow □ 73 27 20N 107 0E
Kweilin 73 25 16N 110 15E
Kweiyang 73 26 30N 106 35E
Kwidzyn 55 54 45N 18 58E
Kwinana 78 32 15S 115 47E
Kyakhta 73 50 30N 106 25E
Kyle 46 55 32N 4 25W
Kyle of Lochalsh 48 57 17N 5 43W
Kyleakin 48 57 16N 5 44W
Kylestrome 48 58 16N 5 02W
Kyōto 76 35 0N 135 45E
Kyūshū □ 76 33 0N 131 0E
Kyzyl 73 51 50N 94 30E
Kyzyl Kum 71 42 0N 65 0E
Kyzyl Orda 71 44 56N 65 30E

L

Labe, R. 54 50 3N 15 20E
Labrador City 99 52 57N 66 55W
Labrador, Coast of 99 53 20N 61 0W
Labuan, I. 72 5 15N 115 38E
Laccadive Is. = Lakshadweep Is. 70 10 0N 72 30E
Lachine 99 45 30N 73 40W
Lachlan, R. 79 34 22S 143 55E
Ladismith 94 33 28S 21 15E
Ladoga, L. 61 61 15N 30 30E
Lady Grey 94 30 43S 27 13E
Ladybank 47 56 16N 3 8W
Ladybrand 94 29 9S 27 29E
Ladysmith 94 28 32S 29 46E
Lae 79 6 40S 147 2E
Lafayette, Ind., U.S.A. 104 40 25N 86 54W
Lafayette, La., U.S.A. 101 30 18N 92 0W
Lafia 90 8 30N 8 34E
Lafiagi 90 8 52N 5 20E
Lagan, R. 50 54 35N 5 55W
Lagoa dos Patos 108 31 15S 51 0W
Lagos, Nigeria 90 6 25N 3 27E
Lagos, Port. 60 37 5N 8 41W
Lahore 71 31 32N 74 22E
Lahti 61 60 58N 25 40E
Laingsburg 94 33 9S 20 52E
Lairg 48 58 1N 4 24W
Lake Charles 101 30 15N 93 10W
Lake District 44 54 30N 3 10W
Lakeland 101 28 0N 82 0W
Lakewood 104 41 28N 81 50W
Lakshadweep Is. 70 10 0N 72 30E
Lamar 100 38 9N 102 35W
Lambert's Bay 94 32 5S 18 17E
Lambeth 41 51 27N 0 7W
Lambourn 40 51 31N 1 31W
Lamlash 46 55 32N 5 8W
Lammermuir Hills 46 55 50N 2 40W
Lampedusa, I. 58 35 36N 12 40E
Lampeter 42 52 6N 4 6W
Lamu 93 2 10S 40 55E
Lanark 47 55 40N 3 48W
Lancashire □ 44 53 40N 2 30W
Lancaster, U.K. 44 54 3N 2 48W
Lancaster, Calif., U.S.A. 101 34 47N 118 8W
Lancaster, Pa., U.S.A. 104 40 4N 76 19W
Lancaster Sd. 99 74 13N 84 0W
Lanchester 44 54 50N 1 44W
Lanchow, China 73 36 4N 103 44E
Landau 52 49 12N 8 7E
Landeck 54 47 9N 10 34E
Landerneau 56 48 28N 4 17W
Landes □ 56 43 57N 0 48W
Landore 43 51 38N 3 55W
Land's End 43 50 4N 5 43W
Landshut 54 48 31N 12 10E
Langeberge, C. Prov., S. Afr. 94 33 55S 21 20E
Langeberge, C. Prov., S. Afr. 94 28 15S 22 33E
Langholm 46 55 9N 2 59W

Langport Lynton and Lynmouth

Langport	43	51 2N	2 51W
Langres	56	47 52N	5 20E
Languedoc	56	43 58N	4 0E
Lansdowne	94	31 48S	152 30E
Lansing	104	42 47N	84 40W
Laoag	72	18 7N	120 34E
Laois □	51	53 0N	7 20W
Laon	56	49 33N	3 35E
Laos ■	72	17 45N	105 0E
Lapland	61	68 7N	24 0E
Laptev Sea	62	76 0N	125 0E
Laragh	51	53 0N	6 20W
Laramie	100	41 15N	105 29W
Laramie Mts.	100	42 0N	105 30W
Larbert	47	56 2N	3 50W
Laredo	100	27 34N	99 29W
Laren	52	52 16N	5 14E
Largs	47	55 48N	4 51W
Larkhall	47	55 44N	3 58W
Larne	50	54 52N	5 50W
Larne □	50	54 55N	5 55W
Larrimah	78	15 35S	133 12E
Larvik	61	59 4N	10 0E
Las Cruces	100	32 25N	106 50W
Las Mercedes	107	9 7N	66 24W
Las Palmas	88	28 10N	15 28W
Las Vegas, Nev., U.S.A.	100	36 10N	115 5W
Las Vegas, N.M., U.S.A.	100	35 35N	105 10W
Lashio	70	22 56N	97 45E
Lassen, Pk.	105	40 35N	121 40W
Lasswade	47	55 53N	3 8W
Latheron	48	58 17N	3 20W
Latium	58	42 10N	12 30E
Latvia, S.S.R. □	61	56 50N	24 0E
Lauder	46	55 43N	2 45W
Lauenburg	54	53 23N	10 33E
Laugharne	42	51 45N	4 28W
Launceston, Austral.	79	41 24S	147 8E
Launceston, U.K.	43	50 38N	4 21W
Laura	79	15 32S	144 32E
Laurel	101	31 50N	89 0W
Laurencekirk	48	56 50N	2 30W
Laurencetown	51	53 14N	8 11W
Laurentian Plat.	96	52 0N	70 0W
Lausanne	54	46 32N	6 38E
Laut, I.	72	3 40S	116 10E
Laval	56	48 4N	0 48W
Laverton	78	28 44S	122 29E
Lavongai, I.	79	2 18S	150 0E
Lawrence, N.Z.	83	45 55S	169 41E
Lawrence, Kans., U.S.A.	101	39 0N	95 10W
Lawrence, Mass., U.S.A.	104	42 40N	71 9W
Lawton	100	34 33N	98 25W
Laxey	42	54 15N	4 23W
Laxford Bridge	48	58 22N	5 2W
Laysan I.	22	25 30N	167 0W
Lea, R.	41	51 30N	0 10W
Leadgate	44	54 52N	1 48W
Leadville	100	39 17N	106 23W
Leamington	42	52 18N	1 32W
Leatherhead	41	51 18N	0 20W
Leavenworth	101	39 25N	95 0W
Lebanon ■	89	34 0N	36 0E
Lebanon Mts.	89	33 45N	35 45E
Lebombo Mts.	94	24 30S	32 0E
Lebrija	60	36 53N	6 5W
Lecce	58	40 20N	18 10E
Lechlade	42	51 42N	1 40W
Ledbury	42	52 3N	2 25W
Ledeberg	52	51 2N	3 45E
Ledmore	48	58 04N	4 58W
Leduc	98	53 15N	113 30W
Lee, R.	51	51 51N	9 2W
Leeds	45	53 48N	1 34W
Leek	44	53 7N	2 2W
Leenaun	51	53 36N	9 41W
Leer	52	53 13N	7 29E
Leeton	79	34 23S	146 23E
Leeuwarden	52	53 15N	5 48E
Leeuwin, C.	78	34 20S	115 9E
Leeward Is.	107	16 30N	63 30W
Leghorn	58	43 32N	10 18E
Legnica	54	51 12N	16 10E
Leh	70	34 15N	77 35E
Leicester	41	52 39N	1 9W
Leicester □	45	52 40N	1 10W
Leiden	52	52 9N	4 30E
Leie, R.	52	51 2N	3 45E
Leigh, Gr. Manch., U.K.	45	53 29N	2 31W
Leigh, Here. & Worcs., U.K.	44	52 10N	2 21W
Leigh Creek	79	30 28S	138 24E
Leighton Buzzard	40	51 55N	0 39W
Leinster □	51	53 0N	7 10W
Leinster, Mt.	51	52 38N	6 47W
Leipzig	54	51 20N	12 23E
Leiston	40	52 13N	1 35E
Leith	47	55 59N	3 10W
Leith Hill	40	51 10N	0 23W
Leitrim	50	54 0N	8 5W
Leixlip	51	53 22N	6 30W
Lek, R.	52	51 54N	4 38E
Lena, R.	62	64 30N	127 0E
Leninabad	71	40 17N	69 37E
Leninakan	71	41 0N	42 50E
Leningrad	61	59 55N	30 20E
Leninogorsk	62	50 20N	83 30E
Leninsk-Kuznetskiy	62	55 10N	86 10E
Lenkoran	71	39 45N	48 50E
Lennoxtown	47	55 58N	4 14W
Lens	56	50 26N	2 50E
Lentini	58	37 18N	15 0E
Leominster	42	52 15N	2 43W
León, Mexico	106	21 7N	101 30W
León, Nic.	106	12 20N	86 51W
León, Spain	60	42 38N	5 34W
León □	60	42 40N	5 55W
Leonora	78	28 49S	121 19E
Lephepe	94	23 22S	25 50E
Lepton	45	53 39N	1 45W
Lerdo	106	25 32N	103 32W
Lere	90	9 43N	9 18W
Lérida	60	41 37N	0 39E
Lerwick	49	60 10N	1 10W
Leslie	47	56 12N	3 12W
Lesmahagow	47	55 38N	3 55W
Lesotho ■	94	29 40S	28 0E
Lesser Antilles	107	12 30N	61 0W
Lessines	52	50 42N	3 50E
Leszno	54	51 50N	16 30E
Letaba, R.	94	23 42S	31 25E
Letchworth	40	51 58N	0 13W
Lethbridge	98	49 45N	112 45W
Leti Is.	72	8 10S	128 0E
Letterkenny	50	54 57N	7 42W
Leuven	52	50 52N	4 42E
Levelland	100	33 38N	102 17W
Leven	47	56 12N	3 0W
Leven, L.	47	56 12N	3 22W
Leverburgh	48	57 46N	7 0W
Leverkusen	52	51 2N	6 59E
Levin	83	40 37S	175 18E
Lévis	99	46 48N	71 9W
Lewes	40	50 53N	0 2E
Lewis, Butt of	48	58 30N	6 12W
Lewis, I.	48	58 10N	6 40W
Lewis Ra.	100	48 15N	114 0W
Lewisham	41	51 27N	0 1W
Lewiston	100	44 3N	70 10E
Lexington	101	38 6N	84 30W
Leyburn	44	54 19N	1 50W
Leyland	45	53 41N	2 42W
Leyte, I.	72	11 0N	125 0E
Leyton	41	51 34N	0 01W
Lhasa	73	29 50N	91 3E
Liao Ho, R.	73	41 0N	121 55E
Liaoning □	73	41 40N	122 30E
Liaotung	73	41 40N	123 0E
Liaoyang	73	41 15N	123 10E
Liaoyüan	73	42 55N	125 10E
Liard, R.	98	61 51N	121 18W
Liberal	100	37 4N	101 0W
Liberec	54	50 47N	15 7E
Liberia ■	88	6 30N	9 30W
Libourne	56	44 55N	0 14W
Libramont	56	49 55N	5 23E
Libreville	88	0 25N	9 26E
Libya ■	88	28 30N	17 30E
Libyan Desert	89	25 0N	25 0E
Libyan Plat.	91	30 40N	26 30E
Licata	58	37 6N	13 55E
Lichfield	41	52 40N	1 50W
Lichtenburg	94	26 8S	26 8E
Lida	55	53 53N	25 15E
Liddel, R.	46	55 03N	2 57W
Liechtenstein ■	54	47 8N	9 35E
Liège	52	50 38N	5 35E
Liège □	52	50 32N	5 35E
Lienz	54	46 50N	12 46E
Liepāja	61	56 30N	21 0E
Lier	52	51 7N	4 34E
Liffey, R.	51	53 21N	6 20W
Lifford	50	54 50N	7 30W
Liguria □	58	44 30N	9 0E
Ligurian Sea	58	43 20N	9 0E
Likasi	92	10 55S	26 48E
Lille	56	50 38N	3 3E
Lillehammer	61	61 8N	10 30E
Lillooet	105	50 44N	121 57W
Lilongwe	92	14 0S	33 48E
Lim Fjord	61	56 38N	8 23E
Lima, Peru	108	12 0S	77 0W
Lima, U.S.A.	104	40 42N	84 5W
Limassol	71	34 42N	33 1E
Limavady	50	55 3N	6 58W
Limavady □	50	55 0N	6 55W
Limbe	92	15 55S	35 2E
Limburg	52	50 22N	8 4E
Limburg □	52	51 20N	5 55E
Limerick	51	52 40N	8 38W
Limerick □	51	52 30N	8 50W
Limoges	56	45 50N	1 15E
Limón	107	10 0N	83 2W
Limousin	56	46 0N	1 0E
Limpopo, R.	94	23 15S	32 5E
Limpsfield	41	51 15N	0 1E
Limuru	93	1 2S	36 35E
Linares, Mexico	106	24 50N	99 40W
Linares, Spain	60	38 10N	3 40W
Lincoln, N.Z.	83	43 38S	172 30E
Lincoln, U.K.	44	53 14N	0 32W
Lincoln, U.S.A.	101	40 50N	96 42W
Lincoln □	44	53 14N	0 32W
Lincoln Sea	96	84 0N	55 0W
Lincoln Wolds	44	53 20N	0 5W
Lindi	93	9 58S	39 38E
Lingen	52	52 32N	7 21E
Lingfield	40	51 11N	0 1W
Lingga Arch.	72	0 10S	104 30E
Linköping	61	58 28N	15 36E
Linlithgow	47	55 58N	3 38W
Linn, Mt.	105	40 0N	123 0W
Linnhe, L.	48	56 36N	5 25W
Linsia	73	35 50N	103 0E
Linz	54	48 18N	14 18E
Lions, G. of	56	43 0N	4 0W
Lipari, Is.	58	38 40N	15 0E
Liphook	40	51 04N	0 48W
Lippe, R.	52	51 40N	7 20E
Lira	93	2 17N	32 57E
Liria	60	39 37N	0 35W
Lisala	92	2 12N	21 38E
Lisboa = Lisbon	60	38 42N	9 10W
Lisbon	60	38 42N	9 10W
Lisburn	50	54 30N	6 9W
Lisburn □	50	54 30N	6 5W
Lisdoonvarna	51	53 2N	9 18W
Lisieux	56	49 10N	0 12E
Liskeard	43	50 27N	4 29W
Lismore, Austral.	79	28 44S	153 21E
Lismore, Ireland	51	52 8N	7 58W
Lismore I.	48	56 30N	5 30W
Lisnaskea	50	54 15N	7 27W
Listowel	51	52 27N	9 30W
Litherland	45	53 29N	3 0W
Lithgow	79	33 25S	150 8E
Lithuania S.S.R. □	61	55 30N	24 0E
Litoměřice	54	50 33N	14 10E
Little Carpathians, mts.	54	48 30N	17 20E
Little Karoo	94	33 45S	21 30E
Little Laut Is.	72	4 45S	115 40E
Little Lever	45	53 33N	2 22W
Little Minch	48	57 35N	6 45W
Little Ouse, R.	40	52 25N	0 50E
Little River	83	43 45S	172 49E
Little Rock	101	34 41N	92 10W
Littleborough	45	53 38N	2 8W
Littlehampton	40	50 48N	0 32W
Littleport	40	52 27N	0 18E
Liuchow	73	24 10N	109 10E
Liverpool, Austral.	79	33 54S	150 58E
Liverpool, U.K.	45	53 25N	3 0W
Liverpool Bay	44	53 30N	3 20W
Liverpool Plains	79	31 15S	150 15E
Liverpool Ra.	79	31 50S	150 30E
Liversedge	45	53 42N	1 42W
Livingston, U.K.	47	55 52N	3 33W
Livingston, U.S.A.	100	45 40N	110 40W
Livingstone	92	17 46S	25 52E
Livingstone Mts.	93	9 40S	34 20E
Livingstonia	93	10 38S	34 5E
Livorno = Leghorn	58	43 32N	10 18E
Liwale	93	9 48S	37 58E
Lizard	43	49 58N	5 10W
Lizard Pt.	43	49 57N	5 11W
Ljubljana	58	46 4N	14 33E
Ljusnan, R.	61	62 0N	15 20E
Llanberis	42	53 7N	4 7W
Llandaff	43	51 29N	3 13W
Llandovery	42	51 59N	3 49W
Llandrindod Wells	42	52 15N	3 23W
Llandudno	42	53 19N	3 51W
Llandyssul	42	52 3N	4 20W
Llanelli	43	51 41N	4 11W
Llanfyllin	42	52 47N	3 17W
Llangefni	42	53 15N	4 20W
Llangollen	42	52 58N	3 10W
Llangurig	42	52 25N	3 36W
Llanhilleth	43	51 43N	3 07W
Llanidloes	42	52 28N	3 31W
Llanishen	43	51 44N	2 45W
Llano Estacado	100	34 0N	103 0W
Llanos	108	3 25N	71 35W
Llanrwst	42	53 8N	3 49W
Llantrisant	43	51 33N	3 22W
Llantwit-Major	43	51 24N	3 29W
Llanwrtyd Wells	42	52 6N	3 39W
Lleyn Peninsula	42	52 55N	4 35W
Llobregat, R.	60	41 19N	2 9E
Llwyn-y-pia	43	51 38N	3 27W
Loanhead	47	55 53N	3 10W
Lobatse	94	25 12S	25 40E
Lobito	92	12 18S	13 35E
Lobstick L.	99	54 0N	65 12W
Locarno	54	46 10N	8 47E
Lochaber	48	56 55N	5 0W
Lochailort	48	56 53N	5 40W
Lochaline	48	56 32N	5 47W
Lochboisdale	49	57 10N	7 20W
Lochearnhead	46	56 24N	4 19W
Lochgelly	47	56 7N	3 18W
Lochgilphead	46	56 2N	5 37W
Lochmaben	46	55 8N	3 27W
Lochmaddy	49	57 36N	7 10W
Lochnagar	48	56 57N	3 14W
Lochranza	46	55 42N	5 18W
Lochwinnoch	47	55 47N	4 39W
Lochy, L.	48	56 58N	4 55W
Lockerbie	46	55 7N	3 21W
Lod	89	31 57N	34 54E
Loddon	40	52 32N	1 29E
Lodwar	93	3 10N	35 40E
Łódź	55	51 45N	19 27E
Loeriesfontein	94	30 56S	19 26E
Lofoten Is.	61	68 30N	15 0E
Lofthouse	45	53 44N	1 30W
Loftus	44	54 33N	0 52W
Logan	100	41 45N	111 50W
Logan, Mt.	98	60 41N	140 22W
Logroño	60	42 28N	2 32W
Loikaw	70	19 40N	97 17E
Loire, R.	56	47 16N	2 10W
Lokeren	52	51 6N	3 59E
Lokichokio	93	4 19N	34 13E
Lokka	61	67 55N	27 35E
Lokoja	90	7 47N	6 45E
Lomami, R.	92	1 0S	24 40E
Lombardy	58	45 35N	9 45E
Lomblen, I.	72	8 30S	123 32E
Lombok, I.	72	8 35S	116 20E
Lomé	88	6 9N	1 20E
Lomond, L.	46	56 8N	4 38W
Łomza	55	53 10N	22 2E
Londiani	93	0 10S	35 33E
London, Can.	104	42 59N	81 15W
London, U.K.	41	51 30N	0 5W
Londonderry	50	55 0N	7 20W
Londonderry, Co.	50	55 0N	7 20W
Long Ashton	43	51 26N	2 39W
Long Beach	105	33 46N	118 12W
Long Crendon	41	51 47N	1 0W
Long Eaton	45	52 54N	1 16W
Long I.	104	40 50N	73 20W
Long, L.	46	56 4N	4 50W
Long Melford	40	52 5N	0 44E
Long Mynd	45	52 35N	2 50W
Longbenton	44	55 00N	1 34W
Longford	50	53 43N	7 50W
Longford □	51	53 42N	7 45W
Longforgan	47	56 28N	3 8W
Longlac	99	49 45N	86 25W
Longmont	100	40 10N	105 4W
Longreach	79	23 28S	144 14E
Longridge	45	53 50N	2 37W
Longton	45	53 43N	2 48W
Longtown	44	55 1N	2 59W
Longview	101	32 30N	94 45W
Löningen	52	52 43N	7 44E
Looe	43	50 24N	4 25W
Loop Hd.	51	52 34N	9 55W
Lop Nor	73	40 20N	90 10E
Lopez C.	88	0 47S	8 40E
Lorain	104	41 20N	82 55W
Lorca	60	37 41N	1 42W
Lord Howe I.	23	31 33S	159 6E
Lordsburg	100	32 15N	108 45W
Lorient	56	47 45N	3 23W
Lorne	46	56 26N	5 10W
Lorraine	56	49 0N	6 0E
Los Alamos	100	35 57N	106 17W
Los Angeles	105	34 0N	118 10W
Los Mochis	106	25 45N	109 5W
Lošinj	58	44 30N	14 30E
Loskop Dam Game Reserve	94	25 25S	29 25E
Lossiemouth	48	57 43N	3 17W
Lot, R.	56	44 18N	0 20E
Lothian □	46	55 55N	3 35W
Loughborough	45	52 46N	1 11W
Loughor	43	51 39N	4 5W
Loughrea	51	53 11N	8 33W
Louis Trichardt	94	23 0S	29 55E
Louisiade Arch.	79	11 10S	153 0E
Louisiana □	101	30 50N	92 0W
Louisville	101	38 15N	85 45W
Loulé	60	37 9N	8 0W
Lourdes	56	43 6N	0 3W
Lourenço-Marques = Maputo	94	25 58S	32 32E
Louth	44	53 23N	0 0W
Louth □	50	53 55N	6 30W
Louvière, La	52	50 27N	4 10E
Lövenich	52	50 56N	6 46E
Lowell	104	42 38N	71 19W
Lower Austria	54	48 25N	15 40E
Lower Cam	43	51 43N	2 22W
Lower Hutt	83	41 10S	174 55E
Lower Largo	47	56 12N	2 56W
Lower Saxony	54	52 45N	9 0E
Lower Tunguska, R.	62	64 20N	93 0E
Lowestoft	40	52 29N	1 44E
Łowicz	55	52 6N	19 55E
Lowther Hills	46	55 20N	3 40W
Lowton Common	45	53 29N	2 32W
Lu-ta	73	39 0N	121 31E
Lualaba, R.	92	5 45S	26 50E
Luanda	92	8 58S	13 9E
Luang Prabang	72	19 45N	102 10E
Luarca	60	43 32N	6 32W
Lubbock	100	33 40N	101 55W
Lübeck	54	53 52N	10 41E
Lublin	55	51 12N	22 38E
Lubumbashi	92	11 32S	27 28E
Lucan	51	53 21N	6 27W
Lucania, Mt.	98	60 48N	141 25W
Lucca	58	43 50N	10 30E
Luce Bay	46	54 45N	4 48W
Lucena	60	37 27N	4 31W
Lučenec	55	48 18N	19 42E
Luchow	73	28 57N	105 26E
Luckenwalde	54	52 5N	13 11E
Lucknow	70	26 50N	81 0E
Lüdenscheid	52	51 13N	7 37E
Lüderitz	92	26 41S	15 8E
Ludgershall	42	51 15N	1 38W
Ludlow	45	52 23N	2 42W
Ludwigsburg	54	48 53N	9 11E
Ludwigshafen	54	49 27N	8 27E
Luga	61	58 40N	29 55E
Lugano	54	46 0N	8 57E
Lugazi	93	0 32N	32 57E
Lugnaquilla	51	52 48N	6 28W
Lugo	60	43 2N	7 35W
Lugoj	55	45 42N	21 57E
Luing I.	46	56 15N	5 40W
Łukow	55	51 58N	22 22E
Lule älv, R.	61	65 35N	22 10E
Luleå	61	65 35N	22 10E
Lulua, R.	92	6 30S	22 50E
Lumbwa	93	0 12S	35 28E
Lumsden	83	45 44S	168 27E
Lund	61	55 44N	13 12E
Lundy, I.	42	51 10N	4 41W
Lune, R.	44	54 0N	2 51W
Lüneburg	54	53 15N	10 23E
Lüneburg Heath	54	53 0N	10 0E
Lünen	52	51 36N	7 31E
Luni, R.	70	25 40N	72 20E
Lurgan	50	54 28N	6 20W
Lusaka	92	15 28S	28 16E
Lusambo	92	4 58S	23 28E
Lushoto □	93	4 45S	38 20E
Luton	40	51 53N	0 24W
Lutsk	55	50 50N	25 15E
Lutterworth	41	52 28N	1 12W
Luvua R.	92	6 50S	27 30E
Luwingu, Mt.	93	10 15S	30 2E
Luxembourg	52	49 37N	6 9E
Luxembourg □	52	49 58N	5 30E
Luxembourg ■	52	50 0N	6 0E
Luxor	91	25 41N	32 38E
Luzern	54	47 3N	8 18E
Luzon, I.	72	16 0N	121 0E
Lvov	55	49 40N	24 0E
Lyakhov Is.	62	73 40N	141 0E
* Lyallpur	71	31 30N	73 5E
Lybster	48	58 18N	3 16W
Lydd	40	50 57N	0 56E
Lydda = Lod	89	31 57N	34 54E
Lydenburg	94	25 10S	30 29E
Lydham	45	52 31N	2 59W
Lydney	43	51 43N	2 32W
Lyell	83	41 48S	172 4E
Lyell Range	83	41 38S	172 20E
Lyme Bay	43	50 36N	2 55W
Lyme Regis	43	50 44N	2 57W
Lymm	45	53 23N	2 30W
Lynchburg	101	37 23N	79 10W
Lyndhurst	40	50 53N	1 33W
Lynn	104	42 28N	70 57W
Lynton and Lynmouth	42	51 14N	3 50W

* *Renamed Faisalabad*

Lyonnais Millom

Lyonnais 56 45 45N 4 15E
Lyons 56 45 46N 4 50E
Lytham St. Anne's 45 53 45N 2 58W
Lyttelton 83 43 35S 172 44E

M

Maam Cross 51 53 28N 9 32W
Ma'an 71 30 12N 35 44E
Maanshan 73 31 40N 118 30E
Maas, R. 52 51 48N 4 55E
Maastricht 52 50 50N 5 40E
Mablethorpe 44 53 21N 0 14E
Mabua 91 30 30N 35 12E
Macau ■ 73 22 16N 113 35E
Macclesfield 44 53 16N 2 9W
McCook 100 40 15N 100 35W
Macdonnell Ranges 78 23 40S 133 0E
Macduff 48 57 40N 2 30W
Maceió 108 9 40S 35 41W
Macerata 58 43 19N 13 28E
Macgillycuddy's Reeks, mts. 51 52 2N 9 45W
Machakos 93 1 30S 37 15E
Machen 43 51 35N 3 07W
Machrihanish 46 55 25N 5 42W
Machynlleth 42 52 36N 3 51W
* Macias Nguema Biyoga 88 3 30N 8 40E
Macintyre, R. 79 28 37S 149 40E
Mackay 79 21 8S 149 11E
Mackay, L. 78 22 30S 129 0E
McKeesport 104 40 21N 79 50W
Mackenzie 98 55 20N 123 05W
Mackenzie Bay 98 69 0N 137 30W
Mackenzie Mts. 98 64 0N 130 0W
Mackenzie, R., Austral. 79 23 38S 149 46E
Mackenzie, R., Can. 98 69 10N 134 20W
McKinley, Mt. 98 63 10N 151 0W
McLaughlin 105 45 50N 100 50W
Maclear 94 31 2S 28 23E
McLennan 98 55 42N 116 50W
McLeod, L. 78 24 0S 113 50E
McLure 98 51 2N 120 13W
McMinnville 100 45 16N 123 11W
Macnean, L. 50 54 19N 7 52W
Mâcon 56 46 19N 4 50E
Macon 101 32 50N 83 37W
McPherson 100 38 25N 97 40W
Macquarie Is. 23 50 0S 160 0E
Macroom 51 51 54N 8 57W
Madagascar, I. 92 20 0S 47 0E
Madang 79 5 12S 145 49E
Madaoua 90 14 5N 6 27E
Madeira, R. 108 5 30S 61 20W
Madera 106 29 15N 107 55W
Madhya Pradesh □ 70 21 50N 81 0E
Madinat al Shaab 71 12 50N 45 0E
Madison 101 43 5N 89 25W
Madiun 72 7 38S 111 32E
Madras 70 13 8N 80 19E
Madre, Sierra 106 16 0N 93 0W
Madrid 60 40 25N 3 45W
Maebashi 76 36 24N 139 4E
Maerdy 43 51 40N 3 29W
Maesteg 43 51 36N 3 40W
Maevatanana 92 16 56N 46 49E
† Mafeking 94 25 50S 25 38E
Mafia I. 93 7 45S 39 50E
Magadan 62 59 30N 151 0E
Magadi 93 1 54S 36 19E
Magdalen Is. 99 47 30N 61 40W
Magdeburg 54 52 8N 11 36E
Magee, I. 50 54 48N 5 44W
Magelang 72 7 29S 110 13E
Magellan's Str. 108 52 30S 75 0W
Maggiore, L. 58 46 0N 8 35E
Maghâgha 91 28 38N 30 50E
Maghera 50 54 51N 6 40W
Magherafelt 50 54 44N 6 37W
Magherafelt □ 50 54 50N 6 40W
Maghull 45 53 31N 2 56W
Magnitogorsk 62 53 27N 59 4E
Mahābād 71 36 50N 45 45E
Mahagi 93 2 20N 31 0E
Mahalapye 94 23 1S 26 51E
Mahanadi R. 70 20 33N 85 0E
Maharashtra □ 70 19 30N 75 30E
Mahari Mts. 93 6 20S 30 0E
Mahé 70 11 42N 75 34E
Mahenge 93 8 45S 36 35E
Maheno 83 45 10S 170 50E
Mahia Pen. 83 39 9S 177 55E
Mahón 60 39 50N 4 18E
Mai-Ndombe, L. 92 2 0S 18 0E
Maiden Newton 43 50 46N 2 35W
Maidenhead 41 51 31N 0 42W
Maidstone 41 51 16N 0 31E
Maiduguri 90 12 0N 13 20E
Maimana 71 35 53N 64 38E
Main Barrier Ra. 79 31 10S 141 20E
Main, R. 54 50 13N 11 0E
Maine □ 101 45 20N 69 0W
Mainland, I., Orkneys, U.K. 49 59 0N 3 10W
Mainland, I., Shetlands, U.K. 49 60 15N 1 22W
Maintirano 92 18 3S 44 1E
Mainz 52 50 0N 8 17E
Maiquetía 107 10 36N 66 57W
Maitland 79 32 44S 151 36E
Maiyema 90 12 5N 4 25E
Maizuru 76 35 25N 135 22E
Majorca, I. = Mallorca, I. 60 39 30N 3 0E
‡ Majunga 92 15 40S 46 25E
Makasar, Str. of 72 1 0S 118 20E
Makeyevka 62 48 0N 38 0E
Makgadikgadi Salt Pans 92 20 40S 25 45E
Makhachkala 71 43 0N 47 15E
Makó 55 46 14N 20 33E
Makurazaki 76 31 15N 130 20E
Makurdi 90 7 43N 8 28E
Mal B. 51 52 50N 9 30W
Malabar Coast 70 11 0N 75 0E
Malacca, Str. of 72 3 0N 101 0E
Malad City 100 42 15N 112 20E
Maladetta, Mt. 60 42 40N 0 30E
Málaga 60 36 43N 4 23W
Malahide 51 53 26N 6 10W
Malakal 89 9 33N 31 50E
Malang 72 7 59S 112 35E
Malanje 92 9 30S 16 17E
Mälaren 61 59 30N 17 10E
Malatya 71 38 25N 38 20E
Malawi ■ 93 13 0S 34 0E
Malaya ■ 72 4 0N 102 0E
Malaya Vishera 61 58 55N 32 25E
Malbork 55 54 3N 19 10E
Malcolm 78 28 51S 121 25E
Maldegem 52 51 14N 3 26E
Maldive Is. ■ 70 2 0N 73 0W
Maldon 41 51 43N 0 41E
Malhão, Sa. do 60 37 25N 8 0W
Mali ■ 88 15 0N 10 0W
Malin Hd. 50 55 18N 7 16W
Malindi 93 3 12S 40 5E
Mallaig 48 57 0N 5 50W
Mallaranny 50 53 55N 9 46W
Mallawi 91 27 44N 30 44E
Mallorca, I. 60 39 30N 3 0E
Mallow 51 52 8N 8 40W
Malmesbury, S. Afr. 94 33 28S 18 41E
Malmesbury, U.K. 42 51 35N 2 5W
Malmö 61 55 36N 12 59E
Malta ■ 58 35 50N 14 30E
Malton 44 54 9N 0 48W
Malvern Hills 42 52 0N 2 19W
Mambasa 93 1 22N 29 3E
Mamfe 90 5 50N 9 15E
Man, I. of 42 54 15N 4 30W
Manaar, Gulf of 70 8 30N 79 0E
Managua 106 12 0N 86 20W
Manakara 92 22 8S 48 1E
Manapouri 83 45 34S 167 39E
Manapouri, L. 83 45 32S 167 32E
Manaus 108 3 0S 60 0W
Mancha, La 60 39 10N 2 54W
Manchester, U.K. 45 53 30N 2 15W
Manchester, U.S.A. 104 42 58N 71 29W
Manchouli 73 49 46N 117 24E
Manda 93 10 30S 34 40E
Mandal 61 58 2N 7 25E
Mandalay 70 22 0N 96 10E
Mandan 100 46 50N 101 0W
Manengouba Mts. 90 5 0N 9 45E
Manfalût 91 27 20N 30 52E
Manfredónia 58 41 40N 15 55E
Mangalore 70 12 55N 74 47E
Mangaweka 83 39 48S 175 47E
Mangole I. 72 1 50S 125 55E
Mangonui 83 35 1S 173 32E
Mangotsfield 43 51 29N 2 29W
Mangyai 73 38 6N 91 37E
Mangyshlak Pen. 71 43 40N 52 30E
Manhattan 101 39 10N 96 40W
Manihiki I. 22 10 24S 161 1W
Manila 72 14 40N 121 3E
Manipur □ 70 24 30N 94 0E
Manitoba □ 98 55 30N 97 0W
Manitoba, L. 98 51 0N 98 45W
Manizales 107 5 5N 75 32W
Manjimup 78 34 15S 116 6E
Mannheim 54 49 28N 8 29E
Mannin B. 51 53 27N 10 04W
Manningtree 40 51 56N 1 3E
Manorhamilton 50 54 19N 8 11W
Mans, Le 56 48 0N 0 10E
Mansel I. 99 62 0N 79 50W
Mansfield, U.K. 44 53 8N 1 12W
Mansfield, U.S.A. 104 40 45N 82 30W
Mantes-la-Jolie 56 49 0N 1 41E
Mantiqueira, Serra da 108 22 0S 44 0W
Mantua 58 45 10N 10 47E
Manukau 83 37 1S 174 55E
Manyara L. 93 3 40S 35 50E
Manyoni 93 5 45S 34 55E
Manzanares 60 39 0N 3 22W
Manzanillo, Cuba 107 20 20N 77 10W
Manzanillo, Mexico 106 19 0N 104 20W
Manzini 94 26 30S 31 25E
Maputo 94 25 58S 32 32E
Maputo R. 92 26 35S 32 30E
Mar del Plata 108 38 0S 57 30W
Mar, Serra do 108 25 30S 49 0W
Mara 93 1 30S 34 32E
Maracaibo 107 10 40N 71 37W
Maracaibo, L. 107 9 40N 71 30W
Maracay 107 10 15N 67 36W
Maradi 90 13 35N 8 10E
Marāgheh 71 37 30N 46 12E
Marajo I. 108 1 0S 49 30W
Maranhão = São Luis 108 2 31S 44 16W
Marañon, R. 108 4 50S 75 35W
Marazion 43 50 8N 5 29W
Marbat 71 17 0N 54 45E
Marbella 60 36 30N 4 57W
Marble Bar 78 21 9S 119 44E
March 40 52 33N 0 5E
Marchena 60 37 18N 5 23W
Marches 58 43 22N 13 10E
Maree L. 48 57 40N 5 30W
Mareeba 79 16 59S 145 28E
Margarita I. 107 11 0N 64 0W
Margate, S. Afr. 94 30 50S 30 20E
Margate, U.K. 40 51 23N 1 24E
Maria van Diemen, C. 83 34 29S 172 40E
Mariana Is. 23 17 0N 145 0E
Marianao 107 23 8N 82 24W
Maribor 58 46 36N 15 40E
Maricourt 99 61 30N 72 0W
Marietta 101 34 0N 84 30W
Marion 101 40 35N 85 40W
Maritime Alps 56 44 10N 7 10E
Market Deeping 45 52 40N 0 20W
Market Drayton 45 52 55N 2 30W
Market Harborough 45 52 29N 0 55W
Market Rasen 44 53 24N 0 20W
Market Weighton 44 53 52N 0 40W
Markethill 50 54 18N 6 31W
Markham Mts. 112 83 0S 164 0E
Markinch 47 56 12N 3 9W
Marl 52 51 39N 7 4E
Marlborough 42 51 26N 1 44W
Marlborough □ 83 41 45S 173 33E
Marlow 41 51 34N 0 47W
Marmande 56 44 30N 0 10E
Marmara, Sea of 71 40 45N 28 15E
Marne, R. 56 48 53N 2 25E
Maroantsetra 92 15 26S 49 44E
Maroua 90 10 40N 14 20E
Marovoay 92 16 6S 46 39E
Marple 45 53 23N 2 5W
Marquesas Is. 22 9 30S 140 0W
Marquette 101 46 30N 87 21W
Marrakech 88 31 40N 8 0W
Marree 79 29 39S 138 1E
Marsabit 93 2 18N 38 0E
Marsala 58 37 48N 12 25E
Marsden 45 53 36N 1 55W
Marseilles 56 43 18N 5 23E
Marsh I. 101 29 35N 91 50W
Marshall 101 39 8N 93 15W
Marshall Is. 23 9 0N 171 0E
Martaban, G. of 70 15 40N 96 30E
Marte 90 12 23N 13 46E
Martha's Vineyard 101 41 25N 70 35W
Martigny 54 46 6N 7 3E
Martigues 56 43 24N 5 4E
Martinique, I. 107 14 40N 61 0W
Marton 83 40 4S 175 23E
Martos 60 37 44N 3 58W
Martova = Mantua 58 45 10N 10 47E
Marugame 76 34 15N 133 55E
Mary 71 37 40N 61 50E
Mary Kathleen 79 20 35S 139 48E
Maryborough, Queens., Austral. 79 25 31S 152 37E
Maryborough, Vic., Austral. 79 37 0S 143 44E
Maryland □ 101 39 10N 76 40W
Maryport 44 54 43N 3 30W
Masai Steppe 93 4 30S 36 30E
Masaka 93 0 21S 31 45E
Masan 73 35 11N 128 32E
Masasi 93 10 45S 38 52E
Masbate, I. 72 12 21N 123 36E
Maseru 94 29 18S 27 30E
Masham 44 54 15N 1 40W
Mashhad 71 36 20N 59 35E
Masindi 93 1 40N 31 43E
Masirah 71 20 25N 58 50E
Masisi 93 1 23S 28 49E
Masjed Soleyman 71 31 55N 49 25E
Mask, L. 51 53 36N 9 24W
Mason City 101 43 9N 93 12W
Massachusetts □ 101 42 25N 72 0W
Massif Central 56 45 30N 2 21E
Masterton 83 40 56S 175 39E
Masuda 76 34 40N 131 51E
Masurian Lakes 55 53 30N 21 30E
Matabeleland North □ 92 20 0S 28 0E
Matadi 92 5 52S 13 31E
Matagalpa 106 13 10N 85 40W
Matagorda I. 101 28 10N 96 40W
Matamoros, Campeche, Mexico 106 25 53N 97 30W
Matamoros, Coahuila, Mexico 106 25 45N 103 1W
Matanzas 107 23 0N 81 40W
Mataranka 78 14 55S 133 4E
Matatiele 94 30 20S 28 49E
Mataura 83 46 11S 168 51E
Matehuala 106 23 40N 100 50W
Matlock 44 53 8N 1 32W
Mato Grosso, Plat. of 108 15 0S 54 0W
Matopo Hills 92 20 36S 28 20E
Matrûh 91 31 19N 27 9E
Matsue 76 35 25N 133 10E
Matsumoto 76 36 15N 138 0E
Matsusaka 76 34 34N 136 32E
Matsuyama 76 33 45N 132 45E
Matterhorn, mt. 54 45 58N 7 39E
Maturín 107 9 45N 63 11W
Mau Ranipur 70 25 16N 79 8E
Maubeuge 56 50 17N 3 57E
Maumere 72 8 38S 122 13E
Maumturk Mts. 51 53 32N 9 42W
Mauritania ■ 88 20 50N 10 0W
Mauritius ■ 23 20 0S 57 0E
Mawlaik 70 23 40N 94 26E
Mawson Base 112 67 30N 65 0E
Mayagüez 107 18 12N 67 9W
Maybole 46 55 21N 4 41W
Mayen 52 50 18N 7 10E
Mayfield 40 51 1N 0 17E
Maykop 71 44 35N 40 25E
Maynooth 51 53 22N 6 38W
Mayo □ 50 53 47N 9 7W
Mazar-i-Sharif 71 36 41N 67 0E
Mazatlán 106 23 10N 106 30W
Mbabane 94 26 18S 31 6E
Mbala 93 8 46S 31 17E
Mbale 93 1 8N 34 12E
Mbandaka 92 0 1S 18 18E
Mbanga 90 4 30N 9 33E
Mbarara 93 0 35S 30 25E
Mberubu 90 6 10N 7 38E
Mbeya 93 8 54S 33 29E
Mbulu 93 3 45S 35 30E
Meath □ 51 53 32N 6 40W
Mecca 71 21 30N 39 54E
Mechelen 52 51 2N 4 29E
Mechernich 52 50 35N 6 39E
Medan 72 3 40N 98 38E
Medellín 107 6 15N 75 35W
Medford 105 42 20N 122 52W
Mediaş 55 46 9N 24 22E
Medicine Hat 98 50 0N 110 45W
Medina 71 24 35N 39 52E
Medina-Sidonia 60 36 28N 5 57W
Mediterranean Sea 88 35 0N 15 0E
Médoc 56 45 10N 0 56W
Medway, R. 40 51 28N 0 45E
Meekatharra 78 26 32S 118 29E
Meerut 70 29 1N 77 50E
Meissen 54 51 10N 13 29E
Meknès 88 33 57N 5 33W
Mekong, R. 70 18 0N 104 15E
Melaka 72 2 15N 102 15E
Melbourne 79 37 50S 145 0E
Melilla 88 35 21N 2 57W
Melk 54 48 13N 15 20E
Melksham 42 51 22N 2 9W
Melrose 46 55 35N 2 44W
Meltham 45 53 35N 1 51W
Melton Mowbray 45 52 46N 0 52W
Melun 56 48 32N 2 39E
Melvich 48 58 33N 3 55W
Melville 98 50 55N 102 50W
Melville I., Austral. 78 11 30S 131 0E
Melville I., Can. 98 75 30N 111 0W
Melville Pen. 99 68 0N 84 0W
Melvin, L. 50 54 26N 8 10W
Memmingen 54 47 59N 10 12E
Memphis 101 35 7N 90 0W
Menai Strait 42 53 7N 4 20W
Mendip Hills 42 51 17N 2 40W
Mendocino 105 39 26N 123 50W
Mendoza 108 32 50S 68 52W
Menen 52 50 47N 3 7E
Mengtsz 73 23 20N 103 20E
Menindee 79 32 20S 142 25E
Menorca, I. 60 40 0N 4 0E
Menston 45 53 53N 1 44W
Mentawai Is. 72 2 0S 99 0E
Menton 58 43 50N 7 29E
Menzies 78 29 40S 120 58E
Meppel 52 52 42N 6 12E
Meppen 52 52 41N 7 20E
Merano 58 46 40N 11 10E
Merced 100 37 18N 120 30W
Mercer 83 37 16S 175 5E
Mercy C. 99 65 0N 62 30W
Mere 42 51 5N 2 16W
Mergui Arch. 70 12 30N 98 35E
Mérida, Mexico 106 20 50N 89 40W
Mérida, Spain 60 38 55N 6 25W
Meriden 41 52 27N 1 36W
Merksem 52 51 16N 4 25E
Merredin 78 31 28S 118 18E
Merrick 46 55 8N 4 30W
Merse 46 55 40N 2 30W
Mersea I. 40 51 48N 0 55E
Mersey, R. 44 53 20N 2 56W
Merseyside □ 44 53 25N 2 55W
Mersin 71 36 51N 34 36E
Merthyr Tydfil 43 51 45N 3 23W
Merton 41 51 25N 0 13W
Meru 93 0 3N 37 40E
Merzig 52 49 26N 6 37E
Mesa 100 33 20N 111 56W
Mesewa 89 15 35N 39 25E
Mesopotamia = Al Jazirah 71 33 30N 44 0E
Messina, Italy 58 38 10N 15 32E
Messina, S. Afr. 94 22 20S 30 12E
Messina, Str. of 58 38 5N 15 35E
Methil 47 56 10N 3 01W
Methven, N.Z. 83 43 38S 171 40E
Methven, U.K. 47 56 25N 3 35W
Metz 56 49 8N 6 10E
Meuse, R. 52 50 45N 5 41E
Mevagissey 43 50 16N 4 48W
Mexborough 45 53 29N 1 18W
Mexicali 106 32 40N 115 30W
México 106 19 20N 99 10W
Mexico ■ 106 20 0N 100 0W
Mexico, G. of 106 25 0N 90 0W
Mey 48 58 38N 3 14W
Miami 101 25 52N 80 15W
Miaoli 73 24 33N 120 42E
Michigan □ 101 44 40N 85 40W
Michigan City 104 41 42N 86 56W
Michigan, L. 104 44 0N 87 0W
Michipicoten I. 99 47 40N 85 50W
Mickle Fell 44 54 38N 2 16W
Micklefield 45 53 48N 1 20W
Mid Glamorgan □ 42 51 40N 3 25W
Middelburg, Neth. 52 51 30N 3 36E
Middelburg, C. Prov., S. Afr. 94 31 30S 25 0E
Middelburg, Trans., S. Afr. 94 25 49S 29 28E
Middlesboro 101 36 40N 83 40W
Middlesbrough 44 54 35N 1 14W
Middleton 45 53 33N 2 12W
Middleton-in-Teesdale 44 54 38N 2 5W
Middlewich 44 53 12N 2 28W
Midhurst 40 50 59N 0 44W
Midland, Mich., U.S.A. 101 43 37N 84 17W
Midland, Tex., U.S.A. 100 32 0N 102 3W
Midland Junction 78 31 50S 115 58E
Midleton 51 51 52N 8 12W
Midsomer Norton 42 51 17N 2 29W
Miercurea Ciuc 55 46 21N 25 48E
Mieres 60 43 18N 5 48W
Mihara 76 34 24N 133 5E
Mikindani 93 10 15S 40 2E
Milan 58 45 28N 9 10E
Milano = Milan 58 45 28N 9 10E
Milazzo 58 38 13N 15 13E
Mildenhall 40 52 20N 0 30E
Mildura 79 34 13S 142 9E
Miles 79 26 40S 150 23E
Miles City 100 46 30N 105 50W
Milford Haven 42 51 43N 5 2W
Milford on Sea 40 50 44N 1 36W
Millau 56 44 8N 3 4E
Millicent 79 37 34S 140 21E
Millom 44 54 13N 3 16W

* *Renamed Bioko*
† *Now Mafikeng*
‡ *Renamed Mahajunga*

Millport New Alresford

Millport	47	55 45N	4 55W
Millstreet	51	52 4N	9 5W
Milltown Malbay	51	52 51N	9 25W
Milnathort	47	56 14N	3 25W
Milnerton	94	33 54S	18 29E
Milngavie	47	55 57N	4 20W
Milnrow	45	53 36N	2 06W
Milton	83	46 7S	169 59E
Milton Keynes	40	52 3N	0 42W
Milverton	43	51 2N	3 15W
Milwaukee	104	43 9N	87 58W
Minamata	76	32 10N	130 30E
Mindanao, I.	72	8 0N	125 0E
*Mindanao Sea	72	9 0N	124 0E
Minden	54	52 18N	8 54E
Mindoro, I.	72	13 0N	121 0E
Minehead	42	51 12N	3 29W
Mineral Wells	100	32 50N	98 5W
Mingan	99	50 20N	64 0W
Mingulay I.	49	56 50N	7 40W
Minho □	60	41 25N	8 20W
Minho, R.	60	41 58N	8 40W
Minna	90	9 37N	6 30E
Minneapolis	101	44 58N	93 20W
Minnesota □	101	46 40N	94 0W
Minot	100	48 10N	101 15W
Minsk	62	53 52N	27 30E
Mińsk Mazowiecki	55	52 10N	21 33E
Mintlaw	48	57 32N	1 59W
Minûf	91	30 26N	30 52E
Minya Konka, mt.	73	29 36N	101 50E
Miquelon, I.	99	47 2N	56 20W
Mirny	112	66 0S	95 0E
Mirzapur	70	25 10N	82 45E
Mishan	73	45 31N	132 2E
Miskolc	55	48 7N	20 50E
Misoöl, I.	72	2 0S	130 0E
Mississippi □	101	33 0N	90 0W
Mississippi, R.	101	29 0N	89 15W
Missoula	100	47 0N	114 0W
Missouri □	101	38 25N	92 30W
Mistassini L.	99	51 0N	73 40W
Misurata	88	32 10N	15 3E
Mît Ghamr	91	30 42N	31 12E
Mitcheldean	43	51 51N	2 29W
Mitchell, Austral.	79	26 29S	147 58E
Mitchell, U.S.A.	100	43 40N	98 0W
Mitchell, R.	79	37 20S	147 0E
Mitchelstown, Ireland	51	52 16N	8 18W
Mito	76	36 20N	140 30E
Mittelland Kanal	52	52 23N	7 45E
Miyako	76	39 40N	141 75E
Miyako-Jima	76	24 45N	125 20E
Miyakonojō	76	31 32N	131 5E
Miyazaki	76	31 56N	131 30E
Mizen Hd.	51	51 27N	9 50W
Mizoram □	70	23 0N	92 40E
Mjanji	93	0 16N	34 0E
Mjøsa	61	60 40N	11 0E
Mkomanzi R.	94	30 13S	30 57E
Mława	55	53 9N	20 25E
Mme	90	6 18N	10 14E
Moate	51	53 25N	7 43W
Moba	93	7 0S	29 48E
Mobile	101	30 41N	88 3W
Mobutu Sese Seko, L.	93	1 30N	31 0E
Mocha	71	13 36N	43 25E
Mochudi	94	24 27S	26 7E
Modbury	43	50 21N	3 53W
Modderrivier	94	29 2S	24 38E
Módena	58	44 39N	10 55E
Modesto	100	37 43N	121 0W
Moe	79	38 12S	146 19E
Moffat	46	55 20N	3 27W
Mogadiscio	89	2 2N	45 25E
Mogadishu = Mogadiscio	89	2 2N	45 25E
Mogami-gawa, R.	76	38 45N	140 0E
Mogollon Mesa	100	35 0N	111 0W
Mohill	50	53 57N	7 52W
Moidart	48	56 49N	5 41W
Mointy	73	47 40N	73 45E
Moisie	99	50 12N	66 1W
Mokai	83	38 32S	175 56E
Mokpo	73	34 50N	126 30E
Mol	52	51 11N	5 5E
Mold	42	53 10N	3 10W
Moldavian S.S.R. □	55	47 0N	28 0E
Molde	61	62 45N	7 9E
Mole, R.	41	51 13N	0 15W
Molepolole	94	24 28S	25 28E
Molfetta	58	41 12N	16 35E
Molise □	58	41 45N	14 30E
Mollendo	108	17 0S	72 0W
Molopo, R.	94	25 40S	24 30E
Molteno	94	31 22S	26 22E
Molucca Sea	72	4 0S	124 0E
Moluccas Is.	72	1 0S	127 0E
Mombasa	93	4 2S	39 43E
Mombetsu	76	42 27N	142 4E
Mona Passage	107	18 0N	67 40W
Monaco ■	56	43 46N	7 23E
Monadhliath Mts.	48	57 10N	4 4W
Monaghan	50	54 15N	6 58W
Monaghan □	50	54 10N	7 0W
Monarch Mt.	105	51 55N	125 57W
Monasterevan	51	53 10N	7 5W
Moncayo, Sierra del	60	41 48N	1 50W
Mönchengladbach	52	51 12N	6 23E
Monclova	106	26 50N	101 30W
Moncton	99	46 7N	64 51W
Mondego, R.	60	40 28N	8 0W
Mondovi	58	44 23N	7 56E
Moneymore	50	54 42N	6 40W
Monforte	60	39 6N	7 25W
Mongalla	89	5 8N	31 55E
Monghyr	70	25 23N	86 30E
Mongolia ■	73	47 0N	103 0E
Mongu	92	15 16S	23 12E
Moniaive	46	55 11N	3 55W
Monifieth	46	56 30N	2 48W
Monmouth	43	51 48N	2 43W
Monópoli	58	40 57N	17 18E
Monroe	101	32 32N	92 4W
Monrovia	88	6 18N	10 47W
Mons	52	50 27N	3 58E
Montagu	94	33 45S	20 8E
Montana □	100	47 0N	110 0W
Montargis	56	48 0N	2 43E
Montauban	56	44 0N	1 21E
Montceau-les-Mines	56	46 40N	4 23E
Monte-Carlo	58	43 46N	7 23E
Monte Cristi	107	19 52N	71 39W
Montego B.	107	18 30N	78 0W
Montélimar	56	44 33N	4 45E
Montemorelos	106	25 11N	99 42W
Monterey	105	36 35N	121 57W
Monterrey	106	25 40N	100 30W
Montes Claros	108	16 30S	43 50W
Montevideo	108	34 50S	56 11W
Montgomery, U.K.	42	52 34N	3 9W
Montgomery, U.S.A.	101	32 20N	86 20W
Montluçon	56	46 22N	2 36E
Monto	79	24 52S	151 12E
Montpelier, Idaho, U.S.A.	100	42 15N	111 20W
Montpelier, Vt., U.S.A.	104	44 15N	72 38W
Montpellier	56	43 37N	3 52E
Montréal	104	45 31N	73 34W
Montreux	54	46 26N	6 55E
Montrose, U.K.	48	56 43N	2 28W
Montrose, U.S.A.	100	38 30N	107 52W
Monzón	60	41 52N	0 10E
Moore, L.	78	29 50S	117 35E
Moorfoot Hills	46	55 44N	3 8W
Moorhead	101	47 0N	97 0W
Moorreesburg	94	33 6S	18 38E
Moose Jaw	98	50 24N	105 30W
Moosehead L.	101	45 40N	69 40W
Moosonee	99	51 17N	80 39W
Moradabad	70	28 50N	78 50E
Morar L.	48	56 57N	5 40W
Morava, R.	54	49 50N	16 50E
Moravian Hts.	54	49 30N	15 40E
Moray Firth	48	57 50N	3 30W
Morecambe	44	54 5N	2 52W
Morecambe B.	44	54 7N	3 0W
Moree	79	29 28S	149 54E
Morelia	106	19 40N	101 11W
Morella	60	40 35N	0 5W
Morena, Sierra	60	38 20N	4 0W
Moreton-in-Marsh	42	51 59N	1 42W
Moretonhampstead	43	50 39N	3 45W
Morgan	79	34 0S	139 35E
Morioka	76	39 45N	141 8E
Morlaix	56	48 36N	3 52W
Morley	45	53 45N	1 36W
Moro G.	72	6 30N	123 0E
Morobe	79	7 49S	147 38E
Morocco ■	88	32 0N	5 50W
Morogoro	93	6 50S	37 40E
Morondava	92	20 17S	44 17E
Morotai, I.	72	2 10N	128 30E
Moroto	93	2 28N	34 42E
Morpeth	44	55 11N	1 41W
Morrinsville	83	37 40S	175 32E
Morristown	101	36 18N	83 20W
Morven	48	56 38N	5 44W
Morwell	79	38 10S	146 22E
Mosborough	45	53 19N	1 22W
Moscow	100	46 45N	116 59W
Moscow = Moskva	62	55 45N	37 35E
Mosel, R.	52	50 22N	7 36E
Moselle, R.	56	50 22N	7 36E
Moses Lake	100	47 16N	119 17W
Mosgiel	83	45 53S	170 21E
Moshi	93	3 22S	37 18E
Mosjøen	61	65 51N	13 12E
*Mossâmedes	92	15 7S	12 11E
Mossburn	83	45 41S	168 15E
Mosselbaai	94	34 11S	22 8E
Mossend	47	55 49N	4 00W
Mossley	45	53 31N	2 1W
Mossman	79	16 28S	145 23E
Mostaganem	88	35 54N	0 5E
Mostar	58	43 22N	17 50E
Mostrim	51	53 42N	7 38W
Mosty	55	53 27N	24 38E
Mosul	71	36 20N	43 5E
Motherwell	47	55 48N	4 0W
Motril	60	36 44N	3 37W
Motueka	83	41 7S	173 1E
Moulmein	70	16 30N	97 40E
Mount Barker	78	34 38S	117 40E
Mount Bellew	51	53 28N	8 31W
Mount Gambier	79	37 50S	140 46E
Mount Isa	79	20 42S	139 26E
Mount Lofty Ra.	79	34 35S	139 5E
Mountain Ash	43	51 42N	3 22W
Mountmellick	51	53 7N	7 20W
Mountrath	51	53 0N	7 30W
Mounts Bay	43	50 3N	5 27W
Mourne Mts.	50	54 10N	6 0W
Mourne, R.	50	54 45N	7 39W
Mouscron	52	50 45N	3 12E
Moutohora	83	38 17S	177 32E
Moville	50	55 11N	7 3W
Moy, R.	50	54 5N	8 50W
Moyale	93	3 30N	39 0E
Moyle □	50	55 10N	6 15W
Mozambique	92	15 3S	40 42E
Mozambique ■	92	19 0S	35 0E
Mozambique Chan.	92	20 0S	39 0E
Mpanda	93	6 23S	31 40E
Mporokoso	93	9 25S	30 5E
Mpwapwa	93	6 30S	36 30E
Mtwara	93	10 20S	40 20E
Mubarraz	71	25 29N	49 40E
Mubende	93	0 33N	31 22E
Mubi	90	10 18N	13 16E
Much Wenlock	45	52 36N	2 34W
Muck, I.	48	56 50N	6 15W
Mudgee	79	32 32S	149 31E
Muêda	93	11 36S	39 28E
Muhammad Râs	91	27 50N	34 0E
Muir of Ord	48	57 30N	4 35W
Muirkirk	46	55 31N	4 6W
Muizenberg	94	34 6S	18 28E
Mukachevo	55	48 27N	22 45E
Mukden = Shenyang	73	41 35N	123 30E
Mulde, R.	54	51 10N	12 48E
Muleba	93	1 50S	31 37E
Mülheim	52	51 26N	6 53E
Mulhouse	56	47 40N	7 20E
Mull I.	48	56 27N	6 0W
Mull, Sound of	48	56 30N	5 50W
Muller Ra.	79	5 30S	143 0E
Mullet Pen.	50	54 10N	10 2W
Mullewa	78	28 29S	115 30E
Mullingar	51	53 31N	7 20W
Multan	71	30 15N	71 30E
Mumbles	43	51 34N	4 0W
Mumbles Hd.	43	51 33N	4 0W
Muna, I.	72	5 0S	122 30E
München = Munich	54	48 8N	11 33E
Muncie	101	40 10N	85 20W
Mundesley	40	52 53N	1 24E
Mungindi	79	28 58S	149 1E
Munich	54	48 8N	11 33E
Münster	52	51 58N	7 37E
Munster □	51	52 20N	8 40W
Mur, R.	54	47 7N	13 55E
Murang'a	93	0 45S	37 9E
Murchison	83	41 49S	172 21E
Murchison, R.	78	26 45S	116 15E
Murchison Ra.	78	20 0S	134 10E
Murcia	60	38 2N	1 10W
Murcia □	60	37 50N	1 30W
Mures R.	55	46 0N	22 0E
Murgon	79	26 15S	151 54E
Müritz, L.	54	53 25N	12 40E
Murmansk	61	68 57N	33 10E
Muroran	76	42 25N	141 0E
Murray Bridge	79	35 6S	139 14E
Murray, R.	79	35 20S	139 22E
Murraysburg	94	31 58S	23 47E
Murrumbidgee, R.	79	34 40S	143 0E
Murshid	91	21 40N	31 10E
Murton	44	54 51N	1 22W
Murupara	83	38 28S	176 42E
Murwara	70	23 46N	80 28E
Murwillumbah	79	28 18S	153 27E
Muş	71	38 45N	41 30E
Musa, G.	91	28 32N	33 59E
Muscat	71	23 40N	58 38E
Musgrave Ras.	78	26 0S	132 0E
Mushin	90	6 32N	3 21E
Muskegon	104	43 15N	86 17W
Muskogee	101	35 50N	95 25W
Musoma	93	1 30S	33 48E
Musselburgh	47	55 57N	3 3W
Musselshell, R.	100	47 21N	107 58W
Muswellbrook	79	32 16S	150 56E
Mût	91	25 28N	28 58E
Mutankiang	73	44 35N	129 30E
Mutsu-Wan	76	41 5N	140 55E
Muzaffarpur	70	26 7N	85 32E
Mwanza	93	2 30S	32 58E
Mwaya	93	9 32S	33 55E
Mweelrea	51	53 37N	9 48W
Mweru, L.	92	9 0S	29 0E
Mwirasandu	93	0 56S	30 22E
Mybster	48	58 27N	3 24W
Myitkyina	70	25 30N	97 26E
Mynydd Prescelly, mt.	42	51 57N	4 48W
Mysore	70	12 17N	76 41E
Mytholmroyd	45	53 43N	1 59W
Mzimvubu, R.	94	31 35S	29 35E

N

Naas	51	53 12N	6 40W
Nababeep	94	29 36S	17 46E
Nabq	91	28 5N	29 23E
Nābulus	89	32 14N	35 15E
Nacozari	106	30 30N	109 50W
Nafada	90	11 8N	11 20E
Nag Hammâdi	91	26 2N	32 18E
Nagaland □	70	26 0N	94 30E
Nagano	76	36 40N	138 10E
Nagaoka	76	37 27N	138 50E
Nagappattinam	70	10 46N	79 51E
Nagasaki	76	32 47N	129 50E
Nagoya	76	35 10N	136 50E
Nagpur	70	21 8N	79 10E
Nagykanizsa	54	46 28N	17 0E
Naha	76	26 13N	127 42E
Nahariya	89	33 1N	35 5E
Nahîya, Wadi	91	28 55N	31 0E
Nailsea	43	51 25N	2 44W
Nailsworth	43	51 41N	2 12W
Nairn	48	57 35N	3 54W
Nairobi	93	1 17S	36 48E
Naivasha	93	0 40S	36 30E
Najafābād	71	32 40N	51 15E
Nakamura	76	33 0N	133 0E
Nakatsu	76	33 40N	131 15E
Nakhichevan A.S.S.R. □	71	39 14N	45 30E
Nakhl	91	29 55N	33 43E
Nakhon Ratchasima (Khorat)	72	14 59N	102 12E
Nakina	99	50 10N	86 40W
Nakuru	93	0 15S	35 5E
Nam Dinh	72	20 25N	106 5E
Nam Tso	73	30 40N	90 30E
Namaland	92	30 0S	18 0E
Namangan	71	41 0N	71 40E
Namasagali	93	1 2N	33 0E
Namatanai	79	3 40S	152 29E
Nambour	79	26 32S	152 58E
Namcha Barwa	73	29 40N	95 10E
Namibia □	92	22 0S	18 9E
Nampa	100	43 40N	116 40W
Nampula	92	15 6S	39 7E
Namur	52	50 27N	4 52E
Namur □	52	50 17N	5 0E
Nan Shan	73	38 30N	99 0E
Nanaimo	105	49 10N	124 0W
Nanango	79	26 40S	152 0E
Nanchang	73	24 26N	117 18E
Nanchung	73	30 47N	105 59E
Nancy	56	48 42N	6 12E
Nander	70	19 10N	77 20E
Nanking	73	32 10N	118 50E
Nannine	78	26 51S	118 18E
Nanning	73	22 48N	108 20E
Nanping	73	26 40N	118 5E
Nantes	56	47 12N	1 33W
Nantucket I.	101	41 16N	70 3W
Nantwich	44	53 5N	2 31W
Nantyglo	43	51 48N	3 10W
Nanyang	73	33 0N	112 32E
Nanyuki	93	0 2N	37 4E
Nao, C. de la	60	38 44N	0 14E
Naoetsu	76	37 12N	138 10E
Napa	100	38 18N	122 17W
Napier	83	39 30S	176 56E
Naples	58	40 50N	14 5E
Napoli = Naples	58	40 50N	14 5E
Naqâda	91	25 53N	32 42E
Nara	76	34 40N	135 49E
Naracoorte	79	36 58S	140 45E
Narberth	42	51 48N	4 45W
Narbonne	56	43 11N	3 0E
Nares Str.	99	81 0N	65 0W
Narmada, R.	70	22 40N	77 30E
Narodnaya, G.	62	65 5N	60 0E
Narok	93	1 20S	33 30E
Narrabri	79	30 19S	149 46E
Narrandera	79	34 42S	146 31E
Narrogin	78	32 58S	117 14E
Narromine	79	32 12S	148 12E
Narva	61	59 10N	28 5E
Narvik	61	68 28N	17 26E
Naseby	83	45 1S	170 10E
Nashua	101	42 50N	71 25W
Nashville	101	36 12N	86 46W
Nasik	70	20 2N	73 50E
Nassau	107	25 0N	77 30W
Nasser City = Kôm Ombo	91	24 25N	32 52E
Nasser, L.	91	23 0N	32 30E
Natal	108	5 47S	35 13W
Natal □	94	28 30S	30 30E
Natashquan	99	50 14N	61 46W
Natchez	101	31 35N	91 25W
Natrûn, W. el.	91	30 25N	30 0E
Natuna Is.	72	4 0N	108 0E
Naturaliste, C.	78	33 32S	115 0E
Nauru I.	23	0 25N	166 0E
Naushahra	71	34 0N	72 0E
Navalcarnero	60	40 17N	4 5W
Navan	51	53 39N	6 40W
Navarra □	60	42 40N	1 40W
Nazareth	89	32 42N	35 17E
Nazas, R.	106	25 20N	104 4W
Naze	76	28 22N	129 27E
Naze, The	40	51 43N	1 19E
Ndala	93	4 45S	33 23E
Ndjamena	88	12 4N	15 8E
Neagh, Lough	50	54 35N	6 25W
Neath	43	51 39N	3 49W
Nebraska □	100	41 30N	100 0W
Nebraska City	101	40 40N	95 52W
Nebrodi Mts.	58	37 55N	14 45E
Neckar, R.	54	48 43N	9 15E
Needles, The	40	50 42N	1 19W
Negoiu, Mt.	55	45 35N	24 31E
Negotin	55	44 16N	22 37E
Negrais C.	70	16 0N	94 30E
Negro, R., Argent.	108	40 0S	64 0W
Negro, R., Boliv.	108	14 11S	63 7W
Negros, I.	72	10 0N	123 0E
Neheim-Hüsten	52	51 27N	7 58E
Neikiang	73	29 35N	105 10E
Neilston	47	55 47N	4 27W
Neisse, R.	54	52 4N	14 46E
Nejd, prov.	71	26 30N	42 0E
Nellore	70	14 27N	79 59E
Nelson, Can.	98	49 30N	117 20W
Nelson, N.Z.	83	41 18S	173 16E
Nelson, U.K.	45	53 50N	2 14W
Nelson □	83	42 11S	172 15E
Nelson Forks	98	59 30N	124 0W
Nelson, R.	98	54 33N	98 2W
Nelspruit	94	25 29S	30 59E
Nemuro	76	43 20N	145 35E
Nemuro-Kaikyō	76	43 30N	145 30E
Nenagh	51	52 52N	8 11W
Nene, R.	40	52 38N	0 7E
Nepal ■	70	28 0N	84 30E
Nepalganj	70	28 0N	81 40E
Nephi	100	39 43N	111 52W
Nephin	50	54 1N	9 21W
Nerchinsk	73	52 0N	116 39E
Neretva, R.	58	43 1N	17 27E
Ness, Loch	48	57 15N	4 30W
Neston	45	53 17N	3 3W
Netherlands ■	52	52 0N	5 30E
Nettilling L.	99	66 30N	71 0W
Neubrandenburg	54	53 33N	13 17E
Neuchâtel	54	47 0N	6 55E
Neuchâtel, L.	54	46 53N	6 50E
Neufchâteau, Belg.	52	49 50N	5 25E
Neufchâteau, France	56	48 21N	5 40E
Neumünster	54	54 4N	9 58E
Neunkirchen	52	49 23N	7 6E
Neusielder, L.	54	47 50N	16 47E
Neuss	52	51 12N	6 39E
Neustadt	52	49 21N	8 10E
Neustrelitz	54	53 22N	13 4E
Neuwied	52	50 26N	7 29E
Nevada □	100	39 20N	117 0W
Nevada, Sierra	60	37 3N	3 15W
Nevel	61	56 0N	29 55E
Nevers	56	47 0N	3 9E
Nevis I.	107	17 0N	62 30W
Nevis, L.	48	57 0N	5 43W
New Alresford	40	51 6N	1 10W

* *Renamed Bohol Sea*

**Renamed Namibe*

New Amsterdam
Otaki

New Amsterdam	**107**	6 15N	57 30W
New Bedford	**104**	41 40N	70 52W
New Braunfels	**100**	29 43N	98 9W
New Brighton, N.Z.	**83**	43 29S	172 43E
New Brighton, U.K.	**45**	53 27N	3 2W
New Britain	**104**	41 41N	72 47W
New Britain, I.	**79**	5 50S	150 20E
New Brunswick □	**99**	46 50N	66 30W
New Bussa	**90**	9 53N	4 31E
New Caledonia, I.	**23**	21 0S	165 0E
New Castile	**60**	39 45N	3 20W
New Castle	**104**	39 55N	85 23W
New Cumnock	**46**	55 24N	4 13W
New Deer	**48**	57 30N	2 10W
New England Ra.	**79**	30 20S	151 45E
New Forest	**40**	50 53N	1 40W
New Guinea, I.	**79**	4 0S	136 0E
New Hampshire □	**101**	43 40N	71 40W
New Haven	**104**	41 20N	72 54W
New Hebrides, Is.	**23**	15 0S	168 0E
New Ireland, I.	**79**	3 20S	151 50E
New Jersey □	**101**	39 50N	74 10W
New Mexico □	**100**	34 30N	106 0W
New Mills	**45**	53 22N	2 0W
New Norfolk	**79**	42 46S	147 2E
New Orleans	**101**	30 0N	90 5W
New Plymouth	**83**	39 4S	174 5E
New Quay	**42**	52 13N	4 21W
New Romney	**40**	50 59N	0 57E
New Sauchie	**47**	56 08N	3 48W
New Scone	**47**	56 25N	3 24W
New Siberian Is.	**62**	75 0N	140 0E
New Silksworth	**44**	54 52N	1 24W
New South Wales □	**79**	33 0S	146 0E
New Tredegar	**43**	51 43N	3 15W
New Westminster	**105**	49 13N	122 55W
New York □	**101**	42 40N	76 0W
New York City	**104**	40 45N	74 0W
New Zealand ■	**83**	40 0S	176 0E
Newark	**104**	40 41N	74 12W
Newark-on-Trent	**44**	53 6N	0 48W
Newbiggin-by-the-Sea	**44**	55 12N	1 31W
Newbridge-on-Wye	**44**	52 13N	3 27W
Newburgh, Fife, U.K.	**47**	56 21N	3 15W
Newburgh, Grampian, U.K.	**48**	57 19N	2 0W
Newburn	**44**	54 57N	1 45W
Newbury	**40**	51 24N	1 19W
Newcastle, Austral.	**79**	33 0S	151 40E
Newcastle, Ireland	**50**	53 5N	6 4W
Newcastle, S. Afr.	**94**	27 45S	29 58E
Newcastle, U.K.	**50**	54 13N	5 54W
Newcastle Emlyn	**42**	52 2N	4 29W
Newcastle-under-Lyme	**44**	53 2N	2 15W
Newcastle-upon-Tyne	**44**	54 59N	1 37W
Newcastle Waters	**78**	17 30S	133 28E
Newcastle West	**51**	52 27N	9 3W
Newdegate	**78**	33 6S	119 0E
Newham	**41**	51 31N	0 2E
Newhaven	**40**	50 47N	0 4E
Newmains	**47**	55 46N	3 53W
Newman, Mt.	**78**	23 20S	119 34E
Newmarket, Ireland	**51**	52 13N	9 0W
Newmarket, U.K.	**40**	52 15N	0 23E
Newmarket-on-Fergus	**51**	52 46N	8 54W
Newmilns	**47**	55 36N	4 20W
Newnham	**43**	51 48N	2 27W
Newport, Ireland	**50**	53 53N	9 32W
Newport, Gwent, U.K.	**43**	51 35N	3 0W
Newport, I. of W., U.K.	**40**	50 42N	1 18W
Newport, U.S.A.	**101**	39 5N	84 23W
Newport B.	**50**	53 52N	9 38W
Newport News	**101**	37 2N	76 30W
Newport on Tay	**47**	56 27N	2 56W
Newport Pagnell	**40**	52 5N	0 42W
Newquay	**43**	50 24N	5 6W
Newry	**50**	54 10N	6 20W
Newry & Mourne □	**50**	54 10N	6 15W
Newton Abbot	**43**	50 32N	3 37W
Newton-Aycliffe	**44**	54 36N	1 33W
Newton le Willows	**45**	53 28N	2 27W
Newton Mearns	**47**	55 46N	4 20W
Newton Stewart	**46**	54 57N	4 30W
Newtonabbey □	**50**	54 45N	6 0W
Newtongrange	**47**	55 52N	3 4W
Newtown	**42**	52 31N	3 19W
Newtown Hamilton	**50**	54 12N	6 35W
Newtownabbey	**50**	54 40N	5 55W
Newtownards	**50**	54 37N	5 40W
Newtownstewart	**50**	54 43N	7 22W
Neyland	**42**	51 43N	4 58W
Neyshābūr	**71**	36 10N	58 20E
Ngapara	**83**	44 57S	170 46E
Ngozi	**93**	2 54S	29 50E
Nguru	**90**	12 56N	10 29E
Niagara Falls	**104**	43 7N	79 5W
Niamey	**90**	13 27N	2 6E
Niangara	**92**	3 50N	27 50E
Nias, I.	**72**	1 0N	97 40E
Nicaragua ■	**106**	11 40N	85 30W
Nicastro	**58**	39 0N	16 18E
Nice	**56**	43 42N	7 14E
Nicobar Is.	**72**	9 0N	93 0E
Nicosia	**71**	35 10N	33 25E
Nidd, R.	**44**	54 1N	1 32W
Niers, R.	**52**	51 35N	6 13E
Nigel	**94**	26 27S	28 25E
Niger ■	**88**	13 30N	10 0E
Niger Delta	**90**	4 0N	5 30W
Niger, R.	**90**	10 0N	4 40E
Nigeria ■	**90**	8 30N	8 0E
Nightcaps	**83**	45 57S	168 14E
Niigata	**76**	37 58N	139 0E
Niihama	**76**	33 55N	133 10E
Nijkerk	**52**	52 13N	5 30E
Nijmegen	**52**	51 50N	5 52E
Nikkō	**76**	36 45N	139 35E
Nikolayev	**62**	46 58N	32 7E
Nikolayevski	**62**	50 10N	45 35E
Nile, R.	**91**	27 30N	30 30E
Nilgiri Hills	**70**	11 30N	76 30E
Nîmes	**56**	43 50N	4 23E
Ningpo	**73**	29 53N	121 33E
Ningsia Hui A.R. □	**73**	37 45N	106 0E
Ningteh	**73**	26 45N	120 0E
Ninove	**52**	50 51N	4 2E
Niort	**56**	46 19N	0 29W
Nipigon, L.	**98**	49 50N	88 30W
Nishinoomote	**76**	30 43N	130 59E
Niterói	**108**	22 52S	43 0W
Nith, R.	**46**	55 20N	3 5W
Nithsdale	**46**	55 14N	3 50W
Nivelles	**52**	50 35N	4 20E
Nivernais	**56**	47 0N	3 40E
Nizamghat	**70**	28 20N	95 45E
Nizhniy Tagil	**62**	57 55N	59 57E
Njombe	**93**	9 20S	34 50E
Nkhata Bay	**93**	11 33S	34 16E
Nkongsamba	**90**	4 55N	9 55E
Nobeoka	**76**	32 36N	131 41E
Nocera Umbra	**58**	43 8N	12 47E
Nogales, Mexico	**106**	31 36N	94 29W
Nogales, U.S.A.	**100**	31 20N	110 56W
Noirmoutier, Î. de	**56**	46 58N	2 10W
Nome	**96**	64 30N	165 30W
Noord Brabant □	**52**	51 40N	5 0E
Noord Holland □	**52**	52 30N	4 45E
Noordbeveland	**52**	51 45N	3 50E
Nootka I.	**105**	49 40N	126 50W
Nordegg	**98**	52 29N	116 5W
Nordhausen	**54**	51 29N	10 47E
Nordhorn	**52**	52 27N	7 4E
Nordkinn	**61**	71 3N	28 0E
Nore R.	**51**	52 40N	7 20W
Norfolk	**101**	36 52N	76 15W
Norfolk □	**40**	52 39N	1 0E
Norfolk I.	**23**	28 58S	168 3E
Norham	**46**	55 44N	2 9W
Norilsk	**62**	69 20N	88 0E
Norman Wells	**98**	65 17N	126 45W
Normandy	**56**	48 45N	0 10E
Normanton, Austral.	**79**	17 40S	141 10E
Normanton, U.K.	**45**	53 41N	1 26W
Norrköping	**61**	58 37N	16 11E
Norrland □	**61**	66 50N	18 0E
Norseman	**78**	32 8S	121 43E
North Battleford	**98**	52 50N	108 17W
North Bay	**99**	46 20N	79 30W
North Bend	**100**	43 28N	124 7W
North Berwick	**46**	56 4N	2 44W
North C.	**83**	34 23S	173 4E
North Cape	**61**	71 15N	25 40E
North Carolina □	**101**	35 30N	80 0W
North Channel	**32**	55 0N	5 30W
North Dakota □	**100**	47 30N	100 0W
N. Dorset Downs	**43**	50 50N	2 30W
North Down □	**50**	54 40N	5 45W
North Downs	**41**	51 17N	0 30E
North Esk, R.	**48**	56 44N	2 25W
North European Plain	**24**	55 0N	20 0E
N. Foreland	**40**	51 22N	1 28E
North Island	**83**	38 0S	176 0E
North Kessock	**48**	57 30N	4 15W
North Korea ■	**73**	40 0N	127 0E
North Minch	**48**	58 5N	5 55W
North Pagai, I.	**72**	2 45S	100 15E
North Platte	**100**	41 10N	100 50W
North Pole	**112**	90 0N	0 0E
North Queensferry	**47**	56 1N	3 22W
North Rhine Westphalia □	**54**	51 55N	7 0E
North Ronaldsay, I.	**49**	59 20N	2 30W
North Sea	**24**	56 0N	4 0E
North Shields	**44**	55 00N	1 26W
N. Taranaki Bt.	**83**	38 45S	174 20E
North Tawton	**43**	50 48N	3 55W
North Tidworth	**42**	51 14N	1 40W
North Uist I.	**49**	57 40N	7 15W
North Vancouver	**105**	49 2N	123 3W
North Walsham	**40**	52 49N	1 22E
North Weald Bassett	**41**	51 42N	0 10E
North West Highlands	**48**	57 35N	5 2W
North West River	**99**	53 30N	60 10W
North York Moors	**44**	54 25N	0 50W
North Yorkshire □	**44**	54 15N	1 25W
Northallerton	**44**	54 20N	1 26W
Northam, Austral.	**78**	31 35S	116 42E
Northam, U.K.	**43**	51 2N	4 13W
Northampton, Austral.	**78**	28 21S	114 33E
Northampton, U.K.	**40**	52 14N	0 54W
Northampton □	**40**	52 16N	0 55W
Northern Ireland □	**50**	54 45N	7 0W
Northern Territory □	**78**	16 0S	133 0E
Northfleet	**41**	51 26N	0 20E
Northiam	**40**	50 59N	0 39E
Northland □	**83**	35 30S	173 30E
Northleach	**42**	51 49N	1 50W
Northowram	**45**	53 44N	1 50W
Northumberland □	**44**	55 12N	2 0W
Northwest Terr. □	**98**	65 0N	100 0W
Northwich	**44**	53 16N	2 30W
Norton	**44**	54 9N	0 48W
Norton Sd.	**98**	64 0N	165 0W
Norway ■	**61**	67 0N	11 0E
Norwich	**40**	52 38N	1 17E
Noshiro	**76**	40 12N	140 0E
Nossob, R.	**94**	25 15S	20 30E
Notec, R.	**54**	52 50N	16 0E
Nottingham	**44**	52 57N	1 10W
Nottingham □	**44**	53 10N	1 0W
Nouadhibou	**88**	21 0N	17 0W
Nouméa	**23**	22 17S	166 30E
Noupoort	**94**	31 10S	24 57E
Nova Scotia □	**99**	45 10N	63 0W
Novara	**58**	45 27N	8 36E
Novaya Zemlya	**62**	75 0N	56 0E
Novgorod	**61**	58 30N	31 25E
Novi Sad	**55**	45 18N	19 52E
Novograd Volynskiy	**55**	50 40N	27 35E
Novokuznetsk	**62**	54 0N	87 10E
Novorossiysk	**62**	44 43N	37 52E
Novosibirsk	**62**	55 0N	83 5E
Novska	**58**	45 19N	17 0E
Nowra	**79**	34 53S	150 35E
Nowy Sacz	**55**	49 40N	20 41E
Nowy Tomyśl	**54**	52 19N	16 10E
Nsukka	**90**	7 0N	7 50E
Nubian Desert	**89**	21 30N	33 30E
Nueva Rosita	**106**	28 0N	101 20W
Nuevo Laredo	**106**	27 30N	99 40W
Nugrus, Gebel	**91**	24 58N	39 34E
Nuhaka	**83**	39 3S	177 45E
Nullagine	**78**	21 53S	120 6E
Nullarbor Plain	**78**	30 45S	129 0E
Numan	**90**	9 29N	12 3E
Numazu	**76**	35 7N	138 51E
Nuneaton	**41**	52 32N	1 29W
Nunivak I.	**96**	60 0N	166 0W
Nunkiang	**73**	49 11N	125 12E
Nuoro	**58**	40 20N	9 20E
Nuremberg	**54**	49 26N	11 5E
Nürnberg = Nuremberg	**54**	49 26N	11 5E
Nusa Tenggara □	**72**	7 30S	117 0E
Nusaybin	**71**	37 3N	41 10E
Nushki	**71**	29 35N	65 65E
Nuweveldberge	**94**	32 10S	21 45E
Nyabing	**78**	33 30S	118 7E
Nyahanga	**93**	2 20S	33 37E
Nyahururu	**93**	0 2N	36 27E
Nyakanazi	**93**	3 2S	31 10E
Nyakanyasi	**93**	1 10S	31 13E
Nyâlâ	**89**	12 2N	24 58E
Nyanza	**93**	4 21S	29 36E
Nyasa, L.	**93**	12 0S	34 30E
Nyenchen, mts.	**73**	30 0N	87 0E
Nyeri	**93**	0 23S	36 56E
Nyíregyháza	**55**	48 0N	21 47E
Nylstroom	**94**	24 42S	28 22E
Nyngan	**79**	31 30S	147 8E
Nzega	**93**	4 10S	33 12E
Nzubuka	**93**	4 45S	32 50E

O

Oadby	**41**	52 37N	1 7W
Oahu I.	**22**	21 30N	158 0W
Oak Ridge	**101**	36 1N	84 5W
Oakdale	**43**	51 40N	3 13W
Oakengates	**45**	52 42N	2 29W
Oakham	**45**	52 40N	0 43W
Oakland	**105**	37 50N	122 18W
Oakley	**47**	56 04N	3 33W
Oakworth	**45**	53 50N	1 58W
Oamaru	**83**	45 5S	170 59E
Oaxaca	**106**	17 2N	96 40W
Ob, G. of	**62**	70 0N	73 0E
Ob, R.	**62**	62 40N	66 0E
Oba	**99**	49 4N	84 7W
Oban, N.Z.	**83**	46 55S	168 10E
Oban, U.K.	**46**	56 25N	5 30W
Oberhausen	**52**	51 28N	6 50E
Obi, Is.	**72**	1 30S	127 30E
Obiaruku	**90**	5 51N	6 9E
Obihiro	**76**	42 25N	143 12E
Obluchye	**73**	49 10N	130 50E
Ocala	**101**	29 11N	82 5W
Ocaña	**60**	39 55N	3 30W
Ochil Hills	**46**	56 14N	3 40W
October Revolution I.	**62**	79 30N	97 0E
Odate	**76**	40 16N	140 34E
Odendaalsrus	**94**	27 48S	26 43E
Odense	**61**	55 22N	10 23E
Oder, R.	**54**	53 33N	14 38E
Odessa, U.S.A.	**100**	31 51N	102 23W
Odessa, U.S.S.R.	**55**	46 30N	30 45E
Odra, R.	**54**	53 33N	14 38E
Offa	**90**	8 13N	4 42E
Offaly □	**51**	53 15N	7 30W
Offenbach	**54**	50 6N	8 46E
Ogbomosho	**90**	8 1N	3 29E
Ogden	**100**	41 13N	112 1W
Ogdensburg	**101**	44 40N	75 27W
Ogoja	**90**	6 38N	8 39E
Ogun □	**90**	7 0N	3 0E
Oguta	**90**	5 44N	6 44E
Ogwashi-Uku	**90**	6 15N	6 30E
Ohai	**83**	44 55S	168 0E
Ohakune	**83**	39 24S	175 24E
Ohio □	**101**	40 20N	83 0W
Ohio, R.	**104**	38 0N	86 0W
Ohrigstad	**94**	24 41S	30 36E
Oil City	**101**	41 26N	79 40W
Oise, R.	**56**	49 53N	3 50E
Oita	**76**	33 14N	131 36E
Ojos del Salado	**108**	27 0S	68 40W
Oka, R.	**62**	56 20N	43 59E
Okarito	**83**	43 15S	170 9E
Okayama	**76**	34 40N	133 54E
Okazaki	**76**	34 57N	137 10E
Oke-Iho	**90**	8 1N	3 18E
Okehampton	**43**	50 44N	4 1W
Okha	**62**	53 40N	143 0E
Okhotsk	**62**	59 20N	143 10E
Okhotsk, Sea of	**62**	55 0N	145 0E
Oki, Is.	**76**	36 15N	133 15E
Okija	**90**	5 54N	6 55E
Okinawa-Jima	**76**	26 32N	128 0E
Okinoerabu-Jima	**76**	27 21N	128 33E
Okitipupa	**90**	6 31N	4 50E
Oklahoma □	**100**	35 20N	97 30W
Oklahoma City	**101**	35 25N	97 30W
Okrika	**90**	4 47N	7 4E
Okuru	**83**	43 55S	168 55E
Öland	**61**	56 45N	16 50E
Ólbia	**58**	40 55N	9 30E
Old Castile, reg.	**60**	41 55N	4 0W
Old Castle	**51**	53 46N	7 10W
Old Windsor	**41**	51 27N	0 35W
Oldbury	**41**	52 30N	2 0W
Oldcastle	**50**	53 46N	7 10W
Oldenburg	**52**	53 10N	8 10E
Oldenzaal	**52**	52 19N	6 53E
Oldham	**45**	53 33N	2 8W
Oldmeldrum	**48**	57 20N	2 19W
Olekminsk	**62**	60 40N	120 30E
Olenek, R.	**62**	71 0N	123 50E
Oléron, I. d'	**56**	45 55N	1 15W
Olifants, R.	**94**	24 5S	31 20E
Olifantshoek	**94**	27 57S	22 42E
Ollerton	**44**	53 12N	1 1W
Olney	**40**	52 9N	0 42W
Olomouc	**54**	49 38N	17 12E
Oloron-Ste.-Marie	**56**	43 11N	0 38W
Olovyannaya	**73**	50 50N	115 10E
Olpe	**52**	51 2N	7 50E
Olsztyn	**55**	53 48N	20 29E
Olt, R.	**55**	43 50N	24 40E
Oltenița	**55**	44 7N	26 42E
Olympic Nat. Park	**100**	47 48N	123 30W
Olympus, Mt.	**105**	47 52N	123 40W
Omagh	**50**	54 36N	7 20W
Omagh □	**50**	54 35N	7 15W
Omaha	**101**	41 15N	96 0W
Oman, G. of	**71**	24 30N	58 30E
Omdurmân	**89**	15 40N	32 28E
Ometepec	**106**	16 39N	98 23W
Ōmiya	**76**	35 54N	139 38E
Omsk	**62**	55 0N	73 38E
Ōmuta	**76**	33 0N	130 26E
Ondo	**90**	7 4N	4 47E
Onega	**61**	64 0N	38 10E
Onega, L.	**61**	62 0N	35 30E
Onega, R.	**61**	63 0N	39 0E
Onehunga	**83**	36 55S	174 30E
Ongarue	**83**	38 42S	175 19E
Onitsha	**90**	6 6N	6 42E
Onomichi	**76**	34 25N	133 12E
Onslow	**78**	21 40S	115 0E
Ontake, Mt.	**76**	35 50N	137 15E
Ontario	**100**	44 1N	117 1W
Ontario □	**99**	52 0N	88 10W
Ontario, L.	**104**	43 40N	78 0W
Oodnadatta	**79**	27 33S	135 30E
Ooldea	**78**	30 27S	131 50E
Oostende = Ostend	**52**	51 15N	2 50E
Oosterhout	**52**	51 39N	4 52E
Opava	**55**	49 57N	17 58E
Ophthalmia Ra.	**78**	23 15S	119 30E
Opi	**90**	6 36N	7 28E
Opobo	**90**	4 35N	7 34E
Opole	**55**	50 42N	17 58E
Oporto	**60**	41 8N	8 40W
Opotiki	**83**	38 1S	177 19E
Opua	**83**	35 19S	174 9E
Opunake	**83**	39 26S	173 52E
Oradea	**55**	47 2N	21 58E
Oran	**88**	35 37N	0 39W
Orange, Austral.	**79**	33 15S	149 7E
Orange, France	**56**	44 8N	4 47E
Orange, U.S.A.	**101**	30 10N	93 50W
Orange Free State □	**94**	28 30S	27 0E
Orange, R.	**94**	28 30S	18 0E
Oranienburg	**54**	52 45N	13 15E
Oranjefentein	**94**	23 28S	27 42E
Oranmore	**51**	53 16N	8 57W
Orbetello	**58**	42 26N	11 11E
Orbost	**79**	37 40S	148 29E
Ord, Mt.	**78**	17 20S	125 34E
Ord, R.	**78**	15 33S	128 35E
Ordos	**73**	39 25N	108 45E
Ordzhonikidze	**71**	43 0N	44 35E
Örebro	**61**	59 20N	15 18E
Orel	**62**	52 57N	36 3E
Orenburg	**62**	51 45N	55 6E
Orense	**60**	42 19N	7 55W
Orepuki	**83**	46 19S	167 46E
Orford Ness	**40**	52 6N	1 31E
Orinoco, R.	**107**	5 45N	67 40W
Orissa □	**70**	21 0N	85 0E
Oristano	**58**	39 54N	8 35E
Oristano, G. of	**58**	39 50N	8 22E
Orizaba	**106**	18 50N	97 10W
Orkney	**94**	26 42S	26 40E
Orkney Is.	**49**	59 0N	3 0W
Orlando	**101**	28 30N	81 25W
Orléanais	**56**	48 0N	2 0E
Orléans	**56**	47 54N	1 52E
Ormara	**71**	25 16N	64 33E
Ormoc	**72**	11 0N	124 37E
Ormond	**83**	38 33S	177 56E
Ormskirk	**45**	53 35N	2 53W
Örnsköldsvik	**61**	63 17N	18 40E
Orodo	**90**	5 34N	7 4E
Oron	**90**	4 48N	8 14E
Oronsay I.	**46**	56 0N	6 14W
Orsk	**62**	51 12N	58 34E
Orşova	**55**	44 41N	22 25E
Ortegal, C.	**60**	43 43N	7 52W
Ortona	**58**	42 21N	14 24E
Oruro	**108**	18 0S	67 19W
Orvieto	**58**	42 43N	12 8E
Orwell, R.	**40**	52 2N	1 12E
Ōsaka	**76**	34 30N	135 30E
Osh	**71**	40 37N	72 49E
Oshawa	**104**	43 50N	78 50W
Oshogbo	**90**	7 48N	4 37E
Osijek	**58**	45 34N	18 41E
Oskarshamn	**61**	57 15N	16 27E
Oslo	**61**	59 55N	10 45E
Oslo Fjord	**61**	58 30N	10 0E
Osnabrück	**52**	52 16N	8 2E
Oss	**52**	51 46N	5 32E
Ossa, Mt.	**79**	41 52S	146 3E
Ossett	**45**	53 40N	1 35W
Ostend	**52**	51 15N	2 50E
Östersund	**61**	63 10N	14 38E
Ostia Lido	**58**	41 43N	12 17E
Ostrava	**55**	49 51N	18 18E
Ostróda	**55**	53 42N	19 58E
Ostrołeka	**55**	53 4N	21 38E
Ostrów Mazowiecka	**55**	52 50N	21 51E
Ostrów Wielkopolski	**55**	51 36N	17 44E
Osumi Channel	**76**	30 55N	131 0E
Osumi, Is.	**76**	30 30N	130 45E
Osuna	**60**	37 14N	5 8W
Oswaldtwistle	**45**	53 44N	2 27W
Oswego	**104**	43 29N	76 30W
Oswestry	**45**	52 52N	3 3W
Otago □	**83**	45 20S	169 20E
Otaki	**83**	40 45S	175 10E

Otaru Pratt

Otaru 76 43 10N 141 0E
Otavi 92 19 40S 17 24E
Otford 41 51 18N 0 11E
Otira Gorge 83 42 53S 171 33E
Otley 45 53 54N 1 41W
Otoineppu 76 44 44N 142 16E
Otorohanga 83 38 12S 175 14E
Otranto, Str. of 58 40 15N 18 40E
Ottawa 104 45 27N 75 42W
Ottawa Is. 99 59 35N 80 16W
Ottery St. Mary 43 50 45N 3 16W
Otukpa 90 7 9N 7 41E
Oturkpo 90 7 10N 8 15E
Otwock 55 52 5N 21 20E
Ouachita Mts. 101 34 50N 94 30W
Ouagadougou 88 12 25N 1 30W
Oude Rijn, R. 52 52 12N 4 24E
Oudtshoorn 94 33 35S 22 14E
Oughter, L. 50 54 2N 7 30W
Ougrée 52 50 36N 5 32E
Ouidah 90 6 25N 2 0E
Oujda □ 88 33 18N 1 25W
Oulton Broad 40 52 28N 1 43E
Oulu 61 65 1N 25 29E
Oulu, L. 61 64 25N 27 0E
Oundle 40 52 28N 0 28W
Our, R. 52 49 55N 6 5E
Ourthe, R. 52 50 29N 5 35E
Ouse, Great, R. 40 52 12N 0 7E
Ouse, Little, R. 40 52 25N 0 20E
Ouse, R., Sussex, U.K. 40 50 43N 0 3E
Ouse, R., Yorks., U.K. 44 54 3N 0 7E
Outer Hebrides, Is. 49 57 30N 7 40W
Ouyen 79 35 1S 142 22E
Ovar 60 40 51N 8 40W
Overflakkee 52 51 44N 4 10E
Overijssel □ 52 52 25N 6 35E
Oviedo 60 43 25N 5 50W
Owaka 83 46 27S 169 40E
Owambo 92 17 20S 16 30E
Owase 76 34 7N 136 5E
Owatonna 101 44 3N 93 17W
Owen Falls 93 0 30N 33 5E
Owen Stanley Range 79 8 30S 147 0E
Owens L. 105 36 20N 118 0W
Owerri 90 5 29N 7 0E
Owo 90 7 18N 5 30E
Owosso 101 43 0N 84 10W
Oxenhope 45 53 48N 1 57W
Oxford, N.Z. 83 43 18S 172 11E
Oxford, U.K. 40 51 45N 1 15W
Oxford □ 40 51 45N 1 15W
Oxted 41 51 14N 0 01W
Oykel, R. 48 57 55N 4 26W
Oyo 90 7 46N 3 56E
Oyonnax 56 46 16N 5 40E
Ozamis 72 8 15N 123 50E
Ozark Plateau 101 37 20N 91 40W

P

Pa-an 73 16 45N 97 40E
Paarl 94 33 45S 18 56E
Pabbay I. 49 57 46N 7 12W
Pacaraima, Sierra 107 4 0N 63 0W
Pacific Ocean 22 10 0N 140 0W
Padang 72 1 0S 100 20E
Padiham 45 53 48N 2 20W
Padova = Padua 58 45 24N 11 52E
Padre I. 101 27 0N 97 20W
Padstow 43 50 33N 4 57W
Padua 58 45 24N 11 52E
Paeroa 83 37 23S 175 41E
Pag 58 44 30N 14 50E
Pagalu, I. 88 1 35S 3 35E
Pahiatua 83 40 27S 175 50E
Paignton 43 50 26N 3 33W
Painted Desert 100 36 40N 111 30W
Paisley 47 55 51N 4 27W
Paiyin 73 36 45N 104 4E
Paiyünopo 73 41 46N 109 58E
Pakanbaru 72 0 30N 101 15E
Pakhoi 73 21 30N 109 10E
Pakistan ■ 71 30 0N 70 0E
Pakse 72 15 5N 105 52E
Palagruza 58 42 24N 16 15E
Palapye 92 22 30S 27 7E
Palawan, I. 72 10 0N 119 0E
Palembang 72 3 0S 104 50E
Palencia 60 42 1N 4 34W
Palermo 58 38 8N 13 20E
Paletwa 70 21 30N 92 50E
Palk Strait 70 10 0N 80 0E
Pallas Green 51 52 35N 8 22W
Palma 60 39 33N 2 39E
Palma, Bay of 60 39 30N 2 39E
Palma, La, Panama 107 8 15N 78 0W
Palma, La, Spain 60 37 21N 6 38W
Palmas, C. 88 4 27N 7 46W
Palmas, G. of 58 39 0N 8 30E
Palmerston 83 45 29S 170 43E
Palmerston North 83 40 21S 175 39E
Palmi 58 38 21N 15 51E
Palmira 107 3 32N 76 16W
Palmyra Is. 22 5 52N 162 5W
Palo Alto 105 37 25N 122 8W
Palos, C. 60 37 38N 0 40W
Pamiers 56 43 7N 1 39E
Pamirs 71 37 40N 73 0E
Pampa 100 35 35N 100 58W
Pampas 108 34 0S 64 0W
Pamplona, Colomb. 107 7 23N 72 39W
Pamplona, Spain 60 42 48N 1 38W
Panamá 107 9 0N 79 25W
Panama ■ 107 8 48N 79 55W
Panama Canal Zone 107 9 10N 79 56W
Panama, G. of 96 8 4N 79 20W
Panay I. 72 11 10N 122 30E
Pančevo 55 44 52N 20 41E
Pancorbo Pass 60 42 32N 3 5W
Pangani 93 5 25S 38 58E
Pangbourne 40 51 28N 1 5W
Pangola R. 94 23 40S 27 43E
Pantar, I. 72 8 28S 124 10E
Pantelleria, I. 58 36 52N 12 0E
Panuco 106 22 0N 98 25W
Panuco, R. 106 21 30N 98 30W
Panyam 90 9 27N 9 8E
Paoki 73 34 25N 107 15E
Paoting 73 38 50N 115 30E
Paotow 73 40 45N 110 0E
Papakura 83 37 4S 174 59E
Papantla 106 20 45N 97 21W
Papenburg 52 53 7N 7 25E
Papua, Gulf of 79 9 0S 144 50E
Papua New Guinea ■ 79 8 0S 145 0E
Pará □ 108 3 20S 52 0W
Paragua, R. 107 6 30N 63 30W
Paraguay ■ 108 23 0S 57 0W
Paraguay, R. 108 27 18S 58 38W
Parakou 90 9 25N 2 40E
Paramaribo 108 5 50N 55 10W
Paraná 108 32 0S 60 30W
Paraná, R. 108 33 43S 59 15W
Pardubice 54 50 3N 15 45E
Pare Pare 72 4 0S 119 45E
Parima, Serra 107 2 30N 64 0W
Paris 56 48 50N 2 20E
Park Range 100 40 0N 106 30W
Parkersburg 104 39 18N 81 31W
Parkes 79 33 9S 148 11E
Parma 58 44 50N 10 20E
Parnaiba, R. 108 3 35S 43 0W
Paroo, R. 79 30 0S 144 5E
Parry Is. 98 77 0N 110 0W
Parry Sound 99 45 20N 80 0W
Partington 45 53 25N 2 25W
Partry Mts. 51 53 40N 9 28W
Pasadena, Calif., U.S.A. 105 34 5N 118 9W
Pasadena, Tex., U.S.A. 101 29 45N 95 14W
Passage East 51 52 15N 7 0W
Passage West 51 51 52N 8 20W
Passau 54 48 34N 13 27E
Passero, C. 58 36 42N 15 8E
Patagonia 108 45 0S 69 0W
Patchway 43 51 32N 2 34W
Patea 83 39 45S 174 30E
Pategi 90 8 50N 5 45E
Pateley Bridge 44 54 5N 1 45W
Patensie 94 33 46S 24 49E
Paternò 58 37 34N 14 53E
Paterson 104 40 55N 74 10W
Pathfinder Res. 100 42 30N 107 0W
Patiala 70 30 23N 76 26E
Patna 70 25 35N 85 18E
Patrickswell 51 52 36N 8 42W
Patrington 44 53 41N 0 1W
Patti 58 38 8N 14 57E
Pau 56 43 19N 0 25W
Pauillac 56 45 11N 0 46W
Paulpietersburg 94 27 23S 30 50E
Pavia 58 45 10N 9 10E
Pavlodar 62 52 33N 77 0E
Pawtucket 104 41 51N 71 22W
Paz, La, Boliv. 108 16 20S 68 10W
Paz, La, Mexico 106 24 10N 110 20W
Peace River 98 56 15N 117 18W
Peak Hill 78 32 39S 148 11E
Peak Range 79 22 50S 148 20E
Peak, The 44 53 24N 1 53W
Pechenga 61 69 30N 31 25E
Pechora G. 62 68 40N 54 0E
Pecos 100 31 25N 103 35W
Pecos, R. 100 29 42N 102 30W
Pécs 55 46 5N 18 15E
Peebles 47 55 40N 3 12W
Peel 42 54 14N 4 40W
Peel Fell, mt. 46 55 17N 2 35W
Pegasus Bay 83 43 20S 173 10E
Pegu Yoma, mts. 70 19 0N 96 0E
Pehan 73 48 17N 120 31E
Pehpei 73 29 44N 106 29E
Peiping 73 39 50N 116 20E
Pekalongan 72 6 53S 109 40E
Peking = Peiping 73 39 45N 116 25E
Peleng, I. 72 1 20S 123 30E
Pelly, R. 98 62 15N 133 30W
Peloro, C. 58 38 15N 15 40E
Pelvoux, Massif de 56 44 52N 6 20E
Pematang Siantar 72 2 57N 99 5E
Pemba, I. 93 5 0S 39 45E
Pemberton 78 34 30S 116 0E
Pembroke 42 51 41N 4 57W
Pen-y-Ghent 44 54 10N 2 15W
Pen-y-groes 42 53 3N 4 18W
Penarth 43 51 26N 3 11W
Pendine 42 51 44N 4 33W
Pendle Hill 45 53 53N 2 18W
Pendlebury 45 53 31N 2 20W
Pendleton 105 45 35N 118 50W
Pengpu 73 33 0N 117 25E
Penistone 45 53 31N 1 38W
Penketh 45 53 22N 2 37W
Penki 73 41 20N 132 50E
Pennines 44 54 50N 2 20W
Pennsylvania □ 101 40 50N 78 0W
Penong 78 31 59S 133 5E
Penrhyn Is. 22 9 0S 150 30W
Penrith, Austral. 79 33 43S 150 38E
Penrith, U.K. 44 54 40N 2 45W
Penryn 43 50 10N 5 7W
Pensacola 101 30 30N 87 10W
Pensacola Mts. 112 84 0S 40 0W
Penticton 105 49 30N 119 30W
Pentland 79 20 32S 145 25E
Pentland Firth 48 58 43N 3 10W
Pentland Hills 46 55 48N 3 25W
Pentre Foelas 42 53 2N 3 41W
Penygraig 43 51 36N 3 26W
Penza 62 53 15N 45 5E
Penzance 43 50 7N 5 32W
Peoria 101 40 40N 89 40W
Perche 56 48 31N 1 1E
Perdido, Mte. 60 42 40N 0 50E
Pereira 107 4 49N 75 43W
Peribonca, R. 99 49 0N 72 25W
Périgueux 56 45 10N 0 42E
Perm (Molotov) 62 58 0N 57 10E
Pernambuco = Recife 108 8 0S 35 0W
Perpignan 56 42 42N 2 53E
Perranporth 43 50 21N 5 9W
Perryton 100 36 28N 100 48W
Pershore 42 52 7N 2 4W
Persian Gulf 71 27 0N 50 0E
Perth, Austral. 78 31 57S 115 52E
Perth, U.K. 47 56 24N 3 27W
Peru ■ 108 8 0S 75 0W
Perúgia 58 43 6N 12 24E
Pésaro 58 43 55N 12 53E
Pescara 58 42 28N 14 13E
Peshawar 71 34 2N 71 37E
Petange 52 49 33N 5 55E
Peterborough, Austral. 79 32 58S 138 51E
Peterborough, U.K. 40 52 35N 0 14W
Peterculter 48 57 5N 2 18W
Peterhead 48 57 30N 1 49W
Peterlee 44 54 45N 1 18W
Petersburg 101 37 17N 77 26W
Petersfield 40 51 0N 0 56W
Peto 106 20 10N 89 0W
Petone 83 41 13S 174 53E
Petropavlovsk-Kamchatskiy 62 53 16N 159 0E
Petrovaradin 55 45 16N 19 55E
Petrovsk 62 52 22N 45 19E
Petrozavodsk 61 61 41N 34 20E
Petton 44 54 52N 1 36W
Petworth 40 50 59N 0 37W
Pforzheim 54 48 53N 8 43E
Phan Rang 72 11 40N 109 9E
Phan Thiet 72 11 1N 108 9E
Phanom Dang Raek, mts. 72 14 45N 104 0E
Phenix City 101 32 30N 85 0W
Philadelphia 104 40 0N 75 10W
Philippines ■ 72 12 0N 123 0E
Philippolis 94 30 15S 25 16E
Philipstown 94 30 28S 24 30E
Phnom Penh 72 11 33N 104 55E
Phoenix 100 33 30N 112 10W
Phoenix Is. 22 3 30S 172 0W
Piacenza 58 45 2N 9 42E
Picardy 56 50 0N 2 15E
Pickering 44 54 15N 0 46W
Picton 83 41 18S 174 3E
Pidurutalagala, mt. 70 7 10N 80 50E
Piedmont 58 45 0N 7 30E
Piedmont Plat. 101 34 0N 81 30W
Piedras Negras 106 28 35N 100 35W
Pierre 100 44 23N 100 20W
Piet Retief 94 27 1S 30 50E
Pietermaritzburg 94 29 35S 30 25E
Pietersburg 94 23 54S 29 25E
Pietrosul 55 47 35N 24 43E
Pikes Peak 100 38 50N 105 10W
Piketberg 94 32 55S 18 40E
Pilanesberg 94 25 14S 27 4E
Pilbara Cr. 78 21 15S 118 22E
Pilcomayo, R. 108 25 21S 57 42W
Pilica, R. 55 51 25N 20 45E
Pilling 45 53 55N 2 54W
Pilsen = Plzen 54 49 45N 13 22E
Pimba 79 31 18S 136 46E
Pine Bluff 101 34 10N 92 0W
Pine Creek 78 13 50S 131 49E
Pinetown 94 29 48S 30 54E
Pingliang 73 35 20N 106 40E
Pingsiang 73 22 2N 106 55E
Pingtung 73 22 36N 120 30E
Pinjarra 78 32 37S 115 52E
Piombino 58 42 54N 10 30E
Piotrków Trybunalski 55 51 23N 19 43E
Pirmasens 52 49 12N 7 30E
Pisa 58 43 43N 10 23E
Pisciotta 58 40 7N 15 12E
Pisek 54 49 19N 14 10E
Pistóia 58 43 57N 10 53E
Pitcairn I. 22 25 5S 130 5W
Piteå 61 65 20N 21 25E
Piteşti 55 44 52N 24 54E
Pitlochry 48 56 43N 3 43W
Pitt I. 105 53 30N 129 50W
Pittsburgh 104 40 25N 79 55W
Pizzo 58 38 44N 16 10E
Placentia 99 47 20N 54 0W
Plainview 100 34 10N 101 40W
Plasencia 60 40 3N 6 8W
Plata, La 108 35 0S 57 55W
Plata, La, Rio de 108 35 0S 56 40W
Plattsburgh 101 44 41N 73 30W
Plauen 54 50 29N 12 9E
Plenty, Bay of 83 37 45S 177 0E
Plockton 48 57 20N 5 40W
Ploieşti 55 44 57N 26 5E
Plumbridge 50 54 46N 7 15W
Plymouth 43 50 23N 4 9W
Plympton 43 50 24N 4 2W
Plynlimon 42 52 29N 3 47W
Plzen 54 49 45N 13 22E
Po, R. 58 44 57N 12 4E
Pocatello 100 42 50N 112 25W
Pocklington 44 53 56N 0 48W
Pofadder 94 29 10S 19 22E
Pointe-à-Pitre 107 16 10N 61 30W
Pointe-Noire 92 4 48S 12 0E
Poitiers 56 46 35N 0 20E
Poland ■ 55 52 0N 20 0E
Polegate 40 50 49N 0 15E
Polesworth 41 52 37N 1 37W
Polillo I. 72 14 56N 122 0E
Polperro 43 50 19N 4 31W
Pombal 60 39 55N 8 40W
Ponca City 101 36 40N 97 5W
Ponce 107 18 1N 66 37W
Pondicherry 70 11 59N 79 50E
Pondoland 94 31 10S 29 30E
Ponferrada 60 42 32N 6 35W
Pongola, R. 94 27 15S 32 13E
Pont-à-Mousson 56 45 54N 6 1E
Pontardawe 43 51 43N 3 51W
Pontardulais 43 51 42N 4 3W
Pontedera 58 43 40N 10 37E
Pontefract 45 53 42N 1 19W
Ponteland 44 55 03N 1 45W
Pontevedra 60 42 26N 8 40W
Pontianak 72 0 3S 109 15E
Pontnewydd 43 51 40N 3 01W
Pontycymmer 43 51 36N 3 35W
Pontypool 43 51 42N 3 1W
Pontypridd 43 51 36N 3 21W
Poole 43 50 42N 2 2W
Poolewe 48 57 45N 5 38W
Pooley Bridge 44 54 37N 2 49W
Popayán 107 2 27N 76 36W
Poperinge 52 50 51N 2 42E
Popocatepetl, vol. 106 19 10N 98 40W
Porbandar 70 21 44N 69 43E
Porcher I. 105 53 50N 130 30W
Pori 61 61 29N 21 48E
Porkkala 61 59 59N 24 26E
Porlock 42 51 13N 3 36W
Port Alberni 105 49 40N 124 50W
Port Alfred 94 33 36S 26 55E
Port Angeles 105 48 7N 123 30W
Port Arthur 101 30 0N 94 0W
Port Askaig 46 55 51N 6 8W
Port-au-Prince 107 18 40N 72 20W
Port Augusta 79 32 30S 137 50E
Port-Cartier 99 50 2N 66 50W
Port Chalmers 83 45 49S 170 30E
Port Coquitlam 105 49 15N 122 45W
Port Darwin 78 12 24S 130 45E
Port Davey 79 43 16S 145 55E
Port de Paix 107 19 50N 72 50W
Port Elizabeth 94 33 58S 25 40E
Port Erin 42 54 5N 4 45W
Port Étienne = Nouadhibou 88 21 0N 17 0W
Port Fairy 79 38 22S 142 12E
Port Glasgow 46 55 57N 4 40W
Port Harcourt 90 4 40N 7 10E
Port Hedland 78 20 25S 118 35E
Port Huron 104 43 0N 82 28W
Port Kelang 72 3 0N 101 23E
Port Laoise 51 53 2N 7 20W
Port Lincoln 79 34 42S 135 52E
Port Macquarie 79 31 25S 152 54E
Port Moresby 79 9 24S 147 8E
Port Musgrave 79 11 55S 141 50E
Port Nelson 98 57 3N 92 36W
Port Nolloth 94 29 17S 16 52E
Port Nouveau-Quebec 99 58 30N 65 50W
Port of Ness 48 58 29N 6 13W
Port of Spain 107 10 40N 61 20W
Port Phillip B. 79 38 10S 144 50E
Port Pirie 79 33 10S 137 58E
Port Said 91 31 16N 32 18E
Port St. Mary 42 54 5N 4 45W
Port Shepstone 94 30 44S 30 28E
Port Sudan 89 19 32N 37 9E
Port Sunlight 45 53 22N 3 0W
Port Talbot 43 51 35N 3 48W
Port William 46 54 46N 4 35W
Portadown 50 54 27N 6 26W
Portaferry 50 54 23N 5 32W
Portage La Prairie 98 49 58N 98 18W
Portarlington 51 53 10N 7 10W
Portballintrae 50 55 13N 6 32W
Portglenone 50 54 53N 6 30W
Porthmadog 42 52 55N 4 13W
Portishead 43 51 29N 2 46W
Portknockie 48 57 40N 2 52W
Portland, Austral. 79 38 20S 141 35E
Portland, Me., U.S.A. 104 43 40N 70 15W
Portland, Oreg., U.S.A. 105 45 35N 122 40W
Portland, Bill of 43 50 31N 2 27W
Portmahomack 48 57 50N 3 50W
Portmarnock 51 53 25N 6 10W
Portnahaven 46 55 40N 6 30W
Porto = Oporto 60 41 8N 8 40W
Pôrto Alegre 108 30 5S 51 3W
Porto Empédocle 58 37 18N 13 30E
Porto Novo 90 6 23N 2 42E
Porto Tórres 58 40 50N 8 23E
Portoferráio 58 42 50N 10 20E
Portoscuso 58 39 12N 8 22E
Portpatrick 46 54 50N 5 7W
Portree 48 57 25N 6 11W
Portrush 50 55 13N 6 40W
Portsmouth, U.K. 40 50 48N 1 6W
Portsmouth, Ohio, U.S.A. 101 38 45N 83 0W
Portsmouth, Va., U.S.A. 101 36 50N 76 20W
Portstewart 50 55 12N 6 43W
Porttipahta 61 68 5N 26 30E
Portugal ■ 60 40 0N 7 0W
Portuguesa R. 107 9 0N 68 20W
Portumna 51 53 5N 8 12W
Postmasburg 94 28 18S 23 5E
Potchefstroom 94 26 41S 27 7E
Potenza 58 40 40N 15 50E
Potgietersrus 94 24 10S 29 3E
Potomac, R. 101 38 0N 76 23W
Potow 73 38 8N 116 31E
Potsdam 54 52 23N 13 4E
Potters Bar 41 51 42N 0 11W
Poulaphouca Res. 51 53 8N 6 30W
Poulton le Fylde 45 53 51N 2 59W
Póvoa de Varzim 60 41 25N 8 46W
Powell 100 44 45N 108 45W
Powell Creek 78 18 6S 133 46E
Powys □ 42 52 20N 3 20W
Poyang Hu 73 29 10N 116 10E
Poynton 45 53 21N 2 07W
Požarevac 55 44 35N 21 18E
Poznan 54 52 25N 16 55E
Prague 54 50 5N 14 22E
Praha = Prague 54 50 5N 14 22E
Prato 58 43 53N 11 5E
Pratt 100 37 40N 98 45W

Preesall Ryukyu Is

Preesall 45 53 55N 2 58W
Premier Downs 78 30 30S 126 30E
Prenzlau 54 53 19N 13 51E
Přerov 55 49 28N 17 27E
Prescot 45 53 27N 2 49W
Prescott 100 34 35N 112 30W
Presidio 100 29 30N 104 20W
Prestatyn 42 53 20N 3 24W
Presteigne 42 52 17N 3 0W
Preston, U.K. 45 53 46N 2 42W
Preston, U.S.A. 100 42 10N 111 55W
Preston, C. 78 20 51S 116 12E
Prestonpans 47 55 58N 3 0W
Prestwich 45 53 32N 2 18W
Prestwick 46 55 30N 4 38W
Pretoria 94 25 44S 28 12E
Price 100 39 40N 110 48W
Prieska 94 29 40S 22 42E
Prince Albert 98 53 15N 105 50W
Prince Albert Pen. 98 72 30N 116 0W
Prince Charles I. 99 67 47N 76 12W
Prince Edward I. □. 99 46 30N 63 30W
Prince Edward Is. 23 45 15S 39 0E
Prince George 98 53 55N 122 50W
Prince of Wales I. 98 73 0N 99 0W
Prince Patrick I. 98 77 0N 120 0W
Prince Rupert 98 54 20N 130 20W
Princes Risborough 41 51 43N 0 50W
Princess Charlotte B. 79 14 25S 144 0E
Princetown 43 50 33N 4 0W
Prins Albert 94 33 12S 22 2E
Pripyat, R. 55 51 30N 30 0E
Progreso 106 21 20N 89 40W
Prokopyevsk 62 54 0N 87 3E
Provence 56 43 40N 5 46E
Providence 104 41 41N 71 15W
Provo 100 40 16N 111 37W
Prudhoe 44 54 57N 1 52W
Prudhoe Bay 98 70 20N 148 20W
Pruszków 55 52 9N 20 49E
Prut, R. 55 46 3N 28 10E
Przemyśl 55 49 50N 22 45E
Przeworsk 55 50 6N 22 32E
Przhevalsk 71 42 30N 78 20E
Pskov 61 57 50N 28 25E
Puddletown 43 50 45N 2 21W
Pudsey 45 53 47N 1 40W
Puebla □ 106 18 30N 98 0W
Pueblo 100 38 20N 104 40W
Pueblonuevo 60 38 16N 5 16W
Puerto de Santa Maria 60 36 36N 6 13W
Puerto Montt 108 41 22S 72 40W
Puerto Rico ■ 107 18 15N 66 45W
Puertollano 60 38 43N 4 7W
Puget Sd. 105 47 15N 122 30W
Puigcerdá 60 42 24N 1 50E
Pukekohe 83 37 12S 174 55E
Pula 58 44 54N 13 57E
Pulantien 73 39 25N 122 0E
Pulborough 40 50 58N 0 30W
Pullman 100 46 49N 117 10W
Punakha 70 27 42N 89 52E
Pune 70 18 29N 73 57E
Punjab □ 70 31 0N 76 0E
Punta Arenas 108 53 0S 71 0W
Purfleet 41 51 29N 0 15E
Puri 70 19 50N 85 58E
Purísima, La 106 26 10N 112 4W
Purley 41 51 29N 1 4W
Purus, R. 108 5 25S 64 0W
Pusan 73 35 5N 129 0E
Putaruru 83 38 2S 175 50E
Putumayo, R. 108 1 30S 70 0W
Puy-de-Dôme 56 45 46N 2 57E
Puy-de-Sancy 56 45 32N 2 41E
Puy, Le 56 45 2N 3 53E
Puyallup 100 47 10N 122 22W
Pwllheli 42 52 54N 4 26W
Pyatigorsk 71 44 2N 43 0E
Pyŏngyang 73 39 0N 125 30E
Pyramid L. 105 40 0N 119 30W
Pyrenees 56 42 45N 0 18E

Q

Qal'at el Mudauwara 71 29 28N 36 3E
Qalyûb 91 30 12N 31 11E
Qâra 91 29 38N 26 30E
Qasr Farâfra 91 27 0N 28 1E
Qatar ■ 71 25 30N 51 15E
Qazvin 71 36 15N 50 0E
Qena 91 26 10N 32 43E
Qena, Wadi 91 26 12N 32 44E
Qom 71 34 40N 51 0E
Quackenbrück 52 52 40N 7 59E
Quang Tri 72 16 45N 107 13E
Quantock Hills, The 42 51 8N 3 10W
Queanbeyan 79 35 17S 149 14E
Québec 99 46 52N 71 13W
Québec □ 99 50 0N 70 0W
Queen Charlotte 105 53 15N 132 2W
Queen Charlotte Is. 98 53 20N 132 10W
Queen Elizabeth Is. 98 76 0N 95 0W
Queen Maud G. 98 68 15N 102 30W
Queenborough 41 51 24N 0 46E
Queensbury 45 53 46N 1 50W
Queensferry 47 56 0N 3 25W
Queensland □ 79 15 0S 142 0E
Queenstown, Austral. 79 42 4S 145 35E
Queenstown, N.Z. 83 45 1S 168 40E
Queenstown, S. Afr. 94 31 52S 26 52E
Quelimane 92 17 53S 36 58E
Querétaro 106 20 40N 100 23W
Quesnel 98 53 0N 122 30W
Quetta 71 30 15N 66 55E
Quezon City 72 14 38N 121 0E
Qui Nhon 72 13 40N 109 13E
Quibdó 107 5 42N 76 40W
Quilon 70 8 50N 76 38E
Quilpie 79 26 35S 144 11E
Quimper 56 48 0N 4 9W
Quimperlé 56 47 53N 3 33W
Quincy 104 42 14N 71 0W
Quintanar de la Sierra 60 41 57N 2 55W
Quito 108 0 15S 78 35W
Quneitra 89 33 7N 35 48E
Quoich, L. 48 57 4N 5 20W
Quorn 79 32 25S 138 0E
Quruq Tagh, mts. 73 41 30N 90 0E
Qûs 91 25 55N 32 50E
Quseir 91 26 7N 34 16E

R

Raahe 61 64 40N 24 28E
Raasay I. 48 57 25N 6 4W
Raba 72 8 36S 118 55E
Rabat 88 34 2N 6 48W
Rabaul 79 4 24S 152 18E
Rabigh 71 22 50N 39 5E
Raciborz 55 50 7N 18 18E
Racine 104 42 41N 87 51W
Radcliffe 45 53 35N 2 19W
Radekhov 55 50 25N 24 32E
Radium Hill 79 32 30S 140 42E
Radlett 41 51 41N 0 19W
Radnor Forest 42 52 17N 3 10W
Radom 55 51 23N 21 12E
Radomsko 55 51 5N 19 28E
Radstock 42 51 17N 2 25W
Radyr 43 51 32N 3 16W
Raetihi 83 39 25S 175 17E
Rafah 91 31 18N 34 14E
Raglan 83 37 55S 174 55E
Ragusa 58 36 56N 14 42E
Raichur 70 16 10N 77 20E
Raigarh 70 21 56N 83 25E
Rainford 45 53 31N 2 48W
Rainham 41 51 22N 0 36E
Rainhill 45 53 24N 2 46W
Rainier, Mt. 100 46 50N 121 50W
Raipur 70 21 17N 81 45E
Rajahmundry 70 17 1N 81 48E
Rajasthan □ 70 26 45N 73 30E
Rajkot 70 22 15N 70 56E
Raleigh 101 35 46N 78 38W
Ramallah 89 31 55N 35 10E
Rambouillet 56 48 40N 1 48E
Ramla 89 31 55N 34 52E
Ramnad 70 9 25N 78 55E
Ramoutsa 94 24 50S 25 52E
Rampart 98 65 0N 150 15W
Ramsbottom 45 53 36N 2 20W
Ramsey, Cambs., U.K. 40 52 27N 0 6W
Ramsey, I. of M., U.K. 42 54 20N 4 21W
Ramsey I. 42 51 52N 5 21W
Ramsgate 40 51 20N 1 25E
Ranchi 70 23 19N 85 27E
Randers 61 56 29N 10 1E
Randfontein 94 26 8S 27 45E
Rangitaiki, R. 83 37 54S 176 49E
Rangoon 70 16 45N 96 20E
Rangwe 93 0 38S 34 35E
Rannoch 48 56 41N 4 20W
Rannoch, L. 48 56 41N 4 20W
Rantemario 72 3 15S 119 57E
Rapid City 100 44 0N 103 0W
Ras al Hadd 71 22 30N 59 50E
Ras Bânâs 91 23 57N 35 59E
Ras en Naqb 91 30 0N 35 37E
Rashid = Rosetta 91 31 21N 30 22E
Rasht 71 37 20N 49 40E
Rath Luirc (Charleville) 51 52 21N 8 40W
Rathcoole 51 53 17N 6 29W
Rathdowney 51 52 52N 7 36W
Rathdrum 51 52 57N 6 13W
Rathkeale 51 52 32N 8 57W
Rathlin I. 50 55 18N 6 14W
Rathmelton 50 55 3N 7 35W
Rathmore, Cork, Ireland 51 51 30N 9 21W
Rathmore, Kerry, Ireland 51 52 5N 9 12W
Rathnew 51 53 00N 6 05W
Ratlam 70 23 20N 75 0E
Rattray Hd. 48 57 38N 1 50W
Raukumara Ra. 83 38 5S 177 55E
Ravenglass 44 54 21N 3 25W
Ravenna 58 44 28N 12 15E
Ravensburg 54 47 48N 9 38E
Ravenshoe 79 17 37S 145 29E
Ravensthorpe 78 33 35S 120 2E
Rawalpindi 71 33 38N 73 8E
Rawdon 45 53 52N 1 40W
Rawene 83 35 25S 173 32E
Rawlinna 78 30 58S 125 28E
Rawlins 100 41 50N 107 20W
Rawlinson Range 78 24 40S 128 30E
Rawmarsh 45 53 27N 1 20W
Rawtenstall 45 53 42N 2 18W
Ray, C. 99 47 33N 59 15W
Rayleigh 41 51 36N 0 38E
Raz, Pte. du 56 48 2N 4 47W
Ré, Île de 56 46 12N 1 30W
Reading, U.K. 41 51 27N 0 57W
Reading, U.S.A. 104 40 20N 75 53W
Rebun-Tō 76 45 23N 141 2E
Recife 108 8 0S 35 0W
Recklinghausen 52 51 36N 7 10E
Red Deer 98 52 20N 113 50W
Red, R. 101 31 0N 91 40W
Red Sea 71 25 0N 36 0E
Redbourne 41 51 47N 0 23W
Redbridge 41 51 35N 0 7E
Redcar 44 54 37N 1 4W
Redcliff Bay 43 51 27N 2 50W
Redding 105 40 30N 122 25W
Redditch 42 52 18N 1 57W
Redhill 41 51 14N 0 10W
Redland 49 59 6N 3 4W
Redlands 100 34 0N 117 11W
Redondela 60 42 15N 8 38W
Redruth 43 50 14N 5 14W
Ree, L. 51 53 35N 8 0W
Reefton 83 42 6S 171 51E
Reepham 40 52 46N 1 6E
Regensburg 54 49 1N 12 7E
Regina 98 50 27N 104 35W
Registan □ 71 30 15N 65 0E
Reichenbach 54 50 36N 12 19E
Reigate 41 51 14N 0 11W
Reims 56 49 15N 4 0E
Reinga, C. 83 34 25S 172 43E
Reitz 94 27 48S 28 29E
Remscheid 52 51 11N 7 12E
Renfrew 47 55 52N 4 24W
Reni 55 45 28N 28 15E
Renishaw 45 53 18N 1 21W
Renkum 52 51 58N 5 43E
Renmark 79 34 11S 140 43E
Rennes 56 48 7N 1 41W
Reno 105 39 30N 119 50W
Reno, R. 58 44 37N 12 17E
Renton 47 55 58N 4 35W
Requena 60 39 30N 1 4W
Resolution I., Can. 99 61 30N 65 0W
Resolution I., N.Z. 83 45 40S 166 40E
Réunion, I. 23 22 0S 56 0E
Reus 60 41 10N 1 5E
Revelstoke 98 51 0N 118 10W
Revilla Gigedo, Is. de 22 18 40N 112 0W
Rewari 70 28 15N 76 40E
Rexburg 100 43 55N 111 50W
Reykjavik 96 64 10N 21 57E
Reynolds Ra. 78 22 30S 133 0E
Rheine 52 52 17N 7 25E
Rheinland-Pfalz □ 54 50 50N 7 0E
Rheydt 52 51 10N 6 24E
Rhine, R. 54 51 52N 6 20E
Rhode Island □ 101 41 38N 71 37W
* Rhodesia ■ 92 20 0S 30 0E
Rhondda 42 51 39N 3 30W
Rhône, R. 56 43 28N 4 42E
Rhossilli 42 51 34N 4 18W
Rhyl 42 53 19N 3 29W
Rhymney 43 51 45N 3 17W
Rhynie 48 57 20N 2 50W
Riau Arch. 72 0 30N 104 20E
Ribatejo □ 60 39 15N 8 30W
Ribble, R. 44 54 13N 2 20W
Ribeirão Prêto 108 21 10S 47 50W
Riccarton 83 43 32S 172 37E
Richards B. 94 28 48S 32 6E
Richfield 100 38 50N 112 0W
Richland 105 46 15N 119 15W
Richmond, Austral. 79 20 43S 143 8E
Richmond, N.Z. 83 41 4S 173 12E
Richmond, S. Afr. 94 29 51S 30 18E
Richmond, N. Yorks., U.K. 44 54 24N 1 43W
Richmond, Surrey, U.K. 41 51 28N 0 18W
Richmond, Calif., U.S.A. 105 38 0N 122 21W
Richmond, Va., U.S.A. 101 37 33N 77 27W
Rickmansworth 41 51 38N 0 28W
Ried 54 48 14N 13 30E
Rietfontein 94 26 44S 20 1E
Rieti 58 42 23N 12 50E
Riga 61 56 53N 24 8E
Riga, G. of 61 57 40N 23 45E
Rijau 90 11 8N 5 17E
Rijeka 58 45 20N 14 21E
Rijssen 52 52 19N 6 30E
Rijswijk 52 52 4N 4 22E
Rimini 58 44 3N 12 33E
Rimouski 99 48 27N 68 30W
Ringwood 40 50 50N 1 48W
Rio de Janeiro 108 23 0S 43 12W
Rio Grande del Norte, R. 106 26 0N 97 0W
Rio Grande do Sul □ 108 30 0S 53 0W
Rio Muni □ 88 1 30N 10 0E
Riom 56 45 54N 3 7E
Ripley 44 54 3N 1 34W
Ripon 44 54 8N 1 31W
Risca 43 51 36N 3 6W
Rishton 45 53 46N 2 26W
Riva del Garda 58 45 53N 10 50E
Riversdal 94 34 7S 21 15E
Riverside 100 34 0N 117 22W
Riverton, Can. 98 51 1N 97 0W
Riverton, N.Z. 83 46 21S 168 0E
Riviera 54 44 0N 8 30E
Riviera di Levante 58 44 23N 9 15E
Rivière-du-Loup 99 47 50N 69 30W
Riyadh 71 24 41N 46 42E
Rizzuto, C. 58 38 54N 17 5E
Roanne 56 46 3N 4 4E
Roanoke 101 37 19N 79 55W
Robertson 94 33 46S 19 50E
Robertson Ra. 78 23 15S 121 0E
Roberttown 45 53 41N 1 42W
Robinson Ranges 78 25 40S 118 0E
Robla, La 60 42 50N 5 41W
Robson, Mt. 98 53 10N 119 10W
Roca, C. 60 38 40N 9 31W
Rochdale 45 53 36N 2 10W
Roche-sur-Yon, La 56 46 40N 1 26W
Rochefort 56 45 56N 0 57W
Rochelle, La 56 46 10N 1 9W
Rochester, Kent, U.K. 41 51 22N 0 30E
Rochester, Northum., U.K. 46 55 16N 2 16W
Rochester, Minn., U.S.A. 101 44 1N 92 28W
Rochester, N.Y., U.S.A. 104 43 10N 77 40W
Rochford 41 51 36N 0 42E
Rochfortbridge 51 53 25N 7 19W
Rock Hill 101 34 55N 81 2W
Rock Island 101 41 30N 90 35W
Rock Sprs. 100 41 40N 109 10W
Rockford 101 42 20N 89 0W
Rockhampton 79 23 22S 150 32E
Rockingham Forest 44 52 28N 0 42W
Rockland 101 44 0N 69 0W
Rocky Ford 100 38 7N 103 45W
* Renamed Zimbabwe
Rocky Mount 100 35 55N 77 48W
Rocky Mts. 98 55 0N 121 0W
Rodel 48 57 45N 6 57W
Ródhos 71 36 15N 28 10E
Roding R. 41 51 31N 0 7E
Roebourne 78 20 44S 117 9E
Roermond 52 51 12N 6 0E
Roeselare 52 50 57N 3 7E
Roggeveldberge 94 32 10S 20 10E
Rojo, C. 106 21 33N 97 20W
Roma 79 26 32S 148 49E
Roma = Rome 58 41 54N 12 30E
Roman 55 46 57N 26 55E
Romania ■ 55 46 0N 25 0E
Romans 56 45 3N 5 3E
Rome, Italy 58 41 54N 12 30E
Rome, Ga., U.S.A. 101 34 20N 85 0W
Rome, N.Y., U.S.A. 104 43 14N 75 29W
Romiley 45 53 24N 2 08W
Romilly 56 48 31N 3 44E
Romney Marsh 40 51 0N 1 0E
Romsey 40 51 0N 1 29W
Romsley 41 52 25N 2 03W
Rona I. 48 57 33N 6 0W
Roncesvalles, Pass 60 43 1N 1 19W
Ronda 60 36 46N 5 12W
Ronse 52 50 45N 3 35E
Roodepoort-Maraisburg 94 26 8S 27 52E
Roosendaal 52 51 32N 4 29E
Roosevelt I. 112 79 0S 161 0W
Roosevelt, R. 108 7 35S 60 20W
Roraima, Mt. 107 5 10N 60 40W
Rosa, Monte 54 45 57N 7 53E
Rosario, Argent. 108 33 0S 60 50W
Rosario, Venez. 106 10 19N 72 19W
Roscommon 51 53 38N 8 11W
Roscommon □ 50 53 40N 8 15W
Roscrea 51 52 58N 7 50W
Roseburg 105 43 10N 123 10W
Rosehearty 48 57 42N 2 8W
Rosenheim 54 47 51N 12 9E
Rosetown 98 51 35N 107 59W
Rosetta 91 31 21N 30 22E
Rosetta Mouth 91 31 30N 30 20E
Rosneath 47 56 1N 4 49W
Ross 83 42 53S 170 49E
Ross on Wye 42 51 55N 2 34W
Ross Sea 112 74 0S 178 0E
Rossan Pt. 50 54 42N 8 47W
Rosslare 51 52 17N 6 23W
Rostock 54 54 4N 12 9E
Rostov 62 57 14N 39 25E
Roswell 100 33 26N 104 32W
Rosyth 47 56 2N 3 26W
Rothbury 46 55 19N 1 55W
Rother, R. 40 50 59N 0 40E
Rotherham 45 53 26N 1 21W
Rothes 48 57 31N 3 12W
Rothesay 46 55 50N 5 3W
Rothwell 45 53 46N 1 29W
Roto 79 33 0S 145 30E
Rotoroa Lake 83 41 55S 172 39E
Rotorua 83 38 9S 176 16E
Rotorua, L. 83 38 5S 176 18E
Rotterdam 52 51 55N 4 30E
Rotuma, I. 23 12 25S 177 5E
Roubaix 56 50 40N 3 10E
Rouen 56 49 27N 1 4E
Rousay, I. 49 59 10N 3 2W
Roussillon 56 45 24N 4 49E
Rouxville 94 30 11S 26 50E
Rouyn 99 48 20N 79 0W
Rovaniemi 61 66 29N 25 41E
Rovereto 58 45 53N 11 3E
Rovigo 58 45 4N 11 48E
Rovno 55 50 40N 26 10E
Rowlands Gill 44 54 55N 1 44W
Roxburgh, N.Z. 83 45 33S 169 19E
Roxburgh, U.K. 46 55 34N 2 30W
Royston, U.K. 40 52 3N 0 1W
Royston, U.K. 45 53 36N 1 27W
Royton 45 53 34N 2 7W
Ruabon 42 53 0N 3 3W
Ruahine Ra. 83 39 55S 176 2E
Ruapehu 83 39 17S 175 35E
Ruapuke I. 83 46 46S 168 31E
Rubery 41 52 24N 1 59W
Rubha Hunish, C. 48 57 42N 6 20W
Rudok 73 33 30N 79 40E
Rufiji, R. 93 7 50S 38 15E
Rugby 41 52 23N 1 16W
Rugeley 45 52 47N 1 56W
Rügen 54 54 22N 13 25E
Ruhr, R. 54 51 25N 6 44E
Rum Jungle 78 13 0S 130 59E
Rumania ■ 55 46 0N 25 0E
Rumford 101 44 30N 70 30W
Rumoi 76 43 56N 141 39W
Rumuruti 93 0 17N 36 32E
Runanga 83 42 25S 171 15E
Runcorn 45 53 20N 2 44W
Runka 90 12 28N 7 20E
Rupat, I. 72 1 45N 101 40E
Rur, R. 52 50 54N 6 24E
Ruschuk = Ruse 55 43 48N 25 59E
Ruse 55 43 48N 25 59E
Rush 51 53 31N 6 7W
Rushden 40 52 17N 0 37W
Russellville 101 35 15N 93 0W
Rustenburg 94 25 41S 27 14E
Rutherglen 47 55 50N 4 11W
Ruthin 42 53 7N 3 20W
Rutshuru 93 1 13S 29 25E
Ruzomberok 55 49 3N 19 17E
Rwanda ■ 93 2 0S 30 0E
Ryan, L. 46 55 0N 5 2W
* Rybinsk 62 58 5N 38 50E
† Rybinsk Res. 62 58 30N 38 0E
Ryde 40 50 44N 1 9W
Rye 40 50 57N 0 46E
Rye, R. 44 54 12N 0 53W
Ryukyu Is. 76 26 0N 128 0E
* Renamed Andropov
† Renamed Andropov Res.

Rzeszów Shawinigan

Rzeszów 55 50 5N 21 58E
Rzhev 61 56 20N 34 20E

S

's Gravenhage = Hague, The 52 52 7N 4 17E
Saale, R. 54 51 57N 11 56E
Saar (Sarre), □ 52 49 20N 6 45E
Saarbrücken 52 49 15N 6 58E
Saarburg 52 49 36N 6 32E
Saaremaa 61 58 30N 22 30E
Saarlouis 52 49 19N 6 45E
Sabadell 60 41 28N 2 7E
Sabah □ 72 6 0N 117 0E
Sabi, R. 92 18 50S 31 40E
Sabie 94 25 4S 30 48E
Sabinas 106 27 50N 101 10W
Sabinas Hidalgo 106 26 40N 100 10W
Sabine Mts. 58 42 15N 12 50E
Sable, C., Can. 99 43 29N 65 38W
Sable, C., U.S.A. 101 25 5N 81 0W
Sable I. 99 44 0N 60 0W
Sabzevār 71 36 15N 57 40E
Sacramento 105 38 39N 121 30E
Sacramento Mts. 100 32 30N 105 30W
Sacramento, R. 105 38 3N 121 56W
Sacriston 44 54 49N 1 38W
Sadaba 60 42 19N 1 12W
Sadiya 70 27 50N 95 40E
Sado 76 38 0N 138 25E
Sadon 70 25 28N 98 0E
Safad 89 32 58N 35 28E
Safâga 91 26 42N 34 0E
Saffron Walden 40 52 2N 0 15E
Safi 88 31 2N 35 28E
Saga 76 33 15N 130 16E
Sagaing 70 23 30N 95 30E
Saginaw 104 43 26N 83 55W
Saguenay, R. 99 48 22N 71 0W
Sagunto 60 39 42N 0 18W
Sahagún 60 42 18N 5 2W
Sahara 88 23 0N 5 0E
Saharan Atlas 88 34 9N 3 29E
Saharanpur 70 29 58N 77 33E
Sahiwal 71 30 45N 73 8E
Saigon = Ho Chi Minh City 72 10 58N 106 40E
Saiki 76 32 58N 131 57E
Saimaa. 61 61 15N 28 15E
St. Abb's Head 46 55 55N 2 10W
St. Agnes 43 50 18N 5 13W
St. Albans, U.K. 41 51 44N 0 19W
St. Albans, U.S.A. 101 44 49N 73 7W
St. Alban's Head 43 50 34N 2 3W
St. Andrews, N.Z. 83 44 33S 171 10E
St. Andrews, U.K. 46 56 20N 2 48W
St. Anne's 45 53 45N 3 2W
St. Asaph 42 53 15N 3 27W
St. Austell 43 50 20N 4 48W
St. Bee's Hd. 44 54 30N 3 38E
St. Boniface 98 49 53N 97 5W
St. Bride's B. 42 51 48N 5 15W
St-Brieuc 56 48 30N 2 46W
St. Catharines 104 43 10N 79 15W
St. Catherine's Pt. 40 50 34N 1 18W
St. Charles 101 38 46N 90 30W
St-Claude 56 46 22N 5 52E
St. Clears 42 51 48N 4 30W
St. Cloud 101 45 30N 94 11W
St. Columb Major 43 50 26N 4 56W
St. Combs 48 57 40N 1 55W
St. Croix, I. 107 17 45N 64 45W
St. David's 42 51 54N 5 16W
St. David's Head 42 51 54N 5 16W
St-Dizier 56 48 40N 5 0E
St. Elias, Mt. 98 60 20N 141 59W
St-Étienne 56 45 27N 4 22E
St. Francis C. 94 34 14S 24 49E
St. Gallen 54 47 25N 9 20E
St-Gaudens 56 43 6N 0 44E
St. George, Austral. 79 28 1S 148 41E
St. George, U.S.A. 100 37 10N 113 35W
St-Georges 52 50 37N 4 20E
St. George's 107 12 5N 61 43W
St. George's Channel 32 52 0N 6 0W
St. Gotthard P. 54 46 33N 8 33E
St. Govan's Hd. 42 51 35N 4 56W
St. Helena B. 94 32 40S 18 10E
St. Helena, I. 22 15 55S 5 44W
St. Helens, U.K. 45 53 28N 2 44W
St. Helens, U.S.A. 100 45 55N 122 50W
St. Helier 43 49 11N 2 6W
St-Hyacinthe 104 45 40N 72 58W
St. Ives, Cambs., U.K. 40 52 20N 0 5W
St. Ives, Cornwall, U.K. 43 50 13N 5 29W
St. John 99 45 20N 66 8W
St. John's 99 47 35N 52 40W
St. Joseph 101 39 40N 94 50W
St. Just 43 50 7N 5 41W
St. Kilda 83 45 53S 170 31E
St. Kitts-Nevis ■ 107 17 20N 62 40W
St. Lawrence, Gulf of 99 48 25N 62 0W
St. Lawrence, I. 96 63 0N 170 0W
St. Lawrence, R. 99 49 30N 66 0W
St. Louis, Senegal 88 16 8N 16 27W
St. Louis, U.S.A. 101 38 40N 90 12W
St. Lucia, C. 94 28 32S 32 29E
St. Lucia ■ 107 14 0N 60 50W
St. Lucia, Lake 94 28 5S 32 30E
St. Magnus B. 49 60 25N 1 35W
St-Malo 56 48 39N 2 1W
St.-Martin, I. 107 18 0N 63 0W
St. Marys 79 41 32S 148 11E
St. Mary's I. 43 49 55N 6 17W
St. Mawes 43 50 10N 5 1W
St. Monance 46 56 13N 2 46W
St. Moritz 54 46 30N 9 51E
St-Nazaire 56 47 17N 2 12W
St. Neots 40 52 14N 0 16W
St-Niklaas 52 51 10N 4 8E
St. Paul 101 44 54N 93 5W
St. Peter Port 43 49 27N 2 31W
St. Petersburg 101 27 45N 82 40W
St.-Pierre, I. 99 46 48N 56 12W
St-Quentin 56 49 50N 3 16E
St-Raphaël 56 43 25N 6 46E
St.-Servan-sur-Mer 56 48 38N 2 0W
St. Thomas, I. 107 18 21N 64 55W
St.-Trond 52 50 48N 5 12E
St-Tropez 56 43 17N 6 38E
St.-Vallier 56 45 11N 4 50E
St. Vincent ■ 107 13 10N 61 10W
Saintes 56 45 45N 0 37W
Saintfield 50 54 28N 5 50W
Saintonge 56 45 40N 0 50W
Sākahka 71 30 0N 40 8E
Sakai 76 34 30N 135 30E
Sakata 76 36 38N 138 19E
Sakhalin, I. 62 51 0N 143 0E
Sala 61 59 58N 16 35E
Salālah 71 16 56N 53 59E
Salamanca 60 40 58N 5 39W
Saldaña 60 42 32N 4 48W
Saldanha 94 33 0S 17 58E
Saldanha Bay 94 33 6S 18 0E
Sale, Austral. 79 38 6S 147 6E
Sale, U.K. 45 53 26N 2 19W
Salekhard 62 66 30N 66 25E
Salem, India 70 11 40N 78 11E
Salem, U.S.A. 105 45 0N 123 0W
Salen 48 56 42N 5 48W
Salerno 58 40 40N 14 44E
Salford 45 53 30N 2 17W
Salida 100 38 35N 106 0W
Salima 92 13 47S 34 28E
Salina 100 38 50N 97 40W
Salina Cruz 106 16 10N 95 10W
Salina, I. 58 38 35N 14 50E
Salinas, R. 105 36 45N 121 48W
*Salisbury, Zimb. 92 17 50S 31 2E
Salisbury, U.K. 42 51 4N 1 48W
Salisbury, Md., U.S.A. 101 38 20N 75 38W
Salisbury, N.C., U.S.A. 101 35 42N 80 29W
Salisbury Plain 42 51 13N 1 50W
Salmon, R. 100 45 51N 116 46W
Salonta 55 46 49N 21 42E
Salop □ 45 52 36N 2 45W
Salt Lake City 100 40 45N 111 58W
Salta 108 24 47S 65 25W
Saltash 43 50 25N 4 13W
Saltburn by the Sea 44 54 35N 0 58W
Saltcoats 47 55 38N 4 47W
Saltfleet 44 53 25N 0 11E
Saltillo 106 25 30N 100 57W
Salton Sea 100 33 20N 115 50W
Salûm 91 31 31N 25 7E
Salûm, G. of 91 31 30N 25 9E
Saluzzo 58 44 39N 7 29E
Salvador 108 13 0S 38 30W
Salvador ■ 106 13 50N 89 0W
Salween, R. 70 16 31N 97 37E
Salzburg 54 47 48N 13 2E
Salzburg □ 54 47 15N 13 0E
Salzgitter 54 52 2N 10 22E
Samâlût 91 28 20N 30 42E
Samar, I. 72 12 0N 125 0E
Samarkand 71 39 40N 66 55E
Sambiase 58 38 58N 16 16E
Sambor 55 49 30N 23 10E
Sambre, R. 52 50 27N 4 52E
Same 93 4 2S 37 38E
Samshui 73 23 7N 112 58E
Samsun 71 41 15N 36 15E
San Andres Mts. 100 33 0N 106 45W
San Angelo 100 31 30N 100 30W
San Antonio 100 29 30N 98 30W
San Antonio, C. 106 21 50N 84 57W
San Antônio Falls 108 9 30S 65 0W
San Benedetto 58 45 2N 10 57E
San Bernardino 105 34 7N 117 18W
San Carlos 106 29 0N 101 10W
San Cristóbal 107 7 46N 72 14W
San Diego 105 32 43N 117 10W
San Felipe 107 10 20N 68 44W
San Fernando, Mexico 106 30 0N 115 10W
San Fernando, Trin. 107 10 20N 61 30W
San Francisco 105 37 47N 122 30W
San Francisco de Macorîs 107 19 19N 70 15W
San Joaquin R. 105 37 4N 121 51W
San Jorge, G. of, Spain 60 40 50N 0 55W
San Jorge, G. of, Argent. 108 46 0S 66 0W
San José, C. Rica 107 10 0N 84 2W
San José, Guat. 106 14 0N 90 50W
San Jose 105 37 20N 121 53W
San Juan 107 18 28N 66 37W
San Juan Mts. 100 38 30N 108 30W
San Lucas C. 106 22 50N 110 0W
San Luis Obispo 100 35 21N 120 38W
San Luis Potosi 106 22 9N 100 59W
San Marcos 100 29 53N 98 0W
San Marino ■ 58 43 56N 12 25E
San Mateo 105 37 32N 122 19W
San Matias, G. of 108 41 30S 64 0W
San Miguel 106 9 40N 65 11W
San Pedro Sula 106 15 30N 88 0W
San, R. 55 50 25N 22 20E
San Remo 58 43 48N 7 47E
San Salvador 106 13 40N 89 20W
San Salvador (Watlings) I. 107 24 0N 74 40W
San Sebastián 60 43 17N 1 58W
San Severo 58 41 41N 15 23E
San Vicente de la Barquera 60 43 30N 4 29W
San'a 71 15 27N 44 12E
Sanandaj 71 35 25N 47 7E
Sancti-Spíritus 107 21 52N 79 33W
Sandakan 72 5 53N 118 10E
Sanday, I. 49 59 15N 2 30W
Sandbach 44 53 9N 2 23W
Sandbank 47 55 58N 4 57W
Sandhurst 41 51 21N 0 48W

* *Renamed Harare*

Sandoa 92 9 48S 23 0E
Sandomierz 55 50 40N 21 43E
Sandoway 70 18 20N 94 30E
Sandown 40 50 39N 1 9W
Sandpoint 100 48 20N 116 40W
Sandstone 78 27 59S 119 16E
Sandusky 104 41 25N 82 40W
Sandwich 40 51 16N 1 21E
Sandy 40 52 07N 0 17W
Sanford Mt. 98 62 30N 143 0W
Sangli 70 16 55N 74 33E
Sangre de Cristo Mts. 100 37 0N 105 0W
Sangsang 73 29 30N 86 0E
Sankuru, R. 92 4 17S 20 25E
Sanlucár la Mayor 60 37 26N 6 18W
Sanok 55 49 35N 22 10E
Sanquhar 46 55 21N 3 56W
Santa Ana 105 33 48N 117 55W
Santa Barbara 105 34 25N 119 40W
Santa Catalina, I. 100 33 20N 118 30W
Santa Clara, Cuba 107 22 20N 80 0W
Santa Clara, U.S.A. 100 37 21N 122 0W
Santa Cruz 105 36 55N 122 1W
Santa Cruz I. 105 34 0N 119 45W
Santa Cruz, Is. 23 10 30S 166 0E
Santa Fe, Argent. 108 31 35S 60 41W
Santa Fe, U.S.A. 100 35 40N 106 0W
Santa Lucia Range 105 36 0N 121 20W
Santa Maria 100 34 58N 120 29W
Santa Marta 107 11 15N 74 13W
Santa Monica 100 34 0N 118 30W
Santa Rosa 105 38 26N 122 43W
Santa Rosa I. 100 34 0N 120 6W
Santander 60 43 27N 3 51W
Santarém, Brazil 108 2 25S 54 42W
Santarém, Port. 60 39 12N 8 42W
Santiago, Chile 108 33 24S 70 50W
Santiago, Dom. Rep. 107 19 30N 70 40W
Santiago, Spain 60 42 52N 8 37W
Santiago de Cuba 107 20 0N 75 49W
Santo Domingo 107 18 30N 70 0W
Santos 108 24 0S 46 20W
Santry 51 53 24N 6 15W
São Francisco, R. 108 10 30S 36 24W
São Luis 108 2 39S 44 15W
São Paulo 108 23 40S 46 50W
Sao Roque, C. 108 5 30S 35 10W
São Tomé, I. 88 0 10N 7 0E
Sâone, R. 56 46 25N 4 50E
Sapporo 76 43 0N 141 15E
Sarajevo 58 43 52N 18 26E
Sarasota 101 27 10N 82 30W
Saratoga Springs 104 43 5N 73 47W
Saratov 62 51 30N 46 2E
Sarawak □ 72 2 0N 113 0E
Sardinia, I. 58 40 0N 9 0E
Sarina 79 21 22S 149 13E
Sark, I. 43 49 25N 2 20W
Sarny 55 51 17N 26 40E
Sarrebourg 56 48 43N 7 3E
Sarreguemines 56 49 1N 7 4E
Sarthe, R. 56 47 33N 0 31W
Sasebo 76 33 10N 129 43E
Saskatchewan □ 98 54 40N 106 0W
Saskatchewan, R. 98 53 12N 99 16W
Saskatoon 98 52 10N 106 38W
Sasolburg 94 26 46S 27 49E
Sássari 58 40 44N 8 33E
Sassnitz 54 54 29N 13 39E
Sátoraljaújhely 55 48 25N 21 41E
Satpura Ra. 70 21 40N 75 0E
Satsuna-Shotō 76 30 0N 130 0E
Satu Mare 55 47 46N 22 55E
Saudi Arabia ■ 71 26 0N 44 0E
Sault Ste. Marie 99 46 30N 84 20W
Saumur 56 47 15N 0 5W
Saundersfoot 42 51 43N 4 42W
Sauri 90 11 50N 6 44E
Sava, R. 55 44 50N 20 26E
Savalou 90 7 57N 2 4E
Savannah 101 32 4N 81 4W
Savé 90 8 2N 2 17E
Savona 58 44 19N 8 29E
Savoy □ 56 45 26N 6 35E
Sawahlunto 72 0 52S 100 52E
Sawara 76 35 55N 140 30E
Sawatch Mts. 100 38 30N 106 30W
Sawbridgeworth 40 51 49N 0 10E
Sawel, Mt. 50 54 48N 7 5W
Sawu, I. 72 10 35S 121 50E
Sawu Sea 72 9 30S 121 50E
Saxmundham 40 52 13N 1 29E
Sayda 89 33 35N 35 25E
Saynshand 73 44 55N 110 11E
Sazin 70 35 35N 73 30E
Sca Fell 44 54 27N 3 14W
Scalby 44 54 18N 0 26W
Scalloway 49 60 9N 1 16W
Scalpay, I. 48 57 18N 6 0W
Scammon Bay 98 62 0N 165 49W
Scandinavia 61 64 0N 12 0E
Scapa Flow 49 58 52N 3 6W
Scarba, I. 46 56 10N 5 42W
Scarborough 44 54 17N 0 24W
Scariff 51 52 55N 8 32W
Scarinish 48 56 30N 6 48W
Scarp, I. 48 58 1N 7 8W
Schaffhausen 54 47 42N 8 39E
Schefferville 99 54 48N 66 50W
Schelde, R. 52 51 10N 4 20E
Schenectady 104 42 50N 73 58W
Schiedam 52 51 55N 4 25E
Schiermonnikoog, I. 52 53 30N 6 15E
Schio 58 45 42N 11 21E
Schleswig 54 54 32N 9 34E
Schleswig-Holstein □ 54 54 10N 9 40E
Schouten Is. 72 1 0S 136 0E
Schouwen, I. 52 51 43N 3 45E
Schwangyashan 73 46 35N 131 15E
Schwarzrand 94 26 0S 17 0E
Schweinfurt 54 50 3N 10 12E
Schweizer Reneke 94 27 11S 25 18E
Schwerin 54 53 37N 11 22E
Schwyz 54 47 2N 8 39E
Sciacca 58 37 30N 13 3E
Scilla 58 38 18N 15 44E
Scilly, Isles of 43 49 55N 6 15W
Scone 46 56 25N 3 26W
Scotia Sea 22 56 5S 56 0W
Scotland □ 46 57 0N 4 0W
Scott, I. 112 67 0S 179 0E
Scottsbluff 100 41 55N 103 35W
Scottsdale 79 41 9S 147 31E
Scourie 48 58 20N 5 10W
Scrabster 48 58 36N 3 31W
Scranton 104 41 22N 75 41W
Scunthorpe 44 53 35N 0 38W
Seaford 40 50 46N 0 8E
Seaforth, L. 48 57 52N 6 36W
Seaham 44 54 51N 1 20W
Seahouses 46 55 35N 1 39W
Seaton 43 50 42N 3 3W
Seaton Burn 44 55 03N 1 37W
Seaton Delaval 44 55 5N 1 33W
Seattle 105 47 41N 122 15W
Secretary I. 83 45 15S 166 56E
Secunderabad 70 17 28N 78 30E
Sedalia 101 38 40N 93 18W
Sedbergh 44 54 20N 2 31W
Seddon 83 41 40S 174 7E
Seddonville 83 41 33S 172 1E
Sedgefield 44 54 40N 1 27W
Seeheim 94 26 32S 17 52E
Segovia 60 40 57N 4 10W
Segura, R. 60 38 9N 0 40W
Seil, I. 46 56 17N 5 37W
Seine, R. 56 49 28N 0 15E
Sekenke 93 4 18S 34 11E
Sekondi-Takoradi 88 5 0N 1 48W
Sekuma 94 24 36S 23 57E
Selaru, I. 72 8 18S 131 0E
Selby 44 53 47N 1 5W
Selkirk 46 55 33N 2 50W
Selkirk Mts. 98 51 15N 117 40W
Selma 101 32 30N 87 0W
Selsey 40 50 44N 0 47W
Selsey Bill 40 50 44N 0 47W
Selvas 108 6 30S 67 0W
Selwyn 79 21 30S 140 29E
Selwyn Ra. 79 21 10S 140 0E
Semarang 72 7 0S 110 26E
Semipalatinsk 62 50 30N 80 10E
Semois, R. 52 49 53N 4 44E
Sendai, Kagoshima, Japan 76 31 50N 130 20E
Sendai, Miyagi, Japan 76 38 15N 141 0E
Senegal ■ 88 14 30N 14 30W
Senekal 94 28 18S 27 36E
Senga Hill 93 9 19S 31 11E
Senigállia 58 43 42N 13 12E
Senja I. 61 69 15N 17 30E
Sennâr 89 13 30N 33 35E
Senta 55 45 55N 20 3E
Sept-Îles 99 50 13N 66 22W
Sequoia Nat. Park 100 36 30N 118 30W
Seraing 52 50 35N 5 32E
Seram, I. 72 3 10S 129 0E
Seremban 72 2 43N 101 53E
Serengeti Plain 93 2 40S 35 0E
Serov 62 59 36N 60 35E
Serowe 92 22 25S 26 43E
Sesheke 92 17 29S 24 13E
Sestao 60 43 18N 3 0W
Setana 76 42 26N 139 51E
Sète 56 43 25N 3 42E
Sètif 88 36 9N 5 26E
Seto Naikai 76 34 20N 133 30E
Settle 44 54 5N 2 18W
Setúbal 60 38 30N 8 58W
Setúbal, B. of 60 38 40N 8 56W
Sevastopol 62 44 35N 33 30E
Sevenoaks 41 51 16N 0 11E
Severn, R. 42 51 35N 2 38W
Severnaya Zemlya 62 79 0N 100 0E
Seville 60 37 23N 6 0W
Seward 98 60 0N 149 40W
Seward Pen. 98 65 0N 164 0W
Seychelles, Is. 23 5 0S 56 0E
Seyne 56 44 21N 6 22E
Sfax 88 34 49N 10 48E
Sfîntu Gheorghe 55 45 52N 25 48E
Sgurr Mor 48 57 42N 5 0W
Shaba 92 8 0S 25 0E
Shackleton 112 78 30S 36 1W
Shaftesbury 43 51 0N 2 12W
Shagamu 90 6 51N 3 39E
Shahjahanpur 70 27 54N 79 57E
Shāhrūd 71 36 30N 55 0E
Shaki 90 8 41N 3 21E
Shan □ 70 21 30N 98 30E
Shanga 90 9 1N 5 2E
Shanghai 73 31 10N 121 25E
Shangjao 73 28 25N 117 57E
Shangkiu 73 34 28N 115 42E
Shangshui 73 33 42N 114 34E
Shanklin 40 50 39N 1 9W
Shannon 83 40 33S 175 25E
Shannon, R. 51 53 10N 8 10W
Shansi □ 73 37 30N 112 15E
Shantar Is. 62 55 9N 137 40E
Shantow (Swatow) 73 23 25N 116 40E
Shantung □ 73 36 0N 117 30E
Shaohing 73 30 0N 120 32E
Shaoyang 73 27 10N 111 30E
Shap 44 54 32N 2 40W
Shapinsay, I. 49 59 2N 2 50W
Sharjah 71 25 23N 55 26E
Shark B. 78 11 20S 130 35E
Sharlston 45 53 42N 1 23W
Sharma 91 27 52N 35 27E
Sharpness 43 51 43N 2 28W
Shasi 73 30 16N 112 20E
Shasta, Mt. 105 41 30N 122 0W
Shasta Res. 105 40 50N 122 15W
Shaw 45 53 34N 2 05W
Shawinigan 104 46 35N 72 50W

Shawnee **Sugarloaf Pt**

Shawnee **101** 35 15N 97 0W
Sheboygan **104** 43 46N 87 45W
Sheelin, Lough **50** 53 48N 7 20W
Sheerness **41** 51 26N 0 47E
Sheffield **45** 53 23N 1 28W
Shefford **40** 52 2N 0 20W
Shelburne **99** 43 47N 65 20W
Shelby **100** 48 30N 111 59W
Shelekhov G. **62** 59 30N 157 0E
Shellharbour **79** 34 31S 150 51E
Shenandoah **101** 40 50N 95 25W
Shendam **90** 9 10N 9 30E
Shensi □ **73** 34 50N 109 25E
Shenyang (Mukden) **73** 41 35N 123 30E
Shepetovka **55** 50 10N 27 10E
Shephelah **89** 31 30N 34 43E
Shepparton **79** 36 23S 145 26E
Shepton Mallet **42** 51 11N 2 31W
Sherborne **43** 50 56N 2 31W
Sherbro I. **88** 7 30N 12 40W
Sherbrooke **104** 45 28N 71 57W
Sherburn **45** 53 47N 1 15W
Sheridan **100** 44 50N 107 0W
Sheringham **40** 52 56N 1 11E
Sherman **101** 33 40N 96 35W
Sheslay **98** 58 17N 131 45W
Shetland Is. **49** 60 30N 1 30W
Shevchenko **71** 44 25N 51 20E
Shibata **76** 37 57N 139 20E
Shibetsu **76** 44 10N 142 23E
Shibîn El Kôm **91** 30 31N 30 55E
Shiel, L. **48** 56 48N 5 32W
Shieldaig **48** 57 31N 5 39W
Shigatse **73** 29 10N 89 0E
Shihkiachwang **73** 38 0N 114 32E
Shikarpur **71** 27 57N 68 39E
Shikoku □ **76** 33 30N 133 30E
Shildon **44** 54 37N 1 39W
Shillelagh **51** 52 46N 6 32W
Shimabara **76** 32 48N 130 20E
Shimada **76** 34 49N 138 19E
Shimanovsk **73** 52 15N 127 30E
Shimizu **76** 35 0N 138 30E
Shimo-Jima **76** 32 15N 130 7E
Shimoga **70** 13 57N 75 32E
Shimonoseki **76** 33 58N 131 0E
Shin, L. **48** 58 7N 4 30W
Shin, R. **48** 57 58N 4 26W
Shiney Row **44** 54 53N 1 29W
Shingu **76** 33 40N 135 55E
Shinjō **76** 38 46N 140 18E
Shinyanga **93** 3 45S 33 27E
Shiogama **76** 38 19N 141 1E
Shipki La **70** 31 45N 78 40E
Shipley **45** 53 50N 1 47W
Shipston-on-Stour **42** 52 4N 1 38W
Shir Kūh **71** 31 45N 53 30E
Shirāz **71** 29 42N 52 30E
Shirehampton **43** 51 29N 2 41W
Shiremoor **44** 55 01N 1 28W
Shirwa, L. **92** 15 55S 35 40E
Shiukwan **73** 24 58N 113 3E
Shiyata **91** 29 25N 25 7E
Shizuoka **76** 35 0N 138 30E
Shoeburyness **40** 51 31N 0 49E
Sholapur **70** 17 43N 75 56E
Shoreham-by-Sea **40** 50 50N 0 17W
Shoshone **100** 43 0N 114 27W
Shoshone Mts. **105** 39 30N 117 30W
Shoshong **92** 22 56S 26 31E
Shotton Colliery **44** 54 44N 1 18W
Shotts **47** 55 49N 3 47W
Shreveport **101** 32 30N 93 50W
Shrewsbury **45** 52 42N 2 45W
Shwebo **70** 22 30N 95 45E
Si Kiang, R. **73** 22 20N 113 20E
Siakwan **73** 25 45N 100 10E
Sialkot **71** 32 32N 74 30E
*Siam, G. of **72** 11 30N 101 0E
Sian **73** 34 2N 109 0E
Siang K. **73** 27 10N 112 45E
Siangfan **73** 32 15N 112 2E
Siangtan **73** 28 0N 112 55E
Siao Hingan Ling **73** 49 0N 127 0E
Sibâi, Gebel el **91** 25 45N 34 10E
Sibaya, L. **94** 27 20S 32 45E
Sibenik **58** 43 48N 15 54E
Siberut, I. **72** 1 30S 99 0E
Sibiu **55** 45 45N 24 9E
Sibolga **72** 1 50N 98 45E
Sibuyan, I. **72** 12 25N 122 40E
Sichang **73** 28 0N 102 10E
Sîdi Abd el Rahmân **91** 30 55N 28 41E
Sîdi Barrâni **91** 31 32N 25 58E
Sidi-Bel-Abbès **88** 35 13N 0 10W
Sidi Haneish **91** 31 10N 27 35E
Sidi Omar **91** 31 24N 24 57E
Sidlaw Hills **48** 56 32N 3 10W
Sidmouth **43** 50 40N 3 13W
Sidney **100** 47 51N 104 7W
Sidra, G. of **88** 31 40N 18 30E
Siedlce **55** 52 10N 22 20E
Siegburg **52** 50 48N 7 12E
Siegen **52** 50 52N 8 2E
Siena **58** 43 20N 11 20E
Sienyang **73** 34 20N 108 48E
Sierra Leone ■ **88** 9 0N 12 0W
Sikhote Alin Ra. **62** 46 0N 136 0E
Sikkim □ **70** 27 50N 88 50E
Sil, R. **60** 42 23N 7 30W
Silchar **70** 24 49N 92 48E
Silesia **54** 51 0N 16 30E
Silloth **44** 54 53N 3 25W
Silsden **45** 53 55N 1 55W
Silver City **100** 32 50N 108 18W
Silvermine Mts. **51** 52 47N 8 15W
Simeulue, I. **72** 2 45N 95 45E
Simikot **70** 30 0N 81 50E
Simla **70** 31 2N 77 15E
Simonstown **94** 34 14S 18 26E
Simplon Pass **54** 46 15N 8 0E
Simpson Des. **79** 25 0S 137 0E
Sinai **91** 29 0N 34 0E
Sinai, Mt. = Musa, G. **91** 28 32N 33 59E
Sinaloa **106** 25 50N 108 20W
Sines **60** 37 56N 8 51W
Singapore ■ **72** 1 17N 103 51E
Singida **93** 4 49S 34 48E
Singtai **73** 37 2N 114 30E
Sining **73** 36 35N 101 50E
Sinkiang-Uighur □ **73** 42 0N 86 0E
Sinnûris **91** 29 26N 30 31E
Sinop **71** 42 1N 35 11E
Sinsiang **73** 35 15N 113 55E
Sintai **73** 30 59N 105 0E
Sintra **60** 38 47N 9 25W
Sinŭiju **73** 40 5N 124 24E
Sinyang **73** 32 6N 114 2E
Sioux City **101** 42 32N 96 25W
Sioux Falls **101** 43 35N 96 40W
Sipora, I. **72** 2 15S 99 44E
Siracusa **58** 37 4N 15 17E
Siret, R. **55** 47 58N 26 5E
Sirsa **70** 29 33N 75 4E
Sisak **58** 45 30N 16 21E
Sitka **96** 57 9N 134 58W
Sittard **52** 51 0N 5 52E
Sittingbourne **41** 51 20N 0 43E
Siwa **91** 29 11N 25 31E
Siwa Oasis **91** 29 10N 25 30E
Sizewell **40** 52 13N 1 38E
Sjælland **61** 55 30N 11 30E
Skagen **61** 68 37N 14 27E
Skagerrak **61** 57 30N 9 0E
Skagway **98** 59 30N 135 20W
Skeena, R. **98** 54 9N 130 5W
Skegness **44** 53 9N 0 20E
Skellefte, R. **61** 65 30N 18 30E
Skellefteå **61** 64 45N 20 58E
Skelmanthorpe **45** 53 35N 1 39W
Skelmersdale **45** 53 34N 2 49W
Skelmorlie **47** 55 52N 4 53W
Skerries **51** 53 35N 6 7W
Skibbereen **51** 51 33N 9 16W
Skiddaw **44** 54 39N 3 9W
Skien **61** 59 12N 9 35E
Skierniewice **55** 51 58N 20 19E
Skikda **88** 36 50N 6 58E
Skipton **45** 53 57N 2 1W
Skokholm, I. **42** 51 42N 5 16W
Skomer, I. **42** 51 44N 5 19W
Skye, I. **48** 57 15N 6 10W
Slaithwaite **45** 53 37N 1 53W
Slaney, R. **51** 52 52N 6 45W
Slavkov = Austerlitz **54** 49 10N 16 52E
Slea Hd. **51** 52 7N 10 30W
Sleaford **44** 53 0N 0 22W
Sleat, Sd. of **48** 57 5N 5 47W
Sliedrecht **52** 51 50N 4 45E
Slieve Aughty **51** 53 4N 8 30W
Slieve Bloom **51** 53 4N 7 40W
Slieve Donard **50** 54 10N 5 57W
Slieve Gamph **50** 54 6N 9 0W
Slieve Gullion **50** 54 8N 6 26W
Slieve League **50** 54 40N 8 42W
Slieve Mish **51** 52 12N 9 50W
Slievenamon **51** 52 25N 7 37W
Sligo **50** 54 17N 8 28W
Sligo □ **50** 54 10N 8 35W
Sligo B. **50** 54 20N 8 40W
Slough **41** 51 30N 0 35W
Slovakian Ore Mts. **55** 50 25N 13 0E
Slovensko **55** 48 30N 19 0E
Slyne Hd. **51** 53 25N 10 10W
Smederevo **55** 44 40N 20 57E
Smethwick **41** 52 29N 1 58W
Smithers **105** 54 45N 127 10W
Smithfield **94** 30 13S 26 32E
Smolensk **62** 54 45N 32 0E
Snaefell **44** 54 18N 4 26W
Snake, R. **105** 46 12N 119 2W
Sneek **52** 53 2N 5 40E
Sneem **51** 51 50N 9 55W
Sneeuberge **94** 32 0S 24 55E
Snizort, L. **48** 57 33N 6 28W
Snodland **41** 51 19N 0 26E
Snohetta **61** 62 19N 9 16E
Snowdon **42** 53 4N 4 8W
Snowy, R. **79** 37 46S 148 30E
Sobat, R. **89** 8 32N 32 40E
Soche (Yarkand) **73** 38 24N 77 20E
Socorro **100** 34 3N 106 58W
Socotra, I. **89** 12 30N 54 0E
Söderhamn **61** 61 18N 17 10E
Soekmekaar **94** 23 30S 29 55E
Soest **52** 52 9N 5 19E
Sohâg **91** 26 27N 31 43E
Soham **40** 52 20N 0 20E
Soignies **52** 50 35N 4 5E
Soissons **56** 49 25N 3 19E
Sokółka **55** 53 25N 23 30E
Sokoto **90** 13 2N 5 16E
Solai **93** 0 2N 36 12E
Soledad **107** 10 55N 74 46W
Solent, The **40** 50 45N 1 25W
Solihull **41** 52 26N 1 47W
Solingen **52** 51 10N 7 4E
Solomon Is. **79** 6 0S 155 0E
Solomon Sea **79** 7 0S 150 0E
Solway Firth **32** 54 45N 3 38W
Sombor **55** 45 46N 19 17E
Sombrerete **106** 23 40N 103 40W
Somerset **101** 37 5N 84 40W
Somerset □ **42** 51 9N 3 0W
Somerset East **94** 32 42S 25 35E
Somerset, I. **98** 73 30N 93 0W
Somerset West **94** 34 8S 18 50E
Somerton **43** 51 3N 2 45W
Someş, R. **55** 47 15N 23 45E
Songea **93** 10 40S 35 40E
Songkhla **72** 7 13N 100 37E
Sonning Common **41** 51 28N 0 54W
Sonora, R. **106** 28 30N 111 33W
Soochow **73** 31 18N 120 41E
Sopron **54** 47 41N 16 37E
Sorgono **58** 40 0N 9 0E
Soria **60** 41 43N 2 32W
Soroti **93** 1 43N 33 35E
Soröya **61** 70 35N 22 45E
Sorrento **58** 40 38N 14 23E
Sorsogon **72** 13 0N 124 0E
Sosnowiec **55** 50 20N 19 10E
Sŏul **73** 37 31N 127 6E
Sound, The **61** 56 7N 12 30E
South Africa, Rep. of, ■ **94** 30 0S 25 0E
South Auckland & Bay of Plenty □ **83** 38 30S 177 0E
South Australia □ **78** 32 0S 139 0E
South Bend **104** 41 38N 86 20W
South Benfleet **41** 51 33N 0 34E
South Carolina □ **101** 33 45N 81 0W
South China Sea **72** 7 0N 107 0E
South Dakota □ **100** 45 0N 100 0W
South Dorset Downs **43** 50 40N 2 26W
South Downs **40** 50 53N 0 10W
South Elmsall **45** 53 36N 1 17W
South Esk, R. **48** 56 44N 3 3W
South Foreland **40** 51 7N 1 23E
South Georgia **112** 54 30S 37 0W
South Glamorgan □ **42** 51 30N 3 20W
South Hayling **40** 50 47N 0 56W
South Hetton **44** 54 48N 1 24W
South Hiendley **45** 53 36N 1 21W
South Invercargill **83** 46 26S 168 23E
South Island **83** 44 0S 170 0E
South Kirkby **45** 53 35N 1 25W
South Korea ■ **73** 36 0N 128 0E
South Ockendon **41** 51 30N 0 18E
South Orkney Is. **112** 63 0S 45 0W
South Oxhey **41** 51 37N 0 23W
South Pagai, I. **72** 3 28S 100 20E
South Pole **112** 90 0S 0 0E
South Ronaldsay, I. **49** 58 46N 2 58W
S. Sandwich Is. **112** 57 0S 27 0W
South Shetland Is. **112** 62 0S 59 0W
South Shields **44** 54 59N 1 26W
South Taranaki Bight **83** 39 40S 174 5E
South Tyne, R. **44** 54 46N 2 25W
South West Africa ■ = Namibia **92** 22 0S 18 9E
South West Cape **83** 47 16S 167 31E
South Yemen ■ **71** 15 0N 48 0E
South Yorkshire □ **44** 53 30N 1 20W
Southampton **40** 50 54N 1 23W
Southampton I. **99** 64 30N 84 0W
Southborough **40** 51 10N 0 15E
Southbridge **83** 43 48S 172 16E
Southend-on-Sea **41** 51 32N 0 42E
Southern Alps **83** 43 41S 170 11E
Southern Cross **78** 31 12S 119 15E
Southern Ocean **23** 62 0S 160 0W
Southern Uplands **46** 55 30N 3 3W
Southland □ **83** 45 51S 168 13E
Southport, Austral. **79** 27 58S 153 25E
Southport, U.K. **45** 53 38N 3 1W
Southwark **41** 51 29N 0 5W
Southwell **44** 53 4N 0 57W
Southwold **40** 52 19N 1 41E
Sovetsk **61** 55 6N 21 50E
Sowerby Bridge **45** 53 42N 1 55W
Spa **52** 50 29N 5 53E
Spain ■ **60** 40 0N 5 0W
Spalding **45** 52 47N 0 9W
Spandau **54** 52 35N 13 7E
Spanish Fork **100** 40 10N 111 37W
Sparks **100** 39 30N 119 45W
Spartivento, C. **58** 37 56N 16 4E
Spean Bridge **48** 56 53N 4 55W
Spean, R. **48** 56 55N 4 59W
Speke **45** 53 21N 2 51W
Spencer G. **79** 34 0S 137 20E
Spennymoor **44** 54 43N 1 35W
Spenser Mts. **83** 42 15S 172 45E
Sperrin Mts. **50** 54 50N 7 0W
Spey, R. **48** 57 26N 3 25W
Speyer, R. **52** 49 18N 7 52E
Spézia, La **58** 44 8N 9 50E
Spiddal **51** 53 14N 9 19W
Spilsby **44** 53 10N 0 6E
Spinazzola **58** 40 58N 16 5E
Spithead **40** 50 43N 0 56W
Split **58** 43 31N 16 26E
Spokane **105** 47 45N 117 25W
Spree, R. **54** 52 32N 13 13E
Springburn **83** 43 40S 171 32E
Springfield, N.Z. **83** 43 19S 171 56E
Springfield, Ill., U.S.A. **101** 39 48N 89 40W
Springfield, Mass., U.S.A. **104** 42 8N 72 37W
Springfield, Mo., U.S.A. **101** 37 15N 93 20W
Springfield, Ohio, U.S.A. **104** 39 58N 83 48W
Springfield, Oreg., U.S.A. **105** 44 2N 123 0W
Springfontein **94** 30 15S 25 40E
Springs **94** 26 13S 28 25E
Springsure **79** 24 8S 148 6E
Springville **100** 40 14N 111 35W
Spurn Hd. **44** 53 34N 0 8E
Sredinnyy Ra. **62** 57 0N 160 0E
Srepok, R. **72** 13 33N 106 16E
Sretensk **73** 52 10N 117 40E
Sri Lanka ■ **70** 7 30N 80 50E
Srinagar **70** 34 12N 74 50E
Stadskanaal **52** 53 4N 6 48E
Staffa, I. **48** 56 26N 6 21W
Stafford **45** 52 49N 2 9W
Stafford □ **45** 52 53N 2 10W
Staincross **45** 53 35N 1 30W
Staines **41** 51 26N 0 30W
Stainland **45** 53 40N 1 53W
Stalbridge **43** 50 57N 2 22W
Stalybridge **45** 53 29N 1 56W
Stamford **45** 52 39N 0 29W
Standerton **94** 26 55S 29 13E
Standish **45** 53 35N 2 39W
Stanger **94** 29 18S 31 21E
Stanley, Falk. Is. **108** 51 40S 58 0W
Stanley, U.K. **44** 54 53N 1 42W
Stannington **45** 53 23N 1 33W
Stanovoy Ra. **62** 55 0N 130 0E
Stanthorpe **79** 28 36S 151 59E
Stapleford **45** 52 56N 1 16W
Staplehurst **40** 51 9N 0 35E
Staraya Russa **61** 57 58N 31 10E
Stargard **54** 53 29N 13 19E
Start Pt. **43** 50 13N 3 38W
Staten, I. **108** 54 40S 64 0W
Staunton **101** 38 7N 79 4W
Stavelot **52** 50 23N 5 55E
Stawell **79** 37 5S 142 47E
Steenwijk **52** 52 47N 6 7E
Steinkjer **61** 63 59N 11 31E
Stella Land **94** 26 45S 24 50E
Stellenbosch **94** 33 58S 18 50E
Stelvio P. **58** 46 32N 10 27E
Stendal **54** 52 36N 11 50E
Stenhousemuir **47** 56 2N 3 46W
Stepps **47** 55 53N 4 09W
Sterkstroom **94** 31 32S 26 32E
Sterling **100** 40 40N 103 15W
Stettin = Szczecin **54** 53 27N 14 27E
Stettler **98** 52 19N 112 40W
Stevenage **40** 51 54N 0 11W
Stevenston **47** 55 38N 4 46W
Stewart I. **83** 46 58S 167 54E
Stewarton **47** 55 40N 4 30W
Steyning **40** 50 54N 0 19W
Steynsburg **94** 31 15S 25 49E
Steytlerville **94** 33 17S 24 19E
Stikine, R. **98** 58 0N 131 12W
Stillwater **101** 36 5N 97 3W
Stirling **47** 56 7N 3 57W
Stirling Ra. **78** 34 0S 118 0E
Stockbridge **40** 51 7N 1 30W
Stockerau **54** 48 24N 16 12E
Stockholm **61** 59 20N 18 3E
Stockport **45** 53 25N 2 11W
Stocksbridge **45** 53 30N 1 36W
Stockton Heath **45** 53 22N 2 35W
Stockton-on-Tees **44** 54 34N 1 20W
Stoke-on-Trent **44** 53 1N 2 11W
Stoke Poges **41** 51 31N 0 35W
Stokenchurch **41** 51 39N 0 54W
Stolberg **52** 50 48N 6 13E
Stone **45** 52 55N 2 10W
Stonehaven **48** 56 58N 2 11W
Stonehenge **40** 51 9N 1 45W
Stonehouse, Glos., U.K. **43** 51 45N 2 18W
Stonehouse, Strathclyde, U.K. **47** 55 42N 4 0W
Stonewall **98** 50 10N 97 19W
Storavan **61** 65 45N 18 10E
Stormberg **94** 31 16S 26 17E
Stornoway **48** 58 12N 6 23W
Storrington **40** 50 54N 0 27W
Storsjön **61** 60 35N 16 45E
Storuman, L. **61** 65 5N 17 10E
Stour (Gt. Stour), R. **40** 51 15N 0 57E
Stour, R., Dorset, U.K. **43** 50 48N 2 7W
Stour, R., Heref. & Worcs., U.K. **42** 52 25N 2 13W
Stour, R., Suffolk, U.K. **40** 51 55N 1 5E
Stourbridge **41** 52 28N 2 8W
Stourport **42** 52 21N 2 18W
Stow-on-the-Wold **42** 51 55N 1 42W
Stowmarket **40** 52 11N 1 0E
Strabane **50** 54 50N 7 28W
Strabane □ **50** 54 45N 7 25W
Strachur **46** 56 10N 5 5W
Stradbally, Laois, Ireland **51** 53 2N 7 10W
Stradbally, Waterford, Ireland **51** 52 7N 7 28W
Stralsund **54** 54 17N 13 5E
Strand **94** 34 9S 18 48E
Strangford **50** 54 23N 5 34W
Strangford, L. **50** 54 30N 5 37W
Stranorlar **50** 54 52N 7 47W
Stranraer **46** 54 54N 5 0W
Strasbourg **56** 48 35N 7 42E
Stratford **83** 39 20S 174 19E
Stratford-on-Avon **42** 52 12N 1 42W
Strath Earn **47** 56 20N 3 50W
Strath Spey **48** 57 15N 3 40W
Strathaven **47** 55 40N 4 4W
Strathbogie, Dist. **48** 57 25N 2 45W
Strathclyde □ **46** 56 0N 4 50W
Strathmore **48** 58 20N 4 40W
Stratton **43** 50 49N 4 31W
Street **42** 51 7N 2 43W
Stretford **45** 53 27N 2 19W
Strokestown **50** 53 47N 8 6W
Strómboli, I. **58** 38 48N 15 12E
Stromeferry **48** 57 20N 5 33W
Stronsay, I. **49** 59 8N 2 38W
Stroud **43** 51 44N 2 12W
Stuart L. **105** 54 30N 124 30W
Sturminster Newton **43** 50 56N 2 18W
Stutterheim **94** 32 33S 27 28E
Stuttgart, Ger. **54** 48 46N 9 10E
Stuttgart, U.S.A. **101** 34 30N 91 33W
Styr, R. **55** 51 4N 25 20E
Styria **54** 47 26N 15 0E
Suakin **89** 19 0N 37 20E
Suanhwa **73** 40 35N 115 0E
Subotica **55** 46 6N 19 29E
Suchou **73** 31 15N 120 40E
Suck, R. **51** 53 17N 8 10W
Sucre **108** 19 0S 65 15W
Sudan ■ **89** 15 0N 30 0E
Sudan, The **88** 11 0N 9 0E
Sudbury, Can. **99** 46 30N 81 0W
Sudbury, U.K. **40** 52 2N 0 44E
Sudeten Highlands **54** 50 20N 16 45E
Sudr **91** 29 40N 32 42E
Sueca **60** 39 12N 0 21W
Suez **91** 29 58N 32 31E
Suez Canal **91** 31 0N 32 20E
Suez, G. of **91** 28 40N 33 0E
Suffolk □ **40** 52 16N 1 0E
Sugarloaf Pt. **79** 32 22S 152 30E

** Renamed Thailand, G. of*

Sühbaatar □ Torremolinos

Sühbaatar □ 73 46 54N 113 25E
Suihwa 73 46 40N 126 57E
Suir, R. 51 52 31N 7 59W
Sukhumi 71 43 0N 41 0E
Sukkur 71 27 50N 68 46E
Sulaimaniya 71 35 35N 45 29E
Sulawesi, I. 72 2 0S 120 0E
Sulina 55 45 10N 29 40E
Sulitjelma 61 61 7N 16 8E
Sulu Arch. 72 6 0N 121 0E
Sulu Sea 72 8 0N 120 0E
Suluq 89 31 44N 20 14E
Sumatera, I. 72 0 40N 100 20E
Sumba, I. 72 9 45S 119 35E
Sumbawa, I. 72 8 34S 117 17E
Sumbawanga □ 93 8 0S 31 30E
Sumter 101 33 55N 80 10W
Sunart, L. 48 56 42N 5 43W
Sunbury on Thames 41 51 24N 0 24W
Sunda Str. 72 6 20S 105 30E
Sundarbans, The 70 22 0N 89 0E
Sundays, R. 94 32 10S 24 40E
Sunderland 44 54 54N 1 22W
Sundsvall 61 62 23N 17 17E
Sungari, R. 73 44 30N 126 20E
Sunninghill 41 51 25N 0 40W
Suō-Nada 76 33 50N 131 30E
Superior, Nebr., U.S.A. 100 40 3N 98 2W
Superior, Wis., U.S.A. 101 46 45N 92 5W
Superior, L. 101 47 40N 87 0W
Sūr 89 33 19N 35 16E
Surabaja 72 7 17S 112 45E
Surakarta 72 7 35S 110 48E
Surat 70 21 12N 72 55E
Surinam ■ 108 4 0N 56 15W
Surrey □ 40 51 16N 0 30W
Susa 58 45 8N 7 3E
Susanville 105 40 28N 120 40W
Sutherland 94 32 33S 20 40E
Sutherland Falls 83 44 48S 167 46E
Sutterton 45 52 54N 0 8W
Sutton 41 51 22N 0 13W
Sutton Bridge 45 52 46N 0 12E
Sutton Coldfield 41 52 33N 1 50W
Sutton-in-Ashfield 44 52 8N 1 16W
Suva 23 17 40S 178 8E
Suwa 76 36 2N 138 8E
Svalbard 112 78 0N 17 0E
Svealand □ 61 59 55N 15 0E
Sverdlovsk 62 56 50N 60 30E
Sverdrup Is. 98 79 0N 97 0W
Svobodnyy 73 51 20N 128 0E
Swadlincote 45 52 47N 1 34W
Swaffham 40 52 38N 0 42E
Swakopmund 92 22 37S 14 30E
Swale, R. 44 54 18N 1 20W
Swan Hill 79 35 20S 143 33E
Swan, R. 78 32 3S 115 35E
Swanage 43 50 36N 1 59W
Swanley 41 51 23N 0 10E
Swanlinbar 50 54 11N 7 42W
Swanscombe 41 51 27N 0 13E
Swansea 43 51 37N 3 57W
Swansea Bay 42 51 34N 3 55W
Swartberge 94 33 20S 22 0E
Swaziland ■ 94 26 30S 31 30E
Sweden ■ 61 67 0N 15 0E
Sweetwater 100 32 30N 100 28W
Swellendam 94 34 1S 20 26E
Swift Current 98 50 20N 107 45W
Swilly, L. 50 55 12N 7 35W
Swindon 42 51 33N 1 47W
Swinford 50 53 57N 8 57W
Świnoujście 54 53 54N 14 16E
Swinton 45 53 31N 2 21W
Switzerland ■ 54 46 30N 8 0E
Swords 51 53 27N 6 15W
Sydney, Austral. 79 33 53S 151 10E
Sydney, Can. 99 46 7N 60 7W
Sylhet 70 24 54N 91 52E
Syracuse 104 43 4N 76 11W
Syrdarya, R. 62 45 0N 65 0E
Syre 48 58 22N 4 14W
Syria ■ 89 35 0N 38 0E
Syston 45 52 42N 1 5W
Szczecin 54 53 27N 14 27E
Szczecinek 54 53 43N 16 41E
Szechwan □ 73 30 15N 103 15E
Székesfehérvár 55 47 15N 18 25E
Szolnok 55 47 10N 20 15E
Szombathely 54 47 14N 16 38E

T

Tablas, I. 72 12 25N 122 2E
Table Mt. 94 34 0S 18 22E
Tábor 54 49 25N 14 39E
Tabora 93 5 2S 32 57E
Tabrīz 71 38 7N 46 20E
Tacloban 72 11 15N 124 58E
Tacna 108 18 0S 70 20W
Tacoma 105 47 15N 122 30W
Tadcaster 45 53 53N 1 16W
Tademaït, Plateau du 88 28 30N 2 30E
Tadmor 83 41 27S 172 45E
Tadzhik S.S.R. □ 71 35 30N 70 0E
Taegu 73 35 50N 128 37E
Taejŏn 73 36 20N 127 28E
Taganrog 62 47 12N 38 50E
Taghmon 51 52 19N 6 40W
Tagus = Tajo, R. 60 39 44N 5 50W
Tahakopa 83 46 30S 169 23E
Tahcheng 73 46 50N 83 1E
Tahiti, I. 22 17 37S 149 27W
Tahoe, L. 105 39 0N 120 9W
Tahta 91 26 44N 31 32E
T'ai Hu 73 31 10N 120 0E
Taichung 73 24 10N 120 35E
T'aihang Shan 73 35 40N 113 20E
Taihape 83 39 41S 175 48E
Taimyr Pen. 62 75 0N 100 0E
Tain 48 57 49N 4 4W
Tainan 73 23 0N 120 15E
Taipei 73 25 2N 121 30E
Taitung 73 22 43N 121 4E
Taiwan ■ 73 23 30N 121 0E
Taiyüan 73 38 0N 112 30E
Tajima 76 35 19N 135 8E
Tajo, R. 60 40 35N 1 52W
Tak 72 16 52N 99 8E
Takaka 83 40 51S 172 50E
Takamatsu 76 34 20N 134 5E
Takaoka 76 36 40N 137 0E
Takapuna 83 36 47S 174 47E
Takasaki 76 36 20N 139 0E
Takayama 76 36 18N 137 11E
Takefu 76 35 50N 136 10E
Talai 73 45 30N 124 20E
Talata Mafara 90 12 38N 6 4E
Talaud Is. 72 4 30N 127 10E
Talavera de la Reina 60 39 55N 4 46W
Talca 108 35 20S 71 46W
Taldy Kurgan 73 45 10N 78 45E
Talgarth 42 51 59N 3 15W
Tali 73 25 45N 100 5E
Taliabu, I. 72 1 45S 125 0E
Talkeetna 98 62 20N 150 0W
Tallaght 51 53 17N 6 22W
Tallahassee 101 30 25N 84 15W
Tallinn 61 59 29N 24 58E
Tallow 51 52 6N 8 0W
Talybont 42 52 29N 3 59W
Tama Abu Ra. 72 3 10N 115 0E
Tamale 88 9 22N 0 50W
Tamanrasset 88 22 56N 5 30E
Tamar, R. 43 50 33N 4 15W
* Tamatave 92 18 10S 49 25E
Tambov 62 52 45N 41 20E
Tame, R. 41 52 43N 1 45W
Tamgak, Mts. 88 19 12N 8 35E
Tamil Nadu □ 70 11 0N 77 0E
Tampa 101 27 57N 82 30W
Tampere 61 61 30N 23 50E
Tampico 106 22 20N 97 50W
Tamsagbulag 73 47 14N 117 21E
Tamu 70 24 13N 94 12E
Tamworth, Austral. 79 31 0S 150 58E
Tamworth, U.K. 41 52 38N 1 41W
Tanacross 98 63 40N 143 30W
Tanami Des. 78 18 50S 132 0E
Tananarive □ 92 19 0S 47 0E
Tando Adam 71 25 45N 68 40E
Tandragee 50 54 22N 6 23W
Tane-ga-Shima 76 30 30N 131 0E
Taneatua 83 38 4S 177 1E
Tanezrouft 88 23 9N 0 11E
Tanga 93 5 5S 39 2E
Tanganyika, L. 93 6 40S 30 0E
Tangier 88 35 50N 5 49W
Tanglha Shan 73 33 0N 90 0E
Tangshan 73 39 40N 118 10E
Tanimbar Is. 72 7 30S 131 30E
Tanjungbalai 72 2 55N 99 44E
Tanta 91 30 45N 30 57E
Tanzania ■ 93 6 40S 34 0E
Taonan 73 45 30N 122 20E
Tapa Shan 73 31 45N 109 30E
Tapajós, R. 108 4 30S 56 10W
Tapanui 83 45 56S 169 18E
Tapuaenuku, Mt. 83 41 55S 173 50E
Tarabulus = Tripoli 88 34 31N 33 52E
Taranaki □ 83 39 5S 174 51E
Taransay, I. 48 57 54N 7 0W
Táranto 58 40 30N 17 11E
Taranto, G. of 58 40 0N 17 15E
Tararua Range 83 40 45S 175 25E
Tarawera 83 39 2S 176 36E
Tarbagatai Ra. 62 48 30N 83 0E
Tarbat Ness 48 57 52N 3 48W
Tarbert, Ireland 51 52 34N 9 22W
Tarbert, U.K. 48 57 54N 6 49W
Tarbes 56 43 15N 0 3E
Tarbet 46 56 13N 4 44W
Tarcoola 78 30 44S 134 36E
Taree 79 31 50S 152 30E
Tarf Shaqq al Abd 91 26 50N 36 6E
Tarfa, Wadi el 91 28 16N 31 15E
Tarifa 60 36 1N 5 36W
Tarkastad 94 32 0S 26 16E
Tarleton 45 53 41N 2 50W
Tarn, R. 56 44 5N 1 2E
Tarnobrzeg □ 55 50 40N 22 0E
Tarnów 55 50 3N 21 0E
Tarporley 44 53 10N 2 42W
Tarragona 60 41 5N 1 17E
Tarrasa 60 41 26N 2 1E
Tartu 61 58 25N 26 58E
Tashauz 71 42 0N 59 20E
Tashigong 73 33 0N 79 30E
Tashkent 71 41 20N 69 10E
Tashkurghan 71 36 45N 67 40E
Tasman Bay 83 40 59S 173 25E
Tasman Mts. 83 41 3S 172 25E
Tasman Sea 83 36 0S 160 0E
Tasmania, I., □ 79 49 0S 146 30E
Tatabánya 55 47 32N 18 25E
Tatarsk 62 55 20N 75 50E
Tateyama 76 35 0N 139 50E
Tatsaitan 73 37 55N 95 0E
Tat'ung 73 40 9N 113 19E
Taumarunui 83 38 53S 175 15E
Taung 94 27 33S 24 47E
Taunggyi 70 20 50N 97 0E
Taunton 43 51 1N 3 7W
Taupo 83 38 41S 176 7E
Taupo, L. 83 38 46S 175 55E
Tauranga 83 37 35S 176 11E
Taurianova 58 38 22N 16 1E
Taurus Mts. 71 37 0N 35 0E
Tavani 98 62 10N 93 30W
Tavira 60 37 8N 7 40W
Tavistock 43 50 33N 4 9W
Tavoy 70 14 7N 98 18E
Taw, R. 43 50 58N 3 58W

* *Renamed Toamasina*

Tawau 72 4 20N 117 55E
Tay, Firth of 47 56 25N 3 8W
Tay, L. 48 56 30N 4 10W
Tay, R. 46 56 37N 3 38W
Taylor Mt. 100 35 16N 107 50W
Tayma 71 27 35N 38 45E
Taynuilt 46 56 25N 5 15W
Tayport 47 56 27N 2 52W
Tayside □ 48 56 25N 3 30W
Tbilisi 71 41 50N 44 50E
Te Anau L. 83 45 15S 167 45E
Te Aroha 83 37 32S 175 44E
Te Awamutu 83 38 1S 175 20E
Te Kuiti 83 38 20S 175 11E
Te Puke 83 37 46S 176 22E
Tebay 44 54 25N 2 35W
Tebing Tinggi 72 3 38S 102 1E
Tecuci 55 45 51N 27 27E
Tees, R. 44 54 36N 1 25W
Teesdale 44 54 37N 2 10W
Tegal 72 6 52S 109 8E
Tegina 90 10 5N 6 11E
Tegucigalpa 106 14 10N 87 0W
Tehrān 71 35 44N 51 30E
Tehuantepec 106 16 10N 95 19W
Tehuantepec, Gulf of 106 15 50N 95 0W
Tehuantepec, Isthmus of 106 17 0N 94 30W
Teifi, R. 42 52 4N 4 14W
Teign, R. 43 50 41N 3 42W
Teignmouth 43 50 33N 3 30W
Tekapo, L. 83 43 53S 170 33E
Tel Aviv-Jaffa 89 32 4N 34 48E
Tela 106 15 40N 87 28W
Telford 45 52 42N 2 31W
Telukbetung 72 5 29S 105 17E
Tembuland □ 94 31 35S 28 0E
Teme, R. 42 52 23N 2 15W
Temple 101 31 5N 97 28W
Temple B. 79 12 15S 143 3E
Templemore 51 52 48N 7 50W
Temuco 108 38 50S 72 50W
Temuka 83 44 14S 171 17E
Tenasserim 70 12 6N 99 3E
Tenbury Wells 42 52 18N 2 35W
Tenby 42 51 40N 4 42W
Tenerife, I. 88 28 20N 16 40W
T'enghsien 73 35 8N 117 9E
Tennant Creek 78 19 30S 134 0E
Tennessee □ 101 36 0N 86 30W
Tennessee, R. 101 34 30N 86 20W
Tenryū 76 34 52N 137 55E
Tenterden 40 51 4N 0 42E
Tenterfield 79 29 0S 152 0E
Tepic 106 21 30N 104 54W
Téramo 58 42 40N 13 40E
Teresina 108 5 2S 42 45W
Termez 71 37 0N 67 15E
Términi Imerese 58 37 59N 13 51E
Térmoli 58 42 0N 15 0E
Terne, R. 61 65 50N 24 12E
Terni 58 42 34N 12 38E
Ternopol 55 49 30N 25 40E
Terracina 58 41 17N 13 12E
Terralba 58 39 42N 8 38E
Terschelling, I. 52 53 25N 5 20E
Teruel 60 40 22N 1 8W
Teshio 76 44 53N 141 44E
Teshio-Gawa, R. 76 44 53N 141 45E
Tessaoua 90 13 47N 7 56E
Test, R. 40 51 7N 1 30W
Tetbury 42 51 37N 2 9W
Tete 92 16 13S 33 33E
Teton, R. 100 47 58N 111 0W
Tettenhall 41 52 35N 2 7W
Tetuan 88 35 30N 5 25W
Teviot, R. 46 55 21N 2 51W
Teviotdale 46 55 25N 2 50W
Tewkesbury 42 51 59N 2 8W
Texarkana 101 33 25N 94 3W
Texas □ 100 31 40N 98 30W
Texel, I. 52 53 5N 4 50E
Tezpur 70 26 40N 92 45E
Thaba Nchu 94 29 10S 26 52E
Thaba Putsoa, mt. 94 29 45S 28 0E
Thabana Ntlenyana, Mt. 94 29 30S 29 9E
Thabazimbi 94 24 40S 26 4E
Thailand (Siam) ■ 72 16 0N 102 0E
Thame, R. 40 51 35N 1 8W
Thames 83 37 7S 175 34E
Thanet, I. of 40 51 21N 1 20E
Thanh Hoa 72 19 48N 105 46E
Thar (Great Indian) Desert 70 28 25N 72 0E
Thargomindah 79 27 58S 143 46E
Thatcham 40 51 24N 1 17W
Thaxted 40 51 57N 0 20E
The Dalles 105 45 40N 121 11W
The Pas 98 53 45N 101 15W
Theodore 79 24 55S 150 3E
Thermopolis 100 43 35N 108 10W
Thessaloníki 89 40 38N 23 0E
Thetford 40 52 25N 0 44E
Thetford Mines 104 46 8N 71 18W
Theydon Bois 41 51 40N 0 06E
Thika 93 1 1S 37 5E
Thionville 56 49 20N 6 10E
Thirsk 44 54 15N 1 20W
Thomastown 51 52 32N 7 10W
Thompson, R., Can. 98 50 15N 121 24W
Thompson, R., U.S.A. 105 39 46N 93 37W
Thornaby on Tees 44 54 36N 1 19W
Thornbury 43 51 36N 2 31W
Thorne 44 53 36N 0 56W
Thorney 40 52 37N 0 8W
Thornhill 46 55 15N 3 46W
Thornley 44 54 45N 1 26W
Thornliebank 47 55 48N 4 18W
Thornton 45 53 52N 3 1W
Thrapston 40 52 24N 0 32W
Throckley 44 54 58N 1 49W
Thrybergh 45 53 27N 1 18W
Thuin 52 50 20N 4 17E
Thule 99 77 30N 69 0W
Thun 54 46 45N 7 38E
Thunder B. 98 48 20N 89 0W
Thurcroft 45 53 24N 1 13W
Thurles 51 52 40N 7 53W
Thurlstone 45 53 31N 1 37W
Thurmaston 41 52 40N 1 8W
Thurso 48 58 34N 3 31W
Thurso, R. 48 58 36N 3 30W
Tiber, R. 58 41 44N 12 14E
Tiberias 89 32 47N 35 32E
Tibesti 88 21 0N 17 30E
Tibet 73 32 30N 86 0E
Tibooburra 79 29 26S 142 1E
Tiburón, I. 106 29 0N 112 30W
Ticino, R. 58 45 9N 9 14E
Tideswell 45 53 17N 1 46W
Tiel 52 51 53N 5 26E
Tielt 52 51 0N 3 20E
Tien Shan 73 42 0N 80 0E
Tienen 52 50 48N 4 57E
Tienshui 73 34 30N 105 34E
Tientsin 73 39 10N 117 0E
Tierra del Fuego, I. 108 54 0S 69 0W
Tighnabruaich 46 55 55N 5 13W
Tigris, R. 71 37 0N 42 30E
Tijuana 106 32 30N 117 3W
Tikhvin 61 59 35N 33 30E
Tiko 90 4 4N 9 20E
Tiksi 62 71 50N 129 0E
Tilburg 52 51 31N 5 6E
Tilbury 41 51 27N 0 24E
Tillicoultry 47 56 9N 3 44W
Timaru 83 44 23S 171 14E
Timau 93 0 4N 37 15E
Timbuktu = Tombouctou 88 16 50N 3 0W
Timişoara 55 45 43N 21 15E
Timmins 99 48 28N 81 25W
Timor, I. 72 9 0S 125 0E
Timor Sea 72 10 0S 127 0E
Tindouf 88 27 50N 8 4W
Tingley 45 53 44N 1 35W
Tintagel 43 50 40N 4 45W
Tintern 42 51 42N 2 41W
Tipperary 51 52 28N 8 10W
Tipperary □ 51 52 37N 7 55W
Tipton 41 52 32N 2 4W
Tiptree 40 51 48N 0 46E
Tirân 91 27 56N 34 35E
Tiraspol 55 46 55N 29 35E
Tiree, I. 48 56 31N 6 55W
Tîrgu Mureş 55 46 31N 24 38E
Tiruchchirappalli 70 10 45N 78 45E
Tisa, R. 55 45 15N 20 17E
Tisza, R. 55 47 38N 20 44E
Titicaca, L. 108 15 30S 69 30W
Titilagarh 70 20 15N 83 5E
Titiwa 90 12 14N 12 53E
Titovo Užice 55 43 55N 19 50E
Tiverton 43 50 54N 3 30W
Tlacotalpán 106 18 37N 95 40W
Tlaxcala 106 19 20N 98 14W
Tlaxiaco 106 17 10N 97 40W
Toba 76 34 30N 136 45E
Toba, L. 72 2 40N 98 50E
Tobago, I. 107 11 10N 60 30W
Tobercurry 50 54 3N 8 43W
Tobruk 89 32 7N 23 55E
Tocantins, R. 108 14 30S 49 0W
Tochigi 76 36 25N 139 45E
Todmorden 45 53 43N 2 7W
Togo ■ 88 6 15N 1 35E
Tokaj 55 48 8N 21 27E
Tokanui 83 46 34S 168 56E
Tokara Is. 76 29 0N 129 0E
Tokarahi 83 44 56S 170 39E
Tokelau Is. 22 9 0S 172 0W
Tokunoshima 76 27 56N 128 55E
Tokushima 76 34 4N 134 34E
Tokuyama 76 34 0N 131 50E
Tōkyō 76 35 45N 139 45E
Tolaga Bay 83 38 21S 178 20E
Toledo, Spain 60 39 50N 4 2W
Toledo, U.S.A. 104 41 37N 83 33W
Toledo, Mts. 60 39 33N 4 20W
Tolima □ 107 3 45N 75 15W
Tolosa 60 43 8N 2 5W
Toluca 106 19 20N 99 50W
Tomakomai 76 42 38N 141 36E
Tomatin 48 57 20N 4 0W
Tombouctou 88 16 50N 3 0W
Tomini 72 0 30N 120 30E
Tomintoul 48 57 15N 3 22W
Tomsk 62 56 30N 85 12E
Tonbridge 40 51 12N 0 18E
Tone R. 43 50 59N 3 15W
Tonga Is. ■ 22 20 0S 173 0W
Tongaat 94 29 33S 31 9E
Tongaland 94 27 0S 32 0E
Tongeren 52 50 47N 5 28E
Tongking, G. of 72 20 0N 108 0E
Tonlé Sap 72 13 0N 104 0E
Tonopah 100 38 4N 117 12W
Tonyrefail 43 51 35N 3 26W
Tooele 100 40 30N 112 20W
Toome 50 54 45N 6 28W
Toowoomba 79 27 32S 151 56E
Topeka 101 39 3N 95 40W
Topolobampo 106 25 40N 109 10W
Topsham 43 50 40N 3 27W
Torbay 43 50 26N 3 31W
Tordesillas 60 41 30N 5 0W
Torhout 52 51 5N 3 7E
Tormes, R. 60 41 7N 6 0W
Torne, R. 61 65 50N 24 12E
Tornio 61 65 50N 24 12E
Toronto 104 43 39N 79 20W
Tororo 93 0 45N 34 12E
Torpoint 43 50 23N 4 12W
Torquay 43 50 27N 3 31W
Tôrre de Moncorvo 60 41 12N 7 8W
Torrelavega 60 43 20N 4 5W
Torremolinos 60 36 38N 4 30W

Torreón

Vlissingen

Torreón 106 25 33N 103 25W
Torres 106 28 46N 110 47W
Torres Strait 79 9 50S 142 20E
Torres Vedras 60 39 5N 9 15W
Torridge, R. 43 50 51N 4 10W
Torridon, L. 48 57 35N 5 50W
Tortosa 60 40 49N 0 31E
Tortosa C. 60 40 41N 0 52E
Toruń 55 53 0N 18 39E
Tory I. 50 55 17N 8 12W
Totland 40 50 41N 1 32W
Totley 45 53 18N 1 32W
Tottington 45 53 36N 2 20W
Totton 40 50 55N 1 29W
Tottori 76 35 30N 134 15E
Toul 56 48 40N 5 53E
Toulon 56 43 10N 5 55E
Toulouse 56 43 37N 1 27E
Touraine 56 47 20N 0 30E
Tournai 52 50 35N 3 25E
Tours 56 47 22N 0 40E
Touwsrivier 94 33 20S 20 0E
Towcester 40 52 7N 0 56W
Tower Hamlets 41 51 32N 0 02W
Townshend, C. 79 22 18S 150 30E
Townsville 79 19 15S 146 45E
Toyama 76 36 40N 137 15E
Toyama, B. 76 37 0N 137 30E
Toyohashi 76 34 45N 137 25E
Toyooka 76 35 35N 134 55E
Trabzon 71 41 0N 39 45E
Trafalgar, C. 60 36 10N 6 2W
Trail 98 49 5N 117 40W
Tralee 51 52 16N 9 42W
Tralee B. 51 52 17N 9 55W
Tramore 51 52 10N 7 10W
Tranent 47 55 57N 2 58W
Trang 72 7 33N 99 38E
Trangan, I. 72 6 40S 134 20E
Transkei □ 94 32 15S 28 15E
Transvaal □ 94 25 0S 29 0E
Transylvania 55 46 19N 25 0E
Transylvanian Alps 55 45 30N 25 0E
Trápani 58 38 1N 12 30E
Traralgon 79 38 12S 146 34E
Tras os Montes e Alto-Douro □ 60 41 25N 7 20W
Trasimeno, L. 58 43 10N 12 5E
Travers, Mt. 83 42 1S 172 45E
Traverse City 101 44 45N 85 39W
Trebic 54 49 15N 15 50E
Tredegar 43 51 47N 3 16W
Treharris 43 51 40N 3 17W
Treherbert 43 51 40N 3 32W
Tremadog Bay 42 52 51N 4 18W
Tremp 60 42 10N 0 52E
Trent, R. 44 53 33N 0 44W
Trentino-Alto Adige □ 58 46 5N 11 0E
Trento 58 46 5N 11 8E
Trenton 104 40 15N 74 41W
Treorchy 43 51 39N 3 30W
Treviso 58 45 40N 12 15E
Trevose Hd. 43 50 33N 5 3W
Trier 52 49 45N 6 37E
Trieste 58 45 39N 13 45E
Triglav 58 46 25N 13 45E
Trim 51 53 34N 6 48W
Trimdon 44 54 43N 1 23W
Trincomalee 70 8 38N 81 15E
Tring 41 51 47N 0 39W
Trinidad 100 37 15N 104 30W
Trinidad & Tobago ■ 107 10 30N 61 20W
Trinidad I. 22 20 20S 29 50W
Trinity B. 79 16 30S 146 0E
Tripoli 88 32 49N 13 7E
Tristan da Cunha, I. 22 37 6S 12 20W
Trivandrum 70 8 31N 77 0E
Trois-Rivières 104 46 25N 72 40W
Trollhättan 61 58 17N 12 20E
Tromsø 61 69 40N 18 56E
Trondheim 61 63 25N 10 25E
Trondheim Fjord 61 63 35N 10 30E
Trossachs, The 46 56 14N 4 24W
Trostan 50 55 4N 6 10W
Trowbridge 42 51 18N 2 12W
Troy 104 42 45N 73 39W
Troyes 56 48 19N 4 3E
Trujillo, Peru 108 8 0S 79 0W
Trujillo, Venez. 106 9 22N 70 26W
Truro, Can. 99 45 21N 63 14W
Truro, U.K. 43 50 17N 5 2W
Tsaidam 73 37 0N 95 0E
Tsangpo 73 29 40N 89 0E
Tselinograd 62 51 10N 71 30E
Tshabong 94 26 2S 22 29E
Tsiaotso 73 35 11N 113 37E
Tsin Ling Shan 73 34 0N 107 30E
Tsinan 73 36 32N 117 0E
Tsinghai □ 73 36 0N 96 0E
Tsingkiang 73 27 50N 114 38E
Tsingshih 73 29 43N 112 13E
Tsingtao 73 36 0N 120 25E
Tsining 73 35 30N 116 35E
Tsitsihar 73 47 20N 124 0E
Tsu 76 34 45N 136 25E
Tsuchiura 76 36 12N 140 15E
Tsugaru Str. 76 41 30N 140 30E
Tsuni 73 27 43N 106 52E
Tsuruoka 76 38 44N 139 50E
Tsushima, I. 76 34 20N 129 20E
Tsushima-kaikyō 76 34 20N 130 0E
Tsuyama 76 35 0N 134 0E
Tuam 51 53 30N 8 50W
Tuamotu Arch. 22 17 0S 144 0W
Tuapse 71 44 5N 39 10E
Tuatapere 83 46 8S 167 41E
Tubuai Is. 22 25 0S 150 0W
Tucson 100 32 14N 110 59W
Tucumán □ 108 26 48S 66 2W
Tucumcari 100 35 12N 103 45W
Tucupita 107 9 14N 62 3W
Tudela 60 42 4N 1 39W
Tukuyu 93 9 17S 33 35E
Tula, Mexico 106 23 0N 99 40W
Tula, U.S.S.R. 62 54 13N 37 32E
Tulancingo 106 20 5N 98 22W
Tulare 100 36 15N 119 26W
Tulcea 55 45 13N 28 46E
Tūlkarm 89 32 19N 35 10E
Tullamore 51 53 17N 7 30W
Tullibody 47 56 08N 3 50W
Tullow 51 52 48N 6 45W
Tulsa 101 36 10N 96 0W
Tumeremo 107 7 18N 61 30W
Tummel, L. 48 56 43N 3 55W
Tummel, R. 48 56 42N 4 5W
Tumucumaque, Serra de 108 2 0N 55 0W
Tumut 79 35 16S 148 13E
Tunbridge Wells 40 51 7N 0 16E
Tunduma 93 9 20S 32 48E
Tunduru 93 11 0S 37 25E
Tungchow 73 39 58N 116 50E
Tungchuan 73 35 4N 109 2E
T'unghua 73 41 45N 126 0E
Tungliao 73 43 42N 122 11E
Tungting Hu 73 29 15N 112 30E
Tunhwang 73 40 5N 94 46E
Tunis 88 36 50N 10 11E
Tunisia ■ 88 33 30N 9 10E
Tunja 107 5 40N 73 25W
Tunki 73 29 44N 118 4E
Tura 70 25 30N 90 16E
Turfan 73 43 6N 89 24E
Turfan Depression 73 42 45N 89 0E
Turin 58 45 3N 7 40E
Turkana, L. 93 4 10N 32 10E
Turkestan 71 43 10N 68 10E
Turkey ■ 71 39 0N 36 0E
Turkmen S.S.R. □ 71 39 0N 59 0E
Turks Is. 107 21 20N 71 20W
Turku 61 60 30N 22 19E
Turneffe Is. 106 17 20N 87 50W
Turnhout 52 51 19N 4 57E
Turnu Măgurele 55 43 46N 24 56E
Turnu-Severin 55 44 39N 22 41E
Turriff 48 57 32N 2 28W
Tuscaloosa 101 33 13N 87 31W
Tuscany 60 43 28N 11 15E
Tutikorin 70 8 50N 78 12E
Tuttlingen 54 47 59N 8 50E
Tutuila, I. 22 14 19S 170 50W
Tuva, A.S.S.R. □ 62 51 30N 95 0E
Tuvalu 23 8 0S 176 0E
Tuxpan 106 20 50N 97 30W
Tuxtla Gutiérrez 106 16 50N 93 10W
Tuyun 73 26 15N 107 32E
Tuzla 58 44 34N 18 41E
Tweed, R. 46 55 42N 2 10W
Twin Falls 100 42 30N 114 30W
Twyford 41 51 29N 0 51W
Tyldesley 45 53 31N 2 29W
Tyler 101 32 18N 95 17W
Tyndrum 46 56 26N 4 41W
Tyne & Wear □ 44 54 55N 1 35W
Tyne, R. 44 54 58N 1 28W
Tynemouth 44 55 1N 1 27W
Tynewydd 43 51 40N 3 32W
Tyrol 54 47 3N 10 43E
Tyrone □ 50 54 40N 7 15W
Tyrrhenian Sea 58 40 0N 12 30E
Tyumen 62 57 0N 65 18E
Tywi, R. 43 51 48N 4 20W
Tzaneen 94 23 47S 30 9E
Tzekung 73 29 25N 104 30E
Tzepo 73 36 28N 117 58E

U

Ube 76 33 56N 131 15E
Ubeda 60 38 3N 3 23W
Ubiaja 90 6 41N 6 22E
Ubundi 92 0 22S 25 30E
Ucayali, R. 108 6 0S 75 0W
Uchiura Bay 76 45 25N 140 40E
Uckfield 40 50 58N 0 6E
Udaipur 70 24 36N 73 44E
Uddingston 47 55 50N 4 3W
Udi 90 6 23N 7 21E
Údine 58 46 5N 13 10E
Ueda 76 36 24N 138 16E
Uele, R. 92 3 50N 22 40E
Uelzen 54 53 0N 10 33E
Ufa 62 54 45N 55 55E
Uffculme 43 50 54N 3 19W
Uganda ■ 93 2 0N 32 0E
Uinta Mts. 100 40 45N 110 30W
Uitenhage 94 33 40S 25 28E
Ujjain 70 23 9N 75 43E
Újpest 55 47 22N 19 6E
Ujung Pandang 72 5 10S 119 20E
Ukiah 100 39 10N 123 9W
Ukraine S.S.R. □ 62 48 0N 35 0E
Ulaanbaatar 73 47 54N 106 52E
Ulan Ude 62 52 0N 107 30E
Ulanhot 73 46 5N 122 1E
Ulco 94 28 21S 24 15E
Ulhasnagar 70 19 15N 73 10E
Ullapool 48 57 54N 5 10W
Ullswater, L. 44 54 35N 2 52W
Ulm 54 48 23N 10 0E
Ulsta 49 60 30N 1 09W
Ulster □ 50 54 45N 6 30W
Ulva, I. 48 56 30N 6 12W
Ulverston 44 54 13N 3 7W
Ulverstone 79 41 11S 146 11E
Ulyanovsk 62 54 25N 48 25E
Ulyasutay (Javhlant) 73 47 56N 97 28E
Uman 55 48 40N 30 12E
Umbrella Mts. 83 45 35S 169 5E
Umbria □ 58 42 53N 12 30E
Ume, R. 61 63 45N 20 20E
Umeå 61 63 45N 20 20E
Umm Rumah 91 25 50N 36 30E
Umm Said 71 25 0N 51 40E
*Umtali 92 18 58S 32 38E
Umtata 94 31 36S 28 49E
Umuahia-Ibeku 90 5 33N 7 29E
Umzinto 94 30 15S 30 45E
Unac, R. 58 44 30N 16 9E
Ungava B. 99 59 30N 67 30W
Unggi 73 42 16N 130 28E
Union of Soviet Soc. Rep. ■ 62 60 0N 100 0E
Uniondale 94 33 39S 23 7E
United Arab Emirates ■ 71 23 50N 54 0E
United Kingdom ■ 22 55 0N 3 0W
United States of America ■ 96 37 0N 96 0W
Unna 52 51 32N 7 40E
Unst, I. 49 60 50N 0 55W
Up Holland 45 53 32N 2 43W
Upernavik 96 72 49N 56 20W
Uphall 47 55 55N 3 30W
Upington 94 28 25S 21 15E
Upper Austria 54 48 10N 14 0E
Upper Hutt 83 41 8S 175 5E
Upper Klamath L. 105 42 16N 121 55W
Upper L. Erne 50 54 14N 7 22W
Upper Volta ■ 88 12 0N 0 30W
Uppingham 45 52 36N 0 43W
Uppsala 61 59 53N 17 38E
Upton 43 50 32N 4 26W
Ura-Tyube 71 39 55N 69 1E
Urakawa 76 42 9N 142 47E
Ural Mts. 62 60 0N 59 0E
Ural, R. 62 49 0N 52 0W
Uralsk 62 51 20N 51 20E
Urandangi 79 21 32S 138 14E
Urawa 76 35 50N 139 40E
Ure, R. 44 54 20N 1 25W
Ures 106 29 30N 110 30W
Urfa 71 37 12N 38 50E
Urfahr 54 48 19N 14 17E
Urgench 71 41 40N 60 30E
Urlingford 51 52 43N 7 35W
Urmia, L. = Rezā'īyeh, Daryācheh-ye 71 37 30N 45 30E
Urmston 45 53 28N 2 22W
Uruguay ■ 108 32 30S 55 30W
Uruguay, R. 108 28 0S 56 0W
Urumchi = Wulumuchi 73 43 40N 87 50E
Ushant, I. 56 48 25N 5 5W
Usk 43 51 42N 2 53W
Usk, R. 42 51 37N 2 56W
Üsküdar 71 41 0N 29 5E
Usoro 90 5 33N 6 11E
Ussuriysk 62 43 40N 131 50E
Ust Kamenogorsk 73 50 0N 82 20E
Ust Urt Plat. 71 44 0N 55 0E
Usti nad Labem 54 50 41N 14 3E
Ustica, I. 58 38 42N 13 10E
Usuki 76 33 8N 131 49E
Usumacinta, R. 106 17 0N 91 0W
Utah □ 100 39 30N 111 30W
Utah, L. 100 40 10N 111 58W
Utete 93 8 0S 38 45E
Utica 104 43 5N 75 18W
Utrecht, Neth. 52 52 3N 5 8E
Utrecht, S. Afr. 94 27 38S 30 20E
Utrecht □ 52 52 6N 5 7E
Utrera 60 37 12N 5 48W
Utsunomiya 76 36 30N 139 50E
Uttar Pradesh □ 70 27 0N 80 0E
Uttaradit 72 17 36N 100 5E
Uttoxeter 45 52 53N 1 50W
Uusikaupunki 61 60 47N 21 25E
Uvalde 100 29 15N 99 48W
Uvinza 93 5 5S 30 24E
Uwajima 76 33 10N 132 35E
Uyo 90 5 1N 7 53E
Uzbekistan S.S.R. □ 71 41 30N 65 0E
Uzhgorod 55 48 36N 22 18E
Uznam, I. 54 54 0N 14 0E

V

Vaal, R. 94 27 40S 25 30E
Vaaldam 94 27 0S 28 14E
Vaasa 61 63 6N 21 38E
Vadsø 61 70 3N 29 50E
Váh, R. 55 49 10N 18 20E
Valdai Hills 61 57 0N 33 0E
Valdepeñas 60 38 43N 3 25W
Valdivia □ 108 40 0S 73 0W
Valdosta 101 30 50N 83 20W
Valence 56 44 57N 4 54E
Valencia 107 10 11N 68 0W
Valencia □ 60 39 20N 0 40W
Valencia, G. of 60 39 30N 0 20E
Valenciennes 56 50 20N 3 34E
Valentia I. 51 51 54N 10 22W
Valera 107 9 19N 70 37W
Valga 61 57 41N 26 0E
Valjevo 55 44 18N 19 53E
Valladolid, Mexico 106 20 30N 88 20W
Valladolid, Spain 60 41 38N 4 43W
Valle d'Aosta □ 58 45 45N 7 22E
Vallecas 60 40 23N 3 41W
Vallejo 100 38 12N 122 15W
Valletta 58 35 54N 14 30E
Valley City 100 46 57N 98 0W
Valls 60 41 18N 1 15E
Valparaiso □ 108 33 2S 71 40W
Vals, R. 94 27 28S 26 52E
Valverde del Camino 60 37 35N 6 47W
Van 71 38 30N 43 20E
Van Diemen G. 78 11 45S 131 50E
Vancouver, Can. 105 49 15N 123 10W
Vancouver, U.S.A. 105 45 44N 122 41W
Vancouver I. 105 49 50N 126 0W
Vanderbijlpark 94 26 42S 27 54E
Vanderhoof 105 54 0N 124 0W
Vaner, L. 61 58 47N 13 30E
Vännäs 61 63 58N 19 48E
Vannes 56 47 40N 2 47W

* *Renamed Mutare*

Vanrhynsdorp 94 31 36S 18 44E
Vanwyksvlei 94 30 18S 21 49E
Varanasi 70 25 22N 83 8E
Varangar Fjord 61 70 3N 29 25E
Varberg 61 57 17N 12 20E
Vardø 61 70 23N 31 5E
Varel 52 53 23N 8 9E
Västerås 61 59 37N 16 38E
Västervik 61 57 43N 16 43E
Vasto 58 42 8N 14 40E
Vatersay, I. 49 56 55N 7 32W
Vatter, L. 61 58 25N 14 30E
Vechta 52 52 47N 8 18E
Vechte, R. 52 52 34N 6 6E
Veendam 52 53 5N 6 52E
Vega 61 65 40N 11 55E
Vega, La 107 19 20N 70 30W
Vejer de la Frontera 60 36 15N 5 59W
Velbert 52 51 20N 7 0E
Velebit Planina 58 44 50N 15 20E
Velikiye Luki 61 56 25N 30 32E
Velletri 58 41 43N 12 43E
Véneto □ 58 45 40N 12 0E
Venezia = Venice 58 45 20N 13 0E
Venezuela ■ 107 8 0N 65 0W
Venice 58 45 27N 12 20E
Venlo 52 51 22N 6 11E
Ventnor 40 50 35N 1 12W
Ventspils 61 57 25N 21 32E
Vera 60 37 15N 1 15W
Veracruz 106 19 10N 96 10W
Vercelli 58 45 19N 8 25E
Verde, C. 88 14 40N 17 15W
Verden 54 52 58N 9 18E
Verdun 56 49 12N 5 24E
Vereeniging 94 26 38S 27 57E
Verkhoyansk 62 67 50N 133 50E
Verkhoyansk Ra. 62 66 0N 129 0E
Vermont □ 101 43 40N 72 50W
Verneukpan L. 94 30 0S 21 0E
Vernon, Can. 105 50 20N 119 15W
Vernon, U.S.A. 100 34 10N 99 20W
Verona 58 45 27N 11 0E
Verviers 52 50 37N 5 52E
Vesuvius, Mt. 58 40 50N 14 22E
Vet, R. 94 27 50S 25 55E
Vettore, Mte. 58 44 38N 7 5E
Viana do Castelo 60 41 42N 8 50W
Vicenza 58 45 32N 11 31E
Vich 60 41 58N 2 19E
Vichy 56 46 9N 3 26E
Vicksburg 101 32 22N 90 56W
Victoria, Camer. 90 4 1N 9 10E
Victoria, Can. 105 48 30N 123 25W
Victoria, H. K. 73 22 25N 114 15E
Victoria, Malay. 72 5 20N 115 20E
Victoria □, Austral. 79 37 0S 144 0E
Victoria □, Rhod. 92 21 0S 31 30E
Victoria Falls 92 17 58S 25 45E
Victoria I. 98 71 0N 111 0W
Victoria, L. 93 1 0S 33 0E
Victoria Ld. 112 75 0S 160 0E
Victoria Nile R. 93 2 25N 31 50E
Victoria West 94 31 25S 23 4E
Vidin 55 43 59N 22 28E
Vienna 54 48 12N 16 22E
Vienne 56 45 31N 4 53E
Vienne, R. 56 47 5N 0 30E
Vientiane 72 17 58N 102 36E
Viersen 52 51 15N 6 23E
Vietnam ■ 72 12 0N 105 0E
Vigía Chico 106 19 46N 87 35W
Vigo 60 42 12N 8 41W
Vikna 61 64 55N 10 58E
Vila Franca de Xira 60 38 59N 8 59W
Vila Real 60 41 17N 7 48W
Vilaine, R. 56 47 35N 2 10W
Vilhelmina 61 64 35N 16 39E
Villa Ahumada 106 30 30N 106 40W
Villach 54 46 37N 13 51E
Villahermosa 106 17 45N 92 50W
Villanueva de la Serena 60 38 59N 5 50W
Villarreal 60 39 55N 0 3W
Villarrobledo 60 39 18N 2 36W
Villefranche-de-Rouergue 56 44 21N 2 2E
Villefranche-sur-Saône 56 45 59N 4 43E
Villena 60 38 39N 0 52W
Vilnius 61 54 38N 25 25E
Vilvoorde 52 50 56N 4 26E
Vilyuysk 62 63 40N 121 20E
Viña del Mar 108 33 0S 71 30W
Vinaroz 60 40 30N 0 27E
Vindhya Ra. 70 22 50N 77 0E
Vinh 72 18 45N 105 38E
Vinkovci 55 45 19N 18 48E
Vinnitsa 55 49 15N 28 30E
Virgin Is. 107 18 40N 64 30W
Virginia, Ireland 50 53 50N 7 5W
Virginia, S. Afr. 94 28 8S 26 55E
Virginia, U.S.A. 101 47 30N 92 32W
Virginia □ 101 37 45N 78 0W
Virginia Water 41 51 23N 0 33W
Virton 52 49 35N 5 32E
Vis 58 43 0N 16 10E
Visalia 100 36 25N 119 18W
Visby 61 57 37N 18 18E
Viscount Melville Sd. 98 74 10N 108 0W
Vishakhapatnam 70 17 45N 83 20E
Viso, Mte. 58 44 38N 7 5E
Vitebsk 61 55 10N 30 15E
Viterbo 58 42 25N 12 8E
Vitoria 60 42 50N 2 41W
Vitré 56 48 8N 1 12W
Vitry-le-François 56 48 43N 4 33E
Vittório Véneto 58 45 59N 12 18E
Vivero 60 43 39N 7 38W
Vizianagaram 70 18 6N 83 10E
Vlaardingen 52 51 55N 4 21E
Vladimir Volynskiy 55 50 50N 24 18E
Vladivostok 62 43 10N 131 53E
Vlieland, I. 52 53 30N 4 55E
Vlissingen 52 51 26N 3 34E

Vltava, R Wyndham

Vltava, R. 54 49 35N 14 10E
Vogelkop 72 1 25S 133 0E
Vogels Berg, mt. 54 50 37N 9 30E
Voi 93 3 25S 38 32E
Volga, R. 62 52 20N 48 0E
Volgograd 62 48 40N 44 25E
Völklingen 52 49 15N 6 50E
Volksrust 94 27 24S 29 53E
Vologda 62 59 25N 40 0E
Volsk 62 52 5N 47 28E
Volta, L. 88 7 30N 0 15E
Volta, R. 88 8 0N 0 10W
Voorburg 52 52 5N 4 24E
Vorarlberg □ 54 47 20N 10 0E
Vorkuta 62 67 48N 64 20E
Voronezh 62 51 40N 39 10E
Vosges □ 56 48 12N 6 20E
Vostok I. 22 10 5S 152 23W
Vrbas, R. 58 45 8N 17 29E
Vrede 94 27 24S 29 6E
Vredendal 94 31 41S 18 35E
Vršac 55 45 8N 21 18E
Vryburg 94 26 55S 24 45E
Vryheid 94 27 54S 30 47E
Vulcano, I. 58 38 25N 14 58E
Vyborg 61 60 43N 28 47E
Vyrnwy, L. 42 52 48N 3 30W
Vyrnwy, R. 42 52 43N 3 15W
Vyshniy Volochek 61 57 30N 34 30E

W

Waal, R. 52 51 59N 4 8E
Waalwijk 52 51 42N 5 4E
Wabash 101 40 48N 85 46W
Wabrzeźno 55 53 16N 18 57E
Waco 101 31 33N 97 5W
Wâd Medanî 89 14 28N 33 30E
Waddenzee 52 53 6N 5 10E
Waddington, Mt. 105 51 23N 125 15W
Wadebridge 43 50 31N 4 51W
Wadi Gemâl 91 24 35N 35 10E
Wadi Halfa 91 21 53N 31 19E
Wageningen 52 51 58N 5 40E
Wagga Wagga 79 35 7S 147 24E
Wagin, Austral. 78 33 17S 117 25E
Wagin, Nigeria 90 12 42N 7 10E
Waigeo, I. 72 0 20S 130 40E
Waihi 83 37 23S 175 52E
Waikaremoana L. 83 38 49S 177 9E
Waikari 83 42 58S 172 41E
Waikato, R. 83 37 23S 174 43E
Waikokopu 83 39 3S 177 52E
Waikouaiti 83 45 36S 170 41E
Waimakariri, R. 83 42 23S 172 42E
Waimarino 83 40 40S 175 20E
Waimate 83 44 53S 171 3E
Waiouru 83 39 28S 175 41E
Waipara 83 43 3S 172 46E
Waipawa 83 39 56S 176 38E
Waipiro 83 38 2S 176 22E
Waipu 83 35 59S 174 29E
Waipukurau 83 40 1S 176 33E
Wairakei 83 38 37S 176 6E
Wairarapa I. 83 41 14S 175 15E
Wairau, R. 83 41 32S 174 7E
Wairoa 83 39 3S 177 25E
Waitaki, R. 83 44 23S 169 55E
Waitara 83 38 59S 174 15E
Waiuku 83 37 15S 174 45E
Wajima 76 37 30N 137 0E
Wajir 93 1 42N 40 20E
Wakasa B. 76 35 45N 135 30E
Wakatipu, L. 83 45 5S 168 33E
Wakayama 76 34 15N 135 15E
Wake I. 23 19 18N 166 36E
Wakefield, N.Z. 83 41 24S 173 5E
Wakefield, U.K. 45 53 41N 1 31W
Wakkanai 76 45 28N 141 35E
Wakkerstroom 94 27 24S 30 10E
Wałbrzych 54 50 45N 16 18E
Walbury Hill 40 51 22N 1 28W
Walcheren, I. 52 51 30N 3 35E
Waldbröl 52 50 52N 7 36E
Wales □ 42 52 30N 3 30W
Walgett 79 30 0S 148 5E
Walkden 45 53 37N 2 24W
Walker 44 54 58N 1 32W
Walla Walla 100 46 3N 118 25W
Wallace 100 47 30N 116 0W
Wallachia 55 44 35N 25 0E
Wallaroo 79 33 56S 137 39E
Wallasey 45 53 26N 3 2W
Wallingford 40 51 36N 1 08W
Walls 49 60 14N 1 32W
Wallsend 44 54 59N 1 30W
Walmer, S. Afr. 94 33 57S 25 35E
Walmer, U.K. 40 51 12N 1 23E
Walmley 41 52 31N 1 47W
Walsall 41 52 36N 1 59W
Walsenburg 100 37 42N 104 45W
Walsingham 40 52 53N 0 53E
Waltham Abbey 41 51 40N 0 1E
Waltham Forest 41 51 37N 0 2E
Walton-le-Dale 45 53 45N 2 41W
Walton-on-Thames 41 51 21N 0 22W
Walton-on-the-Naze 40 51 52N 1 17E
Walvis Bay 92 23 0S 14 28E
Wanaka 83 44 42S 169 7E
Wanaka L. 83 44 33S 169 7E
Wandoan 79 26 5S 149 55E
Wandsworth 41 51 28N 0 15W
Wanganui 83 39 35S 175 3E
Wangaratta 79 36 21S 146 19E
Wanhsien 73 36 45N 107 24E
* Wankie 92 18 18S 26 30E
Wantage 40 51 35N 1 25W
Ward, Ireland 51 53 25N 6 19W
Ward, N.Z. 83 41 49S 174 11E
Warden 94 27 50S 29 0E
Wardha 70 20 45N 78 39E
Wareham 43 50 41N 2 8W
Warendorf 52 51 57N 8 0E
Warkworth 83 36 24S 174 41E
Warley 41 52 30N 2 0W
Warlingham 41 51 18N 0 03W
Warmbad 94 24 51S 28 19E
Warminster 42 51 12N 2 11W
Warnemünde 54 54 9N 12 5E
Warner Range, Mts. 105 41 30S 120 20W
Warrego, R. 79 30 24S 145 21E
Warren 101 41 52N 79 10W
Warrenpoint 50 54 7N 6 15W
Warrenton 94 28 9S 24 47E
Warri 90 5 30N 5 41E
Warrina 79 28 12S 135 50E
Warrington 45 53 25N 2 38W
Warrnambool 79 38 25S 142 30E
Warsaw 55 52 13N 21 0E
Warsop 44 53 13N 1 9W
Warszawa = Warsaw 55 52 13N 21 0E
Warta, R. 54 52 35N 14 39E
Warwick, Austral. 79 28 10S 152 1E
Warwick, U.K. 42 52 17N 1 36W
Warwick □ 42 52 20N 1 30W
Wasatch, Mt., Ra. 100 40 30N 111 15W
Wash, The 32 52 58N 0 20W
Washington, U.K. 44 54 55N 1 30W
Washington, U.S.A. 104 38 52N 77 0W
Washington □ 100 47 45N 120 30W
Watchet 42 51 10N 3 20W
Waterbeach 40 52 16N 0 11E
Waterberg 94 24 14S 28 0E
Waterbury 104 41 32N 73 0W
Waterford 51 52 16N 7 8W
Waterford □ 51 52 10N 7 40W
Waterford Harb. 51 52 10N 6 58W
Waterloo 101 42 27N 92 20W
Waterlooville 40 50 52N 1 01W
Watertown 104 43 58N 75 57W
Waterval-Boven 94 25 40S 30 18E
Waterville 51 51 49N 10 10W
Watford 42 51 38N 0 23W
Wath upon Dearne 45 53 30N 1 21W
Watlings I. 107 24 0N 74 35W
Watlington 41 51 38N 1 0W
Watsa 93 3 4N 29 30E
Watson Lake 98 60 6N 128 49W
Watton 40 52 35N 0 50E
Watubella Is. 72 4 28S 131 54E
Wau 89 7 45N 28 1E
Waukegan 101 42 22N 87 54W
Wausau 101 44 57N 89 40W
Wave Hill 78 17 32S 131 0E
Waveney, R. 40 52 24N 1 20E
Waverley 83 39 46S 174 37E
Waxahachie 101 32 22N 96 53W
Waycross 101 31 12N 82 25W
Weald, The 40 51 7N 0 9E
Wear, R. 44 54 55N 1 22W
Weardale 44 54 44N 2 5W
Weatherford 100 32 45N 97 48W
Weaver, R. 45 53 17N 2 35W
Weddell Sea 112 72 30S 40 0W
Wednesbury 41 52 33N 2 1W
Wednesfield 41 52 36N 2 3W
Weenen 94 28 48S 30 7E
Weert 52 51 15N 5 43E
Weifang 73 36 47N 119 10E
Weihai 73 37 30N 122 10E
Weimar 54 51 0N 11 20E
Weipa 79 12 24S 141 50E
Weiser 100 44 10N 117 0W
Welkom 94 28 0S 26 50E
Welland, R. 45 52 43N 0 10W
Wellesley Is. 79 17 20S 139 30E
Wellingborough 40 52 18N 0 41W
Wellington, Austral. 79 32 35S 148 59E
Wellington, N.Z. 83 41 19S 174 46E
Wellington, S. Afr. 94 33 38S 18 57E
Wellington, U.K. 44 52 42N 2 31W
Wellington, U.S.A. 100 37 15N 97 25W
Wellington □ 83 40 8S 175 36E
Wells, Norfolk, U.K. 40 52 57N 0 51E
Wells, Somerset, U.K. 42 51 12N 2 39W
Wels 54 48 9N 14 1E
Welshpool 42 52 40N 3 9W
Welwyn Garden City 41 51 49N 0 11W
Wem 45 52 52N 2 45W
Wemyss Bay 47 55 52N 4 54W
Wenatchee 105 47 30N 120 17W
Wenchow 73 28 0N 120 35E
Wendover 41 51 46N 0 45W
Wensleydale 44 54 18N 2 0W
Wensum, R. 40 52 37N 1 22E
Wentworth, Austral. 79 34 2S 141 54E
Wentworth, U.K. 45 53 28N 1 25W
Wepener 94 29 42S 27 3E
Werne 52 51 38N 7 38E
Werra, R. 54 51 0N 10 0E
Wesel 52 51 39N 6 34E
Weser, R. 54 53 33N 8 30E
West Bengal □ 70 25 0N 90 0E
West Beskids, mts. 55 49 30N 19 20E
West Bromwich 41 52 32N 2 1W
West Calder 47 55 51N 3 34W
West Glamorgan □ 42 51 40N 3 55W
West Indies 96 15 0N 70 0W
West Kilbride 47 55 41N 4 50W
West Kirby 45 53 22N 3 11W
West Linton 47 55 45N 3 24W
West Mersea 40 51 46N 0 55E
West Midlands □ 45 52 30N 1 55W
West Nicholson 92 21 2S 29 20E
West Palm Beach 101 26 44N 80 3W
West Schelde R. 52 51 23N 3 50E
West Siberian Plain 62 62 0N 75 0E
West Sussex □ 40 50 55N 0 30W
West Virginia □ 101 39 0N 81 0W
West Yorkshire □ 44 53 45N 1 40W
Westerdal R. 61 60 30N 14 0E
Westerham 41 51 16N 0 5E
Western Australia □ 78 25 0S 118 0E
Western Desert 91 27 40N 26 30E
Western Germany ■ 54 50 0N 8 0E
Western Ghats 70 15 30N 74 30E
Western Isles □ 49 57 30N 7 10W
† Western Malaysia □ 72 4 0N 102 0E
Western Samoa ■ 22 14 0S 172 0W
Westerwald 54 50 39N 8 0E
Westhoughton 45 53 34N 2 30W
Westland □ 83 43 33S 169 59E
Westland Bight 83 42 55S 170 5E
Westmeath □ 51 53 30N 7 30W
Westminster 41 51 30N 0 07W
Weston 45 53 55N 2 44W
Weston-super-Mare 42 51 20N 2 59W
Weston upon Trent 45 52 50N 2 02W
Westport, Ireland 50 53 44N 9 31W
Westport, N.Z. 83 41 46S 171 37E
Westray Firth 49 59 15N 3 0W
Westray, I. 49 59 18N 3 0W
Westward Ho! 43 51 2N 4 16W
Wetar, I. 72 7 30S 126 30E
Wetherby 45 53 56N 1 23W
Wetteren 52 51 0N 3 53E
Wetzlar 54 50 33N 8 30E
Wewak 79 3 38S 143 41E
Wexford 51 52 20N 6 28W
Wexford □ 51 52 20N 6 25W
Wexford Harb. 51 52 20N 6 25W
Wey, R. 41 51 19N 0 29W
Weybridge 41 51 22N 0 28W
Weyburn 98 49 40N 103 50W
Weymouth 43 50 36N 2 28W
Whakatane 83 37 57S 177 1E
Whaley Bridge 45 53 20N 2 0W
Whalley 45 53 49N 2 25W
Whalsay, I. 49 60 22N 1 0W
Whangamomona 83 39 8S 174 44E
Whangarei 83 35 43S 174 21E
Wharfe, R. 44 53 55N 1 30W
Wheatley Hill 44 54 45N 1 23W
Wheeling 104 40 2N 80 41W
Whernside, Mt. 44 54 14N 2 24W
Whickham 44 54 56N 1 41W
Whiddy, I. 51 51 41N 9 30W
Whiston 45 53 25N 2 45W
Whitburn 47 55 52N 3 41W
Whitby 44 54 29N 0 37W
Whitchurch, Hants., U.K. 40 51 14N 1 20W
Whitchurch, Salop, U.K. 44 52 58N 2 42W
White Cliffs 83 43 26S 171 55E
White Mts., Czech. 55 49 0N 17 50E
White Mts., U.S.A. 100 37 30N 118 15W
White, Mts. 101 44 15N 71 15W
White Nile, R. 89 9 30N 31 40E
White Russia 62 53 30N 27 0E
White Sea 61 66 30N 38 0E
Whitefield 45 53 33N 2 18W
Whitehaven 44 54 33N 3 35W
Whitehead 50 54 45N 5 42W
Whitehorse 98 60 43N 135 3W
Whithorn 46 54 55N 4 25W
Whitianga 83 36 47S 175 41E
Whitley Bay 44 55 4N 1 28W
Whitney, Mt. 105 36 35N 118 14W
Whitstable 40 51 21N 1 2E
Whittington, Derby, U.K. 45 53 17N 1 26W
Whittington, Salop, U.K. 45 52 53N 3 0W
Whittle-le-Woods 45 53 40N 2 37W
Whittlesey 40 52 34N 0 8W
Whitworth 45 53 40N 2 11W
Whyalla 79 33 2S 137 30E
Wichita 101 37 40N 97 29W
Wichita Falls 100 33 57N 98 30W
Wick 48 58 26N 3 5W
Wickersley 45 53 25N 1 17W
Wickford 41 51 37N 0 31E
Wickham Market 40 52 9N 1 21E
Wicklow 51 53 0N 6 2W
Wicklow □ 51 52 59N 6 25W
Wicklow Hd. 51 52 59N 6 3W
Wicklow Mts. 51 53 0N 6 30W
Wide Open 44 55 02N 1 36W
Widnes 45 53 22N 2 44W
Wieliczka 55 50 0N 20 5E
Wien = Vienna 54 48 12N 16 22E
Wiener Neustadt 54 47 49N 16 16E
Wiesbaden 52 50 7N 8 17E
Wigan 45 53 33N 2 38W
Wigmore 41 52 19N 2 51W
Wigston 41 52 35N 1 6W
Wigton 44 54 50N 3 9W
Wigtown 46 54 52N 4 27W
Wigtown B. 46 54 46N 4 15W
Wilcannia 79 31 30S 143 26E
Wilge R. 94 25 40S 29 10E
Wilhelm II Coast 112 67 0S 90 0E
Wilhelmshaven 54 53 30N 8 9E
Wilkes Barre 104 41 15N 75 52W
Wilkes Land 112 69 0S 120 0E
Wilkie 98 52 27N 108 42W
Willebroek 52 51 4N 4 22E
Willemstad 107 12 5N 69 0W
Willenhall 41 52 36N 2 3W
Williams Lake 105 52 10N 122 10W
Williamsport 104 41 18N 77 1W
Willington 44 54 43N 1 42W
Williston, S. Afr. 94 31 20S 20 53E
Williston, U.S.A. 100 48 10N 103 35W
Williton 42 51 9N 3 20W
Willmar 101 45 5N 95 0W
Willowmore 94 33 15S 23 30E
Wilmington, Del., U.S.A. 104 39 45N 75 32W
Wilmington, N.C., U.S.A. 101 34 14N 77 54W
Wilmslow 45 53 19N 2 14W
Wilnecote 41 52 36N 1 40W
Wilson's Promontory 79 38 55S 146 25E
Wilton 42 51 5N 1 52W
Wiltshire □ 42 51 20N 2 0W
Wiluna 78 26 36S 120 14E
Wimborne Minster 43 50 48N 2 0W
Wimmera 79 36 30S 142 0E
Winburg 94 28 30S 27 2E
Wincanton 43 51 3N 2 24W
Winchester, U.K. 40 51 4N 1 19W
Winchester, U.S.A. 101 39 14N 78 8W
Wind River Range, Mts. 100 43 0N 109 30W
Windermere 44 54 24N 2 56W
Windermere, L. 44 54 20N 2 57W
Windhoek 92 22 35S 17 4E
Windorah 79 25 24S 142 36E
Windsor, Can. 104 42 18N 83 0W
Windsor, U.K. 41 51 28N 0 36W
Windward Is. 107 13 0N 63 0W
Windward Passage 107 20 0N 74 0W
Windygates 47 56 12N 3 1W
Wingate 44 54 44N 1 23W
Winkleigh 43 50 49N 3 57W
Winnemucca 100 41 0N 117 45W
Winnipeg 98 49 54N 97 9W
Winnipeg, L. 98 52 0N 97 0W
Winnipegosis L. 98 52 30N 100 0W
Winona 101 44 2N 91 45W
Winschoten 52 53 9N 7 3E
Winsford 44 53 12N 2 31W
Winslow, U.K. 40 51 57N 0 52W
Winslow, U.S.A. 100 35 2N 110 41W
Winston-Salem 101 36 7N 80 15W
Winterswijk 52 51 58N 6 43E
Winterthur 54 47 30N 8 44E
Winton, Austral. 79 22 24S 143 3E
Winton, N.Z. 83 46 8S 168 20E
Wirksworth 44 53 5N 1 34W
Wirral 44 53 25N 3 0W
Wisbech 40 52 39N 0 10E
Wisconsin □ 101 44 30N 90 0W
Wishaw 47 55 46N 3 55W
Wismar 107 5 59N 58 18W
Witbank 94 25 51S 29 14E
Witham 41 51 48N 0 39E
Witheridge 43 50 55N 3 43W
Withernsea 44 53 43N 0 2W
Withnell 45 53 42N 2 33W
Witney 40 51 47N 1 29W
Witten 52 51 26N 7 19E
Wittenberge 54 53 0N 11 44E
Wittenburg 54 53 30N 11 4E
Wittenoom 78 22 15S 118 20E
Witwatersrand 94 26 0S 27 0E
Wiveliscombe 43 51 2N 3 20W
Wivenhoe 40 51 51N 0 59E
Wokam, I. 72 5 45S 134 28E
Woking 41 51 18N 0 33W
Wokingham 41 51 25N 0 50W
Wolin 54 53 50N 14 37E
Wollaston Pen. 98 69 30N 115 0W
Wollongong 79 34 25S 150 54E
Wolmaransstad 94 27 12S 26 13E
Wolverhampton 41 52 35N 2 6W
Wolverton 40 52 3N 0 48W
Wolviston 44 54 39N 1 25W
Wombwell 45 53 31N 1 23W
Wondai 79 26 20S 151 49E
Wonthaggi 79 38 37S 145 37E
Woodbridge 40 52 6N 1 19E
Woodhall Spa 44 53 10N 0 12W
Woodroffe, Mt. 78 26 20S 131 45E
Woodstock 40 51 51N 1 20W
Woodville 83 40 20S 175 53E
Woolacombe 42 51 10N 4 12W
Wooler 46 55 33N 2 0W
Woomera 79 31 11S 136 47E
Woonsockett 104 44 5N 98 15W
Wootton Bassett 42 51 32N 1 55W
Worcester, S. Afr. 94 33 39S 19 27E
Worcester, U.K. 42 52 12N 2 12W
Worcester, U.S.A. 104 42 14N 71 49W
Workington 44 54 39N 3 34W
Worksop 44 53 19N 1 9W
Wormerveer 52 52 30N 4 46E
Wormit 47 56 26N 2 59W
Worms 54 49 37N 8 21E
Worms Head 42 51 33N 4 19W
Worsbrough 45 53 31N 1 29W
Worsley 45 53 30N 2 23W
Worthing 40 50 49N 0 21W
Wotton-under-Edge 43 51 37N 2 20W
Wragby 44 53 17N 0 18W
Wrangel I. 62 71 0N 180 0E
Wrangell 98 56 30N 132 25W
Wrangell Mts. 98 61 40N 143 30W
Wrath, C. 48 58 38N 5 0W
Wrekin, The 42 52 41N 2 35W
Wrexham 42 53 5N 3 0W
Writtle 41 51 44N 0 27E
Wrocław 54 51 5N 17 5E
Wrotham 41 51 18N 0 20E
Wroughton 42 51 31N 1 47W
Wroxham 40 52 42N 1 23E
Wuchow 73 23 26N 111 19E
Wuchung 73 38 4N 106 12E
Wuhan 73 30 35N 114 15E
Wuhu 73 31 18N 118 20E
Wukari 90 7 57N 9 42E
Wulumuchi 73 43 40N 87 50E
Wum 90 6 40N 10 2E
Wuppertal 52 51 15N 7 8E
Würzburg 54 49 46N 9 55E
Wusih 73 31 30N 120 30E
Wusu 73 44 27N 84 37E
Wutunghliao 73 29 25N 104 0E
Wuwei 73 37 55N 102 48E
Wuyi Shan 73 26 40N 116 30E
Wuyun 73 46 16N 129 37E
Wyandra 79 27 12S 145 56E
Wye 40 51 11N 0 56E
Wye, R. 42 51 36N 2 40W
Wymondham 40 52 34N 1 7E
Wynberg 94 34 2S 18 28E
Wyndham, Austral. 78 15 33S 128 3E
Wyndham, N.Z. 83 46 20S 168 51E

* Renamed Hwange

† Now part of Malaysia

Place	Page	Lat	Long
Wyoming □	100	42 48N	109 0W
Wyre, R.	45	53 52N	2 57W

X

Place	Page	Lat	Long
Xingu, R.	108	2 25 s	52 35W

Y

Place	Page	Lat	Long
Yaan	73	30 0N	102 59 E
Yabassi	90	4 30N	9 57 E
Yablonovyy Ra.	62	53 0N	114 0 E
Yakima	105	46 42N	120 30W
Yakima, R.	105	47 0N	120 30W
Yaku-Jima	76	30 20N	130 30 E
Yakutsk	62	62 5N	129 40 E
Yalgoo	78	28 16 s	116 39 E
Yallourn	79	38 10 s	146 18 E
Yalung K.	73	32 0N	100 0 E
Yamagata	76	38 15N	140 15 E
Yamaguchi	76	34 10N	131 32 E
Yamdena	72	7 45 s	131 20 E
Yampi Sd.	78	16 8 s	123 38 E
Yan	90	10 5N	12 11 E
Yanam	70	16 47N	82 15 E
Yangchuan	73	38 0N	113 29 E
Yangtze Chiang, R.	73	27 30N	99 30 E
Yaoundé	88	3 50N	11 35 E
Yaqui, R.	106	28 28N	109 30W
Yaraka	79	24 53 s	144 3 E
Yare, R.	40	52 36N	1 28 E
Yarmouth	40	50 42N	1 29W
Yaroslavl	62	57 35N	39 55 E
Yate	43	51 32N	2 26W
Yatsushiro	76	32 30N	130 40 E
Yawatahama	76	33 27N	132 24 E
Yayama-rettō	76	24 30N	123 40 E
Yazd	71	31 55N	54 27 E
Yeadon	45	53 52N	1 40W
Yedintsy	55	48 5N	27 20 E
Yehsien	73	37 12N	119 58 E
Yell, I.	49	60 35N	1 5W
Yellow Sea	73	35 0N	123 0 E
Yellowknife	98	62 27N	114 21W
Yellowstone National Park	100	44 35N	110 0W
Yellowstone, R.	100	47 58N	103 59W
Yemen ■	71	15 0N	44 0 E
Yenangyaung	70	20 30N	95 0 E
Yenbo'	71	24 0N	38 5 E
Yenisey, R.	62	68 0N	86 30 E
Yeniseysk	62	58 39N	92 4 E
Yent'ai	73	37 35N	121 25 E
Yeovil	43	50 57N	2 38W
Yeppoon	79	23 5 s	150 47 E
Yerevan	71	40 10N	44 20 E
Yes Tor	43	50 41N	3 59W
Yeu, I. d'	56	46 42N	2 20W
Yilan	73	24 47N	121 44 E
Yinchwan	73	38 30N	106 20 E
Yingkow	73	40 43N	122 9 E
Yiyang	73	28 45N	112 16 E
Yogyakarta	72	7 49 s	110 22 E
Yokkaichi	76	35 0N	136 30 E
Yokohama	76	35 27N	139 39 E
Yokosuka	76	35 20N	139 40 E
Yokote	76	39 20N	140 30 E
Yola	90	9 10N	12 29 E
Yonago	76	35 25N	133 19 E
Yonezawa	76	37 57N	140 4 E
Yonkers	104	40 57N	73 51W
York, Austral.	78	31 52 s	116 47 E
York, U.K.	44	53 58N	1 7W
York, U.S.A.	104	39 57N	76 43W
York, C.	79	10 42 s	142 31 E
Yorke Pen.	79	34 50 s	137 40 E
Yorkshire Wolds	44	54 0N	0 30W
Yorkton	98	51 11N	102 28W
Yosemite National Park	100	38 0N	119 30W
Youghal	51	51 58N	7 51W
Youghal Har.	51	51 55N	7 50W
Young	79	34 19 s	148 18 E
Youngstown	104	41 7N	80 41W
Ypres	52	50 50N	2 52 E
Ysabel, I.	79	8 0 s	158 40 E
Ystalyfera	43	51 46N	3 48W
Ystradgynlais	43	51 47N	3 45W
Ythan, R.	48	57 26N	2 12W
Yuba City	100	39 12N	121 37W
Yūbari	76	43 4N	141 59 E
Yucatán □	106	21 30N	86 30W
Yucatán Channel	106	22 0N	86 30W
Yugoslavia ■	58	44 0N	20 0 E
Yukon, R.	98	65 30N	150 0W
Yukon Territory □	98	63 0N	135 0W
Yuma	100	32 45N	114 37W
Yumen	73	41 13N	96 55 E
Yun Ho	73	35 0N	117 0 E
Yungtsi	73	34 50N	110 25 E
Yunnan □	73	25 0N	102 30 E
Yutze	73	37 45N	112 45 E

Z

Place	Page	Lat	Long
Zaandam	52	52 26N	4 49 E
Zabrze	55	50 18N	18 46 E
Zacapa	106	14 59N	89 31W
Zacatecas	106	22 49N	102 34W
Zacoalco	106	20 10N	103 40W
Zadar	58	44 8N	15 8 E
Zafra	60	38 26N	6 30W
Zagań	54	51 39N	15 22 E
Zagazig	91	30 40N	31 12 E
Zagnanado	90	7 18N	2 28 E
Zagreb	58	45 50N	16 0 E
Zagros Mts.	71	33 45N	47 0 E
Zāhedān	71	29 30N	60 50 E
Zahlah	71	33 52N	35 50 E
Zaïre, R.	92	1 30N	28 0 E
Zaïre, Rep. of ■	92	3 0 s	23 0 E
Zambèze, R.	92	18 46 s	36 16 E
Zambia ■	92	15 0 s	28 0 E
Zamboanga	72	6 59N	122 3 E
Zamora, Mexico	106	20 0N	102 21W
Zamora, Spain	60	41 30N	5 45W
Zanesville	104	39 56N	82 2W
Zanjan	71	36 40N	48 35 E
Zanthus	78	31 2 s	123 34 E
Zanzibar	93	6 12 s	39 12 E
Zaporozhye	62	47 50N	35 10 E
Zaragoza	60	41 39N	0 53W
Zaria	90	11 0N	7 40 E
Zary	54	51 37N	15 10 E
Zastron	94	30 18 s	27 7 E
Zawyet Shammâs	91	31 30N	26 37 E
Zâwyet Um el Rakham	91	31 18N	27 1 E
Zâwyet Ungeîla	91	31 23N	26 42 E
Zduńska Wola	55	51 37N	18 59 E
Zeehan	79	41 52 s	145 25 E
Zeeland	52	51 41N	5 40 E
Zeerust	94	25 31 s	26 4 E
Zeist	52	52 5N	5 15 E
Zemun	55	44 51N	20 25 E
Zerbst	54	51 59N	12 8 E
Zhabinka	55	52 13N	24 2 E
Zhdanov	62	47 5N	37 31 E
Zhigansk	62	66 35N	124 10 E
Zhitomir	55	50 20N	28 40 E
Zhmerinka	55	49 2N	28 10 E
Ziel, Mt.	78	23 20 s	132 30 E
Zielona Góra	54	51 57N	15 31 E
Žilina	55	49 12N	18 42 E
Zilling Tso	73	31 40N	89 0 E
Zimbabwe ■	92	20 16 s	31 0 E
Zimbabwe ■ (formerly Rhodesia)	92	19 0 s	29 0 E
Zinder	90	13 48N	9 0 E
Zion Nat. Park	100	37 25N	112 50W
Zolochev	55	49 45N	24 58 E
Zrenjanin	55	45 22N	20 23 E
Zug	54	47 10N	8 31 E
Zuid-Holland □	52	52 0N	4 35 E
Zululand	94	43 19N	2 15 E
Zumbo	92	15 35 s	30 26 E
Zürich	54	47 22N	8 32 E
Zuru	90	11 27N	5 4 E
Zutphen	52	52 9N	6 12 E
Zvolen	55	48 33N	19 10 E
Zweibrücken	52	49 15N	7 20 E
Zwickau	54	50 43N	12 30 E
Zwolle	52	52 31N	6 6 E
Żyrardów	55	52 3N	20 35 E
Zyryanovsk	73	49 50N	84 57 E

Acknowledgement is made to the following for providing the photographs used in this atlas.

Aerofilms Ltd.; Air France; Air India; G. Atkinson; Australian Information Service; Brazilian Embassy, London; Brazilian Tourist Office, London; G. P. Chapman; Chile Tourist Office, London; Danish Embassy, London; Fiat (England) Ltd.; Finnish Tourist Bureau; Harland & Wolff Ltd.; R. J. Harrison Church; Japan Information Centre, London; Meteorological Office, London; Moroccan Tourist Office, London; N.A.S.A.; Netherlands National Tourist Office, London; Novosti Press Agency; M. Rentsch; S.A.S.; W. B. Smith; Society For Anglo-Chinese Understanding, London; Transafrica Pix.; Wiggins Teape Ltd.; B. M. Willett; Z.E.F.A. (U.K.) Ltd.

The Earth from Space

1. ROCKY MOUNTAINS (CANADA)

This is an area of high precipitation, much of which falls as snow which covers the high mountains in this image, emphasizing the drainage pattern. The conspicuous straight valley bisecting the area is part of the Rocky Mountain Trench, a great fault zone that extends from Alaska to Montana.

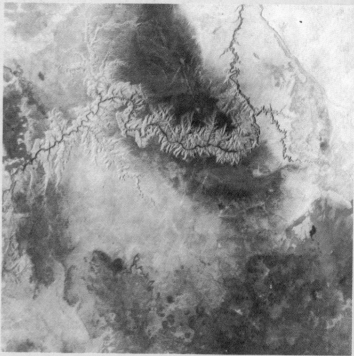

2. GRAND CANYON (U.S.A.)

The Colorado river is shown here flowing through the Grand Canyon in Arizona, which at this point is 1.5km deep and 20km wide. The reddish area distinguishes the Kaibab Plateau, an area over 2700m high, on which higher precipitation permits vegetation growth.

A Landsat satellite launched and controlled by NASA in the USA travels around the earth at a height of 917km, and "photographs" every point of the world once every 18 days. The view from the satellite is broken into four component bands of the spectrum, bands 4, 5, 6, and 7, converted into electrical signals and transmitted

3. TAKLA MAKAN DESERT (CHINA)

Snow cover spreads over the marshland around the Tarim River in the north-east and onto the desert sand-dunes. It is not easy to appreciate the size of these dunes from this image; individual dune ridges are 1½-3km wide and extend 8-32km.

4. MISSISSIPPI DELTA (U.S.A.)

The blue colouring of the farmland in this area is caused by extensive flooding of the Mississippi River. The large quantity of sediment transported by the river flows into the Gulf of Mexico building up the delta and appearing as a light blue mass in the sea.

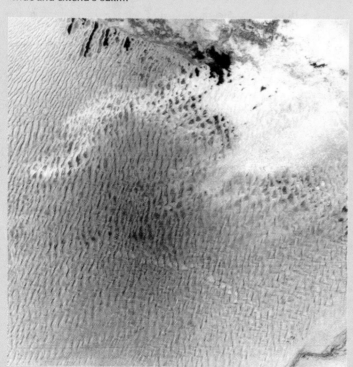

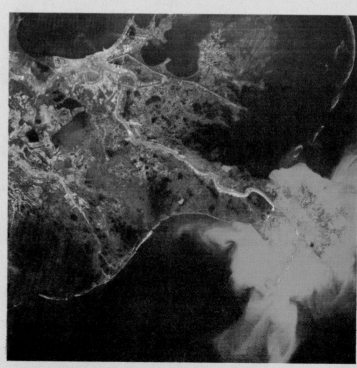